Revolutionary Patriots

of

Worcester and Somerset Counties

Maryland

1775-1783

Henry C. Peden, Jr.

HERITAGE BOOKS
2006

HERITAGE BOOKS
AN IMPRINT OF HERITAGE BOOKS, INC.

Books, CDs, and more—Worldwide

For our listing of thousands of titles see our website
at
www.HeritageBooks.com

Published 2006 by
HERITAGE BOOKS, INC.
Publishing Division
65 East Main Street
Westminster, Maryland 21157-5026

Copyright © 1999 Henry C. Peden, Jr.

All rights reserved. No part of this book may be reproduced or transmitted in any form or by any means, electronic or mechanical, including photocopying, recording or by any information storage and retrieval system without written permission from the author, except for the inclusion of brief quotations in a review.

International Standard Book Number: 978-1-888265-81-7

INTRODUCTION

This book has been compiled for the purpose of serving as a research tool for locating the men and women of Worcester and Somerset Counties, Maryland, including present day Wicomico County, who served in the military, rendered material aid to the army or navy, took the Oath of Allegiance and Fidelity, served in an office or on a committee at the town, county or state level, or in some fashion contributed and supported the fight for freedom by the American colonies from the rule of Great Britain during the Revolutionary War, 1775-1783.

It is hoped that this book, which is the fifteenth in a series on the Revolutionary War patriots and soldiers in Maryland, will encourage and enable interested persons to become members of such patriotic organizations as The Sons of the American Revolution, The Daughters of the American Revolution, The Sons of the Revolution, and The Society of the Cincinnati.

This book contains names and information that have not been previously published. Additional lists were found that were not included in *The Maryland Militia in the Revolutionary War* by S. Eugene Clements and F. Edward Wright (1987). Hundreds of names were found in lists of those who took the Oath of Allegiance in 1778 that were not included in *9000 Men Who Took the Oath of Allegiance and Fidelity to Maryland During the Revolution* by Bettie S. Carothers (1975). Also, some errors discovered in those two books have been corrected herein.

Information for this book has been gleaned from many primary and secondary sources, which makes this book far more than just a listing of names and ranks. Many of the approximately 5,000 persons named herein have genealogical data included with their respective entries, such as places of residence and dates of birth, death, and marriage, names of wives, husbands, children, and other relatives, plus information gleaned from court records, church registers, military muster rolls, and pension files.

Each entry in this book has been documented and a key to that documentation has been implemented within the text to enable the reader to review the cited source. A letter followed by a number is the code used for a source and the page within that source. For example, [Ref: D-555] would indicate that the information can be found on page 555 of Reference D, which is *Archives of Maryland, Volume 18*. The coded sources cited herein are as follows:

A = *Archives of Maryland, Volume XI*. "Journal of the Maryland Conventions, July 26 - August 14, 1775, and Journal and Correspondence of the Maryland Council of Safety, August 29, 1775 - July 6, 1776" (Baltimore: Maryland Historical

Society, 1892)

B = *Archives of Maryland, Volume XII.* "Journal and Correspondence of the Maryland Council of Safety, July 7, 1776 - December 31, 1776" (Baltimore: Maryland Historical Society, 1893)

C = *Archives of Maryland, Volume XVI.* "Journal and Correspondence of the Council of Safety, January 1, 1777 - March 20, 1777" and "Journal and Correspondence of the State Council, March 20, 1777 - March 28, 1778" (Baltimore: Maryland Historical Society, 1897)

D = *Archives of Maryland, Volume XVIII.* "Muster Rolls and Other Records of Service of Maryland Troops in the American Revolution, 1775-1783" (Baltimore: Maryland Historical Society, 1900)

E = *Archives of Maryland, Volume XXI.* "Journal and Correspondence of the Council of Maryland, April 1, 1778 - October 26, 1779" (Baltimore: Maryland Historical Society, 1901)

F = *Archives of Maryland, Volume XLIII.* "Journal and Correspondence of the State Council of Maryland, 1779-1780" (Baltimore: Maryland Historical Society, 1924)

G = *Archives of Maryland, Volume XLV.* "Journal and Correspondence of the State Council of Maryland, 1780-1781" (Baltimore: Maryland Historical Society, 1927)

H = *Archives of Maryland, Volume XLVII.* "Journal and Correspondence of the State Council of Maryland, 1781" (Baltimore: Maryland Historical Society, 1930)

I = *Archives of Maryland, Volume XLVIII.* "Journal and Correspondence of the State Council of Maryland, 1781-1784" (Baltimore: Maryland Historical Society, 1931)

J = *Revolutionary War Military Collection, Manuscript MS.1814.* (Baltimore: Maryland Historical Society, Manuscripts Division)

K = *Draftees from Worcester County on May 10, 1781, reported by Joseph Dashiell* (Annapolis: Maryland State Archives, Accession No. MdHR6636-30)

L = *Draftees from Somerset County in June, July, and August, 1781 reported by George Dashiell* (Annapolis: Maryland State Archives, Accession No. MdHR6636-31)

M = Clements, S. Eugene and Wright, F. Edward. *The Maryland Militia in the*

Revolutionary War (Westminster, Maryland: Family Line Publications, 1987)

N = Carothers, Bettie S. *9000 Men Who Signed the Oath of Allegiance and Fidelity to Maryland During the Revolution* (Baltimore: Published by the Author, 1975)

O = *Calendar of Maryland State Papers, The Red Books, No. 4, Part 1* (Annapolis: The Hall of Records Commission, 1950)

P = Papenfuse, Edward C., et al. *An Inventory of Maryland State Papers, Volume 1*, "The Era of the American Revolution, 1775-1789" (Annapolis: The Hall of Records Commission, 1977)

Q = *Maryland Genealogical Society Bulletin* (as cited)

R = Papenfuse, Edward C., et al. *A Biographical Dictionary of the Maryland Legislature, 1635-1789* (Baltimore: The Johns Hopkins University Press, 1979), 2 volumes

S = *Membership Applications of the Maryland Society, Sons of the American Revolution* (identified by Maryland State Society number) maintained by the University of Baltimore (Langsdale Library)

T = *Oaths of Allegiance in Somerset County in 1778* (Annapolis: Maryland State Archives, MSA No. S990, Blue Book No. 5)

U = *National Genealogical Society Quarterly* (as cited)

V = *DAR Patriot Index, Centennial Edition* (Washington, D. C.: Daughters of the American Revolution, 1990), 3 volumes

W = White, Virgil D. *Genealogical Abstracts of Revolutionary War Pension Files* (Waynesboro, Tennessee: The National Historical Publishing Company, 1990), 4 volumes

X = *Maryland Pension Rolls of 1835: Report from the Secretary of War in Relation to the Pension Establishment of the United States* (Baltimore: Genealogical Publishing Company, 1968, reprint)

Y = Wright, F. Edward. *Maryland Eastern Shore Vital Records, 1751-1775* (Westminster, Maryland: Family Line Publications, 1984)

Z = *Recruits from Worcester County on April 8, 1780 as reported by James Martin* (Annapolis: Maryland State Archives, Accession No. 4594-40)

It must be noted that it is not possible to know who all of the patriots were who served in or from Worcester and Somerset Counties during the entire Revolutionary War period. This is especially true for those who joined the Maryland Line and served in the Continental Army. Due to the constant reorganization of the Maryland troops during the war, it is not easily determinable which soldier served from which county. It appears, however, that many of them served in the 3rd and 5th Maryland Continental Lines.

It is likely that several entries herein may or may not pertain to the same person, so they have been listed separately. When obvious to this compiler, information has been consolidated and attributed to one person. However, in many cases, this was not possible. Therefore, whenever the name appears more than once, additional research may be necessary before drawing conclusions.

Since Worcester and Somerset Counties were "sandwiched in" between Sussex County, Delaware (to the north) and Accomack County, Virginia (to the south), one should also consult my *Revolutionary Patriots of Delaware, 1775-1783* and, Stratton Nottingham's *Soldiers and Sailors of the Eastern Shore of Virginia in the Revolutionary War*, and Pauline Manning Batchelder's *A Somerset Sampler: Families of Old Somerset County, Maryland, 1700-1776*, for more information on soldiers and their families from this part of Maryland's Eastern Shore and the Lower Delmarva.

Further, as may be the case in works such as this, it is possible that some patriots and soldiers may have inadvertently been omitted. Therefore, one should see *Archives of Maryland, Volume 18*, "Muster Rolls of Maryland Troops During the American Revolution, 1775-1783" for perhaps other soldiers who served from Worcester and Somerset Counties in the Maryland Continental Line.

I would like to express my sincere appreciation to Mary E. Herbert, Jennifer Bryan, and Sarah Schmidt of the Manuscripts Division at the Maryland Historical Society, and Constance R. Neale, Assistant Director of State and Local Records at the Maryland State Archives, for their assistance during this compilation.

Henry C. Peden, Jr.
Bel Air, Maryland
January 27, 1999

REVOLUTIONARY PATRIOTS OF
WORCESTER AND SOMERSET COUNTIES
MARYLAND, 1775-1783

ABBOTT (ABBET), George. Private, Somerset Militia, Princess Anne Bn., Capt. Thomas Irving's Monie Co., 1780 [Ref: M-219]. Took the Oath of Allegiance in Somerset County in 1778 before the Hon. Levin Wilson [Ref: T-17, N-50].
ABBOTT (ABBET), John. Private, Somerset Militia, Princess Anne Bn., Capt. Thomas Irving's Monie Co., 1780 [Ref: M-219].
ABBOTT (ABBET), John Jr. Drafted from Somerset County on July 30, 1781 to serve in the Continental Army [Ref: D-406, L-35C].
ABBOTT (ABBET), Levin. Private, Maryland Line, whose name appeared on "a list of recruits from and deserters taken up in Somerset County on Oct 20, 1780" [Ref: D-346].
ABBOTT (ABBET), Loyd. Private, Somerset Militia, Princess Anne Bn., Capt. Thomas Irving's Monie Co., 1780 [Ref: M-219]. Took the Oath of Allegiance in Somerset County in 1778 before the Hon. Levin Wilson [Ref: N-50, and T-17 listed the name as "Loyed Abbett"].
ABBOTT (ABBET), William. Took the Oath of Allegiance in Somerset County in 1778 before the Hon. Levin Wilson [Ref: T-17].
ACKWORTH, Ephraim (1759 -   ). Son of Samuel Acworth *[sic]*, born in Stepney Parish on Oct 17, 1759 [Ref: Y-51]. Corporal, Somerset Militia, Salisbury Bn., Capt. William Turpin's Rewastico Co., 1778/1780 [Ref: M-217].
ACKWORTH, Henry. Sergeant, Somerset Militia, Salisbury Bn., Capt. William Turpin's Rewastico Co., 1778/1780 [Ref: M-217]. Took the Oath of Allegiance in Somerset County in 1778 before the Hon. William Winder [Ref: T-22, and N-50 mistakenly listed the name as Henry Ashworth"].
ACKWORTH, John. Private, Somerset Militia, Salisbury Bn., Capt. William Turpin's Rewastico Co., 1778/1780 [Ref: M-217].
ACKWORTH, Mary. See "James Phillips," q.v.
ACKWORTH, Mattilda. See "Angelo Huffington," q.v.
ACKWORTH, Richard. Corporal, Somerset Militia, Salisbury Bn., Capt. Henry Gale's Quantico Co., 1778/1780 [Ref: M-216].
ACKWORTH, Richard Jr. Took the Oath of Allegiance in Somerset County in 1778 before the Hon. William Winder [Ref: T-22 mistakenly listed the name as "Richard Ashworth, Jr."].
ACKWORTH, Samuel. See "Ephraim Ackworth," q.v.
ACKWORTH, Train. Took the Oath of Allegiance in Somerset County in 1778 before the Hon. William Winder [Ref: T-22 listed the name as "Traine Ackworth" and N-50 mistakenly listed the name as "Levin Ashworth"]. Private, Somerset Militia, Salisbury Bn., Capt. Joseph Venables' Barren Creek Co., 1778/1780 [Ref: M-217]. Drafted from Somerset County into the Continental Army on June 20, 1781, but was subsequently excused [Ref: L-35C].

ACKWORTH, William. Took the Oath of Allegiance in Somerset County on Feb 16, 1778 before the Hon. Joseph Venables [Ref: T-25 listed the name as "Wm. Acworth"].

ADAMS, Alexander. Ensign, Somerset Militia, Princess Anne Bn., Capt. John Jones' Princess Anne Co., Sep 9, 1777 to at least July 24, 1780 [Ref: M-47, M-219, C-381]. Took the Oath of Allegiance in Somerset County in 1778 before the Hon. Peter Waters [Ref: T-18]. See "Peter Collins" and "William Horsey," q.v.

ADAMS, Andrew. Private, Somerset Militia, Salisbury Bn., White Haven Co., 1778/1780 [Ref: M-219]. Took the Oath of Allegiance in Somerset County in 1778 before the Hon. Levin Wilson [Ref: T-17, N-50].

ADAMS, Anne. See "Jacob Adams," q.v.

ADAMS, David. Private, Worcester Militia, Wicomico Bn., Capt. Benjamin Dennis' Co., Eighth Class, July 15, 1780 [Ref: M-256].

ADAMS, Eli. Private, Worcester Militia, Snow Hill Bn., Capt. Samuel Smyley's Co., 1777 [Ref: M-250]. Private, Worcester Militia, Wicomico Bn., Capt. Samuel Smyley's Co., Eighth Class, July 15, 1780 [Ref: M-259].

ADAMS, Elie. Private, Worcester Militia, Wicomico Bn., Capt. Benjamin Dennis' Co., Sixth Class, July 15, 1780 [Ref: M-256].

ADAMS, George. Private, Somerset Militia, Princess Anne Bn., Capt. George Waters' Pocomoke Co., 1780 [Ref: M-220]. Drafted from Somerset County on July 30, 1781 to serve in the Continental Army [Ref: L-35C].

ADAMS (ADDAMS), Hope (1755 -   ). Son of William and Tabitha Addams, born in Coventry Parish on April 7, 1755 [Ref: Y-77]. Sergeant, Somerset Militia, Princess Anne Bn., St. Asaph's Co., 1780 [Ref: M-220].

ADAMS (ADDAMS), Isaac (1757 -   ). Son of William and Tabitha Addams, born in Coventry Parish on Dec 30, 1757 [Ref: Y-77]. Private, Somerset Militia, Princess Anne Bn., St. Asaph's Co., 1780 [Ref: M-221].

ADAMS (ADDAMS), Jacob (1757 -   ). Son of Jacob and Anne Addams, born in Coventry Parish on Dec 1, 1757 [Ref: Y-77]. Private, Somerset Militia, Princess Anne Bn., Capt. George Waters' Pocomoke Co., 1780 [Ref: M-220].

ADAMS, James. Private, Somerset Militia, Salisbury Bn., Capt. Josiah Dashiell's Wicomico Creek Co., 1778/1780 [Ref: M-218].

ADAMS, John. Attended the Maryland Convention in 1776, a delegate from Somerset County [Ref: O-28]. Justice of the Orphans Court, commissioned on June 4, 1777 [Ref: C-274]. Judge of the Court of Appeals for Somerset County, commissioned on May 23, 1778 [Ref: E-109]. "Dr. John Adams" rendered patriotic service by supplying pork in Somerset County for the use of the military on June 4, 1781 [Ref: P-402].

ADAMS, John. Private, Somerset Militia, Salisbury Bn., White Haven Co., 1778/1780 [Ref: M-218].

ADAMS, John (1763-1835). Applied for a pension (R83) in Ross County, Ohio on Oct 16, 1833, age 70, stating he was born in Somerset County, Maryland on

March 5, 1763 and served aboard a privateer during the war. John married Sophia Smith in 1805 and died on May 19, 1835. Sophia died in Fayette County, Ohio on Nov 9, 1847. In 1852 the surviving children were Josiah Adams, Celia Moomaw, and Elizabeth Kerr [Ref: W-12].

ADAMS, Josiah. See "John Adams," q.v.

ADAMS, Levi. Private, Somerset Militia, Princess Anne Bn., Capt. John Williams' Watkins Point Co., 1780 [Ref: M-222].

ADAMS (ADDAMS), Philip. Took the Oath of Allegiance in Worcester County in 1778 before the Hon. James Selby [Ref: J-1814 (Box 4) listed the name as "Phillop Addoms"].

ADAMS, Philip (Phill). Private, Somerset Militia, Princess Anne Bn., Capt. George Waters' Pocomoke Co., 1780 [Ref: M-220]. See "Thomas Adams," q.v.

ADAMS, Philip (of Hope). Private, Somerset Militia, Princess Anne Bn., Capt. George Waters' Pocomoke Co., 1780 [Ref: M-220].

ADAMS (ADDAMS), Philip Collins. Private, Somerset Militia, Princess Anne Bn., Capt. George Waters' Pocomoke Co., 1780 [Ref: M-220 listed the name as "Phill Collens Adams"]. Took the Oath of Allegiance in Somerset County in 1778 before the Hon. Levin Wilson [Ref: N-50, and T-17 listed the name as "Phillip Collins Addams"].

ADAMS, Rachel. See "Thomas Adams," q.v.

ADAMS, Rhoda. See "Fountain Beauchamp," q.v.

ADAMS (ADDAMS), Samuel. Private, Somerset Militia, Salisbury Bn., White Haven Co., 1778/1780 [Ref: M-218]. Private, Somerset Militia, Princess Anne Bn., Capt. George Waters' Pocomoke Co., 1780 [Ref: M-220]. Took the Oath of Allegiance in Somerset County in 1778 before the Hon. John Williams [Ref: N-50, T-21 listed the name as "Samuel Addams"].

ADAMS, Stephen. Took the Oath of Allegiance in Somerset County on Feb 28, 1778 before the Hon. Joseph Venables [Ref: T-25].

ADAMS (ADDAMS), Tabitha (Tabytha). See "William Adams" and "Hope Adams" and "William Adams, Jr." and "Isaac Adams," q.v.

ADAMS, Thomas. Private, Somerset County, Capt. John Gunby's 2nd Independent Maryland Co.; present on May 1, 1776; "deserted" on June 24, 1776; mustered on Aug 21, 1776 [Ref: D-641].

ADAMS (ADDAMS), Thomas (1761 -   ). Son of Phillip and Rachel Addams, born in Coventry Parish on Nov 8, 1761 [Ref: Y-77]. Private, Somerset Militia, Princess Anne Bn., Capt. George Waters' Pocomoke Co., 1780 [Ref: M-220].

ADAMS, William. Private, Somerset Militia, Princess Anne Bn., Capt. George Waters' Pocomoke Co., 1780 [Ref: M-220]. Took the Oath of Allegiance in Somerset County in 1778 before the Hon. Peter Waters [Ref: T-18].

ADAMS, William (c1735-1795). Attended the Maryland Convention in 1775-1776, one of the delegates from Somerset County. Served in the Lower House of the Maryland Legislature, 1762-1770, 1785-1788. William married first to Leah Hath (d. 1760), second to Ann ---- (possibly Sarah Ann Taylor on March

23, 1761), and died in 1795, leaving no surviving children [Ref: O-28, R-99, Y-77, Y-78].

ADAMS (ADDAMS), William (c1723-c1783). Private, Somerset Militia, Princess Anne Bn., St. Asaph's Co., 1780 [Ref: M-221]. Took the Oath of Allegiance in Somerset County in 1778 before the Hon. Levin Wilson [Ref: T-17]. William Adams was born circa 1723 in Maryland, married Tabytha Addams *[sic]*, served as a private during the war, and died after 1783 in Maryland [Ref: V-20].

ADAMS, William Jr. (1752 -   ). Son of William and Tabitha Adams [Tabytha Addams], born in Coventry Parish on Aug 3, 1752 [Ref: Y-77]. Private, Somerset Militia, Salisbury Bn., White Haven Co., 1778/1780 [Ref: M-219]. See "Hope Adams" and "Isaac Adams," q.v.

ADDISON, Thomas Grafton. See "William Mills," q.v.

ADEAR (ODEAR?), Elisha. Private, Worcester Militia, Wicomico Bn., Capt. Samuel Horsey's Co., Seventh Class, July 15, 1780 [Ref: M-257].

ADKINS, Barzlea. See "Henry Dennis," q.v.

ADKINS, John. Private, Worcester Militia, Wicomico Bn., Capt. John Davis' Co., Second Class, July 15, 1780 [Ref: M-254].

ADKINS, Middleton. Private, Worcester Militia, Wicomico Bn., Capt. John Davis' Co., Eighth Class, July 15, 1780 [Ref: M-255].

ADKINS, Milly. See "Henry Dennis," q.v.

ADKINSON, Benjamin. Rendered patriotic service by supplying bacon in Somerset County for the use of the military on June 10, 1781 [Ref: P-403].

ADKINSON, George. Private, Worcester Militia, Wicomico Bn., Capt. Benjamin Dennis' Co., Second Class, July 15, 1780 [Ref: M-255].

AIKMAN, Thomas. Took the Oath of Allegiance in Somerset County in 1778 before the Hon. Levin Wilson [Ref: T-17, N-50].

AIRES, George. See "George Ayres," q.v.

AIREY, Elizabeth. See "John Gale," q.v.

AIREY, Kelloton. Took the Oath of Allegiance in Somerset County in 1778 [Ref: N-50].

AKE, William. Private, Worcester Militia, Sinepuxent Bn., Capt. John Coe's Co., Third Class, 1779/1780 [Ref: M-252].

ALEXANDER (ALLEXANDER), John. Private, Worcester Militia, Wicomico Bn., Capt. Philip Quinton's Co., Fifth Class, July 15, 1780 [Ref: M-256]. Private, Worcester Militia, Capt. John Martin's Co., 1780/1781 [Ref: J-1814 (Box 12)].

ALEXANDER (ALLEXANDER), Mark. Took the Oath of Allegiance in Worcester County in 1778 before the Hon. Joshua Townsend [Ref: J-1814 (Box 4)].

ALIPHANT, Mathias. See "Mathias Oliphant," q.v.

ALLEN, Arthur. Private, 3rd Maryland Independent Co., Worcester County, Capt. John Watkins' Co., enlisted Feb 9, 1776; muster roll dated Aug 20, 1776, absent on furlough [Ref: D-22].

ALLEN, Gilbert. Private, 5th Maryland Line, enlisted March 10, 1777 and reported missing on Aug 16, 1780 after the Battle of Camden, South Carolina [Ref: D-182].

ALLEN, James. Private, 5th Maryland Line, enlisted July 8, 1777 and present as of Nov 1, 1780 [Ref: D-182].

ALLEN, John. Private, Worcester Militia, Wicomico Bn., Capt. Fisher Walton's Co., Eighth Class, July 15, 1780 [Ref: M-258].

ALLEN, John Jr. Took the Oath of Allegiance in Worcester County in 1778 before the Hon. Nehemiah Holland [Ref: J-1814 (Box 4)].

ALLEN, John Sr. Took the Oath of Allegiance in Worcester County in 1778 before the Hon. Nehemiah Holland [Ref: J-1814 (Box 4)].

ALLEN, Joseph. Private, Somerset Militia, Princess Anne Bn., Capt. James Elzey's Co., 1780 [Ref: M-220].

ALLEN, Lydia. See "Samuel Hitch," q.v.

ALLEN, Stephen. Private, 3rd Maryland Independent Co., Worcester County, Capt. John Watkins' Co., enlisted Feb 9, 1776; muster roll dated Aug 20, 1776, present for duty [Ref: D-22]. Sergeant, Worcester Militia, Wicomico Bn., Capt. Fisher Walton's Co., July 15, 1780 [Ref: M-258]. Took the Oath of Allegiance in Worcester County in 1778 before the Hon. Nehemiah Holland [Ref: J-1814 (Box 4)].

ALLEN, William. Private, Worcester Militia, Wicomico Bn., Capt. James Patterson's Co., Seventh Class, July 15, 1780 [Ref: M-258]. Ensign, Worcester Militia, Capt. John Martin's Co., 1780/1781 [Ref: J-1814 (Box 12)].

ALLEN, William. Private, Worcester Militia, Snow Hill Bn., Capt. Samuel Smyley's Co., 1777 [Ref: M-250].

ALLEN, William. Private, Worcester Militia, Snow Hill Bn., Capt. Samuel Smyley's Co., 1777 [Ref: M-250].

ALLEN, William (c1725-1792). Took the Oath of Allegiance in Worcester County in 1778 before the Hon. Nehemiah Holland [Ref: J-1814 (Box 4)]. Rendered patriotic service by supplying corn for the use of the military on Feb 20, 1780 and July 10, 1780, and by supplying beef on Oct 10, 1781 [Ref: P-271, P-446, G-9]. Served as Sheriff of Somerset County, 1755-1758, Justice of Worcester County, 1764-1775, and was "recorded as being delinquent when required for militia service in 1782." He married Patience Marshall and probably died without progeny in 1792 [Ref: R-106].

ALLEN, William (of Aaron). Private, Worcester Militia, Wicomico Bn., Capt. James Patterson's Co., Fifth Class, July 15, 1780 [Ref: M-258].

ALLEN, William Davis (1749-c1800). Private, Somerset Militia, Salisbury Bn., Capt. Josiah Dashiell's Wicomico Creek Co., 1778/1780 [Ref: M-218]. Select Militia, Somerset County, Aug 15, 1781 [Ref: L-35B]. Quartermaster, Somerset

County, September, 1781 to February, 1782 [Ref: P-431]. William Davis Allen was born on Aug 21, 1749, married Mary Jane (Polk) Whittington Strawbridge, served as a private during the war, and died before 1800 [Ref: V-46].

ALLISON, Richard. Took the Oath of Allegiance in Worcester County in 1778 before the Hon. William Hopewell [Ref: J-1814 (Box 4) listed the name as "Richard Ollison"].

ALLISON, William. Private, Worcester Militia, Sinepuxent Bn., Capt. John Coe's Co., Sixth Class, 1779/1780 [Ref: M-252].

ALPHE(?), Joshua. Private, Somerset Militia, Salisbury Bn., Capt. William Turpin's Rewastico Co., 1778/1780 [Ref: M-217].

ALPHE(?), William. Private, Somerset Militia, Salisbury Bn., Capt. William Turpin's Rewastico Co., 1778/1780 [Ref: M-217].

AMOSS, Abel. Private, Maryland Line, whose name appeared on "a list of recruits from and deserters taken up in Somerset County on Oct 20, 1780" and noted as "deserter, not joined '82" [Ref: D-346].

ANDERSON, George (1755 -   ). Son of John and Sarah Anderson, born in Stepney Parish on June 20, 1755 [Ref: Y-44]. Private, Somerset Militia, Salisbury Bn., Capt. William Turpin's Rewastico Co., 1778/1780 [Ref: M-217].

ANDERSON, Ignatius (Ignasius). Private, Worcester Militia, Snow Hill Bn., Capt. Ebenezer Handy's Co., April 9, 1776 [Ref: M-249]. Private, Worcester Militia, Wicomico Bn., Capt. James Perdue's Co., Seventh Class, July 15, 1780 [Ref: M-256].

ANDERSON, James. Corporal, Somerset Militia, Salisbury Bn., Capt. Josiah Dashiell's Wicomico Creek Co., 1778/1780 [Ref: M-218].

ANDERSON, James. Private, Somerset Militia, Salisbury Bn., Capt. James Bennett's Salisbury Co., 1778/1780 [Ref: M-218].

ANDERSON, James. Private, Somerset Militia, Salisbury Bn., Capt. William Turpin's Rewastico Co., 1778/1780 [Ref: M-217].

ANDERSON, James. Private, Select Militia, Somerset County, Aug 15, 1781 [Ref: L-35B].

ANDERSON, John (1752 -   ). Son of John and Sarah Anderson, born in Stepney Parish on Feb 14, 1752 [Ref: Y-44]. Private, Somerset Militia, Salisbury Bn., Capt. William Turpin's Rewastico Co., 1778/1780 [Ref: M-217]. See "George Anderson," q.v.

ANDERSON, Joseph. Private, Somerset Militia, Salisbury Bn., Capt. James Bennett's Salisbury Co., 1778/1780 [Ref: M-218].

ANDERSON, Levin. Private, Worcester Militia, Wicomico Bn., Capt. James Patterson's Co., Fifth Class, July 15, 1780 [Ref: M-258].

ANDERSON, Nathan. Private, Worcester Militia, Wicomico Bn., Capt. Charles Bennett's Co., Second Class, July 15, 1780 [Ref: M-255]. Took the Oath of Allegiance in Worcester County in 1778 before the Hon. John Selby [Ref: J-1814 (Box 4)].

ANDERSON, Robert. Private, Somerset Militia, Salisbury Bn., Capt. Levin Irving's Black Water Co., 1778/1780 [Ref: M-217].

ANDERSON, Sarah. See "John Anderson" and "George Anderson," q.v.

ANNIS, Micajah (1752-1828). Private, Virginia Line, who applied for pension (S34627) in Worcester County on Jan 2, 1819, age 67, and received $96 per annum. He was born in Accomack County, Virginia, married (wife's name not stated; living in 1820), and died on Dec 6, 1828 in Worcester County, Maryland [Ref: X-44, W-68].

ARBUCKLE, Euphame. See "William Purnell (of Eufa)," q.v.

ARDIS, Jacob. Private, 3rd Maryland Independent Co., Worcester County, Capt. John Watkins' Co., enlisted Feb 3, 1776; muster roll dated Aug 20, 1776, present for duty [Ref: D-22 listed the name as "Jacob Ardes"].

ARDIS, Stephen. Took the Oath of Allegiance in Worcester County in 1778 before the Hon. Nehemiah Holland [Ref: J-1814 (Box 4)].

ARDIS, Zadok. Took the Oath of Allegiance in Worcester County in 1778 before the Hon. Nehemiah Holland [Ref: J-1814 (Box 4)].

ARMSTRONG, Jesse. Private, Worcester Militia, Wicomico Bn., Capt. Samuel Smyley's Co., Fourth Class, July 15, 1780 [Ref: M-259]. Took the Oath of Allegiance in Worcester County in 1778 before the Hon. Joshua Townsend [Ref: J-1814 (Box 4)].

ARNOLD, General. See "Thomas Seon," q.v.

ASKELLEY, John. Private, Somerset Militia, Salisbury Bn., Capt. Henry Gale's Quantico Co., 1778/1780 [Ref: M-216].

ATKINS, Nimrod. Private, Worcester Militia, Wicomico Bn., Capt. John Davis' Co., Eighth Class, July 15, 1780 [Ref: M-255 listed the name as "Nimrond Atkins"].

ATKINS, Stanten. Private, Worcester Militia, Wicomico Bn., Capt. John Davis' Co., Fourth Class, July 15, 1780 [Ref: M-254].

ATKINS, Stephen. Private, Worcester Militia, Wicomico Bn., Capt. John Davis' Co., Seventh Class, July 15, 1780 [Ref: M-255].

ATKINS, William. Private, Worcester Militia, Wicomico Bn., Capt. John Davis' Co., Sixth Class, July 15, 1780 [Ref: M-254].

ATKINSON, Angelo. Ensign, Worcester Militia, Capt. Benjamin Dennis' Co., June 21, 1776 [Ref: M-49, A-506]. Took the Oath of Allegiance in Worcester County in 1778 before the Hon. John Selby [Ref: J-1814 (Box 4) listed the name as "Angelle Atkinson"]. Private(?), Worcester Militia, Wicomico Bn., Capt. Charles Bennett's Co., Eighth Class, July 15, 1780 [Ref: M-255]. See "William Atkinson Selby," q.v.

ATKINSON, Charles. See "James Atkinson," q.v.

ATKINSON, Elizabeth. Rendered patriotic service by supplying bacon for the use of the military in Somerset County on Aug 14, 1780 [Ref: P-309]. See "James Atkinson," q.v.

ATKINSON, Harriet. See "James Atkinson," q.v.

ATKINSON, Henry. Private, Worcester Militia, Wicomico Bn., Capt. Charles Bennett's Co., Second Class, July 15, 1780 [Ref: M-255].

ATKINSON, James (1761 -   ). Son of James and Mary Atkinson, born in Coventry Parish, Somerset County, on March 4, 1761 and married Phila Wharton on Nov 8, 1785. Their children were: Sarah (b. Nov 3, 1786); Mary (b. Dec 5, 1790); Harriet (b. March 1, 1791); Thomas (b. May 29, 1793); Elizabeth (b. June 4, 1797, married Thomas D. Holland); Charles (b. Dec 30, 1800); Wheatley (b. March 9, 1802); Phila (b. Oct --, 1803?); Jane (b. April 27, 1805); James (b. May 20, 1810); and, Louisa (no date given). [Ref: Y-69, and Atkinson Family Bible in Raymond B. Clark, Jr.'s *Maryland and Delaware Bible Records* (1990), p. 38]. Private, Somerset Militia, Princess Anne Bn., Capt. George Waters' Pocomoke Co., 1780 [Ref: M-220]. Private, Worcester Militia, Capt. John Martin's Co., 1780/1781 [Ref: J-1814 (Box 12)]. Took the Oath of Allegiance in Worcester County in 1778 before the Hon. Joshua Townsend [Ref: J-1814 (Box 4)].

ATKINSON, Jane. See "James Atkinson," q.v.

ATKINSON, John. Took the Oath of Allegiance in Worcester County in 1778 before the Hon. Joshua Townsend [Ref: J-1814 (Box 4)].

ATKINSON, Joshua. Private, Somerset Militia, Salisbury Bn., Capt. John Span Conway's Nanticoke Point Co., 1778/1780 [Ref: M-216].

ATKINSON, Louisa. See "James Atkinson," q.v.

ATKINSON, Mary. See "William A. Selby" and "James Atkinson," q.v.

ATKINSON, Phila. See "James Atkinson," q.v.

ATKINSON, Samuel. Quartermaster, Worcester Militia, Capt. John Martin's Co., 1780/1781 [Ref: J-1814 (Box 12)].

ATKINSON, Sarah. See "Thomas Barnes, Jr." and "Outten Sturgis, Sr." and "James Atkinson," q.v.

ATKINSON, Thomas. Ensign, Worcester Militia, Capt. Philip Quinton's Co., July 6, 1776 to June 28, 1777, discharged [Ref: M-49, A-553]. Took the Oath of Allegiance in Worcester County in 1778 before the Hon. John Selby [Ref: J-1814 (Box 4)].

ATKINSON, Thomas. Private, Worcester Militia, Wicomico Bn., Capt. Charles Bennett's Co., Third Class, July 15, 1780 [Ref: M-255]. See "James Atkinson," q.v.

ATKINSON, Wheatley. See "James Atkinson," q.v.

ATKINSON, William. Private, Worcester Militia, Wicomico Bn., Capt. Philip Quinton's Co., Fourth Class, July 15, 1780 [Ref: M-256]. Took the Oath of Allegiance in Worcester County in 1778 before the Hon. John Selby [Ref: J-1814 (Box 4)]. Private, Worcester Militia, Capt. John Martin's Co., 1780/1781 [Ref: J-1814 (Box 12)].

AUSTIN, Elijah. Private, Somerset Militia, Salisbury Bn., Capt. James Bennett's Salisbury Co., 1778/1780 [Ref: M-218].

AUSTIN, George (c1745-1807). Private, Somerset Militia, Princess Anne Bn., Capt. Thomas Irving's Monie Co., 1780 [Ref: M-219].
AUSTIN, Hamilton. Private, Somerset Militia, Salisbury Bn., Capt. James Bennett's Salisbury Co., 1778/1780 [Ref: M-218]. Took the Oath of Allegiance in Somerset County on Feb 21, 1778 (made his "X" mark) before the Hon. Joseph Venables [Ref: T-25 listed the name as "Hammelton Austin"].
AUSTIN, Harris. On July 30, 1781, William Hearn recruited Harris Austin from Somerset County to serve in the Continental Army [Ref: L-35C].
AUSTIN, John. Private, Somerset Militia, Salisbury Bn., Capt. James Bennett's Salisbury Co., 1778/1780 [Ref: M-218]. Took the Oath of Allegiance in Somerset County on Feb 21, 1778 before the Hon. Joseph Venables [Ref: T-25].
AUSTIN, Joseph. Private, Somerset Militia, Princess Anne Bn., Capt. Thomas Irving's Monie Co., 1780 [Ref: M-219]. Took the Oath of Allegiance in Somerset County in 1778 before the Hon. Peter Waters [Ref: T-18 listed the name as "Joseph Austen"].
AUSTIN, Mathias. Corporal, Worcester Militia, Snow Hill Bn., Capt. Ebenezer Handy's Co., April 9, 1776 [Ref: M-249 listed the name as "Mathias -?-tin"]. Worcester Militia, Wicomico Bn., Capt. Elijah Shockley's Co., Sixth Class, July 15, 1780 [Ref: M-255]. Took the Oath of Allegiance in Worcester County on Feb 25, 1778 before the Hon. Ebenezer Handy [Ref: J-1814 (Box 4) listed the name as "Matthias Auston"].
AUSTIN, Robert (1708-c1780). Took the Oath of Allegiance in Somerset County in 1778 before the Hon. Levin Wilson [Ref: N-50, T-17 listed the name as "Robert Austen"].
AVERY, Charles. Private, Somerset Militia, Princess Anne Bn., Capt. Isaac Handy's Great Annemessix Co., 1780 [Ref: M-221].
AYDELOTT (AYDOLETT), Benjamin Jr. (c1750-1826). Took the Oath of Allegiance in Worcester County in 1778 before the Hon. Nehemiah Holland [Ref: J-1814 (Box 4)]. Private, Worcester Militia, Snow Hill Bn., Capt. Samuel Smyley's Co., 1777 [Ref: M-250 listed the name without the "Jr."]. "Benjamin Aydelatt" married Martha Sturgis, daughter of Outten Sturgis, and died in 1826 [Ref: R-793].
AYDELOTT (AYDOLETT), Benjamin Sr. Took the Oath of Allegiance in Worcester County in 1778 before the Hon. Nehemiah Holland [Ref: J-1814 (Box 4)]. Rendered patriotic service by providing lodging and provisions for the military on Sep 20, 1781 [Ref: P-439].
AYDELOTT (AYDOLETT), George Howard (1748-1803). Private, Worcester Militia, Sinepuxent Bn., Capt. Josiah Dale's Co., Eighth Class, 1779/1780 [Ref: M-254 listed the name as "Geo: Hayward Aydolett"]. Rendered patriotic service by supplying corn for the use of the military in Worcester County on July 10, 1780 [Ref: G-10 listed the name as "George Howard Aydolett"]. "Howard Aydelott" rendered patriotic service by supplying corn in Worcester

County for the use of the military on June 19, 1780 [Ref: P-296]. "George Howard Aydelotte" was born in Delaware on March 21, 1748, married Mrs. Christian Brittingham Hill, served in the Maryland militia, and died in Kentucky on Sep 19, 1803 [Ref: V-102].

AYDELOTT (AYDOLETT), James. Private, Worcester Militia, Wicomico Bn., Capt. Fisher Walton's Co., Sixth Class, July 15, 1780 [Ref: M-258 listed the name as "James Aydelot"]. Took the Oath of Allegiance in Worcester County in 1778 before the Hon. Nehemiah Holland [Ref: J-1814 (Box 4)].

AYDELOTT (AYDOLETT), John (1715-c1790). Private, Worcester Militia, Sinepuxent Bn., Capt. John Coe's Co., Fifth Class, 1779/1780 [Ref: M-252 listed the name as "John Aydolitt"].

AYDELOTT (AYDOLETT), Obed. Private, Worcester Militia, Sinepuxent Bn., Capt. John Coe's Co., Seventh Class, 1779/1780 [Ref: M-252].

AYDELOTT (AYDOLETT), William. Sergeant, Worcester Militia, Wicomico Bn., Capt. Fisher Walton's Co., July 15, 1780 [Ref: M-258 listed the name as "William Aydelott"]. Took the Oath of Allegiance in Worcester County in 1778 before the Hon. Nehemiah Holland [Ref: J-1814 (Box 4)]. Rendered patriotic service by supplying corn for the use of the military on March 27, 1780 and July 10, 1780 [Ref: G-10, and P-279 listed the name as "William Ayldet"].

AYDELOTT (AYDOLETT), William Jr. Took the Oath of Allegiance in Worcester County in 1778 before the Hon. Nehemiah Holland [Ref: J-1814 (Box 4)].

AYRES, George. Private, Somerset Militia, Capt. George Day Scott's Co., 1775 [Ref: J-1814 (Box 1)]. Took the Oath of Allegiance in Somerset County in 1778 before the Hon. John Span Conway [Ref: N-50, T-14 listed the name as "George Aires"].

AYRES, Henry. First Lieutenant, Worcester Militia, Snow Hill Bn., Capt. John Parramore's Co., Aug 30, 1777 [Ref: M-49, M-250, C-351]. Took the Oath of Allegiance in Worcester County in 1778 before the Hon. John Selby [Ref: J-1814 (Box 4)]. First Lieutenant, Worcester Militia, Wicomico Bn., Capt. John Parramore's Co., July 15, 1780 [Ref: M-259]. Rendered patriotic service by supplying beef for the use of the military on Oct 5, 1781 [Ref: P-444].

AYRES, Henry. Private, Maryland Troops, Worcester County, draughted May 1, 1781 [Ref: K-99, D-372 listed the name as "Henry Ayrs"].

AYRES, Isaac (1754 -   ). Private, Worcester Militia, Sinepuxent Bn., Capt. John Rackliff's Co., Seventh Class, 1779/1780 [Ref: M-251]. Took the Oath of Allegiance in Worcester County in 1778 before the Hon. John Selby [Ref: J-1814 (Box 4)]. Rendered patriotic service by supplying salt for the use of the military on Jan 9, 1781 [Ref: P-353 listed the name as "Isaac Ayers"]. Born in Worcester Parish on Aug 20, 1754 [Ref: Y-29].

AYRES, James. Private, 3rd Maryland Independent Co., Worcester County, Capt. John Watkins' Co., enlisted Feb 28, 1776; muster roll dated Aug 20, 1776, sick in the country [Ref: D-22].

AYRES, John. Ensign, Worcester Militia, Snow Hill Bn., Capt. Samuel Smyley's Co., Aug 30, 1777 [Ref: M-49, M-250, C-351]. Took the Oath of Allegiance in Worcester County in 1778 before the Hon. Nehemiah Holland [Ref: J-1814 (Box 4)]. Ensign, Worcester Militia, Wicomico Bn., Capt. Samuel Smyley's Co., July 15, 1780 [Ref: M-259]. Rendered patriotic service by supplying beef for the use of the military on Sep 20, 1781 [Ref: P-439].

AYRES, Littleton. Private, Somerset Militia, Capt. George Day Scott's Co., 1775 [Ref: J-1814 (Box 1)]. Took the Oath of Allegiance in Somerset County in 1778 before the Hon. John Span Conway [Ref: T-14 listed the name as "Littleton Aires"].

AYRES, Richard. Private, 3rd Maryland Independent Co., Worcester County, Capt. John Watkins' Co., enlisted Feb 10, 1776; muster roll dated Aug 20, 1776, present for duty [Ref: D-21]. Took the Oath of Allegiance in Worcester County in 1778 before the Hon. Nehemiah Holland [Ref: J-1814 (Box 4)].

BA-?-US, Phillip. Private, Somerset Militia, Princess Anne Bn., Capt. James Elzey's Co., 1780 [Ref: M-220].

BACON, William (Worcester County). After being discharged from confinement he appeared before the Council of Maryland on July 1, 1777 and voluntarily took the Oath of Allegiance to the State [Ref: C-303].

BADLEY, Charles. Private, Somerset Militia, Salisbury Bn., Capt. Joseph Venables' Barren Creek Co., 1778/1780 [Ref: M-217]. Drafted from Somerset County on July 30, 1781 to serve in the Continental Army, but was subsequently excused [Ref: L-35C].

BADLEY, James. Private, Somerset Militia, Salisbury Bn., Capt. Joseph Venables' Barren Creek Co., 1778/1780 [Ref: M-217].

BAILEY (BAILY), Benjamin. Took the Oath of Allegiance in Somerset County on Feb 28, 1778 before the Hon. Joseph Venables [Ref: T-25].

BAILEY (BAILY), George. Took the Oath of Allegiance in Somerset County on Feb 28, 1778 before the Hon. Joseph Venables [Ref: T-25].

BAILEY (BAILY), George Sr. Private, Somerset Militia, Salisbury Bn., Capt. Josiah Dashiell's Wicomico Creek Co., 1778/1780 [Ref: M-218].

BAILEY (BAILY), Mills. Private, Somerset Militia, Salisbury Bn., Capt. Josiah Dashiell's Wicomico Creek Co., 1778/1780 [Ref: M-218 listed the name as "Mills Bayley"].

BAILEY (BAILY), Mills. See "George Finch," q.v.

BAILEY (BAILY), Robert. Took the Oath of Allegiance in Somerset County in 1778 before the Hon. John Williams [Ref: T-21, N-50].

BAKER, --?--. Private, Worcester Militia, Sinepuxent Bn., Capt. Josiah Dale's Co., First Class, 1779/1780 [Ref: M-253].

BAKER, Archibald. Private, Worcester Militia, Sinepuxent Bn., Capt. Josiah Dale's Co., Fourth Class, 1779/1780 [Ref: M-254].

BAKER, Benjamin. Private, Somerset Militia, Salisbury Bn., Capt. William Turpin's Rewastico Co., 1778/1780 [Ref: M-217].

BAKER, Elisha. Private, 3rd Maryland Independent Co., Worcester County, Capt. John Watkins' Co., enlisted March 16, 1776; muster roll dated Aug 20, 1776, absent on furlough [Ref: D-23].

BAKER, George. Private, Worcester Militia, Sinepuxent Bn., Capt. Josiah Dale's Co., Fourth Class, 1779/1780 [Ref: M-254].

BAKER, Godfrey. Private, Worcester Militia, Sinepuxent Bn., Capt. John Coe's Co., Second Class, 1779/1780 [Ref: M-251].

BAKER, John. Private, Somerset Militia, Salisbury Bn., Capt. James Bennett's Salisbury Co., 1778/1780 [Ref: M-218].

BAKER, John. Private, Worcester Militia, Wicomico Bn., Capt. James Perdue's Co., First Class, July 15, 1780 [Ref: M-256].

BAKER, Levin. Private, Worcester Militia, Sinepuxent Bn., Capt. John Coe's Co., Second Class, 1779/1780 [Ref: M-251].

BAKER, Levin. Private, Worcester Militia, Sinepuxent Bn., Capt. Josiah Dale's Co., Seventh Class, 1779/1780 [Ref: M-254]. He may have been the "Leven Baker" who took the Oath of Allegiance in Worcester County in 1778 before the Hon. Joshua Townsend [Ref: J-1814 (Box 4)].

BAKER, Saul. Private, Worcester Militia, Wicomico Bn., Capt. James Perdue's Co., Seventh Class, July 15, 1780 [Ref: M-256].

BAKER, Salathiel (c1750-1822). Private, Worcester Militia, Sinepuxent Bn., Capt. Josiah Dale's Co., Eighth Class, 1779/1780 [Ref: M-254 listed the name as "Selathel Baker"]. "Salathiel Baker" was born in Maryland circa 1750, married Leah Evans, was a soldier in Maryland during the war, and died before May, 1822 [Ref: V-127].

BAKER, Zadok. Private, Worcester Militia, Sinepuxent Bn., Capt. Josiah Dale's Co., Eighth Class, 1779/1780 [Ref: M-254].

BALL, Hannah. See "William Ball," q.v.

BALL, Jacob. See "Jacob Bell," q.v.

BALL, John. Ensign, Worcester Militia, June 28, 1777 [Ref: M-50]. Took the Oath of Allegiance in Worcester County in 1778 before the Hon. John Selby [Ref: J-1814 (Box 4)].

BALL, John. Private, Worcester Militia, Snow Hill Bn., Capt. Samuel Smyley's Co., 1777 [Ref: M-250]. Private, Worcester Militia, Wicomico Bn., Capt. William Handy's Co., Second Class, July 15, 1780 [Ref: M-257].

BALL, Levi. Private, Worcester Militia, Wicomico Bn., Capt. James Patterson's Co., Second Class, July 15, 1780 [Ref: M-258]. Took the Oath of Allegiance in Worcester County in 1778 before the Hon. Nehemiah Holland [Ref: J-1814 (Box 4)].

BALL, Samuel. See "William Ball," q.v.

BALL, William (1756 -   ). Son of Samuel and Hannah Ball, born in Coventry Parish on Jan 17, 1756 [Ref: Y-79]. Private, Worcester Militia, Wicomico Bn., Capt. Philip Quinton's Co., Third Class, July 15, 1780 [Ref: M-256].

BALLARD, Alice. See "George Day Scott," q.v.

BALLARD, Arnold. Sergeant, Somerset Militia, Salisbury Bn., White Haven Co., 1778/1780 [Ref: M-218]. Took the Oath of Allegiance in Somerset County in 1778 before the Hon. Levin Wilson [Ref: T-17, N-50].
BALLARD, Benjamin. Private, Somerset Militia, Salisbury Bn., White Haven Co., 1778/1780 [Ref: M-219].
BALLARD, Daniel. Private, Worcester Militia, Wicomico Bn., Capt. Fisher Walton's Co., Third Class, July 15, 1780 [Ref: M-258].
BALLARD, Daniel (molato). Took the Oath of Allegiance in Worcester County in 1778 before the Hon. Nehemiah Holland [Ref: J-1814 (Box 4)].
BALLARD, George. Private, Somerset Militia, Salisbury Bn., Capt. John Span Conway's Nanticoke Point Co., 1778/1780 [Ref: M-216]. Took the Oath of Allegiance in Somerset County in 1778 before the Hon. John Span Conway [Ref: T-14, N-50].
BALLARD, Henry. Private, Worcester Militia, Wicomico Bn., Capt. Fisher Walton's Co., Second Class, July 15, 1780 [Ref: M-258].
BALLARD, Henry (molato). Took the Oath of Allegiance in Worcester County in 1778 before the Hon. Nehemiah Holland [Ref: J-1814 (Box 4)].
BALLARD, James. Private, Worcester Militia, Wicomico Bn., Capt. John Parramore's Co., Seventh Class, July 15, 1780 [Ref: M-259].
BALLARD, James. Private, Somerset Militia, Princess Anne Bn., Capt. John Jones' Princess Anne Co., 1780 [Ref: M-219].
BALLARD, James. Private, Somerset Militia, Princess Anne Bn., Capt. Thomas Irving's Monie Co., 1780 [Ref: M-219].
BALLARD, James (molato). Took the Oath of Allegiance in Worcester County in 1778 before the Hon. Nehemiah Holland [Ref: J-1814 (Box 4)].
BALLARD, Jane. See "Levin Pollitt," q.v.
BALLARD, Jarvis. Took the Oath of Allegiance in Somerset County in 1778 before the Hon. Peter Waters [Ref: T-18].
BALLARD, Levin. Private, Somerset Militia, Princess Anne Bn., Capt. John Jones' Princess Anne Co., 1780 [Ref: M-219].
BALLARD, Samuel. Private, Somerset Militia, Salisbury Bn., Capt. John Span Conway's Nanticoke Point Co., 1778/1780 [Ref: M-216].
BALLARD, William. Corporal, Somerset Militia, Princess Anne Bn., Capt. John Jones' Princess Anne Co., 1780 [Ref: M-219].
BALLARD, William. Private, Somerset Militia, Princess Anne Bn., Capt. Thomas Irving's Monie Co., 1780 [Ref: M-219].
BALLARD, William. Private, Worcester Militia, Wicomico Bn., Capt. Fisher Walton's Co., Fifth Class, July 15, 1780 [Ref: M-258].
BALLARD, William. Took the Oath of Allegiance in Somerset County in 1778 before the Hon. Peter Waters [Ref: T-18].
BALLARD, William (molato). Took the Oath of Allegiance in Worcester County in 1778 before the Hon. Nehemiah Holland [Ref: J-1814 (Box 4)].

BALLARD, William (of Arnold). Private, Somerset Militia, Princess Anne Bn., Capt. Thomas Irving's Monie Co., 1780 [Ref: M-219].

BANES, Dunkin. Took the Oath of Allegiance in Somerset County in 1778 before the Hon. William Winder [Ref: T-22, and N-50 listed the name as "Dunkin Bener"]. See "Duncan Brans," q.v.

BANISTER, Charles. Corporal, Somerset Militia, Princess Anne Bn., Capt. James Elzey's Co., 1780 [Ref: M-220]. Took the Oath of Allegiance in Somerset County in 1778 before the Hon. Levin Wilson [Ref: T-17, N-50]. Select Militia, Somerset County, Aug 15, 1781 [Ref: L-35A].

BANKS, Henry (c1758-1829). Private, Somerset Militia, Salisbury Bn., Capt. Josiah Dashiell's Wicomico Creek Co., 1778/1780 [Ref: M-218]. Took the Oath of Allegiance in Somerset County in 1778 before the Hon. William Winder [Ref: N-50, and T-22 listed the name as "Henrey Banks"]. Henry Banks was born circa 1758, married twice (second wife was Polly Messick), was a soldier during the war, and died before Sep 21, 1829 [Ref: V-143].

BANKS, Robert. Took the Oath of Allegiance in Somerset County on Feb 28, 1778 (made his "X" mark) before the Hon. Joseph Venables [Ref: T-25].

BANUM, William. Private, Worcester Militia, Sinepuxent Bn., Capt. John Postly's Co., First Class, 1779/1780 [Ref: M-251].

BARBER, James. Private, 3rd Maryland Independent Co., Worcester County, Capt. John Watkins' Co., enlisted March 11, 1776; muster roll dated Aug 20, 1776, present for duty [Ref: D-21].

BARKLEY, Henry. Private, Somerset Militia, Salisbury Bn., Capt. John Span Conway's Nanticoke Point Co., 1778/1780 [Ref: M-216].

BARKLEY, Isaac. Private, Somerset Militia, Salisbury Bn., Capt. John Span Conway's Nanticoke Point Co., 1778/1780 [Ref: M-216].

BARKLEY, Joseph. Private, Somerset Militia, Salisbury Bn., Capt. John Span Conway's Nanticoke Point Co., 1778/1780 [Ref: M-216].

BARNES, Amelia. See "Samuel Blades," q.v.

BARNES, Thomas Jr. (1759-1811). Son of Thomas and Rebecca Barnes (Barns), born in Coventry Parish on March 30, 1759, married (wife unknown), and died in April, 1811. His son Thomas (3rd) was born circa 1785, married Sarah Atkinson on May 28, 1807, and died in 1819 [Ref: S-3008, Y-80]. Private, Worcester Militia, Wicomico Bn., Capt. Philip Quinton's Co., Fourth Class, July 15, 1780 [Ref: M-256].

BARNICASTLE, Frederick. Private, Worcester Militia, Wicomico Bn., Capt. Elijah Shockley's Co., Seventh Class, July 15, 1780 [Ref: M-255].

BARRET, Joseph. Private, Somerset Militia, Princess Anne Bn., St. Asaph's Co., 1780 [Ref: M-220].

BARTLET, Abraham. Private, Somerset Militia, Salisbury Bn., Capt. John Span Conway's Nanticoke Point Co., 1778/1780 [Ref: M-216].

BASSETT, John. Private, Worcester Militia, Wicomico Bn., Capt. John Davis' Co., Second Class, July 15, 1780 [Ref: M-254]. Took the Oath of Allegiance in

Worcester County in 1778 before the Hon. Joshua Townsend [Ref: J-1814 (Box 4)].
BASSETT, William. Took the Oath of Allegiance in Worcester County in 1778 before the Hon. Joshua Townsend [Ref: J-1814 (Box 4)]. Private, Worcester Militia, Sinepuxent Bn., Capt. Matthew Purnell's Co., Eighth Class, July 25, 1780 [Ref: M-252 listed the name as "William Bassitt"].
BASSETT, William (of John). Took the Oath of Allegiance in Worcester County in 1778 before the Hon. Joshua Townsend [Ref: J-1814 (Box 4)].
BAYLEY (BAYLY), Benjamin. Corporal, Somerset Militia, Salisbury Bn., White Haven Co., 1778/1780 [Ref: M-218].
BAYLEY (BAYLY), Elias. Private, Somerset Militia, Salisbury Bn., White Haven Co., 1778/1780 [Ref: M-218].
BAYLEY (BAYLY), Esme (1740-1801). Major, Somerset Militia, Salisbury Bn., Aug 30, 1777 [Ref: M-51, C-381]. Took the Oath of Allegiance in Somerset County in 1778 before the Hon. Levin Wilson [Ref: T-17, N-50]. Esme Bayley was born on Dec 27, 1740, married Sinah ----, served as a major during the war, and died on Nov 10, 1801 [Ref: V-116].
BAYLEY (BAYLY), George. Private, Somerset Militia, Salisbury Bn., White Haven Co., 1778/1780 [Ref: M-218].
BAYLEY (BAYLY), Littleton. Private, Somerset Militia, Salisbury Bn., White Haven,Co., 1778/1780 [Ref: M-219 listed the name as "Lill. Bayly"].
BAYLEY (BAYLY), Miles. Took the Oath of Allegiance in Somerset County in 1778 before the Hon. William Winder [Ref: T-22, N-50].
BAYLEY (BAYLY), Robert. Second Lieutenant, Somerset Militia, Princess Anne Bn., St. Asaph's Co., 1780 [Ref: M-220].
BAYLEY (BAYLY), Sinah. See "Esme Bayley," q.v.
BAYLEY (BAYLY), Stephen. Private, Somerset Militia, Salisbury Bn., White Haven Co., 1778/1780 [Ref: M-218].
BEACH, Benjamin Peirce. Recruited by Capt. Levin Handy and enlisted in the Continental Army in Worcester County on Feb 4, 1780 for the duration of the war, stating he was born in America [Ref: Z-40]. "Benjamin Beach" was a private in the 5th Maryland Line who was listed as a recruit among others from Worcester County who were entitled to clothing from the Commissary of Stores on April 24, 1780 [Ref: F-150]. "Benjamin Beachbeach" was reported missing on Aug 16, 1780 after the Battle of Camden, South Carolina [Ref: D-186].
BEACHAM, Steven. See "Stephen Beauchamp," q.v.
BEACHBOARD, Joshua. Private, Worcester Militia, Snow Hill Bn., Capt. Samuel Smyley's Co., 1777 [Ref: M-250 listed the name as "Joshua Beachborad"]. Private, Worcester Militia, Wicomico Bn., Capt. Fisher Walton's Co., Fourth Class, July 15, 1780 [Ref: M-258].
BEARD, James (1752 -   ). Son of James and Sarah Beard, born in Stepney Parish on March 14, 1752 [Ref: Y-42]. Private, Somerset Militia, Salisbury Bn., Capt. Henry Gale's Quantico Co., 1778/1780 [Ref: M-216]. See "Thomas Beard," q.v.

BEARD, John (1751-1836). Born in Maryland, possibly Somerset County, on April 7, 1751, married Ann Doughty, served as a private during the war, and died in Virginia on March 8, 1836 [Ref: V-201].

BEARD, Sarah. See "James Beard" and "Thomas Beard," q.v.

BEARD, Thomas (1755-1803?). Private, Somerset Militia, Salisbury Bn., Capt. Josiah Dashiell's Wicomico Creek Co., 1778/1780 [Ref: M-218]. Drafted from Somerset County on July 30, 1781 to serve in the Continental Army [Ref: D-406, L-35C]. One Thomas Beard was born in Maryland circa 1758, married Ann Chapman, served as a private and rendered other patriotic service during the war, and died before June 14, 1803 [Ref: V-201]. Thomas Beard, son of James and Sarah Beard, was born in Stepney Parish on Nov 6, 1755 [Ref: Y-42]. Additional research will be necessary before drawing conclusions.

BEARD, William. Private, Somerset Militia, Salisbury Bn., Capt. Josiah Dashiell's Wicomico Creek Co., 1778/1780 [Ref: M-218].

BEATHARD, Jarman. See "Jarman Bethards," q.v.

BEAUCHAMP, Daniel. Private, Somerset Militia, Princess Anne Bn., St. Asaph's Co., 1780 [Ref: M-221]. See "John Beauchamp," q.v.

BEAUCHAMP, Easter. See "Levi Beauchamp," q.v.

BEAUCHAMP, Edmond. See "Thomas Beauchamp" and "William Beauchamp" and "Littleton Beauchamp," q.v.

BEAUCHAMP, Edward. Private, Somerset Militia, Princess Anne Bn., St. Asaph's Co., 1780 [Ref: M-221]. See "Littleton Beauchamp," q.v.

BEAUCHAMP, Elizabeth. See "Thomas Beauchamp" and "William Beauchamp" and "Littleton Beauchamp," q.v.

BEAUCHAMP, Fountain. Private, Somerset Militia, Princess Anne Bn., Capt. George Waters' Pocomoke Co., 1780 [Ref: M-220]. Fountain Beauchamp (1727-1782) married Rhoda (Rodey) Adams and their son Fountain Beauchamp was born in Coventry Parish on June 19, 1754 [Ref: Y-79, and V-204 indicates the father, not the son, served as a private in the war]. Additional research may be necessary before drawing conclusions. See "Levi Beauchamp," q.v.

BEAUCHAMP, Isaac. Private, Somerset Militia, Princess Anne Bn., Capt. Isaac Handy's Great Annemessix Co., 1780 [Ref: M-221].

BEAUCHAMP, Isaac. Private, Somerset Militia, Princess Anne Bn., St. Asaph's Co., 1780 [Ref: M-220].

BEAUCHAMP, John. Private, Worcester Militia, Sinepuxent Bn., Capt. John Coe's Co., Sixth Class, 1779/1780 [Ref: M-252 listed the name as "John Beachamp"].

BEAUCHAMP, John. Private, Somerset Militia, Princess Anne Bn., Capt. Isaac Handy's Great Annemessix Co., 1780 [Ref: M-221].

BEAUCHAMP, John (1760 -   ). Son of Daniel Beauchamp and Sarah Lannard, born in Coventry Parish on Sep 18, 1760 [Ref: Y-79]. Private, Somerset Militia, Princess Anne Bn., St. Asaph's Co., 1780 [Ref: M-221].

BEAUCHAMP, Joshua. Private, Somerset Militia, Princess Anne Bn., Capt. Isaac Handy's Great Annemessix Co., 1780 [Ref: M-221].

BEAUCHAMP, Levi. Private, Somerset Militia, Princess Anne Bn., Capt. George Waters' Pocomoke Co., 1780 [Ref: M-220]. There were two men with this name in Coventry Parish: one was the son of Fountain and Rhodie Beauchamp, born April 8, 1751, and the other was the son of Robert and Easter Beauchamp, born Feb 20, 1750 [Ref: Y-69].

BEAUCHAMP, Littleton (1759-1822). Son of Edward [Edmond?] and Elizabeth Beauchamp, born in Coventry Parish on May 25, 1759 [Ref: Y-79]. Private, Worcester Militia, Snow Hill Bn., Capt. Ebenezer Handy's Co., April 9, 1776 [Ref: M-249]. Private, Worcester Militia, Wicomico Bn., Capt. James Perdue's Co., Eighth Class, July 15, 1780 [Ref: M-256 listed the name as "Littleton Becham"]. Littleton Beauchamp was born on May 25, 1759, married Nancy ----, served as a private during the war, and died before July 27, 1822 in Alabama [Ref: V-204].

BEAUCHAMP, Martha. See "William Beauchamp," q.v.

BEAUCHAMP, Nancy. See "Littleton Beauchamp" and "Isaac Mitchell," q.v.

BEAUCHAMP, Newell (1743-1825). Born in Maryland, probably Worcester County, on May 8, 1743, married Annis Downham, served as a captain in Delaware during the war, and died in Kentucky on Aug 10, 1825 [Ref: V-204].

BEAUCHAMP, Rhodie. See "Levi Beauchamp," q.v.

BEAUCHAMP, Robert. See "Levi Beauchamp," q.v.

BEAUCHAMP (BEACHAM), Stephen. Second Lieutenant, Worcester Militia, Capt. Shockley's Co., May 15, 1776 to at least June 28, 1777 [Ref: M-51 listed the name as "Stephen Beacham," M-57 and A-427 listed the name as "Stephen Bucham," and A-405 listed the name as "Stephen Bacham"].

BEAUCHAMP, Steven. Private, Wicomico Bn., Capt. Elijah Shockley's Co., Seventh Class, July 15, 1780 [Ref: M-255 listed the name as "Steven Beacham"].

BEAUCHAMP, Thomas (1752 -   ). Son of Edmond and Elizabeth Beauchamp, born in Coventry Parish on Feb 20, 1752 [Ref: Y-69]. Took the Oath of Allegiance in Somerset County in 1778 before the Hon. John Williams [Ref: T-21, N-50]. Private, Somerset Militia, Princess Anne Bn., Capt. George Waters' Pocomoke Co., 1780 [Ref: M-220].

BEAUCHAMP, William (1754 -   ). Son of Edmond and Elizabeth Beauchamp, born in Coventry Parish on Dec 28, 1754 [Ref: Y-79]. Private, Worcester Militia, Snow Hill Bn., Capt. Ebenezer Handy's Co., April 9, 1776 [Ref: M-249]. Private, Worcester Militia, Wicomico Bn., Capt. Elijah Shockley's Co., Fifth Class, July 15, 1780 [Ref: M-255 listed the name as "William Beacham"].

BEAUCHAMP, William (c1760-c1795). Born in Maryland, probably Worcester County, married Nancy Parker, served as a private in Maryland, and died in Georgia after 1795 [Ref: V-204].

BEAUCHAMP, William (1743-1808). Born in Maryland, probably Worcester County, married first to Elizabeth Manlove and second to Martha ----, served in the navy during the war, and died in Virginia on Oct 11, 1808 [Ref: V-204].

BEAVENS, Charles. Private, Worcester Militia, Capt. John Martin's Co., 1780/1781 [Ref: J-1814 (Box 12)].
BEAVENS, Elizabeth. See "John Beavens," q.v.
BEAVENS, Hezekiah. Private, Worcester Militia, Sinepuxent Bn., Capt. Matthew Purnell's Co., Second Class, July 25, 1780 [Ref: M-252].
BEAVENS, John (1758 -   ). Son of Roland and Elizabeth Beavens, born in Coventry Parish on May 1, 1758 [Ref: Y-80]. Private, Worcester Militia, Wicomico Bn., Capt. Philip Quinton's Co., Sixth Class, July 15, 1780 [Ref: M-256 listed the name as "John Bevans"].
BEAVENS, Roland or Rowland (1740-1809). First Lieutenant, Worcester Militia, Wicomico Bn., Capt. Charles Bennett's Co., Aug 30, 1777 to at least July 15, 1780 [Ref: M-53, C-351 listed the name as "Roland Bevins" and M-255 listed the name as "Rowland Beavans"]. Took the Oath of Allegiance in Worcester County in 1778 before the Hon. John Selby [Ref: J-1814 (Box 4) listed the name as "Rowland Beavins"]. Rowland Beavins (or Roland Beavens) was born on May 10, 1740, married Tabitha Dennis in Coventry Parish on Sep 22, 1765, served as a first lieutenant during the war, and died in 1809 [Ref: Y-93, V-245].
BEAVENS, Rowland. Private, Worcester Militia, Capt. John Martin's Co., 1780/1781 [Ref: J-1814 (Box 12)].
BEAVENS, Thomas. Rendered patriotic service by supplying pork for the use of the military on Jan 4, 1781 [Ref: P-351].
BEAVENS, William. Took the Oath of Allegiance in Worcester County in 1778 before the Hon. John Selby [Ref: J-1814 (Box 4) listed the name as "William Beavins"]. Corporal, Worcester Militia, Capt. John Martin's Co., 1780/1781 [Ref: J-1814 (Box 12)]. See "William Bevans," q.v.
BEDSWORTH, Samuel. See "Samuel Betsworth," q.v.
BELL (BEAL?), Joseph. Private, Somerset Militia, Princess Anne Bn., St. Asaph's Co., 1780 [Ref: M-220].
BELL, Ezekiel. Private, Somerset Militia, Salisbury Bn., Capt. Levin Irving's Black Water Co., 1778/1780 [Ref: M-217].
BELL, Hamilton. Took the Oath of Allegiance in Somerset County in 1778 before the Hon. Levin Wilson [Ref: T-17, N-50].
BELL, Hamilton Jr. Took the Oath of Allegiance in Somerset County in 1778 before the Hon. Levin Wilson [Ref: T-17, N-50].
BELL, Henry. Took the Oath of Allegiance in Worcester County in 1778 before the Hon. Joshua Townsend [Ref: J-1814 (Box 4)].
BELL, Jacob. First Lieutenant, Somerset Militia, 1st Bn., Capt. Robert Hitch's Co., commissioned April 11, 1776 [Ref: A-327, and M-50 mistakenly listed the name as "Jacob Ball" and incorrectly gave the commission date as May 11, 1776].
BELL, John (1760 -   ). Son of Josephas and Sophia Bell, born in Coventry Parish on Oct 18, 1760 [Ref: Y-78]. Private, Somerset Militia, Princess Anne Bn., Capt. John Williams' Watkins Point Co., 1780 [Ref: M-222]. Drafted from

Somerset County on June 20, 1781 to serve in the Continental Army [Ref: L-35C].
BELL, Josephas. See "William Bell" and "Nathaniel Bell" and "John Bell," q.v.
BELL, Levin. Took the Oath of Allegiance in Worcester County in 1778 before the Hon. John Selby [Ref: J-1814 (Box 4)].
BELL, Nathaniel (1762 -   ). Son of Josephas and Sophia Bell, born in Coventry Parish on Dec 31, 1762 [Ref: Y-78]. Private, Somerset Militia, Princess Anne Bn., Capt. John Williams' Watkins Point Co., 1780 [Ref: M-222].
BELL, Sophia. See "William Bell" and "Nathaniel Bell" and "John Bell," q.v.
BELL, William (1755 -   ). Son of Josephas and Sophia Bell, born in Coventry Parish on Oct 28, 1755 [Ref: Y-78]. Took the Oath of Allegiance in Somerset County in 1778 before the Hon. Levin Wilson [Ref: T-17, N-50]. Rendered patriotic service by supplying bacon for the use of the military on Aug 9, 1780 [Ref: P-308].
BENNETT (BENNET), Charles. Captain, Worcester Militia, Wicomico Bn., Aug 30, 1777 to at least July 15, 1780 [Ref: M-52, M-255, C-351]. Took the Oath of Allegiance in Worcester County in 1778 before the Hon. John Selby [Ref: J-1814 (Box 4)].
BENNETT (BENNET), Charles. Private, Worcester Militia, Snow Hill Bn., Capt. John Parramore's Co., 1777 [Ref: M-250]. Private, Worcester Militia, Wicomico Bn., Capt. John Parramore's Co., Fourth Class, July 15, 1780 [Ref: M-259].
BENNETT (BENNET), Charles (of William). Took the Oath of Allegiance in Worcester County in 1778 before the Hon. Joshua Townsend [Ref: J-1814 (Box 4) listed the name as "Charles Bennit, son of Wm."].
BENNETT (BENNET), Edward. Private, Somerset Militia, Salisbury Bn., Capt. William Turpin's Rewastico Co., 1778/1780 [Ref: M-217]. See "Littleton Bennett," q.v.
BENNETT (BENNET), George. Private, Somerset Militia, Salisbury Bn., Capt. Henry Gale's Quantico Co., 1778/1780 [Ref: M-216].
BENNETT (BENNET), James. Private, Somerset Militia, Salisbury Bn., Capt. William Turpin's Rewastico Co., 1778/1780 [Ref: M-217]. Took the Oath of Allegiance in Somerset County in 1778 before the Hon. William Winder [Ref: T-22, N-50].
BENNETT (BENNET), James. Second Lieutenant, Worcester Militia, Wicomico Bn., Capt. Charles Bennett's Co., Aug 30, 1777 [Ref: M-52, C-351]. Captain, Somerset Militia, Salisbury Bn., Salisbury Co., May 27, 1779 to at least July 24, 1780 [Ref: M-52, M-218, E-423].
BENNETT (BENNET), James. Private, Worcester Militia, Snow Hill Bn., Capt. John Parramore's Co., 1777 [Ref: M-250]. Private, Worcester Militia, Wicomico Bn., Capt. William Handy's Co., First Class, July 15, 1780 [Ref: M-257].

BENNETT (BENNET), James (of William). Took the Oath of Allegiance in Worcester County in 1778 before the Hon. Joshua Townsend [Ref: J-1814 (Box 4) listed the name as "James Bennit, son of William"].

BENNETT (BENNET), Jane. See "Littleton Bennett," q.v.

BENNETT (BENNET), Jesse (Jessy). Private, Worcester Militia, Snow Hill Bn., Capt. John Parramore's Co., 1777. Private, Worcester Militia, Wicomico Bn., Capt. John Parramore's Co., Second Class, July 15, 1780 [Ref: M-250, M-259].

BENNETT, Jesse. See "Edward Vandame (Vondome)," q.v.

BENNETT (BENNET), John. Private, Somerset Militia, Salisbury Bn., Capt. William Turpin's Rewastico Co., 1778/1780 [Ref: M-217].

BENNETT (BENNET), Littleton (1759 -   ). Son of Edward and Jane Bennet, born in Stepney Parish on Oct 21, 1759 [Ref: Y-46]. Private, Somerset Militia, Salisbury Bn., Capt. Henry Gale's Quantico Co., 1778/1780 [Ref: M-216 listed the name as "Lill. Bennet"].

BENNETT (BENNITT), Samuel. Private, Worcester Militia, Capt. John Martin's Co., 1780/1781 [Ref: J-1814 (Box 12)].

BENNETT (BENNET), William Sr. Took the Oath of Allegiance in Worcester County in 1778 before the Hon. John Selby [Ref: J-1814 (Box 4)].

BENNETT (BENNET), William. Private, Worcester Militia, Snow Hill Bn., Capt. John Parramore's Co., 1777. Private, Worcester Militia, Wicomico Bn., Capt. John Parramore's Co., Seventh Class, July 15, 1780 [Ref: M-259, M-259].

BENNETT (BENNET), William. Private, Worcester Militia, Snow Hill Bn., Capt. John Parramore's Co., 1777. Private, Worcester Militia, Wicomico Bn., Capt. John Parramore's Co., First Class, July 15, 1780 [Ref: M-250, M-259].

BENNETT (BENNET), William (of William). Took the Oath of Allegiance in Worcester County in 1778 before the Hon. John Selby [Ref: J-1814 (Box 4)].

BENNETT (BENNET), William (of William). Took the Oath of Allegiance in Worcester County in 1778 before the Hon. John Selby [Ref: J-1814 (Box 4)].

BENSON, John. Private, Worcester Militia, Snow Hill Bn., Capt. Samuel Smyley's Co., 1777. Private, Worcester Militia, Wicomico Bn., Capt. Samuel Smyley's Co., Sixth Class, July 15, 1780 [Ref: M-250, M-259]. Took the Oath of Allegiance in Worcester County in 1778 in Buckingham Hundred before the Hon. Thomas Purnell [Ref: J-1814 (Box 4)].

BENSON, Joseph. Took the Oath of Allegiance in Worcester County in 1778 before the Hon. Joshua Townsend [Ref: J-1814 (Box 4)].

BENSON, Selby. Private, Worcester Militia, Wicomico Bn., Capt. Fisher Walton's Co., Sixth Class, July 15, 1780 [Ref: M-258].

BENSON, William. Took the Oath of Allegiance in Worcester County in 1778 before the Hon. Nathaniel Miller [Ref: J-1814 (Box 4)].

BENSON, Zepheniah. Private, Worcester Militia, Wicomico Bn., Capt. Isaac Layfield's Co., Fifth Class, July 15, 1780 [Ref: M-257]. See "Zepheniah Benston," q.v.

BENSTON, Elias (1759 -   ). Son of Thomas and Sarah Benston, born in Coventry Parish on July 21, 1759 [Ref: Y-79]. Private, Somerset Militia, Princess Anne Bn., Capt. George Waters' Pocomoke Co., 1780 [Ref: M-220]. Private, Worcester Militia, Wicomico Bn., Capt. Charles Bennett's Co., Sixth Class, July 15, 1780 [Ref: M-255].
BENSTON, Gertrude. See "Levin Boston," q.v.
BENSTON, John (1751 -   ). Son of Benjamin and Ann Benston, born in Coventry Parish on Nov 28, 1751 [Ref: Y-79]. Private, Worcester Militia, Sinepuxent Bn., Capt. John Rackliff's Co., Eighth Class, 1779/1780 [Ref: M-251].
BENSTON, Michael. Private, Somerset Militia, Princess Anne Bn., Capt. John Williams' Watkins Point Co., 1780 [Ref: M-222].
BENSTON, Sarah. See "William Benston" and "Elias Benston" and "Thomas Williamson Benston," q.v.
BENSTON, Thomas. See "Elias Benston," q.v.
BENSTON, Thomas Williamson (1757 -   ). Son of Thomas and Sarah Benston, born in Coventry Parish on March 21. 1757 [Ref: Y-79]. Private, Somerset Militia, Princess Anne Bn., Capt. George Waters' Pocomoke Co., 1780 [Ref: M-220].
BENSTON, William (1754 -   ). Son of William and Sarah Benston, born in Coventry Parish on Dec 24, 1754 [Ref: Y-78]. Private, Somerset Militia, Princess Anne Bn., Capt. John Jones' Princess Anne Co., 1780 [Ref: M-219].
BENSTON, William. Took the Oath of Allegiance in Worcester County in 1778 before the Hon. William Hopewell [Ref: J-1814 (Box 4)].
BENSTON, Zephaniah. Took the Oath of Allegiance in Worcester County in 1778 before the Hon. James Selby [Ref: J-1814 (Box 4)]. See "Zepheniah Benson," q.v.
BETHARDS (BETHERDS), Benjamin. Private, Worcester Militia, Sinepuxent Bn., Capt. John Postly's Co., First Class, 1779/1780 [Ref: M-251].
BETHARDS (BETHERDS), Daniel Coe. Private, Worcester Militia, Sinepuxent Bn., Capt. John Postly's Co., Second Class, 1779/1780 [Ref: M-251]. Took the Oath of Allegiance in Worcester County in 1778 before the Hon. Nathaniel Miller [Ref: J-1814 (Box 4) listed the name as "Daniel Coebattered"]. Ensign, March 16, 1781, Capt. Isaac Evans' Co. [Ref: M-56, G-353].
BETHARDS (BETHERDS), Jarman. Private, 3rd Maryland Independent Co., Worcester County, Capt. John Watkins' Co., enlisted March 18, 1776; muster roll dated Aug 20, 1776, absent on furlough [Ref: D-22 listed the name as "Jarman Beatherd"].
BETHARDS (BETHERDS), John. Took the Oath of Allegiance in Worcester County in 1778 before the Hon. Nathaniel Miller [Ref: J-1814 (Box 4)].
BETHARDS (BETHERDS), Samuel. Private, Worcester Militia, Wicomico Bn., Capt. James Perdue's Co., Fifth Class, July 15, 1780 [Ref: M-256].
BETHARDS (BETHERDS), William. Private, Worcester Militia, Wicomico Bn., Capt. James Perdue's Co., Eighth Class, July 15, 1780 [Ref: M-256].

BETHARDS (BETHERDS), William. Private, Worcester Militia, Wicomico Bn., Capt. John Davis' Co., Eighth Class, July 15, 1780 [Ref: M-255].

BETSWORTH (BEDSWORTH), John. Private, Somerset Militia, Salisbury Bn., Capt. Sampson Wheatly's Co., 1780 [Ref: M-216].

BETSWORTH (BEDSWORTH), Samuel. Took the Oath of Allegiance in Somerset County in 1778 before the Hon. John Williams [Ref: N-50, T-21]. Private, Somerset Militia, Princess Anne Bn., St. Asaph's Co., 1780 [Ref: M-221 listed the name as "Samuel Bedsworth"].

BETSWORTH (BEDSWORTH), Thomas. Private, Somerset Militia, Salisbury Bn., Capt. William Turpin's Rewastico Co., 1778/1780 [Ref: M-217].

BETTS, Robert. Private, Worcester Militia, Sinepuxent Bn., Capt. John Rackliff's Co., Third Class, 1779/1780 [Ref: M-251]. Took the Oath of Allegiance in Worcester County in 1778 in Buckingham Hundred before the Hon. Thomas Purnell [Ref: J-1814 (Box 4)]. Rendered patriotic service by supplying beef for the use of the military on Sep 20, 1781 [Ref: P-439 listed the name as "Robert Bets"].

BEVANS, John. See "John Beavens," q.v.

BEVANS, Thomas. Private, Worcester Militia, Wicomico Bn., Capt. Philip Quinton's Co., Fifth Class, July 15, 1780 [Ref: M-256].

BEVANS, William. Private, Worcester Militia, Wicomico Bn., Capt. Philip Quinton's Co., Eighth Class, July 15, 1780 [Ref: M-256].

BEVANS, William. Private, Worcester Militia, Wicomico Bn., Capt. Philip Quinton's Co., Fourth Class, July 15, 1780 [Ref: M-256]. See "William Beavens," q.v.

BIDDLE, Gilbert. Private, Worcester Militia, Sinepuxent Bn., Capt. John Rackliff's Co., Seventh Class, 1779/1780 [Ref: M-251 listed the name as "Gilbert Bedle"]. Took the Oath of Allegiance in Worcester County in 1778 before the Hon. Nathaniel Miller [Ref: J-1814 (Box 4)]. Rendered patriotic service by supplying and collecting cattle for the use of the military on Sep 30, 1781 [Ref: P-442 listed the name as "Gilbert Biddell"].

BIGGER, Jonathan. Private, Somerset Militia, Salisbury Bn., Capt. Sampson Wheatly's Co., 1780 [Ref: M-216].

BIGGER, Stephen. Private, Somerset Militia, Salisbury Bn., Capt. Sampson Wheatly's Co., 1780 [Ref: M-216].

BIGLAND (BIGLANDS), John (1756 -   ). son of Richard and Mary Biglands, born in Stepney Parish on Feb 21, 1756 [Ref: Y-42]. Private, Worcester Militia, Wicomico Bn., Capt. Robert Handy's Co., Seventh Class, July 15, 1780 [Ref: M-254].

BIGLAND (BIGLANDS), William (1758 -   ). Son of Richard and Mary Biglands, born in Stepney Parish on Aug 19, 1758 [Ref: Y-42]. Private, Worcester Militia, Snow Hill Bn., Capt. Ebenezer Handy's Co., April 9, 1776. Private, Worcester Militia, Wicomico Bn., Capt. Robert Handy's Co., First Class, July 15, 1780 [Ref: M-249, M-254].

BING, William. See "William Byng," q.v.
BIRD, Benjamin. Private, Somerset Militia, Salisbury Bn., Capt. Levin Irving's Black Water Co., 1778/1780 [Ref: M-217].
BIRD, Jemima. See "Joseph Bird," q.v.
BIRD, John. Sergeant, Somerset Militia, Salisbury Bn., Capt. Levin Irving's Black Water Co., 1778/1780 [Ref: M-217].
BIRD, Joseph (1757 -   ). Son of Solomon and Jemima Bird, born in Coventry Parish on April 3, 1757 [Ref: Y-79]. Sergeant, Somerset Militia, Princess Anne Bn., Capt. John Williams' Watkins Point Co., 1780 [Ref: M-221].
BIRD, Patty. See "Elijah Laws, Jr.," q.v.
BIRD, Solomon. Private, Somerset Militia, Salisbury Bn., Capt. Sampson Wheatly's Co., 1780 [Ref: M-216]. See "Joseph Bird," q.v.
BIRD, Thomas (1753-1822). Private, Somerset Militia, Salisbury Bn., Capt. Levin Irving's Black Water Co., 1778/1780 [Ref: M-218]. Private, Somerset Militia, Salisbury Bn., Capt. Sampson Wheatly's Co., 1780 [Ref: M-216]. Thomas Bird was born in 1753, married Elizabeh Hearn, was a soldier during the war, and died in 1822 [Ref: V-259].
BIRDWELL, Benjamin. Private, Worcester Militia, Wicomico Bn., Capt. Elijah Shockley's Co., Third Class, July 15, 1780 [Ref: M-255].
BISHOP, Benjamin. Took the Oath of Allegiance in Worcester County in 1778 before the Hon. Joshua Townsend [Ref: J-1814 (Box 4)].
BISHOP, Benjamin. Took the Oath of Allegiance in Worcester County in 1778 before the Hon. Joshua Townsend [Ref: J-1814 (Box 4)].
BISHOP, Charles. Took the Oath of Allegiance in Worcester County in 1778 before the Hon. Joshua Townsend [Ref: J-1814 (Box 4)].
BISHOP, Edward. Private, Worcester Militia, Sinepuxent Bn., Capt. Matthew Purnell's Co., Fourth Class, July 25, 1780 [Ref: M-252]. Private, Maryland Troops, Worcester County, draughted May 1, 1781 [Ref: K-99, D-372]. Discharged on Dec 10, 1781 [Ref: I-17].
BISHOP, George. Private, 3rd Maryland Independent Co., Worcester County, Capt. John Watkins' Co., enlisted Feb 18, 1776; muster roll dated Aug 20, 1776, sick at his father's [Ref: D-21].
BISHOP, Joseph. Private, Worcester Militia, Wicomico Bn., Capt. William Handy's Co., Third Class, July 15, 1780 [Ref: M-257].
BISHOP, Smith (c1720/30-1783). Attended the Maryland Convention in 1776, one of the delegates from Worcester County [Ref: O-28]. Took the Oath of Allegiance in Worcester County in 1778 before the Hon. Joshua Townsend [Ref: J-1814 (Box 4)]. Smith Bishop was a doctor, married (wife's name not known), rendered patriotic service during the war, and died in 1783 [Ref: V-263].
BISHOP, Smith. Took the Oath of Allegiance in Worcester County in 1778 before the Hon. Nehemiah Holland [Ref: J-1814 (Box 4)].

BISHOP, William. Ensign, Worcester Militia, Snow Hill Bn., Capt. George Spence's Co., Aug 30, 1777 [Ref: M-53, C-351]. Took the Oath of Allegiance in Worcester County in 1778 before the Hon. Joshua Townsend [Ref: J-1814 (Box 4) listed the name as "William Bisshop"]. Rendered patriotic service by supplying beef for the use of the military on Oct 10, 1781 [Ref: P-446].

BISHOP, Zachariah. Private, 3rd Maryland Independent Co., Worcester County, Capt. John Watkins' Co., enlisted Feb 8, 1776; muster roll dated Aug 20, 1776, present for duty [Ref: D-22].

BIVINS, William (1748-c1835). Private, Delaware Line, who applied for a pension (R876) in Montgomery County, Indiana on Sep 22, 1834, age 85, and a resident of Ripley, Indiana. He stated that he was born on April 14, 1748 in Somerset County, Maryland, enlisted at Blackford's Town in Sussex County, Delaware, and after the war lived in Maryland, Virginia, Ohio, and Indiana [Ref: W-275].

BLACK, Aaron (Aron). Took the Oath of Allegiance in Worcester County in 1778 before the Hon. Nehemiah Holland [Ref: J-1814 (Box 4)].

BLADES, Eli (c1764-c1845). Private, Maryland Line, who applied for a pension (R908) in Scott County, Indiana on Feb 19, 1841, age 77, stating he was born in Somerset County, Maryland on Feb 21, 1764 and enlisted in Worcester County. In 1789 he moved to Woodford County, Kentucky for 10 years, then moved to Clarmont County, Ohio for 3 years, then to Clark County, Indiana, and then to Lexington Township [Ref: W-283 listed the name as "Eli Blads or Blade"].

BLADES, James. Private, 5th Maryland Line, enlisted March 31, 1777 and reported missing on Aug 1,6, 1780 after the Battle of Camden, South Carolina [Ref: D-185].

BLADES, Jehu. Took the Oath of Allegiance in Worcester County in 1778 before the Hon. James Selby [Ref: J-1814 (Box 4)].

BLADES, John. Private, Somerset Militia, Princess Anne Bn., Capt. George Waters' Pocomoke Co., 1780 [Ref: M-220]. Took the Oath of Allegiance in Worcester County in 1778 before the Hon. James Selby [Ref: J-1814 (Box 4)].

BLADES, John Levy (c1750-1784). Private, Maryland Line, whose widow Sarah applied for a pension (W99502) in Switzerland County, Indiana on Nov 18, 1844, age 89, a resident of Craig Township. She married John Levy Blades in Somerset or Worcester County, Maryland on Jan 17 or Feb 17, 1776 and he died in Jan or Feb, 1784 in Worcester County. A son Zadock Blades was born in May, 1777 and he and his widowed mother moved to Kentucky and lived in Mason and Bracken Counties. Sarah Blades married second to William Lancaster (a soldier in the Virginia Line, pension S16912) in Bracken County, Kentucky on Sep 11, 1813 and he died in Switzerland County, Indiana on Nov 4, 1843 (Sarah was his second wife). In 1844 Catharine Lancaster, wife of Mallory Lancaster (son of William Lancaster by his first wife) lived in Switzerland County, as did William and Catharine J. Lancaster in 1845 (relationship not stated). [Ref: W-283].

BLADES, Levin (1762 -   ). Son of Samuel and Milleston (Millicent) Blades, born in Coventry Parish on Jan 16, 1762 [Ref: Y-80]. Private, Worcester Militia, Wicomico Bn., Capt. Isaac Layfield's Co., Fifth Class, July 15, 1780 [Ref: M-257].

BLADES, Milleston (Millicent). See "Levin Blades," q.v.

BLADES, Samuel (c1727-1826). Private, Worcester Militia, Wicomico Bn., Capt. James Patterson's Co., Fourth Class, July 15, 1780 [Ref: M-258]. Samuel Blades was born circa 1727, married first to Amelia Barnes and second to Mary Pilchard, served as a private and rendered other patriotic service during the war, and died before Aug 25, 1826 [Ref: V-271]. Two men by this name took the Oath of Allegiance in Worcester County in 1778 before the Hon. James Selby [Ref: J-1814 (Box 4)]. Additional research may be necessary before drawing conclusions. See "Levin Blades," q.v.

BLADES, Sarah. See "John Levy Blades," q.v.

BLADES, Zadock. See "John Levy Blades," q.v.

BLAINE, Duncan. Rendered patriotic service by supplying bacon for the use of the military in Somerset County on Aug 12, 1780 [Ref: P-309].

BLAIR, John. Private, Worcester Militia, Snow Hill Bn., Capt. John Parramore's Co., 1777 [Ref: M-250]. Private, Worcester Militia, Wicomico Bn., Capt. John Parramore's Co., Fifth Class, July 15, 1780 [Ref: M-259]. Took the Oath of Allegiance in Worcester County in 1778 before the Hon. William Hopewell [Ref: J-1814 (Box 4)].

BLAKE, Aaron. Private, Worcester Militia, Wicomico Bn., Capt. Fisher Walton's Co., First Class, July 15, 1780 [Ref: M-258].

BLAKE, Edward. Private, Worcester Militia, Wicomico Bn., Capt. Samuel Smyley's Co., Fourth Class, July 15, 1780 [Ref: M-259]. Private, Maryland Line, whose name appeared on "a list of recruits from and deserters taken up in Somerset County on Oct 20, 1780" [Ref: D-346].

BLAKE, Edward. Took the Oath of Allegiance in Worcester County in 1778 before the Hon. John Selby [Ref: J-1814 (Box 4)].

BLAKE, George. Private, Worcester Militia, Wicomico Bn., Capt. Fisher Walton's Co., Fourth Class, July 15, 1780 [Ref: M-258].

BLAKE, George (molato). Took the Oath of Allegiance in Worcester County in 1778 before the Hon. Nehemiah Holland [Ref: J-1814 (Box 4)].

BLAKE, George Jr. Took the Oath of Allegiance in Worcester County in 1778 before the Hon. John Selby [Ref: J-1814 (Box 4)].

BLAKE, George (of Sarah). Private, Worcester Militia, Wicomico Bn., Capt. John Parramore's Co., First Class, July 15, 1780 [Ref: M-259].

BLAKE, Jacob (1756-1826). Private, Maryland Line, who applied for a pension (S34654) in Worcester County on June 20, 1818 and received $96 per annum. He was aged 65 in 1821 with a wife aged 70 and sons aged 19 and 16 (no names were given). He died on Feb 9, 1826 [Ref: X-44, W-287].

BLAKE, James. Private, Worcester Militia, Wicomico Bn., Capt. Fisher Walton's Co., Third Class, July 15, 1780 [Ref: M-258].

BLAKE, James (molato). Took the Oath of Allegiance in Worcester County in 1778 before the Hon. Nehemiah Holland [Ref: J-1814 (Box 4)].

BLAKE, John. Private, Worcester Militia, Wicomico Bn., Capt. John Parramore's Co., Third Class, July 15, 1780 [Ref: M-259].

BLAKE, Levin (Leven). Took the Oath of Allegiance in Worcester County in 1778 before the Hon. Joshua Townsend [Ref: J-1814 (Box 4)]. Private, Worcester Militia, Wicomico Bn., Capt. Philip Quinton's Co., Sixth Class, July 15, 1780 [Ref: M-256]. Rendered patriotic service by collecting cattle for the use of the military on Oct 9 to Nov 6, 1781 [Ref: P-445].

BLAKE, Ned. Rendered patriotic service by butchering beef for the use of the military in Worcester County on Oct 15, 1781 [Ref: P-447].

BLAKE, Oliver. Private, Worcester Militia, Wicomico Bn., Capt. John Parramore's Co., Fourth Class, July 15, 1780 [Ref: M-259].

BLAKE, Oliver (molato). Took the Oath of Allegiance in Worcester County in 1778 before the Hon. Nehemiah Holland [Ref: J-1814 (Box 4)].

BLAKE, Thomas. Took the Oath of Allegiance in Somerset County in 1778 before the Hon. John Williams [Ref: T-21, N-50].

BLAKE, William. Private, Worcester Militia, Wicomico Bn., Capt. Isaac Layfield's Co., Eighth Class, July 15, 1780 [Ref: M-257]. Took the Oath of Allegiance in Worcester County in 1778 before the Hon. James Selby [Ref: J-1814 (Box 4)].

BLIZZARD, Ratcliff. Private, Worcester Militia, Wicomico Bn., Capt. James Perdue's Co., Third Class, July 15, 1780 [Ref: M-256 listed the name as "Ratcliff Blizard"].

BLOAD, John. Private, Somerset Militia, Princess Anne Bn., Capt. George Waters' Pocomoke Co., 1780 [Ref: M-220].

BLOODSWORTH, John. Sergeant, Somerset Militia, Princess Anne Bn., Capt. John Jones' Princess Anne Co., 1780 [Ref: M-219]. Took the Oath of Allegiance in Somerset County in 1778 before the Hon. Peter Waters [Ref: T-18]. Select Militia, Somerset County, Aug 15, 1781 [Ref: L-35B].

BLOODSWORTH, Littleton. See "Smith Sims," q.v.

BLOYCE, William. Private, Somerset Militia, Princess Anne Bn., Capt. George Waters' Pocomoke Co., 1780 [Ref: M-220].

BLOYTH, James. Private, Somerset Militia, Princess Anne Bn., Capt. Henry Miles' Little Annemessex Co., 1780 [Ref: M-221].

BLUETT, Martha. See "Benjamin F. A. C. Dashiell" and "Joseph Dashiell," q.v.

BOLDS, Samuel. See "Samuel Bowles," q.v.

BOLES, Thomas. See "Samuel Bowles," q.v.

BOLEN, John. Private, Somerset Militia, Princess Anne Bn., Capt. James Elzey's Co., 1780 [Ref: M-220].

BONAWELL, Benjamin. Took the Oath of Allegiance in Worcester County in 1778 before the Hon. William Hopewell [Ref: J-1814 (Box 4)]. Private,

Worcester Militia, Wicomico Bn., Capt. Fisher Walton's Co., Eighth Class, July 15, 1780 [Ref: M-258 listed the name as "Benjamin Bonnewell"].

BOOTH, James. Private, Somerset Militia, Salisbury Bn., Capt. James Bennett's Salisbury Co., 1778/1780 [Ref: M-218].

BORDEN, Levi. Took the Oath of Allegiance in Worcester County in 1778 before the Hon. Joshua Townsend [Ref: J-1814 (Box 4)].

BOSTON, Ann. See "Thomas Summers," q.v.

BOSTON, Daniel. Private, Somerset Militia, Princess Anne Bn., St. Asaph's Co., 1780 [Ref: M-221].

BOSTON, Esau (c1753-1795). Private, Somerset Militia, Princess Anne Bn., Capt. James Elzey's Co., 1780 [Ref: M-220]. Esau Boston, son of Lazarus and Grace Boston, was born or baptized in Coventry Parish on Sep 28, 1753, married first to Sarah Ward and second to Priscilla Heath, served as a private during the war, and died before June 23, 1795 [Ref: Y-69, V-311]. See "Southy Roach" and the other "Esau Boston," q.v.

BOSTON, Esau (c1753-1846). Private, Worcester Militia, Wicomico Bn., Capt. Isaac Layfield's Co., First Class, July 15, 1780 [Ref: M-257]. Private, Maryland Troops, Worcester County, draughted May 1, 1781 [Ref: K-99]. Esau Boston was born circa 1753, married Leah ----, served as a soldier in Maryland, and died on Feb 4, 1846 [Ref: V-311 lists two men by this name who were born about the same time]. Additional research may be necessary before drawing conclusions.

BOSTON, Grace. See "Esau Boston" and "Lazarus Boston," q.v.

BOSTON, Isaac (1758 -   ). Son of Matthews and Martha Boston, born in Coventry Parish on June 5, 1758 [Ref: Y-79]. Private, Worcester Militia, Wicomico Bn., Capt. Isaac Layfield's Co., Eighth Class, July 15, 1780 [Ref: M-257]. Private, Maryland Troops, Worcester County, draughted May 1, 1781 (date of return by Lt. Joseph Dashiell). [Ref: D-372].

BOSTON, Jacob. Took the Oath of Allegiance in Worcester County in 1778 before the Hon. James Selby [Ref: J-1814 (Box 4)].

BOSTON, James (1763 -   ). Son of Matthews and Margaret Boston, born in Coventry Parish on Nov 1, 1763 [Ref: Y-80]. Private, Somerset Militia, Princess Anne Bn., Capt. Henry Miles' Little Annemessex Co., 1780 [Ref: M-221].

BOSTON, Joshua. Corporal, Somerset Militia, Princess Anne Bn., Capt. James Elzey's Co., 1780 [Ref: M-220].

BOSTON, Joshua. Sergeant, Somerset Militia, Princess Anne Bn., Capt. James Elzey's Co., 1780 [Ref: M-220].

BOSTON, Joshua. Took the Oath of Allegiance in Somerset County in 1778 before the Hon. Levin Wilson [Ref: N-50, and T-17 listed the name as "Joshuah Boston"].

BOSTON, Lazarus. Took the Oath of Allegiance in Somerset County in 1778 before the Hon. Peter Waters [Ref: T-18]. Lazarus Boston, son of Lazarus and

Grace Boston, was born in Coventry Parish on March 29, 1760 [Ref: Y-79]. See "Esau Boston," q.v.

BOSTON, Leah. See "Esau Boston," q.v.

BOSTON, Levin (1747-c1820). Private, Somerset Militia, Princess Anne Bn., Capt. Isaac Handy's Great Annemessix Co., 1780 [Ref: M-221]. Levin Boston was born on June 22, 1747, married Gertrude Benston, served as a private during the war, and died before Jan 29, 1820 [Ref: V-311].

BOSTON, Margaret. See "James Boston," q.v.

BOSTON, Martha. See "Isaac Boston," q.v.

BOSTON, Matthews. See "James Boston" and "Isaac Boston," q.v.

BOSTON, Naboth. Private, Worcester Militia, Wicomico Bn., Capt. Isaac Layfield's Co., First Class, July 15, 1780 [Ref: M-257].

BOSTON, Richard. Private, Somerset Militia, Princess Anne Bn., St. Asaph's Co., 1780 [Ref: M-220].

BOULDS, Pheme. See "Ananias Warren," q.v.

BOUNDS, Douty. Private, Somerset Militia, Salisbury Bn., Capt. John Span Conway's Nanticoke Point Co., 1778/1780 [Ref: M-216].

BOUNDS, Jones (1753 -   ). Son of Richard Bounds and Mary Stevens, born in Stepney Parish on April 19, 1753 [Ref: Y-44]. Private, Somerset Militia, Salisbury Bn., Capt. Josiah Dashiell's Wicomico Creek Co., 1778/1780 [Ref: M-218].

BOUNDS, Joshua. Took the Oath of Allegiance in Worcester County in 1778 before the Hon. James Selby [Ref: J-1814 (Box 4) listed the name as "Joshua Bouds"].

BOUNDS, Richard Stevens (1759-1812). Born in Somerset County on June 10, 1759, married Rebecca Benson, was a soldier in the war, and died in 1812 [Ref: V-316]. See "Jones Bounds," q.v.

BOUNDS, William. Private, Somerset Militia, Salisbury Bn., Capt. John Span Conway's Nanticoke Point Co., 1778/1780 [Ref: M-216].

BOWEN, Catherine. See "Luke Bowen," q.v.

BOWEN (BOWIN), David. Private, Worcester Militia, Sinepuxent Bn., Capt. Elisha Purnell's Co., Seventh Class, 1779/1780 [Ref: M-253]. Took the Oath of Allegiance in Worcester County in 1778 before the Hon. Joshua Townsend [Ref: J-1814 (Box 4) listed the name as "David Boyen"].

BOWEN, Dolly. See "Luke Bowen," q.v.

BOWEN (BOWIN), Elijah. Private, Worcester Militia, Sinepuxent Bn., Capt. Elisha Purnell's Co., Fifth Class, 1779/1780 [Ref: M-253]. Took the Oath of Allegiance in Worcester County in 1778 in Quepomco Hundred before the Hon. Thomas Purnell [Ref: J-1814 (Box 4)].

BOWEN (BOWIN), Elisha. Private, Worcester Militia, Sinepuxent Bn., Capt. Elisha Purnell's Co., Eighth Class, 1779/1780 [Ref: M-253].

BOWEN (BOWIN), Jeptha. Private, Worcester Militia, Sinepuxent Bn., Capt. Elisha Purnell's Co., Sixth Class, 1779/1780 [Ref: M-253]. Took the Oath of

Allegiance in Worcester County in 1778 before the Hon. Joshua Townsend [Ref: J-1814 (Box 4) listed the name as "Jepthah Boyen"].
BOWEN (BOWIN), Jesse. Private, Worcester Militia, Sinepuxent Bn., Capt. Elisha Purnell's Co., Second Class, 1779/1780 [Ref: M-253]. Took the Oath of Allegiance in Worcester County in 1778 in Quepomco Hundred before the Hon. Thomas Purnell [Ref: J-1814 (Box 4)].
BOWEN (BOWIN), Jethro. Took the Oath of Allegiance in Worcester County in 1778 in Quepomco Hundred before the Hon. Thomas Purnell [Ref: J-1814 (Box 4)]. Rendered patriotic service by supplying corn for the use of the military on Feb 1, 1780 and July 10, 1780 and by supplying beef on Oct 11, 1780 [Ref: G-10 listed the name as "Jethro Bowen" and P-267 and P-325 listed the name as "Jethro Bowing"].
BOWEN (BOWIN), John. Took the Oath of Allegiance in Worcester County in 1778 in Bogerternorton Hundred before the Hon. Thomas Purnell [Ref: J-1814 (Box 4)].
BOWEN (BOWIN), John. Private, Worcester Militia, Sinepuxent Bn., Capt. Elisha Purnell's Co., First Class, 1779/1780 [Ref: M-253]. Took the Oath of Allegiance in Worcester County in 1778 in Quepomco Hundred before the Hon. Thomas Purnell [Ref: J-1814 (Box 4)].
BOWEN (BOWIN), Levin (Leven). Private, Worcester Militia, Sinepuxent Bn., Capt. Elisha Purnell's Co., Second Class, 1779/1780 [Ref: M-253]. Took the Oath of Allegiance in Worcester County in 1778 in Quepomco Hundred before the Hon. Thomas Purnell [Ref: J-1814 (Box 4)].
BOWEN (BOWIN), Luke. Took the Oath of Allegiance in Worcester County in 1778 in Quepomco Hundred before the Hon. Thomas Purnell [Ref: J-1814 (Box 4)]. In Worcester County Court, in August, 1797, a petition to divide the real estate of Luke Bowen was submitted by James Massey and Comfort his wife, Eleanor Runnals (wife of Thomas Runnals), Luke, Catherine, Dolly, and Lydia Bowen (all of age), and Mary and Rachel Bowen (under age), all representatives of Luke Bowen who died seized of a small tract of land (not named). Edward Burbage was appointed guardian to the minors [Ref: Article by William D. Patrick in *Maryland Magazine of Genealogy*, Vol. 4, No. 1 (Spring, 1981), p. 6].
BOWEN, Lydia. See "Luke Bowen," q.v.
BOWEN, Mary. See "Luke Bowen," q.v.
BOWEN, Rachel. See "Luke Bowen," q.v.
BOWEN (BOWIN), Rackliff. Private, Worcester Militia, Sinepuxent Bn., Capt. Elisha Purnell's Co., Fourth Class, 1779/1780 [Ref: M-253]. Took the Oath of Allegiance in Worcester County in 1778 in Quepomco Hundred before the Hon. Thomas Purnell [Ref: J-1814 (Box 4) listed the name as "Rackliffe Bowin"].
BOWEN (BOWIN), Whittington Jr. Took the Oath of Allegiance in Worcester County in 1778 before the Hon. Nathaniel Miller [Ref: J-1814 (Box 4)].

BOWEN (BOWIN), Whittington Sr. Took the Oath of Allegiance in Worcester County in 1778 before the Hon. Nathaniel Miller [Ref: J-1814 (Box 4)].

BOWEN (BOWIN), William. Took the Oath of Allegiance in Worcester County in 1778 in Quepomco Hundred before the Hon. Thomas Purnell [Ref: J-1814 (Box 4)]. Private, Worcester Militia, Wicomico Bn., Capt. Philip Quinton's Co., Third Class, July 15, 1780 [Ref: M-256].

BOWEN (BOWIN), William. Private, Worcester Militia, Sinepuxent Bn., Capt. John Rackliff's Co., Third Class, 1779/1780 [Ref: M-251]. Private, Worcester Militia, Sinepuxent Bn., Capt. John Coe's Co., Fifth Class, 1779/1780 [Ref: M-252].

BOWEN (BOWIN), William, Segr.*[sic]*. Took the Oath of Allegiance in Worcester County in 1778 before the Hon. Nathaniel Miller [Ref: J-1814 (Box 4)].

BOWIE, William. Second Lieutenant, 2nd Independent Maryland Co., Somerset County, Capt. John Gunby's Co.; officers elected by the Maryland Convention, Jan 2, 1776 [Ref: D-20].

BOWLAND, William. Private, Somerset Militia, Salisbury Bn., Capt. William Turpin's Rewastico Co., 1778/1780 [Ref: M-217].

BOWLES, Samuel (1751-1841). Private, Worcester Militia, Sinepuxent Bn., Capt. Elisha Purnell's Co., Second Class, 1779/1780 [Ref: M-253]. "Samuel Boles or Bowles" applied for a pension (one source gave S10444 and another gave W10444 as the pension file number) in Bourbon County, Kentucky on Nov 13, 1832, stating he was born on March 17, 1751 in Sussex County, Delaware. In the winter of 1774 and 1775, at Lewistown, he volunteered for 12 months and served under Capt. David Hall. In 1776 he moved to Worcester County, Maryland and entered the service under Capt. James Corderry for an 8 months cruise on the privateer *Buckskin*. They took prize on Guinea ship on the coast of the West Indies. He concluded his sea service and in 1777 enlisted under Capt. Matthew Purnell for 6 months. In 1778 he was drafted for 9 months under Capt. Solomon Long and was then attached to the 3rd Maryland Regiment commanded by Colonel Hopewell. He fought in the battle of Trenton, when the Hessians were taken, came down with camp fever and was hospitalized at Germantown for about 5 months. On June 24, 1839, at Callaway County, Missouri, he requested his benefits be transferred from Kentucky to Missouri as he had moved there to be near his children (names not given, although a Thomas D. Boles, age 30, is mentioned later in 1854). On Oct 16, 1854, Nancy Boles or Bowles, age 79, of Callaway County, widow of Samuel who died on May 16, 1841, stated that she married him in Worcester County, Maryland on Feb 15, 1815 (by Rev. Robert Watson) and her maiden name was Nancy Powell [Ref: J-1814 (Box 12); A. W. Burns' abstracts on revolutionary soldiers of Maryland in Kentucky (pp. 8-9) at the Maryland Historical Society; and, source W-314 listed the name as "Samuel Boles or Bowles or Bowels"]. He was probably the "Samuel Bolds" who took the Oath of Allegiance in Worcester County in 1778 before the Hon. Nathaniel Miller [Ref: J-1814 (Box 4)].

BOWMAN, Isaac. Sergeant, Somerset Militia, Salisbury Bn., White Haven Co., 1778/1780 [Ref: M-218].
BOYEN, David. See "David Bowen," q.v.
BOYEN, Jepthah. See "Jeptha Bowen," q.v.
BOZMAN, Ballard. Second Lieutenant, Somerset Militia, 17th Bn., Sep 19, 1776. First Lieutenant, Princess Anne Bn., Capt. Isaac Handy's Great Annemessix Co., Dec 7, 1778 to at least July 24, 1780 [Ref: M-54, M-55, M-221, B-285, C-381, E-260]. Took the Oath of Allegiance in Somerset County in 1778 before the Hon. Levin Wilson [Ref: T-17, N-50].
BOZMAN, Doritha (Doratha). See "William Bozman," q.v.
BOZMAN, Eleanor. See "Joseph Gilliss" and "James Elzey," q.v.
BOZMAN, George. Took the Oath of Allegiance in Somerset County in 1778 before the Hon. John Williams [Ref: T-21]. See "William Bozman," q.v.
BOZMAN, Isaac. Took the Oath of Allegiance in Somerset County in 1778 before the Hon. Levin Wilson [Ref: T-17, N-50].
BOZMAN, Isaiah. Private, Select Militia, Somerset County, Aug 15, 1781 [Ref: L-35A].
BOZMAN, John. Private, Select Militia, Somerset County, Aug 15, 1781 [Ref: L-35B].
BOZMAN, Risdon. Private, Somerset Militia, Princess Anne Bn., St. Asaph's Co., 1780 [Ref: M-220]. Took the Oath of Allegiance in Somerset County in 1778 before the Hon. Peter Waters [Ref: T-18]. Select Militia, Somerset County, Aug 15, 1781 [Ref: L-35A].
BOZMAN, Thomas. Private, Somerset Militia, Princess Anne Bn., Capt. Thomas Irving's Monie Co., 1780 [Ref: M-219].
BOZMAN, William (1756 -   ). Son of George and Doritha (Doratha) Bozman, born in Coventry Parish on March 4, 1756 [Ref: Y-79]. Sergeant, Somerset Militia, Princess Anne Bn., St. Asaph's Co., 1780 [Ref: M-220]. Took the Oath of Allegiance in Somerset County in 1778 before the Hon. John Williams [Ref: T-21, N-50].
BRADFORD, Annanias. Private, Worcester Militia, Sinepuxent Bn., Capt. Matthew Purnell's Co., Second Class, July 25, 1780 [Ref: M-252].
BRADFORD, Avery. Private, Worcester Militia, Sinepuxent Bn., Capt. Matthew Purnell's Co., Sixth Class, July 25, 1780 [Ref: M-252].
BRADFORD, Elisha. Private, Worcester Militia, Sinepuxent Bn., Capt. Matthew Purnell's Co., Seventh Class, July 25, 1780 [Ref: M-252].
BRADFORD, Frances. See "John Holloway," q.v.
BRADFORD, Isaac. Private, Worcester Militia, Sinepuxent Bn., Capt. Matthew Purnell's Co., Fourth Class, July 25, 1780 [Ref: M-252].
BRADFORD, James. Private, Worcester Militia, Sinepuxent Bn., Capt. Elisha Purnell's Co., Second Class, 1779/1780 [Ref: M-253]. Took the Oath of Allegiance in Worcester County in 1778 in Quepomco Hundred before the Hon. Thomas Purnell [Ref: J-1814 (Box 4)].

BRADFORD, John. Private, Worcester Militia, Sinepuxent Bn., Capt. Thomas Purnell's Co., Eighth Class, 1779/1780 [Ref: M-253]. Took the Oath of Allegiance in Worcester County in 1778 before the Hon. Nathaniel Miller [Ref: J-1814 (Box 4)].

BRADFORD, Levin (Levan). Private, Worcester Militia, Sinepuxent Bn., Capt. Matthew Purnell's Co., Fourth Class, July 25, 1780 [Ref: M-252]. Took the Oath of Allegiance in Worcester County in 1778 before the Hon. Nathaniel Miller [Ref: J-1814 (Box 4)].

BRADFORD, Mary. Rendered patriotic service by supplying corn for the use of the military in Worcester County on June 14, 1780 and July 10, 1780 [Ref: P-296, G-10].

BRADFORD, Samuel. Private, Worcester Militia, Sinepuxent Bn., Capt. William Purnell's Co., Sixth Class, 1779/1780 [Ref: M-252]. Took the Oath of Allegiance in Worcester County in 1778 in Bogerternorton Hundred before the Hon. Thomas Purnell [Ref: J-1814 (Box 4) listed the name as "Samuel Braford"].

BRADFORD, Solomon. Private, Worcester Militia, Sinepuxent Bn., Capt. Matthew Purnell's Co., Fourth Class, July 25, 1780 [Ref: M-252]. Took the Oath of Allegiance in Worcester County in 1778 before the Hon. Joshua Townsend [Ref: J-1814 (Box 4)].

BRADFORD, Tabitha. See "John Tarr (of John)," q.v.

BRADFORD, William. Took the Oath of Allegiance in Worcester County in 1778 before the Hon. Nathaniel Miller [Ref: J-1814 (Box 4)].

BRADFORD, William (of Samuel). Private, Worcester Militia, Sinepuxent Bn., Capt. William Purnell's Co., Second Class, 1779/1780 [Ref: M-252].

BRADLEY, Ann. See "George Twilley," q.v.

BRADLEY, James. Took the Oath of Allegiance in Somerset County on Feb 21, 1778 (made his "J" mark) before the Hon. Joseph Venables [Ref: T-25].

BRADSHAW, Morgan. Private, Worcester Militia, Wicomico Bn., Capt. Fisher Walton's Co., First Class, July 15, 1780 [Ref: M-258]. Took the Oath of Allegiance in Worcester County in 1778 before the Hon. John Selby [Ref: J-1814 (Box 4)]. Private, Worcester Militia, Snow Hill Bn., Capt. Samuel Smyley's Co., 1777 [Ref: M-250 listed the name as "Morgain Braishier"].

BRANS, Duncan. Rendered patriotic service by supplying pork in Somerset County for the use of the military on June 8, 1781 [Ref: P-402]. See "Dunkin Banes," q.v.

BRASHER, John. Private, 3rd Maryland Independent Co., Worcester County, Capt. John Watkins' Co., enlisted Feb 2, 1776; muster roll dated Aug 20, 1776, absent on furlough 10th instant [Ref: D-21].

BRASTON(?), James. Took the Oath of Allegiance in Worcester County in 1778 before the Hon. William Hopewell [Ref: J-1814 (Box 4)].

BRATCHER, Richard. Private, Somerset Militia, Princess Anne Bn., Capt. Henry Miles' Little Annemessex Co., 1780 [Ref: M-221].

BRATTEN (BRATTON), Adam. Private, Worcester Militia, Sinepuxent Bn., Capt. John Postly's Co., Sixth Class, 1779/1780 [Ref: M-251].

BRATTEN (BRATTON), Belitha. Private, Worcester Militia, Sinepuxent Bn., Capt. Josiah Dale's Co., Fifth Class, 1779/1780. Private, Worcester Militia, Wicomico Bn., Capt. James Perdue's Co., Fifth Class, July 15, 1780 [Ref: M-254, M-256].

BRATTEN (BRATTON), Isaac. Private, Worcester Militia, Sinepuxent Bn., Capt. John Postly's Co., Fifth Class, 1779/1780 [Ref: M-251].

BRATTEN (BRATTON), James (c1760-1792). Born circa 1760 in Ireland, married Mary Polk, served as a lieutenant in Delaware during the war, and died in Maryland on April 22, 1792 [Ref: V-350].

BRATTEN (BRATTON), Jesse. Private, Worcester Militia, Wicomico Bn., Capt. James Perdue's Co., Seventh Class, July 15, 1780 [Ref: M-256]. Private, Maryland Troops, Worcester County, draughted May 1, 1781 [Ref: K-99 listed the name as "Jessey Brattan" and D-372 listed the name as "Jesey Brattan"]. Born between 1743 and 1759, married Mary ----, served in the war, and died before Jan 28, 1826 [Ref: V-350].

BRATTEN (BRATTON), John. Private, Worcester Militia, Wicomico Bn., Capt. Elijah Shockley's Co., Second Class, July 15, 1780 [Ref: M-255]. Took the Oath of Allegiance in Worcester County in 1778 before the Hon. William Hopewell [Ref: J-1814 (Box 4)]. See "John Round (Rounds, Rownds)," q.v.

BRATTEN (BRATTON), Joseph. Private, Worcester Militia, Sinepuxent Bn., Capt. John Coe's Co., Second Class, 1779/1780 [Ref: M-251].

BRATTEN (BRATTON), Mary. See "Jesse Bratten" and "John Round (Rounds, Rownds)," q.v.

BRATTEN (BRATTON), Nathaniel. Took the Oath of Allegiance in Worcester County in 1778 before the Hon. Nehemiah Holland [Ref: J-1814 (Box 4) listed the name as "Nathaniel Brattin"].

BRATTEN (BRATTON), Nehemiah. Private, Worcester Militia, Wicomico Bn., Capt. James Patterson's Co., Sixth Class, July 15, 1780 [Ref: M-258].

BRATTEN (BRATTON), Samuel. Private, Worcester Militia, Sinepuxent Bn., Capt. Josiah Dale's Co., Sixth Class, 1779/1780 [Ref: M-254]. Private, Worcester Militia, Wicomico Bn., Capt. John Parramore's Co., Second Class, July 15, 1780 [Ref: M-259].

BRATTEN (BRATTON), William (1755-c1840). Sailor, Maryland Sea Service, who applied for a pension (R1168) in Brown County, Ohio on April 17, 1838, age 82, stating he was born in Worcester County, Maryland on Dec 5, 1755 and lived there at the time of his enlistment. He entered the service on Aug 9, 1776 for one year and boarded the ship *Virginia* which was lying in the Chesapeake Bay, near Baltimore, under Commodore James Nicholson. The ship remained in the bay, blockaded by the British for the whole 12 months. In 1797 he moved to Davidson County, Tennessee and in 1802 moved to Smith County, Tennessee. In 1825 he moved to Brown County, Ohio for one year, then went back to Tennessee, and in 1837 returned to Ohio [Ref: J-1814 (Box 12), and W-370 listed the name as "William Bratten or Bratton"].

BRATTEN (BRATTON), William. Private, Worcester Militia, Sinepuxent Bn., Capt. John Postly's Co., Eighth Class, 1779/1780 [Ref: M-251 listed the name as "William Brattin"]. Rendered patriotic service by supplying corn for the use of the military on June 3, 1780 and July 10, 1780 [Ref: G-10 listed the name as "William Bratten" and P-294 listed the name as "William Bratton"].

BRATTEN (BRATTON), William Jr. Took the Oath of Allegiance in Worcester County in 1778 before the Hon. Nathaniel Miller [Ref: J-1814 (Box 4)].

BRATTEN (BRATTON), William Sr. Took the Oath of Allegiance in Worcester County in 1778 before the Hon. Nathaniel Miller [Ref: J-1814 (Box 4)].

BRAUGHTON, Elijah. See "Elijah Broughton," q.v.

BRAYTON, Jesse. Second Lieutenant, Worcester Militia, Wicomico Bn., Capt. James Perdue's Co., May 27, 1779 [Ref: M-55].

BRAZER, Beletha. Private, Worcester Militia, Sinepuxent Bn., Capt. John Coe's Co., Second Class, 1779/1780 [Ref: M-251].

BRERETON, John. Private, Somerset Militia, Salisbury Bn., White Haven Co., 1778/1780 [Ref: M-219]. Took the Oath of Allegiance in Somerset County on Feb 28, 1778 (made his "X" mark) before the Hon. Joseph Venables [Ref: T-25 listed the name as "John Brerton"]. On Jun 20, 1781 William Strawbridge recruited John Brereton from Somerset County to serve in the Continental Army for 3 years [Ref: L-35C].

BRERETON, Joseph. Private, Somerset Militia, Salisbury Bn., White Haven Co., 1778/1780 [Ref: M-219].

BRERETON, Presley. Private, Somerset Militia, Salisbury Bn., White Haven Co., 1778/1780 [Ref: M-219].

BRERETON, William. Took the Oath of Allegiance in Worcester County in 1778 before the Hon. William Hopewell [Ref: J-1814 (Box 4)].

BRETHERD, Daniel Coe. See "Daniel Coe Betherds," q.v.

BREVARD, John (c1740-1799). Ensign, Worcester Militia, Sinepuxent Bn., Capt. Elihu or Elisha Briddell's Co., Aug 30, 1777. Second Lieutenant, May 27, 1779, Capt. Joseph Dashiell's Co. [Ref: M-56, C-350, E-423]. John Brevard was born circa 1740, married Sarah Campbell, served as a second lieutenant during the war, and died before July 27, 1799 [Ref: V-356].

BREVARD, John. Private, Worcester Militia, Sinepuxent Bn., Capt. Josiah Dale's Co., Third Class, 1779/1780 [Ref: M-254]. Private, Maryland Troops, Worcester County, draughted May 1, 1781 [Ref: K-99, D-372].

BREWENTON, Pressly. See "Pressly Bruington," q.v.

BRIDELL, David. Private, Worcester Militia, Wicomico Bn., Capt. Elijah Shockley's Co., Sixth Class, July 15, 1780 [Ref: M-255].

BRIDELL, Elihu or Elisha. Captain, Worcester Militia, Sinepuxent Bn., Aug 30, 1777 [Ref: M-56, C-350 listed the name as "Elihu Briddell"]. Reportedly moved from the county, but no date was given [Ref: M-56 listed the name as "Elisha Briddle"].

BRIDELL, Ezar (Ezac?). Private, Worcester Militia, Wicomico Bn., Capt. Benjamin Dennis' Co., Fourth Class, July 15, 1780 [Ref: M-255].

BRIDELL, John. Private, Worcester Militia, Wicomico Bn., Capt. Elijah Shockley's Co., Eighth Class, July 15, 1780 [Ref: M-255].

BRITT, Frederick. Private, Worcester Militia, Wicomico Bn., Capt. Charles Bennett's Co., Eighth Class, July 15, 1780 [Ref: M-255]. Took the Oath of Allegiance in Worcester County in 1778 before the Hon. Joshua Townsend [Ref: J-1814 (Box 4) listed the name as "Frak. Britt"].

BRITTINGHAM, Belitha (c1750-c1797). Ensign, Worcester Militia, Sinepuxent Bn., Capt. William Purnell's Co., Aug 30, 1777 [Ref: M-56, M-252, C-350]. Second Lieutenant, June 13, 1782, Capt. Littleton Robins' Co., Sinepuxent Bn. [Ref: M-56, I-190]. Took the Oath of Allegiance in Worcester County in 1778 in Bogerternorton Hundred before the Hon. Thomas Purnell [Ref: J-1814 (Box 4)]. In Worcester County Court in February, 1797, a petition to divide the real estate of Belitha Brittingham was submitted by Isaac Solomon Brittingham (of full age) and Nancy, Peggy, Samuel, and James Brittingham (minors), children of Belitha Brittingham, who died intestate, possessed of part of a tract called *Nonesuch*, part of *Poplar Ridge*, and part of *Beckford*. McKimmy Porter was appointed guardian of the minor children [Ref: Article by William D. Patrick in *Maryland Magazine of Genealogy*, Vol. 4, No. 1 (Spring, 1981), p. 5].

BRITTINGHAM, Elijah. Private, Worcester Militia, Wicomico Bn., Capt. James Patterson's Co., Fifth Class, July 15, 1780 [Ref: M-258].

BRITTINGHAM, Elijah. Private, Worcester Militia, Snow Hill Bn., Capt. John Parramore's Co., 1777 [Ref: M-250]. Private, Worcester Militia, Wicomico Bn., Capt. John Parramore's Co., Eighth Class, July 15, 1780 [Ref: M-259].

BRITTINGHAM, Elijah. Private, Worcester Militia, Wicomico Bn., Capt. Samuel Smyley's Co., Fifth Class, July 15, 1780 [Ref: M-259]. Took the Oath of Allegiance in Worcester County in 1778 before the Hon. John Selby [Ref: J-1814 (Box 4)].

BRITTINGHAM, Elisha. Took the Oath of Allegiance in Worcester County in 1778 before the Hon. Nehemiah Holland [Ref: J-1814 (Box 4)].

BRITTINGHAM, Isaac. Private, Worcester Militia, Sinepuxent Bn., Capt. Josiah Dale's Co., Seventh Class, 1779/1780 [Ref: M-254]. Private, Maryland Troops, Worcester County, draughted May 1, 1781 [Ref: K-99, and D-372 mistakenly listed the name as "Isaac Brillingham"]. See "Belitha Brittingham," q.v.

BRITTINGHAM, James. See "Belitha Brittingham," q.v.

BRITTINGHAM, Jessey. Took the Oath of Allegiance in Worcester County in 1778 before the Hon. James Selby [Ref: J-1814 (Box 4)].

BRITTINGHAM, John. Private, Worcester Militia, Wicomico Bn., Capt. John Davis' Co., Third Class, July 15, 1780 [Ref: M-254]. Took the Oath of

Allegiance in Worcester County in 1778 before the Hon. John Selby [Ref: J-1814 (Box 4)].

BRITTINGHAM, John. Private, Worcester Militia, Wicomico Bn., Capt. Fisher Walton's Co., First Class, July 15, 1780 [Ref: M-258]. Took the Oath of Allegiance in Worcester County in 1778 before the Hon. Joshua Townsend [Ref: J-1814 (Box 4)].

BRITTINGHAM, Joseph. Private, Worcester Militia, Wicomico Bn., Capt. James Perdue's Co., Sixth Class, July 15, 1780 [Ref: M-256]. Ensign, May 27, 1779 [Ref: M-56, E-423]. Took the Oath of Allegiance in Worcester County in 1778 before the Hon. Joshua Townsend [Ref: J-1814 (Box 4)].

BRITTINGHAM, Joshua. Private, Worcester Militia, Sinepuxent Bn., Capt. William Purnell's Co., Eighth Class, 1779/1780 [Ref: M-252, M-253]. Took the Oath of Allegiance in Worcester County in 1778 in Buckingham Hundred before the Hon. Thomas Purnell [Ref: J-1814 (Box 4)].

BRITTINGHAM, Nancy. See "Belitha Brittingham," q.v.

BRITTINGHAM, Nathan. Took the Oath of Allegiance in Worcester County in 1778 in Bogerternorton Hundred before the Hon. Thomas Purnell [Ref: J-1814 (Box 4)].

BRITTINGHAM, Nathanael. Took the Oath of Allegiance in Worcester County in 1778 before the Hon. Joshua Townsend [Ref: J-1814 (Box 4)].

BRITTINGHAM, Nathaniel. Private, Worcester Militia, Wicomico Bn., Capt. Fisher Walton's Co., Second Class, July 15, 1780 [Ref: M-258]. Took the Oath of Allegiance in Worcester County in 1778 before the Hon. Nehemiah Holland [Ref: J-1814 (Box 4)].

BRITTINGHAM, Orpha. See "Nehemiah Turpin," q.v.

BRITTINGHAM, Peggy. See "Belitha Brittingham," q.v.

BRITTINGHAM, Purnell (Purnall). Private, Worcester Militia, Wicomico Bn., Capt. Isaac Layfield's Co., Third Class, July 15, 1780 [Ref: M-257]. Took the Oath of Allegiance in Worcester County in 1778 before the Hon. James Selby [Ref: J-1814 (Box 4)].

BRITTINGHAM, Samuel. Private, Worcester Militia, Sinepuxent Bn., Capt. William Purnell's Co., Fifth Class, 1779/1780 [Ref: M-252]. Took the Oath of Allegiance in Worcester County in 1778 in Bogerternorton Hundred before the Hon. Thomas Purnell [Ref: J-1814 (Box 4)]. See "Belitha Brittingham," q.v.

BRITTINGHAM, Samuel. Private, Worcester Militia, Snow Hill Bn., Capt. John Parramore's Co., 1777 [Ref: M-250]. Private, Worcester Militia, Wicomico Bn., Capt. Samuel Smyley's Co., Third Class, July 15, 1780 [Ref: M-259].

BRITTINGHAM, Samuel. First Lieutenant, Worcester Militia, Capt. William Holland's Co., June 28, 1777 [Ref: M-56].

BRITTINGHAM, Solomon (1765-1835). Private, 2nd Maryland Line, by April 24, 1780, when listed as a recruit entitled to clothing from the Commissary of Stores; possibly from Worcester County, but not indicated [Ref: F-150]. Solomon Brittingham was born on April 14, 1765 *[sic]*, served as a private during the war, married Leah Brown on Feb 25, 1816, and died in Fairfield County, Ohio on Oct 11 or Nov 7, 1835 (both dates were given). [Ref: V-370, and W-392 should be consulted for additional information]. See "Belitha Brittingham," q.v.

BRITTINGHAM, Thomas. Private, Worcester Militia, Snow Hill Bn., Capt. John Parramore's Co., 1777 [Ref: M-250]. Private, Worcester Militia, Wicomico Bn., Capt. Samuel Smyley's Co., Third Class, July 15, 1780 [Ref: M-259]. Took the Oath of Allegiance in Worcester County in 1778 before the Hon. John Selby [Ref: J-1814 (Box 4)].

BRITTINGHAM, Thomas. Private, Worcester Militia, Sinepuxent Bn., Capt. William Purnell's Co., Sixth Class, 1779/1780 [Ref: M-252]. Took the Oath of Allegiance in Worcester County in 1778 in Bogerternorton Hundred before the Hon. Thomas Purnell [Ref: J-1814 (Box 4)].

BRITTINGHAM, Truitt (Truett). Private, Worcester Militia, Wicomico Bn., Capt. John Davis' Co., Fifth Class, July 15, 1780 [Ref: M-254]. Took the Oath of Allegiance in Worcester County in 1778 before the Hon. Joshua Townsend [Ref: J-1814 (Box 4)].

BRITTINGHAM, William. Private, Worcester Militia, Wicomico Bn., Capt. John Davis' Co., Second Class, July 15, 1780 [Ref: M-254]. Took the Oath of Allegiance in Worcester County in 1778 before the Hon. James Selby [Ref: J-1814 (Box 4)].

BRITTINGHAM, William. Private, Worcester Militia, Wicomico Bn., Capt. Fisher Walton's Co., Fourth Class, July 15, 1780 [Ref: M-258]. Took the Oath of Allegiance in Worcester County in 1778 before the Hon. Nehemiah Holland [Ref: J-1814 (Box 4)].

BRITTINGHAM, William. Private, Worcester Militia, Wicomico Bn., Capt. John Davis' Co., Sixth Class, July 15, 1780 [Ref: M-254]. Took the Oath of Allegiance in Worcester County in 1778 before the Hon. Joshua Townsend [Ref: J-1814 (Box 4)].

BRITTINGHAM, William. Private, Worcester Militia, Sinepuxent Bn., Capt. William Purnell's Co., Eighth Class, 1779/1780 [Ref: M-252]. Took the Oath of Allegiance in Worcester County in 1778 in Bogerternorton Hundred before the Hon. Thomas Purnell [Ref: J-1814 (Box 4)].

BRITTINGHAM, William. Took the Oath of Allegiance in Worcester County in 1778 in Bogerternorton Hundred before the Hon. Thomas Purnell [Ref: J-1814 (Box 4)].

BRITTINGHAM, William (of Natn). Private, Worcester Militia, Sinepuxent Bn., Capt. William Purnell's Co., Second Class, 1779/1780 [Ref: M-252].

BRITTINGHAM, William (Pocomoak). Took the Oath of Allegiance in Worcester County in 1778 before the Hon. Joshua Townsend [Ref: J-1814 (Box 4)].

BROMFIELD (BRUMFIELD), Thomas. On April 25, 1777 the Council of Maryland issued a recruiting warrant "to Thomas Bromfield of Somerset County to enlist men for the ship *Defence*, during the war, the term of three years, or the cruize according to the usual terms of privateers." [Ref: C-229]. "Thomas Brumfield" was a private in the Somerset County Militia, Capt. George Day Scott's Co., 1775 [Ref: J-1814 (Box 1)].

BROOKS, Benjamin. Third Lieutenant, 2nd Independent Maryland Co., Somerset County, Capt. John Gunby's Co.; officers elected by the Maryland Conventon, Jan 2, 1776 [Ref: D-20].

BROOKS, Samuel. Private, Worcester Militia, Wicomico Bn., Capt. Robert Handy's Co., Seventh Class, July 15, 1780 [Ref: M-254].

BROOKS, Thomas. Took the Oath of Allegiance in Somerset County in 1778 before the Hon. Levin Wilson [Ref: T-17].

BROTON, Joseph, Ensign, Worcester Militia, Sinepuxent Bn., March 16, 1781 [Ref: M-57, G-353].

BROUGHTON (BRAUGHTON), Adam. Took the Oath of Allegiance in Worcester County in 1778 before the Hon. Nathaniel Miller [Ref: J-1814 (Box 4)].

BROUGHTON (BRAUGHTON), Charles. Private, Somerset Militia, Princess Anne Bn., Capt. George Waters' Pocomoke Co., 1780 [Ref: M-220].

BROUGHTON (BRAUGHTON), Elijah (1756 -   ). Son of William and Jemis Broughton, born in Coventry Parish on April 4, 1756 [Ref: Y-79]. Private, Somerset Militia, Princess Anne Bn., Capt. George Waters' Pocomoke Co., 1780 [Ref: M-220].

BROUGHTON (BRAUGHTON), Isaac. Took the Oath of Allegiance in Worcester County in 1778 before the Hon. Nathaniel Miller [Ref: J-1814 (Box 4)].

BROUGHTON (BRAUGHTON), Jemis. See "Elijah Broughton," q.v.

BROUGHTON (BRAUGHTON), John. Private, Worcester Militia, Snow Hill Bn., Capt. Ebenezer Handy's Co., April 9, 1776 [Ref: M-249]. Ensign, Worcester Militia, Capt. Samuel H. Round's Co., Select Militia, Aug 23, 1781 [Ref: M-57, G-577].

BROUGHTON (BRAUGHTON), John Jr. Private, Somerset Militia, Princess Anne Bn., Capt. George Waters' Pocomoke Co., 1780 [Ref: M-220].

BROUGHTON (BRAUGHTON), John Sr. Took the Oath of Allegiance in Somerset County in 1778 before the Hon. Levin Wilson [Ref: T-17, and N-50 mistakenly listed the name as "John Bringhton, Sr."]. See "Josiah Broughton," q.v.

BROUGHTON (BRAUGHTON), Josiah (1760 -   ). Son of John and Mary Broughton, born in Coventry Parish on Dec 24, 1760 [Ref: Y-79]. Corporal, Somerset Militia, Princess Anne Bn., Capt. George Waters' Pocomoke Co., 1780 [Ref: M-220].

BROUGHTON (BRAUGHTON), Kellum. Private, Somerset Militia, Princess Anne Bn., Capt. George Waters' Pocomoke Co., 1780 [Ref: M-220]. Drafted from Somerset County on July 30, 1781 to serve in the Continental Army [Ref: L-35C].

BROUGHTON (BRAUGHTON), Mary. See "Josiah Broughton," q.v.

BROUGHTON (BRAUGHTON), William. Private, Somerset Militia, Princess Anne Bn., St. Asaph's Co., 1780 [Ref: M-220]. Drafted from Somerset County on June 20, 1781 to serve in the Continental Army [Ref: L-35C]. See "Elijah Broughton," q.v.

BROWN, Andrew (1754-1815). Private, Worcester Militia, Wicomico Bn., Capt. Philip Quinton's Co., Second Class, July 15, 1780 [Ref: M-256]. See "William Brown," q.v.

BROWN, Captain. See "Josiah Cathell," q.v.

BROWN, David (c1760-c1829). Son of George Brown, of Worcester County. He married Sarah Carey and daughter Polly Brown (1783-1850) married Handy Hayman (1784-1872) in 1808 in Somerset County [Ref: Q-23:3 (Summer, 1982), "Ancestor Table of Willis Clayton Tull, Jr.," pp. 247-255]. Private, Worcester Militia, Wicomico Bn., Capt. Samuel Horsey's Co., Fourth Class, July 15, 1780 [Ref: M-257].

BROWN, G. R. See "John Robertson," q.v.

BROWN, George (c1745-1803). Private, Worcester Militia, Wicomico Bn., Capt. Samuel Horsey's Co., Sixth Class, July 15, 1780 [Ref: M-257].

BROWN, George (c1720-1788). Rendered patriotic service by supplying bacon for the use of the military on Oct 15, 1780 [Ref: P-327]. See "David Brown," q.v.

BROWN, Grace. See "William Brown," q.v.

BROWN, Gustavus. See "Gustavus Scott," q.v.

BROWN, John. Private, Worcester Militia, Wicomico Bn., Capt. Samuel Horsey's Co., Second Class, July 15, 1780 [Ref: M-256]. See "John Henry," q.v.

BROWN, John. Took the Oath of Allegiance in Somerset County on March 1, 1778 before the Hon. Joseph Venables [Ref: T-25].

BROWN, Jonathan. Private, Somerset County, Capt. John Gunby's 2nd Independent Maryland Co.; present on May 14, 1776; mustered on Aug 21, 1776 [Ref: D-641].

BROWN, Leah. See "Solomon Brittingham," q.v.

BROWN, Levi (1752-1824). Private, Somerset Militia, Salisbury Bn., Capt. James Bennett's Salisbury Co., 1778/1780 [Ref: M-218].

BROWN, Polly. See "John Hayman, Jr." and "David Brown," q.v.

BROWN, Robert. Took the Oath of Allegiance in Somerset County on Feb 19, 1778 before the Hon. Joseph Venables [Ref: T-25].

BROWN, Sarah. See "Gustavus Brown," q.v.

BROWN, William (1759-). Son of Andrew and Grace Brown, born in Coventry Parish on Nov 9, 1759 [Ref: Y-79]. Took the Oath of Allegiance in Somerset County on Jan 26, 1778 before the Hon. Joseph Venables [Ref: T-25, N-50]. Private, Worcester Militia, Wicomico Bn., Capt. Philip Quinton's Co., Seventh Class, July 15, 1780 [Ref: M-256].

BROWN, Wilson (1745-1814). Private, Worcester Militia, Wicomico Bn., Capt. Philip Quinton's Co., Fourth Class, July 15, 1780 [Ref: M-256].

BRUFF, James (1762 -   ). Son of Thomas Bruff and Betty White, born in Coventry Parish on July 25, 1762 [Ref: Y-79]. Private, Somerset Militia, Princess Anne Bn., Capt. George Waters' Pocomoke Co., 1780 [Ref: M-220]. Select Militia, Somerset County, Aug 15, 1781 [Ref: L-35A].

BRUFF, Thomas. First Major, Somerset Militia, Jan 6, 1776. Major, Princess Anne Bn., Aug 30, 1777. Lieutenant Colonel by Oct 26, 1780, succeeded [Ref: M-57, E-351, F-342]. Took the Oath of Allegiance in Somerset County in 1778 before the Hon. Peter Waters [Ref: T-18]. Attended the Maryland Convention in 1776 "for the express purpose of forming a new government" [Ref: O-36]. Appointed by the Maryland Convention in November, 1776 to be one of the Judges of Elections in Somerset County [Ref: O-55]. See "James Bruff," q.v.

BRUINGTON, Hannah. See "John Victor," q.v.

BRUINGTON, Henry. Private, Worcester Militia, Snow Hill Bn., Capt. Ebenezer Handy's Co., April 9, 1776 [Ref: M-249].

BRUINGTON, James. Private, Worcester Militia, Wicomico Bn., Capt. Robert Handy's Co., Fifth Class, July 15, 1780 [Ref: M-254].

BRUINGTON, John. Private, Worcester Militia, Snow Hill Bn., Capt. Ebenezer Handy's Co., April 9, 1776 [Ref: M-249]. Private, Worcester Militia, Wicomico Bn., Capt. Robert Handy's Co., Eighth Class, July 15, 1780 [Ref: M-254].

BRUINGTON, Pressly. Private, Somerset County, Capt. John Gunby's 2nd Independent Maryland Co.; sick in barracks on March 4, 1776; mustered on Aug 21, 1776 [Ref: D-641 listed the name as "Pressly Brewenton"].

BRUINGTON, Samuel. Private, Worcester Militia, Snow Hill Bn., Capt. Ebenezer Handy's Co., April 9, 1776 [Ref: M-249]. Private, Worcester Militia, Wicomico Bn., Capt. Robert Handy's Co., Fourth Class, July 15, 1780 [Ref: M-254].

BRUINGTON, Samuel. Private, Worcester Militia, Wicomico Bn., Capt. Robert Handy's Co., Fourth Class, July 15, 1780 [Ref: M-254].

BRUINGTON, William. Private, Worcester Militia, Snow Hill Bn., Capt. Ebenezer Handy's Co., April 9, 1776 [Ref: M-249]. Took the Oath of Allegiance in Worcester County in 1778 before the Hon. William Hopewell [Ref: J-1814 (Box 4)]. Private, Worcester Militia, Wicomico Bn., Capt. Robert Handy's Co., Fourth Class, July 15, 1780 [Ref: M-254].

BRUMBLE (BRUMBLY), Ezekiel (c1742-1793). Took the Oath of Allegiance in Worcester County in 1778 before the Hon. Nehemiah Holland [Ref: J-1814 (Box 4)]. "Ezekiel Brumbly" was born circa 1742, married Tabitha ----, rendered patriotic service during the war, and died before Oct 8, 1793 [Ref: V-407].

BRUMBLE (BRUMBLY), Fassett. Took the Oath of Allegiance in Worcester County in 1778 before the Hon. John Selby [Ref: J-1814 (Box 4)]. Private, Worcester Militia, Wicomico Bn., Capt. John Davis' Co., Eighth Class, July 15, 1780 [Ref: M-255 listed the name as "Fassat Brumbly"].

BRUMBLE (BRUMBLY), Henry. Took the Oath of Allegiance in Worcester County in 1778 before the Hon. John Selby [Ref: J-1814 (Box 4)].

BRUMBLE (BRUMBLY), Henry. Private, Worcester Militia, Sinepuxent Bn., Capt. John Rackliff's Co., Eighth Class, 1779/1780 [Ref: M-251].
BRUMBLE (BRUMBLY), Henry. Private, Worcester Militia, Sinepuxent Bn., Capt. Elisha Purnell's Co., Third Class, 1779/1780 [Ref: M-253].
BRUMBLE (BRUMBLY), John. Took the Oath of Allegiance in Worcester County in 1778 before the Hon. Joshua Townsend [Ref: J-1814 (Box 4)]. Private, Worcester Militia, Wicomico Bn., Capt. James Patterson's Co., Fourth Class, July 15, 1780 [Ref: M-258].
BRUMBLE (BRUMBLY), Tabitha. See "Ezekiel Brumble," q.v.
BRUMBLE (BRUMBLY), William. Took the Oath of Allegiance in Worcester County in 1778 before the Hon. John Selby [Ref: J-1814 (Box 4)].
BRUMFIELD, Thomas. See "Thomas Bromfield," q.v.
BUCKINGHAM, William Selby. Took the Oath of Allegiance in Worcester County in 1778 before the Hon. Nathaniel Miller [Ref: J-1814 (Box 4)].
BULY, Job. Private, Worcester Militia, Wicomico Bn., Capt. Robert Handy's Co., Fifth Class, July 15, 1780 [Ref: M-254].
BULY, Titus. Private, Worcester Militia, Wicomico Bn., Capt. Robert Handy's Co., Eighth Class, July 15, 1780 [Ref: M-254].
BUNDICK, Mary. See "Brittingham Henderson," q.v.
BURBAGE, Edward. Private, Worcester Militia, Sinepuxent Bn., Capt. Elisha Purnell's Co., First Class, 1779/1780 [Ref: M-253]. See "Luke Bowen," q.v.
BURBAGE, Elias. Private, Worcester Militia, Sinepuxent Bn., Capt. Matthew Purnell's Co., First Class, July 25, 1780 [Ref: M-252]. Took the Oath of Allegiance in Worcester County in 1778 before the Hon. Joshua Townsend [Ref: J-1814 (Box 4)].
BURBAGE, Hampton. Private, Worcester Militia, Sinepuxent Bn., Capt. Thomas Purnell's Co., Eighth Class, 1779/1780 [Ref: M-253].
BURBAGE, John. Private, Worcester Militia, Sinepuxent Bn., Capt. Matthew Purnell's Co., First Class, July 25, 1780 [Ref: M-252]. Took the Oath of Allegiance in Worcester County in 1778 before the Hon. Joshua Townsend [Ref: J-1814 (Box 4)].
BURBAGE, Salathiel (Selathell). Took the Oath of Allegiance in Worcester County in 1778 before the Hon. Joshua Townsend [Ref: J-1814 (Box 4)]. Private, Worcester Militia, Sinepuxent Bn., Capt. Elisha Purnell's Co., Seventh Class, 1779/1780 [Ref: M-253].
BURBAGE, Thomas. Private, Worcester Militia, Sinepuxent Bn., Capt. Elisha Purnell's Co., Fifth Class, 1779/1780 [Ref: M-253]. Took the Oath of Allegiance in Worcester County in 1778 before the Hon. Joshua Townsend [Ref: J-1814 (Box 4)].
BURBAGE, William. Private, Worcester Militia, Sinepuxent Bn., Capt. Elisha Purnell's Co., Second Class, 1779/1780 [Ref: M-253].
BURCH, George. Private, Worcester Militia, Wicomico Bn., Capt. John Parramore's Co., Eighth Class, July 15, 1780 [Ref: M-259].

BURGIN, Daniel. Private, Somerset Militia, Salisbury Bn., Capt. Josiah Dashiell's Wicomico Creek Co., 1778/1780 [Ref: M-218]. Drafted from Somerset County into the Continental Army on June 20, 1781, but was subsequently excused [Ref: L-35C listed the name as "Daniel Burgan"].

BURGIN, Thomas. Private, Somerset Militia, Salisbury Bn., White Haven Co., 1778/1780 [Ref: M-218].

BURK (BURKE), George. Private, Worcester Militia, Sinepuxent Bn., Capt. John Postly's Co., Sixth Class, 1779/1780 [Ref: M-251]. Took the Oath of Allegiance in Worcester County in 1778 before the Hon. Nathaniel Miller [Ref: J-1814 (Box 4)].

BURLING, Thomas. Took the Oath of Allegiance in Worcester County in 1778 before the Hon. Joshua Townsend [Ref: J-1814 (Box 4)].

BURNETT (BURNET), Elijah. Took the Oath of Allegiance in Worcester County in 1778 before the Hon. James Selby [Ref: J-1814 (Box 4)]. Private, Worcester Militia, Wicomico Bn., Capt. James Patterson's Co., Third Class, July 15, 1780 [Ref: M-258].

BURNETT (BURNET), James (c1715-1780). Took the Oath of Allegiance in Worcester County in 1778 before the Hon. James Selby [Ref: J-1814 (Box 4)].

BURNETT (BURNET), James. Private, Worcester Militia, Wicomico Bn., Capt. James Patterson's Co., Fourth Class, July 15, 1780 [Ref: M-258].

BUSEY(?), Phillip. Private, Worcester Militia, Wicomico Bn., Capt. Robert Handy's Co., Sixth Class, July 15, 1780 [Ref: M-254].

BUSSELL, James. Private, Worcester Militia, Wicomico Bn., Capt. Charles Bennett's Co., Fifth Class, July 15, 1780 [Ref: M-255].

BUTLER, Joshua. Private, Worcester Militia, Wicomico Bn., Capt. Benjamin Dennis' Co., Second Class, July 15, 1780 [Ref: M-255 listed the name as "Joshua Buttler"].

BUTLER, William. Private, Worcester Militia, Wicomico Bn., Capt. Samuel Horsey's Co., Second Class, July 15, 1780 [Ref: M-256]. Took the Oath of Allegiance in Worcester County in 1778 before the Hon. William Hopewell [Ref: J-1814 (Box 4)]. Private, Maryland Troops, Worcester County, draughted May 1, 1781 [Ref: K-99, D-372].

BYNG (BING), William. Ensign, Somerset Militia, Salisbury Bn., Capt. James Bennett's Salisbury Co., May 27, 1779; on duty 1780. Second Lieutenant, 1781 [Ref: M-59, M-218, E-423, G-575, H-195, J-1814 (Box 8, Dashiell's correspondence), and H-361 listed the name as "Wm. Bynge"]. Took the Oath of Allegiance in Somerset County in 1778 before the Hon. Gillis Polk [Ref: N-50, and T-15 listed the name as "William Bing"].

BYRD, Benjamin. Took the Oath of Allegiance in Somerset County on Feb 14, 1778 before the Hon. Joseph Venables [Ref: T-25].

BYRD, Benjaman Sr. Took the Oath of Allegiance in Somerset County on Feb 14, 1778 before the Hon. Joseph Venables [Ref: T-25].

BYRD, John. Took the Oath of Allegiance in Somerset County on Feb 14, 1778 before the Hon. Joseph Venables [Ref: T-25].
BYRD, Thomas. Took the Oath of Allegiance in Somerset County on Feb 14, 1778 before the Hon. Joseph Venables [Ref: T-25].
C--?--, John. Private, Somerset Militia, Salisbury Bn., Capt. John Span Conway's Nanticoke Point Co., 1778/1780 [Ref: M-216].
CACEY, Levin. See "Levin Casey," q.v.
CAHOON, Ephraim. See "Ephraim Cohoon," q.v.
CAILE, Margaret. See "Gustavus Scott," q.v.
CAIN, John. Private, Worcester Militia, Wicomico Bn., Capt. Isaac Layfield's Co., Fifth Class, July 15, 1780 [Ref: M-257]. Took the Oath of Allegiance in Worcester County in 1778 before the Hon. James Selby [Ref: J-1814 (Box 4)].
CALBERT, Isaac. Private, Somerset Militia, Princess Anne Bn., Capt. Isaac Handy's Great Annemessix Co., 1780 [Ref: M-221].
CALDWELL, John. Private, Worcester Militia, Wicomico Bn., Capt. Robert Handy's Co., Second Class, July 15, 1780 [Ref: M-254].
CALHOON, Ephraim. See "Ephraim Cohoon," q.v.
CALPIN, Glenn. Took the Oath of Allegiance in Worcester County in 1778 before the Hon. Nehemiah Holland [Ref: J-1814 (Box 4)].
CALVERT, Alexander. See "Neal Calvert," q.v.
CALVERT, Neal. Private, Somerset Militia, Princess Anne Bn., St. Asaph's Co., 1780 [Ref: M-221]. "Alexander Neal Calvert" was the son of Alexander and Mary Calvert, born in Coventry Parish on Jan 14, 1753 [Ref: Y-69].
CALVERT, Mary. See "Neal Calvert," q.v.
CAMEL, James. See "James Campbell," q.v.
CAMEL, Jno. See "John Campbell," q.v.
CAMERON, Bartlet. Took the Oath of Allegiance in Worcester County in 1778 before the Hon. John Selby [Ref: J-1814 (Box 4)].
CAMERON, William. Private, Somerset Militia, Princess Anne Bn., Capt. George Waters' Pocomoke Co., 1780 [Ref: M-220 listed the name as "William Camneron"].
CAMM, John. Rendered patriotic service by supplying cattle for the military in Worcester County on Dec 16, 1781 [Ref: P-462].
CAMPBELL, Bartholomew. Private, Worcester Militia, Wicomico Bn., Capt. Samuel Smyley's Co., First Class, July 15, 1780 [Ref: M-258].
CAMPBELL, Bartley. Private, Worcester Militia, Snow Hill Bn., Capt. John Parramore's Co., 1777 [Ref: M-250 listed the name as "Bartley Cambell"].
CAMPBELL, Duncan. Private, 5th Maryland Line, enlisted June 6, 1778 and discharged on March 1, 1779 [Ref: D-192 listed the name as "Dunk Camble"].
CAMPBELL, James. Private, Worcester Militia, Wicomico Bn., Capt. Isaac Layfield's Co., Fourth Class, July 15, 1780 [Ref: M-257].

CAMPBELL, James. Recruited from Somerset County by Robert Jenkins Henry on July 30, 1781 to serve in the Continental Army until Dec 10, 1781 [Ref: L-35C listed the name as "James Camel"].
CAMPBELL, John. Private, Worcester Militia, Wicomico Bn., Capt. John Davis' Co., First Class, July 15, 1780 [Ref: M-254].
CAMPBELL, John. Private, Somerset Militia, Princess Anne Bn., St. Asaph's Co., 1780 [Ref: M-220]. On June 20, 1781 Samuel Collins (Collens) recruited John Campbell from Somerset County to serve in the Continental Army for 3 years [Ref: L-35C listed the name as "Jno. Camel"].
CAMPBELL, Sarah. See "John Brevard," q.v.
CAMPBELL, Solomon. Private, Worcester Militia, Sinepuxent Bn., Capt. John Rackliff's Co., Third Class, 1779/1780 [Ref: M-251]. Took the Oath of Allegiance in Worcester County in 1778 before the Hon. Nathaniel Miller [Ref: J-1814 (Box 4)]. Rendered patriotic service by supplying corn for the use of the military on June 14, 1780 and July 10, 1780 [Ref: P-296, G-10].
CAMPBELL, Tabitha. See "John Holland" and "Samuel Holland," q.v.
CAMPBELL, William. Private, Worcester Militia, Sinepuxent Bn., Capt. Thomas Purnell's Co., Eighth Class, 1779/1780 [Ref: M-253].
CAMPBELL, William. Private, Worcester Militia, Sinepuxent Bn., Capt. John Postly's Co., Fourth Class, 1779/1780 [Ref: M-251].
CAMPBELL, William. Took the Oath of Allegiance in Worcester County in 1778 before the Hon. Joshua Townsend [Ref: J-1814 (Box 4) listed the name as "William Cambell"]. Rendered patriotic service by supplying corn for the use of the military on Aug 20, 1780 [Ref: P-310].
CANNON, Matthew. Took the Oath of Allegiance in Somerset County in 1778 before the Hon. John Span Conway [Ref: T-14, N-50].
CANNON, Minos (1756-1829). Born in Maryland, possibly Somerset County, in 1756, married Letitia Thompson, served as a soldier in the North Carolina troops during the war, and died in Tennessee on May 10, 1829 [Ref: V-482].
CANNON, Thomas. Private, Somerset Militia, Salisbury Bn., Capt. Henry Gale's Quantico Co., 1778/1780 [Ref: M-216]. Took the Oath of Allegiance in Worcester County in 1778 before the Hon. John Selby [Ref: J-1814 (Box 4)]. One Thomas Cannon was a private in the 5th Maryland Line who enlisted on Aug 28, 1777 and was reported as "left out" in April, 1778 [Ref: D-191].
CANNON, Waitman. Private, Worcester Militia, Sinepuxent Bn., Capt. John Coe's Co., Third Class, 1779/1780 [Ref: M-252].
CANTWELL, Joseph. Private, Somerset Militia, Princess Anne Bn., Capt. Thomas Irving's Monie Co., 1780 [Ref: M-219].
CANTWELL, Nicholas. Sergeant, Somerset Militia, Salisbury Bn., Capt. William Turpin's Rewastico Co., 1778/1780 [Ref: M-217].
CAREY (CARY), Elijah. Ensign, Worcester Militia, Capt. Elijah Shockley's Co., elected May 3, 1776 [Ref: A-405].
CAREY, Elizabeth. See "Solomon Hamblin," q.v.

CAREY (CARY), Hezekiah. Ensign, Worcester Militia, June 28, 1777 and Wicomico Bn., Capt. Elijah Shockley's Co., July 15, 1780 [Ref: M-59, M-255].
CAREY (CARY), Jeremiah. Private, Worcester Militia, Snow Hill Bn., Capt. Samuel Smyley's Co., 1777 [Ref: M-250]. Private, Worcester Militia, Wicomico Bn., Capt. Samuel Smyley's Co., Third Class, July 15, 1780 [Ref: M-259].
CAREY (CARY), John. Took the Oath of Allegiance in Worcester County in 1778 before the Hon. Nehemiah Holland [Ref: J-1814 (Box 4)].
CAREY (CARY), Jonathan. Private, Worcester Militia, Sinepuxent Bn., Capt. Josiah Dale's Co., Second Class, 1779/1780 [Ref: M-254].
CAREY (CARY), Justice. Took the Oath of Allegiance in Worcester County in 1778 before the Hon. Nehemiah Holland [Ref: J-1814 (Box 4)]. Private, Worcester Militia, Wicomico Bn., Capt. Fisher Walton's Co., First Class, July 15, 1780 [Ref: M-258].
CAREY, Karenhappuch. See "William Shockley," q.v.
CAREY (CARY), Levi. Took the Oath of Allegiance in Worcester County in 1778 before the Hon. James Selby [Ref: J-1814 (Box 4)]. Private, Worcester Militia, Wicomico Bn., Capt. Isaac Layfield's Co., Sixth Class, July 15, 1780 [Ref: M-257].
CAREY (CARY), Levin. Private, Worcester Militia, Wicomico Bn., Capt. Elijah Shockley's Co., Eighth Class, July 15, 1780 [Ref: M-255].
CAREY, Mary. See "Solomon Hamblin," q.v.
CAREY, Sarah. See "David Brown," q.v.
CAREY (CARY), Smith. Took the Oath of Allegiance in Worcester County in 1778 before the Hon. Nehemiah Holland [Ref: J-1814 (Box 4)]. Private, Worcester Militia, Wicomico Bn., Capt. Fisher Walton's Co., Eighth Class, July 15, 1780 [Ref: M-258].
CAREY (CARY), Solomon. Private, Worcester Militia, Sinepuxent Bn., Capt. John Postly's Co., Fourth Class, 1779/1780 [Ref: M-251]. Private, Worcester Militia, Sinepuxent Bn., Capt. Josiah Dale's Co., Seventh Class, 1779/1780 [Ref: M-254]. Private, Worcester Militia, Wicomico Bn., Capt. Fisher Walton's Co., Fourth Class, July 15, 1780 [Ref: M-258]. Took the Oath of Allegiance in Worcester County in 1778 before the Hon. Nathaniel Miller [Ref: J-1814 (Box 4)].
CAREY (CARY), Solomon Jr. Took the Oath of Allegiance in Worcester County in 1778 before the Hon. John Selby [Ref: J-1814 (Box 4)].
CAREY (CARY), Solomon Sr. Took the Oath of Allegiance in Worcester County in 1778 before the Hon. Nehemiah Holland [Ref: J-1814 (Box 4)].
CAREY (CARY), William. Took the Oath of Allegiance in Worcester County in 1778 before the Hon. John Selby [Ref: J-1814 (Box 4)].
CARMAN, James. Private, 5th Maryland Line, enlisted on Feb 21, 1777 and reported missing on Aug 16, 1780 after the Battle of Camden [Ref: D-192].

CARMAN, Salathiel. Private, 2nd Maryland Line, whose name first appeared on a list of recruits from and deserters taken up in Somerset County on Oct 20, 1780 and was later listed in Capt. Murdoch's Co. of the Maryland State Regiment on March 15, 1781 [Ref: D-346 listed the name as "Salathiel Carmine" and D-366 listed the name as "Salithiel Carmin"].
CARMAN, William. Private, Somerset Militia, Princess Anne Bn., St. Asaph's Co., 1780 [Ref: M-221].
CARMICHAEL, Benjamin. Private, Somerset Militia, Salisbury Bn., Capt. James Bennett's Salisbury Co., 1778/1780 [Ref: M-218].
CARMICHAEL, John. Private, Somerset Militia, Salisbury Bn., Capt. William Turpin's Rewastico Co., 1778/1780 [Ref: M-217].
CARMICHAEL, Levin. Private, Somerset Militia, Salisbury Bn., Capt. William Turpin's Rewastico Co., 1778/1780 [Ref: M-217].
CARROLL (CARROL), William. Private, Somerset Militia, Princess Anne Bn., Capt. James Elzey's Co., 1780 [Ref: M-220]. Took the Oath of Allegiance in Somerset County in 1778 before the Hon. Levin Wilson [Ref: T-17, N-50].
CARSLEY, Samuel. Private, Somerset Militia, Princess Anne Bn., St. Asaph's Co., 1780 [Ref: M-221].
CARTER, Isaac (1756 -   ). Son of James and Sarah(?) Carter, born in Coventry Parish on Oct 24, 1756 [Ref: Y-69]. Took the Oath of Allegiance in Somerset County in 1778 before the Hon. Levin Wilson [Ref: T-17, N-50].
CARTER, James. See "Isaac Carter," q.v.
CARTER, John. Private, Maryland Line, whose name appeared on "a list of recruits from and deserters taken up in Somerset County on Oct 20, 1780" [Ref: D-346].
CARTER, Sarah. See "Isaac Carter," q.v.
CASE, Barnaby. Private, Maryland Line, whose name appeared on "a list of recruits from and deserters taken up in Somerset County on Oct 20, 1780" [Ref: D-346].
CASEY, Elijah. Ensign, Worcester Militia, Capt. Shockley's Co., June 15, 1776 [Ref: M-60, A-427].
CASEY, Levin. Private, Worcester Militia, Wicomico Bn., Capt. Samuel Horsey's Co., Third Class, July 15, 1780 [Ref: M-256 listed the name as "Levin Cacey"].
CASEY, William. Took the Oath of Allegiance in Somerset County in 1778 before the Hon. William Winder [Ref: T-22, N-50].
CATHELL, Daniel. Ensign, Worcester Militia, June 28, 1777 [Ref: M-60 listed the name as "Daniel Catheel"]. Took the Oath of Allegiance in Worcester County in 1778 before the Hon. William Hopewell [Ref: J-1814 (Box 4)].
CATHELL, Daniel. Private, Wicomico Bn., Capt. Elijah Shockley's Co., Eighth Class, July 15, 1780 [Ref: M-255 listed the name as "Daniel Cathiel"].
CATHELL, David. Private, Worcester Militia, Wicomico Bn., Capt. Samuel Horsey's Co., Second Class, July 15, 1780 [Ref: M-256].

CATHELL, James. Private, 3rd Maryland Independent Co., Worcester County, Capt. John Watkins' Co., enlisted Feb 13, 1776; muster roll dated Aug 20, 1776, present for duty [Ref: D-21].

CATHELL, John. First Lieutenant, Worcester Militia, June 28, 1777 [Ref: M-60 listed the name as "John Catheel"]. Took the Oath of Allegiance in Worcester County in 1778 before the Hon. William Hopewell [Ref: J-1814 (Box 4)].

CATHELL, John (c1750-1812). Private, Worcester Militia, Wicomico Bn., Capt. Samuel Horsey's Co., Third Class, July 15, 1780 [Ref: M-256]. John Cathell was born circa 1750, married Martha Hayman, served as a private during the war, and died before April 21, 1812 [Ref: V-517].

CATHELL, Jonathan (c1759-1801). Ensign, Worcester Militia, Wicomico Bn., Capt. Elijah Shockley's Co., Aug 30, 1777 to at least July 15, 1780 [Ref: M-255; M-60 and C-351 both listed the name as "Jonathan Catheel"]. Took the Oath of Allegiance in Worcester County in 1778 before the Hon. William Hopewell [Ref: J-1814 (Box 4)]. Jonathan Cathell was born in Maryland circa 1759, married Betty Collins, served as an ensign and rendered other patriotic service during the war, and died in Delaware before April 29, 1801 [Ref: V-517].

CATHELL, Josiah. Corporal, 3rd Maryland Independent Co., Worcester County, Capt. John Watkins' Co., enlisted Feb 5, 1776; muster roll dated Aug 20, 1776, sick in barracks [Ref: D-21]. "Josiah Cathel of Capt. Brown's Co. of Matrosses having procured two men to inlist into the said Co. under Captain Brown's promise to endeavor to procure his discharge on his so doing. He is therefore discharged from further service" (proceedings of the Council of Maryland dated Nov 6, 1777). [Ref: C-410]. Took the Oath of Allegiance in Worcester County in 1778 before the Hon. William Hopewell [Ref: J-1814 (Box 4)].

CATHELL, Laban. Private, 3rd Maryland Independent Co., Worcester County, Capt. John Watkins' Co., enlisted Feb 13, 1776; muster roll dated Aug 20, 1776, present for duty [Ref: D-22].

CATHELL, Levi (1754-1815). Private, 3rd Maryland Independent Co., Worcester County, Capt. John Watkins' Co., enlisted Feb 13, 1776; muster roll dated Aug 20, 1776, present for duty [Ref: D-21]. Private, Worcester Militia, Wicomico Bn., Capt. Samuel Horsey's Co., Third Class, July 15, 1780 [Ref: M-256]. Levin Cathell was born on Sep 18, 1754, married Rebecca Porter, served as a private during the war, and died on Nov 26, 1815 [Ref: V-517].

CATHELL, Thomas. Private, Worcester Militia, Wicomico Bn., Capt. Elijah Shockley's Co., Second Class, July 15, 1780 [Ref: M-255]. Took the Oath of Allegiance in Worcester County in 1778 before the Hon. William Hopewell [Ref: J-1814 (Box 4)].

CATHERWOOD, Andrew. Private, Worcester Militia, Wicomico Bn., Capt. William Handy's Co., Third Class, July 15, 1780 [Ref: M-257]. Took the Oath of Allegiance in Worcester County in 1778 before the Hon. Joshua Townsend [Ref: J-1814 (Box 4)].

CATLIN, Joshua. Took the Oath of Allegiance in Somerset County in 1778 before the Hon. John Williams [Ref: T-21, N-50].

CATLIN, William. Private, Somerset Militia, Princess Anne Bn., St. Asaph's Co., 1780 [Ref: M-221].

CATON, Charles (1733-c1815). Born in Maryland, possibly Somerset County, on Aug 20, 1733, married Jemima Summers, was a private during the war, and died in North Carolina before November, 1815 [Ref: V-519].

CATON, John. Private, Somerset Militia, Salisbury Bn., Capt. Sampson Wheatly's Co., 1780 [Ref: M-216].

CATON, Joseph. Private, Somerset Militia, Princess Anne Bn., Capt. John Williams' Watkins Point Co., 1780 [Ref: M-222].

CAUDREY (CAUDRY), Abraham. Took the Oath of Allegiance in Worcester County in 1778 before the Hon. Joshua Townsend [Ref: J-1814 (Box 4)].

CAUDREY (CAUDRY), John. Took the Oath of Allegiance in Worcester County in 1778 before the Hon. Joshua Townsend [Ref: J-1814 (Box 4)]. Private, Worcester Militia, Wicomico Bn., Capt. Benjamin Dennis' Co., Third Class, July 15, 1780 [Ref: M-255].

CAUDREY (CAUDRY), Jonathan. Private, Worcester Militia, Wicomico Bn., Capt. Philip Quinton's Co., Sixth Class, July 15, 1780 [Ref: M-256].

CAUDREY (CAUDRY), William. Private, Worcester Militia, Sinepuxent Bn., Capt. John Rackliff's Co., First Class, 1779/1780 [Ref: M-251]. See "William Cordray (Cordry)," q.v.

CAUSEY, Patrick (1746-1812). Private, Worcester Militia, Wicomico Bn., Capt. Samuel Horsey's Co., Sixth Class, July 15, 1780 [Ref: M-257]. Took the Oath of Allegiance in Worcester County in 1778 before the Hon. William Hopewell [Ref: J-1814 (Box 4) listed the name as "Patrick Carsey"]. Patrick Causey, Sr. was born in 1746 in Worcester County, married Nicey Unicey Lingo (1741-1825), and died in 1812. Their son Patrick Causey, Jr. (1779-1845) married Polly Cropper (1776-1873) on Jan 16, 1807 [Ref: S-3084].

CAUSEY, Saul. Private, Worcester Militia, Wicomico Bn., Capt. Samuel Horsey's Co., First Class, July 15, 1780 [Ref: M-256].

CAVANAUGH, John. Took the Oath of Allegiance in Somerset County in 1778 before the Hon. Levin Wilson [Ref: T-17, N-50].

CAVANAUGH, Robert. Took the Oath of Allegiance in Somerset County in 1778 before the Hon. Levin Wilson [Ref: T-17, N-50].

CAVENDER, John. Private, Somerset Militia, Princess Anne Bn., Capt. Thomas Irving's Monie Co., 1780 [Ref: M-219].

CHAILLE, Comfort. See "Peter Chaille," q.v.

CHAILLE, Elizabeth. See "Samuel Handy," q.v.

CHAILLE, Henrietta. See "Peter Chaille," q.v.

CHAILLE, John. Private, Worcester Militia, Wicomico Bn., Capt. Fisher Walton's Co., Second Class, July 15, 1780 [Ref: M-258]. Took the Oath of Allegiance

in Worcester County in 1778 before the Hon. Joshua Townsend [Ref: J-1814 (Box 4)].
CHAILLE, Margaret. See "Peter Chaille," q.v.
CHAILLE, Mary. See "Peter Chaille," q.v.
CHAILLE, Moses. First Lieutenant, 3rd Maryland Independent Co., Worcester County, Capt. John Watkins' Co., commissioned on Jan 3 or 5, 1776; muster roll dated Aug 20, 1776 indicated "absent, gone to be married." Resigned on Aug 28, 1776 [Ref: D-21, M-61, A-243]. Took the Oath of Allegiance in Worcester County in 1778 in Bogerternorton Hundred before the Hon. Thomas Purnell [Ref: J-1814 (Box 4)]. See "Peter Chaille," q.v.
CHAILLE, Moses. Private, Worcester Militia, Wicomico Bn., Capt. William Handy's Co., Fourth Class, July 15, 1780 [Ref: M-257].
CHAILLE, Peter (c1730/40-1802). Son of Moses Chaillé (d. 1763) and grandson of Dr. Peter Chaillé who immigrated from France circa 1710. Peter married first to Comfort Houston by 1753 and second to Scarborough Holland, widow of "Nehemiah Holland," q.v. Their children were Moses, Zachariah, Mary, Henrietta, Margaret, and Comfort. Peter Chaille served in the Lower House of the Maryland Legislature for most of the time between 1762 and 1790; Maryland Conventions, 1774-1776; Constitution Ratification Convention, 1788; Association of the Freemen of Maryland, 1775; Committee of Observation for Worcester County, 1776-1777; County Court Justice, 1779-1786; Justice of the Orphans Court, 1779-1786; Commissary for Purchases, 1780-1781; Commissary for Horses, 1781; Commissary for Clothing, 1781; Maryland Senate Elector, 1791; and, Associate Justice, Fourth District, 1791. He was a captain by 1762 and colonel, Worcester Militia, 10th Bn., Jan 6, 1776 to at least Aug 4, 1780 [Ref: R-205, M-61, P-347, P-349, P-350, P-454, H-479, I-46, O-4, O-28, A-457, A-viii, and V-524 states he was born in 1740]. Took the Oath of Allegiance in Worcester County in 1778 before the Hon. William Hopewell [Ref: J-1814 (Box 4)]. Rendered patriotic service by supplying corn for the use of the military in 1780 and served as Deputy Superintendent of the Snow Hill Magazine in 1782 [Ref: P-273, P-468]. See "Nehemiah Holland," q.v.
CHAILLE, Peter. Private, Worcester Militia, Wicomico Bn., Capt. William Handy's Co., Eighth Class, July 15, 1780 [Ref: M-258].
CHAILLE, Zachariah. See "Peter Chaille," q.v.
CHAIR (CHAIN?), Alexander. Took the Oath of Allegiance in Somerset County in 1778 before the Hon. Levin Wilson [Ref: T-17, N-50].
CHALLENDER (CHALLENDEN?), John. Took the Oath of Allegiance in Somerset County in 1778 before the Hon. John Williams [Ref: T-21, N-50].
CHAMBERS, John. Private, Worcester Militia, Wicomico Bn., Capt. William Handy's Co., Fifth Class, July 15, 1780 [Ref: M-257].
CHANDLER, William. Private, Worcester Militia, Sinepuxent Bn., Capt. John Coe's Co., Fourth Class, 1779/1780 [Ref: M-252].

CHAPLINE, Susannah. See "John Span Conway," q.v.
CHAPMAN, Ann. See "Thomas Beard," q.v.
CHAPMAN, Pearre. Took the Oath of Allegiance in Worcester County in 1778 before the Hon. James Selby [Ref: J-1814 (Box 4) listed the name as "Peare Chapmon"].
CHAPMAN, Silas. Private, Worcester Militia, Wicomico Bn., Capt. James Patterson's Co., Second Class, July 15, 1780 [Ref: M-258]. Took the Oath of Allegiance in Worcester County in 1778 before the Hon. James Selby [Ref: J-1814 (Box 4) listed the name as "Silas Chapmon"].
CHAVEL, Ezekiel. Rendered patriotic service by cutting beef and guarding a sloop for the military in Worcester County in October, 1781 [Ref: P-442].
CHEARIER(?), James. Took the Oath of Allegiance in Worcester County in 1778 before the Hon. James Selby [Ref: J-1814 (Box 4)].
CHENEY, Andrew Francis. Delegate from Somerset County who attended the Maryland Convention in 1776 "for the express purpose of forming a new government" [Ref: O-36]. Appointed by the Maryland Convention in November, 1776 to be one of the Judges of Elections in Somerset County [Ref: O-55]. Andrew Francis Cheney, chirurgeon (son of James Cheney of Mount Cheney in County of Cork, Ireland, Cost Officer), married Mary Day Scott (daughter of Day Scott) in Stepney Parish, Somerset County, on Tuesday, July 15, 1755 [Ref: Y-42].
CHENICKS(?), Jesse. Private, Worcester Militia, Wicomico Bn., Capt. James Patterson's Co., Sixth Class, July 15, 1780 [Ref: M-258].
CHESSEY, Henry. Private, Somerset County, Capt. John Gunby's 2nd Independent Maryland Co.; sick in barracks on March 9, 1776; mustered on Aug 21, 1776 [Ref: D-641].
CHESWICKS(?), James. Private, Worcester Militia, Wicomico Bn., Capt. Fisher Walton's Co., First Class, July 15, 1780 [Ref: M-258].
CHETAM (CHITTAM), Aquilla. Took the Oath of Allegiance in Somerset County on Feb 28, 1778 before the Hon. Joseph Venables [Ref: T-25].
CHETAM (CHITTAM), John. Private, Somerset County, Capt. John Gunby's 2nd Independent Maryland Co.; present on April 9, 1776; mustered on Aug 21, 1776 [Ref: D-641]. Sergeant, Somerset Militia, Salisbury Bn., Capt. Josiah Dashiell's Wicomico Creek Co., 1778/1780 [Ref: M-218]. Took the Oath of Allegiance in Somerset County on Feb 28, 1778 before the Hon. Joseph Venables [Ref: T-25]. Select Militia, Somerset County, Aug 15, 1781 [Ref: L-35B].
CHETAM (CHITTAM), Walker. Sergeant, Somerset Militia, Salisbury Bn., Capt. Josiah Dashiell's Wicomico Creek Co., 1778/1780 [Ref: M-218].
CHRISTOPHER, Adam. Private, Worcester Militia, Wicomico Bn., Capt. Samuel Horsey's Co., Eighth Class, July 15, 1780 [Ref: M-257]. Took the Oath of Allegiance in Worcester County on Feb 25, 1778 before the Hon. Ebenezer Handy [Ref: J-1814 (Box 4)].

CHRISTOPHER, Elijah. Private, Worcester Militia, Wicomico Bn., Capt. Elijah Shockley's Co., Seventh Class, July 15, 1780 [Ref: M-255]. Took the Oath of Allegiance in Somerset County in 1778 before the Hon. Levin Wilson [Ref: T-17, and N-50 listed the name as "Elizah Christopher"].

CHRISTOPHER, John. Private, Somerset Militia, Salisbury Bn., Capt. Josiah Dashiell's Wicomico Creek Co., 1778/1780 [Ref: M-218]. Took the Oath of Allegiance in Somerset County on Feb 28, 1778 (made his "J" mark) before the Hon. Joseph Venables [Ref: T-25 listed the name as "John Cristopher"].

CHRISTOPHER, Milby. Private, Worcester Militia, Wicomico Bn., Capt. Benjamin Dennis' Co., First Class, July 15, 1780 [Ref: M-255].

CHRISTOPHER, Smith. Private, Worcester Militia, Snow Hill Bn., Capt. Ebenezer Handy's Co., April 9, 1776 [Ref: M-249].

CHRISTOPHER, Stephen. Private, Somerset Militia, Salisbury Bn., Capt. James Bennett's Salisbury Co., 1778/1780 [Ref: M-218].

CHRISTOPHER, Steven. Private, Worcester Militia, Wicomico Bn., Capt. Elijah Shockley's Co., Seventh Class, July 15, 1780 [Ref: M-255].

CHRISTOPHER, Thomas. Took the Oath of Allegiance in Worcester County in 1778 before the Hon. Joshua Townsend [Ref: J-1814 (Box 4)].

CHRISTOPHER, William. Private, Somerset Militia, Salisbury Bn., Capt. Josiah Dashiell's Wicomico Creek Co., 1778/1780 [Ref: M-218].

CHRISTOPHER, William. Private, Somerset Militia, Princess Anne Bn., Capt. John Jones' Princess Anne Co., 1780 [Ref: M-219].

CHRISTOPHER, William. Took the Oath of Allegiance in Somerset County in 1778 (made his "M" mark) before the Hon. Peter Waters [Ref: T-18].

CLARK, Benjamin. Private, Worcester Militia, Sinepuxent Bn., Capt. John Coe's Co., Fourth Class, 1779/1780 [Ref: M-252].

CLARK, Elias Mason. Private, Worcester Militia, Sinepuxent Bn., Capt. Josiah Dale's Co., Fifth Class, 1779/1780 [Ref: M-254].

CLARK, Elizabeth. See "John Satchell," q.v.

CLARK, Gershom. Private, Worcester Militia, Sinepuxent Bn., Capt. John Postly's Co., Second Class, 1779/1780 [Ref: M-251].

CLARKE, Henry. Private, Somerset County, Capt. John Gunby's 2nd Independent Maryland Co.; present on April 8, 1776; mustered on Aug 21, 1776 [Ref: D-641].

CLARKE, Willy. Private, Somerset County, Capt. John Gunby's 2nd Independent Maryland Co.; present on May 29, 1776; mustered on Aug 21, 1776 [Ref: D-641].

CLAVEL, Job. Took the Oath of Allegiance in Worcester County in 1778 before the Hon. Joshua Townsend [Ref: J-1814 (Box 4)].

CLAYWELL, Ezekiel. Took the Oath of Allegiance in Worcester County in 1778 before the Hon. Nehemiah Holland [Ref: J-1814 (Box 4)].

CLAYWELL, Shadrack (1760-1837). Private, Virginia Line, who applied for a pension (S30929) in Cumberland County, Kentucky on Feb 4, 1833, stating he was born in Worcester County, Maryland in 1760, lived in Bedford County, Virginia at the time of his enlistment, and in 1806 moved to Kentucky. He signed his name as Shadrack Claywell, Sr., but no other family information was given in his affidavit, which was witnessed by Nash Glidewell and John Garrett. He died in Kentucky on April 9, 1837 [Ref: V-590; and, W-668 listed the name as "Shadrack or Shadrick Claywell"].

CLOGG, Samuel. Took the Oath of Allegiance in Worcester County in 1778 before the Hon. Nehemiah Holland [Ref: J-1814 (Box 4)].

CLOGG, Walter. Took the Oath of Allegiance in Worcester County in 1778 before the Hon. Nehemiah Holland [Ref: J-1814 (Box 4)].

CLOUDS, Curtis. Private, Worcester Militia, Snow Hill Bn., Capt. John Parramore's Co., 1777 [Ref: M-250].

CLUFF, Jonathan. Private, Somerset Militia, Princess Anne Bn., Capt. George Waters' Pocomoke Co., 1780 [Ref: M-220]. Took the Oath of Allegiance in Somerset County in 1778 before the Hon. Peter Waters [Ref: T-18].

CLUFF, Major. Private, Worcester Militia, Wicomico Bn., Capt. Charles Bennett's Co., Sixth Class, July 15, 1780 [Ref: M-255].

CLUFF, Michael Jr. (1763 -   ). Son of Michael and Sarah Cluff, born in Coventry Parish on Dec 14, 1763 [Ref: Y-81]. Private, Somerset Militia, Princess Anne Bn., Capt. George Waters' Pocomoke Co., 1780 [Ref: M-220]. See "William Cluff," q.v.

CLUFF, Sarah. See "William Cluff" and "Michael Cluff," q.v.

CLUFF, Thomas. Private, Worcester Militia, Wicomico Bn., Capt. Charles Bennett's Co., Seventh Class, July 15, 1780 [Ref: M-255].

CLUFF, William (1761 -   ). Son of Michael and Sarah Cluff, born in Coventry Parish on Dec 11, 1761 [Ref: Y-81]. Private, Somerset Militia, Princess Anne Bn., Capt. George Waters' Pocomoke Co., 1780 [Ref: M-220].

COARSLEY, Hannah. See "Isaac McCready," q.v.

COBB, John. Took the Oath of Allegiance in Worcester County in 1778 before the Hon. Nathaniel Miller [Ref: J-1814 (Box 4)].

COE, Asa (c1748-1787). Private, Worcester Militia, Sinepuxent Bn., Capt. John Coe's Co., Seventh Class, 1779/1780 [Ref: M-252]. Second Lieutenant, March 16, 1781, Capt. John Tull's Co., Sinepuxent Bn. [Ref: M-63, G-353 listed the name as "Assa Coe"]. Asa Coe married Hannah Nelson and served as a second lieutenant in Worcester County during the war [Ref: Q-28:1 (Winter, 1987), "Coe Records of Maryland, 1651-1900," by Carl Robert Coe, pp. 51-84].

COE, John (1744-1807). Captain, Worcester Militia, Sinepuxent Bn., 1779/1780 to March 16, 1781, when succeeded [Ref: M-63, M-251, G-353]. John Coe married Sarah ---- and served as a captain in Worcester County during the war [Ref: Q-28:1, *Ibid.*].

COE, John. Private, Worcester Militia, Sinepuxent Bn., Capt. John Coe's Co., First Class, 1779/1780 [Ref: M-251].

COE, Sarah. See "John Coe," q.v.

COFFEN, Levin. Private, Worcester Militia, Sinepuxent Bn., Capt. John Coe's Co., Fifth Class, 1779/1780 [Ref: M-252].
COHAN, Joseph. See "Thomas Harris," q.v.
COHOON (CAHOON), Benjamin. Private, Worcester Militia, Wicomico Bn., Capt. Elijah Shockley's Co., Fourth Class, July 15, 1780 [Ref: M-255].
COHOON (CAHOON), Ephraim (1750 -   ). Son of Samuel and Margaret Cohoon, born in Coventry Parish on Jan 7, 1750 [Ref: Y-69]. Took the Oath of Allegiance in Worcester County in 1778 before the Hon. Nathaniel Miller [Ref: J-1814 (Box 4)]. "Ephraim Calhoon" was a private in the Worcester Militia, Sinepuxent Bn., Capt. Matthew Purnell's Co., First Class, July 25, 1780 [Ref: M-252].
COHOON (CAHOON), Henry (1760 -   ). Son of Henry and Rachel Cohoon, born in Coventry Parish on June 3, 1760 [Ref: Y-81]. Private, Somerset Militia, Princess Anne Bn., Capt. John Williams' Watkins Point Co., 1780 [Ref: M-222]. See "Nathan Cohoon," q.v.
COHOON, Margaret. See "Ephraim Cohoon," q.v.
COHOON (CAHOON), Nathan (1753 -   ). Son of Henry and Rachel Cohoon, born in Coventry Parish on June 17, 1753 [Ref: Y-81]. Private, Somerset Militia, Princess Anne Bn., Capt. John Williams' Watkins Point Co., 1780 [Ref: M-222].
COHOON, Rachel. See "Nathan Cohoon" and "Henry Cohoon," q.v.
COHOON, Samuel. See "Ephraim Cohoon," q.v.
COHOON (CAHOON), William. Private, 3rd Maryland Independent Co., Worcester County, Capt. John Watkins' Co., enlisted Feb 3, 1776; muster roll dated Aug 20, 1776, present for duty [Ref: D-22].
COLBIRD, William Jr. Took the Oath of Allegiance in Somerset County in 1778 before the Hon. John Williams [Ref: T-21, and N-50 listed the name as "William Colbourd, Jr."]. See "William Coulbourn Jr.," q.v.
COLE, John. Private, Worcester Militia, Wicomico Bn., Capt. James Perdue's Co., Fifth Class, July 15, 1780 [Ref: M-256].
COLL, Edward. Private, 3rd Maryland Independent Co., Worcester County, Capt. John Watkins' Co., enlisted Feb 9, 1776; muster roll dated Aug 20, 1776, sick in barracks [Ref: D-22].
COLLEET, Simon Jr. Took the Oath of Allegiance in Worcester County in 1778 before the Hon. Joshua Townsend [Ref: J-1814 (Box 4)].
COLLEET, Simon Sr. Took the Oath of Allegiance in Worcester County in 1778 before the Hon. William Hopewell [Ref: J-1814 (Box 4)].
COLLEET, William. Took the Oath of Allegiance in Worcester County in 1778 before the Hon. Joshua Townsend [Ref: J-1814 (Box 4)].
COLLIER, ----. See "John Round Morris," q.v.
COLLIER, Dowty. Private, Somerset Militia, Salisbury Bn., Capt. Henry Gale's Quantico Co., 1778/1780 [Ref: M-216]. See "John McGlamery," q.v.
COLLIER, Elizabeth. See "Benjamin Mills," q.v.

COLLIER, Kendall (1763 -   ). Son of Kendall Collier and Sarah Fasset, born in Worcester Parish on April 1, 1763 [Ref: Y-29]. Private, Worcester Militia, Sinepuxent Bn., Capt. John Rackliff's Co., Sixth Class, 1779/1780 [Ref: M-251 listed the name as "Kendle Collier"]. See "Peter Collier," q.v.

COLLIER, Nicholas Evans (1756 -   ). Son of Nicholas Evans Collier and wife Rebecka ----, born in Stepney Parish on Aug 31, 1756 [Ref: Y-44]. Private, Somerset Militia, Salisbury Bn., Capt. Henry Gale's Quantico Co., 1778/1780 [Ref: M-216].

COLLIER, Peter (1760 -   ). Son of Kendall Collier and Sarah Fasset, born in Worcester Parish on Nov 7, 1760 [Ref: Y-29 listed the name as "Petter Collier"]. Private, Worcester Militia, Sinepuxent Bn., Capt. John Rackliff's Co., Seventh Class, 1779/1780 [Ref: M-251].

COLLIER, Rebecka. See "Nicholas Evans Collier," q.v.

COLLIER, Sarah. Rendered patriotic service by supplying corn for the use of the military in Worcester County on June 14, 1780 and July 10, 1780, and by supplying beef on Sep 20, 1780 [Ref: P-296, P-319, G-10].

COLLIER, William. Private, Worcester Militia, Sinepuxent Bn., Capt. Josiah Dale's Co., First Class, 1779/1780 [Ref: M-253].

COLLIER, William. Private, Somerset Militia, Salisbury Bn., Capt. Henry Gale's Quantico Co., 1778/1780 [Ref: M-216].

COLLINGHAM, David. See "David Cottingham," q.v.

COLLINS, Belitha. Private, Worcester Militia, Sinepuxent Bn., Capt. John Postly's Co., Third Class, 1779/1780 [Ref: M-251].

COLLINS, Betty. See "Jonathan Cathell," q.v.

COLLINS, Chambers. Private, Worcester Militia, Sinepuxent Bn., Capt. Elisha Purnell's Co., Third Class, 1779/1780 [Ref: M-253]. Took the Oath of Allegiance in Worcester County in 1778 before the Hon. Joshua Townsend [Ref: J-1814 (Box 4)].

COLLINS, Elijah. Private, Worcester Militia, Wicomico Bn., Capt. Charles Bennett's Co., Fifth Class, July 15, 1780 [Ref: M-255]. Took the Oath of Allegiance in Worcester County in 1778 before the Hon. Joshua Townsend [Ref: J-1814 (Box 4)].

COLLINS, Elisha. Private, Worcester Militia, Sinepuxent Bn., Capt. John Postly's Co., Third Class, 1779/1780 [Ref: M-251].

COLLINS, Ephraim. Private, Worcester Militia, Snow Hill Bn., Capt. Samuel Smyley's Co., 1777 [Ref: M-250]. Private, Worcester Militia, Wicomico Bn., Capt. Samuel Smyley's Co., Third Class, July 15, 1780 [Ref: M-259].

COLLINS, Ephraim. Private, Somerset Militia, Princess Anne Bn., Capt. James Elzey's Co., 1780 [Ref: M-220].

COLLINS, Hannah. See "John Tull," q.v.

COLLINS, Isaac. Took the Oath of Allegiance in Worcester County in 1778 before the Hon. Nathaniel Miller [Ref: J-1814 (Box 4)].

COLLINS, James. Private, Worcester Militia, Snow Hill Bn., Capt. Samuel Smyley's Co., 1777 [Ref: M-250]. Private, Worcester Militia, Wicomico Bn., Capt. Samuel Smyley's Co., Third Class, July 15, 1780 [Ref: M-259]. Took the Oath of Allegiance in Worcester County in 1778 before the Hon. John Selby [Ref: J-1814 (Box 4)]. See "Henry White," q.v.

COLLINS, James. On Aug 15, 1780, along with John Tarr and Benjamin Holland, he petitioned the Council of Maryland with a proposal to manufacture salt in Worcester County for the use of the State [Ref: G-48 listed the name as "James Collings" and indicated he made his "X" mark on the petition].

COLLINS, John. Private, Somerset Militia, Princess Anne Bn., Capt. John Jones' Princess Anne Co., 1780 [Ref: M-219].

COLLINS, John. Private, Worcester Militia, Sinepuxent Bn., Capt. Elisha Purnell's Co., Eighth Class, 1779/1780 [Ref: M-253]. Took the Oath of Allegiance in Worcester County in 1778 in Quepomco Hundred before the Hon. Thomas Purnell [Ref: J-1814 (Box 4) listed the name as "John Collens"].

COLLINS, John. Took the Oath of Allegiance in Worcester County in 1778 before the Hon. Nathaniel Miller [Ref: J-1814 (Box 4)].

COLLINS, Joseph. Private, Somerset Militia, Salisbury Bn., Capt. Joseph Venables' Barren Creek Co., 1778/1780 [Ref: M-217].

COLLINS, Josiah (1757 -   ). Private, Maryland Line, who applied for a pension (S16730) in Decatur County, Indiana on Oct 24, 1832, stating he was born in Worcester County, Maryland on April 19, 1757 and lived there at the time of his enlistment. He later moved to Washington County, Pennsylvania and lived there until 1794 when he moved to Bourbon County, Kentucky. In 1822 he moved to Indiana. He also mentioned a daughter (name not given) in Kentucky in 1832 [Ref: W-716].

COLLINS, Levi. Private, Somerset Militia, Salisbury Bn., Capt. Josiah Dashiell's Wicomico Creek Co., 1778/1780 [Ref: M-218].

COLLINS, Molly. See "Henry White," q.v.

COLLINS, Nehemiah. Took the Oath of Allegiance in Worcester County in 1778 in Quepomco Hundred before the Hon. Thomas Purnell [Ref: J-1814 (Box 4) listed the name as "Nehemiah Collin"].

COLLINS, Parker. Took the Oath of Allegiance in Worcester County in 1778 in Quepomco Hundred before the Hon. Thomas Purnell [Ref: J-1814 (Box 4) listed the name as "Parker Collens"].

COLLINS, Peter. On June 20, 1781 Alexander Adams recruited Peter Collins from Somerset County to serve in the Continental Army for 3 years [Ref: L-35C listed the name as "Peter Collens"].

COLLINS, Samuel. Private, Somerset Militia, Princess Anne Bn., Capt. George Waters' Pocomoke Co., 1780 [Ref: M-220]. See "John Campbell," q.v.

COLLINS, Thomas. Private, Somerset Militia, Princess Anne Bn., Capt. James Elzey's Co., 1780 [Ref: M-220].

COLLINS, Thomas Jr. Private, Somerset Militia, Salisbury Bn., Capt. Josiah Dashiell's Wicomico Creek Co., 1778/1780 [Ref: M-218].

COLLINS, William. Private, Worcester Militia, Sinepuxent Bn., Capt. John Rackliff's Co., Second Class, 1779/1780 [Ref: M-251].

COLLINS, William. Private, Somerset Militia, Salisbury Bn., Capt. Josiah Dashiell's Wicomico Creek Co., 1778/1780 [Ref: M-218].

CONNAWAY, Benjamin. Private, Somerset Militia, Princess Anne Bn., St. Asaph's Co., 1780 [Ref: M-221].

CONNELLY, Priscilla. See "Levi Stevens," q.v.

CONNER, Bartholomew. Private, Worcester Militia, Snow Hill Bn., Capt. Samuel Smyley's Co., 1777 [Ref: M-250]. Private, Worcester Militia, Wicomico Bn., Capt. Samuel Smyley's Co., Eighth Class, July 15, 1780 [Ref: M-259].

CONNER, Dennis. Private, Worcester Militia, Snow Hill Bn., Capt. Samuel Smyley's Co., 1777 [Ref: M-250]. Recruited by Capt. Levin Handy and enlisted on Feb 23, 1780 in the Continental Army in Worcester County for the duration of the war, stating he was born in America [Ref: Z-40]. Private, 5th Maryland Line, listed as a recruit entitled to clothing from the Commissary of Stores on April 24, 1780 [Ref: F-150].

CONNER, Elijah. See "John Conner," q.v.

CONNER, Fradrick. Took the Oath of Allegiance in Worcester County in 1778 before the Hon. Joshua Townsend [Ref: J-1814 (Box 4)].

CONNER, Isabella. See "John Conner," q.v.

CONNER, James. Private, Worcester Militia, Sinepuxent Bn., Capt. John Coe's Co., Fifth Class, 1779/1780 [Ref: M-252].

CONNER, John (1758 -   ). Son of Elijah and Isabella Conner, born in Coventry Parish on July 23, 1758 [Ref: Y-80]. Private, Worcester Militia, Wicomico Bn., Capt. James Patterson's Co., First Class, July 15, 1780 [Ref: M-258].

CONNER, Matthew. Took the Oath of Allegiance in Somerset County in 1778 [Ref: N-50 listed the name as "Matthew Connor"].

CONNER, Sarah. See "Isaac Whittington," q.v.

CONNER, William. Private, Worcester Militia, Wicomico Bn., Capt. James Patterson's Co., Third Class, July 15, 1780 [Ref: M-258]. Private, Maryland Troops, Worcester County, draughted May 1, 1781 [Ref: K-99, D-372]. Took the Oath of Allegiance in Worcester County in 1778 before the Hon. James Selby [Ref: J-1814 (Box 4)].

CONNER, William. Took the Oath of Allegiance in Worcester County in 1778 before the Hon. James Selby [Ref: J-1814 (Box 4)].

CONWAY, John. Private, Somerset Militia, Princess Anne Bn., Capt. John Williams' Watkins Point Co., 1780 [Ref: M-222].

CONWAY, John Span (c1740-1803). Captain, Somerset Militia, Salisbury Bn., Nanticoke Point Co., Sep 22, 1777; on duty July 24, 1780; succeeded on Aug 22, 1781 [Ref: M-64, M-216, C-381, G-575]. Justice who administered the Oath of Allegiance in Somerset County in 1778 and who also took the Oath of

Allegiance before the Hon. John Stewart in 1778 [Ref: T-14, T-19, N-50]. Justice of the Orphans Court and Justice of the Peace, commissioned on Jan 9, 1778 and Nov 21, 1778 and Jan 17, 1782 [Ref: C-464, E-248, I-45]. Rendered patriotic service by supplying bacon for the use of the military on Aug 11, 1780 [Ref: P-309]. "John Spann Conway" was born in Virginia circa 1740, married Susannah Chapline, served as a captain and rendered other civil service in Maryland during the war, and died in August, 1803 in Maryland [Ref: V-646].

COOKSEY, John. Private, Somerset County, Capt. John Gunby's 2nd Independent Maryland Co.; present on March 8, 1776; mustered on Aug 21, 1776 [Ref: D-641]. Private, Somerset Militia, Salisbury Bn., Capt. James Bennett's Salisbury Co., 1778/1780 [Ref: M-218].

COOPER, Abraham. Private, Somerset Militia, Salisbury Bn., Capt. Joseph Venables' Barren Creek Co., 1778/1780 [Ref: M-217]. Took the Oath of Allegiance in Somerset County on Feb 23, 1778 (made his "X mark) before the Hon. Joseph Venables [Ref: T-25].

COOPER, Bennett. Private, Worcester Militia, Wicomico Bn., Capt. Samuel Horsey's Co., Fifth Class, July 15, 1780 [Ref: M-257].

COOPER, Bennett. Private, Worcester Militia, Wicomico Bn., Capt. Charles Bennett's Co., Second Class, July 15, 1780 [Ref: M-255].

COOPER, Eleanor. See "Jonathan Cooper," q.v.

COOPER, John. Private, Somerset Militia, Salisbury Bn., Capt. Joseph Venables' Barren Creek Co., 1778/1780 [Ref: M-217].

COOPER, Jonathan (1756/8-1845). Private, Pennsylvania Line, who applied for a pension in Henry County, Kentucky on Aug 27, 1833, stating he was born in Somerset County, Maryland in 1756 and lived in Westmoreland County, Pennsylvania at the time of his enlistment. About 1788 he moved to Jefferson County, Kentucky and in the fall of 1833 moved to Greene County, Illinois. Jonathan died on Aug 10, 1845 in Jersey County, Illinois and his widow Eleanor (or Nelly) applied for a pension (W6714) on Dec 24, 1850, age 69, stating they were married in Westmoreland County, Pennsylvania on Jan 5, 1798, at which time she was living with James and Polly English at whose home they were married. In 1835 Jonathan had a large family, but no names were given in the affidavit. Supporting statements were given in 1836 by Thomas English (of Jersey County, Illinois, son of James and Polly) and R. Wharton English (of Greene County, Illinois) and in 1850 by Jonathan E. Cooper, David McFain, and James and Polly English, all of Jersey County, Illinois [Ref: W-760]. Another source gives slightly different dates: Jonathan Cooper was born in Maryland in 1758, married twice (second wife was Eleanor English), served as a private in Pennsylvania during the war, and died in Illinois on Sep 10, 1845 [Ref: V-660].

COOPER, Samuel. Private, Somerset Militia, Salisbury Bn., Capt. Joseph Venables' Barren Creek Co., 1778/1780 [Ref: M-217]. Took the Oath of

Allegiance in Somerset County on Feb 28, 1778 before the Hon. Joseph Venables [Ref: T-25].

COOPER, Thomas. Private, Somerset Militia, Salisbury Bn., Capt. Joseph Venables' Barren Creek Co., 1778/1780 [Ref: M-217]. Took the Oath of Allegiance in Somerset County on Feb 28, 1778 before the Hon. Joseph Venables [Ref: T-25].

CORCKWELL (CARCKWELL), Henry. Private, Worcester Militia, Wicomico Bn., Capt. James Perdue's Co., Second Class, July 15, 1780 [Ref: M-256 listed the name as "Henry Cockurll (Corkurll)"]. Private, Maryland Troops, Worcester County, draughted May 1, 1781 [Ref: K-99, D-372].

CORD, William. See "Outten Sturgis, Sr.," q.v.

CORDRAY (CORDREY), Abraham. Private, Worcester Militia, Capt. John Martin's Co., 1780/1781 [Ref: J-1814 (Box 12) listed the name as "Abra. Cordrey"]. See "James Cordray," q.v.

CORDRAY (CORDRY), Daniel. Private, Somerset Militia, Salisbury Bn., Capt. Joseph Venables' Barren Creek Co., 1778/1780 [Ref: M-217 listed the name as "Daniel Condry"]. Took the Oath of Allegiance in Somerset County on Feb 23, 1778 before the Hon. Joseph Venables [Ref: T-25 listed the name as "Daniel Cordry"].

CORDRAY (CORDRY), Elizabeth. See "James Cordray," q.v.

CORDRAY (CORDRY), Henry. Private, Somerset Militia, Salisbury Bn., Capt. John Span Conway's Nanticoke Point Co., 1778/1780 [Ref: M-216].

CORDRAY (CORDRY), James. Took the Oath of Allegiance in Worcester County in 1778 before the Hon. John Selby [Ref: J-1814 (Box 4) listed the name as "Capt. James Cordory"]. "Capt. James Corderry" was captain of the privateer *Buckskin* in 1776 [Ref: A. W. Burns' abstracts on revolutionary soldiers of Maryland in Kentucky (p. 8) at the Maryland Historical Society]. One James Cordrey was the son of Abraham and Elizabeth Cordrey, born in Coventry Parish on May 10, 1753 [Ref: Y-69]. See "Samuel Bowles," q.v.

CORDRAY (CORDRY), Thomas. Private, Somerset Militia, Salisbury Bn., Capt. Joseph Venables' Barren Creek Co., 1778/1780 [Ref: M-217 listed the name as "Thomas Condary"].

CORDRAY (CORDRY), William. Took the Oath of Allegiance in Worcester County in 1778 in Buckingham Hundred before the Hon. Thomas Purnell [Ref: J-1814 (Box 4)]. See "William Caudrey (Caudry)," q.v.

CORNISH, Amas. Took the Oath of Allegiance in Worcester County in 1778 before the Hon. Joshua Townsend [Ref: J-1814 (Box 4)].

CORY, Ann. See "Robert Martin," q.v.

CORY, Dorothy. See "Robert Martin," q.v.

CORY, Jeremiah. See "Robert Martin," q.v.

COSTON (COSTIN, COSTEN), Ahab. Took the Oath of Allegiance in Somerset County on Feb 23, 1778 before the Hon. Joseph Venables [Ref: T-25].

COSTON (COSTIN, COSTEN), Ezekiel. Private, Worcester Militia, Snow Hill Bn., Capt. John Parramore's Co., 1777 [Ref: M-250]. Sergeant, Worcester Militia, Wicomico Bn., Capt. Samuel Smyley's Co., July 15, 1780 [Ref: M-259 listed the name as "Ezekiel Cartor(?)"].

COSTON (COSTIN, COSTEN), Ezekiel (c1725-1784). Took the Oath of Allegiance in Worcester County in 1778 before the Hon. James Selby [Ref: J-1814 (Box 4)].

COSTON (COSTIN, COSTEN), Henry (1762 -   ). Son of Isaac and Sarah Costin, born in Coventry Parish on July 15, 1762 [Ref: Y-81]. Private, Somerset Militia, Princess Anne Bn., Capt. John Jones' Princess Anne Co., 1780 [Ref: M-219].

COSTON (COSTIN), Isaac. See "Henry Coston," q.v.

COSTON (COSTIN, COSTEN), Oliver. Private, Somerset Militia, Princess Anne Bn., Capt. Thomas Irving's Monie Co., 1780 [Ref: M-219]. Took the Oath of Allegiance in Somerset County in 1778 before the Hon. Levin Wilson [Ref: T-17, N-50].

COSTON (COSTIN), Sarah. See "Henry Coston," q.v.

COTTINGHAM, Daniel Private, Worcester Militia, Capt. John Martin's Co., 1780/1781 [Ref: J-1814 (Box 12)].

COTTINGHAM, David (1742/3-1785). Took the Oath of Allegiance in Somerset County in 1778 before the Hon. John Williams [Ref: T-21, N-50]. Private, Somerset Militia, Princess Anne Bn., St. Asaph's Co., 1780 [Ref: M-221 listed the name as "David Collingham"]. David Cottingham was born on March 17, 1742/3 in Maryland, married Mary Gunby, served as a private during the war, and died before Sep 2, 1785 [Ref: V-675].

COTTINGHAM, Elijah. Private, Worcester Militia, Wicomico Bn., Capt. Benjamin Dennis' Co., Sixth Class, July 15, 1780 [Ref: M-256].

COTTINGHAM, Elisha. Private, Worcester Militia, Capt. John Martin's Co., 1780/1781 [Ref: J-1814 (Box 12)].

COTTINGHAM, Elizabeth. See "William Mills," q.v.

COTTINGHAM, Esther. See "William Cottingham," q.v.

COTTINGHAM, John (1754-1829). Son of Daniel and Anne Cottingham, born in Coventry Parish on June 14 *[sic]*, 1754 [Ref: Y-69]. Private, 3rd Maryland Independent Co., Worcester County, Capt. John Watkins' Co., enlisted Feb 3, 1776; muster roll dated Aug 20, 1776, present for duty [Ref: D-22]. John Cottingham was born on June 24 *[sic]*, 1754, married Priscilla Fleming, served as a private during the war, and died on Jan 6, 1829 [Ref: V-675].

COTTINGHAM, John (1759-c1816). Son of John and Mary Cottingham, born in Coventry Parish on Nov 28, 1759 [Ref: Y-81]. Private, Worcester Militia, Wicomico Bn., Capt. Philip Quinton's Co., Eighth Class, July 15, 1780 [Ref: M-256].

COTTINGHAM, John (c1765-1816). Private, Worcester Militia, Capt. John Martin's Co., 1780/1781 [Ref: J-1814 (Box 12)]. This may be the John

Cottingham who was born in Maryland circa 1765, married Margaret Townsend, served as a private during the war, and died in Ohio circa 1816 [Ref: V-675]. Since there two other men by this name, additional research will be necessary before drawing conclusions. See "William Cottingham," q.v.

COTTINGHAM, Mary. See "John Cottingham," q.v.

COTTINGHAM, Thomas (c1718-1783). Took the Oath of Allegiance in Somerset County in 1778 before the Hon. John Williams [Ref: T-21, N-50]. Thomas Cottingham was born in Maryland circa 1718, married Mary Long, rendered patriotic service during the war, and died before June 3, 1783 [Ref: V-675].

COTTINGHAM, Thomas Jr. (1740-c1815). Private, Worcester Militia, Wicomico Bn., Capt. Benjamin Dennis' Co., Sixth Class, July 15, 1780 [Ref: M-256 listed the name without the "Jr."]. Took the Oath of Allegiance in Worcester County in 1778 before the Hon. Joshua Townsend [Ref: J-1814 (Box 4) listed the name as "Jr."]. "Thomas Cottingham" was born circa 1740, married Comfort ----, served as a sergeant during the war, and died after June 15, 1815 [Ref: V-675].

COTTINGHAM, William (1734-1784). Private, Worcester Militia, Wicomico Bn., Capt. Philip Quinton's Co., Seventh Class, July 15, 1780 [Ref: M-256]. Private, Worcester Militia, Capt. John Martin's Co., 1780/1781 [Ref: J-1814 (Box 12)]. William Cottingham was born in Maryland in 1734, married Bettey or Betty Toadvine in Coventry Parish on May 28, 1761, served as a private during the war, and died in 1784 [Ref: Y-81, V-675].

COTTINGHAM, William (1751 -   ). Son of John and Esther Cottingham, born in Coventry Parish on Jan 14, 1753 [Ref: Y-69]. Private, Somerset Militia, Princess Anne Bn., Capt. John Williams' Watkins Point Co., 1780 [Ref: M-222].

COTTMAN (COTMAN), Benjamin. Took the Oath of Allegiance in Somerset County in 1778 before the Hon. Levin Wilson [Ref: T-17, N-50]. Rendered patriotic service by supplying corn for the use of the military on Jan 24, 1780 [Ref: P-265].

COTTMAN (COTMAN), Joseph. First Lieutenant, Somerset Militia, Salisbury Bn., Capt. George Wilson's Co., Sep 9, 1777. First Lieutenant, White Haven Co., 1778/1780. Captain, 1781 [Ref: M-65, M-218, C-382, G-575, J-1814 (Box 8, Dashiell's correspondence), H-195]. Took the Oath of Allegiance in Somerset County in 1778 before the Hon. Levin Wilson [Ref: T-17].

COTTMAN (COTMAN), William. Private, Somerset Militia, Salisbury Bn., White Haven Co., 1778/1780. Second Lieutenant, Capt. Joseph Cottman's Co., 1781 [Ref: M-65, M-218, J-1814 (Box 8, Dashiell's correspondence), G-575, H-195].

COTTMAN (COTMAN), William. Private, Somerset Militia, Princess Anne Bn., Capt. George Waters' Pocomoke Co., 1780 [Ref: M-220].

COULBOURN, Isaac (Somerset County). Took the Oath of Allegiance before the Council of Maryland on March 14, 1778 [Ref: C-536].

COULBOURN, John (d. 1798). Private, Somerset Militia, Princess Anne Bn., Capt. John Williams' Watkins Point Co., 1780 [Ref: M-222]. Took the Oath of

Allegiance in Worcester County in 1778 before the Hon. Joshua Townsend [Ref: J-1814 (Box 4) listed the name as "John Coulbern"]. John Coulbourn was a private in the Snow Hill Bn., Worcester Militia, Capt. Patterson's Co., 6th Class, on July 15, 1780. He married Rachel Laws and died in 1798 [Ref: S-1019A].

COULBOURN, John Jr. Drafted from Somerset County on June 20, 1781 to serve in the Continental Army [Ref: L-35C].

COULBOURN, Robert. Private, Somerset Militia, Princess Anne Bn., Capt. John Williams' Watkins Point Co., 1780 [Ref: M-222].

COULBOURN, Solomon. Private, Somerset Militia, Princess Anne Bn., Capt. John Williams' Watkins Point Co., 1780 [Ref: M-222].

COULBOURN, Stephen. Private, Somerset Militia, Princess Anne Bn., St. Asaph's Co., 1780 [Ref: M-221].

COULBOURN, William. Corporal, Somerset Militia, Princess Anne Bn., Capt. John Williams' Watkins Point Co., 1780 [Ref: M-221].

COULBOURN, William. Private, Somerset Militia, Princess Anne Bn., Capt. Henry Miles' Little Annemessex Co., 1780 [Ref: M-221].

COULBOURN, William Jr. Took the Oath of Allegiance in Somerset County in 1778 before the Hon. John Williams [Ref: T-21, N-50 listed the name as "William Colbourne Jr."].

COVINGTON, Abraham. Private, Somerset Militia, Salisbury Bn., White Haven Co., 1778/1780 [Ref: M-218].

COVINGTON, Levin. Private, Somerset Militia, Salisbury Bn., White Haven Co., 1778/1780 [Ref: M-218].

COVINGTON, Phillip. Private, Somerset Militia, Salisbury Bn., White Haven Co., 1778/1780 [Ref: M-218].

COVINGTON, Samuel. Private, Somerset Militia, Salisbury Bn., Capt. John Span Conway's Nanticoke Point Co., 1778/1780 [Ref: M-216].

COVINGTON, Thomas. Private, Somerset Militia, Salisbury Bn., White Haven Co., 1778/1780 [Ref: M-219].

COVINGTON, William. Private, Worcester Militia, Sinepuxent Bn., Capt. John Postly's Co., Eighth Class, 1779/1780 [Ref: M-251].

COVINGTON, William Sr. (c1720-1789). Born in Maryland circa 1720, probably Worcester County, married first to Sarah Newman and second to Rachel Thomas, rendered patriotic service in North Carolina during the war, and died there circa March 25, 1789 [Ref: V-682].

COWLEY, Hinman. Private, Worcester Militia, Snow Hill Bn., Capt. John Parramore's Co., 1777 [Ref: M-250]. Private, Worcester Militia, Wicomico Bn., Capt. John Parramore's Co., Fifth Class, July 15, 1780 [Ref: M-259 listed the name as "Hinnan(?) Cowly"].

COWLEY, William. Private, 3rd Maryland Independent Co., Worcester County, Capt. John Watkins' Co., enlisted Feb 14, 1776; muster roll dated Aug 20, 1776, sick at his father's [Ref: D-22]. Private, Worcester Militia, Wicomico Bn.,

Capt. John Parramore's Co., Sixth Class, July 15, 1780 [Ref: M-259]. Private, Maryland Troops, Worcester County, draughted May 1, 1781 [Ref: K-99, D-372].

COX, Benjamin. Took the Oath of Allegiance in Worcester County in 1778 before the Hon. Joshua Townsend [Ref: J-1814 (Box 4)].

COX, Clarkson. Private, Somerset Militia, Salisbury Bn., Capt. Levin Irving's Black Water Co., 1778/1780 [Ref: M-217]. On July 30, 1781 Ebenezer Waller recruited Clarkson Cox from Somerset County to serve in the Continental Army until Dec 10, 1781 [Ref: L-35C].

COX, John. Captain, Worcester Militia, Sinepuxent Bn., Aug 30, 1777 [Ref: M-65]. Took the Oath of Allegiance in Worcester County in 1778 before the Hon. Joshua Townsend [Ref: J-1814 (Box 4)].

COX, John. Private, Somerset Militia, Princess Anne Bn., Capt. John Williams' Watkins Point Co., 1780 [Ref: M-222]. See "Horsey Summers," q.v.

COX, Samuel. Private, Worcester Militia, Wicomico Bn., Capt. William Handy's Co., Seventh Class, July 15, 1780 [Ref: M-257]. Took the Oath of Allegiance in Worcester County in 1778 before the Hon. Joshua Townsend [Ref: J-1814 (Box 4)].

COX, Thomas. Private, Somerset Militia, Salisbury Bn., Capt. Levin Irving's Black Water Co., 1778/1780 [Ref: M-218].

COX, Thomas. Private, Somerset Militia, Princess Anne Bn., Capt. John Williams' Watkins Point Co., 1780 [Ref: M-222].

COX, William. Corporal, Somerset Militia, Princess Anne Bn., St. Asaph's Co., 1780 [Ref: M-220].

COY, William (1756-1833). Private, Maryland Line, who applied for a pension (S31614) in Switzerland County, Indiana on Sep 18, 1832, stating he was born in Somerset County, Maryland on March 10, 1756 and lived in Montgomery County, Maryland. His wife was not named, but children shown in his affidavit were Thomas, Nancy, Susannah, Samuel, Esther, Elizabeth, Ann, William, Sarah, Mary, Seely, and Frances. William died on July 10, 1833 [Ref: W-791].

CRACKEL, Elizabeth. See "Kirk Gunby," q.v.

CRAFFORD, William. Private, Worcester Militia, Snow Hill Bn., Capt. John Parramore's Co., 1777 [Ref: M-250]. Private, Worcester Militia, Wicomico Bn., Capt. Samuel Smyley's Co., Sixth Class, July 15, 1780 [Ref: M-259].

CRAIG, Thomas. See "Moses Greer," q.v.

CRAIG, William. Private, Somerset County, Capt. John Gunby's 2nd Independent Maryland Co.; present on March 4, 1776; mustered on Aug 21, 1776 [Ref: D-641].

CRAPPER, Ezekiah (Ezekiel). See "Ananias Warren," q.v.

CRAPPER, Jesse, et al. See "Jesse Cropper, et al," q.v.

CRAWFORD, William. Took the Oath of Allegiance in Worcester County in 1778 before the Hon. John Selby [Ref: J-1814 (Box 4)].

CRESTMORE, George. See "Benjamin Scott," q.v.

CRESTMORE, Lotty. See "Benjamin Scott," q.v.
CROCKETT, John. Took the Oath of Allegiance in Somerset County in 1778 before the Hon. John Span Conway [Ref: T-14, N-50].
CROCKETT, John. Took the Oath of Allegiance in Worcester County in 1778 before the Hon. William Hopewell [Ref: J-1814 (Box 4)].
CROCKETT, Josiah. Took the Oath of Allegiance in Somerset County in 1778 before the Hon. John Stewart [Ref: T-19].
CROOK, Shadery. Took the Oath of Allegiance in Worcester County in 1778 before the Hon. Nathaniel Miller [Ref: J-1814 (Box 4) listed the name as "Shadery Crook" and then wrote a large "R" over the "C" to make it look like "Rrook"?].
CROPPER (CRAPPER), Bela. Private, Worcester Militia, Wicomico Bn., Capt. Samuel Horsey's Co., Eighth Class, July 15, 1780 [Ref: M-257]. Took the Oath of Allegiance in Worcester County in 1778 before the Hon. Nehemiah Holland [Ref: J-1814 (Box 4)].
CROPPER (CRAPPER), Ebenezer. Took the Oath of Allegiance in Worcester County in 1778 before the Hon. Joshua Townsend [Ref: J-1814 (Box 4)].
CROPPER (CRAPPER), Edmond. Took the Oath of Allegiance in Worcester County in 1778 before the Hon. Joshua Townsend [Ref: J-1814 (Box 4)].
CROPPER (CRAPPER), Edmund. Private, Worcester Militia, Sinepuxent Bn., Capt. Thomas Purnell's Co., Sixth Class, 1779/1780 [Ref: M-253]. Private, Worcester Militia, Wicomico Bn., Capt. Benjamin Dennis' Co., Fourth Class, July 15, 1780 [Ref: M-255]. Took the Oath of Allegiance in Worcester County in 1778 before the Hon. Nathaniel Miller [Ref: J-1814 (Box 4)].
CROPPER (CRAPPER), Edmund (Edmond). Took the Oath of Allegiance in Worcester County in 1778 before the Hon. Nathaniel Miller [Ref: J-1814 (Box 4)].
CROPPER (CRAPPER), Edward. Private, Maryland Troops, Worcester County, draughted May 1, 1781 [Ref: K-99, D-372].
CROPPER (CRAPPER), James. Private, Worcester Militia, Sinepuxent Bn., Capt. Thomas Purnell's Co., Third Class, 1779/1780 [Ref: M-253].
CROPPER (CRAPPER), James. Private, 3rd Maryland Independent Co., Worcester County, Capt. John Watkins' Co., enlisted Feb 9, 1776; muster roll dated Aug 20, 1776, present for duty [Ref: D-21].
CROPPER (CRAPPER), Jesse. Private, Worcester Militia, Sinepuxent Bn., Capt. John Rackliff's Co., Eighth Class, 1779/1780 [Ref: M-251]. Took the Oath of Allegiance in Worcester County in 1778 in Buckingham Hundred before the Hon. Thomas Purnell [Ref: J-1814 (Box 4)].
CROPPER (CRAPPER), Jesse. Private, Worcester Militia, Sinepuxent Bn., Capt. Elisha Purnell's Co., Sixth Class, 1779/1780 [Ref: M-253]. Took the Oath of Allegiance in Worcester County in 1778 in Quepomco Hundred before the Hon. Thomas Purnell [Ref: J-1814 (Box 4)].

CROPPER (CRAPPER), Jesse Jr. Took the Oath of Allegiance in Worcester County in 1778 before the Hon. Nathaniel Miller [Ref: J-1814 (Box 4)]. Rendered patriotic service by collecting cattle for the use of the military in Worcester County on Oct 23, 1781 [Ref: P-450]. Private, Worcester Militia, Sinepuxent Bn., Capt. John Postly's Co., Seventh Class, 1779/1780 [Ref: M-251 listed the name without the "Jr."].

CROPPER (CRAPPER), Labin. Private, Worcester Militia, Sinepuxent Bn., Capt. Thomas Purnell's Co., Fourth Class, 1779/1780 [Ref: M-253].

CROPPER (CRAPPER), Levi. Private, Worcester Militia, Sinepuxent Bn., Capt. John Rackliff's Co., Fourth Class, 1779/1780 [Ref: M-251].

CROPPER (CRAPPER), Levi. Private, Worcester Militia, Sinepuxent Bn., Capt. Elisha Purnell's Co., Seventh Class, 1779/1780 [Ref: M-253].

CROPPER (CRAPPER), Levi (of Natt.). Private, Maryland Troops, Worcester County, draughted May 1, 1781 [Ref: K-99, D-372]. On July 21, 1781 "Levi Crapper" was deposed concerning his family responsibilities [Ref: P-413].

CROPPER (CRAPPER), Levin. Private, Worcester Militia, Sinepuxent Bn., Capt. John Coe's Co., Fifth Class, 1779/1780 [Ref: M-252].

CROPPER (CRAPPER), Major. Private, Worcester Militia, Sinepuxent Bn., Capt. Thomas Purnell's Co., Fifth Class, 1779/1780 [Ref: M-253]. Took the Oath of Allegiance in Worcester County in 1778 before the Hon. Nathaniel Miller [Ref: J-1814 (Box 4)].

CROPPER (CRAPPER), Nathan. Rendered patriotic service by supplying beef in Worcester County for the use of the military on Oct 12, 1780 [Ref: P-325].

CROPPER (CRAPPER), Nathaniel. Took the Oath of Allegiance in Worcester County in 1778 before the Hon. Nathaniel Miller [Ref: J-1814 (Box 4)].

CROPPER (CRAPPER), Nathaniel Jr. Took the Oath of Allegiance in Worcester County in 1778 before the Hon. Nathaniel Miller [Ref: J-1814 (Box 4)].

CROPPER (CRAPPER), Noble. Took the Oath of Allegiance in Worcester County in 1778 before the Hon. Nathaniel Miller [Ref: J-1814 (Box 4)]. Private, Worcester Militia, Sinepuxent Bn., Capt. John Rackliff's Co., Fifth Class, 1779/1780 [Ref: M-251].

CROPPER (CRAPPER), Polly. See "Patrick Causey," q.v.

CROPPER (CRAPPER), Reuben (Ruben). Private, Worcester Militia, Sinepuxent Bn., Capt. John Rackliff's Co., Seventh Class, 1779/1780 [Ref: M-251]. Private, Maryland Troops, Worcester County, draughted May 1, 1781 [Ref: K-99, D-372]. Took the Oath of Allegiance in Worcester County in 1778 in Buckingham Hundred before the Hon. Thomas Purnell [Ref: J-1814 (Box 4)]. On July 21, 1781 he gave a "deposition concerning health" [Ref: P-413].

CROPPER (CRAPPER), Vincent. Took the Oath of Allegiance in Worcester County in 1778 before the Hon. Nathaniel Miller [Ref: J-1814 (Box 4)]. Rendered patriotic service by supplying beef for the use of the military on Sep 21, 1781 [Ref: P-347].

CROPPER (CRAPPER), William. Took the Oath of Allegiance in Worcester County in 1778 before the Hon. Joshua Townsend [Ref: J-1814 (Box 4)].
CROPPER (CRAPPER), William Jr. Private, Worcester Militia, Sinepuxent Bn., Capt. Thomas Purnell's Co., Eighth Class, 1779/1780 [Ref: M-253].
CROPPER (CRAPPER), Zadok. Private, Worcester Militia, Sinepuxent Bn., Capt. John Coe's Co., Fifth Class, 1779/1780 [Ref: M-252].
CROSWELL, George. Private, Somerset Militia, Princess Anne Bn., Capt. Henry Miles' Little Annemessex Co., 1780 [Ref: M-221].
CROSWELL, George Jr. Private, Somerset Militia, Princess Anne Bn., Capt. Henry Miles' Little Annemessex Co., 1780 [Ref: M-221].
CROSWELL, Lawson. Private, Somerset Militia, Princess Anne Bn., Capt. Henry Miles' Little Annemessex Co., 1780 [Ref: M-221].
CROUCH, Daniel. Took the Oath of Allegiance in Somerset County in 1778 [Ref: N-50].
CROUCH, David. Took the Oath of Allegiance in Somerset County in 1778 (made his "X" mark) before the Hon. John Span Conway [Ref: T-14].
CROUCH, Shadrick (Shadrach). Private, Worcester Militia, Snow Hill Bn., Capt. Ebenezer Handy's Co., April 9, 1776 [Ref: M-249]. Took the Oath of Allegiance in Worcester County in 1778 before the Hon. William Hopewell [Ref: J-1814 (Box 4)]. Private, Worcester Militia, Wicomico Bn., Capt. Robert Handy's Co., Fourth Class, July 15, 1780 [Ref: M-254].
CROUCH, Thomas. Private, Worcester Militia, Wicomico Bn., Capt. Robert Handy's Co., Fifth Class, July 15, 1780 [Ref: M-254]. Took the Oath of Allegiance in Worcester County in 1778 before the Hon. William Hopewell [Ref: J-1814 (Box 4)].
CULBER, Ann. See "Robert Scroggin," q.v.
CULLEN, Daniel. See "Samuel Cullen," q.v.
CULLEN (CULLINS), Samuel (1762 -   ). Son of Daniel and Winnifort Cullen, born in Coventry Parish on March 18, 1762 [Ref: Y-81]. Private, Somerset Militia, Princess Anne Bn., Capt. John Williams' Watkins Point Co., 1780 [Ref: M-222].
CULLEN (CULLING), Thomas. Private, Somerset Militia, Salisbury Bn., Capt. Sampson Wheatly's Co., 1780 [Ref: M-216].
CULLEN (CULLIN), William. Private, Somerset Militia, Princess Anne Bn., Capt. Isaac Handy's Great Annemessix Co., 1780 [Ref: M-221].
CULLEN (CULLIN), William Sr. Took the Oath of Allegiance in Somerset County in 1778 before the Hon. Peter Waters [Ref: T-18].
CULLEN, Winnifort. See "Samuel Cullen," q.v.
CULVER, Charles. Private, Somerset Militia, Salisbury Bn., Capt. Joseph Venables' Barren Creek Co., 1778/1780 [Ref: M-217].
CULVER, Levin. Private, Somerset Militia, Salisbury Bn., Capt. Levin Irving's Black Water Co., 1778/1780 [Ref: M-218].

CULVER, Nathan. Took the Oath of Allegiance in Somerset County on Feb 7, 1778 before the Hon. Joseph Venables [Ref: T-25].
CURLIS (CURLES), Benjaman. Took the Oath of Allegiance in Worcester County in 1778 in Buckingham Hundred before the Hon. Thomas Purnell [Ref: J-1814 (Box 4)].
CURLIS (CURLES), Eading. Took the Oath of Allegiance in Worcester County in 1778 in Buckingham Hundred before the Hon. Thomas Purnell [Ref: J-1814 (Box 4)].
CURLIS (CURLES), Joseph. Took the Oath of Allegiance in Worcester County in 1778 before the Hon. Nathaniel Miller [Ref: J-1814 (Box 4)].
CURREN, John. Private, Worcester Militia, Sinepuxent Bn., Capt. John Rackliff's Co., Eighth Class, 1779/1780 [Ref: M-251].
CURTIS, Amelia. See "Isaac Handy," q.v.
CURTIS, Benjamin. Private, 3rd Maryland Independent Co., Worcester County, Capt. John Watkins' Co., enlisted Feb 10, 1776; muster roll dated Aug 20, 1776, present for duty [Ref: D-22].
CURTIS, Isaac. Ensign, Somerset Militia, Princess Anne Bn., Capt. Thomas King's Co., Dec 7, 1778. Ensign, St. Asaph's Co., 1780. Select Militia, Aug 15, 1781. Lieutenant, Select Militia, Capt. John Williams' Co., Aug 23, 1781 [Ref: M-220, E-260, G-577, L-35A, M-67]. Took the Oath of Allegiance in Somerset County in 1778 before the Hon. John Williams [Ref: T-21, N-50].
CURTIS, James. Ensign, Somerset Militia, 17th Bn., Sep 9, 1776. Ensign, Princess Anne Bn., Capt. William Waters' Co., Sep 22, 1777. Second Lieutenant, Salisbury Bn., Jan 7, 1778. Ensign(?), Princess Anne Bn., Capt. Isaac Handy's Great Annemessix Co., 1780 [Ref: M-67, M-221, B-285, C-381, E-381]. Took the Oath of Allegiance in Somerset County in 1778 before the Hon. John Williams [Ref: T-21, N-50]. Since there may have been two men by this name, additional research will be necessary before drawing conclusions.
CURTIS, Samuel. Private, Somerset Militia, Princess Anne Bn., St. Asaph's Co., 1780 [Ref: M-221].
CUSTIS, Peggy (Margaret). See "Samuel Wilson," q.v.
DAILY, William. Private, Somerset Militia, Salisbury Bn., Capt. Levin Irving's Black Water Co., 1778/1780 [Ref: M-218].
DAKES (DAKUS?), Jesse. Private, Somerset Militia, Princess Anne Bn., St. Asaph's Co., 1780 [Ref: M-221].
DALE, Campbell. Private, Worcester Militia, Sinepuxent Bn., Capt. Josiah Dale's Co., Seventh Class, 1779/1780 [Ref: M-254].
DALE, Ebenezer. Private, Worcester Militia, Sinepuxent Bn., Capt. Josiah Dale's Co., Sixth Class, 1779/1780 [Ref: M-254].
DALE, Jacob. See "James Dale," q.v.
DALE, James. Private, Worcester Militia, Sinepuxent Bn., Capt. John Postly's Co., Eighth Class, 1779/1780 [Ref: M-251]. Took the Oath of Allegiance in

Worcester County in 1778 before the Hon. Nehemiah Holland [Ref: J-1814 (Box 4)]. See the other "James Dale," q.v.

DALE, James. Private, Worcester Militia, Sinepuxent Bn., Capt. Josiah Dale's Co., Fourth Class, 1779/1780 [Ref: M-254]. Took the Oath of Allegiance in Worcester County in 1778 before the Hon. Nathaniel Miller [Ref: J-1814 (Box 4)]. One James Dale died by June, 1796, when a petition was submitted to the Worcester County Court for a commission to divide the real estate of James Dale who had died intestate leaving six children: Joshua Dale, Jacob Dale, John P. Dale (minor), Margaret Dale (minor), Martha Truitt (wife of George), and Mary McGrigor (wife of William). William Dale was appointed guardian to the minors [Ref: Article by William D. Paatrick in *Maryland Magazine of Genealogy*, Vol. 4, No. 1 (Spring, 1981), p. 3].

DALE, Jesse. Private, Worcester Militia, Sinepuxent Bn., Capt. Josiah Dale's Co., Third Class, 1779/1780 [Ref: M-254].

DALE, John. Private, Worcester Militia, Sinepuxent Bn., Capt. Josiah Dale's Co., Second Class, 1779/1780 [Ref: M-254].

DALE, John (of John). Took the Oath of Allegiance in Worcester County in 1778 before the Hon. Nehemiah Holland [Ref: J-1814 (Box 4)].

DALE, John P. See "James Dale," q.v.

DALE, Jonathan. Rendered patriotic service by hauling provisions for the military in Worcester County on Oct 1, 1780 [Ref: P-322].

DALE, Joshua. See "James Dale," q.v.

DALE, Josiah. Captain, Worcester Militia, Sinepuxent Bn., 1780 [Ref: M-254]. Rendered patriotic service by supplying corn for the use of the military on June 14, 1780 and July 10, 1780 [Ref: P-296, G-10]. See "Joshua or Josiah Deal," q.v.

DALE, Margaret. See "James Dale," q.v.

DALE, Matthew (c1760-c1814). Took the Oath of Allegiance in Worcester County in 1778 before the Hon. Nehemiah Holland [Ref: J-1814 (Box 4)]. "Mathew Dale" was born in Maryland circa 1762, married Catherine (Keaty) Purnell, rendered patriotic service in Maryland during the war, and died in Kentucky before July 25, 1814 [Ref: V-750]. If this is one and the same person, he would have been born in 1760 or earlier since signers of the oath in 1778 were aged 18 and older. Additional research may be necessary before drawing conclusions.

DALE, Samuel. Took the Oath of Allegiance in Worcester County in 1778 before the Hon. Nathaniel Miller [Ref: J-1814 (Box 4)].

DALE, Thomas (1744-1812). Private, Worcester Militia, Sinepuxent Bn., Capt. John Postly's Co., Fourth Class, 1779/1780 [Ref: M-251]. Second Lieutenant, Worcester Militia, Capt. Isaac Evans' Co., March 16, 1781 [Ref: M-67, G-353]. Took the Oath of Allegiance in Worcester County in 1778 before the Hon. Nathaniel Miller [Ref: J-1814 (Box 4)]. Thomas Dale was born in Maryland on

March 5, 1744, married Elizabeth Evans, served as a second lieutenant during the war, and died in Tennessee on Jan 6, 1812 [Ref: V-750].

DALF(?), David. Private, Somerset Militia, Salisbury Bn., White Haven Co., 1778/1780 [Ref: M-219].

DANE, William. Took the Oath of Allegiance in Somerset County in 1778 [Ref: N-50].

DANIELS, John. See "William Mills," q.v.

DARBY, Benjamin (1745-1787). Son of Walter Darby and Sarah Rolph. Benjamin was born in Somerset County, married Sarah Twiford on Nov 30, 1775, and died in Dorchester County on Dec 25, 1787. Their son John Darby (1788-1829) married Amelia Catherine Russell (1789-1856) in Dorchester County in 1809 and they lived and died in Sussex County, Delaware [Ref: S-2784, S-3033, V-759]. Took the Oath of Allegiance in Somerset County on Feb 28, 1778 before the Hon. Joseph Venables [Ref: T-25 listed the name as "Benjaman Darby"]. Private, Somerset Militia, Capt. Joseph Venables' Barren Creek Co., Salisbury Bn., 1778/1780 [Ref: Maryland Historical Society Militia Lists Manuscript (photocopy of the original) listed the name as "Ben. Darby" and source M-217 mistakenly listed the name as "Ben. Davis(?)"].

DARBY, Daniel. Son of Walter Darby and Sarah Rolph, and a brother of "Benjamin Darby," q.v. [Ref: *Maryland Calender of Wills*, Vol. 12, p. 180]. Private, Somerset Militia, Salisbury Bn., Capt. Joseph Venables' Barren Creek Co., 1778/1780 [Ref: Maryland Historical Society Militia Lists Manuscript (photocopy of the original) listed the name as "Daniel Darby" and source M-217 listed the name as "Daniel Da--ey"].

DARBY, John. Private, Somerset Militia, Salisbury Bn., Capt. Levin Irving's Black Water Co., 1778/1780 [Ref: M-217]. Took the Oath of Allegiance in Somerset County on Feb 28, 1778 before the Hon. Joseph Venables [Ref: T-25]. See "Benjamin Darby," q.v.

DARBY, Mary. See "Levin Moore," q.v.

DARBY, Walter. See "Benjamin Darby" and "Daniel Darby," q.v.

DARCUS, William. Private, Somerset Militia, Princess Anne Bn., Capt. John Williams' Watkins Point Co., 1780 [Ref: M-222].

DASHIELL, Ann. See "Levin Dashiell" and "John Dashiell," q.v.

DASHIELL, Arasy (Arosy). See "James F. Dashiell," q.v.

DASHIELL, Arthur (1734-1802). First Lieutenant, Somerset Militia, 1st Bn., Capt. John Philips' Co., Aug 19, 1776 [Ref: M-67, B-220]. Arthur Dashiell was born on July 29, 1734, married first to Rachel Cordray and second to Mrs. Elizabeth Phillips, served as a first lieutenant during the war, and died in September, 1802 [Ref: V-763].

DASHIELL, Benjamin (1736-1799). Born in Maryland, probably Somerset County, in 1736, married twice (second wife was Ann Yoe), served as a naval commander during the war, and died on Sep 30, 1799 [Ref: V-763].

DASHIELL, Benjamin (1745 -   ). Brother of "John Dashiell," q.v. Never married [Ref: R-255]. Private, Somerset Militia, Salisbury Bn., Capt. Levin Irving's Black Water Co., 1778/1780 [Ref: M-217].

DASHIELL, Benjamin Frederick Augustus Caesar (1763-1820). Son of Joseph Dashiell (1736-1787) and Martha Bluett, born in Stepney Parish on Sunday, May 22, 1763, and married Henrietta ---- (1757-1791). Children: Theodore Gunby, Elizabeth Leah, and Henrietta Ann. Benjamin served in the Lower House of the Maryland Legislature between 1789 and 1803 and died in Somerset County on April 5, 1820 [Ref: R-251, R-252, V-763]. Private, Worcester Militia, Wicomico Bn., Capt. Robert Handy's Co., Sixth Class, July 15, 1780 [Ref: M-254]. See "Joseph Dashiell," q.v.

DASHIELL, Bridget. See "John Dashiell" and "Levin Dashiell," q.v.

DASHIELL, Clement. See "Josiah Dashiell," q.v.

DASHIELL, Easter. See "Henry Lowes," q.v.

DASHIELL, Eleanor. See "Joseph Dashiell" and "John Dashiell," q.v.

DASHIELL, Elizabeth. See "Benjamin F. A. C. Dashiell" and "George Dashiell" and "John Dashiell" and "John Stewart," q.v.

DASHIELL, Eunice. See "John Dashiell," q.v.

DASHIELL, George (1743-c1805). Son of George and Elizabeth Dashiell. George married first to Rose (Arosy) Fisher on Aug 6, 1760 and second to Sally Dennis by 1803. Children: James Fairfax, Tubman, John, Josiah, Robert (physician), George (reverend), William D., and Fisher. He served as Sheriff of Somerset County, 1770-1773; County Court Justice, 1775-1777; Judge of the Court of Appeals for Tax Assessment, 1786 [Ref: R-252, R-253]. Colonel, Somerset Militia, Jan 6, 1776; County Lieutenant, July 1, 1777 to at least July 24, 1780 [Ref: M-67, M-222, J-1814 (Box 8, Dashiell's correspondence), C-304]. Appointed as Collector of Cloathing for the American Army in Somerset County on Nov 27, 1777, and Commissary of Purchases in 1780 [Ref: C-426, P-261, P-263, P-297, P-301, P-363]. Attended the Maryland Conventions in 1774, 1775 and 1776, and signed the Association of the Freemen of Maryland on July 26, 1775 [Ref: O-1, O-4, O-28, A-67]. Took the Oath of Allegiance in Somerset County on Feb 7, 1778 before the Hon. Joseph Venables [Ref: T-25]. It must be noted that there were three men by this name who served during the war: George Dashiell, born circa 1729, died before Dec 26, 1809, married Elizabeth Jones, and served as county lieutenant; George Dashiell (1740-1825) married Priscilla Jones and served as a private; and, George Dashiell, born on Aug 28, 1743, died after Nov 17, 1783, married Rose Fisher, and rendered patriotic service [Ref: V-763, V-764]. Some of the aforegoing information appears to be in error and could apply to any one of them. Additional research will be necessary before drawing conclusions. See "John Dashiell" and "Aaron Sterling," q.v.

DASHIELL, Henney. See "Josiah Dashiell," q.v.

DASHIELL, Henrietta. See "Benjamin F. A. C. Dashiell" and "Isaac Wright," q.v.

DASHIELL, Isaac (1759 -   ). Private, Somerset Militia, Salisbury Bn., Capt. Levin Irving's Black Water Co., 1778/1780 [Ref: M-217]. Brother of "John Dashiell (1757-1818)," q.v.

DASHIELL, Isabell. See "Robert Dashiell," q.v.

DASHIELL, James (1740-1796). Private, Somerset Militia, Salisbury Bn., Capt. John Span Conway's Nanticoke Point Co., 1778/1780 [Ref: M-216]. James Dashiell was born on Aug 20, 1740, married Sarah Evans, served as a private during the war, and died before Feb 9, 1796 [Ref: V-764]. Brother of "John Dashiell," q.v.

DASHIELL, James Fairfax (1761 -   ). Son of George and Arasy (Arosy) Dashiell, born in Stepney Parish on May 6, 1761 [Ref: Y-44]. Private, Somerset Militia, Salisbury Bn., Capt. Josiah Dashiell's Wicomico Creek Co., 1778/1780 [Ref: M-218]. See "George Dashiell," q.v.

DASHIELL, Jane (Jean). See "William Winder," q.v.

DASHIELL, Jesse or Jessie (1716-1778). Took the Oath of Allegiance in Somerset County in 1778 before the Hon. John Stewart [Ref: T-19, R-254]. See "John Dashiell, of Winder," q.v.

DASHIELL, John (c1740-1817). Son of Levin and Bridget Dashiell. John married Elizabeth Killet on Dec 29, 1762. Children: Levin, John, Robert Killet Washington, Eunice, Leah Washington, and Sarah Anne [Ref: R-254]. Second Lieutenant, Somerset Militia, 1st Bn., Aug 19, 1776. First Lieutenant, Princess Anne Bn., Capt. Thomas Irving's Monie Co., Sep 22, 1777 to at least July 24, 1780 [Ref: M-67, M-219, B-220, C-381]. See "John Dashiell, of Winder," q.v.

DASHIELL, John (1757-1818). Son of Jesse Dashiell and Susanna Townsend. John married Eleanor Dashiell by 1795 and had at least three children: George, Eleanor T., and Betsy (Elizabeth). He may have served in the Maryland Legislature. He was a captain by 1798 and major by 1803 [Ref: R-254, R-255]. Second Lieutenant, Somerset Militia, Capt. Robert Dashiell's Co., Sep 22, 1777, and First Lieutenant, Salisbury Bn., April 20, 1778 [Ref: M-67, C-382, E-42]. First Lieutenant, Worcester Militia, Wicomico Bn., Capt. Robert Handy's Co., May 27, 1779 to at least July 15, 1780 [Ref: M-67, M-254, E-423]. John Dashiell was born on Aug 11, 1757, married first to Anne or Nancy ---- and second to Eleanor ----, served as a lieutenant during the war, and died on March 25, 1818 [Ref: V-764]. See "John Dashiell, of Winder" and "George Dashiell" and "James Dashiell," q.v.

DASHIELL, John. Sergeant, Somerset Militia, Salisbury Bn., Capt. John Span Conway's Nanticoke Point Co., 1778/1780 [Ref: M-216].

DASHIELL, John. Took the Oath of Allegiance in Somerset County in 1778 before the Hon. William Winder [Ref: T-22 listed the name as "John Dashiele"].

DASHIELL, John. Took the Oath of Allegiance in Somerset County in 1778 before the Hon. Levin Wilson [Ref: T-17 listed the name as "John Dashiel"].

DASHIELL, John (of Winder). Son of Winder and Ann Dashiell. John married Ann or Nancy ----, but had no children. His first cousin was John Dashiell

(1757-1818), son of Jesse Dashiell (1716-1778), and his third cousin was John Dashiell (c1740-1817), son of Levin Dashiell (1711-1795). "Jno. Dashiell (of Winder)" was a corporal in the Somerset Militia, Salisbury Bn., Capt. John Span Conway's Nanticoke Point Co., 1778/1780 [Ref: M-216]. "John Dashiell" was born on April 17, 1751, married Sarah (Killam) Handy, served as a corporal during the war, and died on Dec 15, 1816 [Ref: V-764]. There were at least three men named John Dashiell who were eligible to represent Somerset County in the Maryland Legislature in 1784 [Ref: R-253, R-254]. Due to this identification problem, additional research will be necessary before drawing conclusions

DASHIELL, Joseph. See "John Henry" and "Uriah Forrest," q.v.

DASHIELL, Joseph (1736-1787). Lieutenant Colonel, Worcester Militia, 10th Bn., Jan 6, 1776. Colonel, Feb 3, 1777. County Lieutenant, Worcester County, July 1, 1777 [Ref: M-67, M-249, M-250, C-110, C-304, P-322]. Took the Oath of Allegiance in Worcester County in 1778 before the Hon. William Hopewell [Ref: J-1814 (Box 4) listed the name as "Joseph Dayshield"]. On Aug 6, 1778 the Council of Maryland commissioned a Letter of Marque and Reprisal to Joseph Dashiell, master of the sloop *Dolphin*, mounting two swivels and 16 small arms, navigated by 10 men, burthen 10 tons, belonging to John Fassett & Co. [Ref: E-178]. Collector of Cloathing for the American Army in Worcester County, appointed on Nov 27, 1777 [Ref: C-426]. Commissary of Purchases for Worcester County, 1778-1780 [Ref: C-551, P-256, P-330, F-215]. As Worcester County Lieutenant he signed a return for men draughted into service with the Maryland Troops on May 1, 1781 [Ref: K-99, D-372]. On Oct 15, 1780 Joseph Dashiell wrote to the Governor stating that he "has been unable to take his seat in the Assembly because of difficulty forwarding cattle procured." [Ref: P-327]. Attended the Maryland Convention in 1776 [Ref: O-28]. Joseph married first to Martha Bluett on May 18, 1757 and second to Susannah --- by 1774. Children: William Pitt, Benjamin F. A. C., Martha Bluett, and Eleanor Matilda. He was a captain by 1757, lieutenant colonel by 1776, County Court Justice, 1766-1787, and member of the Lower House of the Maryland Legislature, 1768-1785. He died intestate by February, 1787 [Ref: R-255, V-764].

DASHIELL, Joseph. Sergeant, Somerset Militia, Salisbury Bn., Capt. John Span Conway's Nanticoke Point Co., 1778/1780 [Ref: M-216]. Took the Oath of Allegiance in Somerset County in 1778 before the Hon. William Winder [Ref: N-50, and T-22 listed the name sa "Joseph Dashiele"].

DASHIELL, Josiah (1746-1784). Son of Capt. Clement Dashiell and Sarah Piper. Josiah married his first cousin Henney Dashiell, daughter of Thomas, and died without progeny [Ref: R-255, R-256]. Captain, Somerset Militia, Salisbury Bn., Wicomico Creek Co., Sep 22, 1777 to at least July 24, 1780 [Ref: M-67, M-218, C-382, E-423]. Sheriff of Somerset County, 1773-1775, member of the Lower House of the Maryland Legislature, 1779-1782, and County Court

Justice, 1778-1784 [Ref: R-256]. Rendered patriotic service by supplying wheat for the use of the military on May 14, 1781 [Ref: P-394]. See "George Dashiell," q.v.

DASHIELL, Leah. See "John Dashiell," q.v.

DASHIELL, Levi. Private, Somerset Militia, Salisbury Bn., Capt. Joseph Venables' Barren Creek Co., 1778/1780 [Ref: M-217].

DASHIELL, Levin (1711-1795). Son of Thomas and Ann Dashiell. Levin married Bridget ---- in 1738 [Ref: R-256]. Justice of the Orphans Court for Somerset County, commissioned on June 4, 1777 [Ref: C-274]. Took the Oath of Allegiance in Somerset County in 1778 before the Hon. Peter Waters [Ref: T-18]. Rendered patriotic service by supplying corn for the use of the military in Somerset County on Jan 15, 1780 [Ref: P-261]. See "John Dashiell (of Winder)," q.v.

DASHIELL, Martha. See "Joseph Dashiell," q.v.

DASHIELL, Matthew(?). Private, Somerset Militia, Salisbury Bn., Capt. Josiah Dashiell's Wicomico Creek Co., 1778/1780 [Ref: M-218].

DASHIELL, Nancy. See "John Dashiell," q.v.

DASHIELL, Rebecca. See "John Stewart," q.v.

DASHIELL, Robert. Captain, Somerset Militia, Salisbury Co., Salisbury Bn., from Sep 22, 1777 to at least May 26, 1781 [Ref: M-67, C-283, I-151]. Rendered patriotic service by supplying pork for the use of the military on May 26, 1781 [Ref: P-398]. See the other "Robert Dashiell," q.v.

DASHIELL, Robert. Ensign, Somerset Militia, Salisbury Bn., Capt. Henry Gale's Quantico Co., from Sep 22, 1777 to 1780 [Ref: M-67, M-216, G-575]. See the other "Robert Dashiell," q.v.

DASHIELL, Robert. Took the Oath of Allegiance in Somerset County in 1778 before the Hon. Gillis Polk [Ref: T-15, N-50]. One Robert Dashiell was born on Sep 29, 1745, married Isabell ---- (1745-1833), died on March 4, 1814, and is buried in the Dashiell-Huston-Rider Family Graveyard on the south side of Tony Tank Lake between Camden Avenue and South Salisbury Blvd. in Wicomico County [Ref: *Graveyards and Gravestones of Wicomico*, by John E. Jacob (1996), p. 104]. Since there were other men by this name, additional research will be necessary before drawing conclusions. See "George Dashiell" and "John Dashiell," q.v.

DASHIELL, Sarah. See "John Dashiell" and "William F. Dashiell" and "William Robertson," q.v.

DASHIELL, Susanna. See "Joseph Dashiell," q.v.

DASHIELL, Theodore. See "Benjamin F. A. C. Dashiell," q.v.

DASHIELL, Thomas. See "Josiah Dashiell" and "Levin Dashiell," q.v.

DASHIELL, Tubman. See "George Dashiell," q.v.

DASHIELL, William. Private, Somerset Militia, Capt. George Day Scott's Co., 1775 [Ref: J-1814 (Box 1)]. See "John Stewart" and "George Dashiell," q.v.

DASHIELL, William Francis (1750-1790). Son of William and Sarah Dashiell, born in Stepney Parish on Jan 26, 1750 [Ref: Y-51]. Took the Oath of Allegiance in Somerset County in 1778 before the Hon. John Stewart [Ref: T-19]. Private, Somerset Militia, Salisbury Bn., Capt. John Span Conway's Nanticoke Point Co., 1778/1780. Ensign, Capt. John McCloster's Co., July 21, 1781 [Ref: M-67, M-216, G-575, J-1814 (Box 8, Dashiell's correspondence), H-361]. William Francis Dashiell was born on Jan 26, 1750, married Priscilla Evans, served as a private during the war, and died in 1790 [Ref: V-764].

DASHIELL, William Pitt. See "Joseph Dashiell," q.v.

DASHIELL, Winder. Took the Oath of Allegiance in Somerset County in 1778 before the Hon. John Span Conway [Ref: T-14, N-50].

DAUGHERTY, Isaac. Private, Somerset Militia, Salisbury Bn., White Haven Co., 1778/1780 [Ref: M-219].

DAUGHERTY, Jesse. Private, Somerset Militia, Princess Anne Bn., Capt. Henry Miles' Little Annemessex Co., 1780 [Ref: M-221].

DAUGHERTY, John. Private, Somerset Militia, Salisbury Bn., Capt. Sampson Wheatly's Co., 1780 [Ref: M-216].

DAUGHERTY, Nathaniel. Private, Somerset Militia, Salisbury Bn., Capt. Sampson Wheatly's Co., 1780 [Ref: M-216].

DAUGHERTY, Peter. Private, Somerset Militia, Salisbury Bn., Capt. Sampson Wheatly's Co., 1780 [Ref: M-216]. Drafted from Somerset County on June 20, 1781 to serve in the Continental Army [Ref: L-35C].

DAUGHERTY, Stephen. Private, Somerset Militia, Salisbury Bn., Capt. Sampson Wheatly's Co., 1780 [Ref: M-216].

DAVIS, Abijah (1750 -   ). Son of Benjamin and Mary Davis, born in Worcester Parish on March 8, 1750 [Ref: Y-30]. Private, Worcester Militia, Sinepuxent Bn., Capt. John Postly's Co., Fifth Class, 1779/1780 [Ref: M-251 listed the name as "Abisha(?) Davis"]. Took the Oath of Allegiance in Worcester County in 1778 before the Hon. Nathaniel Miller [Ref: J-1814 (Box 4)].

DAVIS, Annanias. Private, Worcester Militia, Sinepuxent Bn., Capt. Josiah Dale's Co., Second Class, 1779/1780 [Ref: M-254].

DAVIS, Arthur. Took the Oath of Allegiance in Worcester County in 1778 before the Hon. Nehemiah Holland [Ref: J-1814 (Box 4)].

DAVIS, Beauchamp. Private, Somerset Militia, Princess Anne Bn., Capt. Isaac Handy's Great Annemessix Co., 1780 [Ref: M-221].

DAVIS, Benjamin. Took the Oath of Allegiance in Worcester County in 1778 before the Hon. James Selby [Ref: J-1814 (Box 4)]. See "Abijah Davis," q.v.

DAVIS, Benjamin. Private, Worcester Militia, Sinepuxent Bn., Capt. Elisha Purnell's Co., Fifth Class, 1779/1780 [Ref: M-253]. Took the Oath of Allegiance in Worcester County in 1778 before the Hon. Joshua Townsend [Ref: J-1814 (Box 4)]. Private, Worcester Militia, Wicomico Bn., Capt. John Davis' Co., Fourth Class, July 15, 1780 [Ref: M-254].

DAVIS, Charles. Private, Worcester Militia, Capt. John Martin's Co., 1780/1781 [Ref: J-1814 (Box 12) listed the name as "Chas. Davis"].

DAVIS, Edward. Private, Worcester Militia, Sinepuxent Bn., Capt. Thomas Purnell's Co., Third Class, 1779/1780 [Ref: M-253]. Took the Oath of Allegiance in Worcester County in 1778 in Quepomco Hundred before the Hon. Thomas Purnell [Ref: J-1814 (Box 4) listed the name as "Edward Davise"].

DAVIS, Edward. Took the Oath of Allegiance in Worcester County in 1778 before the Hon. Nathaniel Miller [Ref: J-1814 (Box 4)].

DAVIS, Eli. Private, Worcester Militia, Sinepuxent Bn., Capt. Thomas Purnell's Co., Sixth Class, 1779/1780 [Ref: M-253].

DAVIS, Elisha. Corporal, Worcester Militia, Snow Hill Bn., Capt. Ebenezer Handy's Co., April 9, 1776 [Ref: M-249].

DAVIS, George. Private, Worcester Militia, Snow Hill Bn., Capt. Ebenezer Handy's Co., April 9, 1776 [Ref: M-249]. Private, Worcester Militia, Wicomico Bn., Capt. James Perdue's Co., First Class, July 15, 1780 [Ref: M-256].

DAVIS, Henry. Private, Somerset Militia, Princess Anne Bn., Capt. James Elzey's Co., 1780 [Ref: M-220]. Took the Oath of Allegiance in Somerset County in 1778 before the Hon. Peter Waters [Ref: T-18].

DAVIS, Hezekiah. Took the Oath of Allegiance in Worcester County in 1778 before the Hon. Joshua Townsend [Ref: J-1814 (Box 4)].

DAVIS, James. Private, Virginia Militia, made the declaration on Sep 24, 1832, age 69, that he "was born in Maryland 4 March 1762; his father moved to Accomack County, Virginia when he was about 12 years old where he has lived here ever since. He was called into service in a Co. commanded by Capt. Thomas Marshall, attached to the 2nd Regiment, Virginia Militia. He entered the service and went on guard in July, 1777, the first time at Wallops Island where he was stationed most of the time. He also did duty at Musqueto Point on Pocomoke River and on Onancock Creek and other places." (Court Orders, 1832-1836). [Ref: Stratton Nottingham's *Soldiers and Sailors of the Eastern Shore of Virginia in the Revolutionary War*, p. 41]. It should be noted that a longer declaration by James Davis on July 29, 1833, age 71, is contained in the aforementioned book, adding that he "joined the militia when he was about 15 years old with his father's consent. His age is recorded in a book which his brother Major Davis had at the death of his father. His brother has now been dead for 10 years." [Ref: *Ibid.*, pp. 44-45]. See "Major Davis," q.v.

DAVIS, James. Private, Worcester Militia, Wicomico Bn., Capt. John Davis' Co., First Class, July 15, 1780 [Ref: M-254].

DAVIS, James. Took the Oath of Allegiance in Worcester County in 1778 before the Hon. William Hopewell [Ref: J-1814 (Box 4)].

DAVIS, James. Took the Oath of Allegiance in Worcester County in 1778 before the Hon. Nathaniel Miller [Ref: J-1814 (Box 4)].

DAVIS, James. Took the Oath of Allegiance in Worcester County in 1778 before the Hon. Joshua Townsend [Ref: J-1814 (Box 4)].
DAVIS, James. Took the Oath of Allegiance in Worcester County in 1778 before the Hon. John Selby [Ref: J-1814 (Box 4)].
DAVIS, James (of Ben). Private, Worcester Militia, Wicomico Bn., Capt. James Patterson's Co., Seventh Class, July 15, 1780 [Ref: M-258].
DAVIS, Jesse. First Lieutenant, Worcester Militia, 10th Bn., Capt. Jesse Gray's Co., May 15, 1776 [Ref: M-68, A-426].
DAVIS, Jesse. Private, Worcester Militia, Sinepuxent Bn., Capt. Josiah Dale's Co., Third Class, 1779/1780 [Ref: M-254].
DAVIS, Jesse. Took the Oath of Allegiance in Worcester County in 1778 before the Hon. Nathaniel Miller [Ref: J-1814 (Box 4)].
DAVIS, John. Ensign, Worcester Militia, Wicomico Bn., June 28, 1777. First Lieutenant, Wicomico Bn., Capt. Isaac Houston's Co., Aug 30, 1777. Captain, May 27, 1779 to at least July 15, 1780 [Ref: M-68, M-254, C-351, E-423]. Took the Oath of Allegiance in Worcester County in 1778 before the Hon. Nathaniel Miller [Ref: J-1814 (Box 4)].
DAVIS, John. Private, Worcester Militia, Snow Hill Bn., Capt. Ebenezer Handy's Co., April 9, 1776 [Ref: M-249].
DAVIS, John. Private, Worcester Militia, Sinepuxent Bn., Capt. Thomas Purnell's Co., Fourth Class, 1779/1780 [Ref: M-253].
DAVIS, John. Private, Worcester Militia, Wicomico Bn., Capt. James Patterson's Co., Fourth Class, July 15, 1780 [Ref: M-258].
DAVIS, John (Broad Creek). Took the Oath of Allegiance in Somerset County in 1778 before the Hon. Levin Wilson [Ref: T-17, N-50].
DAVIS, John (miller). Took the Oath of Allegiance in Worcester County in 1778 before the Hon. Nehemiah Holland [Ref: J-1814 (Box 4)].
DAVIS, John (of George). Took the Oath of Allegiance in Worcester County in 1778 before the Hon. Joshua Townsend [Ref: J-1814 (Box 4)].
DAVIS, John (of John). Took the Oath of Allegiance in Worcester County in 1778 before the Hon. Nehemiah Holland [Ref: J-1814 (Box 4)].
DAVIS, John G. See "William Davis," q.v.
DAVIS, Joseph. Private, Worcester Militia, Snow Hill Bn., Capt. Samuel Smyley's Co., 1777 [Ref: M-250]. Took the Oath of Allegiance in Worcester County in 1778 before the Hon. Nehemiah Holland [Ref: J-1814 (Box 4)].
DAVIS, Joshua. Private, Somerset Militia, Princess Anne Bn., Capt. John Jones' Princess Anne Co., 1780 [Ref: M-219]. Took the Oath of Allegiance in Somerset County in 1778 before the Hon. Peter Waters [Ref: T-18].
DAVIS, Joshua. Took the Oath of Allegiance in Worcester County in 1778 before the Hon. Joshua Townsend [Ref: J-1814 (Box 4)].
DAVIS, Levi. Private, Worcester Militia, Sinepuxent Bn., Capt. Josiah Dale's Co., Eighth Class, 1779/1780 [Ref: M-254].

DAVIS, Levin (Levan). Private, Worcester Militia, Sinepuxent Bn., Capt. Thomas Purnell's Co., Seventh Class, 1779/1780 [Ref: M-253]. Took the Oath of Allegiance in Worcester County in 1778 before the Hon. Nathaniel Miller [Ref: J-1814 (Box 4)]. Rendered patriotic service by supplying pork for the use of the military on Oct 1, 1780 [Ref: P-322].

DAVIS, Levin. Private, 3rd Maryland Independent Co., Worcester County, Capt. John Watkins' Co., enlisted May 6, 1776; muster roll dated Aug 20, 1776 indicated "deceased 20 July" [Ref: D-22].

DAVIS, Major (Mager). Took the Oath of Allegiance in Worcester County in 1778 before the Hon. James Selby [Ref: J-1814 (Box 4)]. Private, Worcester Militia, Wicomico Bn., Capt. James Patterson's Co., Seventh Class, July 15, 1780 [Ref: M-258]. See "James Davis," q.v.

DAVIS, Mary. See "Abijah Davis," q.v.

DAVIS, Matthew. Private, Worcester Militia, Sinepuxent Bn., Capt. William Purnell's Co., Fifth Class, 1779/1780 [Ref: M-252].

DAVIS, Matthias. Private, Worcester Militia, Sinepuxent Bn., Capt. John Postly's Co., First Class, 1779/1780 [Ref: M-251]. Took the Oath of Allegiance in Worcester County in 1778 before the Hon. Nathaniel Miller [Ref: J-1814 (Box 4)]. Private, Worcester Militia, Capt. John Martin's Co., 1780/1781 [Ref: J-1814 (Box 12) listed the name as "Maths. Davis].

DAVIS, Nathaniel. Private, Worcester Militia, Wicomico Bn., Capt. Fisher Walton's Co., First Class, July 15, 1780 [Ref: M-258]. Took the Oath of Allegiance in Worcester County in 1778 before the Hon. Nehemiah Holland [Ref: J-1814 (Box 4)].

DAVIS, Nehemiah. Private, Worcester Militia, Sinepuxent Bn., Capt. Thomas Purnell's Co., Fourth Class, 1779/1780 [Ref: M-253]. Took the Oath of Allegiance in Worcester County in 1778 before the Hon. Nathaniel Miller [Ref: J-1814 (Box 4) listed the name as "Nemiah Davis"].

DAVIS, Nixon. Took the Oath of Allegiance in Worcester County in 1778 before the Hon. Joshua Townsend [Ref: J-1814 (Box 4)].

DAVIS, Phillip. Private, Worcester Militia, Wicomico Bn., Capt. John Davis' Co., Fifth Class, July 15, 1780 [Ref: M-254]. Took the Oath of Allegiance in Worcester County in 1778 before the Hon. Joshua Townsend [Ref: J-1814 (Box 4)].

DAVIS, Robert. Private, Worcester Militia, Wicomico Bn., Capt. John Davis' Co., Sixth Class, July 15, 1780 [Ref: M-254].

DAVIS, Robert (of Thomas). Took the Oath of Allegiance in Worcester County in 1778 before the Hon. Joshua Townsend [Ref: J-1814 (Box 4)].

DAVIS, Samuel. Private, Somerset Militia, Salisbury Bn., Capt. Joseph Venables' Barren Creek Co., 1778/1780 [Ref: M-217].

DAVIS, Samuel. Took the Oath of Allegiance in Worcester County in 1778 before the Hon. Joshua Townsend [Ref: J-1814 (Box 4)].

DAVIS, Samuel (of Walker). Took the Oath of Allegiance in Worcester County in 1778 before the Hon. Nehemiah Holland [Ref: J-1814 (Box 4)].

DAVIS, Sarah. See "Littleton Williams" and "John Williams," q.v.

DAVIS, Saul. Private, Worcester Militia, Wicomico Bn., Capt. Elijah Shockley's Co., Fourth Class, July 15, 1780 [Ref: M-255].

DAVIS, Shadrick. Private, Worcester Militia, Wicomico Bn., Capt. John Davis' Co., Second Class, July 15, 1780 [Ref: M-254].

DAVIS, Solomon. Took the Oath of Allegiance in Worcester County in 1778 in Buckingham Hundred before the Hon. Thomas Purnell [Ref: J-1814 (Box 4) listed the name as "Soloman Davise"].

DAVIS, Spencer. Private, Worcester Militia, Snow Hill Bn., Capt. Ebenezer Handy's Co., April 9, 1776 [Ref: M-249]. Private, Worcester Militia, Wicomico Bn., Capt. Robert Handy's Co., First Class, July 15, 1780 [Ref: M-254].

DAVIS, Thomas. Private, Somerset Militia, Princess Anne Bn., Capt. John Jones' Princess Anne Co., 1780 [Ref: M-219]. Took the Oath of Allegiance in Somerset County in 1778 before the Hon. Levin Wilson [Ref: T-17].

DAVIS, Thomas. Private, Somerset Militia, Princess Anne Bn., Capt. Isaac Handy's Great Annemessix Co., 1780 [Ref: M-221]. Took the Oath of Allegiance in Somerset County in 1778 before the Hon. John Williams [Ref: T-21].

DAVIS, Thomas. Private, Worcester Militia, Capt. John Martin's Co., 1780/1781 [Ref: J-1814 (Box 12)].

DAVIS, Thomas. Took the Oath of Allegiance in Worcester County in 1778 before the Hon. Joshua Townsend [Ref: J-1814 (Box 4)].

DAVIS, Walton. Took the Oath of Allegiance in Worcester County in 1778 before the Hon. Nehemiah Holland [Ref: J-1814 (Box 4)].

DAVIS, William (1761-   ). Private, 3rd Maryland Independent Co., Worcester County, Capt. John Watkins' Co., enlisted April 16, 1776; muster roll dated Aug 20, 1776, present for duty [Ref: D-22]. He applied for a pension (S32202) in Bourbon County, Kentucky on Nov 28, 1833, stating he was born in Worcester County, Maryland on Jan 12, 1761 and lived there at the time of his enlistment. He later moved to Kentucky (date not given) and in 1834 moved to Parke County, Indiana to be near his only sister (name not given). In 1834 a John G. Davis lived in Parke County, but no relationship was given [Ref: W-912].

DAVIS, William. Private, Somerset Militia, Salisbury Bn., Capt. William Turpin's Rewastico Co., 1778/1780 [Ref: M-217].

DAVIS, William (Matapony). Took the Oath of Allegiance in Worcester County in 1778 before the Hon. Nehemiah Holland [Ref: J-1814 (Box 4)].

DAVIS, Zephaniah. Private, Worcester Militia, Wicomico Bn., Capt. James Patterson's Co., Fifth Class, July 15, 1780 [Ref: M-258].

DAWS, James. Private, Worcester Militia, Sinepuxent Bn., Capt. John Postly's Co., Eighth Class, 1779/1780 [Ref: M-251].

DAWSON, Joseph. Private, Somerset Militia, Princess Anne Bn., Capt. Isaac Handy's Great Annemessix Co., 1780 [Ref: M-221].

DAY, John. Private, Somerset Militia, Salisbury Bn., Capt. Joseph Venables' Barren Creek Co., 1778/1780 [Ref: M-217].

DAZEY, Eliphas. Private, Worcester Militia, Sinepuxent Bn., Capt. John Coe's Co., Fourth Class, 1779/1780 [Ref: M-252].

DEAL, Isaac. Took the Oath of Allegiance in Worcester County in 1778 before the Hon. Joshua Townsend [Ref: J-1814 (Box 4)].

DEAL, Joshua or Josiah. Second Lieutenant, Worcester Militia, Sinepuxent Bn., Capt. Elihu or Elisha Briddell's Co., Aug 30, 1777. First Lieutenant, May 23, 1779, when he reportedly moved from the county [Ref: C-350 listed the name as "Josiah Deal" and M-68 listed the name as "Joshua Deal"].

DEAN, James. Private, Somerset Militia, Salisbury Bn., Capt. Joseph Venables' Barren Creek Co., 1778/1780 [Ref: M-217]. Drafted from Somerset County on June 20, 1781 to serve in the Continental Army [Ref: L-35C].

DEAN, Steven. Private, Worcester Militia, Wicomico Bn., Capt. Elijah Shockley's Co., Sixth Class, July 15, 1780 [Ref: M-255].

DEAN, William. Private, Somerset Militia, Princess Anne Bn., Capt. George Waters' Pocomoke Co., 1780 [Ref: M-220 listed the name as "William Dear"]. On July 30, 1781 Thomas Harriss recruited William Dean from Somerset County to serve in the Continental Army until Dec 10, 1781 [Ref: L-35C].

DEAVER, William. See "William Devereaux," q.v.

DECATUR, Stephen. Took the Oath of Allegiance in Worcester County in 1778 in Buckingham Hundred before the Hon. Thomas Purnell [Ref: J-1814 (Box 4)].

DEGAN, John. Took the Oath of Allegiance in Worcester County on Feb 25, 1778 before the Hon. Ebenezer Handy [Ref: J-1814 (Box 4)].

DELASTATIUS, Joseph (c1755-1808). Served as a sergeant in the Virginia Continental Line, married Eleanor ----, and died before Sep 23, 1808 in Maryland, probably Worcester County [Ref: V-810].

DELASTATIUS, William. Rendered patriotic service in Worcester County by driving cattle for the military in 1781 [Ref: P-349 listed the name as "William Delestatius"]. Peter, John and William Delastatious were all soldiers in the Virginia Line in Accomack County. Heirs in 1834 were William Walton, Sally Hayward, Peter Delastatious, and John Delastitious [Ref: Stratton Nottingham's *Soldiers and Sailors of the Eastern Shore of Virginia in the Revolutionary War*, pp. 48, 51, 52].

DEMMICK, Edward. Private, Worcester Militia, Sinepuxent Bn., Capt. John Rackliff's Co., Fifth Class, 1779/1780 [Ref: M-251].

DEMMICK, William. Ensign, Somerset Militia, 1st Bn., Aug 19, 1776 [Ref: M-69, B-220].

DENNIS, Adkins. Private, Worcester Militia, Wicomico Bn., Capt. Samuel Horsey's Co., Third Class, July 15, 1780 [Ref: M-256]. Private, Maryland Troops, Worcester County, draughted May 1, 1781 [Ref: K-99, D-372].

DENNIS, Ann. See "William Polk," q.v.

DENNIS, Anna. See "John Dennis, Jr.," q.v.

DENNIS, Benjamin (c1748-1808). Captain, Worcester Militia, Wicomico Bn., June 21, 1776 to at least July 15, 1780 [Ref: M-69, M-255, A-506, C-351]. Took the Oath of Allegiance in Worcester County in 1778 before the Hon. Nehemiah Holland [Ref: J-1814 (Box 4)]. Served in the Lower House of the Maryland Legislature, 1788-1792, and was a Justice of Worcester County, 1791-1800 [Ref: R-260].

DENNIS, Dunnick (Dunnock). Private, 3rd Maryland Independent Co., Worcester County, Capt. John Watkins' Co., enlisted March 9, 1776; muster roll dated Aug 20, 1776, sick in the country [Ref: D-22]. Private, Worcester Militia, Sinepuxent Bn., Capt. William Purnell's Co., First Class, 1779/1780 [Ref: M-252].

DENNIS, George. Private, Worcester Militia, Wicomico Bn., Capt. William Handy's Co., Third Class, July 15, 1780 [Ref: M-257]. Took the Oath of Allegiance in Worcester County in 1778 before the Hon. Joshua Townsend [Ref: J-1814 (Box 4)].

DENNIS, Henry (c1752-1785). Son of Littleton Dennis (1728-1774) and Susanna Upshur (1733-1784). He married Ann Purnell on Nov 23, 1783 and they had a son Littleton Dennis (born 1784). Henry served in the Lower House of the Maryland Legislature, 1779-1783, and was a militia recruiter in Worcester County in 1781. Second Lieutenant, Worcester Militia, Snow Hill Bn., Capt. Thomas Marshall's Co., Aug 30, 1777. Second or First Lieutenant, Wicomico Bn., Capt. Isaac Layfield's Co., July 15, 1780 [Ref: R-360, C-351, M-69, M-257, R-260]. Took the Oath of Allegiance in Worcester County in 1778 before the Hon. Joshua Townsend [Ref: J-1814 (Box 4)]. Rendered patriotic service by hauling corn for the use of the military in 1780 [Ref: P-256]. Apprehended Robert Pitts at Pitts Landing (Virginia), seized his vessel, and took him prisoner for trial before the Special Court of Maryland in July, 1781 [Ref: H-364 listed the name as "Henry Denness"].

DENNIS, Henry (c1750-c1849). Private, Worcester Militia, Wicomico Bn., Capt. John Davis' Co., Third Class, July 15, 1780 [Ref: M-254]. Took the Oath of Allegiance in Worcester County in 1778 before the Hon. James Selby [Ref: J-1814 (Box 4)]. Private, 3rd Maryland Line, who applied for a pension (R2876) under the Act of June 7, 1832, stating he served in Maryland and at one time lived in Worcester County. On Jan 24, 1848, affidavits by Barzlea and Milly Adkins were mentioned [Ref: W-949]. Although this application was rejected, there was a Henry Dennis who was a private in the Maryland Line, Rawlings Regiment, from 1777 through 1780, having enlisted for three years [Ref: D-105, D-303, D-350]. Henry Dennis was born circa 1750, married first to Ann

Lewis and second to Mrs. Elizabeth (Purnell) Smack [Smock], served as a private during the war, and died before July 31, 1849 [Ref: V-816].

DENNIS, Henry. See "William Polk," q.v.

DENNIS, James. Private, Worcester Militia, Wicomico Bn., Capt. James Perdue's Co., Sixth Class, July 15, 1780 [Ref: M-256]. Took the Oath of Allegiance in Worcester County in 1778 before the Hon. Joshua Townsend [Ref: J-1814 (Box 4)].

DENNIS, John. Private, Worcester Militia, Wicomico Bn., Capt. John Davis' Co., Sixth Class, July 15, 1780 [Ref: M-254].

DENNIS, John. Private, Worcester Militia, Wicomico Bn., Capt. James Perdue's Co., Third Class, July 15, 1780 [Ref: M-256].

DENNIS, John Jr. (c1724-1782). Son of John Dennis and possibly Mary Purnell. John married Anna Maria ---- and they had sons John and Robert [Ref: R-261 listed the name as "John Dennis, Jr."]. He was a captain by 1758; served as a Justice of Somerset County, 1746-1748, 1762; Justice of Worcester County, 1751-1755, 1764-1782; member of the Lower House of the Maryland Legislature from Worcester County, 1754-1755; and, Justice of the Orphans Court of Worcester County, 1777-1782 [Ref: R-261]. Took the Oath of Allegiance in Worcester County in 1778 before the Hon. Joshua Townsend [Ref: J-1814 (Box 4) listed the name without the "Jr."]. Justice of the Peace and Justice of the Orphans Court, commissioned on June 4, 1777 and Nov 29, 1777 and Nov 21, 1778 and Nov 25, 1780 and Jan 17, 1782 [Ref: C-274, C-428, E-249, G-225, and I-46 listed the name without the "Jr."]. Commissioned by the Council of Maryland on Aug 19, 1779 to receive subscriptions for the Continental Loan Office [Ref: E-499].

DENNIS, John Jr. or 3rd. Private, Worcester Militia, Sinepuxent Bn., Capt. Josiah Dale's Co., Third Class, 1779/1780 [Ref: M-254]. Probable son of "John Dennis, Jr.," q.v. [Ref: R-261].

DENNIS, John (of Valentine). Took the Oath of Allegiance in Worcester County in 1778 before the Hon. Joshua Townsend [Ref: J-1814 (Box 4)].

DENNIS, Johnson. Took the Oath of Allegiance in Worcester County in 1778 before the Hon. Joshua Townsend [Ref: J-1814 (Box 4)].

DENNIS, Joseph. Private, Worcester Militia, Wicomico Bn., Capt. James Perdue's Co., Fifth Class, July 15, 1780 [Ref: M-256].

DENNIS, Josiah (1755/6-c1840). Private, Maryland Line, who applied for a pension (R2877) in Morgan County, Georgia on Sep 5, 1838, "age 83 years and 3 months on Sep 3, 1838," stating he was born in Worcester County, Maryland on June 3, 1756 *[sic]* and lived there at the time of his enlistment. He married on Jan 21, 1778 (wife's name not given) and later moved to Henry County, Virginia for 4 years and about 1790 moved to Georgia and lived in Hancock and Morgan Counties [Ref: W-949, W-950].

DENNIS, Joshua. Private, Worcester Militia, Wicomico Bn., Capt. John Davis' Co., Eighth Class, July 15, 1780 [Ref: M-255]. Took the Oath of Allegiance in

Worcester County in 1778 before the Hon. Joshua Townsend [Ref: J-1814 (Box 4)].

DENNIS, Littleton. See "Henry Dennis," q.v.

DENNIS, Mary. See "Samuel Handy," q.v.

DENNIS, Mathias. Private, Worcester Militia, Wicomico Bn., Capt. John Davis' Co., Sixth Class, July 15, 1780 [Ref: M-254].

DENNIS, Robert. Clerk of the Committee of Observation for Worcester County on May 3, 1776 [Ref: A-405 listed the name as "R. Dennis Clk."]. See "John Dennis, Jr.," q.v.

DENNIS, Sally. See "George Dashiell," q.v.

DENNIS, Shalmanezar (Shalmanzar). Private, Worcester Militia, Snow Hill Bn., Capt. Samuel Smyley's Co., 1777 [Ref: M-250]. Took the Oath of Allegiance in Worcester County in 1778 before the Hon. Nehemiah Holland [Ref: J-1814 (Box 4)].

DENNIS, Solomon. Took the Oath of Allegiance in Worcester County in 1778 before the Hon. Joshua Townsend [Ref: J-1814 (Box 4)].

DENNIS, Susannah. Rendered patriotic service by supplying beef for the use of the military on Oct 5, 1780 [Ref: P-323].

DENNIS, Tabitha. See "Roland Beavens," q.v.

DENNIS, Valentine (c1738-1782). Took the Oath of Allegiance in Worcester County in 1778 in Buckingham Hundred before the Hon. Thomas Purnell [Ref: J-1814 (Box 4) listed the name as "Volientine Dennes"]. Valentine Dennis was born after 1738, married (name of wife not known), served as a soldier and rendered other patriotic service during the war, and died before Dec 19, 1782 [Ref: V-816].

DENNIS, William. Ensign, Worcester Militia, Wicomico Bn., Capt. Isaac Houston's Co., Aug 30, 1777. Second Lieutenant, May 27, 1779, Capt. John Davis' Co. [Ref: M-69, C-351, E-423].

DENNIS, William. Private, Worcester Militia, Wicomico Bn., Capt. John Davis' Co., First Class, July 15, 1780 [Ref: M-254].

DENNIS, William Jr. Took the Oath of Allegiance in Worcester County in 1778 before the Hon. Joshua Townsend [Ref: J-1814 (Box 4)].

DENNIS, Zadock. Took the Oath of Allegiance in Worcester County in 1778 before the Hon. Joshua Townsend [Ref: J-1814 (Box 4)].

DENSTON, Abraham. Private, Worcester Militia, Wicomico Bn., Capt. Charles Bennett's Co., Eighth Class, July 15, 1780 [Ref: M-255].

DENSTON, William. Private, Somerset Militia, Princess Anne Bn., Capt. John Jones' Princess Anne Co., 1780 [Ref: M-219].

DENTSON, Levin. Private, Worcester Militia, Wicomico Bn., Capt. Charles Bennett's Co., Fifth Class, July 15, 1780 [Ref: M-255].

DENWOOD, Arthur. Private, Somerset Militia, Salisbury Bn., Capt. Henry Gale's Quantico Co., 1778/1780 [Ref: M-216]. Took the Oath of Allegiance in Somerset County in 1778 before the Hon. William Winder [Ref: T-22, N-50].

DENWOOD, John. On July 22, 1776 the Council of Maryland ordered the Treasurer to pay £300 to John Denwood for the use of the Committee of Observation for Somerset County [Ref: B-88]. First Lieutenant, Somerset Militia, Princess Anne Bn., Capt. John Jones' Princess Anne Co., Sep 22, 1777 to at least July 24, 1780 [Ref: M-69, M-219, C-381]. Took the Oath of Allegiance in Somerset County in 1778 before the Hon. Levin Wilson [Ref: T-17].

DENWOOD, Mary. See "William Winder," q.v.

DENWOOD, Thomas. See "William Winder," q.v.

DEVERIX (DEVEREAUX), Cornelous. Took the Oath of Allegiance in Worcester County in 1778 before the Hon. Joshua Townsend [Ref: J-1814 (Box 4)].

DEVERIX (DEVEREAUX), John. Private, Worcester Militia, Sinepuxent Bn., Capt. William Purnell's Co., Fourth Class, 1779/1780 [Ref: M-252]. Took the Oath of Allegiance in Worcester County in 1778 in Bogerternorton Hundred before the Hon. Thomas Purnell [Ref: J-1814 (Box 4) listed the name as "John Devereux"].

DEVERIX (DEVEREAUX), William (1760/1-1821). Private, Maryland Line, who pensioned (S34736) in Worcester County at $96 per annum effective July 28, 1820, age 60, and died in 1821 [Ref: X-44 listed the name as "William Deaver, alias Devereaux" and W-957 listed the name as "William Devenix or Deverex" and stated he was age 59 in 1820].

DEWEY, Eleanor. See "John Tarr (of John)," q.v.

DICKESON, Sarah. See "Jesse Dickerson," q.v.

DICKERSON, Cornelius (1748-1816). Private, Worcester Militia, Wicomico Bn., Capt. Philip Quinton's Co., Second Class, July 15, 1780 [Ref: M-256]. Private, Worcester Militia, Capt. John Martin's Co., 1780/1781 [Ref: J-1814 (Box 12) listed the name as "Corns. Dickerson"].

DICKERSON, Edward. Private, Somerset Militia, Salisbury Bn., Capt. James Bennett's Salisbury Co., 1778/1780 [Ref: M-218].

DICKERSON, Esau Merrell. Private, Worcester Militia, Wicomico Bn., Capt. Isaac Layfield's Co., Seventh Class, July 15, 1780 [Ref: M-257].

DICKERSON, Isaac. Private, Somerset Militia, Salisbury Bn., Capt. John Span Conway's Nanticoke Point Co., 1778/1780 [Ref: M-216]. Drafted from Somerset County on June 20, 1781 to serve in the Continental Army [Ref: L-35C].

DICKERSON, James. Private, Worcester Militia, Wicomico Bn., Capt. Isaac Layfield's Co., Third Class, July 15, 1780 [Ref: M-257].

DICKERSON, James. Private, Somerset Militia, Princess Anne Bn., Capt. George Waters' Pocomoke Co., 1780 [Ref: M-220].

DICKERSON, Jesse (1760 -   ). Son of William and Sarah Dickeson *[sic]*, born in Coventry Parish on Jan 16, 1760 [Ref: Y-82]. Private, Worcester Militia, Snow Hill Bn., Capt. John Parramore's Co., 1777 [Ref: M-250]. Private, Worcester Militia, Wicomico Bn., Capt. John Parramore's Co., Eighth Class,

July 15, 1780 [Ref: M-259]. Took the Oath of Allegiance in Worcester County in 1778 before the Hon. Nehemiah Holland [Ref: J-1814 (Box 4)].

DICKERSON (DICKENSON), Thomas. Private, Maryland Line, drafted in 1781. Joseph Dashiell, of Worcester County, wrote to the Council of Maryland on Sep 5, 1781, stating, in part, "you will see by my returns by Capt. McClaster who carried up the men from heare that among the inlistment their is a ceartin Thomas Dickenson inlisted during the war, this young man was sick when our other men marched, since he has got well and the Sheriff of Somerset County has taken him into custody and I am informed he is indighted for joining the enemy sum time past. That he was with the enemy I have no doubt but I verily believe it was to please a vile Tory father that he went at all. I submit it to your Excellency, whether an noli proseque had not better isshuw that we may have the use of the man, he is a very young man and I am certain that they have one hundred more proper objects in Somerset then him to make examples of." [Ref: H-477, H-478].

DICKERSON, William. Private, Worcester Militia, Wicomico Bn., Capt. Benjamin Dennis' Co., Sixth Class, July 15, 1780 [Ref: M-256]. See "Jesse Dickerson," q.v.

DICKERY, John. Took the Oath of Allegiance in Somerset County in 1778 [Ref: N-50].

DICKES, Daniel. See "Daniel Dikes," q.v.

DIES, Daniel (1752 -   ). Son of Daniel and Leah Dies, born in Coventry Parish on June 4, 1752 [Ref: Y-70]. Private, Somerset Militia, Princess Anne Bn., Capt. Henry Miles' Little Annemessex Co., 1780 [Ref: M-221].

DIES, Daniel. Private, Somerset Militia, Salisbury Bn., Capt. Sampson Wheatly's Co., 1780 [Ref: M-216].

DIES, John. Private, Somerset Militia, Princess Anne Bn., Capt. Henry Miles' Little Annemessex Co., 1780 [Ref: M-221].

DIES, Leah. See "Daniel Dies," q.v.

DIES, Philip. Private, Somerset Militia, Salisbury Bn., Capt. Sampson Wheatly's Co., 1780 [Ref: M-216 listed the name as "Phillip Dyes"].

DIES, Robert. Private, Somerset Militia, Princess Anne Bn., Capt. Henry Miles' Little Annemessex Co., 1780 [Ref: M-221].

DIGMAN, William. Private, 3rd Maryland Independent Co., Worcester County, Capt. John Watkins' Co., enlisted Feb 3, 1776; muster roll dated Aug 20, 1776, present for duty [Ref: D-23].

DIGNEN (DIGNER), Frederick. Private, Somerset Militia, Princess Anne Bn., Capt. John Jones' Princess Anne Co., 1780 [Ref: M-219]. See "Jesse Johnson," q.v.

DIKES (DICKES), Daniel. Private, Worcester Militia, Wicomico Bn., Capt. Elijah Shockley's Co., Fifth Class, July 15, 1780 [Ref: M-255 listed the name as "Daniel Dikis(?)"]. Private, Worcester Militia, Capt. John Martin's Co., 1780/1781 [Ref: J-1814 (Box 12) listed the name as "Danl. Dickes"].

DIKES, Stephen. Private, Worcester Militia, Wicomico Bn., Capt. Robert Handy's Co., Second Class, July 15, 1780 [Ref: M-254].
DIKES, William. Private, Worcester Militia, Wicomico Bn., Capt. Elijah Shockley's Co., Third Class, July 15, 1780 [Ref: M-255].
DISHAROON, Amelia (Milly). See "Thomas Stanford," q.v.
DISHAROON, Constant. Took the Oath of Allegiance in Somerset County on Feb 14, 1778 before the Hon. Joseph Venables [Ref: T-25].
DISHAROON, Ebby. See "Joshua Disharoon," q.v.
DISHAROON, Francis. Private, Somerset Militia, Salisbury Bn., Capt. Josiah Dashiell's Wicomico Creek Co., 1778/1780 [Ref: M-218].
DISHAROON, George. Private, Worcester Militia, Wicomico Bn., Capt. Samuel Horsey's Co., First Class, July 15, 1780 [Ref: M-256].
DISHAROON, James. Private, Somerset Militia, Salisbury Bn., Capt. Josiah Dashiell's Wicomico Creek Co., 1778/1780 [Ref: M-218]. Took the Oath of Allegiance in Somerset County in 1778 before the Hon. Levin Wilson [Ref: T-17, N-50].
DISHAROON, Joshua (1749/5001819). Private, Somerset Militia, Salisbury Bn., Capt. Josiah Dashiell's Wicomico Creek Co., 1778/1780 [Ref: M-218]. Joshua Disharoon was born on Jan 2, 1749/50, married Ebby ----, served as a private in Maryland, and died in 1819 [Ref: V-843].
DISHAROON, Levin. Private, Worcester Militia, Wicomico Bn., Capt. Robert Handy's Co., Eighth Class, July 15, 1780 [Ref: M-254].
DISHAROON, Nutor. Private, Somerset Militia, Salisbury Bn., Capt. Josiah Dashiell's Wicomico Creek Co., 1778/1780 [Ref: M-218].
DISHAROON, Stephen. Private, Somerset Militia, Salisbury Bn., Capt. Josiah Dashiell's Wicomico Creek Co., 1778/1780 [Ref: M-218].
DISHAROON, Thomas. Took the Oath of Allegiance in Somerset County in 1778 before the Hon. William Winder [Ref: T-22, N-50].
DIXON, Ambrose Jr. Sergeant, Somerset Militia, Princess Anne Bn., St. Asaph's Co., 1780 [Ref: M-220 listed the name without the "Jr."]. Took the Oath of Allegiance in Somerset County in 1778 before the Hon. John Williams [Ref: T-21, N-50].
DIXON, Ambrose Sr. Took the Oath of Allegiance in Somerset County in 1778 before the Hon. John Williams [Ref: T-21, N-50].
DIXON, David. Private, Worcester Militia, Wicomico Bn., Capt. Fisher Walton's Co., Third Class, July 15, 1780 [Ref: M-258]. Took the Oath of Allegiance in Worcester County in 1778 before the Hon. Nehemiah Holland [Ref: J-1814 (Box 4)].
DIXON, Grace. See "William Dixon," q.v.
DIXON, Isaac Sr. Took the Oath of Allegiance in Somerset County in 1778 before the Hon. John Williams [Ref: T-21, N-50]. Rendered patriotic service by supplying bacon for the use of the military in Somerset County on Sep 7, 1780

[Ref: P-315]. Private, Somerset Militia, Princess Anne Bn., St. Asaph's Co., 1780 [Ref: M-220 listed the name without the "Sr."]. See "Thomas Dixon," q.v.

DIXON, Isaac. Ensign, Worcester Militia, Wicomico Bn., Capt. Samuel Horsey's Co., May 27, 1779 to at least July 15, 1780 [Ref: M-70, M-256, E-423]. Took the Oath of Allegiance in Worcester County in 1778 before the Hon. William Hopewell [Ref: J-1814 (Box 4)]. Select Militia, Somerset County, Aug 15, 1781 [Ref: L-35A].

DIXON, Mary. See "William Horsey," q.v.

DIXON, Nathaniel. Sergeant, Worcester Militia, Snow Hill Bn., Capt. Ebenezer Handy's Co., April 9, 1776; Wicomico Bn., Capt. Elijah Shockley's Co., July 15, 1780 [Ref: M-255, M-248]. Took the Oath of Allegiance in Worcester County in 1778 before the Hon. William Hopewell [Ref: J-1814 (Box 4)].

DIXON, Nehemiah. Took the Oath of Allegiance in Worcester County in 1778 before the Hon. James Selby [Ref: J-1814 (Box 4) listed the name as "Nehemiah Dickson"].

DIXON, Outerbridge. Private, Worcester Militia, Snow Hill Bn., Capt. Ebenezer Handy's Co., April 9, 1776 [Ref: M-249]. Private, Worcester Militia, Wicomico Bn., Capt. Elijah Shockley's Co., Fifth Class, July 15, 1780 [Ref: M-255]. Took the Oath of Allegiance in Worcester County in 1778 before the Hon. William Hopewell [Ref: J-1814 (Box 4) and which signature on this list looked like "Outher Credy Dixon"].

DIXON, Samuel. Second Lieutenant, Somerset Militia, 17th Bn., Capt. Schoolfield's Co., Sep 19, 1776. First Lieutenant, Princess Anne Bn., Capt. Waters' Co., Sep 22, 1777. Second Lieutenant, Capt. Waters' Co., July 1, 1778 [Ref: M-70, B-285, C-381, C-457]. Took the Oath of Allegiance in Somerset County in 1778 before the Hon. Levin Wilson [Ref: T-17, N-50].

DIXON, Sarah. See "Thomas Dixon" and "John Turpin," q.v.

DIXON, Thomas (1754-1819). Son of Isaac and Sarah Dixon, born in Coventry Parish on Dec 9, 1754, married Susanna Pollitt, and died on Oct 9, 1819 [Ref: Y-70, V-846]. Second Lieutenant, Somerset Militia, Princess Anne Bn., Capt. John Williams' Watkins Point Co., Dec 7, 1778 to at least July 24, 1780 [Ref: M-70, M-221, E-260]. Took the Oath of Allegiance in Somerset County in 1778 before the Hon. John Williams [Ref: T-21, N-50]. Rendered patriotic service by supplying pork for the use of the military on Jan 3, 1781 [Ref: P-351]. Select Militia, Somerset County, Aug 15, 1781 [Ref: L-35A].

DIXON, Thomas. Took the Oath of Allegiance in Somerset County in 1778 (made his "X" mark) before the Hon. John Williams [Ref: T-21]. See "William Dixon," q.v.

DIXON, William (1750 -   ). Son of Thomas and Grace Dixon, born in Coventry Parish on Dec 27, 1750 [Ref: Y-82]. Ensign, Somerset Militia, Princess Anne Bn., Capt. Henry Miles' Little Annemessex Co., Sep 22, 1777 to at least July 24, 1780 [Ref: M-70, M-221, C-381]. Took the Oath of Allegiance in Somerset County in 1778 before the Hon. John Williams [Ref: T-21, N-50].

DOCKERY, William. Private, Somerset Militia, Salisbury Bn., White Haven Co., 1778/1780 [Ref: M-219]. Took the Oath of Allegiance in Somerset County in 1778 before the Hon. John Span Conway [Ref: T-14].

DOGAN, Abraham. On July 30, 1781 Joseph Wails (Wailes) recruited Abraham Dogan from Somerset County to serve in the Continental Army for the duration of the war [Ref: L-35C].

DONALDSON, John. Private, 3rd Maryland Independent Co., Worcester County, Capt. John Watkins' Co., enlisted Feb 3, 1776; muster roll dated Aug 20, 1776, present for duty [Ref: D-23].

DONALDSON, Samuel. Private, 3rd Maryland Independent Co., Worcester County, Capt. John Watkins' Co., enlisted April 15, 1776; muster roll dated Aug 20, 1776, sick in the country [Ref: D-22].

DONALDSON, Thomas. Private, 3rd Maryland Independent Co., Worcester County, Capt. John Watkins' Co., enlisted Feb 24, 1776; muster roll dated Aug 20, 1776, present for duty [Ref: D-22].

DONALY, Aaron. Private, Somerset Militia, Salisbury Bn., Capt. Josiah Dashiell's Wicomico Creek Co., 1778/1780 [Ref: M-218].

DONAWAY, Thomas. Private, Worcester Militia, Wicomico Bn., Capt. James Perdue's Co., Second Class, July 15, 1780 [Ref: M-256].

DONE, James. Sergeant, 3rd Maryland Independent Co., Worcester County, Capt. John Watkins' Co., enlisted April 7, 1776; muster roll dated Aug 20, 1776, absent on furlough 29th June [Ref: D-21].

DONE, John. First Major, Worcester Militia, 10th Bn., Jan 6, 1776. Lieutenant Colonel, Feb 3, 1777. Colonel, Snow Hill Bn., Aug 30, 1777 to Sep 29, 1778 (resigned). Recommended as colonel of the Somerset Militia, Princess Anne Bn., on July 21, 1781 [Ref: M-70, G-575, C-110, C-350, E-256, J-1814 (Box 8, Dashiell's correspondence), H-361]. Took the Oath of Allegiance in Worcester County in 1778 before the Hon. Nehemiah Holland [Ref: J-1814 (Box 4)]. Attended the Maryland Convention and served on the Committee of Observation in 1776 [Ref: O-28, A-457].

DONE, John. Private, Somerset Militia, Salisbury Bn., White Haven Co., 1778/1780 [Ref: M-219]. See "William Waters," q.v.

DONE, Robert. Second Major, Worcester Militia, 10th Bn., Jan 6, 1776. First Major, Feb 3, 1777. Lieutenant Colonel, Snow Hill Bn., Aug 30, 1777. Colonel, Dec 3, 1778 [Ref: M-70, C-110, C-350, E-256]. Took the Oath of Allegiance in Worcester County in 1778 before the Hon. Nehemiah Holland [Ref: J-1814 (Box 4)]. Appointed by the Maryland Convention in November, 1776 to be one of the Judges of Elections in Worcester County [Ref: O-55]. On July 2, 1781 He wrote to Joseph Dashiell, County Lieutenant, about the "conditions of prisoners, presumably Loyalists." [Ref: P-408]. Rendered patriotic service by supplying beef for the use of the military on Oct 1, 1781 [Ref: P-443]. See "Joseph Handy," q.v.

DONE, William. Private, Worcester Militia, Wicomico Bn., Capt. William Handy's Co., Eighth Class, July 15, 1780 [Ref: M-258].
DONE, William. Took the Oath of Allegiance in Somerset County in 1778 before the Hon. Levin Wilson [Ref: T-17].
DONOHO, Richardson. Private, Somerset Militia, Salisbury Bn., Capt. Henry Gale's Quantico Co., 1778/1780 [Ref: M-216].
DONOHO, William Sr. Private, Somerset Militia, Salisbury Bn., Capt. Henry Gale's Quantico Co., 1778/1780 [Ref: M-216].
DONOHOE, Daniel. Private, Worcester Militia, Capt. John Martin's Co., 1780/1781 [Ref: J-1814 (Box 12)].
DONOHOE, John. Private, Worcester Militia, Capt. John Martin's Co., 1780/1781 [Ref: J-1814 (Box 12)].
DORITY, Dickerson. See "Dickerson Douty," q.v.
DORMAN, Catherine. See "Zadock Dorman," q.v.
DORMAN, Chane(?). Private, Somerset Militia, Princess Anne Bn., Capt. John Jones' Princess Anne Co., 1780 [Ref: M-219].
DORMAN, George. Private, Somerset Militia, Princess Anne Bn., Capt. Thomas Irving's Monie Co., 1780 [Ref: M-219].
DORMAN, Isaiah. Sergeant, Somerset Militia, Princess Anne Bn., Capt. John Jones' Princess Anne Co., 1780 [Ref: M-219]. Took the Oath of Allegiance in Somerset County in 1778 before the Hon. Peter Waters [Ref: T-18].
DORMAN, Jesse. Private, Somerset Militia, Salisbury Bn., White Haven Co., 1778/1780 [Ref: M-218].
DORMAN, John. Private, Somerset Militia, Princess Anne Bn., Capt. John Jones' Princess Anne Co., 1780 [Ref: M-219]. See "Zadock Dorman," q.v.
DORMAN, John. Private, Worcester Militia, Wicomico Bn., Capt. Philip Quinton's Co., Sixth Class, July 15, 1780 [Ref: M-256].
DORMAN, Levin. Private, Somerset Militia, Princess Anne Bn., Capt. John Jones' Princess Anne Co., 1780 [Ref: M-219].
DORMAN, Major. Private, Worcester Militia, Wicomico Bn., Capt. Charles Bennett's Co., First Class, July 15, 1780 [Ref: M-255].
DORMAN, Mathew. Private, Worcester Militia, Wicomico Bn., Capt. Charles Bennett's Co., Second Class, July 15, 1780 [Ref: M-255].
DORMAN, Michael. Private, Somerset Militia, Salisbury Bn., White Haven Co., 1778/1780 [Ref: M-218].
DORMAN, Milby. Private, Worcester Militia, Wicomico Bn., Capt. Elijah Shockley's Co., First Class, July 15, 1780 [Ref: M-255].
DORMAN, Nehemiah. Private, Worcester Militia, Wicomico Bn., Capt. William Handy's Co., Sixth Class, July 15, 1780 [Ref: M-257]. Took the Oath of Allegiance in Worcester County in 1778 before the Hon. Joshua Townsend [Ref: J-1814 (Box 4)].
DORMAN, Rachel. See "John Hayman, Jr.," q.v.

DORMAN, Robert. Private, Somerset Militia, Salisbury Bn., Capt. William Turpin's Rewastico Co., 1778/1780 [Ref: M-217].
DORMAN, Samuel. Private, Worcester Militia, Wicomico Bn., Capt. Philip Quinton's Co., Third Class, July 15, 1780 [Ref: M-256]. Took the Oath of Allegiance in Worcester County in 1778 before the Hon. Joshua Townsend [Ref: J-1814 (Box 4)].
DORMAN, William. Private, Somerset Militia, Salisbury Bn., Capt. William Turpin's Rewastico Co., 1778/1780 [Ref: M-217].
DORMAN, Zadock (1762 -   ). Son of John and Catherine Dorman, born in Coventry Parish on Feb 27, 1762 [Ref: Y-95]. Private, Somerset Militia, Princess Anne Bn., Capt. George Waters' Pocomoke Co., 1780 [Ref: M-220].
DORSEY, Eli. Third Lieutenant, 3rd Maryland Independent Co., Worcester County, Capt. John Watkins' Co., commissioned Jan 5, 1776; muster roll dated Aug 20, 1776, present for duty [Ref: D-21].
DORY(?), Jesse. Private, Somerset Militia, Princess Anne Bn., Capt. Isaac Handy's Great Annemessix Co., 1780 [Ref: M-221].
DORY(?), John. Private, Worcester Militia, Snow Hill Bn., Capt. John Parramore's Co., 1777 [Ref: M-250].
DOUGLAS, Elizabeth. See "Louther Hitch," q.v.
DOUGLAS, William. Private, Somerset Militia, Salisbury Bn., Capt. John Span Conway's Nanticoke Point Co., 1778/1780 [Ref: M-216].
DOUTY (DOUGHTY), Ann. See "John Beard," q.v.
DOUTY (DOUGHTY, DAUGHTY), Isaac. Private, Somerset Militia, Salisbury Bn., Capt. Sampson Wheatly's Co., 1780 [Ref: M-216 listed the name as "Isaac Daughty"].
DOUTY (DOUGHTY, DORITY), Dickerson. Private, Somerset Militia, Salisbury Bn., Capt. John Span Conway's Nanticoke Point Co., 1778/1780 [Ref: M-216 listed the name as "Dickerson Dority"]. Private, Somerset Militia, Princess Anne Bn., Capt. John Williams' Watkins Point Co., 1780 [Ref: M-222 listed the name as "Dickerson Douty"].
DOVE, John. Took the Oath of Allegiance in Somerset County in 1778 before the Hon. Levin Wilson [Ref: T-17, N-50].
DOWNHAM, Annis. See "Newell Beauchamp," q.v
DOWNS, George. Private, Worcester Militia, Wicomico Bn., Capt. William Handy's Co., First Class, July 15, 1780 [Ref: M-257]. Took the Oath of Allegiance in Worcester County in 1778 before the Hon. Nehemiah Holland [Ref: J-1814 (Box 4)].
DOWNS (DOWNES), Mitchell. Took the Oath of Allegiance in Worcester County in 1778 before the Hon. Joshua Townsend [Ref: J-1814 (Box 4)].
DOWSE, John. Private, Somerset County, Capt. John Gunby's 2nd Independent Maryland Co.; sick in barracks on Aug 1, 1776; mustered on Aug 21, 1776 [Ref: D-642].
DREADEN (DREDDEN), William. See "William Dryden," q.v.

89

DREADEN (DRYDEN), Nancy. See "Samuel Tilghman," q.v.
DRISKELL, Adam. Private, Worcester Militia, Wicomico Bn., Capt. Elijah Shockley's Co., Seventh Class, July 15, 1780 [Ref: M-255 listed the name as "Adam Driskill"].
DRISKELL, Dennis. Private, 3rd Maryland Independent Co., Worcester County, Capt. John Watkins' Co., enlisted Feb 5, 1776; muster roll dated Aug 20, 1776, present for duty [Ref: D-21].
DRISKELL, Elgett or Elgate. Private, Worcester Militia, Wicomico Bn., Capt. Samuel Horsey's Co., Eighth Class, July 15, 1780 [Ref: M-257]. "Elgate Driskell" was born in Maryland (no date was given), married Naomiah ----, served as a private during the war, and died before May 15, 1794 [Ref: V-878].
DRISKELL, George. Private, Worcester Militia, Wicomico Bn., Capt. Samuel Horsey's Co., Seventh Class, July 15, 1780 [Ref: M-257].
DRISKELL, John. Private, Worcester Militia, Wicomico Bn., Capt. Elijah Shockley's Co., Sixth Class, July 15, 1780 [Ref: M-255].
DRISKELL, Lovey. See "Moses Driskell," q.v.
DRISKELL, Moses Sr. Private, Worcester Militia, Wicomico Bn., Capt. Samuel Horsey's Co., Eighth Class, July 15, 1780 [Ref: M-257].
DRISKELL, Moses (c1747-1827). Private, Worcester Militia, Wicomico Bn., Capt. Samuel Horsey's Co., Fifth Class, July 15, 1780 [Ref: M-257]. "Moses Driscoll, Jr." was born in Maryland circa 1747, married Lovey ----, was a soldier in the war, and died before June 12, 1827 [Ref: V-878].
DRISKELL, Naomiah. See "Elgett or Elgate Driskell," q.v.
DRISKELL, Shadrick. Private, Worcester Militia, Wicomico Bn., Capt. Samuel Horsey's Co., Eighth Class, July 15, 1780 [Ref: M-257].
DRUM, George. See "Moses Greer," q.v.
DRUMMAN, Bur-?-ll. Private, Worcester Militia, Wicomico Bn., Capt. Charles Bennett's Co., Seventh Class, July 15, 1780 [Ref: M-255].
DRUMMOND, Anne. See "John Selby," q.v.
DRYDEN (DREDDEN), Ephraim. Private, Somerset Militia, Princess Anne Bn., Capt. George Waters' Pocomoke Co., 1780 [Ref: M-220].
DRYDEN (DREADON), Isaac. Private, Worcester Militia, Wicomico Bn., Capt. William Handy's Co., Seventh Class, July 15, 1780 [Ref: M-257].
DRYDEN (DREDEN), Isaac. Private, Worcester Militia, Wicomico Bn., Capt. Benjamin Dennis' Co., Fourth Class, July 15, 1780 [Ref: M-255].
DRYDEN (DREADEN), James. Private, Somerset Militia, Princess Anne Bn., Capt. George Waters' Pocomoke Co., 1780 [Ref: M-220].
DRYDEN (DREADEN), John. Private, Worcester Militia, Wicomico Bn., Capt. Charles Bennett's Co., Third Class, July 15, 1780 [Ref: M-255].
DRYDEN (DRYDDEN), John. Took the Oath of Allegiance in Worcester County in 1778 before the Hon. Joshua Townsend [Ref: J-1814 (Box 4)].
DRYDEN (DREADEN), Jonathan. Private, Somerset Militia, Princess Anne Bn., Capt. George Waters' Pocomoke Co., 1780 [Ref: M-220].

DRYDEN (DREDDEN), Joshua. Private, Worcester Militia, Wicomico Bn., Capt. Philip Quinton's Co., Eighth Class, July 15, 1780 [Ref: M-256].

DRYDEN (DREDDON), Littleton. Corporal, Somerset Militia, Princess Anne Bn., Capt. George Waters' Pocomoke Co., 1780 [Ref: M-220 listed the name as "Lill. Dreddon"].

DRYDEN (DREDON), Moses. Private, Worcester Militia, Sinepuxent Bn., Capt. Thomas Purnell's Co., Second Class, 1779/1780 [Ref: M-253]. Took the Oath of Allegiance in Worcester County in 1778 before the Hon. Joshua Townsend [Ref: J-1814 (Box 4) listed the name as "Moses Drydden"].

DRYDEN (DREADON), Noble. Sergeant, Worcester Militia, Wicomico Bn., Capt. James Patterson's Co., July 15, 1780 [Ref: M-258]. Took the Oath of Allegiance in Worcester County in 1778 before the Hon. William Hopewell [Ref: J-1814 (Box 4)]. Recommended for promotion to ensign on Aug 4, 1780 "as there is a want of officers in Capt. Patterson's Co." [Ref: G-41].

DRYDEN (DREADEN), Samuel. Private, Worcester Militia, Sinepuxent Bn., Capt. William Purnell's Co., Second Class, 1779/1780 [Ref: M-252 listed the name as "Sam Dredon"]. Private, Worcester Militia, Wicomico Bn., Capt. Benjamin Dennis' Co., First Class, July 15, 1780 [Ref: M-255].

DRYDEN, Samuel (of John). Took the Oath of Allegiance in Worcester County in 1778 before the Hon. Joshua Townsend [Ref: J-1814 (Box 4)].

DRYDEN (DREDDEN), Sewell. Private, Worcester Militia, Wicomico Bn., Capt. Benjamin Dennis' Co., Third Class, July 15, 1780 [Ref: M-255].

DRYDEN (DREADEN), Thomas. Private, Somerset Militia, Princess Anne Bn., Capt. George Waters' Pocomoke Co., 1780 [Ref: M-220].

DRYDEN (DREDDEN), William. Private, Worcester Militia, Wicomico Bn., Capt. Benjamin Dennis' Co., Third Class, July 15, 1780 [Ref: M-255]. There were at least three men with this name who served in the revolution (see below). One William Dryden was born before 1755, married Rachel Morgan, served as a private during the war, and died in Ohio before 1820 [Ref: V-880]. Additional research will be necessary before drawing conclusions.

DRYDEN (DREADON), William. Private, Worcester Militia, Snow Hill Bn., Capt. Samuel Smyley's Co., 1777 {Ref: M-250]. Private, Worcester Militia, Wicomico Bn., Capt. Samuel Smyley's Co., Sixth Class, July 15, 1780 [Ref: M-259]. Took the Oath of Allegiance in Worcester County in 1778 before the Hon. Joshua Townsend [Ref: J-1814 (Box 4)].

DRYDEN (DREADEN), William. Private, Somerset Militia, Princess Anne Bn., Capt. James Elzey's Co., 1780 [Ref: M-220 listed the name as "Will Dreaden"]. Took the Oath of Allegiance in Somerset County in 1778 before the Hon. Peter Waters [Ref: T-18].

DUBBERLY (DUBERLY), Eliakim. Private, Worcester Militia, Snow Hill Bn., Capt. Samuel Smyley's Co., 1777 [Ref: M-250]. Private, Worcester Militia, Wicomico Bn., Capt. James Patterson's Co., Fifth Class, July 15, 1780 [Ref: M-258].

DUBBERLY (DUBERLY), John. Private, Worcester Militia, Sinepuxent Bn., Capt. Elisha Purnell's Co., First Class, 1779/1780 [Ref: M-253]. Took the Oath of Allegiance in Worcester County in 1778 in Quepomco Hundred before the Hon. Thomas Purnell [Ref: J-1814 (Box 4)]. Rendered patriotic service by supplying corn for the use of the military on June 14, 1780 and July 10, 1780 [Ref: G-10 listed the name as "John Dubberly" and P-296 mistakenly listed the name as "John Daberly"].

DUBBERLY (DUBERLY), William. Private, Worcester Militia, Wicomico Bn., Capt. James Patterson's Co., Fifth Class, July 15, 1780 [Ref: M-258].

DUER, James. Private, Worcester Militia, Wicomico Bn., Capt. William Handy's Co., Sixth Class, July 15, 1780 [Ref: M-257]. Took the Oath of Allegiance in Worcester County in 1778 before the Hon. Joshua Townsend [Ref: J-1814 (Box 4)].

DUER, James Jr. Rendered patriotic service by supplying salt for the use of the military in Worcester County on Oct 10, 1781 [Ref: P-446].

DUER, Joshua. Ensign, Worcester Militia, Snow Hill Bn., Capt. William Holland's Co., Aug 30, 1777 to Aug 3, 1781, resigned [Ref: M-72, C-351]. Took the Oath of Allegiance in Worcester County in 1778 before the Hon. John Selby [Ref: J-1814 (Box 4)].

DUER, Joshua. Private, Worcester Militia, Wicomico Bn., Capt. Fisher Walton's Co., Eighth Class, July 15, 1780 [Ref: M-258].

DUFF, David. Took the Oath of Allegiance in Somerset County in 1778 before the Hon. Peter Waters [Ref: T-18].

DUKES, Davis. See "Isaac Dukes," q.v.

DUKES, Elizabeth. See "Isaac Dukes," q.v.

DUKES, Isaac (1761/2-1835). Private, Maryland Line and Privateer Service, who applied for a pension (R3111) on Oct 17, 1832 in Ross County, Ohio, a resident of Concord Township where he had moved in 1812. Isaac married Elizabeth King in April, 1793, in Worcester County, Maryland (she was born on July 12, 1772) and he died on April 17, 1835 in Clinton County, Indiana. Elizabeth Dukes applied for a pension on Feb 11, 1840, age 68, stating their children were Davis (b. Jan 18, 1794, and made affidavit in 1840), Mary (b. May, 1796), James (b. 1798), Isaac (b. 1800), Elizabeth (b. July, 1802), Katharine (b. 1806), Spencer (b. 1808), and Samuel (b. 1811). [Ref: W-1034, V-887].

DUKES, Jacob. Took the Oath of Allegiance in Worcester County in 1778 before the Hon. William Hopewell [Ref: J-1814 (Box 4)].

DUKES, James. See "Isaac Dukes," q.v.

DUKES, John. Private, Worcester Militia, Snow Hill Bn., Capt. Samuel Smyley's Co., 1777 [Ref: M-250]. Private, Worcester Militia, Wicomico Bn., Capt. Samuel Smyley's Co., Fourth Class, July 15, 1780 [Ref: M-259].

DUKES, John. Private, Worcester Militia, Wicomico Bn., Capt. Charles Bennett's Co., Sixth Class, July 15, 1780 [Ref: M-255].

DUKES, Katharine. See "Isaac Dukes," q.v.

DUKES, Mary. See "Isaac Dukes," q.v.
DUKES, Parker. Private, Worcester Militia, Snow Hill Bn., Capt. Samuel Smyley's Co., 1777 [Ref: M-250]. Private, Worcester Militia, Wicomico Bn., Capt. Samuel Smyley's Co., Second Class, July 15, 1780 [Ref: M-259]. Took the Oath of Allegiance in Worcester County in 1778 before the Hon. John Selby [Ref: J-1814 (Box 4)].
DUKES, Robert. Private, Worcester Militia, Wicomico Bn., Capt. Benjamin Dennis' Co., Second Class, July 15, 1780 [Ref: M-255]. Took the Oath of Allegiance in Worcester County in 1778 before the Hon. Joshua Townsend [Ref: J-1814 (Box 4)].
DUKES, Robert. Private, Somerset Militia, Salisbury Bn., Capt. Sampson Wheatly's Co., 1780 [Ref: M-216].
DUKES, Robert. Private, Somerset Militia, Princess Anne Bn., Capt. James Elzey's Co., 1780 [Ref: M-220].
DUKES, Samuel. See "Isaac Dukes," q.v.
DUKES, Spencer. See "Isaac Dukes," q.v.
DUKES, William. Private, Worcester Militia, Snow Hill Bn., Capt. Samuel Smyley's Co., 1777 [Ref: M-250]. Private, Worcester Militia, Wicomico Bn., Capt. Samuel Smyley's Co., Fourth Class, July 15, 1780 [Ref: M-259].
DUNCAN, Charles. Took the Oath of Allegiance in Worcester County in 1778 before the Hon. Nehemiah Holland [Ref: J-1814 (Box 4)].
DUNCAN, Isaac. Took the Oath of Allegiance in Worcester County in 1778 before the Hon. Nathaniel Miller [Ref: J-1814 (Box 4)]. Private, Worcester Militia, Sinepuxent Bn., Capt. John Coe's Co., Second Class, 1779/1780 [Ref: M-251 listed the name as "Isaac Dunkin"].
DUNCAN, Jesse. Private, Worcester Militia, Sinepuxent Bn., Capt. John Rackliff's Co., Second Class, 1779/1780 [Ref: M-251 listed the name as "Jesse Dunkin"].
DUNCAN, John. Private, Worcester Militia, Wicomico Bn., Capt. John Davis' Co., Fourth Class, July 15, 1780 [Ref: M-254].
DUNCAN, Levin. Took the Oath of Allegiance in Worcester County in 1778 before the Hon. Joshua Townsend [Ref: J-1814 (Box 4)].
DUNCAN, Thomas. Took the Oath of Allegiance in Worcester County in 1778 before the Hon. John Selby [Ref: J-1814 (Box 4)].
DUNN, Gilbert. Private, Somerset Militia, Salisbury Bn., Capt. John Span Conway's Nanticoke Point Co., 1778/1780 [Ref: M-216].
DUNN, John. See "John Done," q.v.
DURHAM, John. Private, Somerset Militia, Princess Anne Bn., Capt. James Elzey's Co., 1780 [Ref: M-220]. Took the Oath of Allegiance in Somerset County in 1778 before the Hon. Levin Wilson [Ref: T-17 listed the name as "John Durram" and N-51 listed the name as "John Durran"].
DUTTON, James. Drafted from Somerset County on June 20, 1781 to serve in the Continental Army [Ref: L-35C].

DUVALL, G--?--. Muster Master, Capt. John Gunby's Second Independent Co., Somerset County, Aug 21, 1776 [Ref: D-642].

DYES, Phillip. See "Phillip Dies," q.v.

DYMOCK (DYMACK), William. Private, Somerset Militia, Salisbury Bn., Capt. James Bennett's Salisbury Co., 1778/1780 [Ref: M-218]. Took the Oath of Allegiance in Somerset County in 1778 [Ref: N-51]. Rendered patriotic service by supplying wheat for the use of the military on May 14, 1781 [Ref: P-394 listed the name as "William Dymack"]. Took the Oath of Allegiance in Somerset County in 1778 before the Hon. Gillis Polk [Ref: T-15].

ELENSWORTH, Richard. Private, Somerset Militia, Salisbury Bn., Capt. John Span Conway's Nanticoke Point Co., 1778/1780 [Ref: M-216].

ELLIOT, Jacob. Private, Worcester Militia, Wicomico Bn., Capt. James Perdue's Co., Eighth Class, July 15, 1780 [Ref: M-256 listed the name as "Jacob Elliott"].

ELLIOT, John. Private, Somerset Militia, Princess Anne Bn., Capt. John Jones' Princess Anne Co., 1780 [Ref: M-219].

ELLIOT, Thomas. Took the Oath of Allegiance in Worcester County in 1778 before the Hon. Joshua Townsend [Ref: J-1814 (Box 4) listed the name as "Thomas Elliat"].

ELLIS, Edward. Took the Oath of Allegiance in Somerset County on Feb 28, 1778 before the Hon. Joseph Venables [Ref: T-25 listed the name sa "Edward Elliss"].

ELLIS, Jesse. Private, Worcester Militia, Wicomico Bn., Capt. James Patterson's Co., Eighth Class, July 15, 1780 [Ref: M-258 listed the name as "Jesse Elliss"]. Took the Oath of Allegiance in Worcester County in 1778 before the Hon. James Selby [Ref: J-1814 (Box 4) listed the name as "Jessey Ellis"].

ELLIS, Levi. Private, Worcester Militia, Wicomico Bn., Capt. James Patterson's Co., Fifth Class, July 15, 1780 [Ref: M-258]. Took the Oath of Allegiance in Worcester County in 1778 before the Hon. Nehemiah Holland [Ref: J-1814 (Box 4)].

ELLIS, William. Private, Worcester Militia, Wicomico Bn., Capt. Fisher Walton's Co., Second Class, July 15, 1780 [Ref: M-258]. Took the Oath of Allegiance in Worcester County in 1778 before the Hon. James Selby [Ref: J-1814 (Box 4)].

ELLIS, William Jr. Took the Oath of Allegiance in Worcester County in 1778 before the Hon. Nehemiah Holland [Ref: J-1814 (Box 4)].

ELLISON, Luke. Private, Worcester Militia, Sinepuxent Bn., Capt. John Coe's Co., Fourth Class, 1779/1780 [Ref: M-252].

ELMORE, Clifford. Rendered patriotic service by supplying corn for the use of the military in Worcester County on April 21, 1780 [Ref: P-286].

ELMORE, Comfort. Rendered patriotic service by supplying corn for the use of the military in Worcester County on July 10, 1780 [Ref: G-10].

ELMORE, John. Took the Oath of Allegiance in Worcester County in 1778 in Quepomco Hundred before the Hon. Thomas Purnell [Ref: J-1814 (Box 4)].

ELZEY, Arnold (d. 1777). Surveyor of Somerset County who died in 1777 and was replaced by James Polk on May 16, 1777 [Ref: C-255].

ELZEY, Arnold (c1754-1818). Private, Somerset Militia, Princess Anne Bn., Capt. James Elzey's Co., 1780. Select Militia, Somerset County, Aug 15, 1781 [Ref: M-220, L-35A]. A member of the American Whig Society in 1775, he married Henrietta Wilson by 1796 and they had a daughter Elizabeth M. Elzey. Arnold served in the Lower House of the Maryland Legislature in 1784 and was a physician and a founder of the Maryland Medical and Chirurgical Faculty of Maryland in 1799. He served as Surgeon, 23rd Regiment, Maryland Militia, 1794-1800, Garrison Surgeon's Mate, U. S. Army, 5th District, appointed 1814, and Post Surgeon, Washington, D. C., appointed 1816 [Ref: R-304, R-305].

ELZEY, Elizabeth. See "Arnold Elzey," q.v.

ELZEY, Henrietta. See "Levin Handy," q.v.

ELZEY, James (c1747-1791). Ensign, Somerset Militia, Princess Anne Bn., Capt. David Wilson's Co., Sep 22, 1777. Second Lieutenant, Jan 7, 1778. Captain, from Dec 7, 1778 to at least July 24, 1780 [Ref: M-73, M-220, C-381, C-457, E-260]. Took the Oath of Allegiance in Somerset County in 1778 before the Hon. Levin Wilson [Ref: T-17, N-51]. James Elzey was born before 1747, married Eleanor (Nelly) Bozman, served as a captain in the war, and died in 1791 [Ref: V-954].

ELZEY, John. See "William Elzey," q.v.

ELZEY, Mary. See "William Elzey," q.v.

ELZEY, Robert. Private, Somerset Militia, Salisbury Bn., White Haven Co., 1778/1780 [Ref: M-219]. Took the Oath of Allegiance in Somerset County in 1778 before the Hon. Levin Wilson [Ref: T-17, N-51].

ELZEY, William (1761 -   ). Son of John and Mary Elzey, born in Stepney Parish on Feb 28, 1761 [Ref: Y-46]. Private, Somerset Militia, Princess Anne Bn., Capt. James Elzey's Co., 1780 [Ref: M-220].

ENGLISH, Eleanor (Nelly). See "Jonathan Cooper," q.v.

ENGLISH, James and Polly. See "Jonathan Cooper," q.v.

ENGLISH, Thomas and Wharton. See "Jonathan Cooper," q.v.

ENNIS, Cornelous Jr. Took the Oath of Allegiance in Worcester County in 1778 before the Hon. Joshua Townsend [Ref: J-1814 (Box 4)]. "Cornelius Ennis" was a private in the Worcester Militia, Sinepuxent Bn., Capt. William Purnell's Co., Sixth Class, 1779/1780 [Ref: M-252].

ENNIS, Cornelous Sr. Took the Oath of Allegiance in Worcester County in 1778 before the Hon. Joshua Townsend [Ref: J-1814 (Box 4)].

ENNIS, George. Private, Worcester Militia, Sinepuxent Bn., Capt. Elisha Purnell's Co., Sixth Class, 1779/1780 [Ref: M-253]. Took the Oath of Allegiance in Worcester County in 1778 before the Hon. Joshua Townsend [Ref: J-1814 (Box 4)].

ENNIS, Jesse. Second Lieutenant, Worcester Militia, Snow Hill Bn., Capt. George Spence's Co., Aug 30, 1777, and Capt. Samuel Smyley's Co., 1777 [Ref: M-74, M-250, C-351]. Took the Oath of Allegiance in Worcester County in 1778 before the Hon. Joshua Townsend [Ref: J-1814 (Box 4)].

ENNIS, Joseph. Second Lieutenant, Worcester Militia, Sinepuxent Bn., Capt. William Purnell's Co., Aug 30, 1777. First Lieutenant, June 13, 1782, Capt. Littleton Robins' Co. [Ref: M-74, M-252, C-350, I-190]. Took the Oath of Allegiance in Worcester County in 1778 in Bogerternorton Hundred before the Hon. Thomas Purnell [Ref: J-1814 (Box 4) listed the name as "Joseph Enniss"].

ENNIS, Joshua. Private, Worcester Militia, Sinepuxent Bn., Capt. John Rackliff's Co., Third Class, 1779/1780 [Ref: M-251].

ENNIS, Laben. Private, Worcester Militia, Sinepuxent Bn., Capt. Elisha Purnell's Co., First Class, 1779/1780 [Ref: M-253]. Took the Oath of Allegiance in Worcester County in 1778 before the Hon. Joshua Townsend [Ref: J-1814 (Box 4)].

ENNIS, Luke. Took the Oath of Allegiance in Worcester County in 1778 before the Hon. Joshua Townsend [Ref: J-1814 (Box 4)].

ENNIS, Nathanael. Took the Oath of Allegiance in Worcester County in 1778 before the Hon. Joshua Townsend [Ref: J-1814 (Box 4)].

ENNIS, William. Took the Oath of Allegiance in Worcester County in 1778 before the Hon. Joshua Townsend [Ref: J-1814 (Box 4) listed the name as "William Enniss"].

ENNIS, Zadock. Private, Worcester Militia, Wicomico Bn., Capt. Samuel Horsey's Co., Sixth Class, July 15, 1780 [Ref: M-257]. Took the Oath of Allegiance in Worcester County on Feb 25, 1778 before the Hon. Ebenezer Handy [Ref: J-1814 (Box 4)].

ERVIN, Abraham. Private, Somerset County, Capt. John Gunby's 2nd Independent Maryland Co.; sick in barracks on March 20, 1776; mustered on Aug 21, 1776 [Ref: D-641].

ESHOM, Daniel. Private, Worcester Militia, Wicomico Bn., Capt. Benjamin Dennis' Co., Sixth Class, July 15, 1780 [Ref: M-256 listed the name as "Daniel Esom"]. Private, Maryland Troops, Worcester County, draughted May 1, 1781 [Ref: K-99, D-372 listed the name as "Daniel Eashom"].

ESHOM, Jonathan. Private, Worcester Militia, Wicomico Bn., Capt. Benjamin Dennis' Co., First Class, July 15, 1780 [Ref: M-255].

ESHOM, Joseph. Private, Worcester Militia, Wicomico Bn., Capt. Benjamin Dennis' Co., Third Class, July 15, 1780 [Ref: M-255].

ESHOM, Solomon. Private, Worcester Militia, Wicomico Bn., Capt. Benjamin Dennis' Co., Third Class, July 15, 1780 [Ref: M-255].

EUBANKS, John (of Nicholas). Took the Oath of Allegiance in Somerset County in 1778 [Ref: N-51].

EVAN, George. Private, Somerset Militia, Salisbury Bn., Capt. John Span Conway's Nanticoke Point Co., 1778/1780 [Ref: M-216].

EVANS, Dale. Private, Worcester Militia, Sinepuxent Bn., Capt. Josiah Dale's Co., Third Class, 1779/1780 [Ref: M-254].

EVANS, Ebenezer (c1738-1793). Private, Worcester Militia, Sinepuxent Bn., Capt. John Rackliff's Co., Second Class, 1779/1780 [Ref: M-251].

EVANS, Elizabeth. Rendered patriotic service by supplying beef in Worcester County for the use of the military on Oct 12, 1780 [Ref: P-325]. See "Thomas Dale," q.v.

EVANS, Gamage. Private, Worcester Militia, Sinepuxent Bn., Capt. John Coe's Co., First Class, 1779/1780 [Ref: M-251]. Took the Oath of Allegiance in Worcester County in 1778 before the Hon. Nehemiah Holland [Ref: J-1814 (Box 4)].

EVANS, George. Private, Worcester Militia, Sinepuxent Bn., Capt. John Postly's Co., Seventh Class, 1779/1780 [Ref: M-251].

EVANS (EVENS), Hannah. See "Jesse Evans," q.v.

EVANS, Isaac. First Lieutenant, Worcester Militia, Sinepuxent Bn., Capt. William Purnell's Co., Aug 30, 1777. Captain, Aug 9, 1780 [Ref: M-74, M-251, C-350, F-251]. Took the Oath of Allegiance in Worcester County in 1778 before the Hon. Nathaniel Miller [Ref: J-1814 (Box 4)]. Rendered patriotic service by supplying corn for the use of the military on June 14, 1780 [Ref: P-296].

EVANS, Isaac. Lieutenant, Select Militia, Capt. Samuel H. Round's Co., Worcester County, Aug 23, 1781 [Ref: M-74, G-577].

EVANS, Jacob. Private, Worcester Militia, Wicomico Bn., Capt. James Perdue's Co., First Class, July 15, 1780 [Ref: M-256].

EVANS, James. Private, Somerset Militia, Salisbury Bn., Capt. John Span Conway's Nanticoke Point Co., 1778/1780 [Ref: M-216].

EVANS, Jesse (1761 -   ). Son of John and Hannah Evens [sic], born in Coventry Parish on July 20, 1761 [Ref: Y-83]. Private, Somerset Militia, Princess Anne Bn., Capt. Henry Miles' Little Annemessex Co., 1780 [Ref: M-221].

EVANS, John Sr. (c1717-1795). Rendered patriotic service by supplying bacon for the use of the military in Somerset County on Aug 17, 1780 [Ref: P-310]. See "Jesse Evans," q.v.

EVANS, John (1740-1788). Private, Worcester Militia, Sinepuxent Bn., Capt. John Coe's Co., Seventh Class, 1779/1780 [Ref: M-252]. Private, Worcester Militia, Wicomico Bn., Capt. William Handy's Co., Fourth Class, July 15, 1780 [Ref: M-257].

EVANS, John. Private, Somerset Militia, Salisbury Bn., Capt. John Span Conway's Nanticoke Point Co., 1778/1780 [Ref: M-216]. Private, Somerset Militia, Princess Anne Bn., Capt. Thomas Irving's Monie Co., 1780 [Ref: M-219].

EVANS, John (of Nicholas). Second Lieutenant, Somerset Militia, Salisbury Bn., Capt. John Span Conway's Nanticoke Point Co., 1778/1780. First Lieutenant, April 17, 1781 [Ref: M-216, H-195]. Took the Oath of Allegiance in Somerset County in 1778 before the Hon. John Span Conway [Ref: T-14].

EVANS, Joseph. Took the Oath of Allegiance in Worcester County in 1778 before the Hon. Nathaniel Miller [Ref: J-1814 (Box 4)].
EVANS, Leah. See "Salathiel Baker," q.v.
EVANS, Levin. Took the Oath of Allegiance before the Governor and Council of Maryland on March 26, 1777 [Ref: C-190]. Private, Somerset Militia, Princess Anne Bn., Capt. Henry Miles' Little Annemessex Co., 1780 [Ref: M-221].
EVANS, Owen. Private, Somerset Militia, Princess Anne Bn., Capt. Isaac Handy's Great Annemessix Co., 1780 [Ref: M-221].
EVANS, Priscilla. See "William Francis Dashiell," q.v.
EVANS, Richard. Private, Somerset Militia, Princess Anne Bn., Capt. Henry Miles' Little Annemessex Co., 1780 [Ref: M-221].
EVANS, Sarah. See "John Dashiell," q.v.
EVANS, Thomas. Private, Somerset Militia, Princess Anne Bn., Capt. Henry Miles' Little Annemessex Co., 1780 [Ref: M-221].
EVANS, Thomas. Private, Somerset Militia, Princess Anne Bn., Capt. Isaac Handy's Great Annemessix Co., 1780 [Ref: M-221].
EVANS, William. Private, Worcester Militia, Sinepuxent Bn., Capt. John Rackliff's Co., Sixth Class, 1779/1780 [Ref: M-251]. Took the Oath of Allegiance in Worcester County in 1778 in Buckingham Hundred before the Hon. Thomas Purnell [Ref: J-1814 (Box 4) listed the name as "William Eavines"].
EVANS, William. Took the Oath of Allegiance in Worcester County in 1778 in Buckingham Hundred before the Hon. Thomas Purnell [Ref: J-1814 (Box 4) listed the name as "William Eavanes"].
EVANS, William. Private whose name appeared on "a list of recruits from and deserters taken up in Somerset County on Oct 20, 1780" and noted as "deserter belonging to the Delaware State" [Ref: D-346]. See "Ruben Washbourn," q.v.
EVANS, William Mister. Private, Somerset Militia, Princess Anne Bn., Capt. Henry Miles' Little Annemessex Co., 1780 [Ref: M-221].
EWENS, John (of Joshua). Private, Maryland Troops, Worcester County, draughted May 1, 1781 [Ref: K-99, D-372].
EWELL, George. See "Richard Summers," q.v.
EWING, John. Ensign, Somerset Militia, Princess Anne Bn., Capt. William Waters' Co., Sep 22, 1777 [Ref: M-74, C-381].
FALKNER, James. Took the Oath of Allegiance in Worcester County in 1778 before the Hon. Nathaniel Miller [Ref: J-1814 (Box 4)].
FALKNER, John. Private, Worcester Militia, Sinepuxent Bn., Capt. John Coe's Co., Sixth Class, 1779/1780 [Ref: M-252].
FALL, Ananios. Took the Oath of Allegiance in Worcester County in 1778 in Buckingham Hundred before the Hon. Thomas Purnell [Ref: J-1814 (Box 4)].
FALL, Levi. Private, Worcester Militia, Sinepuxent Bn., Capt. John Postly's Co., Fourth Class, 1779/1780 [Ref: M-251].
FALLIN (FOLLIN), Levin. Corporal, Somerset Militia, Salisbury Bn., Capt. William Turpin's Rewastico Co., 1778/1780 [Ref: M-217 listed the name as

"Levin Follin"]. Took the Oath of Allegiance in Somerset County in 1778 before the Hon. William Winder [Ref: N-51, T-22 listed the name as "Levin Fallin"].

FANING, John. Took the Oath of Allegiance in Worcester County in 1778 in Buckingham Hundred before the Hon. Thomas Purnell [Ref: J-1814 (Box 4)].

FARLOW, Benjamin (1756-1821). Private, Worcester Militia, Wicomico Bn., Capt. James Perdue's Co., Second Class, July 15, 1780 [Ref: M-256]. "Ben: Farlow" was born in Maryland on July 4, 1756, married Elizabeth Parsons, served as a private during the war, and died in November, 1821 [Ref: V-988].

FARLOW, George. Private, Worcester Militia, Wicomico Bn., Capt. James Perdue's Co., Seventh Class, July 15, 1780 [Ref: M-256].

FARLOW, John. Private, Worcester Militia, Wicomico Bn., Capt. James Perdue's Co., Sixth Class, July 15, 1780 [Ref: M-256].

FARLOW, William. Private, Worcester Militia, Wicomico Bn., Capt. James Perdue's Co., First Class, July 15, 1780 [Ref: M-256].

FARRELL, John. Took the Oath of Allegiance in Worcester County in 1778 in Buckingham Hundred before the Hon. Thomas Purnell [Ref: J-1814 (Box 4)].

FASSITT (FASSETT), Daniel. Took the Oath of Allegiance in Worcester County in 1778 before the Hon. Joshua Townsend [Ref: J-1814 (Box 4) listed the name as "Daniel Farsett"].

FASSITT (FASSETT), Catherine. See "James Fassitt," q.v.

FASSITT (FASSETT), David. Private, Worcester Militia, Sinepuxent Bn., Capt. John Rackliff's Co., Second Class, 1779/1780 [Ref: M-251]. Took the Oath of Allegiance in Worcester County in 1778 before the Hon. Nathaniel Miller [Ref: J-1814 (Box 4) listed the name as "David Fosset"]. Rendered patriotic service by supplying corn for the use of the military on April 15, 1780 and May 19, 1780 and July 10, 1780 [Ref: P-284 listed the name as "David Fossett" and P-292 listed the name as "David Fassett" and G-10 listed the name as "David Fassitt"].

FASSITT (FASSETT), James (1741-1825). First Lieutenant, Worcester Militia, Sinepuxent Bn., Capt. Elihu or Elisha Briddell's Co., Aug 30, 1777. First Lieutenant, Capt. Joseph Dashiell's Co., May 27, 1778 [Ref: M-75, C-350, and E-423 listed the name as "James Fasset"]. Took the Oath of Allegiance in Worcester County in 1778 before the Hon. John Selby [Ref: J-1814 (Box 4)]. James Fassett or Fassitt was born in Maryland on May 15, 1741, married Catherine ----, served as a first lieutenant during the war, and died in 1825 [Ref: V-995].

FASSITT (FASSETT), James. Private, Worcester Militia, Sinepuxent Bn., Capt. Josiah Dale's Co., Fifth Class, 1779/1780 [Ref: M-254].

FASSITT (FASSETT), John (captain). Took the Oath of Allegiance in Worcester County in 1778 before the Hon. Nathaniel Miller [Ref: J-1814 (Box 4)]. On June 14, 1780, Joseph Dashiell, Commissary of Purchases, issued a receipt to

"Capt. John Fassett" for supplying corn and on Oct 12, 1780 for supplying beef for the use of the military in Worcester County [Ref: P-296, P-325, P-326].

FASSITT (FASSETT), John (1759-c1820). Private, Worcester Militia, Sinepuxent Bn., Capt. John Rackliff's Co., Fifth Class, 1779/1780 [Ref: M-251]. Private, Maryland Line, who applied for a pension (S34826) in Worcester County on Nov 19, 1819, age 60, stating he had enlisted at Annapolis. He received $96 per annum effective June 29, 1818, but was dropped from the rolls under the Act of May 1, 1820; no reason was stated [Ref: X-44]. Rendered patriotic service by supplying corn for the use of the military in Worcester County on July 10, 1780 [Ref: G-10]. See "Joseph Dashiell," q.v.

FASSITT (FASSETT), Juliana. See "Isaac Henry," q.v.

FASSITT (FASSETT), Mary. See "William Purnell," q.v.

FASSITT (FASSETT), Rouse. Private, Worcester Militia, Sinepuxent Bn., Capt. John Rackliff's Co., Fourth Class, 1779/1780 [Ref: M-251 listed the name as "Rouse Fassett"]. Took the Oath of Allegiance in Worcester County in 1778 before the Hon. John Selby [Ref: J-1814 (Box 4)].

FASSITT (FASSET), Sarah. See "Kendall Collier," q.v.

FASSITT (FASSETT), William. Private, Worcester Militia, Sinepuxent Bn., Capt. John Rackliff's Co., Third Class, 1779/1780 [Ref: M-251]. Took the Oath of Allegiance in Worcester County in 1778 before the Hon. Nathaniel Miller [Ref: J-1814 (Box 4)]. Rendered patriotic service by supplying corn for the use of the military on June 14, 1780 and July 10, 1780 [Ref: P-296 listed the name as "William Fassett" and G-10 listed the name as "William Fassitt"]. One "William Fassitt of John" died intestate in Worcester County before August, 1798, leaving his real estate to descend to his brothers and sisters [Ref: Article by William D. Patrick in *Maryland Magazine of Genealogy*, Vol. 4, No. 2 (Fall, 1981), pp. 76-77].

FELCHETT (FITCHETT), Thomas. Private, Somerset Militia, Princess Anne Bn., Capt. James Elzey's Co., 1780 [Ref: M-220 listed the name as "Thomas Fitchett"]. Took the Oath of Allegiance in Somerset County in 1778 before the Hon. Levin Wilson [Ref: T-17 listed the name as "Thomas Felchett" and N-52 listed the name as "Thomas Tolchett"].

FIGGEN, Francis. Private, Somerset County, Capt. John Gunby's 2nd Independent Maryland Co.; present on April 19, 1776; mustered on Aug 21, 1776 [Ref: D-641].

FINCH, George. Private, Somerset County, Capt. John Gunby's 2nd Independent Maryland Co.; present on April 8, 1776; mustered on Aug 21, 1776 [Ref: D-641]. On July 30, 1781 Mills Baily recruited George Finch from Somerset County to serve in the Continental Army until Dec 10, 1781 [Ref: L-35C].

FINCH, John. Took the Oath of Allegiance in Worcester County on Feb 25, 1778 before the Hon. Ebenezer Handy [Ref: J-1814 (Box 4)].

FINLEY, Ebenezer. Second Lieutenant, Somerset Militia, 17th Bn., Capt. Planner Williams' Co., Feb 24, 1776 [Ref: M-75, A-182].

FISHER, Rose (Arosy). See "George Dashiell," q.v.
FISHER, Thomas. Private, Somerset Militia, Princess Anne Bn., Capt. James Elzey's Co., 1780 [Ref: M-220]. Took the Oath of Allegiance in Somerset County in 1778 (made his "X" mark) before the Hon. Peter Waters [Ref: T-18].
FISHER, William. Took the Oath of Allegiance in Somerset County in 1778 before the Hon. Levin Wilson [Ref: T-17, and N-51 listed the name as "William Fishes"].
FITZGERALD, David. Private, Worcester Militia, Sinepuxent Bn., Capt. Thomas Purnell's Co., Third Class, 1779/1780 [Ref: M-253]. Took the Oath of Allegiance in Worcester County in 1778 before the Hon. Nathaniel Miller [Ref: J-1814 (Box 4) listed the name as "David Fitzgerrald"].
FITZJARRALD, John. Private, Somerset Militia, Salisbury Bn., White Haven Co., 1778/1780 [Ref: M-219]. Drafted from Somerset County on July 30, 1781 to serve in the Continental Army [Ref: L-35C]. Discharged on Nov 29, 1781 [Ref: I-7].
FITZJARROLD, James. Private, Somerset Militia, Salisbury Bn., White Haven Co., 1778/1780 [Ref: M-218].
FLEMING, John (1753 -   ). Son of William Fleming and Jean Handy, born in Coventry Parish on Aug 11, 1753 [Ref: Y-70]. Ensign in the Somerset Militia, Princess Anne Bn., Capt. David Wilson's Co., Jan 7, 1778. Ensign, Capt. James Elzey's Co., from Dec 7, 1778 to at least July 24, 1780 [Ref: M-75, M-220, C-457, E-260 listed the name as "John Flemming"].
FLEMING, John. Private, Worcester Militia, Wicomico Bn., Capt. Philip Quinton's Co., Sixth Class, July 15, 1780 [Ref: M-256 listed the name as "John Flemin"]. Private, Worcester Militia, Capt. John Martin's Co., 1780/1781 [Ref: J-1814 (Box 12) listed the name as "Jno. Flemming"].
FLEMING, John Jr. Took the Oath of Allegiance in Somerset County in 1778 before the Hon. Levin Wilson [Ref: T-17, N-51].
FLEMING, Joshua. Private, Worcester Militia, Capt. John Martin's Co., 1780/1781 [Ref: J-1814 (Box 12) listed the name as "Joshua Flemming"].
FLEMING, Priscilla. See "John Cottingham," q.v.
FLEMING, William. Took the Oath of Allegiance in Somerset County in 1778 before the Hon. Peter Waters [Ref: T-18]. See "John Fleming," q.v.
FLETCHER, George. Private, Somerset Militia, Salisbury Bn., Capt. Levin Irving's Black Water Co., 1778/1780 [Ref: M-218]. Rendered patriotic service by supplying corn for the use of the military in Somerset County on Feb 10, 1780 [Ref: P-269].
FLETCHER, John. See "Thomas Fletcher," q.v.
FLETCHER, Levin. Private, Somerset Militia, Salisbury Bn., Capt. Levin Irving's Black Water Co., 1778/1780 [Ref: M-218]. See "Isaac Owens," q.v.
FLETCHER, Rachel. See "Thomas Fletcher" and "William Moore, Sr.," q.v.
FLETCHER, Samuel. Private, Somerset Militia, Salisbury Bn., Capt. Levin Irving's Black Water Co., 1778/1780 [Ref: M-218].

FLETCHER, Thomas (1759 -   ). Son of John and Rachel Fletcher, born in Stepney Parish on Sep 26, 1759 [Ref: Y-46]. Private, Somerset Militia, Salisbury Bn., Capt. James Bennett's Salisbury Co., 1778/1780 [Ref: M-218].

FLINT, John (1756-1841). Private, Worcester Militia, Snow Hill Bn., Capt. Ebenezer Handy's Co., April 9, 1776 [Ref: M-249]. Private, Worcester Militia, Wicomico Bn., Capt. Robert Handy's Co., Fourth Class, July 15, 1780 [Ref: M-254 listed the name as "John Flintt"]. Took the Oath of Allegiance in Worcester County in 1778 before the Hon. William Hopewell [Ref: J-1814 (Box 4)]. He applied for a pension (R3614) on Oct 13, 1835 in Franklin County, Indiana, resident of Bath Township, stating he was born in Worcester County, Maryland on July 6, 1756 and lived there at the time of his enlistment [Ref: W-1217]. John Flint was born in Maryland on July 6, 1756, married Elizabeth (Betty) Johnson, served as a private during the war, and died in Indiana on Aug 13, 1841 [Ref: V-1041].

FLOYD, Aaron. Took the Oath of Allegiance in Somerset County on Feb 25, 1778 (made his "X" mark) before the Hon. Joseph Venables [Ref: T-25].

FLOYD, Hugh. Private, Somerset Militia, Salisbury Bn., Capt. Henry Gale's Quantico Co., 1778/1780 [Ref: M-217].

FLOYD, John. Private, Worcester Militia, Wicomico Bn., Capt. Fisher Walton's Co., Sixth Class, July 15, 1780 [Ref: M-258].

FLOYD, William. Private, Worcester Militia, Snow Hill Bn., Capt. Samuel Smyley's Co., 1777 [Ref: M-250]. Took the Oath of Allegiance in Worcester County in 1778 before the Hon. James Selby [Ref: J-1814 (Box 4) listed the name as "William Floyed"].

FLUELLIN, Samuel. Private, Somerset Militia, Salisbury Bn., Capt. John Span Conway's Nanticoke Point Co., 1778/1780 [Ref: M-216].

FOLLIN, Levin. See "Levin Fallin," q.v.

FOOKS, Ann. See "William Laws" and "William Fooks," q.v.

FOOKS, Daniel (1737-1793). Private, Worcester Militia, Wicomico Bn., Capt. James Perdue's Co., Seventh Class, July 15, 1780 [Ref: M-256]. Daniel Fooks was born on May 29, 1737, married Violetta Tyndall, served as a private during the war, and died before Feb 19, 1793 [Ref: V-1051].

FOOKS, Jesse (c1730-1807). Private, Worcester Militia, Wicomico Bn., Capt. Samuel Horsey's Co., First Class, July 15, 1780 [Ref: M-256]. Took the Oath of Allegiance in Worcester County in 1778 before the Hon. William Hopewell [Ref: J-1814 (Box 4) listed the name as "Jesse Fookse"]. Jesse Fooks was born circa 1730, married Mary ----, served in the militia during the war, and died before May 23, 1807 [Ref: V-1051].

FOOKS, Mary. See "Joshua Stanford" and "Jesse Fooks," q.v.

FOOKS, Thomas. Private, Worcester Militia, Wicomico Bn., Capt. Samuel Horsey's Co., First Class, July 15, 1780 [Ref: M-256]. Took the Oath of Allegiance in Worcester County in 1778 before the Hon. William Hopewell [Ref: J-1814 (Box 4) listed the name as "Thomas Fookse"]. Rendered patriotic service by supplying corn for the use of the military on March 10, 1780 and July 10, 1780 [Ref: P-275, G-10, listed the name as "Thomas Fookes"].

FOOKS, William. Private, Worcester Militia, Wicomico Bn., Capt. Samuel Horsey's Co., First Class, July 15, 1780 [Ref: M-256]. One William Fooks was born before 1764, married Ann ----, served as a private in the war, and died before Feb 22, 1833 [Ref: V-1051]. One William Fooks was born on Jan 27, 1765, died on Aug 22, 1823, and is buried in the William Fooks Family Graveyard at the northwest corner of Ennis Workman Road in Wicomico County [Ref: *Graveyards and Gravestones of Wicomico*, by John E. Jacob (1996), p. 36]. Additional research will be necessary before drawing conclusions.

FORD, Gilbert. Private, Somerset Militia, Princess Anne Bn., Capt. George Waters' Pocomoke Co., 1780 [Ref: M-220].

FORD, Nehemiah. Private, Somerset Militia, Princess Anne Bn., Capt. Isaac Handy's Great Annemessix Co., 1780 [Ref: M-221].

FORD, Thomas. Private, Somerset Militia, Princess Anne Bn., Capt. Isaac Handy's Great Annemessix Co., 1780 [Ref: M-221].

FORD, William. Drafted from Somerset County into the Continental Army on June 20, 1781, but was subsequently excused [Ref: D-408, L-35C].

FORMAN, John. See "William Ironshire," q.v.

FORREST, Uriah. First Lieutenant, 2nd Independent Maryland Co., Somerset County, Capt. John Gunby's Co., officers elected by the Maryland Convention, Jan 2, 1776 [Ref: D-20].

FOSKEY, Ezekiel. Private, Somerset Militia, Princess Anne Bn., Capt. Thomas Irving's Monie Co., 1780 [Ref: M-219].

FOSSET, Sarah. See "Stephen Horsey," q.v.

FOSSETT, David. See "David Fassitt," q.v.

FOUNTAIN, Collin. Ensign, Somerset Militia, 17th Bn., Capt. William Fountain's Co., Feb 24, 1776 [Ref: M-76, A-182].

FOUNTAIN, John. Private, Somerset Militia, Princess Anne Bn., Capt. Isaac Handy's Great Annemessix Co., 1780 [Ref: M-221].

FOUNTAIN, Stephen. Private, Worcester Militia, Wicomico Bn., Capt. Elijah Shockley's Co., First Class, July 15, 1780 [Ref: M-255]. Took the Oath of Allegiance in Worcester County in 1778 before the Hon. Nehemiah Holland [Ref: J-1814 (Box 4) listed the name as "Stevens Fountain"].

FOUNTAIN, Thomas. Ensign, Somerset Militia, Salisbury Bn., Capt. Josiah Dashiell's Wicomico Creek Co., Sep 22, 1777 to at least July 24, 1780 [Ref: M-76, M-218, C-382]. Rendered patriotic service by supplying bacon for the use of the military on Aug 9, 1780 [Ref: P-308].

FOUNTAIN, Thomas G. Took the Oath of Allegiance in Somerset County in 1778 before the Hon. Levin Wilson [Ref: T-17, N-51].

FOUNTAIN, William. Captain, Somerset Militia, 17th Bn., Feb 24, 1776 [Ref: M-76, A-182]. Took the Oath of Allegiance in Somerset County in 1778 before the Hon. Peter Waters [Ref: T-18].

FOWLER, Edward. Private, Somerset Militia, Salisbury Bn., White Haven Co., 1778/1780 [Ref: M-219].

FOWLER, John. Private, Somerset Militia, Salisbury Bn., Capt. James Bennett's Salisbury Co., 1778/1780 [Ref: M-218].

FOX, Elijah Jr. Private, Worcester Militia, Wicomico Bn., Capt. James Perdue's Co., First Class, July 15, 1780 [Ref: M-256].

FRANKLIN, Ebenezer. Private, Worcester Militia, Sinepuxent Bn., Capt. Thomas Purnell's Co., Sixth Class, 1779/1780 [Ref: M-253]. Took the Oath of Allegiance in Worcester County in 1778 before the Hon. Nathaniel Miller [Ref: J-1814 (Box 4) listed the name as "Ebenezar Franklin"].

FRANKLIN, Edward. Took the Oath of Allegiance in Worcester County in 1778 before the Hon. Nathaniel Miller [Ref: J-1814 (Box 4)].

FRANKLIN, Henry. Private, Worcester Militia, Sinepuxent Bn., Capt. Thomas Purnell's Co., Sixth Class, 1779/1780 [Ref: M-253]. Took the Oath of Allegiance in Worcester County in 1778 before the Hon. Nathaniel Miller [Ref: J-1814 (Box 4) listed the name as "Henry Franklyn"]. Rendered patriotic service by supplying corn for the use of the military on July 10, 1780 [Ref: G-10].

FRANKLIN, John. Private, 3rd Maryland Independent Co., Worcester County, Capt. John Watkins' Co., enlisted Feb 8, 1776; muster roll dated Aug 20, 1776, present for duty [Ref: D-22].

FRANKLIN, John. Private, Worcester Militia, Sinepuxent Bn., Capt. Thomas Purnell's Co., Second Class, 1779/1780 [Ref: M-253].

FRANKLIN, John. Private, Worcester Militia, Sinepuxent Bn., Capt. Thomas Purnell's Co., Seventh Class, 1779/1780 [Ref: M-253].

FRANKLIN, John Jr. Took the Oath of Allegiance in Worcester County in 1778 before the Hon. Nathaniel Miller [Ref: J-1814 (Box 4)].

FRANKLIN, John, Segr.*[sic]*. Took the Oath of Allegiance in Worcester County in 1778 before the Hon. Nathaniel Miller [Ref: J-1814 (Box 4)].

FRANKLIN, Lemuel. Private, Worcester Militia, Sinepuxent Bn., Capt. Thomas Purnell's Co., Fifth Class, 1779/1780 [Ref: M-253]. Took the Oath of Allegiance in Worcester County in 1778 before the Hon. Nathaniel Miller [Ref: J-1814 (Box 4)].

FRANKLIN, Peal. Private, Worcester Militia, Sinepuxent Bn., Capt. Thomas Purnell's Co., First Class, 1779/1780 [Ref: M-253]. Took the Oath of Allegiance in Worcester County in 1778 before the Hon. Nathaniel Miller [Ref: J-1814 (Box 4)].

FRANKLIN, Peter. See "Isaac Henry," q.v.

FRANKLIN, William. Private, Worcester Militia, Sinepuxent Bn., Capt. Matthew Purnell's Co., Seventh Class, July 25, 1780 [Ref: M-252].

FRANKLIN, William (of Edward). Took the Oath of Allegiance in Worcester County in 1778 before the Hon. Nathaniel Miller [Ref: J-1814 (Box 4)].

FRANKLIN, William (of William). Took the Oath of Allegiance in Worcester County in 1778 before the Hon. Nathaniel Miller [Ref: J-1814 (Box 4)].

FRASHER, Daniel. Private, Somerset Militia, Salisbury Bn., Capt. John Span Conway's Nanticoke Point Co., 1778/1780 [Ref: M-216].

FREEMAN, John. Private, 3rd Maryland Independent Co., Worcester County, Capt. John Watkins' Co., enlisted March 12, 1776; muster roll dated Aug 20, 1776, sick in barracks [Ref: D-22].

FREONEY, Joshua. Private, Worcester Militia, Snow Hill Bn., Capt. Ebenezer Handy's Co., April 9, 1776 [Ref: M-249]. Private, Worcester Militia, Wicomico Bn., Capt. Robert Handy's Co., Third Class, July 15, 1780 [Ref: M-254].

FRUCE(?), Alexander. Took the Oath of Allegiance in Somerset County in 1778 before the Hon. John Stewart [Ref: T-19].

FULLERTON, Charles. Took the Oath of Allegiance in Somerset County in 1778 before the Hon. William Winder [Ref: T-22, N-51].

FULLERTON, Joshua. Private, Somerset Militia, Salisbury Bn., Capt. Josiah Dashiell's Wicomico Creek Co., 1778/1780 [Ref: M-218 listed the name as "Joshua Fullirton"]. Took the Oath of Allegiance in Somerset County in 1778 before the Hon. William Winder [Ref: T-22, N-51].

FURGESON, Isaac. See "Benjamin Scott," q.v.

FURGESON, Lotty. See "Benjamin Scott," q.v.

FURNISS (FURNIS), George (c1747-1807). Private, Worcester Militia, Wicomico Bn., Capt. Fisher Walton's Co., First Class, July 15, 1780 [Ref: M-258]. Took the Oath of Allegiance in Worcester County in 1778 before the Hon. Nehemiah Holland [Ref: J-1814 (Box 4)].

FURNISS, John and Josiah. See "Levi Stevens," q.v.

FURNISS, Littleton and Mary. See "Levi Stevens," q.v.

FURNISS, Sarah and William. See "Levi Stevens," q.v.

FURROW, Samuel. Private, Maryland Line, whose name appeared on "a list of recruits from and deserters taken up in Somerset County on Oct 20, 1780" [Ref: D-346].

GALE, Amelia. See "John Gale," q.v.

GALE, Anna Maria. See "George Gale," q.v.

GALE, Elizabeth. See "Lambert Hyland" and "George Gale, Jr.," q.v.

GALE, George (1756-1815). Son of Levin Gale and Leah Littleton. George was born on June 3, 1756 in Somerset County, married Anna Maria Hollyday, and died on Jan 2, 1815 in Cecil County. Children: Levin (U. S. Congressman), George, Anna Maria, Leah, Henrietta Maria Elizabeth, Sarah Hollyday, Harriet, Margaret, and Georgiana. George served in the Maryland Senate, 1781-1791, in the Lower House, 1784, and was a Justice of Orphans Court in Somerset County in 1785 and in Cecil County in 1799. He attended the Constitution Ratification Convention in 1788 and was a U. S. Congressman, 1789-1791. He was appointed Supervisor of Distilled Liquors for the District of Maryland by President George Washington in 1791 [Ref: R-335, R-336]. See "John Gale" and "Levin Gale," q.v.

GALE, George Jr. (1756-). Son of George and Elizabeth Gale, born in Stepney Parish on May 9, 1756 [Ref: Y-45]. Took the Oath of Allegiance in Somerset County in 1778 before the Hon. Levin Wilson [Ref: T-17, N-51]. Private, Somerset Militia, Salisbury Bn., Capt. Henry Gale's Quantico Co., 1778/1780. Recommended for promotion to ensign on July 21, 1781 [Ref: M-77, M-216, G-575, J-1814 (Box 8, Dashiell's correspondence) and H-361 listed the name as "George Gale, of George"].

GALE, Georgiana. See "George Gale," q.v.

GALE, Harriet. See "Isaac Henry" and "George Gale," q.v.

GALE, Henrietta. See "George Gale," q.v.

GALE, Henry (c1740-). Son of John Gale and Milcah Hill [Ref: R-336]. Captain, Somerset Militia, Salisbury Bn., Quantico Co., Sep 22, 1777 to at least July 24, 1780 [Ref: M-77, M-216, C-381]. Took the Oath of Allegiance in Somerset County in 1778 before the Hon. William Winder [Ref: N-51, and T-22 listed the name as "Henrey Gale"].

GALE, John (1753-1813). Son of George Gale and Elizabeth Airey. John was born in Stepney Parish on Sep 25, 1753, married Amelia Williams, and died testate before March 3, 1813. Children: John Planner, Mary, Milcah, and Amelia Caroline. John served in the Lower House of the Maryland Legislature, 1785-1789, 1806-1809, attended the Constitution Ratification Convention in 1788, and was an Associate Justice, Fourth District, 1794 [Ref: R-337, Y-45]. Service: Second lieutenant, 2nd Maryland Line, 1776; first lieutenant, April 10, 1777; prisoner at Staten Island in August, 1777, and exchanged in December, 1777; captain, Dec 10, 1777; transferred to 5th Maryland Line, January, 1781; aide-de-camp to Gen. Mordecai Gist, December, 1782 to the end of the war; brevet major, September, 1783; colonel, Maryland Militia, by 1794; brigadier general, Tenth Brigade, Maryland Militia, 1801. He received bounty land warrant #422-300 in 1808 at which time he lived at Princess Anne in Somerset County, Maryland [Ref: W-1299, R-337, D-113, D-364]. See "Henry Gale," q.v.

GALE, Leah. See "George Gale" and "Levin Gale," q.v.

GALE, Levin (c1730-1791). Son of Capt. Matthias Gale and Margaret Gordon. Levin was born circa 1730, married his first cousin Leah Littleton, and died on Oct 9, 1791. Children: Robert, Littleton, George, Levin, and Leah Littleton. Levin served as a member of the Lower House from Somerset County, 1756-1771; County Justice, 1766-1777; Trustee for the Nanticoke Indians, 1768; Justice of the Court of Oyer and Terminer and Gaol Delivery, 1770-1772; Justice of the Court of Appeals, 1777-1779; Justice of the Orphans Court, 1777; and, Judge of the Court of Appeals for Tax Assessment, 1786 [Ref: R-338, C-

274]. Took the Oath of Allegiance in Somerset County in 1778 before the Hon. Levin Wilson [Ref: T-17]. See "George Gale," q.v.

GALE, Levin Jr. Took the Oath of Allegiance in Somerset County in 1778 before the Hon. Levin Wilson [Ref: T-17, and N-51 mistakenly listed the name as "Lem Gale, Jr."].

GALE, Littleton. See "Levin Gale," q.v.

GALE, Margaret. See "George Gale," q.v.

GALE, Mary. See "Samuel Wilson" and "John Gale," q.v.

GALE, Matthias. See "Levin Gale," q.v.

GALE, Milcah. See "John Gale" and "Henry Gale," q.v.

GALE, Robert. See "Levin Gale," q.v.

GALE, Sarah. See "George Gale," q.v.

GALE, William. Private, Somerset Militia, Salisbury Bn., White Haven Co., 1778/1780. First Lieutenant, Capt. Joseph Cottman's White Haven Co., 1781 [Ref: M-77, G-575, M-218, J-1814 (Box 8, Dashiell's correspondence), H-195].

GALE, William (of Levin). Drafted from Somerset County on June 20, 1781 to serve in the Continental Army [Ref: L-35C].

GALLOWAY, Benjamin. See "Luther Martin," q.v.

GALLOWAY, James. Private, Somerset Militia, Princess Anne Bn., Capt. Thomas Irving's Monie Co., 1780 [Ref: M-219].

GALLOWAY, John. On May 30, 1776 the Maryland Council of Safety wrote to the Committee of Observation for Worcester County: "The bearer hereof Mr. John Galloway is with some other gentleman in partnership about setting up and carrying on a salt work under the encouragement of the last Convention. He is in great measure unacquainted in your county, and as the work will be of the greatest public utility, we take the liberty of recommending him to your notice and countenance, and shall be much obliged to you for any assistance you may give him, or any favors you will pleased to confer upon him." [Ref: A-448].

GARNET, Michel. Took the Oath of Allegiance in Somerset County on Feb 28, 1778 (made his "X" mark) before the Hon. Joseph Venables [Ref: T-25].

GARRETT, John. See "Shadrack Claywell," q.v.

GATES, Charles. Private, Somerset Militia, Salisbury Bn., Capt. Henry Gale's Quantico Co., 1778/1780 [Ref: M-216]. Took the Oath of Allegiance in Somerset County in 1778 (made his "X" mark) before the Hon. John Span Conway [Ref: T-14, N-51].

GATES, William. Took the Oath of Allegiance in Somerset County in 1778 (made his "W" mark) before the Hon. John Span Conway [Ref: T-14].

GAULT, Archibald Johnson. Took the Oath of Allegiance in Worcester County in 1778 before the Hon. Nathaniel Miller [Ref: J-1814 (Box 4)].

GAULT, David. Took the Oath of Allegiance in Worcester County in 1778 before the Hon. Nathaniel Miller [Ref: J-1814 (Box 4)].

GAULT, William. Ensign, Worcester Militia, Sinepuxent Bn., Capt. Thomas Purnell's Co., Aug 30, 1777 [Ref: M-78, M-253, C-350]. Took the Oath of Allegiance in Worcester County in 1778 before the Hon. Nathaniel Miller [Ref: J-1814 (Box 4)].

GERMAN, John. Private, Worcester Militia, Wicomico Bn., Capt. John Davis' Co., Fourth Class, July 15, 1780 [Ref: M-254].

GERMAN, William. Private, Worcester Militia, Wicomico Bn., Capt. James Perdue's Co., Fourth Class, July 15, 1780 [Ref: M-256].

GETTETT, John. Rendered patriotic service by supplying corn for the use of the military in Worcester County on April 12, 1780 [Ref: P-283].

GIBBENS, Ezekiel. Private, Somerset Militia, Princess Anne Bn., Capt. James Elzey's Co., 1780 [Ref: M-220]. Select Militia, Somerset County, Aug 15, 1781 [Ref: L-35B].

GIBBENS, James. Private, Somerset Militia, Princess Anne Bn., Capt. James Elzey's Co., 1780 [Ref: M-220]. Select Militia, Somerset County, Aug 15, 1781 [Ref: L-35A].

GIBBENS, John. Took the Oath of Allegiance in Somerset County in 1778 before the Hon. John Williams [Ref: T-21, and N-51 listed the name as "John Gibbon"].

GIBBENS, Josiah. Private, Somerset Militia, Princess Anne Bn., Capt. James Elzey's Co., 1780 [Ref: M-220].

GIBBENS, Thomas Jr. Private, Somerset Militia, Princess Anne Bn., Capt. James Elzey's Co., 1780 [Ref: M-220 listed the name as "Thomas Gibbens, of Thomas"]. Took the Oath of Allegiance in Somerset County in 1778 before the Hon. John Williams [Ref: T-21, and N-51 listed the name as "Thomas Gibbon, Jr."].

GIBBENS, Thomas Sr. Private, Somerset Militia, Princess Anne Bn., Capt. James Elzey's Co., 1780 [Ref: M-220]. Took the Oath of Allegiance in Somerset County in 1778 before the Hon. John Williams [Ref: T-21, and N-51 listed the name as "Thomas Gibbins"].

GIBBENS, William. Took the Oath of Allegiance in Somerset County in 1778 before the Hon. John Williams [Ref: T-21].

GIBBENS, William Jr. Private, Somerset Militia, Princess Anne Bn., Capt. James Elzey's Co., 1780 [Ref: M-220].

GIBBENS, William Sr. Private, Somerset Militia, Princess Anne Bn., Capt. James Elzey's Co., 1780 [Ref: M-220].

GIBBS, Abraham. Private, Worcester Militia, Wicomico Bn., Capt. Philip Quinton's Co., Eighth Class, July 15, 1780 [Ref: M-256]. See "John Gibbs," q.v.

GIBBS, Elizabeth. See "John Gibbs," q.v.

GIBBS, John (1753 -   ). Son of Abraham and Elizabeth Gibbs, born in Coventry Parish on March 22, 1753 [Ref: Y-70]. Private, Worcester Militia, Wicomico Bn., Capt. Philip Quinton's Co., First Class, July 15, 1780 [Ref: M-256].

GIBBS, Robert. Private, Worcester Militia, Wicomico Bn., Capt. Fisher Walton's Co., First Class, July 15, 1780 [Ref: M-258]. Took the Oath of Allegiance in Worcester County in 1778 before the Hon. Nehemiah Holland [Ref: J-1814 (Box 4)].

GIBSON, Isaac. Private, Somerset Militia, Princess Anne Bn., Capt. Thomas Irving's Monie Co., 1780 [Ref: M-219].

GIBSON, Jacob. Private, Somerset Militia, Salisbury Bn., Capt. William Turpin's Rewastico Co., 1778/1780 [Ref: M-217].

GIBSON, John. Private, Somerset Militia, Princess Anne Bn., Capt. Isaac Handy's Great Annemessix Co., 1780 [Ref: M-221].

GILES, Anney. See "Isaac Giles," q.v.

GILES, Elizabeth. See "Isaac Giles," q.v.

GILES, Eunice. See "Isaac Giles," q.v.

GILES, Isaac (c1734-1790/1). Son of Thomas Giles and Ann Harris, of Stepney Parish, Somerset County. He married Elizabeth ---- and their children were: Peggy (b. Oct 6, 1764); Anney (b. July 28, 1771); Thomas (b. Jan 13, 1776, married Elizabeth Leatherbury); and, Sarah (b. July 19, 1778). "In 1787 Isaac Giles and his wife Elizabeth agreed by mutual assent to live separate and apart from each other and maintain that estate and those articles each had at the time of marriage." He died testate before Jan 27, 1791 (date of probate). [Ref: Q-28:2 (Spring, 1987), "The Giles Family of Old Somerset," by Louis F. Giles III, pp. 226-232]. Private, Somerset Militia, Salisbury Bn., Capt. Joseph Venables' Barren Creek Co., 1778/1780 [Ref: M-217]. Took the Oath of Allegiance in Somerset County on Feb 19, 1778 before the Hon. Joseph Venables [Ref: T-25].

GILES, Isaac (1762-1810/1). Son of Jacob and Eunice Giles. He was born on July 30, 1762 in Stepney Parish, Somerset County, married Nelly Phillips, and died intestate before March 5, 1811 (date of filing of inventory). Their sons were William Giles (1795-1872) and John Phillips Giles (b. 1799). [Ref: Q-28:2, *Ibid.*]. Private, Somerset Militia, Salisbury Bn., Capt. Levin Irving's Black Water Co., 1778/1780 [Ref: M-218].

GILES, Jacob. See "Isaac Giles," q.v.

GILES, John (1746 -   ). Son of Thomas Giles and Ann Harris, born in Stepney Parish, Somerset County, on April 27, 1746 [Ref: Q-28:2, *Ibid.*]. He was probably the John Giles who was a private in the Worcester Militia, Wicomico Bn., Capt. Robert Handy's Co., First Class, on July 15, 1780 [Ref: M-254]. See "Isaac Giles," q.v.

GILES, Major. See "Thomas Seon," q.v.

GILES, Peggy. See "Isaac Giles," q.v.

GILES, Sarah. See "Isaac Giles," q.v.

GILES, Thomas. See "John Giles" and "Isaac Giles," q.v.

GILES, William. See "Isaac Giles," q.v.

GILLETT, Ayres. Private, Worcester Militia, Wicomico Bn., Capt. James Patterson's Co., Sixth Class, July 15, 1780 [Ref: M-258].
GILLETT, John. Rendered patriotic service by supplying corn for the use of the military in Worcester County on July 10, 1780 [Ref: G-10 listed the name as "John Gillitt"].
GILLETT (GILLET), Nancy. See "Samuel McMaster," q.v.
GILLETT, William. Private, Worcester Militia, Wicomico Bn., Capt. James Patterson's Co., First Class, July 15, 1780 [Ref: M-258].
GILLIS, Elizabeth. See "David Polk" and "Gillis Polk" and "Josiah Polk" and "William Polk," q.v.
GILLIS, Esther. See "Levin Winder" and "William Winder" and "William Winder, Jr.," q.v.
GILLISS, Ezekiel. Lieutenant, Somerset Militia, Princess Anne Bn., Capt. David Wilson's Co., Sep 22, 1777 [Ref: M-78, C-381]. Took the Oath of Allegiance in Somerset County in 1778 before the Hon. Levin Wilson [Ref: T-17, N-51]. Select Militia, Somerset County, Aug 15, 1781 [Ref: L-35B].
GILLISS, George. Ensign, Somerset Militia, Salisbury Bn., Capt. Joseph Venables' Co., Sep 22, 1777 [Ref: M-78, C-381]. Took the Oath of Allegiance in Somerset County on Feb 28, 1778 before the Hon. Joseph Venables [Ref: T-25]. See "Joseph Gilliss, Sr.," q.v.
GILLISS, John. Took the Oath of Allegiance in Worcester County in 1778 before the Hon. Joshua Townsend [Ref: J-1814 (Box 4) listed the name as "John Gilles"]. See "Joseph Gilliss," q.v.
GILLISS, Joseph Sr. (c1706-c1786). Son of John and Mary Gillis or Gilliss. Joseph married Eleanor Bozman by 1736 and their sons were George and William. Joseph attended the Lower House from Somerset County, 1751-1754, was a County Justice, 1754-1774, a Justice of the Court of Oyer and Terminer and Gaol Delivery in 1771, and a captain in the military by 1755 [Ref: R-353]. Took the Oath of Allegiance in Somerset County in 1778 before the Hon. William Winder [Ref: T-22].
GILLISS, Joseph (c1739-c1796). Second Lieutenant, Somerset Militia, Salisbury Bn., Capt. Josiah Dashiell's Wicomico Creek Co., Sep 22, 1777 to at least July 24, 1780 [Ref: M-78, M-218, C-382]. Took the Oath of Allegiance in Somerset County in 1778 before the Hon. Levin Wilson [Ref: T-17, N-51]. Joseph Gillis was born circa 1738-1740, married first to Anne Handy and second to Elizabeth Irving, was a second lieutenant during the war, and died before May 20, 1796 [Ref: V-1164]. Joseph Gilliss married Elizabeth (Betty) Irving (1747-1816) between 1772 and 1777, and died in 1798 *[sic]*. A daughter Nelly Irving Gillis married Levin Gillis Pollitt (1760-1829) and died in 1841 [Ref: S-1513].
GILLISS, Joseph. Private, Somerset Militia, Salisbury Bn., Capt. Joseph Venables' Barren Creek Co., 1778/1780 [Ref: M-217]. Took the Oath of Allegiance in Somerset County on Feb 27, 1778 before the Hon. Joseph Venables [Ref: T-

25]. On July 30, 1781 David Hickman recruited Joseph Gilliss from Somerset County to serve in the Continental Army until Dec 10, 1781 [Ref: L-35C].

GILLISS, Joseph Jr. Private, Somerset Militia, Salisbury Bn., Capt. Joseph Venables' Barren Creek Co., 1778/1780 [Ref: M-217]. Took the Oath of Allegiance in Somerset County on Feb 27, 1778 (made his "X mark) before the Hon. Joseph Venables [Ref: T-25].

GILLISS, Levin (c1761-1815). Private, Somerset Militia, Salisbury Bn., Capt. Josiah Dashiell's Wicomico Creek Co., 1778/1780 [Ref: M-218]. Select Militia, Somerset County, Aug 15, 1781 [Ref: L-35B]. Levin Gilliss was born circa 1761, married Elinor Morris, was a private during the war, and died before July 24, 1815 [Ref: V-1164].

GILLISS, Mary. See "Joseph Gilliss," q.v.

GILLISS, Nellie. See "George Handy" and "Joseph Gilliss," q.v.

GILLISS, Priscilla. See "John Round," q.v.

GILLISS, Thomas. Private, Somerset Militia, Salisbury Bn., Capt. Josiah Dashiell's Wicomico Creek Co., 1778/1780 [Ref: M-218]. Took the Oath of Allegiance in Somerset County on Feb 24, 1778 (made his "X" mark) before the Hon. Joseph Venables [Ref: T-25].

GILLISS, Thomas Sr. Took the Oath of Allegiance in Somerset County in 1778 before the Hon. William Winder [Ref: T-22].

GILLISS, William. Private, Somerset Militia, Salisbury Bn., Capt. Joseph Venables' Barren Creek Co., 1778/1780 [Ref: M-217]. On July 30, 1781 William Gilliss was "recruited by the class" to serve in the Continental Army until Dec 10, 1781 [Ref: L-35C].

GILLISS, William. Quartermaster, Somerset Militia, 17th Bn., Jan 6, 1776 [Ref: M-78]. Sheriff of Somerset County, 1777-1778 [Ref: C-255, P-169]. Took the Oath of Allegiance in Somerset County in 1778 before the Hon. Levin Wilson [Ref: T-17, N-51].

GILLISS, William. See "Joseph Gilliss, Sr.," q.v.

GIST, Mordecai. See "John Gale," q.v.

GIVENS (GIVAN), Day. Took the Oath of Allegiance in Somerset County in 1778 before the Hon. William Winder [Ref: T-22, and N-51 mistakenly listed the name as "Day Gwins"].

GIVENS (GIVAN), George. First Lieutenant, Worcester Militia, Wicomico Bn., Capt. John Davis' Co., May 27, 1779 to at least July 15, 1780 [Ref: M-255, and M-81, E-423 mistakenly listed the name as "George Gwins"]. Took the Oath of Allegiance in Worcester County in 1778 before the Hon. Joshua Townsend [Ref: J-1814 (Box 4)].

GIVENS (GIVAN), James. Private, Worcester Militia, Sinepuxent Bn., Capt. William Purnell's Co., Fourth Class, 1779/1780 [Ref: M-252]. Took the Oath of Allegiance in Worcester County in 1778 in Bogerternorton Hundred before the Hon. Thomas Purnell [Ref: J-1814 (Box 4)].

GIVENS (GIVAN), John Sr. Took the Oath of Allegiance in Worcester County in 1778 before the Hon. Joshua Townsend [Ref: J-1814 (Box 4)].
GIVENS (GIVAN), John. Took the Oath of Allegiance in Worcester County in 1778 before the Hon. Joshua Townsend [Ref: J-1814 (Box 4)].
GIVENS (GIVAN), Jonathan. Private, Worcester Militia, Wicomico Bn., Capt. Elijah Shockley's Co., Third Class, July 15, 1780 [Ref: M-255 listed the name as "Jonathan Givins"].
GIVENS (GIVAN), Rounds. Private, Worcester Militia, Wicomico Bn., Capt. John Davis' Co., Second Class, July 15, 1780 [Ref: M-254]. Took the Oath of Allegiance in Worcester County in 1778 before the Hon. John Selby [Ref: J-1814 (Box 4) listed the name as "Rownd Givans"].
GLADDEN, Joseph. Private, Somerset Militia, Salisbury Bn., White Haven Co., 1778/1780 [Ref: M-219].
GLADSON, Thomas. Private, Worcester Militia, Sinepuxent Bn., Capt. William Purnell's Co., Second Class, 1779/1780 [Ref: M-252].
GLADSTON (GLASTIN), John. Took the Oath of Allegiance in Worcester County in 1778 in Bogerternorton Hundred before the Hon. Thomas Purnell [Ref: J-1814 (Box 4) listed the name as "John Gladston"]. Private, Somerset Militia, Salisbury Bn., Capt. Joseph Venables' Barren Creek Co., 1778/1780 [Ref: M-217 listed the name as "John Glastin"].
GLASCO, Peter. Took the Oath of Allegiance in Somerset County in 1778 before the Hon. Levin Wilson [Ref: T-17].
GLASGOW, Patrick. Ensign, Worcester Militia, 10th Bn., Capt. James Martin's Co., May 25, 1776. First Lieutenant, Wicomico Bn., Capt. William Handy's Co., Aug 30, 1777 to at least July 15, 1780 [Ref: M-79, M-257, A-444, and C-350 listed the name as "Patrick Glassgow"]. Took the Oath of Allegiance in Worcester County in 1778 before the Hon. John Selby [Ref: J-1814 (Box 4)].
GLASS, Christopher. Private, Worcester Militia, Wicomico Bn., Capt. Elijah Shockley's Co., First Class, July 15, 1780 [Ref: M-255]. Took the Oath of Allegiance in Worcester County in 1778 before the Hon. Joshua Townsend [Ref: J-1814 (Box 4)].
GLASS, Levin. Took the Oath of Allegiance in Worcester County in 1778 before the Hon. Joshua Townsend [Ref: J-1814 (Box 4)].
GLIDEWELL, Nash. See "Shadrack Claywell," q.v.
GODDARD (GODDERD), William. Private, Somerset Militia, Salisbury Bn., Capt. James Bennett's Salisbury Co., 1778/1780 [Ref: M-218]. Rendered patriotic service by supplying corn for the use of the military in Somerset County on Jan 29, 1780 [Ref: P-266].
GODFREY, Belitha. Private, Worcester Militia, Sinepuxent Bn., Capt. John Coe's Co., Fourth Class, 1779/1780 [Ref: M-252].
GODFREY, Charles. Took the Oath of Allegiance in Worcester County in 1778 before the Hon. Joshua Townsend [Ref: J-1814 (Box 4)]. Private, Worcester Militia, Sinepuxent Bn., Capt. John Coe's Co., Third Class, 1779/1780 [Ref: M-

252 listed the name as "Chs. Godfrey"]. Rendered patriotic service by supplying bacon for the use of the military on Sep 19, 1780 [Ref: P-318]. Private, Worcester Militia, Capt. John Martin's Co., 1780/1781 [Ref: J-1814 (Box 12)].

GODFREY, James. Private, Worcester Militia, Sinepuxent Bn., Capt. John Coe's Co., First Class, 1779/1780 [Ref: M-251]. Took the Oath of Allegiance in Worcester County in 1778 before the Hon. Joshua Townsend [Ref: J-1814 (Box 4)].

GODFREY, Polly. See "Purnall Truitt," q.v.

GOODWIN, --?--. See "Matthew Nutter," q.v.

GORDON, Margaret. See "Levin Gale," q.v.

GORDY, Joshua. Private, Somerset County, Capt. John Gunby's 2nd Independent Maryland Co.; present on April 15, 1776; mustered on Aug 21, 1776 [Ref: D-641 listed the name as "Joshua Gordey"].

GORDY, Peter. Corporal, Worcester Militia, Snow Hill Bn., Capt. Ebenezer Handy's Co., April 9, 1776 [Ref: M-249]. Corporal(?), Worcester Militia, Wicomico Bn., Capt. Robert Handy's Co., Third Class, July 15, 1780 [Ref: M-254]. Took the Oath of Allegiance in Worcester County on Feb 25, 1778 before the Hon. Ebenezer Handy [Ref: J-1814 (Box 4)].

GORDY, William. Private, Worcester Militia, Snow Hill Bn., Capt. Ebenezer Handy's Co., April 9, 1776 [Ref: M-249]. Private, Worcester Militia, Wicomico Bn., Capt. Robert Handy's Co., Seventh Class, July 15, 1780 [Ref: M-254].

GORE, John. Private, Somerset Militia, Salisbury Bn., Capt. Josiah Dashiell's Wicomico Creek Co., 1778/1780 [Ref: M-218]. Took the Oath of Allegiance in Worcester County in 1778 before the Hon. Joshua Townsend [Ref: J-1814 (Box 4)].

GORE, Mary. See "Samuel Handy," q.v.

GORNWELL, John. Private, Worcester Militia, Sinepuxent Bn., Capt. William Purnell's Co., Third Class, 1779/1780 [Ref: M-252]. Took the Oath of Allegiance in Worcester County in 1778 before the Hon. Joshua Townsend [Ref: J-1814 (Box 4) listed the name as "John Gornall"].

GORNWELL, Major. Private, Worcester Militia, Wicomico Bn., Capt. William Handy's Co., Fifth Class, July 15, 1780 [Ref: M-257].

GOSLEE, Daniel. See "George Goslee," q.v.

GOSLEE, Elizabeth. See "George Goslee," q.v.

GOSLEE, George (1751 -   ). Son of Daniel and Elizabeth Goslee, born in Stepney Parish on Jan 30, 1753 [Ref: Y-45]. Private, Somerset Militia, Salisbury Bn., Capt. Josiah Dashiell's Wicomico Creek Co., 1778/1780 [Ref: M-218].

GOSLEE, John (c1750-1795). Private, Somerset Militia, Salisbury Bn., Capt. Josiah Dashiell's Wicomico Creek Co., 1778/1780 [Ref: M-218]. Drafted from Somerset County on June 20, 1781 to serve in the Continental Army [Ref: L-35C]. "John Gosley" was born circa 1750, married Hannah Tull, was a private during the war, and died in 1795 [Ref: V-1195].

GOSLEE, Joseph. Private, Somerset Militia, Salisbury Bn., Capt. Josiah Dashiell's Wicomico Creek Co., 1778/1780 [Ref: M-218].
GOSLEE, Thomas. Private, Somerset Militia, Salisbury Bn., Capt. William Turpin's Rewastico Co., 1778/1780 [Ref: M-217].
GOSLEE, William. Private, Somerset Militia, Salisbury Bn., Capt. William Turpin's Rewastico Co., 1778/1780 [Ref: M-217].
GOSLEN (GOSLIN), James. Took the Oath of Allegiance in Somerset County in 1778 before the Hon. William Winder [Ref: T-22, N-51].
GOSLEN (GOSLIN), Levin. Took the Oath of Allegiance in Somerset County in 1778 before the Hon. William Winder [Ref: T-22, N-51].
GOSWELLING, Nelly. See "Isaac Mitchell," q.v.
GOTTING, Philip. Rendered patriotic service by providing coopering services for the military in Worcester County in 1781 [Ref: P-405].
GRACE, Richard. Sergeant, 3rd Maryland Independent Co., Worcester County, Capt. John Watkins' Co., enlisted Jan 25, 1776; muster roll dated Aug 20, 1776, present for duty [Ref: D-21].
GRAHAM, Benjamin. Private, Somerset Militia, Salisbury Bn., Capt. Joseph Venables' Barren Creek Co., 1778/1780 [Ref: M-217].
GRAHAM, Ezekiel. Private, Somerset Militia, Salisbury Bn., Capt. Joseph Venables' Barren Creek Co., 1778/1780 [Ref: M-217].
GRAHAM, James. Private, Somerset Militia, Salisbury Bn., Capt. Sampson Wheatly's Co., 1780 [Ref: M-216].
GRAHAM, William. Took the Oath of Allegiance in Somerset County in 1778 (made his "G" mark) before the Hon. Gillis Polk [Ref: T-15].
GRAHAM, William. Took the Oath of Allegiance in Worcester County in 1778 before the Hon. Joshua Townsend [Ref: J-1814 (Box 4)].
GRANT, Cassia. See "Robert Martin," q.v.
GRAVENOR, Thomas. Drafted from Somerset County on July 30, 1781 to serve in the Continental Army [Ref: L-35C].
GRAY, Benjamin Sr. Private, Worcester Militia, Sinepuxent Bn., Capt. Josiah Dale's Co., Eighth Class, 1779/1780 [Ref: M-254].
GRAY, Benjamin. Private, Worcester Militia, Sinepuxent Bn., Capt. Josiah Dale's Co., Fifth Class, 1779/1780 [Ref: M-254].
GRAY, David. Private, Worcester Militia, Sinepuxent Bn., Capt. Josiah Dale's Co., First Class, 1779/1780 [Ref: M-253].
GRAY, Isaac. Private, Worcester Militia, Sinepuxent Bn., Capt. Thomas Purnell's Co., Sixth Class, 1779/1780 [Ref: M-253].
GRAY, Jerrediah. Private, Worcester Militia, Sinepuxent Bn., Capt. Josiah Dale's Co., Third Class, 1779/1780 [Ref: M-254].
GRAY, Jesse. Captain, Worcester Militia, 10th Bn., May 15, 1776 [Ref: M-80, A-426].
GRAY, Jesse. Private, 3rd Maryland Independent Co., Worcester County, Capt. John Watkins' Co., enlisted May 16, 1776; muster roll dated Aug 20, 1776

indicated "deserted 30 June" [Ref: D-23]. Private, Worcester Militia, Sinepuxent Bn., Capt. Josiah Dale's Co., First Class, 1779/1780 [Ref: M-253].

GRAY, Jesse. Private, Worcester Militia, Wicomico Bn., Capt. James Perdue's Co., Third Class, July 15, 1780 [Ref: M-256].

GRAY, John. Private, Somerset Militia, Princess Anne Bn., Capt. John Jones' Princess Anne Co., 1780 [Ref: M-219].

GRAY, John. Private, Worcester Militia, Wicomico Bn., Capt. John Davis' Co., Seventh Class, July 15, 1780 [Ref: M-255]. Private, Maryland Troops, Worcester County, draughted May 1, 1781 [Ref: K-99, D-372].

GRAY, John. Took the Oath of Allegiance in Worcester County in 1778 before the Hon. Joshua Townsend [Ref: J-1814 (Box 4)].

GRAY, Johnson. Private, Worcester Militia, Sinepuxent Bn., Capt. Josiah Dale's Co., Sixth Class, 1779/1780 [Ref: M-254].

GRAY, Joseph. Private, Worcester Militia, Sinepuxent Bn., Capt. Josiah Dale's Co., Second Class, 1779/1780 [Ref: M-254].

GRAY, Joseph. Private, Worcester Militia, Wicomico Bn., Capt. Benjamin Dennis' Co., Eighth Class, July 15, 1780 [Ref: M-256].

GRAY, Mary. See "Whittey Gray," q.v.

GRAY, Thomas. Private, Worcester Militia, Sinepuxent Bn., Capt. Josiah Dale's Co., Sixth Class, 1779/1780 [Ref: M-254].

GRAY, Thomas Jr. Rendered patriotic service by supplying corn for the use of the military in Worcester County on June 14, 1780 and July 10, 1780 [Ref: P-296, G-10].

GRAY, Thomas Sr. Rendered patriotic service by supplying corn for the use of the military in Worcester County on July 10, 1780 [Ref: G-10].

GRAY, Whittey (Whittington?). "Whittey Gray" was a private in the Somerset Militia, Princess Anne Bn., Capt. James Elzey's Co., in 1780 [Ref: M-220]. "Whittington Gray" was the son of William and Mary Gray of Coventry Parish, born on Nov 10, 1759 [Ref: Y-70].

GRAY, William. Private, Worcester Militia, Sinepuxent Bn., Capt. Thomas Purnell's Co., Fourth Class, 1779/1780 [Ref: M-253]. See "Whittey Gray," q.v

GREEN, Abednego. Private, Somerset Militia, Salisbury Bn., Capt. John Span Conway's Nanticoke Point Co., 1778/1780 [Ref: M-216].

GREEN, Ayres. Took the Oath of Allegiance in Worcester County in 1778 before the Hon. John Selby [Ref: J-1814 (Box 4)].

GREEN, Elisha. Private, Somerset Militia, Salisbury Bn., Capt. Henry Gale's Quantico Co., 1778/1780 [Ref: M-216].

GREEN, Elijah. Drafted from Somerset County on June 20, 1781 to serve in the Continental Army [Ref: L-35C].

GREEN, Ezekiel. Private, Somerset Militia, Salisbury Bn., Capt. James Bennett's Salisbury Co., 1778/1780 [Ref: M-218].

GREEN, George. Drafted from Somerset County on June 20, 1781 to serve in the Continental Army [Ref: L-35C].

GREEN, Hillary. Took the Oath of Allegiance in Worcester County in 1778 before the Hon. Nathaniel Miller [Ref: J-1814 (Box 4)].
GREEN, Joseph. Took the Oath of Allegiance in Worcester County in 1778 before the Hon. Nathaniel Miller [Ref: J-1814 (Box 4)].
GREEN, Louisa. See "Kemp Holder," q.v.
GREEN, Michael. Private, Somerset Militia, Salisbury Bn., Capt. Henry Gale's Quantico Co., 1778/1780 [Ref: M-217].
GREEN, Moses. Private, Somerset Militia, Salisbury Bn., White Haven Co., 1778/1780 [Ref: M-219].
GREER, Ayres. Private, Worcester Militia, Wicomico Bn., Capt. John Parramore's Co., Fourth Class, July 15, 1780 [Ref: M-259].
GREER, Henry. Took the Oath of Allegiance in Worcester County in 1778 before the Hon. Joshua Townsend [Ref: J-1814 (Box 4) listed the name as "Henry Grear"].
GREER, James. Private, Somerset Militia, Salisbury Bn., Capt. William Turpin's Rewastico Co., 1778/1780 [Ref: M-217 listed the name as "James Grear"].
GREER, John. Private, Worcester Militia, Sinepuxent Bn., Capt. William Purnell's Co., Seventh Class, 1779/1780 [Ref: M-252]. Took the Oath of Allegiance in Worcester County in 1778 before the Hon. Nehemiah Holland [Ref: J-1814 (Box 4)].
GREER, Levan. Took the Oath of Allegiance in Worcester County in 1778 before the Hon. Nathaniel Miller [Ref: J-1814 (Box 4)].
GREER, Moses (c1752-1832). Private, Pennsylvania Line, who applied for a pension (S34906) at Snow Hill, Worcester County, Maryland, on April 10, 1818, age 67 (on July 28, 1820 he also said he was age 67 and his wife was nearly his age). He stated that he enlisted in Philadelphia and served in the 3rd Pennsylvania Regiment commanded by Col. Thomas Craig for nearly 5 years. He was in the battles of Monmouth, Germantown, Trenton, Princeton, and Siege of Stony Point under Colonel Wayne. In 1820 his wife (not named) "resided with him and she was nearly as old as he." In an earlier application on April 10, 1818 he also gave his age as 67. On Nov 6, 1846, E. I. Maddux, of Baltimore, wrote to the Pension Bureau stating "that heirs of Moses Greer suppose money due them; that he had a pension and had died about 29 Nov 1832; that George Drum on behalf of heirs had promised to prosecute claim. (Names of heirs not given). File indicates a letter of 8 Aug 1839, not in the file, was received from Sylvester Greer, of Dixiana, Alabama." [Ref: W-1431; U-34:2 (1955), p. 77]. Moses Greer pensioned in Worcester County at $96 per annum effective April 10, 1818 and died on Nov 29, 1832 [Ref: X-44]. See "Moses Greyer," q.v.
GREER, Sylvester. See "Moses Greer," q.v.
GREER, Thomas. Private, Worcester Militia, Sinepuxent Bn., Capt. Thomas Purnell's Co., Eighth Class, 1779/1780 [Ref: M-253]. Took the Oath of

Allegiance in Worcester County in 1778 before the Hon. Nathaniel Miller [Ref: J-1814 (Box 4)].

GREER, William. Private, Worcester Militia, Sinepuxent Bn., Capt. Elisha Purnell's Co., Eighth Class, 1779/1780 [Ref: M-253].

GREER, William. Private, Worcester Militia, Sinepuxent Bn., Capt. Elisha Purnell's Co., Seventh Class, 1779/1780 [Ref: M-253].

GREER, William. Took the Oath of Allegiance in Worcester County in 1778 in Quepomco Hundred before the Hon. Thomas Purnell [Ref: J-1814 (Box 4)].

GREYER, Moses. Private, Maryland Line, from Worcester County, who was discharged on Dec 3, 1781 [Ref: I-11]. See "Moses Greer," q.v.

GRIFFIN (GRIFFEN), Beletha (Bilitha). Private, Worcester Militia, Sinepuxent Bn., Capt. Matthew Purnell's Co., Third Class, July 25, 1780 [Ref: M-252]. Took the Oath of Allegiance in Worcester County in 1778 before the Hon. Nathaniel Miller [Ref: J-1814 (Box 4)].

GRIFFIN (GRIFFEN), William. Private, Worcester Militia, Sinepuxent Bn., Capt. Elisha Purnell's Co., Fourth Class, 1779/1780 [Ref: M-253]. Took the Oath of Allegiance in Worcester County in 1778 before the Hon. Joshua Townsend [Ref: J-1814 (Box 4)].

GROOMS (GROOMES), David. Private, Worcester Militia, Snow Hill Bn., Capt. Samuel Smyley's Co., 1777 [Ref: M-250]. Private, Worcester Militia, Wicomico Bn., Capt. Samuel Smyley's Co., Eighth Class, July 15, 1780 [Ref: M-259]. Took the Oath of Allegiance in Worcester County in 1778 before the Hon. John Selby [Ref: J-1814 (Box 4)].

GRUMBLE, John. Private, Somerset Militia, Salisbury Bn., Capt. William Turpin's Rewastico Co., 1778/1780 [Ref: M-217].

GULLETT (GULLITT), Abraham. Private, Somerset Militia, Salisbury Bn., Capt. James Bennett's Salisbury Co., 1778/1780 [Ref: M-218]. Took the Oath of Allegiance in Somerset County in 1778 before the Hon. Gillis Polk [Ref: T-15, N-51].

GUNBY, Benjamin (1762-1823). Son of James and Sarah Gunby, born in Coventry Parish on Feb 15, 1762 [Ref: Y-70]. Private, Somerset Militia, Princess Anne Bn., Capt. John Williams' Watkins Point Co., 1780 [Ref: M-222]. Benjamin Gunby married Esther Sturgis, daughter of Outten Sturgis, and died in 1823 [Ref: R-793].

GUNBY, Isaac. Private, Somerset Militia, Princess Anne Bn., Capt. John Williams' Watkins Point Co., 1780 [Ref: M-222].

GUNBY, James. See "Joseph Gunby" and "Benjamin Gunby," q.v.

GUNBY, John. Captain, Maryland Line, Second Independent Maryland Co., Somerset County; elected by the Maryland Convention on Jan 2, 1776 [Ref: D-20]. Took the Oath of Allegiance in Worcester County in 1778 before the Hon. James Selby [Ref: J-1814 (Box 4)]. Rose to the rank of colonel. See "Kirk Gunby" and Horsey Summers" and "John Selby," q.v.

GUNBY, John (1760 -   ). Son of John and Sarah Gunby, born in Coventry Parish on Jan 1, 1760 [Ref: Y-83]. Private, Somerset Militia, Salisbury Bn., Capt. Sampson Wheatly's Co., 1780 [Ref: M-216]. Private, Worcester Militia, Wicomico Bn., Capt. Isaac Layfield's Co., Seventh Class, July 15, 1780 [Ref: M-257].
GUNBY, Joseph (1757 -   ). Son of James and Sarah Gunby, born in Coventry Parish on Jan 18, 1757 [Ref: Y-70]. Drafted from Somerset County on July 30, 1781 to serve in the Continental Army [Ref: L-35C].
GUNBY, Kirk (1756 -   ). Son of John and Sarah Gunby, born in Coventry Parish on Nov 18, 1756 [Ref: Y-83]. Private, Somerset Militia, Princess Anne Bn., Capt. John Williams' Watkins Point Co., 1780 [Ref: M-222]. Kirk Gunby married Elizabeth Crackel in Coventry Parish on Dec 25, 1766 [Ref: Y-70].
GUNBY, Levin. Private, Somerset Militia, Salisbury Bn., Capt. Josiah Dashiell's Wicomico Creek Co., 1778/1780 [Ref: M-218].
GUNBY, Mary. See "David Cottingham," q.v.
GUNBY, Sarah. See "Joseph Gunby" and "Benjamin Gunby" and "John Gunby," q.v.
GUNN, John. Private, Worcester Militia, Wicomico Bn., Capt. William Handy's Co., Eighth Class, July 15, 1780 [Ref: M-258].
GUNN, Samuel. Took the Oath of Allegiance in Worcester County in 1778 before the Hon. William Hopewell [Ref: J-1814 (Box 4)].
GUPTON (GUPSTON?), William. Private, Somerset Militia, Salisbury Bn., Capt. Levin Irving's Black Water Co., 1778/1780 [Ref: M-217].
GUPTON (GUPSTON?), William. Private, Somerset Militia, Salisbury Bn., Capt. William Turpin's Rewastico Co., 1778/1780 [Ref: M-217].
GURLEY, Francis. Took the Oath of Allegiance in Worcester County in 1778 before the Hon. Joshua Townsend [Ref: J-1814 (Box 4)]. Private, Worcester Militia, Wicomico Bn., Capt. Robert Handy's Co., Seventh Class, July 15, 1780 [Ref: M-254 listed the name as "Frank Gurly"].
GUTHERY (GUTTERY), Caleb. Private, Worcester Militia, Wicomico Bn., Capt. Samuel Smyley's Co., Second Class, July 15, 1780 [Ref: M-259].
GUTHERY (GUTTERY), James. Private, Worcester Militia, Snow Hill Bn., Capt. Samuel Smyley's Co., 1777 [Ref: M-250].
GUTHERY (GUTTERY), Joshua. Took the Oath of Allegiance in Worcester County in 1778 before the Hon. Joshua Townsend [Ref: J-1814 (Box 4)].
GUTHERY (GUTTERY), Moses. Took the Oath of Allegiance in Worcester County in 1778 before the Hon. Joshua Townsend [Ref: J-1814 (Box 4)].
GUTHERY (GUTTERY), Philip. Took the Oath of Allegiance in Worcester County in 1778 before the Hon. Joshua Townsend [Ref: J-1814 (Box 4)].
GWIN, James. Second Lieutenant, Worcester Militia, June 28, 1777 [Ref: M-81].
GWINS, George. See "George Givens" q.v.
HACK, Mary. See "John Waters" and "Peter Waters," q.v.

HADDER, John. Private, Worcester Militia, Sinepuxent Bn., Capt. John Postly's Co., Eighth Class, 1779/1780 [Ref: M-251]. Took the Oath of Allegiance in Worcester County in 1778 before the Hon. Nathaniel Miller [Ref: J-1814 (Box 4)].

HADDER, Nehemiah. Private, Worcester Militia, Sinepuxent Bn., Capt. Matthew Purnell's Co., Seventh Class, July 25, 1780 [Ref: M-252].

HADDER, Shadrick. Private, Worcester Militia, Sinepuxent Bn., Capt. Thomas Purnell's Co., First Class, 1779/1780 [Ref: M-253]. Took the Oath of Allegiance in Worcester County in 1778 in Quepomco Hundred before the Hon. Thomas Purnell [Ref: J-1814 (Box 4) listed the name as "Shadrick Hador"].

HADDER, Warren (Warran). Private, Worcester Militia, Sinepuxent Bn., Capt. John Postly's Co., Fourth Class, 1779/1780 [Ref: M-251]. Took the Oath of Allegiance in Worcester County in 1778 before the Hon. Nathaniel Miller [Ref: J-1814 (Box 4)].

HADDOCK, James. Private, Somerset Militia, Princess Anne Bn., Capt. James Elzey's Co., 1780 [Ref: M-220].

HAILE, John. Private, Somerset Militia, Princess Anne Bn., Capt. Isaac Handy's Great Annemessix Co., 1780 [Ref: M-221].

HAILE, Robert. Private, Somerset Militia, Princess Anne Bn., Capt. Isaac Handy's Great Annemessix Co., 1780 [Ref: M-221].

HAILS, Charles Lucas. Private, Somerset Militia, Salisbury Bn., Capt. James Bennett's Salisbury Co., 1778/1780 [Ref: M-218]. Drafted from Somerset County on June 20, 1781 to serve in the Continental Army, but was subsequently excused [Ref: L-35C].

HAINEY, James. See "James Haynie," q.v.

HAINS, Thomas. Private, Somerset Militia, Salisbury Bn., White Haven Co., 1778/1780 [Ref: M-219].

HALE, William. Took the Oath of Allegiance in Somerset County in 1778 before the Hon. William Winder [Ref: T-22, N-51].

HALEMAN, John. Took the Oath of Allegiance in Somerset County in 1778 before the Hon. William Winder [Ref: T-22, N-51].

HALES, Charles. See "Charles Lucas Hails," q.v.

HALES, Jeremiah. Private, Worcester Militia, Sinepuxent Bn., Capt. William Purnell's Co., Third Class, 1779/1780 [Ref: M-252].

HALES, John. Took the Oath of Allegiance in Worcester County in 1778 in Bogerternorton Hundred before the Hon. Thomas Purnell [Ref: J-1814 (Box 4)].

HALL, Babel. Took the Oath of Allegiance in Somerset County in 1778 before the Hon. Peter Waters [Ref: T-18].

HALL, Charles Sr. Took the Oath of Allegiance in Somerset County in 1778 before the Hon. Peter Waters [Ref: T-18].

HALL, Charles (1761 -   ). Son of John and Ellis Hall, born in Coventry Parish on March 6, 1761 [Ref: Y-84]. Private, Somerset Militia, Princess Anne Bn., Capt. Isaac Handy's Great Annemessix Co., 1780 [Ref: M-221]. He may have been the Charles Hall who took the Oath of Allegiance in Somerset County in 1778 before the Hon. Peter Waters although he was not yet 18 years of age, but he was in his 18th year nonetheless [Ref: T-18].

HALL, David. See "Samuel Lockwood," q.v.

HALL, Elijah. Corporal, Somerset Militia, Princess Anne Bn., Capt. James Elzey's Co., 1780 [Ref: M-220].

HALL, Ellis. See "Charles Hall," q.v.

HALL, George. Private, Somerset Militia, Princess Anne Bn., Capt. Isaac Handy's Great Annemessix Co., 1780 [Ref: M-221].

HALL, James. Private, 3rd Maryland Independent Co., Worcester County, Capt. John Watkins' Co., enlisted Feb 12, 1776; muster roll dated Aug 20, 1776, present for duty [Ref: D-21]. Private, Somerset Militia, Princess Anne Bn., Capt. Isaac Handy's Great Annemessix Co., 1780 [Ref: M-221]. Took the Oath of Allegiance in Somerset County in 1778 before the Hon. John Williams [Ref: T-21, N-51].

HALL, John Sr. Took the Oath of Allegiance in Somerset County in 1778 before the Hon. Peter Waters [Ref: T-18]. See "Charles Hall," q.v.

HALL, John. Drafted from Somerset County on July 30, 1781 to serve in the Continental Army [Ref: L-35C].

HALL, John. Private, Worcester Militia, Wicomico Bn., Capt. William Handy's Co., Fifth Class, July 15, 1780 [Ref: M-257].

HALL, John. Private, Worcester Militia, Wicomico Bn., Capt. Robert Handy's Co., Eighth Class, July 15, 1780 [Ref: M-254].

HALL, Joshua. Took the Oath of Allegiance in Worcester County in 1778 in Buckingham Hundred before the Hon. Thomas Purnell [Ref: J-1814 (Box 4)].

HALL, Peter. Corporal, 3rd Maryland Independent Co., Worcester County, Capt. John Watkins' Co., enlisted Jan 29, 1776; muster roll dated Aug 20, 1776, present for duty [Ref: D-21].

HALL, Philip. Private, 3rd Maryland Independent Co., Worcester County, Capt. John Watkins' Co., enlisted Feb 3, 1776; muster roll dated Aug 20, 1776, present for duty [Ref: D-21].

HALL, Richard. Private, Worcester Militia, Sinepuxent Bn., Capt. John Rackliff's Co., Fifth Class, 1779/1780 [Ref: M-251]. Took the Oath of Allegiance in Worcester County in 1778 before the Hon. Nathaniel Miller [Ref: J-1814 (Box 4)].

HALL, Samuel. Private, Somerset Militia, Princess Anne Bn., Capt. John Williams' Watkins Point Co., 1780 [Ref: M-221]. Took the Oath of Allegiance in Somerset County in 1778 before the Hon. John Williams [Ref: T-21, N-51].

HALL, Sarah. See "James Tull," q.v.

HALL, Thomas. Private, Somerset Militia, Princess Anne Bn., Capt. Isaac Handy's Great Annemessix Co., 1780 [Ref: M-221].

HALL, William. Private, Worcester Militia, Sinepuxent Bn., Capt. John Postly's Co., Second Class, 1779/1780 [Ref: M-251 listed the name as "William(?) Hall(?)"].

HALL, William. Private, Somerset Militia, Salisbury Bn., Capt. Henry Gale's Quantico Co., 1778/1780 [Ref: M-216].

HALL, William. Private, Somerset Militia, Princess Anne Bn., Capt. George Waters' Pocomoke Co., 1780 [Ref: M-220].

HAMBLEN, Benjamin. See "Solomon Hamblin" and "Pierce Dant Hamblen," q.v.

HAMBLEN, Betsey. See "Pierce Dant Hamblen," q.v.

HAMBLEN, James. See "Solomon Hamblin," q.v.

HAMBLEN, Eliakim. See "Solomon Hamblin" and "Job Hamblen," q.v.

HAMBLEN, Ellender. See "Job Hamblen," q.v.

HAMBLEN, Franky. See "Pierce Dant Hamblen," q.v.

HAMBLEN, George. See "Solomon Hamblin" and "Job Hamblen" and "Pierce Dant Hamblen," q.v.

HAMBLEN (HAMBLIN), Job (1762-1833). Private, Virginia Line, who applied for a pension in Jennings County, Indiana on Oct 12, 1818, stating he was born on July 14, 1762 [in Worcester County, Maryland, brother of "Pierce Dant Hamblen," q.v.] and enlisted in Charlotte County, Virginia. He married Eleanor Mullings (or Nelly Mullins) on Sep 3 or Oct 6, 1782 in Pittsylvania County, Virginia and in 1827 they were in Bartholomew County, Indiana. Eleanor Hamblin applied for a pension (W10085) on June 9, 1845 in Brown County, Indiana, stating she was born on March 30, 1765 and Job had died on Sep 1, 1833. Their children were: John (b. Sep 3, 1783); Uriah (b. May 3, 1787); George (b. May 23, 1789, killed in the Battle of Mackinaw); William (b. March 29, 1793); Eliakim (b. July 26, 1796); Ellender (b. May 29, 1799); Sarah or Sally (b. May 26, 1802); and, Polly (no date was given). [Ref: W-1492].

HAMBLEN, John. See "Job Hamblen" and "Pierce Dant Hamblen," q.v.

HAMBLEN, Peter. See "Pierce Dant Hamblen," q.v.

HAMBLEN (HAMBLIN), Pierce Dant (1756 -   ). Private, Virginia Line, who applied for a pension (S2264) in Knox County, Kentucky on June 22, 1833, stating he was born in Worcester County, Maryland on March 24, 1756 and lived with his father George in Charlotte County, Virginia at the time of his enlistment. In 1820 he had eight children: Sally, age 35; George, age 33; John, age 29; Thomas, age 27; Vincent, age 25; Peter, age 23; Betsey, age 17; and, Franky, age 17. In 1833 his brother Benjamin Hamblen and sister Elizabeth T---- were also mentioned [Ref: W-1492 listed the name as "Pierce Dant Hamblin" and Q-29:2 (Spring, 1988), "The Benjamin Hamblens of Cecil, Kent and Worcester Cos., Maryland and Henry, Calloway and Whitely Cos., Kentucky," by John W. Hamblen (pp. 112-118) listed the name as "Pierce Dant Hamblen"]. See "Job Hamblen," q.v.

HAMBLEN, Piercy. See "Solomon Hamblin," q.v.
HAMBLEN, Polly. See "Job Hamblen," q.v.
HAMBLEN, Sally. See "Pierce Dant Hamblen" and "Job Hamblen," q.v.
HAMBLEN, Thomas. See "Pierce Dant Hamblen," q.v.
HAMBLEN, Uriah. See "Job Hamblen," q.v.
HAMBLEN, Vincent. See "Pierce Dant Hamblen," q.v.
HAMBLEN, William. See "Job Hamblen," q.v.
HAMBLIN, Eleanor. See "Job Hamblen," q.v.
HAMBLIN, John. Private, Worcester Militia, Sinepuxent Bn., Capt. Josiah Dale's Co., First Class, 1779/1780 [Ref: M-253].
HAMBLIN, Solomon. Private, Worcester Militia, Sinepuxent Bn., Capt. John Rackliff's Co., Sixth Class, 1779/1780 [Ref: M-251]. The will of Elizabeth Carey (neé Holloway) was probated in Sussex County, Delaware in 1774. She mentioned her daughters Mary Carey, Piercy Hamlin (Hamblin), Keziah Ridley, and Kerenhappuck Shockley, and son Solomon Hamblin. "George and Piercy Hamblen had already sold their Worcester County, Maryland land in 1771. Where they went next is still unknown. However, their grandson James Hamblen, of Transylvania, North Carolina, reported in the 1880 census that his father, Eliakim, was born in Pennsylvania. Eliakim's older brothers, Pierce Dant and Job, both served in the Revolutionary War and reported that they were born in Worcester County, Maryland in 1756 and 1762 respectively. The family was in Charlotte County, Virginia by 1777, Pittsylvania County, Virginia by 1780, and probably in Rockingham County, North Carolina circa 1795. Pierce Dant settled in Knox County, Kentucky, brother Benjamin and sister Elizabeth Hamblen Powers Tye settled first in Stokes County, North Carolina and then Whiteley County, Kentucky, brother George died in Shelby County, Kentucky, brother Job died in Brown County, Indiana in 1833, brother Eliakim was in South Carolina and North Carolina and later disappeared in the Southwest Territory, and sister Piercy married Jesse Powers and settled in Wayne County, Kentucky." [Ref: Q-29:3 (Summer, 1988), "A Hamblen-Carey-Holloway Connection in Worcester County, MD, 1700's," by John W. Hamblen, pp. 303-304].
HAMILTON, Sarah. See "Thomas Holbrook, Sr.," q.v.
HAMLIN, Maddux. Private, Worcester Militia, Wicomico Bn., Capt. James Perdue's Co., Seventh Class, July 15, 1780 [Ref: M-256].
HAMMOND, Edward. Private, Worcester Militia, Sinepuxent Bn., Capt. Elisha Purnell's Co., Sixth Class, 1779/1780 [Ref: M-253].
HAMMOND, Edward. Private, Worcester Militia, Sinepuxent Bn., Capt. William Purnell's Co., Sixth Class, 1779/1780 [Ref: M-252].
HAMMOND, Edward. Private, Worcester Militia, Sinepuxent Bn., Capt. Elisha Purnell's Co., Fourth Class, 1779/1780 [Ref: M-253].
HAMMOND, Edward. Took the Oath of Allegiance in Worcester County in 1778 in Quepomco Hundred before the Hon. Thomas Purnell [Ref: J-1814 (Box 4)].

Rendered patriotic service by supplying corn for the use of the military on April 28, 1780 and July 10, 1780 [Ref: P-287, G-10].

HAMMOND, Edward (of William). Took the Oath of Allegiance in Worcester County in 1778 before the Hon. Joshua Townsend [Ref: J-1814 (Box 4)].

HAMMOND, Edward (of William). Took the Oath of Allegiance in Worcester County in 1778 before the Hon. John Selby [Ref: J-1814 (Box 4)].

HAMMOND, Isaac Jr. Took the Oath of Allegiance in Worcester County in 1778 before the Hon. Joshua Townsend [Ref: J-1814 (Box 4)]. Private, Worcester Militia, Sinepuxent Bn., Capt. Thomas Purnell's Co., Second Class, 1779/1780 [Ref: M-253 listed the name without the "Jr."].

HAMMOND, Isaac Sr. Took the Oath of Allegiance in Worcester County in 1778 before the Hon. Joshua Townsend [Ref: J-1814 (Box 4)]. Private, Worcester Militia, Sinepuxent Bn., Capt. Thomas Purnell's Co., Fifth Class, 1779/1780 [Ref: M-253 listed the name without the "Sr."].

HAMMOND, James. Private, Somerset Militia, Princess Anne Bn., Capt. John Jones' Princess Anne Co., 1780 [Ref: M-219]. Took the Oath of Allegiance in Somerset County in 1778 (made his "H" mark) before the Hon. Peter Waters [Ref: T-18 listed the name as "James Hammon"].

HAMMOND, Sarah. See "Zedakiah Hammond," q.v.

HAMMOND, William. Private, Somerset Militia, Princess Anne Bn., Capt. Isaac Handy's Great Annemessix Co., 1780 [Ref: M-221]. Took the Oath of Allegiance in Worcester County in 1778 in Quepomco Hundred before the Hon. Thomas Purnell [Ref: J-1814 (Box 4)].

HAMMOND, Wilson (c1750-1796). Private, Somerset Militia, Princess Anne Bn., Capt. Isaac Handy's Great Annemessix Co., 1780 [Ref: M-221].

HAMMOND, Zedakiah (c1750-1787). Private, Worcester Militia, Sinepuxent Bn., Capt. Elisha Purnell's Co., Eighth Class, 1779/1780 [Ref: M-253]. Zedakiah Hammond was born circa 1759, married Sarah ----, was a private during the war, and died in October, 1787 [Ref: V-1294].

HANCOCK, Daniel Jr. Took the Oath of Allegiance in Worcester County in 1778 before the Hon. Nehemiah Holland [Ref: J-1814 (Box 4) listed the name as "Daniel Handcock, Jur."]. Private, Worcester Militia, Wicomico Bn., Capt. Fisher Walton's Co., Third Class, July 15, 1780 [Ref: M-258 listed the name without the "Jr."].

HANCOCK, Daniel Sr. Took the Oath of Allegiance in Worcester County in 1778 before the Hon. Nehemiah Holland [Ref: J-1814 (Box 4) listed the name as "Daniel Handcock, Senr."]

HANCOCK, Ebenezer. Private, Worcester Militia, Snow Hill Bn., Capt. John Parramore's Co., 1777 [Ref: M-250]. Private, Worcester Militia, Wicomico Bn., Capt. John Parramore's Co., First Class, July 15, 1780 [Ref: M-259]. Took the Oath of Allegiance in Worcester County in 1778 before the Hon. Nehemiah Holland [Ref: J-1814 (Box 4) listed the name as "Ebenezer Handcock"].

HANCOCK, Elijah. Private, Worcester Militia, Wicomico Bn., Capt. Elijah Shockley's Co., Second Class, July 15, 1780 [Ref: M-255].
HANCOCK, Henry. Private, Worcester Militia, Sinepuxent Bn., Capt. Josiah Dale's Co., Eighth Class, 1779/1780 [Ref: M-254].
HANCOCK, John Jr. Took the Oath of Allegiance in Worcester County in 1778 before the Hon. Nehemiah Holland [Ref: J-1814 (Box 4) listed the name as "John Handcock, Jur."]. Private, Worcester Militia, Snow Hill Bn., Capt. John Parramore's Co., 1777 [Ref: M-250]. Private, Worcester Militia, Wicomico Bn., Capt. John Parramore's Co., Second Class, July 15, 1780 [Ref: M-259 listed the name without the "Jr."].
HANCOCK, John Sr. Took the Oath of Allegiance in Worcester County in 1778 before the Hon. Nehemiah Holland [Ref: J-1814 (Box 4) listed the name as "John Handcock, Senr."]. Private, Worcester Militia, Sinepuxent Bn., Capt. Elisha Purnell's Co., Sixth Class, 1779/1780 [Ref: M-253 listed the name without the "Sr."].
HANCOCK, Joshua. Private, Worcester Militia, Wicomico Bn., Capt. Elijah Shockley's Co., Fifth Class, July 15, 1780 [Ref: M-255].
HANCOCK, Micajah. Private, Worcester Militia, Wicomico Bn., Capt. Elijah Shockley's Co., First Class, July 15, 1780 [Ref: M-255].
HANCOCK, Templin. Private, Worcester Militia, Sinepuxent Bn., Capt. Josiah Dale's Co., Fifth Class, 1779/1780 [Ref: M-254].
HANCOCK, Whittington. Private, Worcester Militia, Sinepuxent Bn., Capt. Elisha Purnell's Co., Eighth Class, 1779/1780 [Ref: M-253].
HANCOCK, William. Private, Worcester Militia, Wicomico Bn., Capt. Fisher Walton's Co., Fourth Class, July 15, 1780 [Ref: M-258]. Took the Oath of Allegiance in Worcester County in 1778 before the Hon. Nehemiah Holland [Ref: J-1814 (Box 4) listed the name as "William Handcock"].
HANCOCK, William Jr. Took the Oath of Allegiance in Worcester County in 1778 before the Hon. Nehemiah Holland [Ref: J-1814 (Box 4) listed the name as "William Handcock, Jur."].
HANDLY, Thomas. Private, Worcester Militia, Snow Hill Bn., Capt. Ebenezer Handy's Co., April 9, 1776 [Ref: M-249 listed the name as "Thomas Hanley"]. Private, Worcester Militia, Wicomico Bn., Capt. Robert Handy's Co., Second Class, July 15, 1780 [Ref: M-254]. Private, Maryland Troops, Worcester County, draughted May 1, 1781 [Ref: K-99, D-372 listed the name as "Thomas Handley"].
HANDLY, William. Private, Worcester Militia, Sinepuxent Bn., Capt. Thomas Purnell's Co., Seventh Class, 1779/1780 [Ref: M-253].
HANDY, Anne. See "Benjamin Wailes" and "Joseph Gilliss," q.v.
HANDY, Betty. See "Samuel Handy," q.v.
HANDY, Charles. See "Levin Handy," q.v.
HANDY, Ebenezer. Captain, Worcester Militia, 10th Bn., April 9, 1776 or June 15, 1776 (both dates were given). Major, Wicomico Bn., Aug 30, 1777. Lieutenant

Colonel, May 27, 1779. Colonel, June 12, 1782 [Ref: M-83, M-249, A-426, C-351, E-423, I-189]. Commissioned a Justice of the Orphans Court on June 4, 1777 [Ref: C-274]. Took the Oath of Allegiance in Worcester County in 1778 before the Hon. William Hopewell [Ref: J-1814 (Box 4)]. Justice who administered the Oath of Allegiance in Worcester County in 1778 [Ref: J-1814 (Box 4)]. Commissioned a Judge of the Court of Appeals for Worcester County on May 27, 1778 [Ref: E-112]. Justice of the Peace for Worcester County, commissioned on Nov 29, 1777 and Nov 21, 1778 and Jan 17, 1782 [Ref: C-428, E-249, I-45]. Rendered patriotic service by storing pork for the use of the military on July 28, 1781 [Ref: P-417]. Special Commission of Judge of the Court of Oyer and Terminer and Gaol Delivery issued to him and five others in Worcester County by the Governor and Council of Maryland on Dec 10, 1783 [Ref: I-488].

HANDY, Elizabeth. See "George Day Scott" and "Levin Handy," q.v.

HANDY, Esther. See "Levin Handy" and "William Polk," q.v.

HANDY, George (1727-1782). Took the Oath of Allegiance in Somerset County in 1778 before the Hon. Gillis Polk [Ref: T-15, N-51]. George Handy was born on Oct 10, 1727 in Maryland, married Nellie Gillis, rendered patriotic service during the war, and died on Nov 6, 1782 [Ref: V-1298].

HANDY, George Jr. (1756-1820). Second Lieutenant, Somerset Militia, Salisbury Bn., Capt. Conway's Co., Sep 22, 1777 [Ref: M-83 and C-381 listed the name without the "Jr."]. Took the Oath of Allegiance in Somerset County in 1778 before the Hon. John Span Conway [Ref: T-14, N-51]. George Handy was born on Nov 23, 1756, married Elizabeth Wilson, was a captain in the war, and died on July 19, 1820 [Ref: V-1298].

HANDY, Harriet. See "Samuel Handy," q.v.

HANDY, Henry (1747-1787). Ensign, Somerset Militia, Salisbury Bn., April 20, 1778 [Ref: M-83, E-42]. Rendered patriotic service by supplying wheat for the use of the military on May 14, 1781 [Ref: P-394]. Took the Oath of Allegiance in Somerset County on Feb 7, 1778 before the Hon. Joseph Venables [Ref: T-25]. Henry Winder was born in 1747, married Jane Winder, was an ensign during the war, and died in 1787 [Ref: V-1298].

HANDY, Isaac (1746-1826). First Lieutenant, Somerset Militia, Princess Anne Bn., Capt. William Waters' Co., Sep 22, 1777. Captain, Great Annemessix Co., from Dec 7, 1778 to Aug 22, 1781, succeeded [Ref: M-83, M-221, C-381, E-260, G-575]. Isaac Handy was born on June 17, 1746, married Amelia Curtis, was a captain during the war, and died in 1826 [Ref: V-1298].

HANDY, Isaac. Private, Somerset Militia, Salisbury Bn., Capt. Levin Irving's Black Water Co., 1778/1780 [Ref: M-218]. Select Militia, Somerset County, Aug 15, 1781 [Ref: L-35B].

HANDY, Isaac. See "William Polk," q.v.

HANDY, Jean. See "John Fleming," q.v.

HANDY, John. Took the Oath of Allegiance in Somerset County on Feb 28, 1778 before the Hon. Joseph Venables [Ref: T-25].
HANDY, John Sr. Took the Oath of Allegiance in Somerset County in 1778 before the Hon. Peter Waters [Ref: T-18].
HANDY, John Custis. See "Samuel Handy," q.v.
HANDY, Joseph. Private, Somerset Militia, Princess Anne Bn., Capt. George Waters' Pocomoke Co., 1780 [Ref: M-220]. On April 21, 1781 (rank or position not stated) he wrote to Col. George Dashiell (Somerset County) about "difficulty incurred while acquiring flagship." [Ref: P-385]. Select Militia, Somerset County, Aug 15, 1781 [Ref: L-35A]. He stated in a deposition on Nov 27, 1781 in Fairfax County, Virginia that he served in a party of light horse commanded by Col. Done in Somerset County, Maryland in June, 1781 when they apprehended a schooner on Colborn's Creek [Ref: H-559].
HANDY, Levin (1754-1799). Captain, 5th Maryland Line, Dec 10, 1776 to at least 1780 [Ref: D-212, F-150]. Took the Oath of Allegiance in Somerset County in 1778 before the Hon. Gillis Polk [Ref: T-15, N-51]. Levin Handy married Nancy Wilson on Feb 24, 1785 and died on June 5, 1799 in Worcester County. She applied for a pension (W9475) on Aug 13, 1838, age 69, and again on Aug 8, 1843, age 74, and the claim was allowed at $480 per annum from March 4, 1843. She filed a certificate from the Maryland Land Office showing that Levin Handy was appointed captain in the 5th Maryland Line on Dec 10, 1776. Mrs. Elizabeth Handy (nee Ker), age 70, deposed that Levin Handy and Nancy Wilson were married by Rev. Jacob Ker, her father, on Feb 24, 1785. Mrs. Henrietta Elzey, of Washington, was present at the wedding. A daughter Elizabeth Martin Handy was born on Nov 30, 1786 and was baptized by Rev. Ker on Feb 25, 1787. A daughter Esther W. Handy was living in 1846. On May 28, 1845, E. K. Wilson stated that Mrs. Handy died in May, 1845 and he applied in behalf of "my cousin, Miss Esther W. Handy, her mother's heir." On March 3, 1851, Charles W. Handy wrote to the Pension Bureau to examine the papers of his grandmother [Ref: W-1506, W-1507; U-39:4 (1951), p. 130]. Levin Handy was born on Aug 20, 1754, married E. Nancy Wilson, was a captain during the war, and died on June 5, 1799 [Ref: V-1298].
HANDY, Levin. Private, Somerset Militia, Salisbury Bn., Capt. Joseph Venables' Barren Creek Co., 1778/1780 [Ref: M-217].
HANDY, Levin. Ensign, Somerset Militia, Salisbury Bn., Capt. Henry Gale's Co., from Jan 7, 1778 to May 12, 1778, resigned [Ref: M-83, C-457, G-575]. Rendered patriotic service by storing flour and corn for the military on April 12, 1780 and Feb 19, 1781 [Ref: P-283, P-363].
HANDY, Martin Luther. Private, Somerset Militia, Salisbury Bn., Capt. Levin Irving's Black Water Co., 1778/1780 [Ref: M-218].
HANDY, Mary. See "Samuel Handy," q.v.
HANDY, Matthias. Private, Worcester Militia, Wicomico Bn., Capt. William Handy's Co., Eighth Class, July 15, 1780 [Ref: M-258]. Took the Oath of

Allegiance in Worcester County in 1778 before the Hon. John Selby [Ref: J-1814 (Box 4)].

HANDY, Robert. Captain, Worcester Militia, Wicomico Bn., Aug 30, 1777 to at least July 15, 1780 [Ref: M-83, M-254, C-351]. Took the Oath of Allegiance in Worcester County in 1778 before the Hon. William Hopewell [Ref: J-1814 (Box 4)].

HANDY, Samuel (1741-1828). Son of Samuel Handy. Born on Aug 15, 1741 in Coventry Parish and married Mary Gore on Nov 27, 1767 [Ref: Y-70; however, source R-403 states Samuel Handy, son of Samuel Handy and Mary Dennis, was born on March 5, 1751/2, died before June 10, 1828, and married Mary ---- by 1768; if so, he would have been only 16 or 17 years old (Samuel Handy, son of Samuel and Betty Handy, was born on Aug 15, 1741); source V-1298 states he was born circa 1741 and died on May 27, 1828; source S-3186 states he was born Aug 15, 1741 in Somerset County, married Mary Gore (1749-1825) on Nov 27, 1767, and died on May 25, 1828 at Snow Hill]. His children were: John Custis Handy (1768-1840) married Elizabeth Chaille (1770-1840); Harriet G.; Mary D.; and, a daughter (name unknown). Samuel attended the Maryland Conventions, 1774-1776, and signed the Association of the Freemen of Maryland on July 26, 1775. He served in the Lower House of the Maryland Legislature from Worcester County, 1781-1782; County Justice, 1775-1778; and, Commissioner of the Tax, 1777-1798 [Ref: R-403, R-404, O-4, O-23, A-67]. First Major, Worcester Militia, 24th Bn., Jan 6, 1776. Lieutenant Colonel, Sinepuxent Bn., Aug 30, 1777. Colonel, March 23, 1778 [Ref: M-83, C-350, and C-547 referred to him as "Esq."]. Took the Oath of Allegiance in Worcester County in 1778 before the Hon. John Selby [Ref: J-1814 (Box 4)]. Rendered patriotic service by supplying salt for the use of the military circa 1781 [Ref: P-464]. Due to the above confusion in his year of birth (1741 vs. 1751), plus there being another Samuel who was a private in the war, additional research will be necessary before drawing conclusions.

HANDY, Samuel. Private, Somerset Militia, Princess Anne Bn., Capt. Isaac Handy's Great Annemessix Co., 1780 [Ref: M-221]. Took the Oath of Allegiance in Somerset County on Feb 7, 1778 before the Hon. Joseph Venables [Ref: T-25]. This may be the Samuel Handy born in 1751. See the other "Samuel Handy," q.v.

HANDY, Sarah. See "Isaac Henry" and "Thomas Irving" and "John Dashiell (of Winder)," q.v.

HANDY, Thomas. Ensign, Somerset Militia, Princess Anne Bn., Capt. John Williams' Watkins Point Co., Dec 7, 1778 to at least July 24, 1780 [Ref: M-83, M-221, E-260]. Lieutenant, Worcester Militia, Capt. John Martin's Co., 1780/1781 [Ref: J-1814 (Box 12)]. Captain by June 10, 1781 when he supplied pork for the use of the military [Ref: P-403]. See "Isaac Henry," q.v.

HANDY, Thomas Jr. Took the Oath of Allegiance in Somerset County in 1778 before the Hon. John Williams [Ref: T-21, N-51].

HANDY, Thomas R. See "Samuel Tilghman," q.v.
HANDY, William. Private, Worcester Militia, Wicomico Bn., Capt. Philip Quinton's Co., First Class, July 15, 1780 [Ref: M-256]. Private, Maryland Troops, Worcester County, draughted May 1, 1781 [Ref: K-99, D-372].
HANDY, William. Took the Oath of Allegiance in Worcester County in 1778 before the Hon. William Hopewell [Ref: J-1814 (Box 4)]. Rendered patriotic service by supplying corn for the use of the military on March 7, 1780 and storing corn on Feb 21, 1781 [Ref: P-274, P-364].
HANDY, William. Took the Oath of Allegiance in Somerset County in 1778 before the Hon. William Winder [Ref: T-22]. Private, Select Militia, Somerset County, Aug 15, 1781 [Ref: L-35B].
HANDY, William Jr. First Lieutenant, Worcester Militia, 10th Bn., Capt. James Martin's Co., May 25, 1776. Captain, Snow Hill Bn., Aug 30, 1777. Captain, Wicomico Bn., July 15, 1780 [Ref: M-83, M-257, C-350, A-444].
HANDY, William (of Samuel). Justice of the Peace for Worcester County, commissioned on Nov 29, 1777 and Nov 21, 1778 and March 27, 1779 [Ref: C-429, E-249, E-327].
HANDY, William (of Thomas). Took the Oath of Allegiance in Worcester County in 1778 before the Hon. Joshua Townsend [Ref: J-1814 (Box 4)].
HANNAN, William. Private, Worcester Militia, Wicomico Bn., Capt. Elijah Shockley's Co., Fifth Class, July 15, 1780 [Ref: M-255].
HANWICK, Elie. Private, Maryland Line, from Worcester County, who was discharged on Dec 3, 1781 [Ref: I-11].
HARGIS, Thomas. Took the Oath of Allegiance in Worcester County in 1778 before the Hon. Nehemiah Holland [Ref: J-1814 (Box 4)].
HARMANSON, Rose Ann. See "Richard Waters, Jr." and "William Waters, Sr.," q.v.
HARMES, George. Took the Oath of Allegiance in Somerset County in 1778 [Ref: N-51].
HARMON, Abel. Private, Worcester Militia, Wicomico Bn., Capt. Samuel Smyley's Co., Fifth Class, July 15, 1780 [Ref: M-259]. Took the Oath of Allegiance in Worcester County in 1778 before the Hon. Joshua Townsend [Ref: J-1814 (Box 4)].
HARMON, Betsy. See "Lazarus Harmon," q.v.
HARMON, Jeremiah. Private, Worcester Militia, Wicomico Bn., Capt. John Parramore's Co., Sixth Class, July 15, 1780 [Ref: M-259]. Took the Oath of Allegiance in Worcester County in 1778 before the Hon. Joshua Townsend [Ref: J-1814 (Box 4)].
HARMON, Lazarus (c1758-1829). Private, 1st Maryland Line, who applied for a pension (S34911) on April 10, 1818, age 60, and in 1820 had a wife Betsy and sons John (age 18) and Joseph (age 12). [Ref: W-1522 listed the name as "Lazarus Harman or Harmon"]. Lazarus Harmon pensioned in Worcester County at $96 per annum effective April 10, 1818 and was dropped from roll

under Act of May 1, 1820 (reason not stated). He was reinstated on Sep 9, 1828 and died on June 18, 1829 (represented by Nathaniel Harmon, administrator). [Ref: U-45:4 (1957), p. 194; X-44, X-54].

HARMON, John. See "Lazarus Harmon," q.v.

HARMON, Joseph. See "Lazarus Harmon," q.v.

HARMON, Middleton (Midleton). Private, Worcester Militia, Wicomico Bn., Capt. Samuel Smyley's Co., Fifth Class, July 15, 1780 [Ref: M-259]. Private, Maryland Troops, Worcester County, draughted May 1, 1781 [Ref: K-99, D-372].

HARMON, Nathaniel. See "Lazarus Harmon," q.v.

HARMON, Nimrod. Took the Oath of Allegiance in Worcester County in 1778 before the Hon. Joshua Townsend [Ref: J-1814 (Box 4)].

HARPER, James. Private, Somerset Militia, Princess Anne Bn., Capt. George Waters' Pocomoke Co., 1780 [Ref: M-220].

HARPER, John. Private, Worcester Militia, Snow Hill Bn., Capt. Samuel Smyley's Co., 1777 [Ref: M-250]. Private, Worcester Militia, Wicomico Bn., Capt. Samuel Smyley's Co., Seventh Class, July 15, 1780 [Ref: M-259].

HARPER, Samuel A. (1762-1819). Private, Maryland Line, who applied for a pension (S34910) in Worcester County on May 13, 1818, age 56, received $96 per annum, and died on Oct 16, 1819 [Ref: X-44, W-1525].

HARPER, Samuel. Private, Worcester Militia, Wicomico Bn., Capt. John Parramore's Co., Eighth Class, July 15, 1780 [Ref: M-259].

HARPER, Sarah. See "John Tarr (of John)," q.v.

HARRIS (HAINES?), John. Private, Somerset Militia, Princess Anne Bn., Capt. James Elzey's Co., 1780 [Ref: M-220].

HARRIS, Ann. See "Isaac Giles" and "John Giles," q.v.

HARRIS, Barnaby. Private, Somerset Militia, Princess Anne Bn., Capt. Isaac Handy's Great Annemessix Co., 1780 [Ref: M-221].

HARRIS, Barton. See "Benton Harris," q.v.

HARRIS, Benton (c1716-1777). Probable son of John Harris, of Somerset County. Benton married Betty Hopkins Whittington, widow of William Whittington and daughter of Hampton Hopkins, but had no children, and died testate before September, 1777. He held many public offices in Worcester County, including Sheriff, 1745-1746, County Justice, 1762-1777, Deputy Commissary, 1743-1777, Lower House of the Maryland Legislature, 1757-1766, Justice of the Court of Oyer and Terminer and Gaol Delivery, 1770-1771, Chairman of the Committee of Observation, 1776, and Register of Wills, 1777 [Ref: R-412, A-457 referred to him as "Esq." and B-54 listed the name as "Barton Harris" and since there was a Barton Harris (c1760-1825) in Maryland during the war, additional research will be necessary before drawing conclusions]. Benton attended the Maryland Convention in 1776 and was appointed by the Maryland Convention in November, 1776 to be one of the Judges of Elections in Worcester County [Ref: O-36, O-55].

HARRIS, Charles. Private, Worcester Militia, Snow Hill Bn., Capt. Ebenezer Handy's Co., April 9, 1776 [Ref: M-249]. Private, Worcester Militia, Wicomico Bn., Capt. Robert Handy's Co., Second Class, July 15, 1780 [Ref: M-254].

HARRIS, George. Took the Oath of Allegiance in Somerset County in 1778 before the Hon. William Winder [Ref: T-22 listed the name as "George Harriss"].

HARRIS, George. Took the Oath of Allegiance in Worcester County in 1778 before the Hon. Joshua Townsend [Ref: J-1814 (Box 4) listed the name as "George Hariss"].

HARRIS, John. See "Benton Harris" and "Thomas Harris," q.v.

HARRIS, John (Pocomoke). Took the Oath of Allegiance in Somerset County in 1778 before the Hon. John Williams [Ref: T-21]. One John Harris married Mary Marshel in Coventry Parish on May 26, 1757 and their son John was born on March 29, 1760 [Ref: Y-83].

HARRIS, Littleton (1756 -   ). Son of Spencer and Sinah Harris, born in Coventry Parish on May 12, 1756 [Ref: Y-71]. Private, Somerset Militia, Princess Anne Bn., Capt. John Jones' Princess Anne Co., 1780 [Ref: M-219 listed the name as "Lill. Harris"]. Took the Oath of Allegiance in Somerset County in 1778 before the Hon. John Williams [Ref: T-21 listed the name as "Littleton Harriss"].

HARRIS, Littleton Jr. Took the Oath of Allegiance in Somerset County in 1778 [Ref: N-51].

HARRIS, Mary. See "Thomas Harris," q.v.

HARRIS, Spencer. Took the Oath of Allegiance in Somerset County in 1778 before the Hon. Peter Waters [Ref: T-18 listed the name as "Spencer Harriss"]. See "Littleton Harris," q.v.

HARRIS, Thomas (1755-c1845). Private, Maryland Line, who applied for a pension (S4686) in Newport, Campbell County, Kentucky on Nov 4, 1834, age 79, stating that he was born in Somerset County, Maryland on May 26, 1755 and lived there at the time of his enlistment. He served as a second sergeant when called to duty in April, 1781 in the Co. of Capt. Joseph Cohan. He had resided in Newport, Kentucky for more than 27 years and was well known to all the old settlers in that town, according to Col. R. M. Johnson, of Scott County (no date was given). On Oct 10, 1845, Thomas Woolen, of Marion County, Indiana, stated he knew Thomas Harris for more than 40 years and witnessed his marriage to Nancy Woolen, daughter of Edward Woolen, of Scott County, Kentucky some time prior to 1794. Johnston Woolen and several others were present, but now were all deceased. Also, a later entry (no date was given) mentioned Miss Marietta Kremm, granddaughter of Thomas Harris, who made an inquiry about "whether he was ever in the war of the revolution." Reference was also made to a Thomas Harris in Queen Anne's County, Maryland [Ref: A. W. Burns' abstracts on revolutionary soldiers of Maryland in Kentucky (pp. 17-18) at the Maryland Historical Society]. Additional research may be necessary before drawing conclusions. See "William Dean," q.v.

HARRIS, Thomas (1762 -   ). Son of John and Mary Harris, born in Coventry Parish on Aug 27, 1762 [Ref: Y-84]. Private, Somerset Militia, Princess Anne Bn., Capt. James Elzey's Co., 1780 [Ref: M-220].

HARRIS, William. Private, Somerset Militia, Salisbury Bn., White Haven Co., 1778/1780 [Ref: M-218].

HARRIS, William. Private, Somerset Militia, Salisbury Bn., Capt. Henry Gale's Quantico Co., 1778/1780 [Ref: M-216].

HARRIS, William. Private, Somerset Militia, Salisbury Bn., Capt. William Turpin's Rewastico Co., 1778/1780 [Ref: M-217].

HARRISON, Eramus. Private, Worcester Militia, Sinepuxent Bn., Capt. Josiah Dale's Co., First Class, 1779/1780 [Ref: M-253].

HARRISON, John. Private, Worcester Militia, Wicomico Bn., Capt. Samuel Horsey's Co., Third Class, July 15, 1780 [Ref: M-256].

HARRISON, Levi (Levie). Private, Somerset Militia, Salisbury Bn., Capt. Joseph Venables' Barren Creek Co., 1778/1780 [Ref: M-217]. Took the Oath of Allegiance in Somerset County in 1778 [Ref: N-51].

HARRISON, Levin. Took the Oath of Allegiance in Somerset County in 1778 before the Hon. William Winder [Ref: T-22].

HARRISON, Rouse. Private, Worcester Militia, Sinepuxent Bn., Capt. Josiah Dale's Co., Second Class, 1779/1780 [Ref: M-254].

HARRISON, William. Private, Worcester Militia, Snow Hill Bn., Capt. Samuel Smyley's Co., 1777 [Ref: M-250]. Took the Oath of Allegiance in Worcester County in 1778 before the Hon. Joshua Townsend [Ref: J-1814 (Box 4) listed the name as "William Harison"].

HART, Richard. Took the Oath of Allegiance in Somerset County in 1778 before the Hon. Levin Wilson [Ref: T-17].

HARTING, Solomon. Private, Worcester Militia, Snow Hill Bn., Capt. Ebenezer Handy's Co., April 9, 1776 [Ref: M-249].

HASTINGS, Joshua. Drafted from Somerset County on June 20, 1781 to serve in the Continental Army [Ref: L-35C].

HATH, Jacob. Private, Worcester Militia, Wicomico Bn., Capt. John Davis' Co., Eighth Class, July 15, 1780 [Ref: M-255].

HATH, James. Private, Worcester Militia, Wicomico Bn., Capt. James Perdue's Co., Second Class, July 15, 1780 [Ref: M-256].

HATH, Leah. See "William Adams," q.v.

HATH, Smith. Private, Worcester Militia, Wicomico Bn., Capt. Elijah Shockley's Co., Fifth Class, July 15, 1780 [Ref: M-255].

HATH, William. Took the Oath of Allegiance in Somerset County in 1778 before the Hon. Levin Wilson [Ref: T-17, N-51].

HATTON, Esther. See "James Phillips," q.v.

HATTON, Robert. Took the Oath of Allegiance in Somerset County in 1778 before the Hon. William Winder [Ref: T-22, N-51].

HATTON, William. Rendered patriotic service by driving cattle for the military in Somerset County on July 28, 1781 [Ref: P-417].
HAUZE, Barnaby. Drafted from Somerset County on June 20, 1781 to serve in the Continental Army [Ref: L-35C].
HAYCOCK, Daniel. Private, Somerset Militia, Princess Anne Bn., Capt. Isaac Handy's Great Annemessix Co., 1780 [Ref: M-221].
HAYDON, George. Recruited by Capt. Levin Handy and enlisted in the Continental Army in Worcester County on Feb 24, 1780 for 3 years, stating he was born in England [Ref: Z-40, and D-21 listed the name as "George Hadin" and stated he enlisted on Feb 12, 1780]. Private, 5th Maryland Line, listed as a recruit among others from Worcester County who were entitled to clothing from the Commissary of Stores on April 24, 1780 [Ref: F-150 listed the name as "George Heydon"].
HAYMAN, Charles Jr. Private, Worcester Militia, Wicomico Bn., Capt. Samuel Horsey's Co., Eighth Class, July 15, 1780 [Ref: M-257 listed the name without the "Jr."]. Rendered patriotic service by supplying bacon in Worcester County for the use of the military on Aug 5, 1781 [Ref: P-420 listed the name with the "Jr."].
HAYMAN, Charles Sr. Rendered patriotic service by supplying bacon in Worcester County for the use of the military on Oct 15, 1780 [Ref: P-326].
HAYMAN, Elizabeth. See "Benjamin Johnson," q.v.
HAYMAN, Handy. See "John Hayman, Jr." and "David Brown," q.v.
HAYMAN, Isaac. Private, Somerset Militia, Salisbury Bn., Capt. Josiah Dashiell's Wicomico Creek Co., 1778/1780 [Ref: M-218]. Private, Worcester Militia, Wicomico Bn., Capt. Samuel Horsey's Co., Eighth Class, July 15, 1780 [Ref: M-257].
HAYMAN, James. Private, Worcester Militia, Wicomico Bn., Capt. Samuel Horsey's Co., Fifth Class, July 15, 1780 [Ref: M-257].
HAYMAN, John Harris. Private, Somerset Militia, Salisbury Bn., Capt. Josiah Dashiell's Wicomico Creek Co., 1778/1780 [Ref: M-218].
HAYMAN, John Jr. (c1745-1824/34). Son of John Hayman (c1709-c1760) and Rachel Dorman (1712-1782/5). He married Edith (Ede) Riggin and a son Handy Hayman (1784-1872) married Polly Brown (1783-1850) in Somerset County in 1808 [Ref: Q-23:3 (Summer, 1982), "Ancestor Table of Willis Clayton Tull, Jr.," pp. 247-255]. Private, Somerset Militia, Princess Anne Bn., Capt. John Jones' Princess Anne Co., 1780 [Ref: M-219].
HAYMAN, Joshua. Private, Somerset Militia, Salisbury Bn., Capt. Josiah Dashiell's Wicomico Creek Co., 1778/1780 [Ref: M-218]. Private, Worcester Militia, Wicomico Bn., Capt. Samuel Horsey's Co., Seventh Class, July 15, 1780 [Ref: M-257].
HAYMAN, Martha. See "John Cathell," q.v.
HAYMAN, Rachel. Rendered patriotic service by supplying pork in Worcester County for the use of the military on Oct 15, 1780 [Ref: P-326].

HAYMAN, Revel. Private, Somerset Militia, Salisbury Bn., Capt. Josiah Dashiell's Wicomico Creek Co., 1778/1780 [Ref: M-218].

HAYMAN, Richard. Took the Oath of Allegiance in Worcester County in 1778 before the Hon. John Selby [Ref: J-1814 (Box 4)].

HAYNIE, Ezekiel. Assistant Surgeon, 2nd Maryland Line, 1781, who was paid for services on Jan 17, 1782; place of residence not stated [Ref: I-43].

HAYNIE (HAINEY), James. Second Lieutenant, Somerset Militia, Salisbury Bn., Capt. Levin Irving's Black Water Co., Sep 22, 1777. First Lieutenant, Black Water Co., April 17, 1781 [Ref: C-381, M-86 listed the name as "James Hayner" and M-217, H-195 listed the name as "James Hainey"]. Took the Oath of Allegiance in Somerset County on Feb 14, 1778 before the Hon. Joseph Venables [Ref: T-25]. Elected Sheriff of Somerset County and commissioned on Oct 22, 1779 [Ref: E-564]. Rendered patriotic service by supplying pork for the use of the military on May 26, 1781 [Ref: P-398 listed the name as "James Hainey"].

HAYNIE (HAINEY), Richard. Took the Oath of Allegiance in Somerset County on Feb 21, 1778 before the Hon. Joseph Venables [Ref: T-25]. Private, Somerset Militia, Salisbury Bn., Capt. Levin Irving's Black Water. Co., 1778/1780 [Ref: M-217 listed the name as "Richard Hainey"].

HAYNIE, Samuel. Took the Oath of Allegiance in Somerset County on Feb 28, 1778 before the Hon. Joseph Venables [Ref: T-25].

HAYWARD, John. Took the Oath of Allegiance in Somerset County in 1778 before the Hon. Peter Waters [Ref: T-18].

HAYWARD, John. Took the Oath of Allegiance in Somerset County on Feb 21, 1778 before the Hon. Joseph Venables [Ref: T-25].

HAYWARD, John. Justice of the Peace for Somerset County, commissioned on Jan 9, 1778 [Ref: C-464].

HAYWARD, John B. Private, Worcester Militia, Sinepuxent Bn., Capt. John Coe's Co., Eighth Class, 1779/1780 [Ref: M-252].

HAYWARD, Sarah. Rendered patriotic service by supplying beef for the use of the military in Worcester County on Oct 25, 1781 [Ref: P-450]. See "William Delastatious," q.v.

HAYWARD, Thomas. Colonel, Somerset Militia, 17th Bn., Jan 6, 1776. Colonel, Princess Anne Bn., Aug 30, 1777 to Jan 29, 1781, when he resigned his commission, stating "it not being in my power to execute that commission as I could wish the disaffection of the people is not to be bore with and not in my power to alter." [Ref: M-86, C-351, H-40]. Took the Oath of Allegiance in Somerset County in 1778 before the Hon. Peter Waters [Ref: T-18]. Attended the Maryland Convention in 1776 "for the express purpose of forming a new government" [Ref: O-36]. Appointed by the Maryland Convention in November, 1776 to be one of the Judges of Elections in Somerset County [Ref: O-55].

HAYWARD, Thomas. Private, 3rd Maryland Independent Co., Worcester County, Capt. John Watkins' Co., enlisted Feb 3, 1776; muster roll dated Aug 20, 1776, absent on furlough [Ref: D-22].

HAYWARD, William. Private, Worcester Militia, Sinepuxent Bn., Capt. John Coe's Co., Eighth Class, 1779/1780 [Ref: M-252].

HAYWARD, William. Second Lieutenant, Somerset Militia, Princess Anne Bn., Capt. George Waters' Co., Sep 22, 1777 [Ref: M-86, C-381]. Took the Oath of Allegiance in Somerset County in 1778 before the Hon. Peter Waters [Ref: T-18].

HAZARD, Elihu. Ensign, Worcester Militia, 10th Bn., Capt. Jesse Gray's Co., May 15, 1776, and Sinepuxent Bn., Capt. Josiah Dale's Co., 1779/1780 [Ref: M-86, M-254, A-426].

HAZZARD, Esther. See "Levin Oakey (Okey)," q.v.

HEARN, Benjamin (c1725-1802). Rendered patriotic service by supplying pork in Somerset County for the use of the military on May 2, 1781 and supplying bacon on June 10, 1781 [Ref: P-390, P-403].

HEARN, Ebenezer (1760-1840). Born in Maryland on Oct 11, 1760, married Dovey Walker, served as a private in North Carolina during the war, and died there on Jan 16, 1840 [Ref: V-1378]. "Ebenezer Hearne" applied for a pension (S6997) in Montgomery County, North Carolina on Jan 8, 1833, stating he was born in Somerset County, Maryland and lived in North Carolina at the time of his enlistment. Also mentioned in 1833 was a brother William Hearne and in 1834 a brother Stephen Hearne, Sr. made affidavit in Montgomery County [Ref: W-1589].

HEARN, Elijah. Private, Worcester Militia, Snow Hill Bn., Capt. Ebenezer Handy's Co., April 9, 1776 [Ref: M-249]. Private, Worcester Militia, Wicomico Bn., Capt. Robert Handy's Co., Fifth Class, July 15, 1780 [Ref: M-254].

HEARN, Elisha (1755-1812). Born in Maryland in 1755, married Fereby Johnson, served as a sailor and private in Georgia during the war, and died there in January, 1812 [Ref: V-1378]. "Elisha Hearne" was probably from Somerset or Worcester County. Additional research will be necessary before drawing conclusions.

HEARN, Elizabeth. See "Thomas Bird," q.v.

HEARN, Hannah. See "Samuel Parsons," q.v.

HEARN, John. Private, Worcester Militia, Snow Hill Bn., Capt. Ebenezer Handy's Co., April 9, 1776 [Ref: M-249]. Private, Worcester Militia, Wicomico Bn., Capt. James Perdue's Co., Fifth Class, July 15, 1780 [Ref: M-256]. Took the Oath of Allegiance in Worcester County in 1778 before the Hon. James Selby [Ref: J-1814 (Box 4) listed the name as "John Harne"].

HEARN, Stephen. See "Ebenezer Hearn," q.v.

HEARN, Tabitha. See "William Hearn," q.v.

HEARN, William (1746-1832). Born in Maryland in 1746, married Tabitha ----, served as a private in North Carolina during the war, and died in Alabama on

Sep 21, 1832 [Ref: V-1378]. "William Hearne" was a brother of "Ebenezer Hearn," q.v. Also see "Harris Austin," q.v.

HEATH, Priscilla. See "Esau Boston," q.v.

HEATH, Stephen. Private, Somerset Militia, Princess Anne Bn., Capt. John Jones' Princess Anne Co., 1780 [Ref: M-219]. Took the Oath of Allegiance in Worcester County in 1778 before the Hon. James Selby [Ref: J-1814 (Box 4)].

HEATH, William. Rendered patriotic service by supplying bacon for the use of the military in Somerset County on Aug 1, 1780 [Ref: P-305, V-1380].

HEATH, William Jr. Took the Oath of Allegiance in Somerset County in 1778 before the Hon. William Winder [Ref: T-22]. Private, Somerset Militia, Salisbury Bn., White Haven Co., 1778/1780 [Ref: M-219 listed the name without the "Jr."].

HEATH, Wilson (1733/4-1785). Private, Somerset Militia, Princess Anne Bn., Capt. John Jones' Princess Anne Co., 1780 [Ref: M-219]. Took the Oath of Allegiance in Somerset County in 1778 before the Hon. Levin Wilson [Ref: T-17, N-51]. Drafted from Somerset County on July 30, 1781 to serve in the Continental Army [Ref: L-35C]. Wilson Heath was born in 1733/4 in Maryland, married Rachel (Heath) Gibbons, served as a private during the war, and died in April, 1785 [Ref: V-1380].

HEATHER, Ephraim. Private, Worcester Militia, Sinepuxent Bn., Capt. Elisha Purnell's Co., Third Class, 1779/1780 [Ref: M-253].

HEATT, William R. Jr. Took the Oath of Allegiance in Somerset County in 1778 [Ref: N-51].

HENDERSON, Benjamin (1758 -   ). Private, Maryland Line and Sea Service, who applied for a pension (S31119) in Bracken County, Kentucky on Sep 16, 1833, stating he was born in Worcester County, Maryland on Jan 1, 1758 and lived there at the time of his enlistment. He moved to Accomack County, Virginia (date not given) and from there to Bracken County, Kentucky [Ref: W-1600]. "Benjaman Henderson" took the Oath of Allegiance in Worcester County in 1778 before the Hon. James Selby [Ref: J-1814 (Box 4)].

HENDERSON, Betty. See "John Paden (Peden)," q.v.

HENDERSON, Bishop. Private, Worcester Militia, Sinepuxent Bn., Capt. Thomas Purnell's Co., Second Class, 1779/1780 [Ref: M-253].

HENDERSON, Brittingham. Private, Worcester Militia, Snow Hill Bn., Capt. John Parramore's Co., 1777 [Ref: M-250]. Private, Worcester Militia, Wicomico Bn., Capt. John Parramore's Co., Sixth Class, July 15, 1780 [Ref: M-259]. Took the Oath of Allegiance in Worcester County in 1778 before the Hon. Nehemiah Holland [Ref: J-1814 (Box 4)]. The following appeared in the court records of Accomack County, Virginia (Court Orders, 1842-1845, p. 149) on March 27, 1843: "William Henderson, a lieutenant and captain in the Revolutionary War on Continental Establishment, has since died intestate and without issue, leaving his brother Brittingham Henderson his only heir at law who has since died intestate leaving five children: Edward Henderson, James Henderson, John

135

Henderson, Joseph Henderson and Nancy Henderson, his only heirs at law. Edward Henderson, James Henderson and John Henderson are still alive; Joseph Henderson died intestate leaving two children: Sebastian Henderson and Sally Henderson his only heirs at law. Nancy Henderson married Bundick Taylor and died intestate leaving four children: William, Sally, Henney, and Mary Bundick *[sic]* her only heirs at law." [Ref: Stratton Nottingham's *Soldiers and Sailors of the Eastern Shore of Virginia in the Revolutionary War*, pp. 64-65].

HENDERSON, Charles. Private, Somerset Militia, Salisbury Bn., Capt. William Turpin's Rewastico Co., 1778/1780 [Ref: M-217].

HENDERSON, Curtis. Private, Worcester Militia, Sinepuxent Bn., Capt. William Purnell's Co., Fourth Class, 1779/1780 [Ref: M-252]. Private, Worcester Militia, Wicomico Bn., Capt. Samuel Smyley's Co., Second Class, July 15, 1780 [Ref: M-259]. Took the Oath of Allegiance in Worcester County in 1778 in Bogerternorton Hundred before the Hon. Thomas Purnell [Ref: J-1814 (Box 4) listed the name as "Curtis Hendoson"].

HENDERSON, Edeth. See "Samuel Henderson," q.v.

HENDERSON, Edward. See "Brittingham Henderson," q.v.

HENDERSON, Ephraim. Private, Worcester Militia, Wicomico Bn., Capt. John Parramore's Co., Seventh Class, July 15, 1780 [Ref: M-259]. Took the Oath of Allegiance in Worcester County in 1778 before the Hon. James Selby [Ref: J-1814 (Box 4)].

HENDERSON, Isaac. Private, Worcester Militia, Wicomico Bn., Capt. Isaac Layfield's Co., Third Class, July 15, 1780 [Ref: M-257]. Took the Oath of Allegiance in Worcester County in 1778 before the Hon. Nehemiah Holland [Ref: J-1814 (Box 4)].

HENDERSON, Jacob. Private, Worcester Militia, Wicomico Bn., Capt. Isaac Layfield's Co., Eighth Class, July 15, 1780 [Ref: M-257]. Took the Oath of Allegiance in Worcester County in 1778 before the Hon. James Selby [Ref: J-1814 (Box 4)].

HENDERSON, James. Private, Worcester Militia, Wicomico Bn., Capt. Isaac Layfield's Co., Second Class, July 15, 1780 [Ref: M-257].

HENDERSON, James. See "Brittingham Henderson," q.v.

HENDERSON, Jenkins. Private, Worcester Militia, Wicomico Bn., Capt. Isaac Layfield's Co., Sixth Class, July 15, 1780 [Ref: M-257 listed the name as "Jenckins Henderson"]. Took the Oath of Allegiance in Worcester County in 1778 before the Hon. James Selby [Ref: J-1814 (Box 4)].

HENDERSON, Jesse. Private, Worcester Militia, Sinepuxent Bn., Capt. William Purnell's Co., First Class, 1779/1780 [Ref: M-252]. Took the Oath of Allegiance in Worcester County in 1778 in Bogerternorton Hundred before the Hon. Thomas Purnell [Ref: J-1814 (Box 4) listed the name as "Jesse Hendason"].

HENDERSON, John. See "Brittingham Henderson," q.v.

HENDERSON, John. Private, Worcester Militia, Sinepuxent Bn., Capt. Matthew Purnell's Co., Eighth Class, July 25, 1780 [Ref: M-252].

HENDERSON, John Trehearn (1755 -   ). Son of William and Mary Henderson, born in Coventry Parish on April 28, 1755 [Ref: Y-84]. Sergeant, Worcester Militia, Wicomico Bn., Capt. Isaac Layfield's Co., July 15, 1780 [Ref: M-257 listed the name as "John Trehorn Henderson"].

HENDERSON, Joseph. Sergeant, Worcester Militia, Wicomico Bn., Capt. Isaac Layfield's Co., July 15, 1780 [Ref: M-257]. Took the Oath of Allegiance in Worcester County in 1778 before the Hon. James Selby [Ref: J-1814 (Box 4)].

HENDERSON, Joseph. See "Brittingham Henderson," q.v.

HENDERSON, Leven. Took the Oath of Allegiance in Worcester County in 1778 before the Hon. Joshua Townsend [Ref: J-1814 (Box 4)].

HENDERSON, Levi. Private, Worcester Militia, Wicomico Bn., Capt. Isaac Layfield's Co., Sixth Class, July 15, 1780 [Ref: M-257].

HENDERSON, Mary. See "John Trehearn Henderson" and "William Merrell Henderson," q.v.

HENDERSON, Nancy. See "Brittingham Henderson," q.v.

HENDERSON, Sally. See "Brittingham Henderson," q.v.

HENDERSON, Samuel (1754 -   ). Son of Samuel and Edeth Henderson, born in Coventry Parish on Feb 4, 1754 [Ref: Y-84]. Private, Worcester Militia, Wicomico Bn., Capt. John Parramore's Co., Second Class, July 15, 1780 [Ref: M-259].

HENDERSON, Sebastian. See "Brittingham Henderson," q.v.

HENDERSON, Smart. Private, Worcester Militia, Wicomico Bn., Capt. Isaac Layfield's Co., Fifth Class, July 15, 1780 [Ref: M-257].

HENDERSON, Thomas. Private, Worcester Militia, Wicomico Bn., Capt. Isaac Layfield's Co., Sixth Class, July 15, 1780 [Ref: M-257]. Took the Oath of Allegiance in Worcester County in 1778 before the Hon. James Selby [Ref: J-1814 (Box 4)].

HENDERSON, William. Private, Worcester Militia, Wicomico Bn., Capt. John Parramore's Co., Eighth Class, July 15, 1780 [Ref: M-259]. Took the Oath of Allegiance in Worcester County in 1778 before the Hon. James Selby [Ref: J-1814 (Box 4)].

HENDERSON, William. Private, Worcester Militia, Sinepuxent Bn., Capt. Matthew Purnell's Co., Third Class, July 25, 1780 [Ref: M-252]. Took the Oath of Allegiance in Worcester County in 1778 before the Hon. Nathaniel Miller [Ref: J-1814 (Box 4)].

HENDERSON, William. See "Brittingham Henderson" and "John Trehearn Henderson" and "William Merrell Henderson," q.v.

HENDERSON, William Holland. Private, Worcester Militia, Wicomico Bn., Capt. Isaac Layfield's Co., Sixth Class, July 15, 1780 [Ref: M-257].

HENDERSON, William Merrell (1757 -   ). Son of William and Mary Henderson, born in Coventry Parish on Feb 10, 1757 [Ref: Y-84]. Private, Worcester

Militia, Wicomico Bn., Capt. Isaac Layfield's Co., Eighth Class, July 15, 1780 [Ref: M-257 listed the name s "William Merrill Henderson"].

HENDRY, William. Took the Oath of Allegiance in Somerset County in 1778 [Ref: N-51].

HENRY, Charles. See "John Henry" and "Isaac Henry," q.v.

HENRY, Charlotte. See "William Winder" and "John Henry," q.v.

HENRY, Dorothy. See "Isaac Henry," q.v.

HENRY, Francis. See "John Henry," q.v.

HENRY, Gertrude. See "William Purnell (of Eufa)," q.v.

HENRY, Hugh. See "Isaac Henry," q.v.

HENRY, Isaac (c1752-1802). Son of Rev. Hugh Henry and Sarah Handy. Isaac married his cousin Dorothy (Dolly) Henry, daughter of John Henry, by 1781, and their children were: Hugh (married Harriet Gale in 1802); Matilda (married Dr. Thomas Handy in 1801); Sarah Ann (married first to George Roberts in 1806 and second to Dr. Thomas Handy); John (married Rebecca ----); Robert (married Mary Mitchell in 1811); William (married Jane Hutton in Wilmington, Delaware in 1833 and died in Cecil County, Maryland in 1841); Charles (married Juliana Fassett in 1820); Mary Ann (married Peter Franklin in 1811); and, James. Isaac Henry served in the Lower House of the Maryland Legislature, 1779-1780, was a trustee of Washington Academy, 1779-1801, and died some time between October, 1801 and November, 1802 [Ref: Q-29:2 (Spring, 1988), pp. 148-149, "Henry Family," by Gale J. Belser; source R-435 did not name his children]. Isaac was an ensign in the Somerset Militia, Salisbury Bn., Capt. Levin Irving's Black Water Co., 1778/1780, and second lieutenant, April 17, 1781 [Ref: N-86, M-217, C-381, H-195]. He took the Oath of Allegiance in Somerset County on Feb 7, 1778 before the Hon. Joseph Venables [Ref: T-25]. See "John Henry," q.v.

HENRY, James. Took the Oath of Allegiance in Somerset County in 1778 before the Hon. Gillis Polk [Ref: T-15, N-51]. See "Isaac Henry," q.v.

HENRY, Jenkins. See "John Henry," q.v.

HENRY, John (c1714-1781). Son of Rev. John Henry (who immigrated to Somerset County from Ireland in 1710) and Mary King Jenkins, widow of Francis Jenkins and daughter of Robert King. John married Dorothy Rider and their sons were Rider Henry (aka Charles Rider Henry), Francis Jenkins Henry (aka Jenkins Henry, married Frances Purnell), John Henry Jr. (resided in Dorchester County, became a delegate to the Continental Congress, 1777-1779, and governor of Maryland, 1797-1798), and Robert Henry. Their daughters were Charlotte (married William Winder), Kiturah (married John Brown), Dorothy or Dolly (married Isaac Henry), Nancy (married Dr. William Wheyland), and Sarah (married John Radcliffe). John Henry was a County Justice in 1742, served in the Lower House of the Maryland Legislature from Worcester County, 1744-1758, was a colonel by 1749, and served in the Lower House from Dorchester County in 1766. He owned 5,700 acres in Dorchester,

Somerset and Worcester Counties and died testate before Sep 13, 1781 in Somerset County [Ref: R-435, R-436 lists one daughter as "Niturah" rather than "Kiturah" and V-1396 states John was born before Oct 1, 1715 and died before Sep 13, 1786]. He also rendered patriotic service by supplying provisions for the use of the military. On Jan 15, 1780 Joseph Dashiell, Commissary of Purchases for Worcester County, issued a receipt for corn to Col. John Henry. On May 14, 1781 William McBryde, Commissary of Purchases for Somerset County, issued a receipt for pork to John Henry [Ref: P-261, P-394]. See "John Noble" and "William Winder, Jr." and "Isaac Henry," q.v.

HENRY, Kiturah. See "John Henry," q.v.

HENRY, Mary. See "Isaac Henry," q.v.

HENRY, Matilda. See "Isaac Henry," q.v.

HENRY, Nancy. See "John Henry," q.v.

HENRY, Rebecca. See "Isaac Henry," q.v.

HENRY, Robert. See "Isaac Henry," q.v.

HENRY, Robert Jenkins (1755 -   ). Son of Robert Jenkins Henry and Gertrude Rousby [Ref: R-437]. Private, Somerset Militia, Princess Anne Bn., Capt. George Waters' Pocomoke Co., 1780 [Ref: M-220]. Drafted from Somerset County on July 30, 1781 to serve in the Continental Army [Ref: L-35C].

HENRY, Rider. Private, Select Militia, Somerset County, Aug 15, 1781 [Ref: L-35B]. See "John Henry," q.v.

HENRY, Sarah. See "John Henry" and "Isaac Henry," q.v.

HENSON, Jonathan. Ensign, Worcester Militia, Snow Hill Bn., Capt. James Patterson's Co., Aug 30, 1777 [Ref: M-87, C-351].

HICKMAN, David. Private, Somerset Militia, Salisbury Bn., Capt. John Span Conway's Nanticoke Point Co., 1778/1780 [Ref: M-216]. See "Joseph Gilliss," q.v.

HICKMAN, Joshua. Private, Worcester Militia, Sinepuxent Bn., Capt. John Postly's Co., Second Class, 1779/1780 [Ref: M-251]. Took the Oath of Allegiance in Worcester County in 1778 before the Hon. Nehemiah Holland [Ref: J-1814 (Box 4)].

HICKMAN, Stephin. Private, Somerset Militia, Salisbury Bn., Capt. Henry Gale's Quantico Co., 1778/1780 [Ref: M-216].

HICKMAN, William. Private, Somerset Militia, Capt. George Day Scott's Co., 1775 [Ref: J-1814 (Box 1)]. Private, Worcester Militia, Sinepuxent Bn., Capt. John Postly's Co., Seventh Class, 1779/1780 [Ref: M-251].

HILL, Broadwater. Private, Worcester Militia, Wicomico Bn., Capt. James Patterson's Co., Eighth Class, July 15, 1780 [Ref: M-258].

HILL, Charles Phillips. Private, Worcester Militia, Wicomico Bn., Capt. Samuel Horsey's Co., Fourth Class, July 15, 1780 [Ref: M-257 listed the name as "Charles Phillips Hill (Liett?)"].

HILL, Christian. See "George Howard Aydelott," q.v.

HILL, Elisha. Private, Worcester Militia, Snow Hill Bn., Capt. Samuel Smyley's Co., 1777 [Ref: M-250]. Private, Worcester Militia, Sinepuxent Bn., Capt. Matthew Purnell's Co., Third Class, July 25, 1780 [Ref: M-252].
HILL, Frederick. Private, Worcester Militia, Snow Hill Bn., Capt. Ebenezer Handy's Co., April 9, 1776. Ensign, Somerset Militia, Capt. Robert Handy's Co., Feb 19, 1777. Ensign, Worcester Militia, Capt. Robert Handy's Co., Aug 30, 1777. First Lieutenant, Somerset Militia, Princess Anne Bn., Capt. Robert Handy's Co., Sep 22, 1777 [Ref: M-87, M-249, C-144, C-351, C-381]. "Fredrick Hill" took the Oath of Allegiance in Worcester County in 1778 before the Hon. William Hopewell [Ref: J-1814 (Box 4)].
HILL, Isaac. Private, Worcester Militia, Sinepuxent Bn., Capt. John Rackliff's Co., First Class, 1779/1780 [Ref: M-251]. Took the Oath of Allegiance in Worcester County in 1778 before the Hon. Nathaniel Miller [Ref: J-1814 (Box 4)].
HILL, Isaac. Private, Worcester Militia, Sinepuxent Bn., Capt. Matthew Purnell's Co., Sixth Class, July 25, 1780 [Ref: M-252]. Took the Oath of Allegiance in Worcester County in 1778 before the Hon. Nathaniel Miller [Ref: J-1814 (Box 4)].
HILL, James. Sergeant, Somerset Militia, Princess Anne Bn., St. Asaph's Co., 1780 [Ref: M-220].
HILL, Johnson. Took the Oath of Allegiance in Worcester County in 1778 before the Hon. Nathaniel Miller [Ref: J-1814 (Box 4)].
HILL, Levin (c1743-1801). Ensign, Worcester Militia, Snow Hill Bn., Capt. John Parramore's Co., Aug 30, 1777. Ensign, Worcester Militia, Wicomico Bn., Capt. John Parramore's Co., July 15, 1780 [Ref: M-87, M-250, M-259, C-351, V-1424]. Took the Oath of Allegiance in Worcester County in 1778 before the Hon. Nehemiah Holland [Ref: J-1814 (Box 4)].
HILL, Micajah. Took the Oath of Allegiance in Worcester County in 1778 before the Hon. Nathaniel Miller [Ref: J-1814 (Box 4)].
HILL, Milcah. See "Henry Gale," q.v.
HILL, Stephen. Private, Worcester Militia, Sinepuxent Bn., Capt. John Rackliff's Co., Fifth Class, 1779/1780 [Ref: M-251]. Took the Oath of Allegiance in Worcester County in 1778 before the Hon. John Selby [Ref: J-1814 (Box 4)].
HILL, William. Private, Somerset Militia, Princess Anne Bn., Capt. John Jones' Princess Anne Co., 1780 [Ref: M-219].
HILL, William. Took the Oath of Allegiance in Worcester County in 1778 before the Hon. Nathaniel Miller [Ref: J-1814 (Box 4)].
HILL, William Stevens. Private, Worcester Militia, Wicomico Bn., Capt. William Handy's Co., Second Class, July 15, 1780 [Ref: M-257].
HILL, Zorababel. Private, Worcester Militia, Wicomico Bn., Capt. James Patterson's Co., Fifth Class, July 15, 1780 [Ref: M-258]. Took the Oath of Allegiance in Worcester County in 1778 before the Hon. James Selby [Ref: J-1814 (Box 4)].
HILLMAN, Betsey and Biddy. See "William Hillman," q.v.

HILLMAN, Esther. See "Jonathan Jenkins," q.v.
HILLMAN, Ezekiel. Private, Somerset Militia, Salisbury Bn., Capt. Josiah Dashiell's Wicomico Creek Co., 1778/1780 [Ref: M-218 listed the name as "Ezekiel Hilman"].
HILLMAN, George. See "William Hillman," q.v.
HILLMAN, John. Private, Somerset Militia, Salisbury Bn., Capt. Josiah Dashiell's Wicomico Creek Co., 1778/1780 [Ref: M-218 listed the name as "John Hilman"].
HILLMAN, Joshua. Took the Oath of Allegiance in Somerset County on Feb 21, 1778 before the Hon. Joseph Venables [Ref: T-25 listed the name as "Joshua Hilmon"]. Sergeant, Somerset Militia, Salisbury Bn., Capt. Josiah Dashiell's Wicomico Creek Co., 1778/1780 [Ref: M-218].
HILLMAN, Nancy and Nelly. See "William Hillman," q.v.
HILLMAN, William (1753-1822). Private, Somerset Militia, Salisbury Bn., White Haven Co., 1778/1780 [Ref: M-218 listed the name as "William Hilman"]. Private, 5th Maryland Line, enlisted on Dec 10, 1776 and discharged on Jan 12, 1780 [Ref: D-212]. He applied for pension on May 14, 1818, age 65, stating he enlisted at Salisbury. He received $96 per annum and died on Aug 16, 1822. His widow Sally (maiden name not given) applied for a pension (W4230) on Aug 23, 1841, age 87, stating she married William on Oct 15, 1785 and he died in Somerset County on Aug 16, 1822. Their children were: Nancy (still living in 1841); Nelly (b. April 1, 1789 and d. about 1830); George (b. in August, 1793 and d. about 1825); Betsey (b. April 1, 1795); Biddy (b. Feb 19, 1796 and still living in 1842); and, William (b. Oct 14, 1799 and d. in November, 1831). [Ref: X-41, W-1643].
HILYARD, William. Took the Oath of Allegiance in Somerset County in 1778 before the Hon. John Williams [Ref: N-51, and T-21 listed the name as "William Hildyard"].
HINMAN, James. Took the Oath of Allegiance in Worcester County in 1778 before the Hon. Joshua Townsend [Ref: J-1814 (Box 4)].
HINSON, James. Second Lieutenant, Worcester Militia, Snow Hill Bn., Capt. James Patterson's Co., Aug 30, 1777 [Ref: M-87, C-351].
HISLUP, Kendall. Private, 3rd Maryland Independent Co., Worcester County, Capt. John Watkins' Co., enlisted Feb 2, 1776; muster roll dated Aug 20, 1776, present for duty [Ref: D-22].
HITCH, --?--. Private, Somerset Militia, Salisbury Bn., Capt. Levin Irving's Black Water Co., 1778/1780 [Ref: M-218].
HITCH, Benjamin. Private, Somerset Militia, Salisbury Bn., Capt. Josiah Dashiell's Wicomico Creek Co., 1778/1780 [Ref: M-218]. Rendered patriotic service by supplying pork for the use of the military on May 17, 1781 [Ref: P-395].
HITCH, Christopher (c1726-1805). Born in Maryland circa 1736, married Susannah or Rebecca ----, rendered patriotic service during the war, and died in Virginia before July 22, 1805 [Ref: V-1436]. He may have been from

Somerset or Worcester County. Additional research will be necessary before drawing conclusions.

HITCH, Elias. Private, Somerset Militia, Salisbury Bn., Capt. Levin Irving's Black Water Co., 1778/1780 [Ref: M-218]. Took the Oath of Allegiance in Somerset County on Feb 21, 1778 (made his "X" mark) before the Hon. Joseph Venables [Ref: T-25].

HITCH, Elijah. Private, Somerset Militia, Salisbury Bn., Capt. Levin Irving's Black Water Co., 1778/1780 [Ref: M-218].

HITCH, Ezekiel (1748-1828). Private, Somerset Militia, Salisbury Bn., Capt. Levin Irving's Black Water Co., 1778/1780 [Ref: M-217]. Drafted from Somerset County on July 30, 1781 to serve in the Continental Army [Ref: L-35C]. Ezekiel Hitch was born in Maryland in 1748, married Betsy Piper, served as a private during the war, and died on Sep 3, 1828 [Ref: V-1436].

HITCH, George. Private, Somerset Militia, Salisbury Bn., Capt. Levin Irving's Black Water Co., 1778/1780 [Ref: M-217].

HITCH, Joshua. Rendered patriotic service by supplying pork in Somerset County for the use of the military on May 14, 1781 [Ref: P-394].

HITCH, Louther (1743-1831). Born in Maryland in 1743, married first to Mary Nicholson and second to Elizabeth Douglas, served as a private during the war, and died in South Carolina in 1831 [Ref: V-1536]. He may have been from Somerset or Worcester County. Additional research will be necessary before drawing conclusions.

HITCH, Robert. Captain, Somerset Militia, 1st Bn., April 11, 1776 [Ref: M-87, A-327].

HITCH, Samuel (1741-1825). Born in Maryland in 1741, married Lydia Allen, served as a corporal during the war in Massachusetts, and died there on March 12, 1825 [Ref: V-1436]. He may have been from Somerset or Worcester County. Additional research will be necessary before drawing conclusions.

HITCH, Severn. Quartermaster, Somerset Militia, 1st Bn., Jan 6, 1776 [Ref: M-87]. Took the Oath of Allegiance in Worcester County in 1778 before the Hon. William Hopewell [Ref: J-1814 (Box 4)].

HITCH, Susanna or Rebecca. See "Christopher Hitch," q.v.

HITCH, Thomas. Sergeant, Somerset Militia, Salisbury Bn., Capt. Levin Irving's Black Water Co., 1778/1780 [Ref: M-217]. Took the Oath of Allegiance in Somerset County on Feb 21, 1778 before the Hon. Joseph Venables [Ref: T-25].

HOBBS, John. Private, Somerset Militia, Salisbury Bn., Capt. William Turpin's Rewastico Co., 1778/1780 [Ref: M-217].

HOBBS, Levin. Private, Worcester Militia, Snow Hill Bn., Capt. Ebenezer Handy's Co., April 9, 1776 [Ref: M-249]. Took the Oath of Allegiance in Worcester County on Feb 25, 1778 before the Hon. Ebenezer Handy [Ref: J-1814 (Box 4)].

HOBBS, Marselliss. Took the Oath of Allegiance in Worcester County on Feb 25, 1778 before the Hon. Ebenezer Handy [Ref: J-1814 (Box 4)].

HOBBS, Matthias (1734-1798). Corporal, Somerset Militia, Salisbury Bn., White Haven Co., 1778/1780 [Ref: M-218]. Born in 1734 in England, married Mary Rencher, served as a corporal during the war, and died in Maryland in 1798 [Ref: V-1442].

HODGE, Joshua. Private, Worcester Militia, Sinepuxent Bn., Capt. Matthew Purnell's Co., Second Class, July 25, 1780 [Ref: M-252].

HOGSHER (HOGSTLER?), Thomas. Took the Oath of Allegiance in Worcester County in 1778 in Bogerternorton Hundred before the Hon. Thomas Purnell [Ref: J-1814 (Box 4)]. Private, Worcester Militia, Sinepuxent Bn., Capt. William Purnell's Co., Second Class, 1779/1780 [Ref: M-252].

HOLBROOK, Henry (1761 -   ). Son of Thomas and Sarah Holbrook, born in Stepney Parish on Nov 1, 1761 [Ref: Y-45]. Private, Somerset Militia, Salisbury Bn., White Haven Co., 1778/1780 [Ref: M-219].

HOLBROOK, John. Private, Somerset Militia, Salisbury Bn., Capt. John Span Conway's Nanticoke Point Co., 1778/1780 [Ref: M-216]. Took the Oath of Allegiance in Somerset County in 1778 before the Hon. John Span Conway [Ref: T-14].

HOLBROOK, John. Private, Somerset Militia, Salisbury Bn., White Haven Co., 1778/1780 [Ref: M-219].

HOLBROOK, Sarah. See "Henry Holbrook" and "Thomas Holbrook" and "Thomas Holbrook, Jr.," q.v.

HOLBROOK, Thomas Jr. (1757 -   ). Son of Thomas and Sarah Holebrook *[sic]*, born in Stepney Parish on July 7, 1757 [Ref: Y-42]. Took the Oath of Allegiance in Somerset County in 1778 before the Hon. John Span Conway [Ref: T-14]. Private, Somerset Militia, Salisbury Bn., White Haven Co., 1778/1780 [Ref: M-219 listed the name without the "Jr."]. Ensign, April 17, 1781 [Ref: H-195].

HOLBROOK, Thomas Sr. Took the Oath of Allegiance in Somerset County in 1778 before the Hon. John Span Conway [Ref: T-14]. Thomas Holebrook *[sic]* married Sarah Hamilton (widow) in Stepney Parish on Aug 20, 1756 [Ref: Y-42]. See "Henry Holbrook," q.v.

HOLDEN (HOLDER), Esther. See "Kemp Holder," q.v.

HOLDEN (HOLDER), Sally. See "Kemp Holder," q.v.

HOLDEN (HOLDER), William, et al. See "Kemp Holder," q.v.

HOLDER, James. Private, Somerset County, Capt. John Gunby's 2nd Independent Maryland Co.; present on March 14, 1776; "deserted" on June 24, 1776; mustered on Aug 21, 1776 [Ref: D-641]. See "Kemp Holder," q.v.

HOLDER, John. Private, Somerset County, Capt. John Gunby's 2nd Independent Maryland Co.; present on April 9, 1776; mustered on Aug 21, 1776 [Ref: D-641]. He may have been the John Holder who was a private in Maryland during the war and died in Delaware in 1792 [Ref: V-1458]. Additional research will be necessary before drawing conclusions. See "Kemp Holder," q.v.

HOLDER, Kemp. Private, Maryland Line, whose great-niece Esther Holden (or Holder) applied for his bounty land (#2268-100) on May 20, 1829 in Somerset County as one of the heirs of Kemp Holden (or Holder), deceased soldier. On Oct 12, 1837 Sally Holden (or Holder), age nearly 65, made affidavit in Somerset County in support of Esther's claim. Other heirs shown were Hetty, William, Zebedee and Amelia Holden (or Holder), Sally Sloyd, and Louisa Green, being the children of William Holden (or Holder), a son of Kemp's deceased brother James Holden (or Holder). A John Holden (or Holder) had enlisted with Kemp Holden (or Holder) on April 7, 1777, but no relationship was given [Ref: W-1676 listed the name as "Kemp Holden or Holder"].

HOLDER, Sally. See "Kemp Holder," q.v.

HOLDER, William, et al. See "Kemp Holder," q.v.

HOLISTON, John. Private, Worcester Militia, Wicomico Bn., Capt. Samuel Smyley's Co., Eighth Class, July 15, 1780 [Ref: M-259].

HOLLAND, Anne. See "Nehemiah Holland," q.v.

HOLLAND, Benjamin. Private, Worcester Militia, Wicomico Bn., Capt. Fisher Walton's Co., Fifth Class, July 15, 1780 [Ref: M-258]. Took the Oath of Allegiance in Worcester County in 1778 before the Hon. Nehemiah Holland [Ref: J-1814 (Box 4)]. On Aug 15, 1780, along with John Tarr and James Collins, he petitioned the Council of Maryland with a proposal to manufacture salt in Worcester County for the use of the State [Ref: G-48].

HOLLAND, Isaac. Took the Oath of Allegiance in Somerset County in 1778 before the Hon. Levin Wilson [Ref: T-17, N-51].

HOLLAND, Israel. See "William Holland," q.v.

HOLLAND, James. Private, Somerset Militia, Princess Anne Bn., Capt. George Waters' Pocomoke Co., 1780 [Ref: M-220].

HOLLAND, John (1746 -   ). Son of Samuel Holland and Tabitha Campbell, born in Worcester Parish on April 26, 1746 [Ref: Y-30]. Private, Worcester Militia, Sinepuxent Bn., Capt. Josiah Dale's Co., Fourth Class, 1779/1780. Ensign, March 16, 1781, Capt. Josiah Dale's Co. [Ref: M-88, M-254, G-353]. Rendered patriotic service by supplying corn for the use of the military on June 14, 1780 and hauling corn on Oct 7, 1780 [Ref: P-296, P-324].

HOLLAND, Levi. Private, Worcester Militia, Wicomico Bn., Capt. Philip Quinton's Co., Third Class, July 15, 1780 [Ref: M-256].

HOLLAND, Levi. Sergeant, Somerset Militia, Princess Anne Bn., Capt. Henry Miles' Little Annemessex Co., 1780 [Ref: M-221]. Took the Oath of Allegiance in Somerset County in 1778 before the Hon. John Williams [Ref: T-21, N-51].

HOLLAND, Levin. Private, Worcester Militia, Sinepuxent Bn., Capt. William Purnell's Co., Third Class, 1779/1780 [Ref: M-252]. Took the Oath of Allegiance in Worcester County in 1778 in Bogerternorton Hundred before the

Hon. Thomas Purnell [Ref: J-1814 (Box 4) listed the name as "Leven Hollond"].

HOLLAND, Mary. See "Michael Holland, Jr.," q.v.

HOLLAND, Michael. Private, Worcester Militia, Sinepuxent Bn., Capt. Elisha Purnell's Co., Sixth Class, 1779/1780 [Ref: M-253].

HOLLAND, Michael Jr. (1752 -   ). Took the Oath of Allegiance in Somerset County in 1778 before the Hon. John Williams [Ref: T-21, N-51]. Michael Holland, son of Michael and Mary Holland, was born in Coventry Parish on Nov 16, 1752 [Ref: Y-71]. He was probably the "Michael Holland" who was a private, Somerset Militia, Salisbury Bn., Capt. Joseph Venables' Barren Creek Co., 1778/1780 [Ref: M-217]. Sergeant, Somerset Militia, Princess Anne Bn., Capt. John Williams' Watkins Point Co., 1780 [Ref: M-221]. See "Michael Holland, Jr.," q.v.

HOLLAND, Nehemiah (c1730-1788). Son of Nehemiah Holland (d. c1760). He married Scarborough ---- by 1771 (she married second to Peter Chaille) and their children were John, William, Nehemiah, Thomas, Peter, and Anne. Nehemiah served in the Lower House of the Maryland Legislature from Worcester County between 1771 and 1783; County Court Justice, 1768-1785; Justice of the Peace and Justice of the Orphans Court, 1777-1785 [Ref: R-446, C-274, C-429, E-249, I-46]. Justice who administered the Oath of Allegiance in Worcester County in 1778 [Ref: J-1814 (Box 4)]. Commissioned by the Council of Maryland on Aug 19, 1779 to receive subscriptions for the Continental Loan Office [Ref: E-499]. Also rendered patriotic service by supplying corn for the use of the military on March 4, 1780 [Ref: P-274]. Special Commission of Judge of the Court of Oyer and Terminer and Gaol Delivery issued to him and five others in Worcester County by the Governor and Council of Maryland on Dec 10, 1783 [Ref: I-488]. See "William Holland," q.v.

HOLLAND, Nehemiah. Sergeant, Worcester Militia, Wicomico Bn., Capt. Samuel Smyley's Co., July 15, 1780 [Ref: M-259].

HOLLAND, Peter. See "Nehemiah Holland," q.v.

HOLLAND, Rebecca. See "William Holland," q.v.

HOLLAND, Samuel (1752 -   ). Son of Samuel Holland and Tabitha Campbell, born in Worcester Parish on Feb 21, 1752 [Ref: Y-30]. Private, Worcester Militia, Sinepuxent Bn., Capt. Josiah Dale's Co., Second Class, 1779/1780 [Ref: M-254]. See "John Campbell," q.v.

HOLLAND, Sarah. See "John Tarr (of John)," q.v.

HOLLAND, Scarborough. See "Nehemiah Holland" and "Peter Chaille," q.v.

HOLLAND, Thomas. See "Nehemiah Holland" and "James Atkinson," q.v.

HOLLAND, William. "There are at least five William Hollands in Worcester County of age by 1777: William Holland (c1707-1786), son of Nehemiah Holland (d. 1721) and uncle of Nehemiah Holland (d. 1788); William Holland, son of Nehemiah Holland (d. 1760) and brother of Nehemiah Holland (d.

1788); William Holland (b. c1735 - d. after 1786), son of William Holland (c1707-1786); William Holland (b. c1740), son of Israel Holland and first cousin of Nehemiah Holland (d. 1788); and, William Holland (b. c1755 - d. after 1788), son of Nehemiah Holland (d. 1788). There is no information in the legislative proceedings that indicates which of these five men was elected to the Lower House in 1778. The *Maryland Archives* and *Inventory of Maryland State Papers* contain references to a Major William Holland who was commissioned a captain in 1777 and a major in 1779 in the Snow Hill Bn. of the Worcester County Militia. Major William Holland is listed with his title in the 1790 census for Worcester County and may be the William Holland who died in 1805 (only the administrative bond in the name of Rebecca Holland exists for his estate). Because of his military service, Major William Holland would have been ineligible to serve in the legislature. Because of his age, family connections, and wealth, it seems probable that William Holland (probably c1755 - d. after 1788), son of Nehemiah Holland (d. 1788), was the Major Holland and hence not the legislator. William Holland (c1707-1786) probably could be eliminated from consideration for this legislative service because of his age. Even if these two men are assumed not to have served, there are, however, still the three others who could have." [Ref: R-446, R-447]. See the William Hollands that follow. Additional research will be necessary before drawing conclusions. Also see "Nehemiah Holland," q.v.

HOLLAND, William. Captain, Worcester Militia, Snow Hill Bn., Aug 30, 1777, and Major, May 27, 1779 [Ref: M-88, C-351, E-423]. He may be the William who rendered patriotic service by supplying corn for the use of the military on March 4, 1780 [Ref: P-274]. See the comments under the other William Holland (above).

HOLLAND, William. Took the Oath of Allegiance in Worcester County in 1778 before the Hon. William Hopewell [Ref: J-1814 (Box 4) listed the name twice].

HOLLAND, William. Private, Worcester Militia, Snow Hill Bn., Capt. Ebenezer Handy's Co., on April 9, 1776 [Ref: M-249]. He may be the William Holland who was a private in the Worcester Militia, Sinepuxent Bn., Capt. Matthew Purnell's Co., Fifth Class, on July 25, 1780 [Ref: M-252].

HOLLAND, William. Took the Oath of Allegiance in Worcester County in 1778 in Quepomco Hundred before the Hon. Thomas Purnell [Ref: J-1814 (Box 4)].

HOLLAND, William (Matapony). Took the Oath of Allegiance in Worcester County in 1778 before the Hon. Nehemiah Holland [Ref: J-1814 (Box 4)].

HOLLOWAY, Aaron. Private, Worcester Militia, Sinepuxent Bn., Capt. Josiah Dale's Co., Seventh Class, 1779/1780 [Ref: M-254].

HOLLOWAY, Ebenezer. Private, Worcester Militia, Sinepuxent Bn., Capt. Josiah Dale's Co., Fifth Class, 1779/1780 [Ref: M-254].

HOLLOWAY, Elijah (1754-c1820). Son of John Holloway and Frances Bradford, born in Worcester Parish on March 11, 1754 [Ref: Y-30]. Private, Worcester Militia, Sinepuxent Bn., Capt. John Postly's Co., Second Class, 1779/1780 [Ref:

M-251]. Elijah Holloway was born in Maryland on March 11, 1754, married (wife's name not known), served as a private during the war, and died in Ohio after 1820 [Ref: V-1463].

HOLLOWAY, Elisha. Private, Worcester Militia, Sinepuxent Bn., Capt. Josiah Dale's Co., Sixth Class, 1779/1780 [Ref: M-254].

HOLLOWAY, Jacob. Private, Worcester Militia, Sinepuxent Bn., Capt. Josiah Dale's Co., Eighth Class, 1779/1780 [Ref: M-254 listed the name as "Jacob Hollaway"].

HOLLOWAY, James. Private, Worcester Militia, Sinepuxent Bn., Capt. Josiah Dale's Co., Fourth Class, 1779/1780 [Ref: M-254 listed the name as "James Halloway"].

HOLLOWAY, Jesse. Private, Worcester Militia, Sinepuxent Bn., Capt. John Postly's Co., Third Class, 1779/1780 [Ref: M-251].

HOLLOWAY, John. See "Elijah Holloway," q.v.

HOLLOWAY, Joshua. Private, Worcester Militia, Wicomico Bn., Capt. Elijah Shockley's Co., Second Class, July 15, 1780 [Ref: M-255].

HOLLOWAY, Levi (1735-c1839). Private, Worcester Militia, Sinepuxent Bn., Capt. Josiah Dale's Co., Fifth Class, 1779/1780 [Ref: M-254 listed the name as "Levi Hollaway"]. He applied for a pension (S32332) in Hamilton County, Indiana on June 1, 1839, age 104, stating he was born in Worcester County, Maryland on April 9, 1735 and lived there at the time of his enlistment. In 1813 he moved to Ohio and in the fall of 1838 he moved to Hamilton County, Indiana [Ref: W-1685].

HOLLOWAY, Moses. Private, Worcester Militia, Wicomico Bn., Capt. Elijah Shockley's Co., Second Class, July 15, 1780 [Ref: M-255 listed the name as "Moses Hollaway"].

HOLLOWAY, William. Private, Worcester Militia, Sinepuxent Bn., Capt. John Rackliff's Co., First Class, 1779/1780 [Ref: M-251]. Took the Oath of Allegiance in Worcester County in 1778 in Buckingham Hundred before the Hon. Thomas Purnell [Ref: J-1814 (Box 4)].

HOLLY, James. Private, Somerset Militia, Salisbury Bn., Capt. Sampson Wheatly's Co., 1780 [Ref: M-216].

HOLSTON, John. See "Whittington Richardson," q.v.

HOLSTON, Robert. Private, 3rd Maryland Independent Co., Worcester County, Capt. John Watkins' Co., enlisted on June 30, 1776; muster roll dated Aug 20, 1776, present for duty [Ref: D-23].

HOOK, Belitha. Private, Worcester Militia, Sinepuxent Bn., Capt. Elisha Purnell's Co., Fourth Class, 1779/1780 [Ref: M-253]. Took the Oath of Allegiance in Worcester County in 1778 in Quepomco Hundred before the Hon. Thomas Purnell [Ref: J-1814 (Box 4)].

HOOK, Roger (Rodger). Private, Worcester Militia, Sinepuxent Bn., Capt. William Purnell's Co., Third Class, 1779/1780 [Ref: M-252]. Took the Oath of

Allegiance in Worcester County in 1778 in Bogerternorton Hundred before the Hon. Thomas Purnell [Ref: J-1814 (Box 4)].

HOOK, William. Private, Worcester Militia, Sinepuxent Bn., Capt. William Purnell's Co., Fifth Class, 1779/1780 [Ref: M-252].

HOOPER, James. See "William Moore," q.v.

HOPEWELL, William. Colonel, Worcester Militia, Wicomico Bn., Aug 30, 1777 to June 3, 1781, resigned [Ref: M-89, C-351, H-269]. Justice who administered the Oath of Allegiance in Worcester County in 1778 [Ref: J-1814 (Box 4)]. Took the Oath of Allegiance in Worcester County on Feb 25, 1778 before the Hon. Ebenezer Handy [Ref: J-1814 (Box 4)]. Justice of the Peace for Worcester County, commissioned on Nov 29, 1777 and Nov 21, 1778 and Jan 17, 1782 [Ref: C-428, E-249, I-46].

HOPKINS, Benjamin. Private, Somerset Militia, Princess Anne Bn., Capt. Henry Miles' Little Annemessex Co., 1780 [Ref: M-221].

HOPKINS, Charles. Private, Somerset Militia, Salisbury Bn., Capt. John Span Conway's Nanticoke Point Co., 1778/1780 [Ref: M-216].

HOPKINS, David. Private, Somerset Militia, Salisbury Bn., Capt. John Span Conway's Nanticoke Point Co., 1778/1780 [Ref: M-216].

HOPKINS, George Collier. Private, Somerset Militia, Salisbury Bn., Capt. John Span Conway's Nanticoke Point Co., 1778/1780 [Ref: M-216]. Rendered patriotic service by supplying pork for the use of the military on Aug 8, 1780 [Ref: P-308]. "George Collair Hopkins" married Betty Leatherbury in Stepney Parish on Aug 27, 1761 and their children were: Prisse (daughter, b. Jan 8, 1762); John (b. Dec 26, 1765); Jeane (b. Dec 7, 1767); and, Luvezan (daughter, b. March 6, 1770). [Ref: Y-52].

HOPKINS, Hampton. Private, Worcester Militia, Sinepuxent Bn., Capt. John Postly's Co., Seventh Class, 1779/1780 [Ref: M-251]. Took the Oath of Allegiance in Worcester County in 1778 before the Hon. Nathaniel Miller [Ref: J-1814 (Box 4)]. Rendered patriotic service by supplying salt for the use of the military on Dec 27, 1781 [Ref: P-464]. See "Benton Harris," q.v.

HOPKINS, James. Took the Oath of Allegiance in Worcester County in 1778 before the Hon. Nathaniel Miller [Ref: J-1814 (Box 4)].

HOPKINS, Jeane. See "George Collier Hopkins," q.v.

HOPKINS, John. Private, Somerset Militia, Salisbury Bn., Capt. Henry Gale's Quantico Co., 1778/1780 [Ref: M-216]. Private, Somerset Militia, Princess Anne Bn., Capt. Thomas Irving's Monie Co., 1780 [Ref: M-219]. See "George Collier Hopkins," q.v.

HOPKINS, Levi. Private, Somerset Militia, Salisbury Bn., Capt. John Span Conway's Nanticoke Point Co., 1778/1780 [Ref: M-216].

HOPKINS, Levin (Leven). Private, Worcester Militia, Snow Hill Bn., Capt. Samuel Smyley's Co., 1777 [Ref: M-250]. Took the Oath of Allegiance in Worcester County in 1778 before the Hon. Joshua Townsend [Ref: J-1814 (Box 4)].

HOPKINS, Luke. Took the Oath of Allegiance in Worcester County in 1778 before the Hon. Joshua Townsend [Ref: J-1814 (Box 4)].
HOPKINS, Luvezan. See "George Collier Hopkins," q.v.
HOPKINS, Matthew. Took the Oath of Allegiance in Worcester County in 1778 before the Hon. Nehemiah Holland [Ref: J-1814 (Box 4)].
HOPKINS, Nathaniel. See "John Selby Purnell," q.v.
HOPKINS, Prisse. See "George Collier Hopkins," q.v.
HOPKINS, Robert. Private, Somerset Militia, Salisbury Bn., Capt. John Span Conway's Nanticoke Point Co., 1778/1780 [Ref: M-216].
HOPKINS, Samuel. Private, Worcester Militia, Wicomico Bn., Capt. John Parramore's Co., First Class, July 15, 1780 [Ref: M-259]. Took the Oath of Allegiance in Worcester County in 1778 before the Hon. Nehemiah Holland [Ref: J-1814 (Box 4)].
HOPKINS, Sinah. See "Stephen Hopkins," q.v.
HOPKINS, Stephen (1753 -   ). Son of William and Sinah Hopkins, born in Coventry Parish on Jan 22, 1753 [Ref: Y-71]. Private, Somerset Militia, Salisbury Bn., Capt. John Span Conway's Nanticoke Point Co., 1778/1780 [Ref: M-216]. Private, Somerset Militia, Princess Anne Bn., Capt. Henry Miles' Little Annemessex Co., 1780 [Ref: M-221].
HOPKINS, William. Private, Somerset Militia, Salisbury Bn., Capt. John Span Conway's Nanticoke Point Co., 1778/1780 [Ref: M-216]. See "Stephen Hopkins," q.v.
HOPKINSON, Thomas. Took the Oath of Allegiance in Somerset County in 1778 before the Hon. John Williams [Ref: T-21, N-51].
HORNER, Benjamin. Private, Somerset Militia, Princess Anne Bn., Capt. Thomas Irving's Monie Co., 1780 [Ref: M-219].
HORNER, John. Private, Somerset Militia, Princess Anne Bn., Capt. Thomas Irving's Monie Co., 1780 [Ref: M-219].
HORNER, William. Private, Somerset Militia, Princess Anne Bn., Capt. Thomas Irving's Monie Co., 1780 [Ref: M-219].
HORSEY, Anthony Smith. See "Smith Horsey," q.v.
HORSEY, George. See "William Horsey," q.v.
HORSEY, Isaac. Private, Select Militia, Somerset County, Aug 15, 1781 [Ref: L-35B]. See "William Horsey," q.v.
HORSEY, John (1750-1810). First Lieutenant, Somerset Militia, Princess Anne Bn., Capt. Henry Miles' Little Annemessex Co., Sep 22, 1777 to at least July 24, 1780 [Ref: M-89, M-221, C-381]. Lieutenant, Somerset Militia, Salisbury Bn., Capt. Sampson Wheatly's Co., 1780 [Ref: M-215]. John Horsey was born in 1750, married Amelia Leatherbury, served as a lieutenant during the war, and died before Dec 13, 1810 [Ref: V-1485].
HORSEY, John. Private, Somerset Militia, Salisbury Bn., Capt. William Turpin's Rewastico Co., 1778/1780 [Ref: M-217 listed the name as "John Horsy"].

HORSEY, John. Sergeant, Somerset Militia, Princess Anne Bttln., Capt. Henry Miles' Little Annemessex Co., 1780. Ensign, Select Militia, Capt. John Williams' Co., Aug 23, 1781 [Ref: M-89, M-221, G-577, L-35B].

HORSEY, John. Justice of the Peace for Somerset County, commissioned on Jan 9, 1778 [Ref: C-464].

HORSEY, John (Pocomoke). Took the Oath of Allegiance in Somerset County in 1778 [Ref: N-51].

HORSEY, John (of John). Took the Oath of Allegiance in Somerset County in 1778 before the Hon. John Williams [Ref: T-21, N-51].

HORSEY, John (of Smith). Took the Oath of Allegiance in Somerset County in 1778 before the Hon. John Williams [Ref: T-21, N-51].

HORSEY, Mary. See "Smith Horsey," q.v.

HORSEY(?), Moses. Private, Somerset Militia, Salisbury Bn., Capt. Joseph Venables' Barren Creek Co., 1778/1780 [Ref: M-217 listed the name as "Moses --rsey"].

HORSEY, Outerbridge. Took the Oath of Allegiance in Somerset County in 1778 before the Hon. John Williams [Ref: T-21, N-51]. It should be noted that an Outerbridge Horsey is mentioned as a captain in the Dorchester County militia in 1778 [Ref: M-89]. Outerbridge Horsey, son of Outerbridge and Mary Horsey, was born in Coventry Parish on March 4, 1751 [Ref: Y-70]. See "William Horsey," q.v.

HORSEY, Revell (Revill). Private, Somerset Militia, Salisbury Bn., Capt. Sampson Wheatly's Co., 1780 [Ref: M-216]. Took the Oath of Allegiance in Somerset County in 1778 before the Hon. John Williams [Ref: T-21 listed the name followed by a word that looked like "damamis" or "demamia" written in small letters. Source N-51 mistakenly listed the name as "Revell Hersey"].

HORSEY, Revell. Took the Oath of Allegiance in Somerset County in 1778 before the Hon. Levin Wilson [Ref: T-17]. Rendered patriotic service by supplying bacon for the use of the military on Aug 15, 1780 [Ref: P-309]. See "Stephen Horsey," q.v.

HORSEY, Samuel. Captain, Worcester Militia, Wicomico Bn., Aug 30, 1777 to at least July 15, 1780 [Ref: M-89, M-256, C-351]. Took the Oath of Allegiance in Worcester County in 1778 before the Hon. William Hopewell [Ref: J-1814 (Box 4)].

HORSEY, Samuel. Private, Worcester Militia, Wicomico Bn., Capt. Samuel Horsey's Co., Seventh Class, July 15, 1780 [Ref: M-257].

HORSEY, Smith. Took the Oath of Allegiance in Somerset County in 1778 before the Hon. John Williams [Ref: T-21, N-51]. Anthony Smith Horsey, son of Smith and Mary Horsey, was born in Coventry Parish on March 3, 1762 [Ref: Y-85].

HORSEY, Smith Jr. Private, Somerset Militia, Princess Anne Bn., Capt. Henry Miles' Little Annemessex Co., 1780 [Ref: M-221]. Select Militia, Somerset County, Aug 15, 1781 [Ref: L-35B listed the name without the "Jr."].

HORSEY, Stephen (1761 -   ). Son of Revel Horsey and Sarah Fosset, born in Coventry Parish on May 29, 1761 [Ref: Y-84]. Private, Somerset Militia, Salisbury Bn., White Haven Co., 1778/1780 [Ref: M-218]. Private, Somerset Militia, Princess Anne Bn., Capt. Henry Miles' Little Annemessex Co., 1780 [Ref: M-221]. He may have been the Stephen Horsey who took the Oath of Allegiance in Worcester County in 1778 before the Hon. William Hopewell although he was not yet 18 years of age, but he was in his 18th year nonetheless [Ref: J-1814 (Box 4)].

HORSEY, William (c1745-1786). Son of Outerbridge Horsey and Mary Dixon. William married first to ---- Adams (daughter of Rev. Alexander Adams, Jr.) and second to Nelly (Eleanor) Wailes by 1775. Children: Outerbridge (b. 1775), Isaac, George Wailes, and William [Ref: R-463]. William was one of the four delegates elected to represent Somerset County at the Maryland Convention in August, 1776 [Ref: O-45]. He took the Oath of Allegiance in Somerset County in 1778 before the Hon. John Williams [Ref: T-21, N-51]. He also served in the Lower House of the Maryland Legislature from Somerset County, 1776-1777, and was a County Court Justice, 1768-1777 [Ref: R-463].

HOSHIER, Edward. Took the Oath of Allegiance in Worcester County in 1778 before the Hon. Joshua Townsend [Ref: J-1814 (Box 4)].

HOSHIER, Ezekiel. Took the Oath of Allegiance in Worcester County in 1778 before the Hon. Joshua Townsend [Ref: J-1814 (Box 4)].

HOSHIER, John. Private, Worcester Militia, Wicomico Bn., Capt. John Davis' Co., First Class, July 15, 1780 [Ref: M-254 listed the name as "John Hosier"].

HOSHIER, Samuel. Took the Oath of Allegiance in Worcester County in 1778 before the Hon. Joshua Townsend [Ref: J-1814 (Box 4)].

HOSHIER, William. Took the Oath of Allegiance in Worcester County in 1778 before the Hon. Joshua Townsend [Ref: J-1814 (Box 4)].

HOSIER, William. Private, Worcester Militia, Sinepuxent Bn., Capt. Matthew Purnell's Co., Second Class, July 25, 1780 [Ref: M-252 listed the name as "William Hozer"]. Took the Oath of Allegiance in Worcester County in 1778 before the Hon. Nathaniel Miller [Ref: J-1814 (Box 4)].

HOUSTON, Amelia. See "Isaac Houston," q.v.

HOUSTON, Benjamin. Took the Oath of Allegiance in Worcester County in 1778 before the Hon. Joshua Townsend [Ref: J-1814 (Box 4)].

HOUSTON, Isaac (c1750-1797). Son of James Houston (d. 1761) and Mary Purnell (widow of Levi Purnell). Isaac married Mary Sturgis (widow of Capt. Joshua Sturgis) by 1776 and their children were James, Jr. ("lunatic" who d. 1814), Mary Dixon (d. 1800), Sarah and Amelia. Isaac served in the Lower House of the Maryland Legislature from Worcester County at various times between 1780 and 1793, and was a County Court Justice in 1777 and 1778. He was called colonel by 1797 [Ref: R-464, R-838]. First Lieutenant, Worcester Militia, Wicomico Bn., June 28, 1777 to Aug 13, 1777, resigned. Captain, Aug 30, 1777 to May 8, 1778, resigned [Ref: M-89, C-351]. Took the Oath of

Allegiance in Worcester County in 1778 before the Hon. Joshua Townsend [Ref: J-1814 (Box 4)]. Justice of the Orphans Court for Worcester County, commissioned on Nov 21, 1778 and March 27, 1779 [Ref: E-250, E-327]. Rendered patriotic service by supplying beef for the use of the military on Oct 10, 1781 and grazing cattle on Nov 8, 1781 [Ref: P-347, P-454]. See "James Houston," q.v.

HOUSTON, James. Ensign, Worcester Militia, Capt. Patterson's Co., June 28, 1777, noted as "deceased" [Ref: M-89].

HOUSTON, James (c1755-1809). Son of James Houston (d. 1761) and Mary Purnell (widow of Levin Purnell). He married first to Martha Purnell by 1791 and second to Gertrude Parker in 1806. Children: James and Isaac. James served in the Lower House of the Maryland Legislature from Worcester County in 1788 and was a County Court Justice in 1799. He was captain, 37th Militia Regiment, 1794, major, 1796, lieutenant colonel, 1800, and was called colonel in 1809 [Ref: R-464, R-838]. He was probably the James Houston who was a private in the Worcester Militia, Wicomico Bn., Capt. Isaac Layfield's Co., Second Class, on July 15, 1780 [Ref: M-257], and a private in Capt. John Martin's Co., 1780/1781 [Ref: J-1814 (Box 12) listed the name as "Jams. Houston"]. He may have rendered patriotic service by supplying corn for the use of the military in Worcester County on Feb 18, 1780 [Ref: P-271]. Since there was at least three men by this name, additional research will be necessary before drawing conclusions.

HOUSTON, James (doctor). Rendered patriotic service by supplying pork in Somerset County for the use of the military on May 14, 1781 [Ref: P-394].

HOUSTON, James Jr. Took the Oath of Allegiance in Worcester County in 1778 before the Hon. William Hopewell [Ref: J-1814 (Box 4)].

HOUSTON, James Sr. Took the Oath of Allegiance in Worcester County in 1778 before the Hon. William Hopewell [Ref: J-1814 (Box 4)].

HOUSTON, John. Private, 3rd Maryland Independent Co., Worcester County, Capt. John Watkins' Co., enlisted Feb 2, 1776; muster roll dated Aug 20, 1776, present for duty [Ref: D-21]. Took the Oath of Allegiance in Worcester County in 1778 before the Hon. James Selby [Ref: J-1814 (Box 4)].

HOUSTON, John. Took the Oath of Allegiance in Worcester County in 1778 before the Hon. Joshua Townsend [Ref: J-1814 (Box 4) listed the name as "John Housten"].

HOUSTON, Joseph. Sergeant, Worcester Militia, Wicomico Bn., Capt. Isaac Layfield's Co., July 15, 1780 [Ref: M-257]. Took the Oath of Allegiance in Worcester County in 1778 before the Hon. James Selby [Ref: J-1814 (Box 4)].

HOUSTON, Levi (1750-1824). Private, Worcester Militia, Wicomico Bn., Capt. Isaac Layfield's Co., Seventh Class, July 15, 1780 [Ref: M-257]. Took the Oath of Allegiance in Worcester County in 1778 before the Hon. Nehemiah Holland [Ref: J-1814 (Box 4)]. Levi Houston was born in Maryland on Aug 20, 1750, married Dolly Schoolfield, served as a private and rendered patriotic service during the war, and died in Kentucky on Feb 11, 1824 [Ref: V-1499].

HOUSTON, Mary. See "Isaac Houston" and "Joshua Townsend," q.v.

HOUSTON, Ralph. Private, Worcester Militia, Sinepuxent Bn., Capt. William Purnell's Co., Eighth Class, 1779/1780 [Ref: M-252]. Took the Oath of Allegiance in Worcester County in 1778 before the Hon. Joshua Townsend [Ref: J-1814 (Box 4)].

HOUSTON, Robert. Private, Worcester Militia, Capt. John Martin's Co., 1780/1781 [Ref: J-1814 (Box 12)].

HOUSTON, Sarah. See "Isaac Houston," q.v.

HOWARD, Charles Wallace. On Aug 21, 1776, Capt. John Gunby, of Somerset County, "certified that the Second Independent Co. under my command was this day mustered by Charles Wallace Howard." [Ref: D-642].

HOWARD, Gillis. Private, Somerset Militia, Salisbury Bn., Capt. James Bennett's Salisbury Co., 1778/1780 [Ref: M-218].

HOWARD, John. Private, Somerset Militia, Princess Anne Bn., Capt. John Jones' Princess Anne Co., 1780 [Ref: M-219].

HOWARD, John. Sergeant, Somerset Militia, Princess Anne Bn., Capt. George Waters' Pocomoke Co., 1780 [Ref: M-220].

HOWARD, Sarah. See "Benjamin Wailes," q.v.

HUDSON, Aaron. Private, Worcester Militia, Wicomico Bn., Capt. James Patterson's Co., Second Class, July 15, 1780 [Ref: M-258]. Took the Oath of Allegiance in Worcester County in 1778 before the Hon. John Selby [Ref: J-1814 (Box 4)].

HUDSON, Annanias. Private, Worcester Militia, Sinepuxent Bn., Capt. John Rackliff's Co., Fourth Class, 1779/1780 [Ref: M-251]. Private, Worcester Militia, Sinepuxent Bn., Capt. Josiah Dale's Co., Second Class, 1779/1780 [Ref: M-254]. Took the Oath of Allegiance in Worcester County in 1778 in Buckingham Hundred before the Hon. Thomas Purnell [Ref: J-1814 (Box 4)]. Private, 5th Maryland Line, by April 24, 1780, when listed as a recruit entitled to clothing from the Commissary of Stores [Ref: F-150].

HUDSON, Annanias Jr. Private, Worcester Militia, Sinepuxent Bn., Capt. John Coe's Co., Fifth Class, 1779/1780 [Ref: M-252].

HUDSON, Archibald. Private, Worcester Militia, Sinepuxent Bn., Capt. William Purnell's Co., Fifth Class, 1779/1780 [Ref: M-252]. Private, Worcester Militia, Wicomico Bn., Capt. Samuel Smyley's Co., First Class, July 15, 1780 [Ref: M-258]. Took the Oath of Allegiance in Worcester County in 1778 in Bogerternorton Hundred before the Hon. Thomas Purnell [Ref: J-1814 (Box 4) listed the name as "Archable Hutson"].

HUDSON, Asariah. See "Solomon Hudson," q.v.

HUDSON, David. Private, Worcester Militia, Sinepuxent Bn., Capt. John Coe's Co., First Class, 1779/1780 [Ref: M-251].

HUDSON, Dennis (c1738-c1810). Private, Worcester Militia, Sinepuxent Bn., Capt. Thomas Purnell's Co., Seventh Class, 1779/1780 [Ref: M-253]. Private, Worcester Militia, Sinepuxent Bn., Capt. John Coe's Co., Seventh Class, 1779/1780 [Ref: M-252]. Dennis Hudson was born circa 1738, married first to Sarah Selby and second to Polly Melvin, served as a private during the war, and died after Aug 20, 1810 [Ref: V-1524].

HUDSON, Dennis Sr. Took the Oath of Allegiance in Worcester County in 1778 before the Hon. Joshua Townsend [Ref: J-1814 (Box 4) listed the name as "Dennis Hutson, Sener"].

HUDSON, Henry. Private, Worcester Militia, Sinepuxent Bn., Capt. Thomas Purnell's Co., Seventh Class, 1779/1780 [Ref: M-253].

HUDSON, Henry (of Major). Took the Oath of Allegiance in Worcester County in 1778 before the Hon. Joshua Townsend [Ref: J-1814 (Box 4) listed the name as "Henry Hutson, son of Major"]

HUDSON, Jesse. Took the Oath of Allegiance in Worcester County in 1778 before the Hon. Joshua Townsend [Ref: J-1814 (Box 4) listed the name as "Jesse Hudson"].

HUDSON, Job. Private, Worcester Militia, Sinepuxent Bn., Capt. John Coe's Co., Seventh Class, 1779/1780 [Ref: M-252].

HUDSON, John. Private, Worcester Militia, Sinepuxent Bn., Capt. Thomas Purnell's Co., Third Class, 1779/1780 [Ref: M-253]. Took the Oath of Allegiance in Worcester County in 1778 before the Hon. Nathaniel Miller [Ref: J-1814 (Box 4)].

HUDSON, John. Private, Worcester Militia, Sinepuxent Bn., Capt. Josiah Dale's Co., Fourth Class, 1779/1780 [Ref: M-254]. Took the Oath of Allegiance in Worcester County in 1778 before the Hon. Nathaniel Miller [Ref: J-1814 (Box 4)].

HUDSON, John Jr. Private, Worcester Militia, Sinepuxent Bn., Capt. John Rackliff's Co., Fourth Class, 1779/1780 [Ref: M-251].

HUDSON, John (of Major). Took the Oath of Allegiance in Worcester County in 1778 before the Hon. Joshua Townsend [Ref: J-1814 (Box 4)].

HUDSON, John (of William). Private, Worcester Militia, Sinepuxent Bn., Capt. Thomas Purnell's Co., Fifth Class, 1779/1780 [Ref: M-253]. Took the Oath of Allegiance in Worcester County in 1778 before the Hon. Joshua Townsend [Ref: J-1814 (Box 4)].

HUDSON, Laban (Laben, Labin). Private, Worcester Militia, Snow Hill Bn., Capt. Samuel Smyley's Co., 1777 [Ref: M-250]. Private, Worcester Militia, Wicomico Bn., Capt. John Parramore's Co., Second Class, July 15, 1780 [Ref: M-259]. Took the Oath of Allegiance in Worcester County in 1778 before the Hon. John Selby [Ref: J-1814 (Box 4)].

HUDSON, Levi. Private, Worcester Militia, Sinepuxent Bn., Capt. William Purnell's Co., Sixth Class, 1779/1780 [Ref: M-252]. Took the Oath of

Allegiance in Worcester County in 1778 before the Hon. Joshua Townsend [Ref: J-1814 (Box 4)].

HUDSON, Lott. Private, Worcester Militia, Sinepuxent Bn., Capt. John Coe's Co., Sixth Class, 1779/1780 [Ref: M-252]. Lott Hudson was born before 1760, married (wife's name not known), was a private during the war, and died after 1780 [Ref: V-1525].

HUDSON, Major. Took the Oath of Allegiance in Worcester County in 1778 before the Hon. Joshua Townsend [Ref: J-1814 (Box 4) listed the name as "Major Hutson"].

HUDSON, McKemmy (McKimmy). Private, Worcester Militia, Sinepuxent Bn., Capt. John Rackliff's Co., Seventh Class, 1779/1780 [Ref: M-251]. Took the Oath of Allegiance in Worcester County in 1778 before the Hon. Joshua Townsend [Ref: J-1814 (Box 4)].

HUDSON, Moses. Private, Worcester Militia, Snow Hill Bn., Capt. John Parramore's Co., 1777 [Ref: M-250]. Sergeant, Worcester Militia, Wicomico Bn., Capt. John Parramore's Co., July 15, 1780 [Ref: M-259]. Took the Oath of Allegiance in Worcester County in 1778 before the Hon. John Selby [Ref: J-1814 (Box 4)].

HUDSON, Richard. Private, Worcester Militia, Sinepuxent Bn., Capt. Josiah Dale's Co., First Class, 1779/1780 [Ref: M-253].

HUDSON, Robert. Private, Worcester Militia, Sinepuxent Bn., Capt. Thomas Purnell's Co., Sixth Class, 1779/1780 [Ref: M-253]. Took the Oath of Allegiance in Worcester County in 1778 before the Hon. Joshua Townsend [Ref: J-1814 (Box 4)].

HUDSON, Samuel. Private, Worcester Militia, Snow Hill Bn., Capt. John Parramore's Co., 1777 [Ref: M-250]. Private, Worcester Militia, Wicomico Bn., Capt. John Parramore's Co., Eighth Class, July 15, 1780 [Ref: M-259]. Took the Oath of Allegiance in Worcester County in 1778 before the Hon. William Hopewell [Ref: J-1814 (Box 4) listed the name as "Samuel Hutson"].

HUDSON, Seth. Private, Worcester Militia, Sinepuxent Bn., Capt. John Coe's Co., First Class, 1779/1780 [Ref: M-251]. Private, Maryland Troops, Worcester County, draughted May 1, 1781 [Ref: K-99, D-372 listed the name as "Seth Hutson"]. Rendered patriotic service by driving cattle for the military on Sep 30, 1781 [Ref: P-442].

HUDSON, Solomon. Took the Oath of Allegiance in Worcester County in 1778 before the Hon. Nathaniel Miller [Ref: J-1814 (Box 4)]. Recruited by Capt. Levin Handy and enlisted in the Continental Army in Worcester County on Feb 15, 1780 for the duration of the war, stating he was born in America [Ref: Z-40]. Private, 5th Maryland Line, listed as a recruit entitled to clothing from the Commissary of Stores on April 24, 1780 [Ref: F-150]. Solomon Hudson and Asariah Hudson were both privates in the 5th Maryland Line and both were listed as "deserted" on July 1, 1780 [Ref: D-214]. Additional research may be necessary before drawing conclusions.

155

HUDSON, Sterling. Private, Worcester Militia, Wicomico Bn., Capt. William Handy's Co., Second Class, July 15, 1780 [Ref: M-257].
HUDSON, Thomas. Private, Worcester Militia, Sinepuxent Bn., Capt. John Rackliff's Co., First Class, 1779/1780 [Ref: M-251].
HUDSON, William. Private, Worcester Militia, Sinepuxent Bn., Capt. Thomas Purnell's Co., Fourth Class, 1779/1780 [Ref: M-253]. Took the Oath of Allegiance in Worcester County in 1778 before the Hon. Joshua Townsend [Ref: J-1814 (Box 4)].
HUET, James. Private, Maryland Line, whose name appeared on "a list of recruits from and deserters taken up in Somerset County on Oct 20, 1780" [Ref: D-346].
HUFFINGTON, Angelo (1757 -   ). Son of Levin Huffington and Mattilda Ackworth, born in Stepney Parish on Jan 3, 1757 [Ref: Y-47]. Private, Somerset Militia, Salisbury Bn., Capt. Joseph Venables' Barren Creek Co., 1778/1780 [Ref: M-217].
HUFFINGTON, John. Private, Somerset Militia, Salisbury Bn., Capt. Joseph Venables' Barren Creek Co., 1778/1780 [Ref: M-217].
HUFFINGTON, Jonathan (c1751-1802). Ensign, Somerset Militia, 1st Bn., Capt. John Philips' Co., Aug 19, 1776 [Ref: M-90, B-220 listed the name as "Jonathan Hupington"]. Private, Somerset Militia, Salisbury Bn., Capt. Joseph Venables' Barren Creek Co., 1778/1780 [Ref: M-217]. Jonathan Huffington was born circa 1751, married Sarah ----, was a private during the war, and died in 1802 [Ref: V-1525].
HUFFINGTON, Joshua. Private, Somerset Militia, Salisbury Bn., Capt. Joseph Venables' Barren Creek Co., 1778/1780 [Ref: M-217].
HUFFINGTON, Levin. See "Angelo Huffington," q.v.
HUFFINGTON, Sarah. See "Jonathan Huffington," q.v.
HUGHS, Jesse. Private, Worcester Militia, Wicomico Bn., Capt. William Handy's Co., Fourth Class, July 15, 1780 [Ref: M-257]. Took the Oath of Allegiance in Worcester County in 1778 before the Hon. John Selby [Ref: J-1814 (Box 4)].
HUGHS, John. Private, Somerset Militia, Salisbury Bn., Capt. John Span Conway's Nanticoke Point Co., 1778/1780 [Ref: M-216].
HULL, Beauchamp. Private, Somerset Militia, Princess Anne Bn., Capt. John Jones' Princess Anne Co., 1780 [Ref: M-219].
HULL, Hope. Private, Somerset Militia, Princess Anne Bn., Capt. John Williams' Watkins Point Co., 1780 [Ref: M-222]. One Hope Hull married Rebeccah Williams in Coventry Parish on Feb 7, 1752 [Ref: Y-71].
HUMPHRIS, Elijah (1760 -   ). Son of Joshua and Esther Humphriss *[sic]*, born in Stepney Parish on Oct 18, 1760 [Ref: Y-47]. Private, Somerset Militia, Salisbury Bn., Capt. James Bennett's Salisbury Co., 1778/1780 [Ref: M-218].
HUMPHRIS, Esther. See "Elijah Humphris," q.v.
HUMPHRIS, Joseph. Private, Somerset Militia, Salisbury Bn., Capt. Henry Gale's Quantico Co., 1778/1780 [Ref: M-216].

HUMPHRIS, Joshua. Private, Somerset Militia, Salisbury Bn., Capt. Josiah Dashiell's Wicomico Creek Co., 1778/1780 [Ref: M-218]. See "Elijah Humphris," q.v.

HUMPHRIS (HUMPHRIES), Thomas. Second Lieutenant, Somerset Militia, 1st Bn., Capt. Robert Hitch's Co., April 11, 1776 [Ref: M-90 listed the name as "Thomas Humphries" and A-327 listed the name as "Thomas Humphreys"]. Took the Oath of Allegiance in Somerset County on Feb 14, 1778 before the Hon. Joseph Venables [Ref: T-25].

HUNT, Bartholomew. Private, Somerset Militia, Princess Anne Bn., Capt. James Elzey's Co., 1780 [Ref: M-220].

HUSTON(?), James. Private, Somerset Militia, Salisbury Bn., Capt. Joseph Venables' Barren Creek Co., 1778/1780 [Ref: M-217 listed the name as "James H----" because the manuscript at the Maryland Historical Society is very difficult to read].

HUTCHINS, Elizabeth. See "John Waters," q.v.

HUTCHINS, William. Private, Somerset Militia, Princess Anne Bn., Capt. George Waters' Pocomoke Co., 1780 [Ref: M-220]. Took the Oath of Allegiance in Somerset County in 1778 before the Hon. Levin Wilson [Ref: T-17, N-51].

HUTCHINSON, Jonathan. Private, Worcester Militia, Wicomico Bn., Capt. William Handy's Co., Second Class, July 15, 1780 [Ref: M-257]. Took the Oath of Allegiance in Worcester County in 1778 before the Hon. Joshua Townsend [Ref: J-1814 (Box 4) listed the name as "Jonathan Hutheson"].

HUTSON, Henry. See "Henry Hudson," q.v.

HUTT, Saul. Took the Oath of Allegiance in Worcester County in 1778 before the Hon. John Selby [Ref: J-1814 (Box 4)].

HUTTON, Jane. See "William Henry," q.v.

HYLAND, Lambert (1751-1819). Second Lieutenant, Somerset Militia, Salisbury Bn., Capt. George Wilson's Co., Sep 9, 1777. Second and/or First Lieutenant, White Haven Co., 1778/1780. Captain, Princess Anne Bn., Aug 22, 1781 [Ref: M-91, M-218, C-382, G-575]. Took the Oath of Allegiance in Somerset County in 1778 before the Hon. Levin Wilson [Ref: T-17]. Lambert Hyland was born in 1751, married first to Eliza Rigby and second to Elizabeth Gale, served as a captain in the war, and died in 1819 [Ref: V-1559].

INGERSOLL, Samuel. Took the Oath of Allegiance in Somerset County in 1778 before the Hon. John Span Conway [Ref: T-14, N-51].

IRONS (IRINS), Daniel. Private, Somerset Militia, Salisbury Bn., Capt. Joseph Venables' Barren Creek Co., 1778/1780 [Ref: M-217].

IRONSHIRE, Joseph. Took the Oath of Allegiance in Worcester County in 1778 before the Hon. Nathaniel Miller [Ref: J-1814 (Box 4)]. Rendered patriotic service by supplying corn for the use of the military on June 17, 1780 and July 10, 1780 [Ref: G-10, and P-296 listed the name as "Joseph Ironshine"].

IRONSHIRE, William. Took the Oath of Allegiance in Worcester County in 1778 before the Hon. Nathaniel Miller [Ref: J-1814 (Box 4)]. Rendered patriotic service by supplying corn for the use of the military on June 1, 1780 [Ref: P-293 listed the name as "William Ironshare"]. The following appeared in *The Pennsylvania Packet, or the General Advertiser*, dated Jan 28, 1778: "William Ironshire offers reward for negro man who ran away from the Widow Nesbury's tavern at New London Cross Roads - who acted as a ostler there from the time Colonel Richardson marched past there to Head Quarters; he called himself Jack; said he belonged to John Forman, of New York, but is the property of the subscriber, of Worcester County, Maryland; his right name is Joe." [Ref: Q-34:2 (Spring, 1993), p. 203].

IRVINE, General. See "Thomas Seon," q.v.

IRVING, Grace. See "Thomas Irving," q.v.

IRVING, Elizabeth. See "Joseph Gilliss," q.v.

IRVING, George. Took the Oath of Allegiance in Somerset County in 1778 before the Hon. Levin Wilson [Ref: T-17, N-51].

IRVING, James. Private, Somerset Militia, Princess Anne Bn., Capt. James Elzey's Co., 1780 [Ref: M-220].

IRVING, James. Private, Somerset Militia, Princess Anne Bn., Capt. James Elzey's Co., 1780 [Ref: M-220].

IRVING, John. Ensign, Somerset Militia, Princess Anne Bn., Capt. William Waters' Co., Sep 22, 1777. First Lieutenant, Jan 7, 1778. First Lieutenant, Capt. James Elzey's Co., Dec 7, 1778 to at least July 24, 1780 [Ref: M-91, M-220, C-457, E-260]. Took the Oath of Allegiance in Somerset County in 1778 before the Hon. Levin Wilson [Ref: T-17, N-51]. Rendered patriotic service by supplying bacon for the use of the military on Aug 16, 1780 [Ref: P-310].

IRVING, Levin (Leaven). Captain, Somerset Militia, Salisbury Bn., Black Water Co., Sep 22, 1777. Major, April 17, 1781 [Ref: M-91, M-217, C-381, H-195]. Took the Oath of Allegiance in Somerset County on Feb 7, 1778 before the Hon. Joseph Venables [Ref: T-25].

IRVING, Sarah. See "Benjamin Purnell," q.v.

IRVING, Thomas (c1734-1784). Captain, Somerset Militia, Princess Anne Bn., Monie Co., Sep 22, 1777, and Major, Oct 28, 1780 [Ref: M-91, M-219, C-381, F-342]. Took the Oath of Allegiance in Somerset County in 1778 before the Hon. Levin Wilson [Ref: T-17, N-51]. Thomas Irving was born circa 1734, married first to Mrs. Sarah Handy and second to Grace ----, served as a captain in the war, and died before March 9, 1784 [Ref: V-1568].

IVES, Walter. Private, 3rd Maryland Independent Co., Worcester County, Capt. John Watkins' Co., enlisted Feb 17, 1776; muster roll dated Aug 20, 1776, present for duty [Ref: D-22].

J--?--, Thomas. Private, Somerset Militia, Salisbury Bn., Capt. John Span Conway's Nanticoke Point Co., 1778/1780 [Ref: M-216].

JACKSON, Ann. See "Henry Jackson," q.v.

JACKSON, Eleanor. See "Henry Jackson," q.v.

JACKSON, George. See "Henry Jackson," q.v.

JACKSON, Henry (c1740-1794). Immigrated by 1771 from Workington, England to Somerset County and married by 1779 to Elizabeth Wilson (daughter of Capt. Samuel Wilson). Children: George Wilson, Robert, Eleanor, Ann Wilson, and Leah. Henry service in the Lower House of the Maryland Legislature from Somerset County, 1777-1783; Maryland Convention, 1775; County Court Justice, 1778-1794; Judge of the Court of Appeals, 1778; Commissioner of the Tax, 1779; Justice of the Peace, 1778-1782; Justice of the Orphans Court, 1780-1789; and, Judge of the Court of Appeals for Tax Assessment, 1786. First Lieutenant, Somerset Militia, Princess Anne Bn., Capt. David Wilson's Back Creek Co., Sep 22, 1777 [Ref: R-479, R-480, M-91, C-381, E-248, C-464, I-45]. Took the Oath of Allegiance in Somerset County in 1778 before the Hon. Levin Wilson [Ref: T-17, N-51]. Commissary of Purchases in Somerset County in 1780 [Ref: P-299, F-215]. Rendered patriotic service by supplying corn for the use of the military on Jan 21, 1780 [Ref: P-264]. Commissioned by the Council of Maryland on Aug 19, 1779 to receive subscriptions for the Continental Loan Office [Ref: E-499].

JACKSON, John. Private, Worcester Militia, Sinepuxent Bn., Capt. Elisha Purnell's Co., Fifth Class, 1779/1780 [Ref: M-253]. Took the Oath of Allegiance in Worcester County in 1778 before the Hon. Joshua Townsend [Ref: J-1814 (Box 4)].

JACKSON, Jonathan. Took the Oath of Allegiance in Somerset County on Feb 28, 1778 before the Hon. Joseph Venables [Ref: T-25].

JACKSON, Jonathan. Took the Oath of Allegiance in Worcester County on Feb 25, 1778 before the Hon. Ebenezer Handy [Ref: J-1814 (Box 4)].

JACKSON, Leah. See "Henry Jackson," q.v.

JACKSON, Mitchell. Private, Somerset Militia, Salisbury Bn., Capt. Levin Irving's Black Water Co., 1778/1780 [Ref: M-217]. Took the Oath of Allegiance in Somerset County on Feb 21, 1778 before the Hon. Joseph Venables [Ref: T-25 listed the name as "Mitchel Jacson"].

JACKSON, Robert. See "Henry Jackson," q.v.

JACKSON, William. Private, Somerset Militia, Salisbury Bn., Capt. John Span Conway's Nanticoke Point Co., 1778/1780 [Ref: M-216]. Took the Oath of Allegiance in Worcester County in 1778 before the Hon. Nathaniel Miller [Ref: J-1814 (Box 4)].

JAMES, Daniel. Private, Somerset Militia, Salisbury Bn., Capt. Joseph Venables' Barren Creek Co., 1778/1780 [Ref: M-217].

JAMES, George. Private, Somerset Militia, Salisbury Bn., Capt. James Bennett's Salisbury Co., 1778/1780. Ensign, Capt. William Turpin's Salisbury Co., 1781 [Ref: M-92, M-218, G-575, J-1814 (Box 8, Dashiell's correspondence), H-195].

JAMES, John. Rendered patriotic service by supplying corn for the use of the military in Worcester County on June 14, 1780 [Ref: P-295].

JAMES, Richard. Drafted from Somerset County on July 30, 1781 to serve in the Continental Army, but was subsequently excused [Ref: L-35C].

JAMES, William. Private, Somerset Militia, Salisbury Bn., Capt. Joseph Venables' Barren Creek Co., 1778/1780 [Ref: M-217]. Drafted from Somerset County on July 30, 1781 to serve in the Continental Army [Ref: L-35C].

JARMAN, Elijah. Private, Worcester Militia, Sinepuxent Bn., Capt. Elisha Purnell's Co., Seventh Class, 1779/1780 [Ref: M-253]. Took the Oath of Allegiance in Worcester County in 1778 before the Hon. Joshua Townsend [Ref: J-1814 (Box 4)].

JARMAN, George. Private, 3rd Maryland Independent Co., Worcester County, Capt. John Watkins' Co., enlisted April 5, 1776; muster roll dated Aug 20, 1776, present for duty [Ref: D-23].

JARMAN, James. Took the Oath of Allegiance in Worcester County in 1778 before the Hon. Joshua Townsend [Ref: J-1814 (Box 4)].

JARMAN, Job. Private, Worcester Militia, Wicomico Bn., Capt. James Perdue's Co., Fourth Class, July 15, 1780 [Ref: M-256 listed the name as "Joab Jerman"].

JARMAN, John. Private, Worcester Militia, Sinepuxent Bn., Capt. Matthew Purnell's Co., Fourth Class, July 25, 1780 [Ref: M-252].

JARMAN, Magdalena. See "William Jarman," q.v.

JARMAN, Robert. Private, 3rd Maryland Independent Co., Worcester County, Capt. John Watkins' Co., enlisted March 28, 1776; muster roll dated Aug 20, 1776, present for duty [Ref: D-22].

JARMAN, Truitt. Private, Worcester Militia, Sinepuxent Bn., Capt. John Postly's Co., Third Class, 1779/1780 [Ref: M-251].

JARMAN, William (c1757-1796). Private, 3rd Maryland Independent Co., Worcester County, Capt. John Watkins' Co., enlisted March 4, 1776; muster roll dated Aug 20, 1776, present for duty [Ref: D-21]. Took the Oath of Allegiance in Worcester County in 1778 in Quepomco Hundred before the Hon. Thomas Purnell [Ref: J-1814 (Box 4) listed the name as "William Jarmon"]. William Jarman was born in Maryland circa 1757, married Magdalena ----, served as a private during the war, and died in Delaware before Nov 26, 1796 [Ref: V-1586].

JARVIS, Solomon. Sergeant, 3rd Maryland Independent Co., Worcester County, Capt. John Watkins' Co., enlisted Jan 25, 1776; muster roll dated Aug 20, 1776, present for duty [Ref: D-21].

JENKINS, David. Private, Somerset Militia, Salisbury Bn., Capt. James Bennett's Salisbury Co., 1778/1780 [Ref: M-218].

JENKINS, Esther. See "Ezekiel Jenkins," q.v.

JENKINS, Ezekiel (1762 -   ). son of Jonathan and Esther Jenkins, born in Stepney Parish on May 12, 1762 [Ref: Y-47]. Private, Somerset Militia, Salisbury Bn., Capt. James Bennett's Salisbury Co., 1780 [Ref: M-218].

JENKINS, Francis. See "Isaac Henry," q.v.

JENKINS, Jarvis. See "Kibble Jenkins," q.v.

JENKINS, John. Private, Somerset Militia, Salisbury Bn., Capt. James Bennett's Salisbury Co., 1778/1780 [Ref: M-218].

JENKINS, Jonathan. Private, Somerset Militia, Salisbury Bn., Capt. James Bennett's Salisbury Co., 1778/1780 [Ref: M-218]. Took the Oath of Allegiance in Somerset County on Feb 28, 1778 (made his "X" mark) before the Hon. Joseph Venables [Ref: T-25 listed the name as "Jonathan Jinkins"]. Jonathan Jenkins married Esther Hillman in Stepney Parish on Aug 5, 1761 [Ref: Y-47]. See "Ezekiel Jenkins," q.v.

JENKINS, Joseph. Private, Somerset Militia, Salisbury Bn., Capt. James Bennett's Salisbury Co., 1778/1780 [Ref: M-218]. Drafted from Somerset County on June 20, 1781 to serve in the Continental Army [Ref: L-35C]. Took the Oath of Allegiance in Somerset County on Feb 28, 1778 (made his "X" mark) before the Hon. Joseph Venables [Ref: T-25 listed the name as "Jos: Jinkins"].

JENKINS, Kibble (1756 -   ). Son of Jarvis and Sarah Jenkins, born in Stepney Parish on Feb 18, 1756 [Ref: Y-42]. Private, Somerset Militia, Salisbury Bn., Capt. James Bennett's Salisbury Co., 1778/1780 [Ref: M-218 mistakenly listed the name as "Zibble Jenkins"]. Drafted from Somerset County on July 30, 1781 to serve in the Continental Army [Ref: L-35C listed the name as "Kibble Jenkins"].

JENKINS, Mary. See "Isaac Henry," q.v.

JENKINS, Sarah. See "Kibble Jenkins," q.v.

JENKINS, William. Private, Somerset Militia, Salisbury Bn., Capt. John Span Conway's Nanticoke Point Co., 1778/1780 [Ref: M-216]. Took the Oath of Allegiance before the Council of Maryland on March 21, 1778 [Ref: C-545].

JESTER, Francis. Private, 3rd Maryland Independent Co., Worcester County, Capt. John Watkins' Co., enlisted Feb 3, 1776; muster roll dated Aug 20, 1776, present for duty [Ref: D-22].

JESTER, Southy (Southey). Private, Worcester Militia, Snow Hill Bn., Capt. Samuel Smyley's Co., 1777 [Ref: M-250]. Private, Worcester Militia, Wicomico Bn., Capt. Samuel Smyley's Co., Sixth Class, July 15, 1780 [Ref: M-259].

JEWEL, William. Sergeant, Somerset Militia, Salisbury Bn., Capt. Sampson Wheatly's Co., 1780 [Ref: M-215].

JOHNSON, Affradoxie. See "Benjamin Johnson," q.v.

JOHNSON, Archibald. Private, Worcester Militia, Sinepuxent Bn., Capt. John Postly's Co., Second Class, 1779/1780 [Ref: M-251].

JOHNSON, Benjamin (c1755-1828). Private, Worcester Militia, Wicomico Bn., Capt. Samuel Horsey's Co., Eighth Class, July 15, 1780 [Ref: M-257]. Benjamin Johnson married Phillis ---- and died testate in Worcester County by April 15, 1828 (date of probate). Their son Affradoxie Johnson (1785-1865) married Elizabeth R. Hayman (1789-1841) on Sep 17, 1806 [Ref: S-2979].

JOHNSON, Daniel. Private, Worcester Militia, Wicomico Bn., Capt. John Parramore's Co., Eighth Class, July 15, 1780 [Ref: M-259]. Took the Oath of

Allegiance in Worcester County in 1778 before the Hon. Nehemiah Holland [Ref: J-1814 (Box 4)].

JOHNSON, David. See "John Selby Purnell," q.v.

JOHNSON, Dennis. See "John Selby Purnell," q.v.

JOHNSON, Eliacam. Private, Worcester Militia, Wicomico Bn., Capt. Charles Bennett's Co., Fourth Class, July 15, 1780 [Ref: M-255].

JOHNSON, Eliakim. Second Lieutenant, Worcester Militia, Snow Hill Bn., Capt. Fisher Waltam [Walton]'s Co., May 27, 1778, and First Lieutenant, Wicomico Bn., Capt. Fisher Walton's Co., July 15, 1780 [Ref: E-423, and M-92, M-258 listed the name as "Eliacam Johnson"]. Took the Oath of Allegiance in Worcester County in 1778 before the Hon. Nehemiah Holland [Ref: J-1814 (Box 4) listed the name as "Eliakim Johnson"].

JOHNSON, Elijah. Private, Somerset Militia, Princess Anne Bn., Capt. John Williams' Watkins Point Co., 1780 [Ref: M-222].

JOHNSON, Elizabeth. See "Hiron Redish" and "John Flint," q.v.

JOHNSON, Fereby. See "Elisha Hearn," q.v.

JOHNSON, Governor. See "Thomas Seon," q.v.

JOHNSON, Henry. Served on the Committee of Observation for Worcester County on May 31, 1776 [Ref: A-457].

JOHNSON, Henry. Private, Worcester Militia, Wicomico Bn., Capt. Charles Bennett's Co., Fifth Class, July 15, 1780 [Ref: M-255].

JOHNSON, Hezekiah. Private, Worcester Militia, Snow Hill Bn., Capt. Samuel Smyley's Co., 1777 [Ref: M-250]. Private, Worcester Militia, Wicomico Bn., Capt. Fisher Walton's Co., Sixth Class, July 15, 1780 [Ref: M-258]. Took the Oath of Allegiance in Worcester County in 1778 before the Hon. Nehemiah Holland [Ref: J-1814 (Box 4)].

JOHNSON, James. First Lieutenant, Worcester Militia, Capt. Elijah Shockley's Co., May 15, 1776 [Ref: M-92, A-405, A-426].

JOHNSON, James. Private, Worcester Militia, Snow Hill Bn., Capt. John Parramore's Co., 1777 [Ref: M-250]. Private, Worcester Militia, Wicomico Bn., Capt. John Parramore's Co., Third Class, July 15, 1780 [Ref: M-259]. Rendered patriotic service by salting beef and driving cattle for the military on Oct 10, 1781 [Ref: P-446].

JOHNSON, Jesse (1756 -   ). Son of William and Tabytha Johnson, born in Coventry Parish on Sep 15, 1756 [Ref: Y-71]. Private, Somerset Militia, Princess Anne Bn., St. Asaph's Co., 1780 [Ref: M-221]. Frederick Digner recruited Jesse Johnson from Somerset County on June 20, 1781 to serve in the Continental Army for 3 years [Ref: L-35C].

JOHNSON, John. Private, Worcester Militia, Sinepuxent Bn., Capt. John Coe's Co., Second Class, 1779/1780 [Ref: M-251]. Private, Maryland Troops, Worcester County, draughted May 1, 1781 [Ref: K-99, D-372].

JOHNSON, John. Private, Worcester Militia, Snow Hill Bn., Capt. John Parramore's Co., 1777 [Ref: M-250]. Private, Worcester Militia, Wicomico Bn., Capt. John Parramore's Co., Fifth Class, July 15, 1780 [Ref: M-259].
JOHNSON, John. Private, Worcester Militia, Snow Hill Bn., Capt. John Parramore's Co., 1777 [Ref: M-250]. Private, Worcester Militia, Sinepuxent Bn., Capt. William Purnell's Co., Third Class, 1779/1780 [Ref: M-252].
JOHNSON, John. Private, Somerset Militia, Salisbury Bn., Capt. Levin Irving's Black Water Co., 1778/1780 [Ref: M-218].
JOHNSON, John. Private, Somerset Militia, Princess Anne Bn., Capt. John Williams' Watkins Point Co., 1780 [Ref: M-222].
JOHNSON, Jonathan. Second Lieutenant, Worcester Militia, Sinepuxent Bn., Capt. William Purnell's Co., Aug 30, 1777 [Ref: M-92, C-350]. Took the Oath of Allegiance in Worcester County in 1778 before the Hon. Nathaniel Miller [Ref: J-1814 (Box 4)].
JOHNSON, Joseph. Private, 3rd Maryland Independent Co., Worcester County, Capt. John Watkins' Co., enlisted Feb 9, 1776; muster roll dated Aug 20, 1776, present for duty [Ref: D-21].
JOHNSON, Lemuel. First Lieutenant, Worcester Militia, June 28, 1777, dismissed [Ref: M-92].
JOHNSON, Lemuel. Private, Worcester Militia, Wicomico Bn., Capt. Fisher Walton's Co., First Class, July 15, 1780 [Ref: M-258].
JOHNSON, Levi. Private, Somerset Militia, Princess Anne Bn., Capt. Thomas Irving's Monie Co., 1780 [Ref: M-219]. Drafted from Somerset County on July 30, 1781 to serve in the Continental Army [Ref: L-35C].
JOHNSON, Littleton. Corporal, 3rd Maryland Independent Co., Worcester County, Capt. John Watkins' Co., enlisted Feb 3, 1776; muster roll dated Aug 20, 1776, present for duty [Ref: D-21]. Private(?), Somerset Militia, Princess Anne Bn., Capt. John Williams' Watkins Point Co., 1780 [Ref: M-222 listed the name as "Lill. Johnson"].
JOHNSON, Peter. Private, Worcester Militia, Wicomico Bn., Capt. Robert Handy's Co., Fourth Class, July 15, 1780 [Ref: M-254].
JOHNSON, Phillis. See "Benjamin Johnson," q.v.
JOHNSON, Purnal. Drafted from Somerset County on June 20, 1781 to serve in the Continental Army [Ref: L-35C].
JOHNSON, R. M. See "Thomas Harris," q.v.
JOHNSON, Robert. Private, Worcester Militia, Sinepuxent Bn., Capt. John Postly's Co., Seventh Class, 1779/1780 [Ref: M-251]. Took the Oath of Allegiance in Worcester County in 1778 before the Hon. Nathaniel Miller [Ref: J-1814 (Box 4)].
JOHNSON, Samuel. Private, Worcester Militia, Sinepuxent Bn., Capt. John Postly's Co., Second Class, 1779/1780 [Ref: M-251]. Took the Oath of Allegiance in Worcester County in 1778 before the Hon. Nathaniel Miller [Ref: J-1814 (Box 4)].

JOHNSON, Samuel. Took the Oath of Allegiance in Worcester County in 1778 before the Hon. Joshua Townsend [Ref: J-1814 (Box 4)].
JOHNSON, Severn. Took the Oath of Allegiance in Worcester County in 1778 before the Hon. Joshua Townsend [Ref: J-1814 (Box 4)].
JOHNSON, Simon. Rendered patriotic service by hauling and storing pork in Worcester County for the use of the military on Oct 13, 1780 [Ref: P-326].
JOHNSON, Smith. Private, Worcester Militia, Wicomico Bn., Capt. Charles Bennett's Co., Fourth Class, July 15, 1780 [Ref: M-255].
JOHNSON, Solomon. Private, Worcester Militia, Wicomico Bn., Capt. Isaac Layfield's Co., Second Class, July 15, 1780 [Ref: M-257]. Took the Oath of Allegiance in Worcester County in 1778 before the Hon. James Selby [Ref: J-1814 (Box 4)].
JOHNSON, Tabytha. See "Jesse Johnson," q.v.
JOHNSON, Thomas. Private, Somerset Militia, Princess Anne Bn., St. Asaph's Co., 1780 [Ref: M-221].
JOHNSON, Thomas. Took the Oath of Allegiance in Worcester County in 1778 before the Hon. Nehemiah Holland [Ref: J-1814 (Box 4), which stated "Affirmations before me but one, vizt., Thomas Johnson only"].
JOHNSON, Whittington. Private, Worcester Militia, Capt. John Martin's Co., 1780/1781 [Ref: J-1814 (Box 12)].
JOHNSON, William. Private, Worcester Militia, Wicomico Bn., Capt. Charles Bennett's Co., Eighth Class, July 15, 1780 [Ref: M-255].
JOHNSON, William. Private, Somerset Militia, Salisbury Bn., Capt. Josiah Dashiell's Wicomico Creek Co., 1778/1780 [Ref: M-218]. See "Jesse Johnson," q.v.
JOHNSON, Zabulon. Took the Oath of Allegiance in Worcester County in 1778 before the Hon. Joshua Townsend [Ref: J-1814 (Box 4)].
JOHNSTON, David. Took the Oath of Allegiance in Worcester County in 1778 before the Hon. Nathaniel Miller [Ref: J-1814 (Box 4)].
JOHNSTON, Dianna. Rendered patriotic service by supplying flour and corn in Worcester County for the use of the military on March 16, 1780 [Ref: P-276].
JONES, Benjamin. Private, Somerset Militia, Salisbury Bn., Capt. Josiah Dashiell's Wicomico Creek Co., 1778/1780 [Ref: M-218]. See "John Jones (of Benjamin)," q.v.
JONES, Benjamin (Forest). Took the Oath of Allegiance in Somerset County in 1778 before the Hon. William Winder [Ref: T-22, and N-51 listed it without the word "Forest" behind his name].
JONES, Charles (Goose Creek). Took the Oath of Allegiance in Somerset County in 1778 before the Hon. Levin Wilson [Ref: T-17, N-51].
JONES, Charles. Sergeant, Somerset Militia, Salisbury Bn., White Haven Co., 1778/1780 [Ref: M-218]. Took the Oath of Allegiance in Somerset County in 1778 before the Hon. Levin Wilson [Ref: T-17, N-51].

JONES, Cotter (1759-1831). Private, Maryland Line, who applied for a pension (S34946) in Worcester County on May 26, 1819, age 60. On Nov 30, 1820 he moved to Somerset County with his wife Nancy (age 38) and four children: Henry (age 13), Francis (age 11), James (age 8), and ---- (fourth child not named). On Jan 14, 1836 a Francis Jones signed a power of attorney as heir at law of the deceased soldier, apparently in regards to bounty land warrant #2250-100 [Ref: W-1869 listed the name as "Cotter Jones"]. "Cotton Jones" pensioned in Somerset County at $96 per annum effective May 26, 1819 and died on Nov 15, 1831 [Ref: X-41].

JONES, Daniel. Private, Worcester Militia, Wicomico Bn., Capt. James Patterson's Co., Fourth Class, July 15, 1780 [Ref: M-258]. Took the Oath of Allegiance in Worcester County in 1778 before the Hon. James Selby [Ref: J-1814 (Box 4) listed the name as "Dannel Jones"]. Rendered patriotic service by supplying pork for the use of the military in Somerset County on Sep 20, 1780 [Ref: P-319].

JONES, Ebenezer. Private, Worcester Militia, Sinepuxent Bn., Capt. John Rackliff's Co., Seventh Class, 1779/1780 [Ref: M-251].

JONES, Elisha. Private, Worcester Militia, Wicomico Bn., Capt. Fisher Walton's Co., First Class, July 15, 1780 [Ref: M-258]. Took the Oath of Allegiance in Worcester County in 1778 before the Hon. James Selby [Ref: J-1814 (Box 4) listed the name as "Elishe Jones"].

JONES, Elisha. Private, Worcester Militia, Snow Hill Bn., Capt. Samuel Smyley's Co., 1777 [Ref: M-250]. Private, Worcester Militia, Wicomico Bn., Capt. Robert Handy's Co., First Class, July 15, 1780 [Ref: M-254]. Took the Oath of Allegiance in Worcester County in 1778 before the Hon. James Selby [Ref: J-1814 (Box 4) listed the name as "Elishe Jones"].

JONES, Elisha. Took the Oath of Allegiance in Worcester County in 1778 before the Hon. Joshua Townsend [Ref: J-1814 (Box 4)].

JONES, Elizabeth. See "George Dashiell," q.v.

JONES, Francis. Private, Somerset Militia, Salisbury Bn., Capt. James Bennett's Salisbury Co., 1778/1780 [Ref: M-218]. See "Cotter Jones," q.v.

JONES, George. Ensign, Somerset Militia, 1st Bn., Capt. John McClester's Co., May 15, 1776 [Ref: M-93, A-426]. Took the Oath of Allegiance in Somerset County in 1778 before the Hon. Levin Wilson [Ref: T-17].

JONES, George. Private, Somerset Militia, Princess Anne Bn., Capt. Thomas Irving's Monie Co., 1780 [Ref: M-219].

JONES, George. Private, Worcester Militia, Sinepuxent Bn., Capt. Elisha Purnell's Co., Sixth Class, 1779/1780 [Ref: M-253]. Took the Oath of Allegiance in Worcester County in 1778 in Quepomco Hundred before the Hon. Thomas Purnell [Ref: J-1814 (Box 4)].

JONES, George (Dames Quarters). Private, Somerset Militia, Princess Anne Bn., Capt. Thomas Irving's Monie Co., 1780 [Ref: M-219 listed the name as "George Jones (DQ)"].

JONES, Giles. Sergeant, Worcester Militia, Wicomico Bn., Capt. Fisher Walton's Co., July 15, 1780 [Ref: M-258]. Took the Oath of Allegiance in Worcester County in 1778 before the Hon. Nehemiah Holland [Ref: J-1814 (Box 4)].

JONES, Henry. See "Cotter Jones," q.v.

JONES, Isaac. See "John Jones (of Benjamin)," q.v.

JONES, James. Private, Worcester Militia, Wicomico Bn., Capt. James Patterson's Co., Eighth Class, July 15, 1780 [Ref: M-258].

JONES, James. Private, Somerset Militia, Salisbury Bn., White Haven Co., 1778/1780 [Ref: M-218]. Took the Oath of Allegiance in Somerset County in 1778 (made his "X" mark) before the Hon. Gillis Polk [Ref: T-15, N-51].

JONES, James (Dames Quarters). Private, Somerset Militia, Princess Anne Bn., Capt. Thomas Irving's Monie Co., 1780 [Ref: M-219 listed the name as "James Jones (DQ)"]. Took the Oath of Allegiance in Somerset County in 1778 [Ref: N-51 listed the name as "James Jones, Jr."].

JONES, James (Somerset County). Took the Oath of Allegiance before the Council of Maryland on March 21, 1778 [Ref: C-545]. See "Cotter Jones," q.v.

JONES, James M. Took the Oath of Allegiance in Somerset County in 1778 before the Hon. John Span Conway [Ref: T-14 listed the name as "James Makn. Jones" and N-51 listed the name as "James Mack Jones"].

JONES, Jesse. First Lieutenant,, Worcester Militia, Sinepuxent Bn., Capt. Elisha Purnell's Co., commissioned Aug 14, 1779 [Ref: M-253, E-493].

JONES, Jesse. Second Lieutenant, Worcester Militia, Sinepuxent Bn., Capt. John Purnell's Co., Aug 30, 1777. First Lieutenant, Aug 14, 1779, Capt. Elisha Purnell's Co. [Ref: M-93, C-350, E-493]. Took the Oath of Allegiance in Worcester County in 1778 in Quepomco Hundred before the Hon. Thomas Purnell [Ref: J-1814 (Box 4)].

JONES, John. Captain, Somerset Militia, Princess Anne Bn., Princess Anne Co., Sep 22, 1777 to at least July 24, 1780 [Ref: M-93, M-219, C-381]. Rendered patriotic service by supplying pork for the use of the military in Somerset County on Aug 3, 1780 [Ref: P-306].

JONES, John. Ensign, Worcester Militia, Sinepuxent Bn., Capt. Matthew Purnell's Co., Aug 30, 1777 to at least July 25, 1780 [Ref: M-93, M-252, C-350].

JONES, John. Private, Somerset Militia, Princess Anne Bn., Capt. Thomas Irving's Monie Co., 1780 [Ref: M-219 listed the name twice]. Select Militia, Somerset County, Aug 15, 1781 [Ref: L-35A].

JONES, John. Private, Somerset Militia, Princess Anne Bn., Capt. Isaac Handy's Great Annemessix Co., 1780 [Ref: M-221]. Select Militia, Somerset County, Aug 15, 1781 [Ref: L-35B].

JONES, John. Private, Worcester Militia, Sinepuxent Bn., Capt. Elisha Purnell's Co., Sixth Class, 1779/1780 [Ref: M-253].

JONES, John. Sergeant, Worcester Militia, Wicomico Bn., Capt. Fisher Walton's Co., July 15, 1780 [Ref: M-258].

JONES, John, Segr.*[sic]*. Took the Oath of Allegiance in Worcester County in 1778 before the Hon. Nathaniel Miller [Ref: J-1814 (Box 4)].

JONES, John Sr. Took the Oath of Allegiance in Worcester County in 1778 before the Hon. John Selby [Ref: J-1814 (Box 4)].

JONES, John Jr. Took the Oath of Allegiance in Worcester County in 1778 before the Hon. Nathaniel Miller [Ref: J-1814 (Box 4)]. Private, Worcester Militia, Sinepuxent Bn., Capt. Matthew Purnell's Co., Seventh Class, July 25, 1780 [Ref: M-252]. Rendered patriotic service by supplying beef for the use of the military on Oct 14, 1780 [Ref: P-326].

JONES, John Jr. (Matapony). Took the Oath of Allegiance in Worcester County in 1778 before the Hon. Nehemiah Holland [Ref: J-1814 (Box 4)].

JONES, John (of Benjamin). Private, Maryland Line, who applied for a pension (R5412) at Nanticoke in Somerset County on May 21, 1833, stating he was born at Wetipguin(?) in Somerset County on Feb 11, 1757, a son of Benjamin Jones, and lived there at the time of his enlistment. In 1833 an Isaac D. Jones of Princess Anne in Somerset County was mentioned, but no relationship was stated [Ref: W-1875]. This was probably the John Jones who was a private in the Somerset Militia, Salisbury Bn., Capt. John Span Conway's Nanticoke Point Co., 1778/1780 [Ref: M-216].

JONES, John (of Robert). Second Lieutenant, Somerset Militia, Princess Anne Bn., Capt. Thomas Irving's Monie Co., Sep 22, 1777 to at least July 24, 1780 [Ref: M-219, M-93, C-381].

JONES, John (Back Creek). Took the Oath of Allegiance in Somerset County in 1778 before the Hon. Levin Wilson [Ref: T-17].

JONES, John (Goose Creek). Ensign, Somerset Militia, Salisbury Bn., Capt. G. Wilson's Co., Sep 22, 1777 [Ref: M-93, C-382 listed the name as "John Jones G.C."]. Took the Oath of Allegiance in Somerset County in 1778 before the Hon. Levin Wilson [Ref: T-17, N-51].

JONES, John (Indian Town). Took the Oath of Allegiance in Worcester County in 1778 before the Hon. Joshua Townsend [Ref: J-1814 (Box 4)].

JONES, John (Monie). Took the Oath of Allegiance in Somerset County in 1778 before the Hon. Levin Wilson [Ref: T-17, and N-51 listed the name as "John Jones of Menie"].

JONES, John (Princess Anne). Took the Oath of Allegiance in Somerset County in 1778 before the Hon. Levin Wilson [Ref: T-17, N-51].

JONES, John Morgan. Drummer, 3rd Maryland Independent Co., Worcester County, Capt. John Watkins' Co., enlisted June 16, 1776; muster roll dated Aug 20, 1776, present for duty [Ref: D-21].

JONES, Joseph. Took the Oath of Allegiance in Worcester County in 1778 before the Hon. Nathaniel Miller [Ref: J-1814 (Box 4)].

JONES, Levin. Corporal, Somerset Militia, Salisbury Bn., White Haven Co., 1778/1780 [Ref: M-218].

JONES, Major (Mager). Took the Oath of Allegiance in Worcester County in 1778 before the Hon. James Selby [Ref: J-1814 (Box 4)]. Private, Worcester Militia, Wicomico Bn., Capt. James Patterson's Co., Fourth Class, July 15, 1780 [Ref: M-258].

JONES, Mathias. Took the Oath of Allegiance in Somerset County in 1778 before the Hon. Peter Waters [Ref: T-18].

JONES, Michael. Took the Oath of Allegiance in Somerset County in 1778 before the Hon. Peter Waters [Ref: T-18].

JONES, Nancy. See "Cotter Jones," q.v.

JONES, Obed. Took the Oath of Allegiance in Worcester County in 1778 before the Hon. Joshua Townsend [Ref: J-1814 (Box 4)].

JONES, Phillip. Private, Somerset Militia, Salisbury Bn., White Haven Co., 1778/1780 [Ref: M-218].

JONES, Priscilla. See "George Dashiell," q.v.

JONES, Robert. Private, Somerset Militia, Princess Anne Bn., Capt. Thomas Irving's Monie Co., 1780 [Ref: M-219].

JONES, Robert (Dames Quarters). Took the Oath of Allegiance in Somerset County in 1778 before the Hon. Levin Wilson [Ref: T-17, N-51].

JONES, Thomas. Ensign, Worcester Militia, Sinepuxent Bn., Capt. Elisha Purnell's Co., commissioned Aug 14, 1779 [Ref: M-94, M-253, C-493].

JONES, Thomas. First Lieutenant, Somerset Militia, 17th Bn., Capt. Benjamin Schoolfield's Co., Sep 19, 1776 [Ref: M-93, B-285].

JONES, Thomas. Private, Somerset Militia, Princess Anne Bn., Capt. Thomas Irving's Monie Co., 1780 [Ref: M-219].

JONES, Thomas. Private, Somerset Militia, Princess Anne Bn., St. Asaph's Co., 1780 [Ref: M-221].

JONES, Thomas. Rendered patriotic service by supplying bacon for the use of the military in Somerset County on Sep 7, 1780 [Ref: P-315]. Took the Oath of Allegiance in Somerset County in 1778 before the Hon. Peter Waters [Ref: T-18].

JONES, Thomas. Took the Oath of Allegiance in Worcester County in 1778 in Quepomco Hundred before the Hon. Thomas Purnell [Ref: J-1814 (Box 4)].

JONES, William. Fidler, 3rd Maryland Independent Co., Worcester County, Capt. John Watkins' Co., enlisted March 19, 1776; muster roll dated Aug 20, 1776, present for duty [Ref: D-21].

JONES, William. Private, Somerset Militia, Salisbury Bn., White Haven Co., 1778/1780 [Ref: M-218].

JONES, William. Private, Worcester Militia, Sinepuxent Bn., Capt. Matthew Purnell's Co., First Class, July 25, 1780 [Ref: M-252].

JONES, William. Private, Somerset County, Capt. John Gunby's 2nd Independent Maryland Co.; present on July 4, 1776; "deserted" on July 9, 1776; mustered on Aug 21, 1776 [Ref: D-642]. This may be the William Jones who applied for a pension (R5755) in Somerset County on Feb 25, 1851, stating he was born in

Somerset County on June 13, 1760 and lived there at the time of his enlistment in the Maryland Line [Ref: W-1884]. However, since there were several men named William Jones in Somerset County, additional research will be necessary before drawing conclusions.

JONES, William. Private, Somerset Militia, Salisbury Bn., Capt. Josiah Dashiell's Wicomico Creek Co., 1778/1780 [Ref: M-218]. Private, Maryland Troops, Worcester County, draughted May 1, 1781 [Ref: K-99, D-372].

JONES, William. Rendered patriotic service by supplying corn for the use of the military in Somerset County on Jan 14 and Jan 15, 1780 [Ref: P-261].

JONES, William. Recommended to Gov. Thomas Johnson by George Dashiell for a commission on May 18, 1778 [Ref: O-99]. Second Lieutenant, Somerset Militia, Princess Anne Bn., Capt. James Elzey's Co., Dec 7, 1778 to at least July 24, 1780 [Ref: M-94, M-220, E-260].

JONES, William. Sergeant, Somerset Militia, Princess Anne Bn., Capt. Thomas Irving's Monie Co., 1780 [Ref: M-219].

JONES, William. Took the Oath of Allegiance in Somerset County on Feb 21, 1778 (made his "X" mark) before the Hon. Joseph Venables [Ref: T-25].

JONES, William. Took the Oath of Allegiance in Worcester County in 1778 before the Hon. Nathaniel Miller [Ref: J-1814 (Box 4), N-51].

JONES, William. Took the Oath of Allegiance in Somerset County in 1778 before the Hon. John Span Conway [Ref: T-14].

JONES, William (of John). Took the Oath of Allegiance in Worcester County in 1778 before the Hon. Joshua Townsend [Ref: J-1814 (Box 4)].

JONES, William (of Thomas), Monie. Private, Select Militia, Somerset County, Aug 15, 1781 [Ref: L-35A].

JOYNES, Edward III (c1763-1830/1). Son of Edward Joynes, Jr. (who died by 1787 in Accomack County, Virginia). He was born circa 1763, served as a seaman in the Virginia State Navy, married Rebecca Watson, and died circa 1830/31 in Worcester County, Maryland [Ref: Q-23:3 (Summer, 1982), "Ancestor Table of Willis Clayton Tull, Jr.," pp. 247-255].

JUET, Nathaniel. Second Lieutenant, Somerset Militia, Princess Anne Bn., Capt. Henry Miles' Little Annemessex Co., Sep 22, 1777 to at least July 24, 1780 [Ref: C-381, M-94, M-221, which latter source questionably listed the name as "Nathaniel --tty?"].

JUSTICE, Elijah. Private, Worcester Militia, Wicomico Bn., Capt. John Parramore's Co., Seventh Class, July 15, 1780 [Ref: M-259].

JUSTICE, John. Private, Worcester Militia, Sinepuxent Bn., Capt. Josiah Dale's Co., Fourth Class, 1779/1780 [Ref: M-254].

KARSLEY, Potter. Private, Somerset Militia, Princess Anne Bn., St. Asaph's Co., 1780 [Ref: M-220].

KELLUM (KILLAM), Edward. Second Lieutenant, Somerset Militia, Salisbury Bn., Capt. William Turpin's Rewastico Co., Jan 7, 1778. First Lieutenant,

Rewastico Co., 1781 [Ref: M-217, M-94, C-457, J-1814 (Box 8, Dashiell's correspondence), G-575].

KELLUM (KILLAM), Isaac Sr. Took the Oath of Allegiance in Worcester County in 1778 before the Hon. Joshua Townsend [Ref: J-1814 (Box 4) listed the name as "Isaac Killam, Sener"].

KELLUM (KILLAM), Isaac. Private, Somerset Militia, Princess Anne Bn., Capt. John Williams' Watkins Point Co., 1780 [Ref: M-222].

KELLUM (KILLAM), Isaac. Private, Worcester Militia, Sinepuxent Bn., Capt. William Purnell's Co., Eighth Class, 1779/1780 [Ref: M-252]. Private, Worcester Militia, Capt. John Martin's Co., 1780/1781 [Ref: J-1814 (Box 12)]. Took the Oath of Allegiance in Worcester County in 1778 in Bogerternorton Hundred before the Hon. Thomas Purnell [Ref: J-1814 (Box 4)].

KELLUM (KILLAM), James. Private, Somerset Militia, Princess Anne Bn., Capt. Isaac Handy's Great Annemessix Co., 1780 [Ref: M-221]. Drafted from Somerset County on June 20, 1781 to serve in the Continental Army [Ref: L-35C].

KELLUM (KILLAM), John. Took the Oath of Allegiance in Worcester County in 1778 before the Hon. James Selby [Ref: J-1814 (Box 4)].

KELLUM (KILLAM), John. Private, Worcester Militia, Wicomico Bn., Capt. Benjamin Dennis' Co., Fourth Class, July 15, 1780 [Ref: M-255].

KELLUM (KILLAM), John. Private, Worcester Militia, Wicomico Bn., Capt. Philip Quinton's Co., Fifth Class, July 15, 1780 [Ref: M-256]. Private, Worcester Militia, Capt. John Martin's Co., 1780/1781 [Ref: J-1814 (Box 12)].

KELLUM (KILLAM), Joseph. Private, Worcester Militia, Wicomico Bn., Capt. William Handy's Co., First Class, July 15, 1780 [Ref: M-257]. Took the Oath of Allegiance in Worcester County in 1778 before the Hon. Joshua Townsend [Ref: J-1814 (Box 4)].

KELLUM (KILLAM), Samuel. Took the Oath of Allegiance in Somerset County in 1778 before the Hon. John Williams [Ref: T-21]. Private, Somerset Militia, Princess Anne Bn., Capt. Isaac Handy's Great Annemessix Co., 1780 [Ref: M-221].

KELLUM (KILLAM), Sarah. See "John Dashiell, of Winder," q.v.

KELLUM (KILLAM), William. Took the Oath of Allegiance in Worcester County in 1778 before the Hon. Joshua Townsend [Ref: J-1814 (Box 4) listed the name as "William Kellem"].

KELLUM (KILLAM), William. Private, Somerset Militia, Princess Anne Bn., Capt. John Williams' Watkins Point Co., 1780 [Ref: M-222].

KELLY, Daniel. Private, Worcester Militia, Wicomico Bn., Capt. Isaac Layfield's Co., Fourth Class, July 15, 1780 [Ref: M-257]. Took the Oath of Allegiance in Worcester County in 1778 before the Hon. James Selby [Ref: J-1814 (Box 4) listed the name as "Dannel Kelley"].

KELLY, George. Took the Oath of Allegiance in Worcester County in 1778 before the Hon. Joshua Townsend [Ref: J-1814 (Box 4)].

KELLY, James. Private, Somerset Militia, Princess Anne Bn., Capt. Thomas Irving's Monie Co., 1780 [Ref: M-219 listed the name as "James Kelley"].

KELLY, Robert. Took the Oath of Allegiance in Worcester County in 1778 before the Hon. Joshua Townsend [Ref: J-1814 (Box 4)].

KELLY(?), John. Private, Worcester Militia, Wicomico Bn., Capt. Isaac Layfield's Co., Fifth Class, July 15, 1780 [Ref: M-257].

KEMP, Natt. Private, Somerset Militia, Salisbury Bn., Capt. Henry Gale's Quantico Co., 1778/1780 [Ref: M-217].

KENELM, Thomas. Took the Oath of Allegiance in Somerset County in 1778 [Ref: N-51].

KENERLY, Everton (c1761-1795). Private, Somerset Militia, Salisbury Bn., Capt. William Turpin's Rewastico Co., 1778/1780 [Ref: M-217]. "Everton Kennerly" was born before 1761, married (wife's name not known), was a soldier in Maryland during the war, and died before June 22, 1795 [Ref: V-1661].

KENNITT, Kendall. Took the Oath of Allegiance in Worcester County in 1778 before the Hon. Nathaniel Miller [Ref: J-1814 (Box 4)].

KENNITT, Presgrave (Prisgrave). Private, Worcester Militia, Sinepuxent Bn., Capt. John Postly's Co., First Class, 1779/1780 [Ref: M-251]. Took the Oath of Allegiance in Worcester County in 1778 before the Hon. Nathaniel Miller [Ref: J-1814 (Box 4)].

KENNITT, Turville. Took the Oath of Allegiance in Worcester County in 1778 before the Hon. Nehemiah Holland [Ref: J-1814 (Box 4)].

KENNITT, William. Private, Worcester Militia, Sinepuxent Bn., Capt. John Postly's Co., Eighth Class, 1779/1780 [Ref: M-251]. Took the Oath of Allegiance in Worcester County in 1778 before the Hon. Nathaniel Miller [Ref: J-1814 (Box 4)].

KER, Jacob. Took the Oath of Allegiance in Somerset County in 1778 before the Hon. Levin Wilson [Ref: T-17]. "Rev. Jacob Ker" married Esther Wilson, daughter of David Wilson, in 1767 [Ref: R-897]. See "Levin Handy," q.v.

KERBY, John. Private, Worcester Militia, Sinepuxent Bn., Capt. John Rackliff's Co., Eighth Class, 1779/1780 [Ref: M-251]. Took the Oath of Allegiance in Worcester County in 1778 before the Hon. Nathaniel Miller [Ref: J-1814 (Box 4)].

KERR, Elizabeth. See "John Adams," q.v.

KILLET, Elizabeth. See "John Dashiell," q.v.

KILLIAM, Isaac. See "Isaac Kellum (Killam)," q.v.

KILPIN, Glenn. Private, Worcester Militia, Snow Hill Bn., Capt. John Parramore's Co., 1777 [Ref: M-250].

KING, Arthur. Private, Somerset Militia, Princess Anne Bn., Capt. John Jones' Princess Anne Co., 1780 [Ref: M-220].

KING, Francis. Rendered patriotic service by supplying bacon for the use of the military in Somerset County on Aug 19, 1780 [Ref: P-310].

KING, James. Second Lieutenant, Worcester Militia, 10th Bn., Capt. Jesse Gray's Co., May 15, 1776 [Ref: M-95, A-426].

KING, Jesse. Corporal, Somerset Militia, Princess Anne Bn., Capt. John Jones' Princess Anne Co., 1780 [Ref: M-219]. Took the Oath of Allegiance in Somerset County in 1778 before the Hon. Peter Waters [Ref: T-18]. Select Militia, Somerset County, Aug 15, 1781 [Ref: L-35A].

KING, Levin. Private, Somerset Militia, Princess Anne Bn., Capt. John Jones' Princess Anne Co., 1780 [Ref: M-219].

KING, Levin Jr. Took the Oath of Allegiance in Somerset County in 1778 before the Hon. John Williams [Ref: T-21, N-51].

KING, Levin (of Babel). Took the Oath of Allegiance in Somerset County in 1778 before the Hon. John Williams [Ref: T-21, N-51].

KING, Nehemiah. Ensign, Somerset Militia, Princess Anne Bn., Capt. William Waters' Co., Jan 7, 1778 [Ref: M-95, C-457]. Took the Oath of Allegiance in Somerset County in 1778 before the Hon. Levin Wilson [Ref: T-17, N-51]. Rendered patriotic service by supplying bacon for the use of the military in Somerset County on Aug 19, 1780 [Ref: P-310].

KING, Philip. Private, Somerset County, Capt. John Gunby's 2nd Independent Maryland Co.; present on April 9, 1776; mustered on Aug 21, 1776 [Ref: D-641].

KING, Planner. Private, Somerset Militia, Princess Anne Bn., Capt. John Jones' Princess Anne Co., 1780 [Ref: M-219].

KING, Robert. See "Isaac Henry," q.v.

KING, Robert Jenkins. Ensign, Somerset Militia, Princess Anne Bn., Capt. George Waters' Pocomoke Co., Sep 22, 1777. Second Lieutenant, 1780 [Ref: M-95, M-220, C-381]. Took the Oath of Allegiance in Somerset County in 1778 before the Hon. Peter Waters [Ref: T-18].

KING, Samuel. Took the Oath of Allegiance in Somerset County in 1778 before the Hon. Levin Wilson [Ref: T-17, N-51].

KING, Thomas. First Lieutenant, Somerset Militia, Princess Anne Bn., Capt. John Williams' Co., Sep 22, 1777. Captain, from Dec 7, 1778 to at least Aug 22, 1781 [Ref: M-95, E-260, G-575]. Took the Oath of Allegiance in Somerset County in 1778 before the Hon. Levin Wilson [Ref: T-17, N-51].

KING, Upshur. Private, Somerset Militia, Princess Anne Bn., Capt. John Jones' Princess Anne Co., 1780 [Ref: M-219]. Took the Oath of Allegiance in Somerset County in 1778 before the Hon. Peter Waters [Ref: T-18].

KING, William. Private, Somerset Militia, Princess Anne Bn., Capt. Thomas Irving's Monie Co., 1780 [Ref: M-219].

KING, William. Private, Somerset Militia, Princess Anne Bn., Capt. John Jones' Princess Anne Co., 1780 [Ref: M-219].

KING, Zorobabel. Took the Oath of Allegiance in Somerset County in 1778 before the Hon. Peter Waters [Ref: T-18].

KNIGHT, James. Private, Somerset Militia, Salisbury Bn., Capt. Josiah Dashiell's Wicomico Creek Co., 1778/1780 [Ref: M-218]. Took the Oath of Allegiance in Somerset County on Feb 28, 1778 (made his "X" mark) before the Hon. Joseph Venables [Ref: T-25].

KNIGHT, Jonathan. Private, Somerset Militia, Salisbury Bn., Capt. Josiah Dashiell's Wicomico Creek Co., 1778/1780 [Ref: M-218].

KNIGHT, Joshua. Private, Somerset Militia, Salisbury Bn., Capt. Josiah Dashiell's Wicomico Creek Co., 1778/1780 [Ref: M-218]. Took the Oath of Allegiance in Somerset County on Feb 28, 1778 (made his "O" mark) before the Hon. Joseph Venables [Ref: T-25].

KNIGHT, Josiah. Private, Somerset Militia, Salisbury Bn., Capt. Josiah Dashiell's Wicomico Creek Co., 1778/1780 [Ref: M-218].

KNIGHT, Nehemiah. Private, Somerset County, Capt. John Gunby's 2nd Independent Maryland Co.; present on March 9, 1776; mustered on Aug 21, 1776 [Ref: D-641].

KNIPS(?), John. Private, Somerset Militia, Princess Anne Bn., Capt. Henry Miles' Little Annemessex Co., 1780 [Ref: M-221].

KNOX, Ezekiel. Private, Worcester Militia, Sinepuxent Bn., Capt. Elisha Purnell's Co., Fifth Class, 1779/1780 [Ref: M-253]. Took the Oath of Allegiance in Worcester County in 1778 in Quepomco Hundred before the Hon. Thomas Purnell [Ref: J-1814 (Box 4) listed the name as "Ezekiell Nox"].

KREMER, Christian (Christien). Took the Oath of Allegiance in Somerset County in 1778 before the Hon. John Williams [Ref: T-20, N-51].

KREMM, Marietta. See "Thomas Harris," q.v.

L--?--K, Carman. Private, Somerset Militia, Salisbury Bn., Capt. James Bennett's Salisbury Co., 1778/1780 [Ref: M-218].

LAMB, Luke. Private, 3rd Maryland Independent Co., Worcester County, Capt. John Watkins' Co., enlisted Feb 10, 1776; muster roll dated Aug 20, 1776, sick in the country [Ref: D-21].

LAMBDEN, Thomas Jr. Took the Oath of Allegiance in Worcester County in 1778 before the Hon. James Selby [Ref: J-1814 (Box 4)]. Private, Worcester Militia, Wicomico Bn., Capt. Isaac Layfield's Co., Second Class, July 15, 1780 [Ref: M-257].

LAMBDEN, Thomas Sr. Took the Oath of Allegiance in Worcester County in 1778 before the Hon. Joshua Townsend [Ref: J-1814 (Box 4) listed the name as "Thomas Lamdon, Sener"].

LAMBERSON, Abraham. Took the Oath of Allegiance in Worcester County in 1778 before the Hon. James Selby [Ref: J-1814 (Box 4)].

LAMBERSON, Levi (1751-1817). Private, Worcester Militia, Wicomico Bn., Capt. Benjamin Dennis' Co., Third Class, July 15, 1780 [Ref: M-255]. Levi Lamberson was born in Maryland in 1751, married Rebecca Parker, served as a soldier in Maryland during the war, and died in Indiana in 1817 [Ref: V-1730].

LAMBERSON, Robert. Private, Worcester Militia, Wicomico Bn., Capt. Fisher Walton's Co., Fourth Class, July 15, 1780 [Ref: M-258]. Took the Oath of Allegiance in Worcester County in 1778 before the Hon. Nehemiah Holland [Ref: J-1814 (Box 4)].

LAMBERSON, Samuel. Private, Worcester Militia, Wicomico Bn., Capt. James Patterson's Co., Sixth Class, July 15, 1780 [Ref: M-258]. Taken prisoner (among others) by the pirate Joseph Mulliner (who was subsequently executed), Samuel Lambson or Lamberson of Worcester County was paroled on May 31, 1781 and dismissed by the Council of Maryland on October 29, 1781 [Ref: H-538].

LAMBERSON, Smith. Private, Worcester Militia, Wicomico Bn., Capt. James Patterson's Co., Third Class, July 15, 1780 [Ref: M-258].

LAMBERSON, Thomas. Private, Worcester Militia, Sinepuxent Bn., Capt. Thomas Purnell's Co., Fifth Class, 1779/1780 [Ref: M-253]. Took the Oath of Allegiance in Worcester County in 1778 before the Hon. Nathaniel Miller [Ref: J-1814 (Box 4)].

LANCASTER, Catharine. See "John Levy Blades," q.v.

LANCASTER, Mallory. See "John Levy Blades," q.v.

LANCASTER, Sarah. See "John Levy Blades," q.v.

LANCASTER, William. See "John Levy Blades," q.v.

LANCE, Walter. Took the Oath of Allegiance in Somerset County in 1778 before the Hon. John Williams [Ref: T-21, N-51].

LANDER, William. See "William Lauder," q.v.

LANDON (LANDEN), John. Took the Oath of Allegiance in Somerset County in 1778 (made his "X" mark) before the Hon. Peter Waters [Ref: T-18].

LANDON (LANDEN), Joseph. Private, Somerset Militia, Princess Anne Bn., Capt. Isaac Handy's Great Annemessix Co., 1780 [Ref: M-221].

LANDON (LANDEN), Littleton. Private, Somerset Militia, Princess Anne Bn., Capt. James Elzey's Co., 1780 [Ref: M-220 listed the name as "Lill. Landen"]. Took the Oath of Allegiance in Somerset County in 1778 before the Hon. Levin Wilson [Ref: T-17]. Select Militia, Somerset County, Aug 15, 1781 [Ref: L-35B].

LANE, Francis. Sergeant, Somerset Militia, Princess Anne Bn., Capt. George Waters' Pocomoke Co., 1780 [Ref: M-220]. Took the Oath of Allegiance in Somerset County in 1778 before the Hon. Peter Waters [Ref: T-18].

LANE, Isaac. Private, 3rd Maryland Independent Co., Worcester County, Capt. John Watkins' Co., enlisted Feb 3, 1776; muster roll dated Aug 20, 1776, present for duty [Ref: D-22 listed the name as "Isaac Lone"].

LANE, Thomas. Private, Worcester Militia, Wicomico Bn., Capt. William Handy's Co., Fifth Class, July 15, 1780 [Ref: M-257].

LANE, William. Took the Oath of Allegiance in Worcester County in 1778 before the Hon. Joshua Townsend [Ref: J-1814 (Box 4) listed the name as "William Lain"].

LANGSDALE, John. Private, Somerset Militia, Salisbury Bn., Capt. William Turpin's Rewastico Co., 1778/1780 [Ref: M-217]. Drafted from Somerset County on July 30, 1781 to serve in the Continental Army [Ref: L-35C].

LANGSDALE, William. Private, Somerset Militia, Salisbury Bn., Capt. William Turpin's Rewastico Co., 1778/1780 [Ref: M-217].

LANK, Francis. Took the Oath of Allegiance in Somerset County on Feb 21, 1778 before the Hon. Joseph Venables [Ref: T-25].

LANKFORD, Benjamin (1758 -   ). Son of Lazarus and Rachel Lankford, born in Coventry Parish on Sep 12, 1758 [Ref: Y-72]. Private, Somerset Militia, Salisbury Bn., Capt. Levin Irving's Black Water Co., 1778/1780 [Ref: M-217]. Private, Somerset Militia, Princess Anne Bn., Capt. John Williams' Watkins Point Co., 1780 [Ref: M-222]. Took the Oath of Allegiance in Somerset County in 1778 before the Hon. William Winder [Ref: N-51, T-22 listed the name as "Benj. Langford"]. See "Killum Lankford" and "Elijah McGlamery," q.v.

LANKFORD, Elijah (1752 -   ). Private, Maryland Line, who applied for a pension (S34953) in Somerset County on April 16, 1818, age 66, stating he lived there at the time of his enlistment. In 1820 Hannah Lankford was mentioned (no relationship stated). Elijah received a payment of $96 per annum. [Ref: W-3012, X-41].

LANKFORD, Ephraim. Private, Somerset Militia, Princess Anne Bn., Capt. James Elzey's Co., 1780 [Ref: M-220].

LANKFORD, Ezekiel. Private, Somerset Militia, Princess Anne Bn., St. Asaph's Co., 1780 [Ref: M-220].

LANKFORD, Hannah. See "Elijah Lankford," q.v.

LANKFORD, Jacob. Private, Somerset Militia, Princess Anne Bn., St. Asaph's Co., 1780 [Ref: M-221].

LANKFORD, Jesse. Private, Somerset Militia, Princess Anne Bn., St. Asaph's Co., 1780 [Ref: M-220].

LANKFORD, Jesse Maddux (1760 -   ). Son of Lazarus and Rachel Lankford, born in Coventry Parish on Oct 4 or 5, 1760 [Ref: Y-72, Y-85]. Private, Somerset Militia, Princess Anne Bn., Capt. John Williams' Watkins Point Co., 1780 [Ref: M-222 listed the name as "Jesse M. Lankford"].

LANKFORD, John. Corporal, Somerset Militia, Salisbury Bn., Capt. William Turpin's Rewastico Co., 1778/1780 [Ref: M-217].

LANKFORD, Joseph. Private, Somerset Militia, Princess Anne Bn., Capt. John Williams' Watkins Point Co., 1780 [Ref: M-222]. Drafted from Somerset County on July 30, 1781 to serve in the Continental Army [Ref: L-35C].

LANKFORD, Joshua. Private, Somerset Militia, Princess Anne Bn., St. Asaph's Co., 1780 [Ref: M-220].

LANKFORD, Killum. Private, Somerset Militia, Princess Anne Bn., Capt. John Williams' Watkins Point Co., 1780 [Ref: M-222]. Killam Lankford married Mary ---- before 1764 and had children Milla (1764-1765), Zeporiah (1766-1770), Noah (b. 1769), and Benjamin (b. 1772) in Coventry Parish [Ref: Y-86].

LANKFORD, Lazarus. See "Benjamin Lankford" and "Jesse Maddux Lankford," q.v.
LANKFORD, Levi. Private, Somerset Militia, Princess Anne Bn., Capt. John Jones' Princess Anne Co., 1780 [Ref: M-219]. Took the Oath of Allegiance in Somerset County in 1778 before the Hon. Peter Waters [Ref: T-18].
LANKFORD, Littleton. See "Puesy Lankford," q.v.
LANKFORD, Mary. See "Killum Lankford," q.v.
LANKFORD, Milla. See "Killum Lankford," q.v.
LANKFORD, Noah. See "Killum Lankford," q.v.
LANKFORD, Puesy (Puza). Took the Oath of Allegiance in Somerset County in 1778 (made his "X" mark" before the Hon. John Williams [Ref: T-21, and N-51 mistakenly listed the name as "Piney Lankford"]. Puza Lankford married Sarah ---- and their son Littleton was born in Coventry Parish on March 9, 1768 [Ref: Y-86].
LANKFORD, Rachel. See "Benjamin Lankford" and "Jesse Maddux Lankford" and "William Lankford," q.v.
LANKFORD, Sarah. See "Puesy Lankford," q.v.
LANKFORD, Thomas. Private, Somerset Militia, Princess Anne Bn., Capt. John Williams' Watkins Point Co., 1780 [Ref: M-222].
LANKFORD, William (1761 -   ). Son of William and Rachel Lankford, born in Coventry Parish on Jan 9, 1761 [Ref: Y-85]. Private, Somerset Militia, Salisbury Bn., Capt. Joseph Venables' Barren Creek Co., 1778/1780 [Ref: M-217]. Private, Somerset Militia, Princess Anne Bn., St. Asaph's Co., 1780 [Ref: M-221].
LANKFORD, Zeporiah. See "Killum Lankford," q.v.
LANNARD, Sarah. See "John Beauchamp," q.v.
LANTENOR, Francis. Recruited by Capt. Levin Handy and enlisted in the Continental Army in Worcester County on Feb 19, 1780 for the duration of the war, stating he was born in France [Ref: Z-40]. Private, 5th Maryland Line, listed as a recruit among others from Worcester County who were entitled to clothing from the Commissary of Stores on April 24, 1780 [Ref: F-150].
LARRAMORE (LARAMOUR), Elijah. Private, Somerset Militia, Salisbury Bn., Capt. John Span Conway's Nanticoke Point Co., 1778/1780 [Ref: M-216].
LARRAMORE (LARAMOUR), Samuel. Private, Somerset Militia, Salisbury Bn., Capt. John Span Conway's Nanticoke Point Co., 1778/1780 [Ref: M-216].
LARRAMORE (LARAMOUR), Thomas. Private, Somerset Militia, Salisbury Bn., Capt. John Span Conway's Nanticoke Point Co., 1778/1780 [Ref: M-216].
LARRAMORE (LARAMOUR), Thomas. Private, Somerset Militia, Salisbury Bn., Capt. John Span Conway's Nanticoke Point Co., 1778/1780 [Ref: M-216].
LATCHAMP, John H. Private, Worcester Militia, Sinepuxent Bn., Capt. John Coe's Co., First Class, 1779/1780 [Ref: M-251].

LATCHAMP, Nehemiah. Private, Worcester Militia, Sinepuxent Bn., Capt. John Coe's Co., Fourth Class, 1779/1780 [Ref: M-252 listed the name as "Nehemiah Lachamp"].
LATCHAMP, Thomas. Private, Worcester Militia, Sinepuxent Bn., Capt. John Coe's Co., First Class, 1779/1780 [Ref: M-251].
LATCHUM, Eleanor or Eleanora. See "John Tarr (of John)," q.v.
LATCHUM, Micajah or Macajah. See "John Tarr (of John)," q.v.
LAUDER (LANDER?), William. Took the Oath of Allegiance in Worcester County in 1778 before the Hon. William Hopewell [Ref: J-1814 (Box 4)].
LAURANCE (LARRANCE), Elisha. Private, Worcester Militia, Sinepuxent Bn., Capt. Josiah Dale's Co., Eighth Class, 1779/1780 [Ref: M-254]. Private, Somerset Militia, Salisbury Bn., Capt. Levin Irving's Black Water Co., 1778/1780 [Ref: M-218].
LAW, John. Private, Somerset Militia, Princess Anne Bn., Capt. John Jones' Princess Anne Co., 1780 [Ref: M-219]. Took the Oath of Allegiance in Somerset County in 1778 before the Hon. Peter Waters [Ref: T-18]. Appointed by the Council of Maryland to be Inspector of Tobacco at Princess Ann Town on Aug 30, 1780 [Ref: F-271].
LAWS, Bolitha (c1720-1783). Born in Maryland, probably Worcester County, circa 1720, married Leah Sturgis, rendered patriotic service in Delaware during the war, and died there circa April 26, 1783 [Ref: V-1755].
LAWS, Comfort. See "Elijah Laws," q.v.
LAWS, Elijah (c1725-1794). Rendered patriotic service by supplying cattle for the use of the military in Worcester County on Sep 26, 1781 [Ref: P-441]. Elijah Laws was born circa 1725 in Maryland, married Comfort ----, rendered civil service during the war, and died before April, 1794 [Ref: V-1755].
LAWS, Elijah Jr. (1744-1814). Took the Oath of Allegiance in Worcester County in 1778 before the Hon. Joshua Townsend [Ref: J-1814 (Box 4)]. Elijah Laws, Jr. was born in 1744, married Patty Bird, served as a private during the war, and died in January, 1814 [Ref: V-1755].
LAWS, Gilbert. Private, Worcester Militia, Wicomico Bn., Capt. William Handy's Co., Sixth Class, July 15, 1780 [Ref: M-257]. Select Militia, Somerset County, Aug 15, 1781 [Ref: L-35B].
LAWS, James. Second Lieutenant, Worcester Militia, Sinepuxent Bn., Capt. John Cox's Co., Aug 30, 1777 [Ref: M-252, and M-96, C-350 listed the name as "John Lawes"].
LAWS, John. First Lieutenant, Worcester Militia, Sinepuxent Bn., Capt. John Tull's Co., March 16, 1781 [Ref: M-96, G-353].
LAWS, John. Private, Somerset Militia, Princess Anne Bn., Capt. Henry Miles' Little Annemessex Co., 1780 [Ref: M-221 listed the name as "John Taws"].
LAWS, John (Dames Quarters). Private, Somerset Militia, Princess Anne Bn., Capt. Thomas Irving's Monie Co., 1780 [Ref: M-219 listed the name as "John Laws (DQ)"].

LAWS, John (Monie). Private, Somerset Militia, Princess Anne Bn., Capt. Thomas Irving's Monie Co., 1780 [Ref: M-219]. Took the Oath of Allegiance in Somerset County in 1778 before the Hon. Levin Wilson [Ref: N-51 listed the name as "John Lawes of Menie" and T-17 listed the name as "John Lawes, Monie"].

LAWS, Joshua. Took the Oath of Allegiance in Worcester County in 1778 before the Hon. Joshua Townsend [Ref: J-1814 (Box 4)].

LAWS, Rachel. See "John Coulbourn," q.v.

LAWS, William. Sergeant, Somerset Militia, Princess Anne Bn., Capt. Thomas Irving's Monie Co., 1780 [Ref: M-219]. Took the Oath of Allegiance in Somerset County in 1778 before the Hon, Levin Wilson [Ref: T-17, N-51 listed the name as "William Lawes"].

LAWS, William. Private, Select Militia, Somerset County, Aug 15, 1781 [Ref: L-35A]. William Laws was born circa 1753, married Ann Fooks, was a private during the war, and died after 1829 [Ref: V-1755].

LAWS, William. Took the Oath of Allegiance in Worcester County in 1778 before the Hon. Joshua Townsend [Ref: J-1814 (Box 4)].

LAWSON, Hance. Private, Somerset Militia, Princess Anne Bn., Capt. Henry Miles' Little Annemessex Co., 1780 [Ref: M-221].

LAWSON, Samuel. Corporal, Somerset Militia, Princess Anne Bn., Capt. Henry Miles' Little Annemessex Co., 1780 [Ref: M-221].

LAYFIELD, -?-len. Private, Somerset Militia, Salisbury Bn., Capt. James Bennett's Salisbury Co., 1778/1780 [Ref: M-218].

LAYFIELD, David. Private, Worcester Militia, Wicomico Bn., Capt. Charles Bennett's Co., Second Class, July 15, 1780 [Ref: M-255]. Took the Oath of Allegiance in Somerset County in 1778 before the Hon. William Winder [Ref: T-22, N-51].

LAYFIELD, Ezekiel. Private, Somerset Militia, Princess Anne Bn., Capt. John Jones' Princess Anne Co., 1780 [Ref: M-219].

LAYFIELD, George. Private, Worcester Militia, Wicomico Bn., Capt. Isaac Layfield's Co., Fourth Class, July 15, 1780 [Ref: M-257].

LAYFIELD, George. Private, Somerset Militia, Salisbury Bn., Capt. Levin Irving's Black Water Co., 1778/1780 [Ref: M-218].

LAYFIELD, George. Second Lieutenant, Worcester Militia, Snow Hill Bn., Capt. William Holland's Co., Aug 30, 1777. First Lieutenant, Wicomico Bn., Capt. Fisher Waltam [Walton]'s Co., May 27, 1779 to at least July 15, 1780. First Lieutenant, Aug 28, 1781, Capt. John Parramore's Co. [Ref: M-258, M-96, C-351, which latter source listed the name as "George Lafield"]. Took the Oath of Allegiance in Worcester County in 1778 before the Hon. Nehemiah Holland [Ref: J-1814 (Box 4)].

LAYFIELD, Isaac. Captain, Worcester Militia, Wicomico Bn., June 28, 1777 to at least July 15, 1780 [Ref: M-96, M-257, C-351, which latter source listed the name as "Isaac Lafield" on Aug 30, 1777]. Took the Oath of Allegiance in

Worcester County in 1778 before the Hon. James Selby [Ref: J-1814 (Box 4)]. Justice of the Peace for Worcester County, commissioned on Nov 29, 1777 and Nov 21, 1778 and Nov 25, 1778 and Jan 17, 1782 [Ref: C-429, E-250, G-225, I-46].

LAYFIELD, James. Private, Somerset Militia, Princess Anne Bn., Capt. Isaac Handy's Great Annemessix Co., 1780 [Ref: M-221].

LAYFIELD, John. Private, Somerset Militia, Princess Anne Bn., Capt. James Elzey's Co., 1780 [Ref: M-220].

LAYFIELD, Robert. Private, Somerset Militia, Salisbury Bn., Capt. James Bennett's Salisbury Co., 1778/1780 [Ref: M-218]. Private, Worcester Militia, Capt. John Martin's Co., 1780/1781 [Ref: J-1814 (Box 12)].

LAYFIELD, Josiah (1758-1855). Born in Maryland, probably Somerset County, in 1758, married Hetty Cauthern, served as a private in Georgia during the war, and died after April 19, 1855 [Ref: V-1757].

LAYFIELD, Saul. Private, Worcester Militia, Wicomico Bn., Capt. James Perdue's Co., Eighth Class, July 15, 1780 [Ref: M-256].

LAYFIELD, Solomon. Private, Worcester Militia, Snow Hill Bn., Capt. Ebenezer Handy's Co., April 9, 1776 [Ref: M-249].

LAYFIELD, Thomas. Private, Worcester Militia, Wicomico Bn., Capt. Isaac Layfield's Co., Third Class, July 15, 1780 [Ref: M-257].

LAYFIELD, Thomas. Private, Worcester Militia, Wicomico Bn., Capt. Charles Bennett's Co., Fourth Class, July 15, 1780 [Ref: M-255].

LAYFIELD, Thomas. Took the Oath of Allegiance in Worcester County in 1778 before the Hon. James Selby [Ref: J-1814 (Box 4)].

LAYFIELD, William. Private, Worcester Militia, Snow Hill Bn., Capt. Ebenezer Handy's Co., April 9, 1776 [Ref: M-249]. Private, Worcester Militia, Wicomico Bn., Capt. John Davis' Co., Fifth Class, July 15, 1780 [Ref: M-254]. Rendered patriotic service by supplying bacon for the use of the military on Oct 7, 1780 [Ref: P-324].

LEATHERBURY, Amelia. See "John Horsey," q.v.

LEATHERBURY, Elizabeth. See "Isaac Giles," q.v.

LEATHERBURY, John. Private, Somerset Militia, Salisbury Bn., White Haven Co., 1778/1780 [Ref: M-218].

LEATHERBURY, John. Private, Somerset Militia, Salisbury Bn., Capt. Levin Irving's Black Water Co., 1778/1780 [Ref: M-217 listed the name as "John Leatherberry"].

LEATHERBURY, John (1744-1784). Second Lieutenant, Somerset Militia, Salisbury Bn., Capt. Henry Gale's Quantico Co., Sep 22, 1777 to at least July 24, 1780 [Ref: M-97, M-216, C-381]. John Leatherbury was born in 1744, married (wife's name not known), served as a second lieutenant during the war, and died before Dec 11, 1784 [Ref: V-1766].

LEATHERBURY, John Jr. Took the Oath of Allegiance in Somerset County in 1778 before the Hon. William Winder [Ref: N-51 listed the name as "John Leatherby Jr." and T-22 listed the name as "John Leatherburey, Jr."].
LEATHERBURY, Jolley. Private, Somerset Militia, Salisbury Bn., White Haven Co., 1778/1780 [Ref: M-219].
LEATHERBURY, Richard. Took the Oath of Allegiance in Somerset County in 1778 before the Hon. John Span Conway [Ref: T-14 listed the name as "R. Leatherbury" and N-51 listed the name as "Richard Leatherbury"].
LECOUNT, James. Private, Somerset Militia, Princess Anne Bn., Capt. Thomas Irving's Monie Co., 1780 [Ref: M-219]. Took the Oath of Allegiance in Worcester County in 1778 before the Hon. Joshua Townsend [Ref: J-1814 (Box 4)].
LENDALL, Thomas. Private, 3rd Maryland Independent Co., Worcester County, Capt. John Watkins' Co., enlisted April 21, 1776; muster roll dated Aug 20, 1776, present for duty [Ref: D-23].
LEONARD, Benjamin. Private, Worcester Militia, Wicomico Bn., Capt. Elijah Shockley's Co., Sixth Class, July 15, 1780 [Ref: M-255]. Took the Oath of Allegiance in Worcester County in 1778 before the Hon. William Hopewell [Ref: J-1814 (Box 4)].
LEONARD, John. Corporal, Somerset Militia, Salisbury Bn., Capt. Levin Irving's Black Water Co., 1778/1780 [Ref: M-217].
LEONARD, Joseph. Private, Somerset Militia, Salisbury Bn., Capt. Levin Irving's Black Water Co., 1778/1780 [Ref: M-217].
LEONARD (LANNARD), Sarah. See "John Beauchamp," q.v.
LESTER, William Jr. Took the Oath of Allegiance in Worcester County in 1778 before the Hon. Nathaniel Miller [Ref: J-1814 (Box 4)].
LESTER, William, Segr.*[sic]*. Took the Oath of Allegiance in Worcester County in 1778 before the Hon. Nathaniel Miller [Ref: J-1814 (Box 4)].
LEVY (LONG?), William. Private, Somerset Militia, Princess Anne Bn., Capt. Isaac Handy's Great Annemessix Co., 1780 [Ref: M-221].
LEWIS, Arthur. Private, Worcester Militia, Wicomico Bn., Capt. John Davis' Co., Eighth Class, July 15, 1780 [Ref: M-255]. Took the Oath of Allegiance in Worcester County in 1778 before the Hon. Joshua Townsend [Ref: J-1814 (Box 4)].
LEWIS, Elizabeth. See "Richard Summers," q.v.
LEWIS, George. Took the Oath of Allegiance in Worcester County in 1778 before the Hon. Joshua Townsend [Ref: J-1814 (Box 4)]. See "Richard Summers," q.v.
LEWIS, James. Private, Worcester Militia, Sinepuxent Bn., Capt. Matthew Purnell's Co., Third Class, July 25, 1780 [Ref: M-252].
LEWIS, James. Private, Worcester Militia, Wicomico Bn., Capt. John Davis' Co., Second Class, July 15, 1780 [Ref: M-254].
LEWIS, James. Took the Oath of Allegiance in Worcester County in 1778 before the Hon. Joshua Townsend [Ref: J-1814 (Box 4)].

LEWIS, Steven. Took the Oath of Allegiance in Worcester County in 1778 before the Hon. Nathaniel Miller [Ref: J-1814 (Box 4)].

LEWIS, Thomas. Private, Worcester Militia, Wicomico Bn., Capt. John Davis' Co., Third Class, July 15, 1780 [Ref: M-254]. Took the Oath of Allegiance in Worcester County in 1778 before the Hon. Nathaniel Miller [Ref: J-1814 (Box 4)].

LEWIS, William. Private, Worcester Militia, Wicomico Bn., Capt. James Perdue's Co., Seventh Class, July 15, 1780 [Ref: M-256]. Took the Oath of Allegiance in Worcester County in 1778 before the Hon. Nathaniel Miller [Ref: J-1814 (Box 4)].

LIETT (HILL?), Charles Phillips. Private, Worcester Militia, Wicomico Bn., Capt. Samuel Horsey's Co., Fourth Class, July 15, 1780 [Ref: M-257].

LINCH, John. Took the Oath of Allegiance in Worcester County in 1778 in Buckingham Hundred before the Hon. Thomas Purnell [Ref: J-1814 (Box 4)].

LINDAL, John. Private, Worcester Militia, Sinepuxent Bn., Capt. John Postly's Co., Sixth Class, 1779/1780 [Ref: M-251].

LINDSAY, James. Private, Worcester Militia, Wicomico Bn., Capt. John Parramore's Co., First Class, July 15, 1780 [Ref: M-259].

LINDSEY, David. Private, Somerset Militia, Princess Anne Bn., Capt. John Williams' Watkins Point Co., 1780 [Ref: M-222].

LINGO, Nicey Unicey. See "Patrick Causey," q.v.

LINGO, Smith. Private, Worcester Militia, Snow Hill Bn., Capt. Ebenezer Handy's Co., April 9, 1776 [Ref: M-249]. Private, Worcester Militia, Sinepuxent Bn., Capt. Josiah Dale's Co., Seventh Class, 1779/1780 [Ref: M-254].

LINNY, James. Private, Worcester Militia, Snow Hill Bn., Capt. John Parramore's Co., 1777 [Ref: M-250].

LINTON, Elijah. Private, Somerset Militia, Princess Anne Bn., Capt. Henry Miles' Little Annemessex Co., 1780 [Ref: M-221].

LISTER, Thomas. Private, Somerset Militia, Princess Anne Bn., Capt. Isaac Handy's Great Annemessix Co., 1780 [Ref: M-221].

LISTER, William. Private, Worcester Militia, Sinepuxent Bn., Capt. Thomas Purnell's Co., Seventh Class, 1779/1780 [Ref: M-253]. Private, Somerset Militia, Princess Anne Bn., Capt. Isaac Handy's Great Annemessix Co., 1780 [Ref: M-221].

LITTLETON, Leah. See "George Gale" and "Levin Gale," q.v.

LIVINGSTON, George. Private, Worcester Militia, Wicomico Bn., Capt. Samuel Horsey's Co., Seventh Class, July 15, 1780 [Ref: M-257 listed the name as "George Levingston"]. Took the Oath of Allegiance in Worcester County in 1778 before the Hon. Nehemiah Holland [Ref: J-1814 (Box 4)].

LIVINGSTON, Stephen Horsey. Second Lieutenant, Worcester Militia, Wicomico Bn., Aug 30, 1777 [Ref: M-98, C-351]. Took the Oath of Allegiance in Worcester County in 1778 before the Hon. William Hopewell [Ref: J-1814 (Box 4) listed the name as "Stephen Livenston"].

LIVINGSTON, Todd. Private, Worcester Militia, Wicomico Bn., Capt. Samuel Horsey's Co., Fourth Class, July 15, 1780 [Ref: M-257 listed the name as "Todd Levingston"]. Took the Oath of Allegiance in Worcester County in 1778 before the Hon. William Hopewell [Ref: J-1814 (Box 4)].

LLOYD, William. Private, Somerset Militia, Salisbury Bn., Capt. William Turpin's Rewastico Co., 1778/1780 [Ref: M-217].

LOCA, John. Private, Somerset Militia, Princess Anne Bn., Capt. James Elzey's Co., 1780 [Ref: M-220].

LOCA, Thomas. Private, Worcester Militia, Wicomico Bn., Capt. Charles Bennett's Co., Second Class, July 15, 1780 [Ref: M-255]. Took the Oath of Allegiance in Worcester County in 1778 before the Hon. William Hopewell [Ref: J-1814 (Box 4)].

LOCKWOOD, Samuel (1755-1834). Private, Delaware Line, who applied for a pension (S13789) in Pendleton County, Kentucky on April 6, 1833, stating he was born in Worcester County, Maryland on July 22, 1755 and about 1761 he moved with his father (not named) to Sussex County, Delaware. He lived there at the time of his enlistment early in 1776 under Capt. David Hall and in 1777 he transferred to the Co. of Capt. William Perry. He served for a time on a rogue galley which attacked a British vessel, but in general his service was guarding along the Delaware shore and at the lighthouse on Cape Henlopen, for a total service of two years. In 1778 he returned to Worcester County where he married (wife's name not given) and in 1791 they moved to Bourbon County, Kentucky (the part which is now Pendleton County). For 15 or 16 years he was a licensed minister of the Methodist Episcopal Church, but not now as he is too infirm. He died on July 28, 1834 [Ref: W-2105]. "Samuel Logwood" was a private in the Worcester Militia, Sinepuxent Bn., Capt. John Postly's Co., Eighth Class, 1779/1780 [Ref: M-251].

LOGAN, Samuel. Took the Oath of Allegiance in Somerset County in 1778 before the Hon. Levin Wilson [Ref: T-17].

LOGWOOD, Samuel. See "Samuel Lockwood," q.v.

LONE, Isaac. See "Isaac Lane," q.v.

LONG, --?--. Private, Somerset Militia, Princess Anne Bn., Capt. John Williams' Watkins Point Co., 1780 [Ref: M-222].

LONG, Anne. See "Solomon Long," q.v.

LONG, Coulborn. Private, Worcester Militia, Sinepuxent Bn., Capt. Thomas Purnell's Co., First Class, 1779/1780 [Ref: M-253]. Took the Oath of Allegiance in Worcester County in 1778 before the Hon. John Selby [Ref: J-1814 (Box 4)].

LONG, Daniel. Private, Worcester Militia, Sinepuxent Bn., Capt. Thomas Purnell's Co., Eighth Class, 1779/1780 [Ref: M-253].

LONG, David. Private, Worcester Militia, Wicomico Bn., Capt. Isaac Layfield's Co., First Class, July 15, 1780 [Ref: M-257]. Took the Oath of Allegiance in Worcester County in 1778 before the Hon. James Selby [Ref: J-1814 (Box 4)].

Rendered patriotic service by supplying beef for the use of the military on Oct 11, 1780 [Ref: P-325]. See "Solomon Long," q.v.

LONG, Elisha. Private, Worcester Militia, Sinepuxent Bn., Capt. Thomas Purnell's Co., Fourth Class, 1779/1780 [Ref: M-253]. Private, Maryland Troops, Worcester County, draughted May 1, 1781 [Ref: K-99, D-372].

LONG, Jesse (1761 -   ). Son of John and Catherine Long, born in Coventry Parish on Aug 28, 1761 [Ref: Y-86]. Private, Worcester Militia, Sinepuxent Bn., Capt. Thomas Purnell's Co., Seventh Class, 1779/1780 [Ref: M-253]. Private, Worcester Militia, Wicomico Bn., Capt. Isaac Layfield's Co., Fifth Class, July 15, 1780 [Ref: M-257]. he may have been the Jesse Long who took the Oath of Allegiance in Worcester County in 1778 before the Hon. Joshua Townsend although he was not yet 18 years of age, but he was in his 18th year nonetheless [Ref: J-1814 (Box 4)].

LONG, Jessey. Took the Oath of Allegiance in Worcester County in 1778 before the Hon. James Selby [Ref: J-1814 (Box 4)].

LONG, Levin. Took the Oath of Allegiance in Somerset County in 1778 before the Hon. Peter Waters [Ref: T-18]. Private, Worcester Militia, Wicomico Bn., Capt. William Handy's Co., Second Class, July 15, 1780 [Ref: M-257]. See "Solomon Long," q.v.

LONG, Littleton. Ensign, Worcester Militia, Snow Hill Bn., Capt. Thomas Marshall's Co., Aug 30, 1777. Ensign, Wicomico Bn., Capt. Isaac Layfield's Co., July 15, 1780 [Ref: M-98, M-257, C-351]. Took the Oath of Allegiance in Worcester County in 1778 before the Hon. James Selby [Ref: J-1814 (Box 4)].

LONG, Mary. See "Thomas Cottingham," q.v.

LONG, Nelly. See "Solomon Long," q.v.

LONG, Rosey. See "Solomon Long," q.v.

LONG, Samuel. Private, Worcester Militia, Sinepuxent Bn., Capt. Thomas Purnell's Co., First Class, 1779/1780 [Ref: M-253]. Took the Oath of Allegiance in Worcester County in 1778 before the Hon. Nathaniel Miller [Ref: J-1814 (Box 4)]. See "Solomon Long," q.v.

LONG, Samuel (of William). Private, Worcester Militia, Sinepuxent Bn., Capt. Thomas Purnell's Co., Fourth Class, 1779/1780 [Ref: M-253].

LONG, Solomon. Private, Somerset Militia, Princess Anne Bn., Capt. John Jones' Princess Anne Co., 1780 [Ref: M-219]. Rendered patriotic service by supplying pork for the use of the military circa 1781-1782 [Ref: P-466]. Took the Oath of Allegiance in Somerset County in 1778 before the Hon. Peter Waters [Ref: T-18].

LONG, Solomon. Son of Solomon Long (d. 1772) and Margaret Maddux, and brother of "Zadock Long," q.v. He died testate in Somerset County in 1798 (will probated on Nov 2, 1798) and his wife was Mary, his daughters were Sarah Ward, Peggy Scott, Nelly Long, Rosey Long, and Anne Long, and his sons were Samuel Long and David Long (and possibly Levin Long, although he was not named in the will of Solomon Long). [Ref: Q-30:3 (Summer, 1989), pp. 253-254, "The Long Family," by Richard P. Baer]. Solomon was a second lieutenant in the 3rd Maryland Independent Co., Worcester County, Capt. John Watkins' Co., commissioned Jan 5, 1776; muster roll dated Aug 20, 1776, present for duty [Ref: D-21]. Captain by October, 1776. Major, Worcester Militia, Wicomico Bn., May 27, 1779. Lieutenant Colonel, June 13, 1782 [Ref: M-98, E-423, I-190, C-389, B-318]. Took the Oath of Allegiance in Worcester County in 1778 before the Hon. Nathaniel Miller [Ref: J-1814 (Box 4)]. Rendered patriotic service by supplying corn for the use of the military on June 14, 1780 and Oct 9, 1781 [Ref: P-295, P-445]. See "Samuel Bowles," q.v.

LONG, William. Private, Worcester Militia, Sinepuxent Bn., Capt. Thomas Purnell's Co., Eighth Class, 1779/1780 [Ref: M-253].

LONG, Zadock. Took the Oath of Allegiance in Somerset County in 1778 before the Hon. Peter Waters [Ref: T-18]. See "Solomon Long," q.v.

LORD, Cateron. See "Henry Lord," q.v.

LORD, Henry (1755 -). Son of Henry and Cateron Lord, born in Coventry Parish on April 27, 1755 [Ref: Y-85]. Private, Somerset Militia, Salisbury Bn., Capt. Sampson Wheatly's Co., 1780 [Ref: M-216].

LORD, John Jr. Rendered patriotic service by supplying pork in Somerset County for the use of the military on June 8, 1781 [Ref: P-402].

LORD, Peter. Private, Somerset Militia, Salisbury Bn., Capt. Sampson Wheatly's Co., 1780 [Ref: M-216].

LORD, Randolph. Private, Somerset Militia, Princess Anne Bn., St. Asaph's Co., 1780 [Ref: M-220].

LORD, Thomas. Corporal, Somerset Militia, Salisbury Bn., Capt. Sampson Wheatly's Co., 1780 [Ref: M-215].

LORD, Thomas. Private, Somerset Militia, Princess Anne Bn., Capt. Henry Miles' Little Annemessex Co., 1780 [Ref: M-221].

LORD, Thomas (of Henry). Private, Somerset Militia, Princess Anne Bn., Capt. Henry Miles' Little Annemessex Co., 1780 [Ref: M-221].

LOVEL, Peter. Took the Oath of Allegiance in Worcester County in 1778 before the Hon. Nathaniel Miller [Ref: J-1814 (Box 4)].

LOWE, Benjamin. Private, Worcester Militia, Wicomico Bn., Capt. Elijah Shockley's Co., Sixth Class, July 15, 1780 [Ref: M-255].

LOWE, George. Private, Worcester Militia, Snow Hill Bn., Capt. Ebenezer Handy's Co., April 9, 1776 [Ref: M-249]. Private, Worcester Militia, Wicomico Bn., Capt. Elijah Shockley's Co., Fourth Class, July 15, 1780 [Ref: M-255].

LOWE, Henry. Private, Somerset Militia, Salisbury Bn., White Haven Co., 1778/1780 [Ref: M-219].

LOWE, Hutson. Private, Somerset Militia, Salisbury Bn., Capt. Levin Irving's Black Water Co., 1778/1780 [Ref: M-218].

LOWE, Levin. See "George Martin," q.v.

LOWE, Thomas. Private, Somerset Militia, Salisbury Bn., Capt. James Bennett's Salisbury Co., 1778/1780 [Ref: M-218].
LOWE, William. Private, Somerset Militia, Salisbury Bn., Capt. William Turpin's Rewastico Co., 1778/1780 [Ref: M-217].
LOWES, Henry. One of four delegates elected to represent Somerset County at the Maryland Convention in August, 1776 [Ref: O-45]. As captain of the vessel *Chatham*, Henry wrote to George Dashiell, Somerset County Lieutenant, about the transportation of supplies by ship on April 20, 1781 [Ref: P-384]. Henry Lowes, Jr., son of Henry and Easther Lowes, married Easter Dashiells in Stepney Parish on July 31, 1759 at 2 o'clock in the afternoon [Ref: Y-48].
LOWRIE, John. Private, 7th Maryland Line, wounded at the Battle of Camden; on Dec 20, 1784 he appeared on a "return of disabled soldiers who have been allowed by the Orphans Court of Somerset County on account their half pay, etc." from the time his full pay ceased; settled up to July 13, 1784, but no amount was stated [Ref: D-634, D-635].
LOYD, James. Private, Somerset Militia, Salisbury Bn., Capt. William Turpin's Rewastico Co., 1778/1780 [Ref: M-217].
LOYD, Levin. Private, Somerset Militia, Salisbury Bn., Capt. William Turpin's Rewastico Co., 1778/1780 [Ref: M-217].
LUCA, John. Private, Somerset Militia, Salisbury Bn., Capt. James Bennett's Salisbury Co., 1778/1780 [Ref: M-218].
LUER(?), Nehemiah. Private, Worcester Militia, Sinepuxent Bn., Capt. John Coe's Co., Fourth Class, 1779/1780 [Ref: M-252].
LUES, James. Took the Oath of Allegiance in Worcester County in 1778 in Buckingham Hundred before the Hon. Thomas Purnell [Ref: J-1814 (Box 4)].
LUKE, Spencer. Private, Somerset Militia, Princess Anne Bn., Capt. John Jones' Princess Anne Co., 1780 [Ref: M-219 listed the name as "Spencer Luk--?"]. Drafted from Somerset County on July 30, 1781 to serve in the Continental Army, but was subsequently excused [Ref: L-35C].
LUKER, William. Took the Oath of Allegiance in Worcester County in 1778 before the Hon. Nehemiah Holland [Ref: J-1814 (Box 4)].
LURMAN (SURMAN?), George. Corporal, Somerset Militia, Salisbury Bn., Capt. Josiah Dashiell's Wicomico Creek Co., 1778/1780 [Ref: M-218].
LURTON, Jacob. Private, Somerset Militia, Salisbury Bn., Capt. James Bennett's Salisbury Co., 1778/1780 [Ref: M-218].
LYNCH, David. Private, Worcester Militia, Sinepuxent Bn., Capt. John Coe's Co., Sixth Class, 1779/1780 [Ref: M-252].
LYNCH, Isaac. Private, Worcester Militia, Sinepuxent Bn., Capt. John Coe's Co., Second Class, 1779/1780 [Ref: M-251].
LYNCH, Jacob. Private, Worcester Militia, Sinepuxent Bn., Capt. John Coe's Co., Third Class, 1779/1780 [Ref: M-252].
LYNN, Catherine. See "Zadok Nutter," q.v.

MACKALLEN, Allexander. Took the Oath of Allegiance in Worcester County in 1778 before the Hon. Joshua Townsend [Ref: J-1814 (Box 4)].
MADDON (MADDOX?), John. Took the Oath of Allegiance in Somerset County in 1778 before the Hon. William Winder [Ref: T-22].
MADDOX, E. I. See "Moses Greer," q.v.
MADDUX, Alexander. Private, Somerset Militia, Salisbury Bn., Capt. Levin Irving's Black Water Co., 1778/1780 [Ref: M-218].
MADDUX, Daniel. First Lieutenant, Somerset Militia, 17th Bn., Capt. William Fountain's Co., Feb 24, 1776 [Ref: M-100, A-182]. Took the Oath of Allegiance in Somerset County in 1778 before the Hon. Peter Waters [Ref: T-18].
MADDUX, Daniel. Sergeant, Somerset Militia, Princess Anne Bn., Capt. Isaac Handy's Great Annemessix Co., 1780 [Ref: M-221].
MADDUX, Elizabeth. See "Thomas Maddux," q.v.
MADDUX, Elizabeth Waters. See "Richard Waters, Jr.," q.v.
MADDUX, Elzey. Private, Somerset Militia, Princess Anne Bn., Capt. Isaac Handy's Great Annemessix Co., 1780 [Ref: M-221].
MADDUX, Elzey. Private, Somerset Militia, Princess Anne Bn., Capt. George Waters' Pocomoke Co., 1780 [Ref: M-220]. Took the Oath of Allegiance in Somerset County in 1778 before the Hon. Peter Waters [Ref: T-18].
MADDUX, Hezekiah. Private, Worcester Militia, Snow Hill Bn., Capt. Ebenezer Handy's Co., April 9, 1776 [Ref: M-249]. Private, Worcester Militia, Wicomico Bn., Capt. James Perdue's Co., First Class, July 15, 1780 [Ref: M-256].
MADDUX, Isaac. Private, Somerset Militia, Salisbury Bn., Capt. Levin Irving's Black Water Co., 1778/1780 [Ref: M-217].
MADDUX, John. Private, Somerset Militia, Salisbury Bn., Capt. James Bennett's Salisbury Co., 1778/1780 [Ref: M-218].
MADDUX, John. Private, Somerset Militia, Salisbury Bn., Capt. Levin Irving's Black Water Co., 1778/1780 [Ref: M-218].
MADDUX, John. Took the Oath of Allegiance in Somerset County in 1778 before the Hon. Peter Waters [Ref: T-18, and N-51 listed the name as "John Maddox"].
MADDUX, John. See "Thomas Maddux," q.v.
MADDUX, Joshua. Private, Somerset Militia, Salisbury Bn., Capt. Levin Irving's Black Water Co., 1778/1780 [Ref: M-218].
MADDUX, Lazarus. Private, Worcester Militia, Wicomico Bn., Capt. Charles Bennett's Co., Fifth Class, July 15, 1780 [Ref: M-255 listed the name as "Lazarus Madux"]. Took the Oath of Allegiance in Worcester County in 1778 before the Hon. Joshua Townsend [Ref: J-1814 (Box 4) listed the name as "Lazarous Maddix"].
MADDUX, Lazarus. Second Lieutenant, Somerset Militia, Princess Anne Bn., Capt. Isaac Handy's Great Annemessix Co., Dec 12, 1778 to at least July 24, 1780 [Ref: M-221 listed the name as "Lazarous Maddux" and M-100, C-260 mistakenly listed the name as "Lazarus Maddon"]. Took the Oath of Allegiance

in Somerset County in 1778 before the Hon. Peter Waters [Ref: T-18]. Drafted from Somerset County on July 30, 1781 to serve in the Continental Army [Ref: L-35C].

MADDUX, Marcy (Mercey). Took the Oath of Allegiance in Worcester County in 1778 before the Hon. Joshua Townsend [Ref: J-1814 (Box 4)]. Private, Worcester Militia, Wicomico Bn., Capt. Philip Quinton's Co., Fourth Class, July 15, 1780 [Ref: M-256].

MADDUX, Margaret. See "Solomon Long," q.v.

MADDUX, Merrell(?). Private, Worcester Militia, Wicomico Bn., Capt. Charles Bennett's Co., Fifth Class, July 15, 1780 [Ref: M-255].

MADDUX, Stoughlin. Second Lieutenant, Somerset Militia, 17th Bn., Capt. William Fountain's Co., Feb 24, 1776 [Ref: M-100, A-182].

MADDUX, Stoughton. Private, Somerset Militia, Princess Anne Bn., Capt. Isaac Handy's Great Annemessix Co., 1780 [Ref: M-221]. Took the Oath of Allegiance in Somerset County in 1778 before the Hon. Peter Waters [Ref: T-18].

MADDUX, Thomas. Private, Somerset Militia, Princess Anne Bn., Capt. Isaac Handy's Great Annemessix Co., 1780 [Ref: M-221].

MADDUX, Thomas (c1750-1783). Son of John Maddux of Somerset County. Thomas took an oath as attorney on May 20, 1777 and by 1782 had married Elizabeth ----; children, if any, unknown. He served in the Lower House of the Maryland Legislature, 1777-1781 [Ref: R-567]. Took the Oath of Allegiance in Somerset County in 1778 before the Hon. John Williams [Ref: T-21, N-51].

MADDUX, Thomas Jr. Second Lieutenant, Somerset Militia, Princess Anne Bn., Capt. John Jones' Co., Sep 22, 1777 [Ref: M-100, C-381]. Took the Oath of Allegiance in Somerset County in 1778 before the Hon. Peter Waters [Ref: T-18]. Second Lieutenant, Somerset Militia, Princess Anne Bn., Capt. John Jones' Princess Anne Co., 1780 [Ref: M-219 listed the name without the "Jr."].

MADDUX, Zoro. Private, Somerset Militia, Princess Anne Bn., Capt. John Williams' Watkins Point Co., 1780 [Ref: M-222].

MAGEE, David. Took the Oath of Allegiance in Worcester County in 1778 before the Hon. William Hopewell [Ref: J-1814 (Box 4)].

MAGEE, Davis. Took the Oath of Allegiance in Worcester County in 1778 before the Hon. William Hopewell [Ref: J-1814 (Box 4)].

MAGEE, Reuben (1754 -   ). Son of David and Mary Megee *[sic]*, born in Stepney Parish on Feb 13, 1754 [Ref: Y-48]. Private, 3rd Maryland Independent Co., Worcester County, Capt. John Watkins' Co., enlisted Feb 21, 1776; muster roll dated Aug 20, 1776, present for duty [Ref: D-22].

MAGILL, Andrew (1758 -   ). Private, North Carolina Line, who applied for a pension (R6826) in Gallatin County, Illinois on May 3, 1837, age 79, stating he was born on May 22, 1758 near Snow Hill [Worcester County], Maryland and lived in Glasgow County, North Carolina (the part that became Edgecombe County) at the time of his enlistment, noting he was the son of a "widow woman." After the war he lived for several years on the Holsten River in Virginia, then for 7 years in Powell's Valley in Virginia, and 21 years in Union County, Kentucky, and finally in Gallatin County, Illinois [Ref: W-2165].

MALCOM (MALCOMB), John. Private, Somerset Militia, Princess Anne Bn., Capt. James Elzey's Co., 1780 [Ref: M-220]. Took the Oath of Allegiance in Somerset County in 1778 before the Hon. Peter Waters [Ref: T-18].

MALLONE, Robert. Private, Somerset Militia, Salisbury Bn., Capt. Josiah Dashiell's Wicomico Creek Co., 1778/1780 [Ref: M-218].

MALLONE, William. Private, Somerset Militia, Salisbury Bn., Capt. Josiah Dashiell's Wicomico Creek Co., 1778/1780 [Ref: M-218].

MALSTON, Jay. Took the Oath of Allegiance in Somerset County in 1778 before the Hon. Peter Waters [Ref: T-18].

MANLOVE, Elizabeth. See "William Beauchamp," q.v.

MARBURY, Colonel. See "Thomas Seon," q.v.

MARCH, John. Took the Oath of Allegiance in Worcester County in 1778 before the Hon. Nehemiah Holland [Ref: J-1814 (Box 4)].

MARCHANT (MERCHANT), John. Took the Oath of Allegiance in Somerset County in 1778 before the Hon. John Williams [Ref: T-21, N-51]. Private, Somerset Militia, Princess Anne Bn., St. Asaph's Co., 1780 [Ref: M-220].

MARCHMENT, Charles. Private, Worcester Militia, Sinepuxent Bn., Capt. Thomas Purnell's Co., Third Class, 1779/1780 [Ref: M-253 listed the name as "Charles Merchment"]. Took the Oath of Allegiance in Worcester County in 1778 before the Hon. Nathaniel Miller [Ref: J-1814 (Box 4) listed the name as "Charles Marchmant"].

MARCHMENT, James. Took the Oath of Allegiance in Worcester County in 1778 before the Hon. John Selby [Ref: J-1814 (Box 4) listed the name as "James Merchment"].

MARCHMENT, Samuel. Private, Worcester Militia, Sinepuxent Bn., Capt. Elisha Purnell's Co., Eighth Class, 1779/1780 [Ref: M-253 listed the name as "Samuel Merchment"]. Took the Oath of Allegiance in Worcester County in 1778 in Quepomco Hundred before the Hon. Thomas Purnell [Ref: J-1814 (Box 4)].

MARCHMENT, Starling. Took the Oath of Allegiance in Worcester County in 1778 before the Hon. Joshua Townsend [Ref: J-1814 (Box 4)].

MARCHMENT, William. Private, 3rd Maryland Independent Co., Worcester County, Capt. John Watkins' Co., enlisted Feb 3, 1776; muster roll dated Aug 20, 1776, sick in the country [Ref: D-21 listed the name as "William Marchmont"].

MARSH, Philip. Private, Worcester Militia, Sinepuxent Bn., Capt. Thomas Purnell's Co., Third Class, 1779/1780 [Ref: M-253]. Took the Oath of Allegiance in Worcester County in 1778 before the Hon. Nathaniel Miller [Ref: J-1814 (Box 4) listed the name as "Philip Mash"].

MARSHALL, Comfort. See "Joshua Merrill," q.v.

MARSHALL, Ephraim. Private, Somerset Militia, Princess Anne Bn., St. Asaph's Co., 1780 [Ref: M-220].
MARSHALL, George. Sergeant, Worcester Militia, Wicomico Bn., Capt. Isaac Layfield's Co., July 15, 1780 [Ref: M-257]. Took the Oath of Allegiance in Worcester County in 1778 before the Hon. James Selby [Ref: J-1814 (Box 4)].
MARSHALL, Isaac. Private, Worcester Militia, Sinepuxent Bn., Capt. Thomas Purnell's Co., Eighth Class, 1779/1780 [Ref: M-253]. Took the Oath of Allegiance in Worcester County in 1778 before the Hon. Nehemiah Holland [Ref: J-1814 (Box 4)]. Private, Somerset Militia, Princess Anne Bn., St. Asaph's Co., 1780 [Ref: M-221]. Private, Maryland Troops, Worcester County, draughted May 1, 1781 [Ref: K-99, D-372].
MARSHALL, John. Sergeant, Somerset Militia, Princess Anne Bn., Capt. George Waters' Pocomoke Co., 1780 [Ref: M-220]. Took the Oath of Allegiance in Worcester County in 1778 before the Hon. James Selby [Ref: J-1814 (Box 4)]. Rendered patriotic service by supplying beef for the use of the military on Oct 5, 1781 [Ref: P-444].
MARSHALL, John Jr. Private, Worcester Militia, Sinepuxent Bn., Capt. Thomas Purnell's Co., Fifth Class, 1779/1780 [Ref: M-253]. Took the Oath of Allegiance in Worcester County in 1778 in Quepomco Hundred before the Hon. Thomas Purnell [Ref: J-1814 (Box 4) listed the name without the "Jr."].
MARSHALL (MARSHEL), Mary. See "John Harris," q.v.
MARSHALL, Patience. See "William Allen," q.v.
MARSHALL, Risdon. Private, Somerset Militia, Princess Anne Bn., St. Asaph's Co., 1780 [Ref: M-221].
MARSHALL, Robert. Private, Somerset Militia, Princess Anne Bn., St. Asaph's Co., 1780 [Ref: M-221]. Took the Oath of Allegiance in Worcester County in 1778 before the Hon. James Selby [Ref: J-1814 (Box 4)].
MARSHALL, Sarah. See "Thomas Purnell, of Thomas," q.v.
MARSHALL, Thomas. Captain, Worcester Militia, Snow Hill Bn., Aug 30, 1777 [Ref: M-101, C-351]. Took the Oath of Allegiance in Worcester County in 1778 before the Hon. James Selby [Ref: J-1814 (Box 4)].
MARSHALL, Thomas. First Lieutenant, Worcester Militia, Snow Hill Bn., Capt. Thomas Marshall's Co., Aug 30, 1777. First Lieutenant, Wicomico Bn., Capt. Isaac Layfield's Co., July 15, 1780 [Ref: M-101, M-257, C-351].
MARSHALL, Thomas. See "James Davis," q.v.
MARSHALL, William. Private, Worcester Militia, Wicomico Bn., Capt. Isaac Layfield's Co., Fifth Class, July 15, 1780 [Ref: M-257]. Private, Maryland Troops, Worcester County, draughted May 1, 1781 [Ref: K-99, D-372].
MARTIN, Ann. See "Robert Martin," q.v.
MARTIN, Cassia. See "Robert Martin," q.v.
MARTIN, Dorothy. See "Robert Martin," q.v.
MARTIN, Elizabeth. See "Robert Martin," q.v.

MARTIN, George. Quartermaster, Worcester Militia, 10th Bn., Jan 1, 1776 [Ref: M-101]. Took the Oath of Allegiance in Worcester County in 1778 before the Hon. Nehemiah Holland [Ref: J-1814 (Box 4)]. On July 30, 1781 Levin Lowe recruited George Martin from Somerset County to serve in the Continental Army until Dec 10, 1781 [Ref: L-35C]. Discharged on Dec 3, 1781 [Ref: I-11]. See "Robert Martin," q.v.

MARTIN, George Jr. Private, Worcester Militia, Wicomico Bn., Capt. William Handy's Co., Sixth Class, July 15, 1780 [Ref: M-257]. Took the Oath of Allegiance in Worcester County in 1778 before the Hon. Joshua Townsend [Ref: J-1814 (Box 4)].

MARTIN, James. Captain, Worcester Militia, 10th Bn., May 25, 1776. Lieutenant Colonel, Wicomico Bn., Aug 30, 1777. Lieutenant Colonel, Snow Hill Bn., May 25, 1779 [Ref: M-101, A-444, C-351, E-423]. On Aug 20, 1780, Joseph Dashiell, Commissary of Purchases for Worcester County, issued a receipt to Col. James Martin for hauling corn for the use of the military [Ref: P-311]. Sheriff of Worcester County, commissioned on Nov 2, 1782 [Ref: I-296].

MARTIN, James. Private, Somerset Militia, Princess Anne Bn., Capt. Thomas Irving's Monie Co., 1780 [Ref: M-219]. Took the Oath of Allegiance in Worcester County in 1778 before the Hon. Nehemiah Holland [Ref: J-1814 (Box 4)]. Rendered patriotic service by storing and hauling provisions for the use of the military in 1782 [Ref: P-467].

MARTIN, John Sr. Took the Oath of Allegiance in Worcester County in 1778 before the Hon. Nehemiah Holland [Ref: J-1814 (Box 4)]. Captain, Worcester Militia, 1780/1781 [Ref: J-1814 (Box 12) listed the name without the "Sr."].

MARTIN, John. Private, Somerset Militia, Princess Anne Bn., Capt. Thomas Irving's Monie Co., 1780 [Ref: M-219]. Took the Oath of Allegiance in Somerset County in 1778 before the Hon. Levin Wilson [Ref: T-17].

MARTIN, John P. See "Robert Martin," q.v.

MARTIN, John Selby. Took the Oath of Allegiance in Worcester County in 1778 before the Hon. Nehemiah Holland [Ref: J-1814 (Box 4)].

MARTIN, Luther. Attorney General of Maryland, appointed by the Council of Maryland on Feb 11, 1778 in place of Benjamin Galloway who had resigned [Ref: C-487]. Took the Oath of Allegiance in Worcester County in 1778 before the Hon. Nehemiah Holland [Ref: J-1814 (Box 4)]. See "Robert Martin," q.v.

MARTIN, Nancy. See "Robert Martin," q.v.

MARTIN, Robert (1755-1836). Private, Maryland Line, who applied for a pension in Pickaway County, Ohio on May 18, 1818, stating he was born in January, 1755, married Nancy Phebus in March, 1780 in Princess Anne, Somerset County, Maryland, and in 1810 lived in Bullitt County, Kentucky. His widow applied for a pension (W9535) in Fountain County, Indiana on April 25, 1845, age 85, stating Robert had died on Nov 13 or 30, 1836 in Pickaway County, Ohio. Her brother (not named) also lived in Indiana on Jan 30, 1846. The children of the deceased soldier were George (d. in infancy), Elizabeth, Luther,

Ann, Dorothy, Cassia, and John P. Martin. The widow Nancy Martin died Sep 19, 1845 in Fountain County at the home of her son John P. Martin (who was then age 51) and she left these children: John P. and Luther Martin, Ann Cory, Dorothy Cory, and Cassia Grant. In 1846 a Jeremiah Cory lived in Fountain County, Indiana [Ref: V-1909, and W-2209 listed the name as "Robert Martin or Martain"].

MARTIN, Thomas. Private, Somerset Militia, Salisbury Bn., Capt. Josiah Dashiell's Wicomico Creek Co., 1778/1780 [Ref: M-218].

MARTIN, Thomas. Private, Somerset Militia, Princess Anne Bn., Capt. Thomas Irving's Monie Co., 1780 [Ref: M-219].

MARTIN, Thomas. Took the Oath of Allegiance in Somerset County in 1778 before the Hon. Levin Wilson [Ref: T-17, N-51].

MARTIN, Thomas. Attended the Maryland Convention in 1776 [Ref: O-36. "Capt. Thomas Martin" took the Oath of Allegiance in Worcester County in 1778 before the Hon. Nehemiah Holland [Ref: J-1814 (Box 4)]. Commissioned a Judge of the Court of Appeals for Worcester County on May 27, 1778 [Ref: E-112].

MARTIN, Thomas. Co. Clerk, Worcester Militia, Capt. John Martin's Co., 1780/1781 [Ref: J-1814 (Box 12)].

MARTIN, Thomas Jr. Took the Oath of Allegiance in Worcester County in 1778 before the Hon. Nehemiah Holland [Ref: J-1814 (Box 4)].

MARTIN, Thomas Jr. Private, Somerset Militia, Princess Anne Bn., Capt. Thomas Irving's Monie Co., 1780 [Ref: M-219].

MARTIN, William. Private, Somerset Militia, Salisbury Bn., Capt. Levin Irving's Black Water Co., 1778/1780 [Ref: M-218].

MARTIN, William. Private, Somerset Militia, Princess Anne Bn., Capt. Thomas Irving's Monie Co., 1780 [Ref: M-219].

MARTIN, William. Took the Oath of Allegiance in Somerset County in 1778 before the Hon. Levin Wilson [Ref: T-17, N-51].

MARTINELL, Francis. Recruited by Capt. Levin Handy and enlisted in the Continental Army in Worcester County on April 7, 1780 for the duration of the war, stating he was born in France [Ref: Z-40].

MASH, Philip. See "Philip Marsh," q.v.

MASON, Bennet. Private, 3rd Maryland Independent Co., Worcester County, Capt. John Watkins' Co., enlisted April 29, 1776; muster roll dated Aug 20, 1776, present for duty [Ref: D-21].

MASON, Daniel. Private, Worcester Militia, Wicomico Bn., Capt. James Patterson's Co., Seventh Class, July 15, 1780 [Ref: M-258].

MASON, Elias. See "Elias Mason Clark," q.v.

MASON, James. Private, 3rd Maryland Independent Co., Worcester County, Capt. John Watkins' Co., enlisted Feb 2, 1776; muster roll dated Aug 20, 1776, present for duty [Ref: D-22].

MASON, John. Took the Oath of Allegiance in Worcester County in 1778 before the Hon. Joshua Townsend [Ref: J-1814 (Box 4)].

MASON, William. Took the Oath of Allegiance in Worcester County in 1778 before the Hon. Joshua Townsend [Ref: J-1814 (Box 4)].

MASSEY, Alexander. Private, Worcester Militia, Sinepuxent Bn., Capt. John Rackliff's Co., Eighth Class, 1779/1780 [Ref: M-251].

MASSEY, Comfort. See "Luke Bowen," q.v.

MASSEY, Ebenezer. Took the Oath of Allegiance in Somerset County in 1778 before the Hon. John Span Conway [Ref: N-51, and T-14 listed the name as "Ebenezer Massy"].

MASSEY, Hezekiah. Private, Worcester Militia, Wicomico Bn., Capt. Samuel Smyley's Co., First Class, July 15, 1780 [Ref: M-258]. Took the Oath of Allegiance in Worcester County in 1778 before the Hon. John Selby [Ref: J-1814 (Box 4)].

MASSEY, James. Private, Worcester Militia, Sinepuxent Bn., Capt. John Rackliff's Co., First Class, 1779/1780 [Ref: M-251]. See "Luke Bowen," q.v.

MASSEY, John. Took the Oath of Allegiance in Worcester County in 1778 before the Hon. Nathaniel Miller [Ref: J-1814 (Box 4) listed the name as "John Massy"]. Rendered patriotic service by supplying corn for the use of the military on June 14, 1780 and July 10, 1780 [Ref: P-296, G-9].

MASSEY, Joshua. Private, Worcester Militia, Sinepuxent Bn., Capt. John Rackliff's Co., First Class, 1779/1780 [Ref: M-251].

MASSEY, Kiah. Private, Worcester Militia, Snow Hill Bn., Capt. John Parramore's Co., 1777 [Ref: M-250].

MATHIS, Jesse. Took the Oath of Allegiance in Somerset County in 1778 before the Hon. Levin Wilson [Ref: T-17, N-51].

MATTHEWS, Baily. Private, Somerset Militia, Princess Anne Bn., St. Asaph's Co., 1780 [Ref: M-221]. Drafted from Somerset County on June 20, 1781 to serve in the Continental Army [Ref: L-35C].

MATTHEWS, Benjamin Holland. Private, Somerset Militia, Princess Anne Bn., St. Asaph's Co., 1780 [Ref: M-220, M-221].

MATTHEWS, David. Private, Somerset Militia, Princess Anne Bn., St. Asaph's Co., 1780 [Ref: M-221].

MATTHEWS, David. Private, Somerset Militia, Princess Anne Bn., St. Asaph's Co., 1780 [Ref: M-221].

MATTHEWS, Denwood. Private, Somerset Militia, Princess Anne Bn., Capt. James Elzey's Co., 1780 [Ref: M-220].

MATTHEWS, Jacob. Private, Somerset Militia, Princess Anne Bn., St. Asaph's Co., 1780 [Ref: M-221].

MATTHEWS, James. Private, Somerset Militia, Princess Anne Bn., Capt. James Elzey's Co., 1780 [Ref: M-220].

MATTHEWS, Jesse. Corporal, Somerset Militia, Princess Anne Bn., Capt. James Elzey's Co., 1780 [Ref: M-220].

MATTHEWS, Levi. Private, Somerset Militia, Princess Anne Bn., Capt. James Elzey's Co., 1780 [Ref: M-220].
MATTHEWS, Nancy. See "Charles Richardson," q.v.
MATTHEWS, Robert. Private, Somerset Militia, Princess Anne Bn., Capt. James Elzey's Co., 1780 [Ref: M-220]. Took the Oath of Allegiance in Somerset County in 1778 before the Hon. Levin Wilson [Ref: T-17, N-51].
MATTHEWS, William Sr. Took the Oath of Allegiance in Somerset County in 1778 (made his "V" mark) before the Hon. Peter Waters [Ref: T-18 listed the name as "Wm. Mathews, Senr."].
MATTHEWS, William. Private, Somerset County, Capt. John Gunby's 2nd Independent Maryland Co.; sick in barracks on March 2, 1776; mustered on Aug 21, 1776 [Ref: D-641]. Took the Oath of Allegiance in Somerset County in 1778 before the Hon. Levin Wilson [Ref: T-17, N-51]. Private, Somerset Militia, Princess Anne Bn., Capt. James Elzey's Co., 1780 [Ref: M-220].
MATTHEWS, William. Sergeant, Somerset Militia, Princess Anne Bn., Capt. James Elzey's Co., 1780 [Ref: M-220]. Took the Oath of Allegiance in Somerset County on Feb 21, 1778 before the Hon. Joseph Venables [Ref: T-25 listed the name as "Wm. Mathews"].
McALLEN, Alexander. Private, Worcester Militia, Wicomico Bn., Capt. William Handy's Co., First Class, July 15, 1780 [Ref: M-257].
McBRIDE, William. Private, Somerset Militia, Salisbury Bn., Capt. Levin Irving's Black Water Co., 1778/1780 [Ref: M-218].
McBRYDE, William. Ensign, Somerset Militia, Salisbury Bn., Capt. Robert Dashiell's Co., Sep 22, 1777 [Ref: M-102, C-382]. Took the Oath of Allegiance in Somerset County in 1778 before the Hon. Levin Wilson [Ref: T-17, N-51]. Commissioned a Justice of the Peace for Somerset County on March 25, 1779 [Ref: E-327 mistakenly listed the name as "William McBird"]. Rendered patriotic service by storing corn for the military in 1780 [Ref: P-295]. Commissary of Purchases for Somerset County between 1777 and 1781 [Ref: P-263, P-544, and C-255 listed the name as "Wm. McBryd"]. See "James Polk, Jr.," q.v.
McCALLY (McLALLY?), Patrick. Private, Somerset Militia, Salisbury Bn., Capt. Joseph Venables' Barren Creek Co., 1778/1780 [Ref: M-217].
McCAULEY, John. Private, Worcester Militia, Sinepuxent Bn., Capt. William Purnell's Co., Eighth Class, 1779/1780 [Ref: M-252].
McCAULEY, William. Private, Worcester Militia, Wicomico Bn., Capt. Philip Quinton's Co., Third Class, July 15, 1780 [Ref: M-256].
McCLAIN, John. Rendered patriotic service by supplying corn in Worcester County for the use of the military on July 10, 1780 [Ref: G-10].
McCLALLAND, Benjamin. Took the Oath of Allegiance in Somerset County on Feb 14, 1778 before the Hon. Joseph Venables [Ref: T-25].
McCLALLAND, Thomas. Took the Oath of Allegiance in Somerset County on Feb 14, 1778 before the Hon. Joseph Venables [Ref: T-25].

McCLANE, James. Took the Oath of Allegiance in Somerset County in 1778 before the Hon. Levin Wilson [Ref: T-17].

McCLEMMEY, Samuel. Sergeant, Somerset Militia, Salisbury Bn., White Haven Co., 1778/1780 [Ref: M-218 listed the name as "Samuel McClammy"]. Took the Oath of Allegiance in Somerset County in 1778 before the Hon. Levin Wilson [Ref: T-17].

McCLEMMEY, Whitty (Whitby). Took the Oath of Allegiance in Somerset County in 1778 before the Hon. Levin Wilson [Ref: N-51, and T-17 listed the name as "Whittey McClemmy"]. Commissioned a Judge of the Court of Appeals for Somerset County on May 23, 1778 [Ref: E-109 listed the name as "Whitby McClemmy"].

McCLEMMEY, William. Took the Oath of Allegiance in Somerset County in 1778 before the Hon. William Winder [Ref: T-22, N-51].

McCLUMMY (McCLEMMY), Martha. See "Benjamin Purnell," q.v.

McCLENNEN, Benjamin. Corporal, Somerset Militia, Salisbury Bn., Capt. Levin Irving's Black Water Co., 1778/1780 [Ref: M-217].

McCLENNEN, Thomas. Private, Somerset Militia, Salisbury Bn., Capt. Levin Irving's Black Water Co., 1778/1780 [Ref: M-217].

McCLESTER, John. First Lieutenant, Salisbury Bn., Capt. John Span Conway's Nanticoke Point Co., Sep 22, 1777. Captain, Nanticoke Point Co., 1781 [Ref: M-102, M-216, A-426, C-381, G-575, J-1814 (Box 8, Dashiell's correspondence), H-195]. Took the Oath of Allegiance in Somerset County in 1778 before the Hon. John Span Conway [Ref: T-14 listed the name as "John McCloster"]. See "Thomas Dickerson (Dickenson)," q.v.

McCLESTER, John. Drafted from Somerset County on July 30, 1781 to serve in the Continental Army [Ref: L-35C].

McCLISH, Thomas. Private, Worcester Militia, Wicomico Bn., Capt. James Perdue's Co., First Class, July 15, 1780 [Ref: M-256].

McCORMICK, Benjamin. Took the Oath of Allegiance in Worcester County in 1778 before the Hon. Nathaniel Miller [Ref: J-1814 (Box 4)].

McCORMICK, John. Private, 3rd Maryland Independent Co., Worcester County, Capt. John Watkins' Co., enlisted April 1, 1776; muster roll dated Aug 20, 1776, absent on furlough 12th instant [Ref: D-21].

McCRAY, James. Took the Oath of Allegiance in Worcester County in 1778 before the Hon. Nathaniel Miller [Ref: J-1814 (Box 4) listed the name as "James Macray"].

McCRAY, John. Private, Worcester Militia, Sinepuxent Bn., Capt. Thomas Purnell's Co., Second Class, 1779/1780 [Ref: M-253].

McCRAY, Robert. Took the Oath of Allegiance in Worcester County in 1778 before the Hon. Nathaniel Miller [Ref: J-1814 (Box 4) listed the name as "Robert McCra"].

McCREADY (McCREDDY), Alexander. Private, Worcester Militia, Wicomico Bn., Capt. Isaac Layfield's Co., Sixth Class, July 15, 1780 [Ref: M-257].

Alexander McCredy married Sarah Randell in Coventry Parish on July 21, 1774 [Ref: Y-86].

McCREADY (McCREDDY), Andrew. Private, Somerset Militia, Princess Anne Bn., St. Asaph's Co., 1780 [Ref: M-220].

McCREADY (McCREDDY), Isaac. Private, Somerset Militia, Princess Anne Bn., St. Asaph's Co., 1780 [Ref: M-221]. Isaac McCrady married Hannah Coarsley in Coventry Parish on April 13, 1774 [Ref: Y-86].

McCREADY (McCREDDY), James. Private, Worcester Militia, Wicomico Bn., Capt. James Patterson's Co., Second Class, July 15, 1780 [Ref: M-258].

McCUDDY, John. Private, Worcester Militia, Capt. John Martin's Co., 1780/1781 [Ref: J-1814 (Box 12)].

McDANIEL, David. Private, Somerset Militia, Princess Anne Bn., Capt. Isaac Handy's Great Annemessix Co., 1780 [Ref: M-221].

McDANIEL, Edward. Private, Somerset Militia, Salisbury Bn., Capt. Joseph Venables' Barren Creek Co., 1778/1780 [Ref: M-217].

McDANIEL, James. Private, Somerset Militia, Salisbury Bn., Capt. Joseph Venables' Barren Creek Co., 1778/1780 [Ref: M-217].

McDANIEL, James. Private, Worcester Militia, Wicomico Bn., Capt. Benjamin Dennis' Co., Eighth Class, July 15, 1780 [Ref: M-256].

McDANIEL, John. Private, Worcester Militia, Wicomico Bn., Capt. Benjamin Dennis' Co., Eighth Class, July 15, 1780 [Ref: M-256].

McDANIEL, William. Private, Somerset Militia, Salisbury Bn., Capt. Joseph Venables' Barren Creek Co., 1778/1780 [Ref: M-217].

McDANIELL, William. Private, Worcester Militia, Wicomico Bn., Capt. Benjamin Dennis' Co., Fifth Class, July 15, 1780 [Ref: M-256].

McDORMAN, William. Corporal, Somerset Militia, Princess Anne Bn., Capt. Thomas Irving's Monie Co., 1780 [Ref: M-219].

McFADDEN, Arthur. Private, Worcester Militia, Snow Hill Bn., Capt. John Parramore's Co., 1777 [Ref: M-250 listed the name as "Arthur McFaddin"]. Private, Worcester Militia, Wicomico Bn., Capt. William Handy's Co., Fifth Class, July 15, 1780 [Ref: M-257]. Took the Oath of Allegiance in Worcester County in 1778 before the Hon. Joshua Townsend [Ref: J-1814 (Box 4)]. Rendered patriotic service by slaughtering beef for the use of the military in October, 1781 [Ref: P-442].

McFADDEN, James. Private, Worcester Militia, Wicomico Bn., Capt. William Handy's Co., Eighth Class, July 15, 1780 [Ref: M-258]. Took the Oath of Allegiance in Worcester County in 1778 before the Hon. Joshua Townsend [Ref: J-1814 (Box 4)].

McFAIN, David. See "Jonathan Cooper," q.v.

McFARLAND, Edward. Took the Oath of Allegiance in Somerset County in 1778 before the Hon. Peter Waters [Ref: T-18 listed the name as "Ephraim McFarlang"].

McGEE, David. See "Reuben Magee," q.v.

McGEE, Daniel. Private, Worcester Militia, Wicomico Bn., Capt. Elijah Shockley's Co., Third Class, July 15, 1780 [Ref: M-255].

McGEE, George. Private, Worcester Militia, Sinepuxent Bn., Capt. John Coe's Co., Third Class, 1779/1780 [Ref: M-252].

McGEE, John. Private, Worcester Militia, Wicomico Bn., Capt. Elijah Shockley's Co., Eighth Class, July 15, 1780 [Ref: M-255].

McGEE, Joshua. Private, Worcester Militia, Wicomico Bn., Capt. Elijah Shockley's Co., Seventh Class, July 15, 1780 [Ref: M-255].

McGEE, Ruben. Private, Worcester Militia, Wicomico Bn., Capt. Samuel Horsey's Co., Sixth Class, July 15, 1780 [Ref: M-257]. See "Reuben Magee," q.v.

McGEE, Samuel. Private, Worcester Militia, Wicomico Bn., Capt. Elijah Shockley's Co., Third Class, July 15, 1780 [Ref: M-255].

McGLAMERY (McGLAMRY), Edward. Private, 3rd Maryland Independent Co., Worcester County, Capt. John Watkins' Co., enlisted Feb 13, 1776; muster roll dated Aug 20, 1776, sick in the country [Ref: D-22 listed the name as "Edward Maglamary"]. Private, Worcester Militia, Wicomico Bn., Capt. Elijah Shockley's Co., Fifth Class, July 15, 1780 [Ref: M-255].

McGLAMERY (McGLAMRY), Elijah. On July 30, 1781 Benjamin Lankford recruited Elijah McGlamry from Somerset County to serve in the Continental Army until Dec 10, 1781 [Ref: L-35C]. Discharged on Dec 3, 1781 [Ref: I-11 listed the name as "Elijah McGlamory" and stated he was from Worcester County].

McGLAMERY (McGLAMRY), John. On June 20, 1781, Dowty Collier recruited John McGlamery from Somerset County to serve in the Continental Army until Dec 10, 1781 [Ref: L-35C listed the name as "Jno. McGlamry"].

McGRATH, Arthur. Private, Somerset Militia, Salisbury Bn., White Haven Co., 1778/1780 [Ref: M-218].

McGRATH, William. Private, Somerset Militia, Princess Anne Bn., Capt. James Elzey's Co., 1780 [Ref: M-220]. Select Militia, Somerset County, Aug 15, 1781 [Ref: L-35A].

McGRIGOR, Mary. See "James Dale," q.v.

McGRIGOR, William. See "James Dale," q.v.

McHENRY, Arthur. Private, 3rd Maryland Independent Co., Worcester County, Capt. John Watkins' Co., enlisted Feb 10, 1776; muster roll dated Aug 20, 1776, present for duty [Ref: D-21].

McHENRY, Urias. Took the Oath of Allegiance in Worcester County in 1778 before the Hon. Nehemiah Holland [Ref: J-1814 (Box 4)]. Private, Worcester Militia, Wicomico Bn., Capt. Fisher Walton's Co., Second Class, July 15, 1780 [Ref: M-258].

McINTIRE, Daniel (1762 -   ). Son of Daniel and Elizabeth McIntyre *[sic]*, born in Stepney Parish on Jan 26, 1762 [Ref: Y-50]. Private, Somerset Militia, Salisbury Bn., Capt. John Span Conway's Nanticoke Point Co., 1780 [Ref: M-216].

McINTIRE, Willen. Private, Somerset Militia, Salisbury Bn., Capt. John Span Conway's Nanticoke Point Co., 1780 [Ref: M-216].
McKENNEN, Benjamin. Private, Select Militia, Somerset County, Aug 15, 1781 [Ref: L-35B].
McKEY, James. Private, Somerset Militia, Salisbury Bn., Capt. James Bennett's Salisbury Co., 1778/1780 [Ref: M-218].
McKINEDEY, Patrick. Private, Somerset Militia, Salisbury Bn., Capt. Sampson Wheatly's Co., 1780 [Ref: M-216].
McLALLY (McCALLY?), Patrick. Private, Somerset Militia, Salisbury Bn., Capt. Joseph Venables' Barren Creek Co., 1778/1780 [Ref: M-217].
McLAUGHLIN, Alexander. Private, Somerset Militia, Salisbury Bn., Capt. Josiah Dashiell's Wicomico Creek Co., 1778/1780 [Ref: M-218].
McLEAN, Enoch. Took the Oath of Allegiance in Somerset County in 1778 before the Hon. Levin Wilson [Ref: T-17, N-51].
McMASTER, Samuel (1744-1811). Born in Scotland on Sep 10, 1744, married Nancy Gillet, rendered patriotic service in Maryland during the war, and died on May 25, 1811 [Ref: V-1980]. "Rev. Samuel McMaster" took the Oath of Allegiance in Worcester County in 1778 before the Hon. Nehemiah Holland [Ref: J-1814 (Box 4)].
McNEILL, Thomas. Private, Worcester Militia, Sinepuxent Bn., Capt. John Coe's Co., Seventh Class, 1779/1780 [Ref: M-252].
McQUE, John. Private, 3rd Maryland Independent Co., Worcester County, Capt. John Watkins' Co., enlisted Feb 3, 1776; muster roll dated Aug 20, 1776, sick in barracks [Ref: D-21].
McVEIGH, Joseph. Private, Somerset Militia, Princess Anne Bn., Capt. John Jones' Princess Anne Co., 1780 [Ref: M-219].
MEARICA, George. Took the Oath of Allegiance in Worcester County in 1778 before the Hon. Joshua Townsend [Ref: J-1814 (Box 4)].
MECCOM, James. Took the Oath of Allegiance in Somerset County in 1778 before the Hon. Peter Waters [Ref: T-18].
MELTON, John. Took the Oath of Allegiance in Worcester County in 1778 before the Hon. James Selby [Ref: J-1814 (Box 4)].
MELVIN (MELVEN), George. Private, Worcester Militia, Wicomico Bn., Capt. Isaac Layfield's Co., Third Class, July 15, 1780 [Ref: M-257]. Took the Oath of Allegiance in Worcester County in 1778 before the Hon. James Selby [Ref: J-1814 (Box 4)].
MELVIN (MELVEN), John. Private, Worcester Militia, Wicomico Bn., Capt. Isaac Layfield's Co., Second Class, July 15, 1780 [Ref: M-257]. Took the Oath of Allegiance in Worcester County in 1778 before the Hon. James Selby [Ref: J-1814 (Box 4)].
MELVIN (MELVEN), Jonathan. Private, Worcester Militia, Wicomico Bn., Capt. James Patterson's Co., Sixth Class, July 15, 1780 [Ref: M-258]. Took the Oath

of Allegiance in Worcester County in 1778 before the Hon. James Selby [Ref: J-1814 (Box 4)].
MELVIN (MELVEN), Joseph. Private, Somerset Militia, Salisbury Bn., Capt. Joseph Venables' Barren Creek Co., 1778/1780 [Ref: M-217].
MELVIN, Leah. See "Nehemiah Redden," q.v.
MELVIN (MELVEN), Littleton. Private, Worcester Militia, Wicomico Bn., Capt. James Patterson's Co., Third Class, July 15, 1780 [Ref: M-258].
MELVIN, Polly. See "Dennis Hudson," q.v.
MELVIN (MELVEN), Robert. Private, Worcester Militia, Wicomico Bn., Capt. Isaac Layfield's Co., Sixth Class, July 15, 1780 [Ref: M-257].
MELVIN (MELVEN), Smith. Private, Worcester Militia, Wicomico Bn., Capt. James Patterson's Co., First Class, July 15, 1780 [Ref: M-258]. Took the Oath of Allegiance in Worcester County in 1778 before the Hon. James Selby [Ref: J-1814 (Box 4)].
MELVIN (MELVEN), William (1750-1807). Private, Worcester Militia, Wicomico Bn., Capt. Isaac Layfield's Co., Fourth Class, July 15, 1780 [Ref: M-257]. Took the Oath of Allegiance in Worcester County in 1778 before the Hon. James Selby [Ref: J-1814 (Box 4) listed the name as "Jr."]. William Melvin or Melven was born in Maryland on May 11, 1750, married Leah Robertson, served as a private and rendered other patriotic service during the war, and died on Feb 20, 1807 [Ref: V-2000].
MERCHMENT, James. See "James Marchment," q.v.
MERRILL (MERRELL), Catte. See "Levin Merrill," q.v.
MERRILL (MERRELL), Comfort. See "Joshua Merrill" and "Jacob Merrill" and "Joshua Merrill," q.v.
MERRILL (MERRELL), Jacob (1756 -   ). Son of John and Comfort Merrell, born in Coventry Parish on Dec 28, 1756 [Ref: Y-88]. Took the Oath of Allegiance in Worcester County in 1778 before the Hon. Joshua Townsend [Ref: J-1814 (Box 4)]. Private, Worcester Militia, Wicomico Bn., Capt. Fisher Walton's Co., Eighth Class, July 15, 1780 [Ref: M-258].
MERRILL (MERRELL), John. Second Lieutenant, Worcester Militia, Capt. Isaac Layfield's Co., June 28, 1777, succeeded [Ref: M-103]. See "Joshua Merrill" and "Jacob Merrill," q.v.
MERRILL (MERRELL), Joseph. Took the Oath of Allegiance in Worcester County in 1778 before the Hon. John Selby [Ref: J-1814 (Box 4)].
MERRILL (MERRELL), Joshua (1757 -   ). Son of William Merrill and Comfort Marshall, born in Coventry Parish on April 12, 1757 [Ref: Y-72]. Private, Somerset Militia, Salisbury Bn., Capt. William Turpin's Rewastico Co., 1778/1780 [Ref: M-217].
MERRILL (MERRELL), Joshua (1754 -   ). Son of John and Comfort Merrell, born in Coventry Parish on July 9, 1754 [Ref: Y-88]. Private, Somerset Militia, Princess Anne Bn., Capt. John Williams' Watkins Point Co., 1780 [Ref: M-222].

MERRILL (MERRELL), Josiah (1758 -   ). Son of Thomas and Leah Merrell, born in Coventry Parish on July 15, 1758 [Ref: Y-73]. Private, Worcester Militia, Wicomico Bn., Capt. Isaac Layfield's Co., Eighth Class, July 15, 1780 [Ref: M-257].

MERRILL, Leah. See "Thomas Merrill, Jr." and "Josiah Merrill," q.v.

MERRILL (MERRELL), Levi (1760 -   ). Son of Simpson and Catte Merrell, born in Coventry Parish on Aug 5, 1760 [Ref: Y-88]. Took the Oath of Allegiance in Worcester County in 1778 before the Hon. Joshua Townsend [Ref: J-1814 (Box 4)]. Rendered patriotic service by supplying beef for the use of the military on Sep 25, 1781 [Ref: P-440].

MERRILL (MERRELL), Levin. Private, Worcester Militia, Wicomico Bn., Capt. Isaac Layfield's Co., Seventh Class, July 15, 1780 [Ref: M-257].

MERRILL (MERRELL), Robert. Private, Somerset Militia, Princess Anne Bn., Capt. George Waters' Pocomoke Co., 1780 [Ref: M-220].

MERRILL (MERRELL), Scarbrough. Took the Oath of Allegiance in Worcester County in 1778 before the Hon. James Selby [Ref: J-1814 (Box 4)].

MERRILL (MERRELL), Simpson (Simson). Took the Oath of Allegiance in Worcester County in 1778 before the Hon. James Selby [Ref: J-1814 (Box 4)]. See "Levi Merrill," q.v.

MERRILL (MERRELL), Thomas Jr. (1756 -   ). Son of Thomas and Leah Merrell, born in Coventry Parish on July 21, 1756 [Ref: Y-73]. Private, Worcester Militia, Wicomico Bn., Capt. Isaac Layfield's Co., Eighth Class, July 15, 1780 [Ref: M-257 listed the name without the "Jr."]. Took the Oath of Allegiance in Worcester County in 1778 before the Hon. James Selby [Ref: J-1814 (Box 4)].

MERRILL (MERRELL), Thomas Sr. Took the Oath of Allegiance in Worcester County in 1778 before the Hon. James Selby [Ref: J-1814 (Box 4)]. See "Josiah Merrill" and "Thomas Merrill, Jr.," q.v.

MERRILL (MERRELL), William. Private, Worcester Militia, Sinepuxent Bn., Capt. Thomas Purnell's Co., Fourth Class, 1779/1780 [Ref: M-253]. Took the Oath of Allegiance in Worcester County in 1778 before the Hon. Nathaniel Miller [Ref: J-1814 (Box 4)].

MERRILL (MERRELL), William. Private, Worcester Militia, Wicomico Bn., Capt. Isaac Layfield's Co., Second Class, July 15, 1780 [Ref: M-257]. Took the Oath of Allegiance in Worcester County in 1778 before the Hon. James Selby [Ref: J-1814 (Box 4)].

MERRILL, William. See "Joshua Merrill," q.v.

MESSICK (MEZICK, MEZECK), Benjamin. Private, Somerset Militia, Salisbury Bn., Capt. William Turpin's Rewastico Co., 1778/1780 [Ref: M-217].

MESSICK (MEZICK, MEZECK), George. Private, Somerset Militia, Salisbury Bn., Capt. John Span Conway's Nanticoke Point Co., 1778/1780 [Ref: M-216].

MESSICK (MEZICK, MEZECK), Jacob. Private, Somerset Militia, Salisbury Bn., Capt. Henry Gale's Quantico Co., 1778/1780 [Ref: M-216]. Drafted from

Somerset County on June 20, 1781 to serve in the Continental Army [Ref: L-35C].
MESSICK (MEZICK, MEZECK), James. Private, Somerset Militia, Salisbury Bn., Capt. John Span Conway's Nanticoke Point Co., 1778/1780 [Ref: M-216].
MESSICK, Polly. See "Henry Banks," q.v.
MIDAR, William. Took the Oath of Allegiance in Somerset County in 1778 [Ref: N-51].
MIDDLETON, John. Took the Oath of Allegiance in Worcester County in 1778 before the Hon. Joshua Townsend [Ref: J-1814 (Box 4)].
MILBOURN, Jacob. Private, Somerset Militia, Princess Anne Bn., Capt. John Williams' Watkins Point Co., 1780 [Ref: M-222]. Drafted from Somerset County on July 30, 1781 to serve in the Continental Army [Ref: L-35C].
MILBOURN, John. Took the Oath of Allegiance in Worcester County in 1778 before the Hon. John Selby [Ref: J-1814 (Box 4)]. Private, Somerset Militia, Princess Anne Bn., St. Asaph's Co., 1780 [Ref: M-221].
MILBOURN, Lodowick. Private, Somerset Militia, Princess Anne Bn., St. Asaph's Co., 1780 [Ref: M-221]. Private, Somerset Militia, Princess Anne Bn., Capt. John Williams' Watkins Point Co., 1780 [Ref: M-222].
MILBOURN, Thomas. Private, Worcester Militia, Wicomico Bn., Capt. John Parramore's Co., Fourth Class, July 15, 1780 [Ref: M-259].
MILES, Bettey. See "Levi Miles," q.v.
MILES, George. Private, Somerset Militia, Princess Anne Bn., Capt. James Elzey's Co., 1780 [Ref: M-220].
MILES, Henry (1752-1796). Captain, Somerset Militia, Princess Anne Bn., Little Annemessex Co., Sep 22, 1777 to at least July 24, 1780 [Ref: M-104, M-221, C-381]. Appointed by the Council of Maryland to be Inspector of Tobacco at Coleburn's Creek on Aug 30, 1780 [Ref: F-271]. Henry Miles was bron in November, 1752, married Elizabeth McLamar, served as a captain during the war, and died before June 21, 1796 [Ref: V-2020]. See "Horsey Summers," q.v.
MILES, Henry. Private, Somerset Militia, Salisbury Bn., Capt. Sampson Wheatly's Co., 1780 [Ref: M-216].
MILES, Henry Walston (c1741-1824). Private, Somerset Militia, Princess Anne Bn., Capt. Thomas Irving's Monie Co., 1780 [Ref: M-219]. One source states Henry Walston Miles was born in 1741, married Mary ---- in Somerset County and their daughter Sarah Walston Miles married James Wallace on May 16, 1795 [Ref: S-3169]. Another states Henry Walston Miles was born circa 1750, married Mary ----, served as a private during the war, and died before Aug 10, 1824 [Ref: V-2020].
MILES, Levi (1763 -   ). Son of William and Bettey Miles, born in Coventry Parish on Feb 11, 1763 [Ref: Y-87]. Private, Somerset Militia, Princess Anne Bn., Capt. Henry Miles' Little Annemessex Co., 1780 [Ref: M-221].
MILES, Levin. Sergeant, Somerset Militia, Princess Anne Bn., Capt. Isaac Handy's Great Annemessix Co., 1780 [Ref: M-221]. See "George Phebus," q.v.
MILES, Mary. See "Henry Walston Miles," q.v.

MILES, Richard. Second Lieutenant, Worcester Militia, Wicomico Bn., Capt. Horsey's Co., May 27, 1779 [Ref: M-104, E-423].
MILES, Samuel. Private, Somerset Militia, Princess Anne Bn., Capt. James Elzey's Co., 1780 [Ref: M-220].
MILES, Samuel (of William). Private, Somerset Militia, Princess Anne Bn., Capt. John Jones' Princess Anne Co., 1780 [Ref: M-219].
MILES, Sarah. See "Henry Walston Miles," q.v.
MILES, William. Private, Somerset Militia, Princess Anne Bn., Capt. Isaac Handy's Great Annemessix Co., 1780 [Ref: M-221].
MILES, William. Private, Somerset Militia, Princess Anne Bn., Capt. Henry Miles' Little Annemessex Co., 1780 [Ref: M-221].
MILES, William. Took the Oath of Allegiance in Worcester County in 1778 before the Hon. William Hopewell [Ref: J-1814 (Box 4)]. See "Levi Miles," q.v.
MILES, William (of James). Private, Somerset Militia, Princess Anne Bn., Capt. James Elzey's Co., 1780 [Ref: M-220].
MILLER, Ayres Smith. Private, Worcester Militia, Wicomico Bn., Capt. James Patterson's Co., Fourth Class, July 15, 1780 [Ref: M-258 listed the name as "Ayres Smith Millor"].
MILLER, John. Private, Worcester Militia, Sinepuxent Bn., Capt. John Coe's Co., Fourth Class, 1779/1780 [Ref: M-252].
MILLER, Nathanel. Took the Oath of Allegiance in Worcester County in 1778 in Buckingham Hundred before the Hon. Thomas Purnell [Ref: J-1814 (Box 4)].
MILLER, Nathaniel. Justice who administered the Oath of Allegiance in Worcester County in 1778 [Ref: J-1814 (Box 4)]. Justice of the Peace for Worcester County, commissioned on Nov 29, 1777 and Nov 21, 1778 [Ref: C-428, E-249].
MILLIGAN (MILIGAN), Isaac. Private, Somerset Militia, Princess Anne Bn., Capt. Isaac Handy's Great Annemessix Co., 1780 [Ref: M-221].
MILLIGAN (MILIGAN), John. Private, Somerset Militia, Princess Anne Bn., Capt. Isaac Handy's Great Annemessix Co., 1780 [Ref: M-221].
MILLS, Benjamin (c1750-1822). Second Lieutenant, Worcester Militia, Sinepuxent Bn., Capt. Matthew Purnell's Co., Aug 30, 1777 [Ref: M-104, C-350]. Took the Oath of Allegiance in Worcester County in 1778 before the Hon. Nathaniel Miller [Ref: J-1814 (Box 4)]. One Benjamin Mills was born before 1750 in England, married Elizabeth Collier, served as a second lieutenant in Maryland during the war, and died in Kentucky on Nov 14, 1822 [Ref: V-2036].
MILLS, Easter. See "William Mills," q.v.
MILLS, Francis. Took the Oath of Allegiance in Worcester County in 1778 before the Hon. Nehemiah Holland [Ref: J-1814 (Box 4)].
MILLS, Hugh. Took the Oath of Allegiance in Worcester County in 1778 before the Hon. James Selby [Ref: J-1814 (Box 4)].

MILLS, John. Private, Worcester Militia, Wicomico Bn., Capt. James Patterson's Co., Eighth Class, July 15, 1780 [Ref: M-258]. Took the Oath of Allegiance in Worcester County in 1778 before the Hon. William Hopewell [Ref: J-1814 (Box 4)].
MILLS, Jonathan. See "Jacob Tull," q.v.
MILLS, Leah. See "Jacob Tull," q.v.
MILLS, Levi. Private, Worcester Militia, Sinepuxent Bn., Capt. John Rackliff's Co., Fifth Class, 1779/1780 [Ref: M-251]. Took the Oath of Allegiance in Worcester County in 1778 before the Hon. Nathaniel Miller [Ref: J-1814 (Box 4)].
MILLS, Richard. Private, Worcester Militia, Wicomico Bn., Capt. Samuel Horsey's Co., Sixth Class, July 15, 1780 [Ref: M-257]. Took the Oath of Allegiance in Worcester County in 1778 before the Hon. William Hopewell [Ref: J-1814 (Box 4)]. Rendered patriotic service by supplying corn for the use of the military on April 5, 1780 and July 10, 1780 [Ref: P-281, G-10].
MILLS, Robert. Private, Worcester Militia, Wicomico Bn., Capt. James Patterson's Co., Second Class, July 15, 1780 [Ref: M-258]. Took the Oath of Allegiance in Worcester County in 1778 before the Hon. James Selby [Ref: J-1814 (Box 4)].
MILLS, Robert. Took the Oath of Allegiance in Worcester County in 1778 before the Hon. James Selby [Ref: J-1814 (Box 4)].
MILLS, Samuel. Private, Worcester Militia, Sinepuxent Bn., Capt. John Rackliff's Co., Sixth Class, 1779/1780 [Ref: M-251]. Took the Oath of Allegiance in Worcester County in 1778 before the Hon. Nehemiah Holland [Ref: J-1814 (Box 4)].
MILLS, Samuel. Private, Worcester Militia, Wicomico Bn., Capt. James Patterson's Co., Seventh Class, July 15, 1780 [Ref: M-258]. Took the Oath of Allegiance in Worcester County in 1778 before the Hon. Nathaniel Miller [Ref: J-1814 (Box 4)].
MILLS, Sarah. See "Levin Parsons," q.v.
MILLS, Stephen. Private, Somerset Militia, Princess Anne Bn., Capt. George Waters' Pocomoke Co., 1780 [Ref: M-220]. Took the Oath of Allegiance in Somerset County in 1778 before the Hon. Levin Wilson [Ref: T-17].
MILLS, Thomas. Private, Somerset Militia, Princess Anne Bn., Capt. Isaac Handy's Great Annemessix Co., 1780 [Ref: M-221].
MILLS, William (c1743-1823). Corporal, Somerset Militia, Salisbury Bn., Capt. Levin Irving's Black Water Co., 1778/1780 [Ref: M-217]. Select Militia, Somerset County, Aug 15, 1781 [Ref: L-35A]. William Mills was born circa 1743, married Elizabeth Cottingham (second wife), was a corporal in the war, and died by July 14, 1823 [Ref: V-2038].
MILLS, William (c1755-c1841). Private, Maryland Line, who applied for a pension (R7251) in Jefferson County, Kentucky on Oct 29, 1838 (1833?), age 82, a resident of Louisville, stating he had lived in Worcester County, Maryland

at the time of enlistment. He was a private in the Worcester Militia, Wicomico [Snow Hill] Bn., Capt. James Patterson's Co., First Class, on July 15, 1780, and also served for 9 months in Col. John Daniel's Regiment. On April 15, 1841 Thomas Grafton Addison of Louisville, Kentucky made inquiry for the heirs (not named) of William Mills, deceased. A son, William P. Mills, served in the Maryland Militia in the War of 1812, moved to Kentucky in 1815, and married Mary E. Moore, daughter of Thomas Moore of Delaware [Ref: W-2370, M-258, H. C. Peden's *Marylanders to Kentucky* (1991), p. 103, and A. W. Burns' abstracts on revolutionary soldiers of Maryland in Kentucky (p. 53) at the Maryland Historical Society]. William (the Revolutionary War soldier) might be the William Mills, son of William and Easter Mills, who was born in Coventry Parish on Sep 3, 1755 [Ref: Y-73]. However, since there were several men with this name (see below), additional research will be necessary before drawing conclusions.

MILLS, William. Private, Somerset Militia, Princess Anne Bn., Capt. George Waters' Pocomoke Co., 1780 [Ref: M-220]. Took the Oath of Allegiance in Somerset County on Feb 26, 1778 before the Hon. Joseph Venables [Ref: T-25].

MILLS, William. Took the Oath of Allegiance in Worcester County in 1778 before the Hon. James Selby [Ref: J-1814 (Box 4)]. Rendered patriotic service by repacking and storing pork for the use of the military on Aug 1, 1781 [Ref: P-419].

MILLS, William Jr. Took the Oath of Allegiance in Worcester County in 1778 before the Hon. Nehemiah Holland [Ref: J-1814 (Box 4)].

MILLS, William Sr. Took the Oath of Allegiance in Worcester County in 1778 before the Hon. Nehemiah Holland [Ref: J-1814 (Box 4)].

MINAB, John. Took the Oath of Allegiance in Worcester County in 1778 before the Hon. Joshua Townsend [Ref: J-1814 (Box 4)].

MISTER, Marmaduke. Private, Somerset Militia, Princess Anne Bn., Capt. Henry Miles' Little Annemessex Co., 1780 [Ref: M-221]. He was deposed regarding a shipwreck circa 1776 [Ref: R-13].

MITCHELL, Eloise. See "John Pope Mitchell," q.v.

MITCHELL, George. Private, Somerset Militia, Princess Anne Bn., Capt. James Elzey's Co., 1780 [Ref: M-220].

MITCHELL, Gertrude. See "John Pope Mitchell," q.v.

MITCHELL, Isaac (1757-1791). Son of Josiah Mitchell and Sophia Hill, born in Worcester Parish on Sep 7, 1757 [Ref: Y-29]. Took the Oath of Allegiance in Worcester County in 1778 before the Hon. Nathaniel Miller [Ref: J-1814 (Box 4)].

MITCHELL, Isaac (c1760 -   ). Son of Isaac and Jennit Mitchell, born in Coventry Parish "---- 1760(?)" [Ref: Y-87]. This may be the Isaac Mitchell, a private in the Maryland Line, whose heirs in Princess Anne (Somerset County) were named as Nancy Beauchamp and Nelly Goswelling in 1839. On May 13th of that year Nancy Richardson of Somerset County made an affidavit regarding bounty land warrant #2257-100 [Ref: W-2378]. Since there were two men named Isaac Mitchell during the Revolutionary era, additional research will be necessary before drawing conclusions. See "James Mitchell" and "John Pope Mitchell," q.v.

MITCHELL, James. Private, Worcester Militia, Sinepuxent Bn., Capt. John Rackliff's Co., Seventh Class, 1779/1780 [Ref: M-251]. One James Mitchell, son of Isaac and Jeanette Mitchell, was born in Coventry Parish on May 16, 1758 [Ref: Y-73].

MITCHELL, James. Took the Oath of Allegiance in Worcester County in 1778 before the Hon. Nathaniel Miller [Ref: J-1814 (Box 4) listed the name as "James Mitchael"].

MITCHELL, James (of Joseph). Took the Oath of Allegiance in Worcester County in 1778 before the Hon. Joshua Townsend [Ref: J-1814 (Box 4)].

MITCHELL, Jeanette. See "James Mitchell," q.v.

MITCHELL, Jennit. See "Isaac Mitchell," q.v.

MITCHELL, John. Private, Maryland Line, whose name appeared on "a list of recruits from and deserters taken up in Somerset County on Oct 20, 1780" [Ref: D-346].

MITCHELL, John. Private, Somerset County, Capt. John Gunby's 2nd Independent Maryland Co.; sick at Princess Anne on June 12, 1776; mustered on Aug 21, 1776 [Ref: D-641]. Private, Somerset Militia, Princess Anne Bn., Capt. John Jones' Princess Anne Co., 1780 [Ref: M-219].

MITCHELL, John. Took the Oath of Allegiance in Worcester County in 1778 before the Hon. William Hopewell [Ref: J-1814 (Box 4)].

MITCHELL, John (Pocomoke). Took the Oath of Allegiance in Somerset County in 1778 before the Hon. Levin Wilson [Ref: T-17].

MITCHELL, John Pope (1751-1810). Son of Col. Joshua Mitchell (d. 1794) and probably Joyce Pope (daughter of John Pope). He married Mary Purnell on May 3, 1773 and their children were Robert, Isaac, John, Rufus, and Eloise Gatty (or Gertrude) Purnell. John was a Justice of Worcester County, 1777-1780, 1784-1800; served in the Lower House of the Maryland Legislature, 1785-1788; Commissioner of the Tax in 1792 and 1798 [Ref: R-598, C-429]. Captain, Worcester Militia, Wicomico Bn., Aug 30, 1777 to May 27, 1779, succeeded [Ref: C-351, M-104, and E-423 listed the name as "J. P. Mitchell"]. Took the Oath of Allegiance in Worcester County in 1778 before the Hon. Joshua Townsend [Ref: J-1814 (Box 4)]. Justice of the Peace for Worcester County, commissioned on Nov 21, 1778 and Nov 25, 1780 [Ref: E-250, G-225]. Rendered patriotic service by supplying beef for the use of the military on Sep 30, 1780 [Ref: P-322 listed the name as "Capt. John P. Mitchell"].

MITCHELL, John Pope. Private(?), Worcester Militia, Sinepuxent Bn., Capt. John Postly's Co., Fourth Class, 1779/1780 [Ref: M-251].

MITCHELL, Joshua (1755 -   ). Son of Josiah Mitchell and Sophia Hill, born in Worcester Parish on Sep 4, 1755 [Ref: Y-29]. Private, Worcester Militia, Wicomico Bn., Capt. James Perdue's Co., Eighth Class, July 15, 1780 [Ref: M-256]. Private, Somerset Militia, Princess Anne Bn., Capt. George Waters' Pocomoke Co., 1780 [Ref: M-220].

MITCHELL, Joshua (c1720-1794). Son of Robert Mitchell (d. 1755). Appointed by the Maryland Convention in November, 1776 to be one of the Judges of Elections in Worcester County [Ref: O-55, and R-598 referred to him as "colonel"]. See "John Pope Mitchell" and "Thomas Muir" and "Josiah Mitchell," q.v.

MITCHELL, Josiah (c1730-1801). Son of Robert Mitchell (d. 1755). Josiah married Sophia Hill on March 7, 1753 in Worcester Parish and their children were Ellen or Elizabeth (b. May 22, 1754), Joshua (b. Sep 4, 1755), Isaac (Sep 7, 1757 - 1791), Robert (b. July 27, 1759), Levin (b. June 20, 1761), Mary (b. April 28, 1763), Sarah (Sep 7, 1766 - 1786), Sophia (b. Dec 14, 1768), and Ann (b. Oct 13, 1770). Josiah served in the Lower House of the Maryland Legislature from Worcester County, 1777-1779, 1786-1787; Justice of the Peace, commissioned on Nov 29, 1777 and March 24, 1779 and Nov 25, 1780 and Jan 17, 1782; Justice of the Orphans Court, 1785-1800; and, Judge of the Court of Appeals for Tax Assessment, appointed in 1786 and 1796 [Ref: R-599, E-327, G-225, Y-29, C-428, I-46].

MITCHELL, Josias. Quartermaster, Worcester Militia, 24th Bn., Jan 6, 1776 [Ref: M-104].

MITCHELL, Levin (1761 -   ). Son of Josiah Mitchell and Sophia Hill, born in Worcester Parish on June 20, 1761 [Ref: Y-29]. Private, Worcester Militia, Sinepuxent Bn., Capt. John Postly's Co., Third Class, 1779/1780 [Ref: M-251].

MITCHELL, Mary. See "Isaac Henry," q.v.

MITCHELL, Robert (1759 -   ). Son of Josiah Mitchell and Sophia Hill, born in Worcester Parish on July 27, 1759 [Ref: Y-29]. Private, Worcester Militia, Sinepuxent Bn., Capt. John Postly's Co., Second Class, 1779/1780 [Ref: M-251]. See "John Pope Mitchell" and "Thomas Purnell, of Thomas," q.v.

MITCHELL, Robert (of Jonathan). Took the Oath of Allegiance in Worcester County in 1778 before the Hon. Nathaniel Miller [Ref: J-1814 (Box 4)].

MITCHELL, Rufus. See "John Pope Mitchell," q.v.

MITCHELL, Samuel. Private, 5th Maryland Line, enlisted on Dec 10, 1776, promoted to corporal on Oct 22, 1778, and discharged on Jan 12, 1780 [Ref: D-227].

MITCHELL, Stephen. Took the Oath of Allegiance in Somerset County on Feb 21, 1778 (made his mark that resembled a "C" curled at both ends) before the Hon. Joseph Venables [Ref: T-25].

MITCHELL, Thomas. Private, Somerset Militia, Salisbury Bn., White Haven Co., 1778/1780 [Ref: M-218].

MITCHELL, Thomas. Private, Somerset Militia, Princess Anne Bn., Capt. John Williams' Watkins Point Co., 1780 [Ref: M-222].
MONCUR, Robert. Took the Oath of Allegiance in Somerset County in 1778 before the Hon. Peter Waters [Ref: T-18].
MONGOMERY, Dennis. Private, Somerset Militia, Princess Anne Bn., Capt. Henry Miles' Little Annemessex Co., 1780 [Ref: M-221].
MOOMAW, Celia. See "John Adams," q.v.
MOORE, Bratshe. Private, Somerset Militia, Salisbury Bn., Capt. Sampson Wheatly's Co., 1780 [Ref: M-216 listed the name as "Bratshe Moor"].
MOORE, Darby. Took the Oath of Allegiance in Somerset County in 1778 (made his "D" mark that resembled an "8") before the Hon. John Williams [Ref: T-21, N-51].
MOORE, Elijah. Private, Somerset Militia, Salisbury Bn., Capt. Levin Irving's Black Water Co., 1778/1780 [Ref: M-217]. Private, Somerset Militia, Princess Anne Bn., St. Asaph's Co., 1780 [Ref: M-220].
MOORE, Grace. See "John Moore," q.v.
MOORE, Isaac. Private, Somerset Militia, Salisbury Bn., Capt. Sampson Wheatly's Co., 1780 [Ref: M-216 listed the name as "Isaac Moor"].
MOORE, Isaac Jr. Private, Somerset Militia, Princess Anne Bn., Capt. Henry Miles' Little Annemessex Co., 1780 [Ref: M-221].
MOORE, Isabella. See "Bennett Phillips," q.v.
MOORE, Jacob. Private, Somerset Militia, Salisbury Bn., Capt. Sampson Wheatly's Co., 1780 [Ref: M-216 listed the name as "Jacob Moor"].
MOORE, James. Took the Oath of Allegiance in Somerset County in 1778 [Ref: N-51 listed the name as "James More"].
MOORE, James (captain). See "William Moore, Sr.," q.v.
MOORE, John (1752 -   ). Son of Thomas and Grace Moore, born in Coventry Parish on Nov 1, 1752 [Ref: Y-72]. Private, Somerset Militia, Princess Anne Bn., Capt. John Williams' Watkins Point Co., 1780 [Ref: M-222 listed the name as "John Moor"].
MOORE, John L. See "Thomas L. Moore," q.v.
MOORE, Joshua. Rendered patriotic service by supplying bacon for the use of the military in Somerset County on Aug 17, 1780 [Ref: P-310].
MOORE, Joshua Evans. Private, Somerset Militia, Salisbury Bn., Capt. John Span Conway's Nanticoke Point Co., 1778/1780 [Ref: M-216 listed the name as "Joshua Evans More"].
MOORE, Levin. Took the Oath of Allegiance in Somerset County on Feb 21, 1778 before the Hon. Joseph Venables [Ref: T-25]. "Levin Moor" married Mary Darby in Stepney Parish on Sep 4, 1757 [Ref: Y-46].
MOORE, Levin (1762 -   ). Son of Levin and Mary Moor *[sic]*, born in Stepney Parish on Aug 16, 1762 [Ref: Y-46]. Private, Somerset Militia, Salisbury Bn., Capt. Henry Gale's Quantico Co., 1780 [Ref: M-216].
MOORE, Mary. See "William Mills" and "Levin Moore," q.v.

MOORE, Samuel. See "William Moore," q.v.

MOORE (MOOR), Stephen. Private, Somerset Militia, Salisbury Bn., Capt. Sampson Wheatly's Co., 1780 [Ref: M-216].

MOORE (MOOR), Thomas. Private, Somerset Militia, Princess Anne Bn., Capt. Thomas Irving's Monie Co., 1780 [Ref: M-219].

MOORE (MOOR), Thomas. Private, Somerset Militia, Princess Anne Bn., St. Asaph's Co., 1780 [Ref: M-220].

MOORE (MOOR), Thomas. Private, Somerset Militia, Salisbury Bn., Capt. Sampson Wheatly's Co., 1780 [Ref: M-216].

MOORE (MOOR), Thomas. Private, Somerset Militia, Princess Anne Bn., Capt. Henry Miles' Little Annemessex Co., 1780 [Ref: M-221]. See "John Moore" and "William Moore" and "William Mills," q.v.

MOORE, Thomas L. (1764 -   ). Private, Maryland Line, who applied for a pension (R7355) on Dec 2, 1833 in Clinton County, Illinois, stating he was born in Somerset County, Maryland in 1764 and lived there at the time of his enlistment. In 1796 or 1797 he moved to Kentucky and in 1819 he moved to Illinois. He further stated that his brother John L. Moore could verify his service [Ref: W-2408].

MOORE, William (1757-1833). Private, 4th Maryland Line, who pensioned in Somerset County at $80 per annum effective May 21, 1833 (retroactive to March 3, 1826) and died on Dec 17, 1833 (James Hooper, agent; Samuel Moore, representative). [Ref: X-54]. Son of Thomas and Ann Moor *[sic]*, born in Stepney Parish on April 18, 1757 [Ref: Y-43]. Private, Somerset Militia, Princess Anne Bn., St. Asaph's Co., 1780 [Ref: M-220 listed the name as "William Moor"].

MOORE, William Jr. Sergeant, Somerset Militia, Salisbury Bn., Capt. Henry Gale's Quantico Co., 1778/1780 [Ref: M-216]. Took the Oath of Allegiance in Somerset County in 1778 [Ref: N-51 listed the name as "William More, Jr."].

MOORE, William Sr. Took the Oath of Allegiance in Somerset County on Feb 14, 1778 before the Hon. Joseph Venables [Ref: T-25 listed the name as "Wm. Moor, Senr."]. Private, Somerset Militia, Salisbury Bn., Capt. Henry Gale's Quantico Co., 1778/1780 [Ref: M-216 listed the name without the "Sr."]. This could be the William Moore who was born in England in 1712, came to America in 1733, married Rachel Fletcher in Maryland, and died in Somerset County in 1788 [Ref: W-2400, which cited bounty land warrant #1472-300-26 by the heirs of Capt. James Moore (1742-1798), Delaware Line, and wife Mary Rider (d. 1812), and "unconfirmed information from another researcher" included therein]. Additional research will be necessary before drawing conclusions.

MOORE, William (of Leaven). Took the Oath of Allegiance in Somerset County on Feb 21, 1778 before the Hon. Joseph Venables [Ref: T-25].

MORGAN, Rachel. See "William Dryden," q.v.

MORRIS, Cornelius. Private, Worcester Militia, Sinepuxent Bn., Capt. Elisha Purnell's Co., Third Class, 1779/1780 [Ref: M-253].
MORRIS, David. See "William Morris," q.v.
MORRIS, Edward. Private, Worcester Militia, Sinepuxent Bn., Capt. Elisha Purnell's Co., First Class, 1779/1780 [Ref: M-253]. Took the Oath of Allegiance in Worcester County in 1778 in Quepomco Hundred before the Hon. Thomas Purnell [Ref: J-1814 (Box 4)]. See "William Morris," q.v.
MORRIS, Elinor. See "Levin Gilliss," q.v.
MORRIS, George. Took the Oath of Allegiance in Worcester County in 1778 before the Hon. Joshua Townsend [Ref: J-1814 (Box 4) listed the name as "George Morriss"].
MORRIS, Isaac. Private, Worcester Militia, Sinepuxent Bn., Capt. Elisha Purnell's Co., Seventh Class, 1779/1780 [Ref: M-253]. Took the Oath of Allegiance in Worcester County in 1778 before the Hon. Joshua Townsend [Ref: J-1814 (Box 4) listed the name as "Isaac Morriss"].
MORRIS, Isaac. Private, Worcester Militia, Sinepuxent Bn., Capt. Thomas Purnell's Co., Sixth Class, 1779/1780 [Ref: M-253 listed the name as "Isaac Morss"].
MORRIS, Jacob. Corporal, Somerset Militia, Salisbury Bn., Capt. Josiah Dashiell's Wicomico Creek Co., 1778/1780 [Ref: M-218]. Took the Oath of Allegiance in Somerset County in 1778 before the Hon. Levin Wilson [Ref: T-17, N-51]. Rendered patriotic service by supplying bacon for the use of the military on Aug 8, 1780 [Ref: P-308]. Drafted from Somerset County on June 20, 1781 to serve in the Continental Army [Ref: L-35C].
MORRIS, James. Private, Worcester Militia, Sinepuxent Bn., Capt. Elisha Purnell's Co., Third Class, 1779/1780 [Ref: M-253].
MORRIS, James Rownd (c1750-1795). Private, Worcester Militia, Wicomico Bn., Capt. William Handy's Co., Third Class, July 15, 1780 [Ref: M-257 listed the name as "James R.(?) Morris"]. Took the Oath of Allegiance in Worcester County in 1778 before the Hon. Nehemiah Holland [Ref: J-1814 (Box 4)]. Clerk of the Worcester County Court from 1778 to 1795. He married Leah Winder (daughter of William) in 1780 [Ref: R-604].
MORRIS, Jethro (Jethrew). Private, Worcester Militia, Sinepuxent Bn., Capt. Elisha Purnell's Co., Fourth Class, 1779/1780 [Ref: M-253]. Took the Oath of Allegiance in Worcester County in 1778 before the Hon. Joshua Townsend [Ref: J-1814 (Box 4) listed the name as "Jethro Morriss"].
MORRIS, John. Private, 3rd Maryland Independent Co., Worcester County, Capt. John Watkins' Co., enlisted March 12, 1776; muster roll dated Aug 20, 1776, present for duty [Ref: D-22]. Private, Worcester Militia, Sinepuxent Bn., Capt. Elisha Purnell's Co., Second Class, 1779/1780 [Ref: M-253]. "John Morris, Quepomco" took the Oath of Allegiance in Worcester County in 1778 before the Hon. John Selby [Ref: J-1814 (Box 4)].

MORRIS, John. Private, Somerset Militia, Salisbury Bn., Capt. Josiah Dashiell's Wicomico Creek Co., 1778/1780 [Ref: M-218 listed the name as "John Morriss"]. Took the Oath of Allegiance in Worcester County in 1778 before the Hon. Joshua Townsend [Ref: J-1814 (Box 4) listed the name as "John Morriss"]. See "Joshua Morris," q.v.

MORRIS, John Round. On Sep 13, 1782 the Council of Maryland gave "permission to John Round Morris of Worcester County to apply to his Excellency George Washington or the Commanding Officers at the out posts of the American Army for leave to go into the City of New York for the purpose of endeavoring to procure the release of ---- [blank] Collier, a prisoner." [Ref: I-262].

MORRIS, Joseph Jr. Private, Somerset Militia, Salisbury Bn., Capt. Josiah Dashiell's Wicomico Creek Co., 1778/1780 [Ref: M-218].

MORRIS, Joshua (1757 -   ). Son of John and Mary Morris, born in Stepney Parish on Jan 18, 1757 [Ref: Y-43]. Private, Worcester Militia, Sinepuxent Bn., Capt. John Postly's Co., Sixth Class, 1779/1780 [Ref: M-251 listed the name as "Joshua Morss"]. Private, Worcester Militia, Wicomico Bn., Capt. Samuel Horsey's Co., Seventh Class, July 15, 1780 [Ref: M-257].

MORRIS, Levi. Private, 3rd Maryland Independent Co., Worcester County, Capt. John Watkins' Co., enlisted March 16, 1776; muster roll dated Aug 20, 1776, sick in barracks [Ref: D-22].

MORRIS, Mary. See "Joshua Morris," q.v.

MORRIS, Philip. Private, Worcester Militia, Sinepuxent Bn., Capt. Elisha Purnell's Co., Eighth Class, 1779/1780 [Ref: M-253]. Took the Oath of Allegiance in Worcester County in 1778 in Quepomco Hundred before the Hon. Thomas Purnell [Ref: J-1814 (Box 4)].

MORRIS, Thomas. Took the Oath of Allegiance in Worcester County in 1778 in Quepomco Hundred before the Hon. Thomas Purnell [Ref: J-1814 (Box 4) listed the name as "Thomas Morres"].

MORRIS, William (1744-c1835). Private, Worcester Militia, Sinepuxent Bn., Capt. Elisha Purnell's Co., Fourth Class, 1779/1780 [Ref: M-253]. Took the Oath of Allegiance in Worcester County in 1778 in Quepomco Hundred before the Hon. Thomas Purnell [Ref: J-1814 (Box 4)]. He applied for a pension (S9040) in Highland County, Ohio on Oct 28, 1833, stating he was born in Worcester County, Maryland on Aug 4, 1744 and lived there at the time of his enlistment. In 1816 he moved to Ohio [Ref: W-2426].

MORRIS, William (c1740-1799). Second Major, Worcester Militia, 24th Bn., Jan 6, 1776. Major, Snow Hill Bn., Aug 30, 1777. Lieutenant Colonel, Sinepuxent Bn., March 23, 1778 [Ref: M-105, A-506, C-350, C-547]. Attended the Maryland Convention in 1775 and signed the Association of the Freemen of Maryland on July 26, 1775 [Ref: O-4, A-67]. Commissioned a Justice of the Orphans Court on June 4, 1777 [Ref: C-274 listed the name as "Wm. Morriss"]. Took the Oath of Allegiance in Worcester County in 1778 before the Hon.

Nehemiah Holland [Ref: J-1814 (Box 4)]. Commissioned a Judge of the Court of Appeals for Worcester County on May 27, 1778 [Ref: E-112]. William was Register of Wills for Worcester County until replaced by John Wise on Aug 16, 1782 since it was reported that he had died. This is an error because William Morris was commissioned a Justice of the Peace and a Justice of the Orphans Court for Worcester County on Dec 10, 1782 and did not die until 1799 (testate). [Ref: I-318, I-325, R-604]. William married first to his cousin Catherine Round (daughter of Capt. Edward Round) by 1780, second to Esther Wilson (daughter of David Wilson) by 1788, and third to Nancy Polk (widow of James Polk) by 1796. His sons were Edward Round Morris, David Wilson Morris, and William Justus Morris [Ref: R-604].

MOSES, George. Private, Somerset Militia, Salisbury Bn., Capt. James Bennett's Salisbury Co., 1778/1780 [Ref: M-218].

MOSS, Isaac. Took the Oath of Allegiance in Worcester County in 1778 before the Hon. Nathaniel Miller [Ref: J-1814 (Box 4)].

MOSS, Joshua. Took the Oath of Allegiance in Worcester County in 1778 before the Hon. Nathaniel Miller [Ref: J-1814 (Box 4)].

MOSS, Richardson. Private, Somerset County, Capt. John Gunby's 2nd Independent Maryland Co.; present on Aug 6, 1776; mustered on Aug 21, 1776 [Ref: D-642].

MUIR, Henry. Took the Oath of Allegiance in Somerset County in 1778 before the Hon. Levin Wilson [Ref: T-17, N-51].

MUIR, James. Private, Somerset Militia, Princess Anne Bn., Capt. Thomas Irving's Monie Co., 1780 [Ref: M-219]. Drafted from Somerset County on July 30, 1781 to serve in the Continental Army, but noted as "incapable of marching" [Ref: L-35C]. One James Muir was born on Oct 2, 1727 in Maryland, married Sarah Nevitt, rendered civil service during the war, and died on Sep 13, 1789 [Ref: V-2102, which did not mention military service so this could be a different James Muir].

MUIR, Joseph. See "Thomas Muir," q.v.

MUIR, Thomas (1754-1837). Private, Maryland Line, who applied for a pension (S8902) in Somerset County on Dec 12, 1832, age 78, stating he lived there at the time of his enlistment [Ref: W-2448]. He also received a pension from the State of Maryland at $80 per annum effective March 4, 1831 and died on Feb 10, 1837. Joseph Muir was the administrator of his estate and received final payment on Feb 25, 1840 [Ref: X-50, W-2448]. On July 30, 1781 Joshua Mitchell recruited Thomas Muir from Somerset County to serve in the Continental Army until Dec 10, 1781 [Ref: L-35C]. Discharged on Dec 3, 1781 [Ref: I-11].

MULLINER, Joseph. See "Samuel Lamberson" and "John Rain," q.v.

MULLINS, Eleanor (Nelly). See "Job Hamblen," q.v.

MUMFORD, Charles. Took the Oath of Allegiance in Worcester County in 1778 before the Hon. Joshua Townsend [Ref: J-1814 (Box 4)].

MUMFORD, George. Private, Worcester Militia, Sinepuxent Bn., Capt. William Purnell's Co., Seventh Class, 1779/1780 [Ref: M-252]. Took the Oath of Allegiance in Worcester County in 1778 in Bogerternorton Hundred before the Hon. Thomas Purnell [Ref: J-1814 (Box 4) listed the name as "Gorge Momford"].

MUMFORD, James Sr. Took the Oath of Allegiance in Worcester County in 1778 before the Hon. Joshua Townsend [Ref: J-1814 (Box 4)].

MUMFORD, James. Private, Worcester Militia, Sinepuxent Bn., Capt. William Purnell's Co., First Class, 1779/1780 [Ref: M-252]. Private, Worcester Militia, Sinepuxent Bn., Capt. Josiah Dale's Co., Sixth Class, 1779/1780 [Ref: M-254]. Private, Worcester Militia, Capt. John Martin's Co., 1780/1781 [Ref: J-1814 (Box 12) listed the name as "Jams. Mumphord"]. Private, Maryland Troops, Worcester County, draughted May 1, 1781 [Ref: K-99, D-372]. On July 21, 1781 he gave his "deposition of physical condition" [Ref: P-413].

MUMFORD, Jesse. Private, Worcester Militia, Sinepuxent Bn., Capt. William Purnell's Co., First Class, 1779/1780 [Ref: M-252]. Private, Worcester Militia, Sinepuxent Bn., Capt. Josiah Dale's Co., Sixth Class, 1779/1780 [Ref: M-254 listed the name as "Jersey Mumford"]. Took the Oath of Allegiance in Worcester County in 1778 before the Hon. Joshua Townsend [Ref: J-1814 (Box 4)].

MUMFORD, John. Private, Worcester Militia, Wicomico Bn., Capt. Benjamin Dennis' Co., Fifth Class, July 15, 1780 [Ref: M-256].

MUMFORD, Major. Private, Worcester Militia, Sinepuxent Bn., Capt. William Purnell's Co., Seventh Class, 1779/1780 [Ref: M-252]. Took the Oath of Allegiance in Worcester County in 1778 before the Hon. Nehemiah Holland [Ref: J-1814 (Box 4)].

MUMFORD, Mathias. Private, Worcester Militia, Sinepuxent Bn., Capt. Elisha Purnell's Co., Fifth Class, 1779/1780 [Ref: M-253 listed the name as "Matthias Munford"]. Took the Oath of Allegiance in Worcester County in 1778 in Quepomco Hundred before the Hon. Thomas Purnell [Ref: J-1814 (Box 4) listed the name as "Matthias Momford"]. Rendered patriotic service by supplying corn for the use of the military on Feb 15, 1780 and July 10, 1780 [Ref: P-270, G-9].

MUMFORD, Sackor. Private, Worcester Militia, Sinepuxent Bn., Capt. John Coe's Co., First Class, 1779/1780 [Ref: M-251].

MUMFORD, Stephen. Private, Worcester Militia, Sinepuxent Bn., Capt. John Coe's Co., Fifth Class, 1779/1780 [Ref: M-252].

MUMFORD, Thomas. Took the Oath of Allegiance in Worcester County in 1778 in Quepomco Hundred before the Hon. Thomas Purnell [Ref: J-1814 (Box 4) listed the name as "Thomas Momford"].

MUMFORD, Zadok. Private, Worcester Militia, Sinepuxent Bn., Capt. Thomas Purnell's Co., Fifth Class, 1779/1780 [Ref: M-253].

MUNGAN, Matthew. Private, Somerset Militia, Salisbury Bn., White Haven Co., 1778/1780 [Ref: M-218].
MUNGAR, John. Private, Somerset Militia, Princess Anne Bn., Capt. John Jones' Princess Anne Co., 1780 [Ref: M-219].
MUNGAR, Thomas. Private, Worcester Militia, Wicomico Bn., Capt. Charles Bennett's Co., Eighth Class, July 15, 1780 [Ref: M-255].
MUNROW, Isaac. Private, Somerset Militia, Princess Anne Bn., Capt. James Elzey's Co., 1780 [Ref: M-220].
MURDEN, Mary. See "Anthony Murphy," q.v.
MURDOCH, Captain. See "Salathaiel Carman," q.v.
MURPHY, Anthony (c1759-1799). Private, Maryland and Virginia Lines, who married Mary West on Aug 27, 1787 at Princess Anne in Somerset County and died in 1799. Mary Murphy, widow, married second to William Portlack (marriage bond dated May 4, 1807 and co-signed by William West, Sr.) and he subsequently died. Mary Portlack, widow, married third to ---- Murden who also died. On March 5, 1849, Mary Murden, age 78, applied for a pension (R7503) in Princess Anne, Maryland. A son, James Portlack, made affidavit on July 9, 1849, also at Princess Anne [Ref: W-2458].
MURPHY, Jeremiah. Took the Oath of Allegiance in Worcester County in 1778 before the Hon. Nathaniel Miller [Ref: J-1814 (Box 4) listed the name as "Jeremiah Murphey"].
MURPHY, Mary. See "Anthony Murphy," q.v.
MURRAY, Duncan (Dunkin). Took the Oath of Allegiance in Worcester County in 1778 before the Hon. Nathaniel Miller [Ref: J-1814 (Box 4)]. Private, Worcester Militia, Sinepuxent Bn., Capt. John Rackliff's Co., Seventh Class, 1779/1780 [Ref: M-251].
MURRAY, John. Private, Worcester Militia, Wicomico Bn., Capt. William Handy's Co., Sixth Class, July 15, 1780 [Ref: M-257]. Took the Oath of Allegiance in Worcester County in 1778 before the Hon. Joshua Townsend [Ref: J-1814 (Box 4)].
MURROW, Dannel. Took the Oath of Allegiance in Worcester County in 1778 before the Hon. James Selby [Ref: J-1814 (Box 4)].
NAIRNE, Esther. See "Southy Whittington," q.v.
NAIRNE, James. Took the Oath of Allegiance in Worcester County in 1778 before the Hon. Joshua Townsend [Ref: J-1814 (Box 4)].
NEARN, John. Private, Worcester Militia, Snow Hill Bn., Capt. Samuel Smyley's Co., 1777 [Ref: M-250].
NEGRO Joe or Jack. See "William Ironshire," q.v.
NELMS, Edmund Nothorn (Edmond Northen?, Edward N.?). Private, Worcester Militia, Snow Hill Bn., Capt. Ebenezer Handy's Co., April 9, 1776 [Ref: M-249 listed the name as "Edmund N. Nelms"]. Second Lieutenant, Somerset Militia, Princess Anne Bn., Capt. Robert Handy's Co., Sep 22, 1777 [Ref: M-106, C-381 listed the name as "Edward Nothorn Nelms"]. Second Lieutenant,

Worcester Militia, Wicomico Bn., Capt. Robert Handy's Co., July 15, 1780 [Ref: M-254 listed the name as "Edmd. Wm. Nelms"]. Took the Oath of Allegiance in 1778 in Worcester County before the Hon. William Hopewell [Ref: J-1814 (Box 4) listed the name as "Edmond Northen Nelloms"]. Rendered patriotic service by supplying corn for the use of the military on March 9, 1780 and July 10, 1780, and supplying beef on Sep 30, 1780 and Oct 15, 1780 [Ref: G-10 listed the name as "Edmd. N. Nelms" and P-275 listed the name as "Edmund N. Nelms" and P-322 and P-326 listed the name as "Edward N. Nelms"].

NELMS, John. Took the Oath of Allegiance in Somerset County in 1778 before the Hon. Gillis Polk [Ref: T-15].

NELSON, Benjamin. Private, Somerset Militia, Salisbury Bn., Capt. Henry Gale's Quantico Co., 1778/1780 [Ref: M-216].

NELSON, Hannah. See "Asa Coe," q.v.

NELSON (NILSON), Hugh. Took the Oath of Allegiance in Worcester County in 1778 before the Hon. John Selby [Ref: J-1814 (Box 4)].

NELSON, James. Private, 3rd Maryland Independent Co., Worcester County, Capt. John Watkins' Co., enlisted Feb 10, 1776; muster roll dated Aug 20, 1776, present for duty [Ref: D-22].

NELSON, Jesse. Private, Worcester Militia, Wicomico Bn., Capt. William Handy's Co., Second Class, July 15, 1780 [Ref: M-257]. Took the Oath of Allegiance in Worcester County in 1778 before the Hon. Joshua Townsend [Ref: J-1814 (Box 4)].

NELSON, John. Took the Oath of Allegiance in Somerset County in 1778 [Ref: N-51].

NELSON, John Jr. Private, Somerset Militia, Salisbury Bn., Capt. Henry Gale's Quantico Co., 1778/1780 [Ref: M-217].

NELSON, Jonathan. Private, Worcester Militia, Wicomico Bn., Capt. William Handy's Co., Fourth Class, July 15, 1780 [Ref: M-257]. Took the Oath of Allegiance in Worcester County in 1778 before the Hon. Joshua Townsend [Ref: J-1814 (Box 4)].

NELSON (NILSON), Moses. Private, Worcester Militia, Wicomico Bn., Capt. William Handy's Co., Fourth Class, July 15, 1780 [Ref: M-257]. Took the Oath of Allegiance in Worcester County in 1778 before the Hon. John Selby [Ref: J-1814 (Box 4) listed the name as "Moses Nilson"]. Rendered patriotic service by salting beef for the use of the military in October, 1781 [Ref: P-442].

NELSON (NILSON), Samuel. Took the Oath of Allegiance in Worcester County in 1778 before the Hon. John Selby [Ref: J-1814 (Box 4)].

NESBURY, Widow. See "William Ironshire," q.v.

NEVITT, Sarah. See "James Muir," q.v.

NEWBOLD, Smart. Took the Oath of Allegiance in Worcester County in 1778 in Buckingham Hundred before the Hon. Thomas Purnell [Ref: J-1814 (Box 4)].

NEWCOMB (NUCOMB), John. Private, Somerset Militia, Salisbury Bn., Capt. John Span Conway's Nanticoke Point Co., 1778/1780 [Ref: M-216].
NEWMAN (NUMAN), John. Private, Somerset Militia, Princess Anne Bn., Capt. Henry Miles' Little Annemessex Co., 1780 [Ref: M-221].
NEWMAN, Sarah. See "William Covington, Sr.," q.v.
NEWMAN (NUMAN), Thomas. Private, Somerset Militia, Salisbury Bn., White Haven Co., 1778/1780 [Ref: M-218 listed the name as "Thomas Numan"].
NEWMAN, Thomas. Private, 3rd Maryland Independent Co., Worcester County, Capt. John Watkins' Co., enlisted May 20, 1776; muster roll dated Aug 20, 1776, present for duty [Ref: D-23].
NEWTON, Abraham. Private, Worcester Militia, Wicomico Bn., Capt. Isaac Layfield's Co., First Class, July 15, 1780 [Ref: M-257]. Took the Oath of Allegiance in Worcester County in 1778 before the Hon. James Selby [Ref: J-1814 (Box 4) listed the name as "Abraham Neuten"].
NEWTON, James. Private, Somerset Militia, Princess Anne Bn., Capt. George Waters' Pocomoke Co., 1780 [Ref: M-220 listed the name as "James Nuton"].
NEWTON, Job. Private, Worcester Militia, Wicomico Bn., Capt. Charles Bennett's Co., Third Class, July 15, 1780 [Ref: M-255].
NEWTON, Levin (1760-1801). Private, Worcester Militia, Snow Hill Bn., Capt. John Parramore's Co., 1777 [Ref: M-250]. Private, Worcester Militia, Wicomico Bn., Capt. Samuel Smyley's Co., Fourth Class, July 15, 1780 [Ref: M-259]. Took the Oath of Allegiance in Worcester County in 1778 before the Hon. Nehemiah Holland [Ref: J-1814 (Box 4)]. Private, Maryland Troops, Worcester County, draughted May 1, 1781 [Ref: K-99, D-372]. Levin Newton was born in Maryland in 1760, married Sarah ----, served as a private during the war, and died in 1801 [Ref: V-2143].
NEWTON, Sarah. See "Levin Newton," q.v.
NEWTON, Selby. Private, Worcester Militia, Wicomico Bn., Capt. Fisher Walton's Co., Third Class, July 15, 1780 [Ref: M-258]. Took the Oath of Allegiance in Worcester County in 1778 before the Hon. John Selby [Ref: J-1814 (Box 4)].
NEWTON, William. Private, Worcester Militia, Wicomico Bn., Capt. Fisher Walton's Co., Fifth Class, July 15, 1780 [Ref: M-258]. Took the Oath of Allegiance in Worcester County in 1778 before the Hon. Nehemiah Holland [Ref: J-1814 (Box 4)].
NIAMBERGH, Thomas. See "Thomas Niember," q.v.
NIBLET, William (1750-1825). Private, Maryland Line, who applied for a pension (S35011) in Worcester County on April 29, 1818, age 68, and had a wife (name not given) mentioned in 1820. In 1789 he received bounty land warrant #11566-100 for his services. In 1818 he received $96 per annum and died in 1825 [Ref: X-44, W-2492].
NICHOLES, Samuel. Private, Worcester Militia, Sinepuxent Bn., Capt. William Purnell's Co., Third Class, 1779/1780 [Ref: M-252].

NICHOLS, Charles. Private, Somerset Militia, Salisbury Bn., Capt. Levin Irving's Black Water Co., 1778/1780 [Ref: M-217].
NICHOLS, Joseph. Private, Somerset Militia, Salisbury Bn., Capt. Levin Irving's Black Water Co., 1778/1780 [Ref: M-217].
NICHOLS, Joshua. Private, Somerset Militia, Salisbury Bn., Capt. Levin Irving's Black Water Co., 1778/1780 [Ref: M-218].
NICHOLSON, Henry. Private, Somerset Militia, Salisbury Bn., Capt. Henry Gale's Quantico Co., 1778/1780 [Ref: M-216].
NICHOLSON, Isaac. Private, Worcester Militia, Wicomico Bn., Capt. Benjamin Dennis' Co., Fifth Class, July 15, 1780 [Ref: M-256].
NICHOLSON, James. See "William Bratten," q.v.
NICHOLSON, John. Private, 3rd Maryland Independent Co., Worcester County, Capt. John Watkins' Co., enlisted June 9, 1776; muster roll dated Aug 20, 1776, present for duty [Ref: D-23].
NICHOLSON, John. Private, Worcester Militia, Wicomico Bn., Capt. Benjamin Dennis' Co., Seventh Class, July 15, 1780 [Ref: M-256].
NICHOLSON, Joseph. Private, Worcester Militia, Capt. John Martin's Co., 1780/1781 [Ref: J-1814 (Box 12)].
NICHOLSON, Mary. See "Louther Hitch," q.v.
NICHOLSON, Mathias. Private, Worcester Militia, Capt. John Martin's Co., 1780/1781 [Ref: J-1814 (Box 12) listed the name as "Maths. Nicholson"].
NICHOLSON, Roger. Private, Somerset Militia, Salisbury Bn., Capt. William Turpin's Rewastico Co., 1778/1780 [Ref: M-217].
NIEMBER (NIAMBERGH), Thomas. Private, 3rd Maryland Independent Co., Worcester County, Capt. John Watkins' Co., enlisted Feb 10, 1776; muster roll dated Aug 20, 1776, present for duty [Ref: D-21 listed the name as "Thos. Niember"]. Soldier in Capt. Long's Independent Co. who was permitted by the Council of Safety on Oct 4, 1776 to go to Worcester County for the recovery of his health [Ref: B-318 listed the name as "Thomas Niambergh"].
NILSON, Moses. See "Moses Nelson," q.v.
NOBBROOTH, Thomas. Took the Oath of Allegiance in Somerset County in 1778 [Ref: N-51].
NOBLE, John. Private, Somerset Militia, Salisbury Bn., Capt. Levin Irving's Black Water Co., 1778/1780 [Ref: M-218]. Took the Oath of Allegiance in Somerset County in 1778 before the Hon. Gillis Polk [Ref: T-15, N-51]. On June 20, 1781 John Henry recruited John Noble from Somerset County to serve in the Continental Army for 3 years [Ref: L-35C].
NOBLE, Jonathan. Private, Worcester Militia, Wicomico Bn., Capt. Elijah Shockley's Co., Eighth Class, July 15, 1780 [Ref: M-255].
NOBLE, Jonathan (of Joseph). Private, Worcester Militia, Wicomico Bn., Capt. Elijah Shockley's Co., Eighth Class, July 15, 1780 [Ref: M-255].
NOBLE, Thomas. Private, Somerset Militia, Princess Anne Bn., Capt. Thomas Irving's Monie Co., 1780 [Ref: M-219].

NOBLE, William. Private, Worcester Militia, Wicomico Bn., Capt. Benjamin Dennis' Co., Fifth Class, July 15, 1780 [Ref: M-256].
NORTH, John. Private, Somerset Militia, Salisbury Bn., Capt. John Span Conway's Nanticoke Point Co., 1778/1780 [Ref: M-216].
NORTH, William. Private, Somerset County, Capt. John Gunby's 2nd Independent Maryland Co.; sick at Princess Anne on May 15, 1776; mustered on Aug 21, 1776 [Ref: D-641].
NOURSE, J. R. See "Thomas Wimbro," q.v.
NUMAN, Thomas. See "Thomas Newman," q.v.
NUTTER, Benjamin. Private, Somerset Militia, Salisbury Bn., Capt. James Bennett's Salisbury Co., 1778/1780 [Ref: M-218].
NUTTER, Huet (Huett). Took the Oath of Allegiance in Somerset County in 1778 before the Hon. William Winder [Ref: T-22, N-51]. The following was sent by George Dashiell, Lieutenant of Somerset County, to the Council of Maryland and recorded on July 31, 1778: "A petition is presented to us from Capt. William Turpin's Co. of Militia complaining of his being appointed and requesting Huet Nutter, who was formerly elected captain, to be put in his place. We see that Mr. Nutter was appointed first lieutenant, on issuing the commissions last fall, and that in January, Mr. John Philips appointed in his stead. We do not claim the power of displacing Captain Turpin but request you'll inform us the occasion of Mr. Nutter's being passed over in the appointment." [Ref: E-173, E-174]. Nothing further was found in the record regarding this issue. An entry on Jan 7, 1779 stated that Huet Nutter (no rank was given) had been paid for his services [Ref: E-276]. Additional research will be necessary before drawing conclusions.
NUTTER, Joseph. Private, Somerset Militia, Salisbury Bn., Capt. Henry Gale's Quantico Co., 1778/1780 [Ref: M-216].
NUTTER, Matthew (1737-1789). Born in Maryland, probably Somerset County, on Nov 26, 1737, married a Goodwin, rendered patriotic service in Virginia during the war, and died on Jan 7, 1789 in Virginia [Ref: V-2169].
NUTTER, William Sr. Private, Somerset Militia, Salisbury Bn., Capt. William Turpin's Rewastico Co., 1778/1780 [Ref: M-217].
NUTTER, Zadok (1759-1839). Born in Maryland, probably Somerset County, on April 20, 1759, married Catherine Lynn, served as a private in Delaware during the war, and died in Virginia in 1839 [Ref: V-2169].
OAK, William. Took the Oath of Allegiance in Somerset County in 1778 [Ref: N-51].
OAKEY (OKEY), Levin (1760-1829). Private, Worcester Militia, Wicomico Bn., Capt. Isaac Layfield's Co., First Class, July 15, 1780 [Ref: M-257 listed the name as "Levin Oakey"]. Took the Oath of Allegiance in Worcester County in 1778 before the Hon. James Selby [Ref: J-1814 (Box 4) listed the name as "Leaven Ockley"]. "Levin Okey" was born in Delaware on Oct 22, 1760,

married Esther Hazzard, served as a private and rendered other patriotic service in Maryland during the war, and died in Ohio on June 21, 1829 [Ref: V-2180].

OCKLY, William. Took the Oath of Allegiance in Worcester County in 1778 before the Hon. James Selby [Ref: J-1814 (Box 4)].

ODEAR, Elisha. Private, Worcester Militia, Wicomico Bn., Capt. Samuel Horsey's Co., Seventh Class, July 15, 1780 [Ref: M-257].

OLIPHANT, John. Private, Worcester Militia, Wicomico Bn., Capt. Robert Handy's Co., Third Class, July 15, 1780 [Ref: M-254]. Took the Oath of Allegiance in Worcester County in 1778 before the Hon. William Hopewell [Ref: J-1814 (Box 4) listed the name as "John Olliphant"].

OLIPHANT, Mathias. Private, Somerset Militia, Salisbury Bn., Capt. Levin Irving's Black Water Co., 1778/1780 [Ref: M-218 listed the name as "Mathias Aliphant"].

OLIPHANT, William. Private, Worcester Militia, Snow Hill Bn., Capt. Ebenezer Handy's Co., April 9, 1776 [Ref: M-249]. Private, Worcester Militia, Wicomico Bn., Capt. James Perdue's Co., Second Class, July 15, 1780 [Ref: M-256 listed the name as "William Oliphan"]. Took the Oath of Allegiance in Worcester County on Feb 25, 1778 before the Hon. Ebenezer Handy [Ref: J-1814 (Box 4) listed the name as "William Ollifant"].

ORAM, William. Private, Somerset Militia, Salisbury Bn., Capt. Levin Irving's Black Water Co., 1778/1780 [Ref: M-218].

ORDIS(?), Zadok. Private, Worcester Militia, Wicomico Bn., Capt. Fisher Walton's Co., Eighth Class, July 15, 1780 [Ref: M-258 listed the name as "Azdok Ordis(?)"].

OTWELL, James. Took the Oath of Allegiance in Worcester County in 1778 before the Hon. Joshua Townsend [Ref: J-1814 (Box 4)].

OUTTEN, Abraham. See "Isaac Outten" and "Obediah Outten," q.v.

OUTTEN, Betty. See "Obediah Outten" and "Isaac Outten," q.v.

OUTTEN (OUTTON), Isaac (1748-1819). Son of Abraham (1722-1769) and Betty Outten, born in Coventry Parish on Sep 13, 1748, married Sarah Waggaman on Jan 11, 1770, and died on Sep 7, 1819 [Ref: Y-88, V-2199]. Private, Somerset Militia, Princess Anne Bn., Capt. John Williams' Watkins Point Co., 1780 [Ref: M-222].

OUTTEN (OUTTON), John. Private, Worcester Militia, Sinepuxent Bn., Capt. Elisha Purnell's Co., Seventh Class, 1779/1780 [Ref: M-253]. Took the Oath of Allegiance in Worcester County in 1778 in Quepomco Hundred before the Hon. Thomas Purnell [Ref: J-1814 (Box 4)].

OUTTEN (OUTTON), Levi. Private, Worcester Militia, Wicomico Bn., Capt. Benjamin Dennis' Co., Seventh Class, July 15, 1780 [Ref: M-256]. Took the Oath of Allegiance in Worcester County in 1778 before the Hon. Joshua Townsend [Ref: J-1814 (Box 4)].

OUTTEN (OUTTON), Levin or Levi (c1744-1825). Ensign, Worcester Militia, Wicomico Bn., Capt. Benjamin Dennis' Co., Aug 30, 1777 [Ref: M-109 and C-

351 listed the name as "Levin Outton"]. "Levi Outten" was born circa 1744, married twice (second wife names Sally), served as an ensign in Maryland during the war, and died on Feb 15, 1825 in Kentucky [Ref: V-2199].

OUTTEN (OUTTON), Mary. See "Thomas Purnell, of Thomas," q.v.

OUTTEN (OUTTON), Matthias. Private, Worcester Militia, Wicomico Bn., Capt. William Handy's Co., First Class, July 15, 1780 [Ref: M-257]. Took the Oath of Allegiance in Worcester County in 1778 before the Hon. Joshua Townsend [Ref: J-1814 (Box 4)].

OUTTEN (OUTTON), Obediah (1760 -   ). Son of Abraham and Betty Outten, born in Coventry Parish on Dec 22, 1760 [Ref: Y-73 listed the name as "Obed Outten"]. Private, Somerset Militia, Princess Anne Bn., Capt. Isaac Handy's Great Annemessix Co., 1780 [Ref: M-221].

OUTTEN, Sally. See "Levin or Levi Outten," q.v.

OUTTEN (OUTTON), Samuel. Took the Oath of Allegiance in Worcester County in 1778 before the Hon. Joshua Townsend [Ref: J-1814 (Box 4)]. It is interesting to note that on Jan 2, 1783, one Samuel Outten, late commander of the British barge *Trimmer*, was paroled and restricted to the City of Annapolis by order of the Council of Maryland. On Jan 4, 1783 the Council granted permission to Samuel Outten "to pass through this State on his way to Accomack County in the State of Virginia for the purpose of visiting his friends, he conducting himself in every respect conformably to his parole of the 2d instant except as to the restriction confining him to the City of Annapolis." [Ref: I-334, I-337]. Additional research will be necessary before drawing conclusions.

OUTTEN (OUTTON), Thomas. Second Lieutenant, Worcester Militia, Capt. Benjamin Dennis' Co., June 21, 1776 [Ref: M-109, A-506].

OWENS, Isaac. Recruited from Somerset County by Levin Fletcher on June 20, 1781 to serve in the Continental Army until Dec 10, 1781 [Ref: L-35C]. Discharged on Dec 3, 1781 [Ref: I-11].

OWENS, James. Private, Somerset Militia, Salisbury Bn., Capt. John Span Conway's Nanticoke Point Co., 1778/1780 [Ref: M-216].

OWENS, Joshua. Private, Worcester Militia, Wicomico Bn., Capt. Elijah Shockley's Co., Fourth Class, July 15, 1780 [Ref: M-255].

OWENS, Levin. Private, Worcester Militia, Wicomico Bn., Capt. Charles Bennett's Co., First Class, July 15, 1780 [Ref: M-255].

OWENS, Levin. Private, Worcester Militia, Wicomico Bn., Capt. Charles Bennett's Co., Sixth Class, July 15, 1780 [Ref: M-255].

OWENS, Levin. Took the Oath of Allegiance in Worcester County in 1778 before the Hon. Joshua Townsend [Ref: J-1814 (Box 4) listed the name as "Leven Owens"].

OWENS, Mary. See "William Owens," q.v.

OWENS, Okly. Private, Worcester Militia, Wicomico Bn., Capt. Charles Bennett's Co., Fourth Class, July 15, 1780 [Ref: M-255].

OWENS, Peter. Private, Worcester Militia, Wicomico Bn., Capt. Charles Bennett's Co., Seventh Class, July 15, 1780 [Ref: M-255].

OWENS, Samuel. Took the Oath of Allegiance in Somerset County in 1778 before the Hon. Levin Wilson [Ref: T-17, N-51].

OWENS, Spencer. Private, Worcester Militia, Wicomico Bn., Capt. Charles Bennett's Co., First Class, July 15, 1780 [Ref: M-255].

OWENS, Thomas. See "William Owens," q.v.

OWENS, William (1757 -   ). Son of Thomas and Mary Owens, born in Coventry Parish on Jan 12, 1757 [Ref: Y-73]. Private, Somerset Militia, Salisbury Bn., Capt. Josiah Dashiell's Wicomico Creek Co., 1778/1780 [Ref: M-218].

OWINGS, Samuel. Private, 3rd Maryland Independent Co., Worcester County, Capt. John Watkins' Co., enlisted Feb 13, 1776; muster roll dated Aug 20, 1776, present for duty [Ref: D-22].

OYSTEN, Elijah. Took the Oath of Allegiance in Worcester County in 1778 before the Hon. William Hopewell [Ref: J-1814 (Box 4)].

PADEN (PEDEN), John (1744-c1796). Son of John and Elizabeth Paden. He was born on Oct 20, 1744 in Coventry Parish, Somerset County, and married Betty Henderson on Sep 2, 1765. Their son Mills was born on Aug 2, 1766 and their son John was born on Feb 1, 1771 [Ref: Y-74, V-2267]. Private, Somerset Militia, Princess Anne Bn., Capt. George Waters' Pocomoke Co., 1780 [Ref: M-220].

PAIN, John. Private, Worcester Militia, Wicomico Bn., Capt. James Patterson's Co., First Class, July 15, 1780 [Ref: M-258]. Took the Oath of Allegiance in Worcester County in 1778 before the Hon. Nehemiah Holland [Ref: J-1814 (Box 4)].

PAIN, Levin (Leven). Private, Worcester Militia, Snow Hill Bn., Capt. Samuel Smyley's Co., 1777 [Ref: M-250]. Private, Worcester Militia, Wicomico Bn., Capt. James Patterson's Co., Third Class, July 15, 1780 [Ref: M-258]. Took the Oath of Allegiance in Worcester County in 1778 before the Hon. Joshua Townsend [Ref: J-1814 (Box 4)].

PAIN, Moses. Took the Oath of Allegiance in Worcester County in 1778 before the Hon. Joshua Townsend [Ref: J-1814 (Box 4)].

PAIN, Samuel. Private, Worcester Militia, Snow Hill Bn., Capt. John Parramore's Co., 1777 [Ref: M-250]. Private, Worcester Militia, Wicomico Bn., Capt. Philip Quinton's Co., Seventh Class, July 15, 1780 [Ref: M-256 listed the name as "Samuel Pane"].

PARKER, Benjamin. Private, Worcester Militia, Snow Hill Bn., Capt. Ebenezer Handy's Co., April 9, 1776 [Ref: M-249]. Private, Worcester Militia, Wicomico Bn., Capt. Robert Handy's Co., Fourth Class, July 15, 1780 [Ref: M-254].

PARKER, Charles. Private, Worcester Militia, Capt. John Martin's Co., 1780/1781 [Ref: J-1814 (Box 12)].

PARKER, Elisha Jr. Private, Worcester Militia, Snow Hill Bn., Capt. Ebenezer Handy's Co., April 9, 1776 [Ref: M-249]. Private, Worcester Militia, Wicomico Bn., Capt. Robert Handy's Co., Sixth Class, July 15, 1780 [Ref: M-254].

PARKER, Elisha Sr. Private, Worcester Militia, Snow Hill Bn., Capt. Ebenezer Handy's Co., April 9, 1776 [Ref: M-249]. Private, Worcester Militia, Wicomico Bn., Capt. Robert Handy's Co., Fifth Class, July 15, 1780 [Ref: M-254].

PARKER, George Jr. Private, Worcester Militia, Wicomico Bn., Capt. Robert Handy's Co., Third Class, July 15, 1780 [Ref: M-254].

PARKER, Gertrude. See "James Houston," q.v.

PARKER, Henry (of Schoolfield). Took the Oath of Allegiance in Worcester County in 1778 before the Hon. Joshua Townsend [Ref: J-1814 (Box 4)].

PARKER, Jacob. Private, Worcester Militia, Snow Hill Bn., Capt. Ebenezer Handy's Co., April 9, 1776 [Ref: M-249]. Private, Worcester Militia, Wicomico Bn., Capt. Robert Handy's Co., Fourth Class, July 15, 1780 [Ref: M-254].

PARKER, Jinkins. Private, Worcester Militia, Snow Hill Bn., Capt. Ebenezer Handy's Co., April 9, 1776 [Ref: M-249].

PARKER, John (1756-1838). Took the Oath of Allegiance in Somerset County in 1778 before the Hon. Levin Wilson [Ref: T-17, N-51]. On March 21, 1778 Capt. John Parker of Somerset County took the Oath of Allegiance before the Council of Maryland [Ref: C-545]. He appears to have been the John Parker who was born on Aug 21, 1756, died on Feb 16, 1838, and is buried in the Parker Family Graveyard on the north side of Dagsboro Road, one and a half miles west of Parsonsburg-Melson Road in Wicomico County [Ref: *Graveyards and Gravestones of Wicomico*, by John E. Jacob (1996), p. 43]. Additional research may be necessary before drawing conclusions. See "Levin Shores," q.v.

PARKER, Nancy. See "William Beauchamp," q.v.

PARKER, Peter. Private, Worcester Militia, Sinepuxent Bn., Capt. Elisha Purnell's Co., Third Class, 1779/1780 [Ref: M-253].

PARKER, Phill. Private, Worcester Militia, Capt. John Martin's Co., 1780/1781 [Ref: J-1814 (Box 12)].

PARKER, Purnell. Private, Worcester Militia, Sinepuxent Bn., Capt. Thomas Purnell's Co., Third Class, 1779/1780 [Ref: M-253].

PARKER, Rebecca. See "Levi Lamberson," q.v.

PARKER, Sacker. Private, Worcester Militia, Sinepuxent Bn., Capt. William Purnell's Co., Fifth Class, 1779/1780 [Ref: M-252 listed the name as "Sacker Paker"]. Took the Oath of Allegiance in Worcester County in 1778 before the Hon. Joshua Townsend [Ref: J-1814 (Box 4)].

PARKER, Samuel. Corporal, Worcester Militia, Capt. John Martin's Co., 1780/1781 [Ref: J-1814 (Box 12)].

PARKER, Scarborough (c1750-c1788). Second Lieutenant, Worcester Militia, Snow Hill Bn., Capt. Benjamin Townsend's Co., March 16, 1781. Ensign, Worcester Militia, Select Militia, Capt. John Parramore's Co., Aug 23, 1781

[Ref: M-110, G-577, G-353, V-2232]. He assisted in "bringing up sundry desartors & draughts, etc." in October, 1781 [Ref: H-514].

PARKER, Scarborough (1756-1839). Took the Oath of Allegiance in Worcester County in 1778 before the Hon. Joshua Townsend [Ref: J-1814 (Box 4)]. Scarborough Parker was born on Aug 10, 1756, died on Sep 15, 1839, and is buried in the Parker Family Graveyard on the north side of Dagsboro Road, one and a half miles west of Parsonsburg-Melson Road in Wicomico County [Ref: *Graveyards and Gravestones of Wicomico*, by John E. Jacob (1996), p. 43].

PARKER, Schoolfield. Took the Oath of Allegiance in Worcester County in 1778 before the Hon. Joshua Townsend [Ref: J-1814 (Box 4)]. Private, Worcester Militia, Capt. John Martin's Co., 1780/1781 [Ref: J-1814 (Box 12) listed the name as "Scophd. Parker"].

PARKER, Selby. Ensign, Worcester Militia, Wicomico Bn., Capt. B. Townsend's Co., June 2, 1781 [Ref: M-110, G-457]. Took the Oath of Allegiance in Worcester County in 1778 before the Hon. Joshua Townsend [Ref: J-1814 (Box 4)].

PARKER, William. Ensign, Worcester Militia, Snow Hill Bn., Capt. John Stewart's Co., Aug 30, 1777 to April 21, 1781, resigned [Ref: M-110, C-351]. Took the Oath of Allegiance in Worcester County in 1778 before the Hon. Joshua Townsend [Ref: J-1814 (Box 4)].

PARKER, William (of Schoolfield). Took the Oath of Allegiance in Worcester County in 1778 before the Hon. Joshua Townsend [Ref: J-1814 (Box 4)].

PARKES, Arthur. Private, Somerset Militia, Princess Anne Bn., Capt. Henry Miles' Little Annemessex Co., 1780 [Ref: M-221].

PARKES, Job. Private, Somerset Militia, Princess Anne Bn., Capt. Henry Miles' Little Annemessex Co., 1780 [Ref: M-221].

PARKES, John. Private, Somerset Militia, Princess Anne Bn., Capt. Henry Miles' Little Annemessex Co., 1780 [Ref: M-221].

PARRADICE, Thomas. Private, Worcester Militia, Snow Hill Bn., Capt. Samuel Smyley's Co., 1777. Private, Worcester Militia, Wicomico Bn., Capt. Samuel Smyley's Co., Second Class, July 15, 1780 [Ref: M-250, M-259].

PARRAMORE (PARAMORE), James. Private, Somerset Militia, Salisbury Bn., Capt. William Turpin's Rewastico Co., 1778/1780 [Ref: M-217].

PARRAMORE (PARAMORE), John (d. 1787). Captain, Worcester Militia, Snow Hill Bn., Aug 30, 1777 [Ref: M-110, M-250, C-351, V-2237]. Captain, Worcester Militia, Wicomico Bn., July 15, 1780 [Ref: M-259 listed the name as "Capt. Parramor"]. Captain, Select Militia, Aug 23, 1781 [Ref: M-110, G-577]. Took the Oath of Allegiance in Worcester County in 1778 before the Hon. Nehemiah Holland [Ref: J-1814 (Box 4)]. Justice of the Peace, commissioned on Nov 21, 1778 and March 27, 1779 and Jan 17, 1782 [Ref: I-46, E-249, and E-327 mistakenly listed the name as "John Panamore"].

PARRAMORE (PARAMORE), John. Private, Worcester Militia, Wicomico Bn., Capt. John Parramore's Co., First Class, July 15, 1780 [Ref: M-259].

PARRAMORE (PARAMORE), Samuel. Private, Somerset Militia, Salisbury Bn., Capt. William Turpin's Rewastico Co., 1778/1780 [Ref: M-217].

PARRAMORE (PARAMORE), Stephen. Corporal, Somerset Militia, Princess Anne Bn., Capt. Henry Miles' Little Annemessex Co., 1780 [Ref: M-221].

PARRAMORE (PARAMORE), Thomas. Private, Somerset County, Capt. John Gunby's 2nd Independent Maryland Co.; present on March 4, 1776; mustered on Aug 21, 1776 [Ref: D-641].

PARRIS, John. Private, Worcester Militia, Sinepuxent Bn., Capt. Thomas Purnell's Co., Sixth Class, 1779/1780 [Ref: M-253]. Took the Oath of Allegiance in Worcester County in 1778 before the Hon. Nathaniel Miller [Ref: J-1814 (Box 4)].

PARSONS, Elizabeth. See "Benjamin Farlow," q.v.

PARSONS, George (1734-1809). First Lieutenant, Worcester Militia, Snow Hill Bn., Capt. Ebenezer Handy's Co., April 9, 1776 or May 15, 1776 (both dates were given). First Lieutenant, Worcester Militia, Wicomico Bn., Capt. Robert Handy's Co., Aug 30, 1777 to May 27, 1779, succeeded [Ref: M-110, M-249, A-426, C-351]. He was born Dec 16, 1734, married Temperance ----, and died Jan 4, 1809 [Ref: V-2239]. See "Jordan Parsons," q.v.

PARSONS, George (1738 -   ). Private, Worcester Militia, Wicomico Bn., Capt. Robert Handy's Co., Fifth Class, July 15, 1780 [Ref: M-254].

PARSONS, George Jr. Rendered patriotic service by supplying bacon for the use of the military on Oct 15, 1780 [Ref: P-326].

PARSONS, John. Private, Worcester Militia, Wicomico Bn., Capt. James Perdue's Co., Fourth Class, July 15, 1780 [Ref: M-256].

PARSONS, John Jr. Private, Worcester Militia, Wicomico Bn., Capt. John Davis' Co., Fourth Class, July 15, 1780 [Ref: M-254].

PARSONS, Jonathan (1739-1808). Sergeant, Worcester Militia, Snow Hill Bn., Capt. Ebenezer Handy's Co., April 9, 1776. Private(?), Worcester Militia, Wicomico Bn., Capt. Robert Handy's Co., Sixth Class, July 15, 1780 [Ref: M-249, M-254]. See "Levin Parsons," q.v.

PARSONS, Jordan (1762 -   ). Son of George Parsons and Temperance Shermon, born in Stepney Parish on Jan 9, 1762 [Ref: Y-48]. Private, Worcester Militia, Wicomico Bn., Capt. Robert Handy's Co., Seventh Class, July 15, 1780 [Ref: M-254].

PARSONS, Levin (1759 -   ). Son of Jonathan Parsons and Sarah Mills, born in Stepney Parish on June 26, 1759 [Ref: Y-48]. Private, Worcester Militia, Wicomico Bn., Capt. Robert Handy's Co., Eighth Class, July 15, 1780 [Ref: M-254].

PARSONS, Porter. Private, Worcester Militia, Wicomico Bn., Capt. John Davis' Co., Seventh Class, July 15, 1780 [Ref: M-255].

PARSONS, Samuel (1757 -   ). Son of William Parsons and Hannah Hearn, born in Stepney Parish on Nov 7, 1757 [Ref: Y-48]. Corporal, Worcester Militia, Snow Hill Bn., Capt. Ebenezer Handy's Co., April 9, 1776 [Ref: M-249].

Private(?), Worcester Militia, Wicomico Bn., Capt. Robert Handy's Co., Third Class, July 15, 1780 [Ref: M-249, M-254].

PARSONS, William. Private, Worcester Militia, Snow Hill Bn., Capt. Ebenezer Handy's Co., April 9, 1776 [Ref: M-249]. Private, Worcester Militia, Wicomico Bn., Capt. Robert Handy's Co., Fifth Class, July 15, 1780 [Ref: M-254]. See "Samuel Parsons," q.v.

PARSONS, Zachariah. Private, Worcester Militia, Wicomico Bn., Capt. John Davis' Co., Seventh Class, July 15, 1780 [Ref: M-255].

PARSONS, Zephaniah. Private, Worcester Militia, Wicomico Bn., Capt. John Davis' Co., Sixth Class, July 15, 1780 [Ref: M-254].

PATRICK, Cornelius. Private, Worcester Militia, Wicomico Bn., Capt. William Handy's Co., Third Class, July 15, 1780 [Ref: M-257].

PATRICK, Daniel. Took the Oath of Allegiance in Worcester County in 1778 before the Hon. Joshua Townsend [Ref: J-1814 (Box 4)].

PATRICK, John. Private, Worcester Militia, Sinepuxent Bn., Capt. William Purnell's Co., Second Class, 1779/1780 [Ref: M-252].

PATTERSON, Anderson (1762 -   ). Son of James and Sarah Patterson, born in Coventry Parish on March 15, 1762 [Ref: Y-88]. Private, Worcester Militia, Wicomico Bn., Capt. James Patterson's Co., Second Class, July 15, 1780 [Ref: M-258].

PATTERSON, James. Captain, Worcester Militia, Wicomico Bn., Capt. James Patterson's Co., July 15, 1780 [Ref: M-258]. Took the Oath of Allegiance in Worcester County in 1778 before the Hon. James Selby [Ref: J-1814 (Box 4)]. See "Anderson Patterson," q.v.

PATTERSON, Sarah. See "Anderson Patterson," q.v.

PATTY (PATTEY), Kendell. Took the Oath of Allegiance in Worcester County in 1778 in Buckingham Hundred before the Hon. Thomas Purnell [Ref: J-1814 (Box 4) listed the name as "Kendell Pattey"]. Private, Worcester Militia, Sinepuxent Bn., Capt. John Rackliff's Co., Third Class, 1779/1780 [Ref: M-251 listed the name as "Kendle Patty"].

PATTY (PATTEY), Powell. Took the Oath of Allegiance in Worcester County in 1778 before the Hon. Nathaniel Miller [Ref: J-1814 (Box 4) listed the name as "Powel Pettey"].

PATTY (PATTEY), Powell Jr. Private, Worcester Militia, Sinepuxent Bn., Capt. John Rackliff's Co., Fourth Class, 1779/1780 [Ref: M-251].

PEACOCK, Israel. Private, Worcester Militia, Wicomico Bn., Capt. Isaac Layfield's Co., First Class, July 15, 1780 [Ref: M-257 listed the name as "Israel Peakock"].

PEACOCK, John. Private, Worcester Militia, Wicomico Bn., Capt. Isaac Layfield's Co., Eighth Class, July 15, 1780 [Ref: M-257]. Took the Oath of Allegiance in Worcester County in 1778 before the Hon. James Selby [Ref: J-1814 (Box 4) listed the name as "John Pacok"].

PEACOCK, John. Took the Oath of Allegiance in Worcester County in 1778 before the Hon. John Selby [Ref: J-1814 (Box 4)].
PEACOCK, Levi. Private, Worcester Militia, Wicomico Bn., Capt. Isaac Layfield's Co., Seventh Class, July 15, 1780 [Ref: M-257]. Took the Oath of Allegiance in Worcester County in 1778 before the Hon. James Selby [Ref: J-1814 (Box 4) listed the name as "Levi Pacok"].
PEACOCK, William. Took the Oath of Allegiance in Worcester County in 1778 before the Hon. James Selby [Ref: J-1814 (Box 4) listed the name as "William Pacok"].
PEAL, Thomas. Private, Worcester Militia, Capt. John Martin's Co., 1780/1781 [Ref: J-1814 (Box 12)].
PEDEN, John. See "John Paden," q.v.
PENEWELL (PENEWILL), Elias. Private, Worcester Militia, Sinepuxent Bn., Capt. William Purnell's Co., First Class, 1779/1780 [Ref: M-252]. Private, Maryland Troops, Worcester County, draughted May 1, 1781 [Ref: K-99, D-372].
PENEWELL (PENEWILL), Elias. Private, Worcester Militia, Sinepuxent Bn., Capt. Thomas Purnell's Co., Seventh Class, 1779/1780 [Ref: M-253]. Took the Oath of Allegiance in Worcester County in 1778 before the Hon. Joshua Townsend [Ref: J-1814 (Box 4)].
PENEWELL (PENEWILL), Elisha. Private, Worcester Militia, Wicomico Bn., Capt. John Davis' Co., Sixth Class, July 15, 1780 [Ref: M-254].
PENEWELL (PENEWILL), Elisha. Private, Worcester Militia, Wicomico Bn., Capt. Elijah Shockley's Co., First Class, July 15, 1780 [Ref: M-255].
PENEWELL (PENEWILL), George. Private, Worcester Militia, Wicomico Bn., Capt. John Davis' Co., Third Class, July 15, 1780 [Ref: M-254].
PENEWELL (PENEWILL), Luke. Private, Worcester Militia, Sinepuxent Bn., Capt. John Postly's Co., Third Class, 1779/1780 [Ref: M-251].
PENEWELL (PENEWILL), Powell. Private, Worcester Militia, Sinepuxent Bn., Capt. John Rackliff's Co., Sixth Class, 1779/1780 [Ref: M-251].
PENEWELL (PENEWILL), Rackliff. Private, Worcester Militia, Sinepuxent Bn., Capt. Thomas Purnell's Co., Eighth Class, 1779/1780 [Ref: M-253].
PENEWELL (PENEWILL), Richard. Private, Worcester Militia, Wicomico Bn., Capt. John Davis' Co., Fourth Class, July 15, 1780 [Ref: M-254].
PENEWELL (PENNEWEL), Thomas. Private, Worcester Militia, Capt. John Martin's Co., 1780/1781 [Ref: J-1814 (Box 12)].
PENEWELL (PENEWILL), William. Private, Worcester Militia, Sinepuxent Bn., Capt. Thomas Purnell's Co., Seventh Class, 1779/1780 [Ref: M-253].
PEPPER, Eli. Took the Oath of Allegiance in Worcester County in 1778 before the Hon. Joshua Townsend [Ref: J-1814 (Box 4)].
PEPPER, Elijah. Took the Oath of Allegiance in Worcester County in 1778 before the Hon. Joshua Townsend [Ref: J-1814 (Box 4)].

PEPPER, Evans. Private, Worcester Militia, Sinepuxent Bn., Capt. Thomas Purnell's Co., Seventh Class, 1779/1780 [Ref: M-253].

PEPPER, John. Took the Oath of Allegiance in Somerset County in 1778 before the Hon. William Winder [Ref: T-22 listed the name as "John Peper"].

PEPPER, Joseph. Took the Oath of Allegiance in Somerset County in 1778 before the Hon. William Winder [Ref: T-22 listed the name as "Joseph Peper"].

PEPPER, Joshua. Private, Worcester Militia, Wicomico Bn., Capt. William Handy's Co., Sixth Class, July 15, 1780 [Ref: M-257].

PEPPER, Levi. Private, Worcester Militia, Sinepuxent Bn., Capt. John Rackliff's Co., Sixth Class, 1779/1780 [Ref: M-251]. Took the Oath of Allegiance in Worcester County in 1778 in Buckingham Hundred before the Hon. Thomas Purnell [Ref: J-1814 (Box 4)].

PEPPER, Solomon. Took the Oath of Allegiance in Worcester County in 1778 before the Hon. Nehemiah Holland [Ref: J-1814 (Box 4)].

PEPPER, Spencer. Private, Worcester Militia, Snow Hill Bn., Capt. Samuel Smyley's Co., 1777 [Ref: M-250]. Private, Worcester Militia, Wicomico Bn., Capt. Samuel Smyley's Co., First Class, July 15, 1780 [Ref: M-258].

PERDUE, Benjamin. Took the Oath of Allegiance in Worcester County in 1778 before the Hon. Nathaniel Miller [Ref: J-1814 (Box 4) listed the name as "Benjamin Purdue"].

PERDUE, George Jr. Private, Worcester Militia, Snow Hill Bn., Capt. Ebenezer Handy's Co., April 9, 1776 [Ref: M-249]. Private, Worcester Militia, Wicomico Bn., Capt. Robert Handy's Co., Second Class, July 15, 1780 [Ref: M-254].

PERDUE, George Sr. Private, Worcester Militia, Wicomico Bn., Capt. Robert Handy's Co., Second Class, July 15, 1780 [Ref: M-254].

PERDUE, James. Private, Worcester Militia, Wicomico Bn., Capt. James Perdue's Co., Fourth Class, July 15, 1780 [Ref: M-256].

PERDUE, James. Private, Worcester Militia, Wicomico Bn., Capt. Robert Handy's Co., Third Class, July 15, 1780 [Ref: M-254].

PERDUE, James. Second Lieutenant, Worcester Militia, 10th or Snow Hill Bn., Capt. Ebenezer Handy's Co., April 9, 1776 or May 15, 1776 (both dates were given). Second Lieutenant, Wicomico Bn., Capt. Robert Handy's Co., Aug 30, 1777. Captain, Worcester Militia, Wicomico Bn., May 27, 1779 to at least July 15, 1780 [Ref: M-113, M-249, M-256, A-426, C-351, E-423]. Took the Oath of Allegiance in Worcester County in 1778 before the Hon. John Selby [Ref: J-1814 (Box 4)].

PERDUE, James Sr. Private, Worcester Militia, Snow Hill Bn., Capt. Ebenezer Handy's Co., April 9, 1776 [Ref: M-249].

PERDUE, John. Private, Worcester Militia, Wicomico Bn., Capt. Robert Handy's Co., Seventh Class, July 15, 1780 [Ref: M-254].

PERDUE, John Jr. Private, Worcester Militia, Wicomico Bn., Capt. Robert Handy's Co., Sixth Class, July 15, 1780 [Ref: M-254].

PERKINS (PURKINS), John. Took the Oath of Allegiance in Somerset County in 1778 before the Hon. Peter Waters [Ref: T-18]. Private, Somerset Militia, Princess Anne Bn., Capt. George Waters' Pocomoke Co., 1780 [Ref: M-220].
PERKINS (PURKINS), John. Took the Oath of Allegiance in Worcester County in 1778 before the Hon. Nathaniel Miller [Ref: J-1814 (Box 4)].
PERKINS (PURKINS), Michael. Took the Oath of Allegiance in Worcester County in 1778 in Quepomco Hundred before the Hon. Thomas Purnell [Ref: J-1814 (Box 4)].
PERKINS (PURKINS), Solomon. Private, Worcester Militia, Sinepuxent Bn., Capt. John Coe's Co., Sixth Class, 1779/1780 [Ref: M-252].
PERKINS (PURKINS), Thomas. Private, Worcester Militia, Sinepuxent Bn., Capt. John Coe's Co., Fourth Class, 1779/1780 [Ref: M-252].
PERRY, William. See "Samuel Lockwood," q.v.
PETTEY, Powel. See "Powell Patty," q.v.
PETTIT, Absolom. Took the Oath of Allegiance in Worcester County in 1778 before the Hon. Joshua Townsend [Ref: J-1814 (Box 4) listed the name as "Absalon Pettit"]. Private, Worcester Militia, Sinepuxent Bn., Capt. William Purnell's Co., Fourth Class, 1779/1780 [Ref: M-252 mistakenly listed the name as "Absolom Pittel"].
PETTIT, Edward. Took the Oath of Allegiance in Worcester County in 1778 before the Hon. Nathaniel Miller [Ref: J-1814 (Box 4)]. Rendered patriotic service by supplying corn for the use of the military on July 10, 1780 [Ref: G-9].
PHEBUS (PHOEBUS), George (1762 -   ). Private, Maryland Line, who applied for a pension (S3683) in Pickaway County, Ohio on Aug 10, 1832, stating he was born in Somerset County, Maryland on July 12, 1762 and lived there at the time of his enlistment. In 1786 he moved to Virginia for 9 years, then to Kentucky for 4 years, and then to Pickaway County, Ohio. Mentioned in 1831 was a Samuel Phebus, also of Ohio [Ref: W-2676]. "George Phebus, Junr." was a private in the Somerset Militia, Princess Anne Bn., Capt. Thomas Irving's Monie Co., in 1780 [Ref: M-219]. On July 30, 1781 Levin Miles recruited "George Phebus" from Somerset County to serve in the Continental Army until Dec 10, 1781 [Ref: L-35C]. "George Febus" was discharged on Dec 3, 1781 [Ref: I-11].
PHEBUS (PHOEBUS), John. Private, Somerset Militia, Princess Anne Bn., Capt. Thomas Irving's Monie Co., 1780 [Ref: M-219]. Took the Oath of Allegiance in Somerset County in 1778 before the Hon. Levin Wilson [Ref: T-17].
PHEBUS (PHOEBUS), John Jr. Private, Somerset Militia, Princess Anne Bn., Capt. Thomas Irving's Monie Co., 1780 [Ref: M-219]. Took the Oath of Allegiance in Somerset County in 1778 before the Hon. Levin Wilson [Ref: T-17].

PHEBUS (PHOEBUS), Josiah. Drafted from Somerset County on June 20, 1781 to serve in the Continental Army, but subsequently noted as "debilitated" [Ref: L-35C].
PHEBUS (PHOEBUS), Nancy. See "Robert Martin," q.v.
PHEBUS (PHOEBUS), Samuel. See "George Phebus," q.v.
PHEBUS (PHOEBUS), William. Corporal, Somerset Militia, Princess Anne Bn., Capt. Thomas Irving's Monie Co., 1780 [Ref: M-219]. Took the Oath of Allegiance in Somerset County in 1778 before the Hon. Levin Wilson [Ref: T-17].
PHILLIPS (PHILIPS), Alice. See "James Phillips," q.v.
PHILLIPS (PHILIPS), Bennett (1763-1842). Private, North Carolina Line, who applied for a pension on May 20, 1834 in Rutherford County, Tennessee, stating he was born in Somerset County, Maryland on Dec 27, 1763, married Miss Isabella Moore in the spring of 1784 in Granville County, North Carolina (where he lived at the time of his enlistment), and moved to Tennessee in 1797. Isabella Phillips applied for a pension (W976) on Nov 20, 1843, stating she was born on Feb 9, 1765, mentioned a son Samuel (other children, if any, were not named), and stated her husband Bennett died on Sep 20, 1842 [Ref: W-2684, V-2300].
PHILLIPS (PHILIPS), Charles. Private, Somerset Militia, Salisbury Bn., Capt. William Turpin's Rewastico Co., 1778/1780 [Ref: M-217].
PHILLIPS (PHILIPS), George. Private, Somerset Militia, Salisbury Bn., Capt. William Turpin's Rewastico Co., 1778/1780 [Ref: M-217].
PHILLIPS (PHILIPS), Isaac. Private, Worcester Militia, Snow Hill Bn., Capt. Ebenezer Handy's Co., April 9, 1776 [Ref: M-249]. Private, Worcester Militia, Wicomico Bn., Capt. James Perdue's Co., Third Class, July 15, 1780 [Ref: M-256]. Took the Oath of Allegiance in Worcester County on Feb 25, 1778 before the Hon. Ebenezer Handy [Ref: J-1814 (Box 4)].
PHILLIPS, Isabella. See "Bennett Phillips," q.v.
PHILLIPS (PHILIPS), Jacob. Took the Oath of Allegiance in Worcester County on Feb 25, 1778 before the Hon. Ebenezer Handy [Ref: J-1814 (Box 4)].
PHILLIPS (PHILLOPS), James (c1725/30 -   ). Took the Oath of Allegiance in Worcester County in 1778 before the Hon. James Selby [Ref: J-1814 (Box 4)]. James Phillips married Leah ---- circa 1750 in Coventry Parish. Their daughter Jane was born on July 10, 1752 and their son James was born on Oct 12, 1756 [Ref: Y-88].
PHILLIPS (PHILIPS), James (1740-1785). Son of Richard and Alice Phillips. James married Mary Ackworth (1744-1799) on March 18, 1762 and died in Somerset County on Sep 12, 1785. Their son James Phillips married Esther Green Hatton on Feb 16, 1813 [Ref: S-2653A, V-2301]. Ensign, Somerset Militia, Salisbury Bn., Capt. William Turpin's Rewastico Co., 1778/1780 to at least Aug 22, 1781 [Ref: M-111, M-217, J-1814 (Box 8, Dashiell's

correspondence), G-575]. Took the Oath of Allegiance in Somerset County in 1778 before the Hon. William Winder [Ref: T-22, N-51].

PHILLIPS (PHILIPS), James Jr. (1756 -   ). Son of James and Leah Phillips, born in Coventry Parish on Oct 12, 1756 [Ref: Y-88]. Private, Worcester Militia, Wicomico Bn., Capt. James Patterson's Co., First Class, July 15, 1780 [Ref: M-258 listed the name without the "Jr."]. Recommended for promotion to ensign in Quantico Co. on April 17, 1781 [Ref: H-195].

PHILLIPS, Jane. See "James Phillips (Phillops), " q.v.

PHILLIPS (PHILIPS), Jesse. Private, Somerset Militia, Salisbury Bn., Capt. John Span Conway's Nanticoke Point Co., 1778/1780 [Ref: M-216].

PHILLIPS (PHILIPS), John. Captain, Somerset Militia, 1st Bn., May 13, 1776 [Ref: M-111, B-220]. Took the Oath of Allegiance in Worcester County on Feb 25, 1778 before the Hon. Ebenezer Handy [Ref: J-1814 (Box 4)]. See "Huet Nutter," q.v.

PHILLIPS (PHILIPS), John. Second Lieutenant, Somerset Militia, Salisbury Bn., Capt. William Turpin's Co., Sep 22, 1777. First Lieutenant, Jan 7, 1778 to at least July 31, 1778 [Ref: M-111, C-382, C-173, C-457]. Took the Oath of Allegiance in Somerset County in 1778 before the Hon. William Winder [Ref: T-22, N-51].

PHILLIPS (PHILIPS), John. Private, Somerset Militia, Salisbury Bn., Capt. John Span Conway's Nanticoke Point Co., 1778/1780 [Ref: M-216]. Private, Somerset Militia, Princess Anne Bn., Capt. James Elzey's Co., 1780 [Ref: M-220]. Drafted from Somerset County on July 30, 1781 to serve in the Continental Army [Ref: L-35C].

PHILLIPS (PHILIPS), Jonah. Private, Somerset Militia, Salisbury Bn., Capt. John Span Conway's Nanticoke Point Co., 1778/1780 [Ref: M-216].

PHILLIPS, Leah. See "James Phillips (Phillops)," q.v.

PHILLIPS, Nelly. See "Isaac Giles," q.v.

PHILLIPS (PHILIPS), Patrick. Private, Somerset County, Capt. John Gunby's 2nd Independent Maryland Co.; sick at Princess Anne on March 12, 1776; mustered on Aug 21, 1776 [Ref: D-641].

PHILLIPS, Richard. See "James Phillips," q.v.

PHILLIPS, Samuel. See "Bennett Phillips," q.v.

PILCHARD, Elijah. Took the Oath of Allegiance in Worcester County in 1778 before the Hon. Nehemiah Holland [Ref: J-1814 (Box 4)].

PILCHARD, Esau. Private, Worcester Militia, Snow Hill Bn., Capt. Samuel Smyley's Co., 1777 [Ref: M-250]. Private, Worcester Militia, Wicomico Bn., Capt. James Patterson's Co., Third Class, July 15, 1780 [Ref: M-258]. Took the Oath of Allegiance in Worcester County in 1778 before the Hon. James Selby [Ref: J-1814 (Box 4) listed the name as "Ezer Pilcher"].

PILCHARD, Jabez. Private, Worcester Militia, Snow Hill Bn., Capt. Samuel Smyley's Co., 1777 [Ref: M-250]. Private, Worcester Militia, Wicomico Bn., Capt. James Patterson's Co., Fourth Class, July 15, 1780 [Ref: M-258]. Took the Oath of Allegiance in Worcester County in 1778 before the Hon. Nehemiah Holland [Ref: J-1814 (Box 4)].

PILCHARD, Levi. Private, Worcester Militia, Wicomico Bn., Capt. James Patterson's Co., Eighth Class, July 15, 1780 [Ref: M-258]. Took the Oath of Allegiance in Worcester County in 1778 before the Hon. Joshua Townsend [Ref: J-1814 (Box 4) listed the name as "Levi Pilsher"].

PILCHARD, Mary. See "Samuel Blades," q.v.

PINTER, Thomas. See "Thomas Pointer," q.v.

PIPER, Ann. See "Joseph Piper," q.v.

PIPER, Betsy. See "Ezekiel Hitch," q.v.

PIPER, John. Justice of the Peace in Somerset County, commissioned on Jan 9, 1778 [Ref: C-464]. See "Joseph Piper," q.v.

PIPER, Joseph (1756 -). Son of John and Ann Piper, born in Stepney Parish on Feb 8, 1756 [Ref: Y-48]. Ensign, Somerset Militia, Salisbury Bn., Capt. William Turpin's Rewastico Co., Sep 22, 1777. Second Lieutenant, Rewastico Co., 1781 [Ref: M-111, M-217, C-382, G-575, J-1814 (Box 8, Dashiell's correspondence), H-195].

PIPER, Priscilla. See "John Round," q.v.

PIPER, Sarah. See "Josiah Dashiell," q.v.

PITTS (PITT), Hillery or Hillary. Private, Worcester Militia, Sinepuxent Bn., Capt. John Postly's Co., First Class, 1779/1780 [Ref: M-251]. Rendered patriotic service by supplying corn for the use of the military on May 3, 1780 [Ref: P-288]. Took the Oath of Allegiance in Worcester County in 1778 before the Hon. Nathaniel Miller [Ref: J-1814 (Box 4)].

PITTS, Robert. See "Henry Dennis," q.v.

PITTS, William. Took the Oath of Allegiance in Worcester County in 1778 before the Hon. Nathaniel Miller [Ref: J-1814 (Box 4)].

POINTER, John. Took the Oath of Allegiance in Worcester County in 1778 before the Hon. Joshua Townsend [Ref: J-1814 (Box 4)].

POINTER, Thomas. Private, Worcester Militia, Sinepuxent Bn., Capt. Matthew Purnell's Co., First Class, July 25, 1780 [Ref: M-252]. Private, Maryland Line, from Worcester County, who was discharged on Dec 3, 1781 [Ref: I-11 listed the name as "Thomas Pinter"].

POINTER (POYNTER), Thomas. Took the Oath of Allegiance in Worcester County in 1778 before the Hon. Joshua Townsend [Ref: J-1814 (Box 4) listed the name as "Thomas Poynter"].

POLK, Ann. See "William Polk," q.v.

POLK, Benjamin. Took the Oath of Allegiance in Somerset County in 1778 before the Hon. Levin Wilson [Ref: T-17, N-51].

POLK, Benjamin Jr. Private, Somerset Militia, Princess Anne Bn., Capt. John Jones' Princess Anne Co., 1780 [Ref: M-219]. Select Militia, Somerset County, Aug 15, 1781 [Ref: L-35A].

POLK, Cata (Caty). See "Gillis Polk," q.v.

POLK, David. Private, Select Militia, Somerset County, Aug 15, 1781 [Ref: L-35B]. See "Gillis Polk" and "Josiah Polk," q.v.

POLK, David (c1705-1783). Took the Oath of Allegiance in Somerset County on Feb 6, 1778 before the Hon. Joseph Venables [Ref: T-25]. He married Elizabeth Gillis and their children were Gillis, Josiah, William, James, and Sinah [Ref: R-653].

POLK, Elizabeth. See "Gillis Polk" and "William Polk," q.v.

POLK, Esther (Hester). See "William Polk," q.v.

POLK, Eunice Jane. See "John Scroggin," q.v.

POLK, Gertrude. See "William Polk," q.v.

POLK, Gillis or Gilliss (c1745-1793). Son of David Polk and Elizabeth Gillis. He married Hannah ---- and their children were Gillis Washington Morris Rounds, Josiah, Nancy, Elizabeth, Sarah, and Cata or Caty. Gillis served in the Lower House of the Maryland Legislature from Somerset County, 1782-1783, 1786-1788; Commissioner of the Tax, 1781-1782; Justice of the Orphans Court, 1786-1791; and, County Court Justice, 1777-1791 [Ref: R-653]. First Lieutenant, Somerset Militia, Salisbury Bn., Capt. Levin Irving's Black Water Co., Sep 22, 1777. Captain, April 17, 1781 [Ref: M-111, M-217, C-381, R-653, H-195]. Justice who administered the Oath of Allegiance in Somerset County in 1778 [Ref: T-15, N-51]. Justice of the Peace, commissioned on Jan 7, 1778 and Nov 21, 1778 and Jan 17, 1782 [Ref: C-464, E-248, I-45]. Served as Commissary of Purchases and also rendered patriotic service by supplying corn for the use of the military in 1780 [Ref: P-266, P-267, P-295]. See "David Polk," q.v.

POLK, Hanna. See "Gillis Polk," q.v.

POLK, James. On May 16, 1777 the Council of Maryland appointed and commissioned James Polk as Surveyor of Somerset County in the room of Arnold Elzey, deceased [Ref: C-255]. First Lieutenant, Somerset Militia, Salisbury Bn., Capt. Henry Gale's Quantico Co., Sep 22, 1777 to at least July 24, 1780 [Ref: M-111, M-216, C-381]. Rendered patriotic service by supplying bacon for the use of the military in Somerset County on Aug 18, 1780 [Ref: P-310]. See "David Polk" and "William Morris," q.v.

POLK, James Jr. On May 16, 1777 the Council of Maryland ordered "that the Western Shore Treasurer pay to James Polk Junior for the use of Wm. McBryd [McBryde] one hundred pounds, to be expended in purchasing peas for the public." [Ref: C-255]. Took the Oath of Allegiance in Somerset County in 1778 before the Hon. Levin Wilson [Ref: T-17, N-51]. Private, Somerset Militia, Salisbury Bn., White Haven Co., 1778/1780 [Ref: M-219 listed the name without the "Jr."].

POLK, James Sr. Took the Oath of Allegiance in Somerset County in 1778 before the Hon. Levin Wilson [Ref: T-17, N-51].

POLK, James (of William). Private, Select Militia, Somerset County, Aug 15, 1781 [Ref: L-35A].

POLK, Jane. See "William Strawbridge," q.v.

POLK, John. Private, Somerset Militia, Salisbury Bn., White Haven Co., 1778/1780 [Ref: M-219]. Select Militia, Somerset County, Aug 15, 1781 [Ref: L-35B].

POLK, Joshua. Private, Somerset Militia, Princess Anne Bn., Capt. John Jones' Princess Anne Co., 1780 [Ref: M-219].

POLK, Josiah (c1740-1784). Son of David Polk and Elizabeth Gillis. Attended the Maryland Convention, 1774-1775, from Somerset County; signed the Association of the Freemen of Maryland in 1775; served on the Executive Council, 1777, and Special Council, Eastern Shore, 1780-1781 [It may be of interest to note that he wrote to the Special Council on June 12, 1781: "From a very severe parixism of the gout I am incapable of attending the Council on Wednesday and cannot determine when I shall be able to attend."] Served in the Lower House of the Maryland Legislature, 1778-1783, Senate, Eastern Shore, 1781-1783, and died testate by Feb 17, 1784. Never married [Ref: R-653, R-654, O-4, H-285, A-viii]. Took the Oath of Allegiance in Somerset County on Feb 6, 1778 before the Hon. Joseph Venables [Ref: T-25]. See "Gillis Polk" and "David Polk" and "William Polk," q.v.

POLK, Mary. See "William Davis Allen" and "William Polk" and "James Bratten," q.v.

POLK, Nancy. See "Gillis Polk" and "William Morris," q.v.

POLK, Priscilla. See "William Whittington," q.v.

POLK, Sarah. See "Gillis Polk," q.v.

POLK, Sinah. See "David Polk," q.v.

POLK, William (1752-1812). Son of David Polk and Elizabeth Gillis. He married first to Esther Winder Handy (widow of Isaac Handy and daughter of William Winder), second to Ann Purnell Dennis (widow of Henry Dennis and daughter of Capt. John Purnell), and third to Mary Hubbell (who subsequently married William Savage). Children: Josiah, William Winder, Elizabeth, Esther (Hester), Gertrude, and Ann Fromentin. William served in the Lower House of the Maryland Legislature in 1777 and 1797, and although elected to the Senate, Eastern Shore in 1801, did not attend. He was a Judge of the Court of Appeals, 1806-1812, and Chief Justice, 4th Judicial District, 1802-1812. William died testate by Dec 14, 1812 [Ref: R-654, R-655, and V-2331 states he was born on Dec 11, 1752 and died in 1814]. Took the Oath of Allegiance in Somerset County in 1778 before the Hon. Levin Wilson [Ref: T-17, N-51]. Rendered patriotic service by supplying pork for the use of the military on Aug 7, 1780 [Ref: P-307]. See "David Polk," q.v.

POLK, William Sr. (1705-1788). Took the Oath of Allegiance in Somerset County in 1778 before the Hon. Levin Wilson [Ref: T-17, N-51]. Born in Maryland in 1705, married Mary (Vaughan) Woodgate, rendered patriotic service and died in Delaware in October, 1788 [Ref: V-2331].

POLLITT (POLLIT), George. Private, Somerset Militia, Princess Anne Bn., Capt. John Jones' Princess Anne Co., 1780 [Ref: M-219]. Took the Oath of Allegiance in Somerset County in 1778 before the Hon. Levin Wilson [Ref: T-17, N-51]. Rendered patriotic service by supplying bacon for the use of the military on Aug 8, 1780 [Ref: P-308].

POLLITT (POLLIT), George Jr. Took the Oath of Allegiance in Somerset County in 1778 before the Hon. Levin Wilson [Ref: T-17, N-51].

POLLITT (POLLIT), John. Private, Somerset Militia, Princess Anne Bn., Capt. John Jones' Princess Anne Co., 1780 [Ref: M-219]. Rendered patriotic service by supplying bacon for the use of the military on Aug 3, 1780 [Ref: P-306]. Took the Oath of Allegiance in Somerset County in 1778 before the Hon. Peter Waters [Ref: T-18]. Select Militia, Somerset County, Aug 15, 1781 [Ref: L-35A].

POLLITT (POLLIT), John Jr. Took the Oath of Allegiance in Somerset County in 1778 [Ref: N-51].

POLLITT (POLLIT), Jonathan. Took the Oath of Allegiance in Somerset County in 1778 before the Hon. Levin Wilson [Ref: T-17, N-51].

POLLITT (POLLIT), Jonathan Jr. Private, Somerset Militia, Princess Anne Bn., Capt. John Jones' Princess Anne Co., 1780 [Ref: M-219]. Took the Oath of Allegiance in Somerset County in 1778 before the Hon. Levin Wilson [Ref: T-17, N-51]. Select Militia, Somerset County, Aug 15, 1781 [Ref: L-35A listed the name without the "Jr."].

POLLITT (POLLIT), Joshua. Private, Somerset Militia, Princess Anne Bn., Capt. John Jones' Princess Anne Co., 1780 [Ref: M-219]. Select Militia, Somerset County, Aug 15, 1781 [Ref: L-35B].

POLLITT (POLLIT), Levin (1760-1829). Corporal, Somerset Militia, Princess Anne Bn., Capt. George Waters' Pocomoke Co., 1780 [Ref: M-220]. Select Militia, Somerset County, Aug 15, 1781 [Ref: L-35A]. "Levin Gillis Pollitt" was born in 1760, married Nelly Irving Gillis circa 1796/1798, and died in 1829. A son Gillis Pollitt married Jane Ballard [Ref: S-1513]. See "Joseph Gillis," q.v.

POLLITT (POLLIT), Littleton. Private, Somerset Militia, Princess Anne Bn., Capt. John Jones' Princess Anne Co., 1780 [Ref: M-219 listed the name as "Lill. Pollitt"].

POLLITT (POLLIT), Nehemiah. Private, Somerset Militia, Princess Anne Bn., Capt. John Jones' Princess Anne Co., 1780 [Ref: M-220]. Select Militia, Somerset County, Aug 15, 1781 [Ref: L-35A].

POLLITT (POLLIT), Samuel. Private, Somerset Militia, Princess Anne Bn., Capt. John Jones' Princess Anne Co., 1780 [Ref: M-219].

POLLITT (POLLIT), Samuel (of Thomas). Took the Oath of Allegiance in Somerset County in 1778 before the Hon. Levin Wilson [Ref: T-17, N-51].

POLLITT (POLLIT), Severn. Took the Oath of Allegiance in Somerset County in 1778 before the Hon. Peter Waters [Ref: T-18].

POLLITT (POLLIT), Stephen. Private, Somerset Militia, Princess Anne Bn., Capt. John Jones' Princess Anne Co., 1780 [Ref: M-219]. Select Militia, Somerset County, Aug 15, 1781 [Ref: L-35A].
POLLITT (POLLIT), Susannah. See "Thomas Dixon," q.v.
POLLITT (POLLIT), Thomas. Private, Somerset Militia, Princess Anne Bn., Capt. John Jones' Princess Anne Co., 1780 [Ref: M-219]. Took the Oath of Allegiance in Somerset County in 1778 before the Hon. Levin Wilson [Ref: T-17, N-51].
POLLITT (POLLIT), Thomas Jr. Rendered patriotic service by supplying pork for the use of the military in Somerset County on Aug 30, 1780 [Ref: P-313].
POLLITT (POLLIT), Thomas (of Thomas). Took the Oath of Allegiance in Somerset County in 1778 before the Hon. Levin Wilson [Ref: T-17, N-51].
POLLITT (POLLIT), Thomas (of William). Private, Somerset Militia, Princess Anne Bn., Capt. John Jones' Princess Anne Co., 1780 [Ref: M-219].
POLLITT (POLLIT), William. Private, Somerset Militia, Princess Anne Bn., Capt. John Jones' Princess Anne Co., 1780 [Ref: M-219]. Took the Oath of Allegiance in Somerset County in 1778 before the Hon. Levin Wilson [Ref: T-17, N-51].
POLLITT (POLLIT), William (of Thomas). Private, Somerset Militia, Princess Anne Bn., Capt. John Jones' Princess Anne Co., 1780 [Ref: M-219].
POLLOCK, James (Irish). Took the Oath of Allegiance in Worcester County in 1778 before the Hon. John Selby [Ref: J-1814 (Box 4)].
POPE, James. Took the Oath of Allegiance in Somerset County in 1778 before the Hon. Levin Wilson [Ref: T-17, N-51].
POPE, John. Private, Worcester Militia, Capt. John Martin's Co., 1780/1781 [Ref: J-1814 (Box 12)]. See "John Pope Mitchell," q.v.
POPE, Joyce. See "John Pope Mitchell," q.v.
POPE, Samuel. Private, Worcester Militia, Wicomico Bn., Capt. Elijah Shockley's Co., Fourth Class, July 15, 1780 [Ref: M-255]. Took the Oath of Allegiance in Worcester County in 1778 before the Hon. Joshua Townsend [Ref: J-1814 (Box 4)].
PORTER, Alexander. Private, Worcester Militia, Wicomico Bn., Capt. Samuel Horsey's Co., Fifth Class, July 15, 1780 [Ref: M-257]. Private, Maryland Troops, Worcester County, draughted May 1, 1781 [Ref: K-99, D-372].
PORTER, Ann. See "William Porter, Jr.," q.v.
PORTER, Claywell. Took the Oath of Allegiance in Somerset County in 1778 [Ref: N-51].
PORTER, Elizabeth. See "James Tull," q.v.
PORTER, James. Private, Somerset Militia, Salisbury Bn., Capt. John Span Conway's Nanticoke Point Co., 1778/1780 [Ref: M-216].
PORTER, John. Took the Oath of Allegiance in Somerset County in 1778 before the Hon. Levin Wilson [Ref: T-17].

PORTER, John. Took the Oath of Allegiance in Worcester County in 1778 before the Hon. Joshua Townsend [Ref: J-1814 (Box 4)].
PORTER, Joseph. Private, Worcester Militia, Sinepuxent Bn., Capt. William Purnell's Co., Seventh Class, 1779/1780 [Ref: M-252].
PORTER, Mary. See "Matthew Porter," q.v.
PORTER, Matthew. Took the Oath of Allegiance in Worcester County in 1778 before the Hon. Nehemiah Holland [Ref: J-1814 (Box 4)]. "Matthews Porter, son of Matthews and Mary Porter" was born in Coventry Parish on July 13, 1753 [Ref: Y-74].
PORTER, McKemmy (McKimmy). Private, Worcester Militia, Wicomico Bn., Capt. William Handy's Co., Eighth Class, July 15, 1780 [Ref: M-258 listed the name as "McKemmy Porter"]. Took the Oath of Allegiance in Worcester County in 1778 before the Hon. Joshua Townsend [Ref: J-1814 (Box 4) listed the name as "McKimmy Porter"]. Corporal, Worcester Militia, Capt. John Martin's Co., 1780/1781 [Ref: J-1814 (Box 12) listed the name as "McKemmey Porter"]. See "Belitha Brittingham," q.v.
PORTER, McKimmey (McCimmey). Private, Somerset Militia, Salisbury Bn., Capt. Joseph Venables' Barren Creek Co., 1778/1780. Ensign, Barren Creek Co., 1781 [Ref: M-111, M-217, G-575, J-1814 (Box 8, Dashiell's correspondence), H-195]. Took the Oath of Allegiance in Somerset County on Feb 2, 1778 before the Hon. Joseph Venables [Ref: T-25 listed the name as "Mu:Cimmey Porter" and N-51 listed the name as "McCinney Porter"]. "McKimmey Porter" rendered patriotic service by supplying corn for the use of the military in Somerset County on Jan 20, 1780 [Ref: P-264].
PORTER, Rebecca. See "Jonathan Cathell," q.v.
PORTER, Solomon Claywell. Took the Oath of Allegiance in Somerset County in 1778 before the Hon. Gillis Polk [Ref: T-15].
PORTER, William. Private, Somerset Militia, Princess Anne Bn., St. Asaph's Co., 1780 [Ref: M-220].
PORTER, William Jr. (1760 -   ). Son of William and Ann Porter, born in Coventry Parish on Nov 6, 1760 [Ref: Y-74]. Private, Somerset Militia, Salisbury Bn., Capt. John Span Conway's Nanticoke Point Co., 1778/1780 [Ref: M-216].
PORTLACK, James. See "Anthony Murphy," q.v.
PORTLACK, Mary. See "Anthony Murphy," q.v.
PORTLACK, William. See "Anthony Murphy," q.v.
POSTLY (POSTLEY), John. Captain, Worcester Militia, Sinepuxent Bn., Aug 30, 1777. Major, Aug 9, 1780. Colonel, June 13, 1782 [Ref: M-112, M-251, C-350, F-251, I-190 listed the name as "John Postley"]. Appointed as one of three Purchasers of Cattle in Worcester County for the use of the Continental Army on Jan 7, 1778 [Ref: C-456]. Took the Oath of Allegiance in Worcester County in 1778 before the Hon. Nehemiah Holland [Ref: J-1814 (Box 4)]. Justice of the Peace, commissioned on Nov 21, 1778 and Jan 17, 1782 [Ref: E-249, I-46].

Rendered patriotic service by supplying corn for the use of the military on March 29, 1780 and June 1, 1780 [Ref: P-293, and P-279 mistakenly listed the name as "Capt. John Portly"].

POSTLY, John. Private(?), Worcester Militia, Sinepuxent Bn., Capt. Postly's Co., Fifth Class, 1779/1780 [Ref: M-251].

POTTER, Henry (1754 -   ). Son of Henry and Molly Potter, born in Coventry Parish on April 9, 1754 [Ref: Y-74]. Private, Somerset Militia, Princess Anne Bn., Capt. John Williams' Watkins Point Co., 1780 [Ref: M-222].

POTTER, Henry (1752 -   ). Son of Thomas and Sarah Potter, born in Coventry Parish on Feb 9, 1752 [Ref: Y-74]. Private, Somerset Militia, Princess Anne Bn., Capt. James Elzey's Co., 1780 [Ref: M-220].

POTTER, Molly. See "Henry Potter," q.v.

POTTER, Sarah. See "Henry Potter," q.v.

POWELL, Annanias (c1755 -   ). Son of Thomas Powell, born in Worcester Parish on "Dec 31, 1755(?)" [Ref: Y-28]. Private, Worcester Militia, Sinepuxent Bn., Capt. Josiah Dale's Co., First Class, 1779/1780 [Ref: M-253].

POWELL, Belitha (1755 -   ). Son of Samuel and Rachel Powel *[sic]*, born in Worcester Parish on Jan 24, 1755 [Ref: Y-29]. Private, Worcester Militia, Sinepuxent Bn., Capt. John Postly's Co., Seventh Class, 1779/1780 [Ref: M-251].

POWELL, Brittain. Ensign, Somerset Militia, 17th Bn., Sep 19, 1776; Private, Princess Anne Bn., Capt. George Waters' Pocomoke Co., 1780 [Ref: M-112, M-220, B-285].

POWELL, Elihu. Private, Worcester Militia, Sinepuxent Bn., Capt. John Postly's Co., Third Class, 1779/1780 [Ref: M-251].

POWELL, Elijah. Private, Worcester Militia, Sinepuxent Bn., Capt. Matthew Purnell's Co., Second Class, July 25, 1780 [Ref: M-252].

POWELL, Elijah. Private, Worcester Militia, Wicomico Bn., Capt. Philip Quinton's Co., Second Class, July 15, 1780 [Ref: M-256].

POWELL, Elijah. Took the Oath of Allegiance in Worcester County in 1778 before the Hon. John Selby [Ref: J-1814 (Box 4)].

POWELL, Gabriel. Private, Worcester Militia, Wicomico Bn., Capt. James Perdue's Co., Fourth Class, July 15, 1780 [Ref: M-256].

POWELL, Jesse (1757 -   ). Private, Worcester Militia, Sinepuxent Bn., Capt. Josiah Dale's Co., Fifth Class, 1779/1780 [Ref: M-254]. Born in Worcester Parish on July 5, 1757 [Ref: Y-28].

POWELL, Jesse. Private, Somerset Militia, Princess Anne Bn., Capt. George Waters' Pocomoke Co., 1780 [Ref: M-220].

POWELL, John. Private, Worcester Militia, Sinepuxent Bn., Capt. Josiah Dale's Co., Fifth Class, 1779/1780 [Ref: M-254]. Private, Worcester Militia, Wicomico Bn., Capt. Charles Bennett's Co., Seventh Class, July 15, 1780 [Ref: M-255]. Rendered patriotic service by supplying corn for the use of the military on May 3, 1780 [Ref: P-288].

POWELL, John (of Samuel). Son of Samuel and Rachel Powel *[sic]*, born in Worcester Parish on March 27, 1761 [Ref: Y-29]. Private, Worcester Militia, Sinepuxent Bn., Capt. John Postly's Co., Fifth Class, 1779/1780 [Ref: M-251].
POWELL, Levi. Private, Somerset Militia, Princess Anne Bn., Capt. George Waters' Pocomoke Co., 1780 [Ref: M-220].
POWELL, Levi. Private, Worcester Militia, Sinepuxent Bn., Capt. Josiah Dale's Co., Eighth Class, 1779/1780 [Ref: M-254]. Private, Maryland Troops, Worcester County, draughted May 1, 1781 [Ref: K-99, D-372]. Took the Oath of Allegiance in Worcester County in 1778 before the Hon. John Selby [Ref: J-1814 (Box 4)].
POWELL, Levin. Private, Somerset Militia, Princess Anne Bn., Capt. George Waters' Pocomoke Co., 1780 [Ref: M-220 listed the name as "Levin Powell"].
POWELL, Mordica. Private, Worcester Militia, Sinepuxent Bn., Capt. Josiah Dale's Co., Seventh Class, 1779/1780 [Ref: M-254].
POWELL, Nancy. See "Samuel Bowles," q.v.
POWELL, Rachel. See "Belitha Powell" and "John Powell," q.v.
POWELL, Samuel. See "John Powell" and "Belitha Powell," q.v.
POWELL, Thomas. Private, Worcester Militia, Wicomico Bn., Capt. Elijah Shockley's Co., Third Class, July 15, 1780 [Ref: M-255].
POWELL, Thomas. Private, Worcester Militia, Sinepuxent Bn., Capt. Josiah Dale's Co., Sixth Class, 1779/1780 [Ref: M-254].
POWELL, William. Private, Somerset Militia, Princess Anne Bn., Capt. George Waters' Pocomoke Co., 1780 [Ref: M-220].
POWELL, William. Private, Worcester Militia, Wicomico Bn., Capt. John Davis' Co., Third Class, July 15, 1780 [Ref: M-254].
POWELL, William. Private, Worcester Militia, Wicomico Bn., Capt. Philip Quinton's Co., Third Class, July 15, 1780 [Ref: M-256].
POWELL, William. Private, Worcester Militia, Sinepuxent Bn., Capt. John Postly's Co., Fifth Class, 1779/1780 [Ref: M-251].
POWELL, Zadock (of Thomas). Private, Worcester Militia, Sinepuxent Bn., Capt. John Postly's Co., Eighth Class, 1779/1780 [Ref: M-251].
POWELL, Zadok (of William). Private, Worcester Militia, Sinepuxent Bn., Capt. John Postly's Co., Fourth Class, 1779/1780 [Ref: M-251].
POWELL, Zadok. Private, Worcester Militia, Sinepuxent Bn., Capt. Matthew Purnell's Co., Second Class, July 25, 1780 [Ref: M-252].
POWER, Thomas. Private, Somerset County, Capt. John Gunby's 2nd Independent Maryland Co.; present on Aug 13, 1776; mustered on Aug 21, 1776 [Ref: D-642].
POWERS, Jesse. See "Solomon Hamblin," q.v.
PRACICE(?), Alexander. Private, Somerset Militia, Salisbury Bn., White Haven Co., 1778/1780 [Ref: M-219].

PRICE, Arthur. Private, Worcester Militia, Snow Hill Bn., Capt. Samuel Smyley's Co., 1777 [Ref: M-250]. Private, Worcester Militia, Wicomico Bn., Capt. Samuel Smyley's Co., Seventh Class, July 15, 1780 [Ref: M-259].

PRICE, Edmond. Private, Somerset Militia, Princess Anne Bn., Capt. Thomas Irving's Monie Co., 1780 [Ref: M-219].

PRICE, George. Private, Worcester Militia, Wicomico Bn., Capt. Robert Handy's Co., Sixth Class, July 15, 1780 [Ref: M-254].

PRICE, Holland. Private, Worcester Militia, Wicomico Bn., Capt. James Patterson's Co., Eighth Class, July 15, 1780 [Ref: M-258]. Took the Oath of Allegiance in Worcester County in 1778 before the Hon. James Selby [Ref: J-1814 (Box 4) listed the name as "Hollan Price"].

PRICE, James. Private, Select Militia, Somerset County, Aug 15, 1781 [Ref: L-35A].

PRICE, John. Private, Somerset Militia, Princess Anne Bn., Capt. James Elzey's Co., 1780 [Ref: M-220]. Select Militia, Somerset County, Aug 15, 1781 [Ref: L-35A].

PRICE, John. Took the Oath of Allegiance in Worcester County in 1778 before the Hon. Nehemiah Holland [Ref: J-1814 (Box 4)].

PRICE, Thomas. Took the Oath of Allegiance in Worcester County in 1778 before the Hon. John Selby [Ref: J-1814 (Box 4)].

PRICE, William. Private, Worcester Militia, Snow Hill Bn., Capt. John Parramore's Co., 1777 [Ref: M-250]. Took the Oath of Allegiance in Worcester County in 1778 before the Hon. John Selby [Ref: J-1814 (Box 4)].

PRIDEAUX, John. Took the Oath of Allegiance in Worcester County in 1778 in Quepomco Hundred before the Hon. Thomas Purnell [Ref: J-1814 (Box 4)]. Private, Worcester Militia, Sinepuxent Bn., Capt. Elisha Purnell's Co., First Class, 1779/1780 [Ref: M-253 listed the name as "John Pridix"].

PRIDEAUX, Thomas. Took the Oath of Allegiance in Worcester County in 1778 in Buckingham Hundred before the Hon. Thomas Purnell [Ref: J-1814 (Box 4)].

PRIOR, David. Private, Somerset Militia, Salisbury Bn., Capt. Josiah Dashiell's Wicomico Creek Co., 1778/1780 [Ref: M-218 listed the name as "David P-?-r"]. Private, Somerset Militia, Princess Anne Bn., Capt. John Jones' Princess Anne Co., 1780 [Ref: M-219]. Took the Oath of Allegiance in Somerset County in 1778 before the Hon. Peter Waters [Ref: T-18].

PROBERT (PROBART), Yelverton Peyton. Took the Oath of Allegiance in Worcester County in 1778 before the Hon. John Selby [Ref: J-1814 (Box 4)]. Private, Worcester Militia, Wicomico Bn., Capt. William Handy's Co., Eighth Class, July 15, 1780 [Ref: M-258 listed the name as "Yelverton P. Probart"].

PRUITT, Benjamin. Private, Worcester Militia, Wicomico Bn., Capt. Fisher Walton's Co., First Class, July 15, 1780 [Ref: M-258]. Took the Oath of Allegiance in Worcester County in 1778 before the Hon. Nehemiah Holland [Ref: J-1814 (Box 4)].

PRUITT, Walter. Private, Worcester Militia, Wicomico Bn., Capt. Fisher Walton's Co., Second Class, July 15, 1780 [Ref: M-258].
PURBUSH, George. Private, Somerset Militia, Salisbury Bn., Capt. John Span Conway's Nanticoke Point Co., 1778/1780 [Ref: M-216].
PURDY, John. Corporal, 3rd Maryland Independent Co., Worcester County, Capt. John Watkins' Co., enlisted Jan 25, 1776; muster roll dated Aug 20, 1776, sick in barracks [Ref: D-21].
PURKINS, John. See "John Perkins," q.v.
PURNELL, Andasia. See "John Selby Purnell," q.v.
PURNELL, Ann. See "Henry Dennis" and "Thomas Purnell, of John," q.v.
PURNELL, Arralanta. See "John Selby Purnell," q.v.
PURNELL, Assariah. Took the Oath of Allegiance in Worcester County in 1778 in Buckingham Hundred before the Hon. Thomas Purnell [Ref: J-1814 (Box 4)].
PURNELL, Benjamin (1740 -   ). Son of Matthew Purnell and Martha McClummy [McClemmy]. He married Sarah Irving (born Sep 21, 1750) on July 3, 1771 and a son John Irving Purnell was born on April 21, 1776 [Ref: S-1530]. Benjamin was an ensign, Worcester Militia, Sinepuxent Bn., Capt. John Purnell's Co., Aug 30, 1777, and second lieutenant in Capt. Elisha Purnell's Co., Aug 14, 1779 [Ref: M-113, C-350 listed the name as "Benjamin Purnal" and E-493 listed the name as "Benjamin Purnall"].
PURNELL, Benjamin. Private, Worcester Militia, Sinepuxent Bn., Capt. Elisha Purnell's Co., Seventh Class, 1779/1780 [Ref: M-253]. Took the Oath of Allegiance in Worcester County in 1778 in Quepomco Hundred before the Hon. Thomas Purnell [Ref: J-1814 (Box 4)]. See "William Selby, Jr.," q.v.
PURNELL, Benjamin (of Walter). Justice of the Peace for Worcester County, appointed Nov 29, 1777 [Ref: C-429].
PURNELL, Catherine (Keaty). See "Matthew Dale," q.v.
PURNELL, Comfort. See "Thomas Purnell, of John," q.v.
PURNELL, Dryden. See "John Purnell," q.v.
PURNELL, Elisha. First Lieutenant, Worcester Militia, Sinepuxent Bn., Capt. John Purnell's Co., Aug 30, 1777, and commissioned captain on Aug 14, 1779 [Ref: M-113, M-253, and C-350 listed the name as "Elisha Purnal" and E-493 listed the name as "Elisha Purnall"]. See "William Purnell," q.v.
PURNELL, Elisha. Private, Worcester Militia, Sinepuxent Bn., Capt. Elisha Purnell's Co., Fourth Class, 1779/1780 [Ref: M-253].
PURNELL, Elizabeth. See "Thomas Purnell, of John" and "Henry Dennis," q.v.
PURNELL, Esther. See "William Purnell" and "Thomas Purnell, of John," q.v.
PURNELL, Frances. See "John Henry," q.v.
PURNELL, George. See "William Purnell," q.v.
PURNELL, James. Private, Worcester Militia, Sinepuxent Bn., Capt. John Rackliff's Co., Fifth Class, 1779/1780 [Ref: M-251]. Took the Oath of

Allegiance in Worcester County in 1778 in Buckingham Hundred before the Hon. Thomas Purnell [Ref: J-1814 (Box 4)].

PURNELL, John. Captain, Worcester Militia, Sinepuxent Bn., Aug 30, 1777 to Aug 14, 1779, when he either succeeded or died (both reasons were cited). [Ref: M-113, C-350 listed the name as "John Purnal" and E-493 listed the name as "John Purnall"]. Took the Oath of Allegiance in Worcester County in 1778 in Quepomco Hundred before the Hon. Thomas Purnell [Ref: J-1814 (Box 4) listed the name as "John Purnell"]. Served on the Committee of Observation in 1776 [Ref: A-457]. Justice of the Peace, appointed Nov 29, 1777 [Ref: C-428, C-429]. See "William Polk" and "Thomas Purnell" and "Thomas Purnell, of Thomas" and "William Purnell" and "Zadock Purnell" and "John Purnell" and "Outten Sturgis, Sr.," q.v.

PURNELL, John (1755-c1845). Private, Worcester Militia, Wicomico Bn., Capt. Fisher Walton's Co., Fifth Class, July 15, 1780 [Ref: M-258]. One John Purnell, age 85, was a pensioner in 1840 in the 3rd Division of Somerset County and resided in the household of Dryden Purnell [Ref: Q-28:4, p. 445].

PURNELL, John (of Hezekiah). Took the Oath of Allegiance in Worcester County in 1778 before the Hon. Nehemiah Holland [Ref: J-1814 (Box 4)].

PURNELL, John (of John). Private, Worcester Militia, Wicomico Bn., Capt. Fisher Walton's Co., Sixth Class, July 15, 1780 [Ref: M-258 listed the name as "John Parnell, of John"].

PURNELL, John Irving. See "Benjamin Purnell," q.v.

PURNELL, John Selby (c1760-1799). Son of Lemuel Purnell and Dennis Hopkins Johnson (widow of David Johnson and daughter of Nathaniel Hopkins). He married Arralanta (Lanta) Robins and their children were John Selby, Andasia R., Arralanta R., and Mary Ann (Nancy). John served in the Lower House of the Maryland Legislature from Worcester County, 1787-1789, and in the Senate, Eastern Shore, 1796-1799. He was an Associate Judge, Fourth District, 1791, and a captain in the 9th Militia Regiment, 1794-1796 [Ref: R-663]. Private, Worcester Militia, Sinepuxent Bn., Capt. William Purnell's Co., Sixth Class, 1779/1780 [Ref: M-252].

PURNELL, Lambert. Private, 3rd Maryland Independent Co., Worcester County, Capt. John Watkins' Co., enlisted May 7, 1776; muster roll dated Aug 20, 1776, sick at his mother's [Ref: D-23]. Took the Oath of Allegiance in Worcester County in 1778 in Quepomco Hundred before the Hon. Thomas Purnell [Ref: J-1814 (Box 4)].

PURNELL, Levi. Took the Oath of Allegiance in Worcester County in 1778 in Quepomco Hundred before the Hon. Thomas Purnell [Ref: J-1814 (Box 4)]. See "Isaac Houston" and "James Houston," q.v.

PURNELL, Levin. Private, Worcester Militia, Sinepuxent Bn., Capt. Elisha Purnell's Co., Second Class, 1779/1780 [Ref: M-253].

PURNELL, Littleton. See "William Purnell," q.v.

PURNELL, Martha. See "Outten Sturgis, Sr.," q.v.

PURNELL, Mary. Rendered patriotic service by supplying beef for the use of the military in Worcester County on Sep 20, 1781 [Ref: P-439]. See "John Dennis, Jr." and "Isaac Houston" and "James Houston" and "John Pope Mitchell" and "John Selby Purnell" and "Thomas Purnell, of Thomas" and "William Purnell" and "Joshua Townsend," q.v.

PURNELL, Matthew (c1750-1791). Captain, Worcester Militia, Sinepuxent Bn., Aug 30, 1777 to at least July 25, 1780 [Ref: M-252, M-113, and C-350 listed the name as "Matthew Purnal"]. Took the Oath of Allegiance in Worcester County in 1778 before the Hon. Nathaniel Miller [Ref: J-1814 (Box 4)]. He married Mary Houston who married second to Joshua Townsend circa 1793 [Ref: R-838]. See "Joshua Townsend" and "Benjamin Purnell," q.v.

PURNELL, Matthew. Private, Worcester Militia, Sinepuxent Bn., Capt. Elisha Purnell's Co., Seventh Class, 1779/1780 [Ref: M-253]. Took the Oath of Allegiance in Worcester County in 1778 in Quepomco Hundred before the Hon. Thomas Purnell [Ref: J-1814 (Box 4)]. See "Samuel Bowles," q.v.

PURNELL, Nancy. See "William Purnell," q.v.

PURNELL, Peter. Private, Worcester Militia, Sinepuxent Bn., Capt. John Rackliff's Co., Sixth Class, 1779/1780 [Ref: M-251].

PURNELL, Robert. Private, Worcester Militia, Wicomico Bn., Capt. Fisher Walton's Co., First Class, July 15, 1780 [Ref: M-258].

PURNELL, Samuel. Private, 7th Maryland Line, enlisted on Feb 11, 1777 and discharged on Feb 9, 1780 [Ref: D-239].

PURNELL, Sarah. Rendered patriotic service by supplying corn for the use of the military in Worcester County on Feb 15, 1780 and July 10, 1780, and by supplying beef on Oct 10, 1781 [Ref: P-270, P-446, G-9]. See "Thomas Purnell, of John," q.v.

PURNELL, Stephen. See "Charles Taylor," q.v.

PURNELL, Thomas. Rendered patriotic service by supplying corn for the use of the military on March 19, 1780 and June 14, 1780 and by supplying beef on Sep 19, 1780 and Sep 20, 1781 [Ref: P-296, P-277, P-318, P-439]. See "William Purnell," q.v.

PURNELL, Thomas, Segr.*[sic]*. Took the Oath of Allegiance in Worcester County in 1778 before the Hon. Nathaniel Miller [Ref: J-1814 (Box 4)].

PURNELL, Thomas (Sinepuxent). Justice of the Peace for Worcester County, commissioned on Nov 29, 1777 and Nov 21, 1778 and March 27, 1779 and I-46 [Ref: C-428, E-249, E-327, I-46]. Special Commission of Judge of the Court of Oyer and Terminer and Gaol Delivery issued to him and five others in Worcester County by the Governor and Council of Maryland on Dec 10, 1783 [Ref: I-488].

PURNELL, Thomas (of John). Son of John Purnell and Elizabeth Rackliffe. He married his first cousin Comfort Purnell, daughter of Thomas, and their children were Thomas, Zadock, John, Elizabeth, Sarah, Zipporah, Esther, and Ann. Thomas served in the Lower House of the Maryland Legislature from

Worcester County, 1777-1779; County Court Justice, 1777-1790; Commissioner of the Tax, appointed in 1777; and, captain by 1790. He died testate by March 21, 1796 [Ref: R-664].

PURNELL, Thomas (of Mat? or Wat?). Private, Worcester Militia, Sinepuxent Bn., Capt. John Rackliff's Co., Second Class, 1779/1780 [Ref: M-251].

PURNELL, Thomas (1745-1790). Son of Thomas Purnell and Mary Outten, (widow of Daniel Selby). He was born on Feb 28, 1745 and died testate on May 8, 1790. He married Sarah Marshall (who later married Robert Mitchell) and their children were Zadock, John, Thomas Marshall, and Mary Outten (all minors in 1788). Thomas was elected to serve in the Lower House of the Maryland Legislature from Worcester County in 1778, but did not attend. He was a County Court Justice, 1777, Commissioner of the Tax, 1778-1790, and was called colonel in 1783. [Ref: R-665, V-2384]. Took the Oath of Allegiance in Worcester County in 1778 before the Hon. Nathaniel Miller [Ref: J-1814 (Box 4) listed the name as "Thomas Purnell, of Thomas"]. He was a captain in the Worcester Militia, Sinepuxent Bn., Aug 30, 1777, and lieutenant colonel on June 13, 1782 [Ref: M-253, M-113, I-190, and C-350 listed the name as "Thomas Purnal"]. Justice who administered the Oath of Allegiance in Worcester County in 1778 [Ref: J-1814 (Box 4)]. Commissioned a Judge of the Court of Appeals for Worcester County on May 27, 1778 [Ref: E-112].

PURNELL, Walter. Took the Oath of Allegiance in Worcester County in 1778 before the Hon. Nathaniel Miller [Ref: J-1814 (Box 4)].

PURNELL, William. "There were at least two candidates for the legislative service of William Purnell in the Lower House from 1773-1774 and in the third convention of December 1774. Both men, who were first cousins, were large landowners and military men. It was not possible to determine which one served, hence both biographies have been included and the same legislative service is assigned to both. See also William Purnell (1739-1796). The man who served in the later assemblies from 1785-1788, William Purnell (d. 1798), was apparently too young to have served in 1773-1774 or in the third convention. The man elected to the 1785 assembly was described in the election returns as 'captain' and since William Purnell (1739-1796) was a major in 1785, it has been assumed the legislator was William Purnell (d. 1798). This assumption is strengthened by a letter in 1791 recommending William Purnell 'of Cropper's Neck' for a justiceship and referring to his frequent service in the legislature. There is, however, the possibility that some of the service assigned to William Purnell (d. 1798) may have been held by William Purnell (1739-1796) ... See also William Purnell (d. 1777)." [Ref: R-665, R-666, R-667]. Additional research will be necessary before drawing conclusions.

PURNELL, William (c1735-1777). Son of John Purnell and Elizabeth Rackliffe. He married Mary Elizabeth Fassitt by 1763 and their children were John, Thomas, and Nancy. William served in the Lower House of the Maryland Legislature from Worcester County, 1773-1774, and was a colonel in the

Worcester Militia, 24th Bn., Jan 6, 1776 [Ref: R-665, M-113, I-190]. See above comments under the other "William Purnell," q.v.

PURNELL, William (1739-1796). Son of Elisha Purnell and Mary Ann Selby. He married Mary Robins by 1762 and their children were Elisha, Thomas Robins, John, Littleton Robins, George Washington, Esther Robins, and Mary Selby. William served in the Lower House of the Maryland Legislature from Worcester County, 1773-1774, attended the Maryland Convention, 1774, and was a County Court Justice, 1786-1795. Captain, Worcester Militia, Sinepuxent Bn., Aug 30, 1777. Major, June 13, 1782. Died testate before Dec 2, 1796 [Ref: R-666, M-252, M-113, V-2384, and C-350 listed the name as "William Purnal"]. Rendered patriotic service by supplying corn for the use of the military on April 28, 1780 [Ref: P-287]. See above comments under the other "William Purnell," q.v.

PURNELL, William (of Eufa). Son of Capt. John Purnell (d. 1761) and Euphame Arbuckle (b. 1734). He married Gertrude Henry by 1791, had five children (names unknown), and died in early 1798 in Worcester County [Ref: R-666, R-667]. Private, Worcester Militia, Sinepuxent Bn., Capt. John Rackliff's Co., Fourth Class, 1779/1780 [Ref: M-251 listed the name as "William Purnell (of Eupa?)"]. He may have been the William Purnell who took the Oath of Allegiance in Worcester County in 1778 in Bogernorton Hundred before the Hon. Thomas Purnell [Ref: J-1814 (Box 4)]. He also served in the Lower House of the Maryland Legislature, 1785-1793, as County Court Justice in 1793, and captain, 9th Militia Regiment, commissioned in 1794 [Ref: R-667]. See comments above.

PURNELL, William (Quepomco). Private, Worcester Militia, Sinepuxent Bn., Capt. John Rackliff's Co., Eighth Class, 1779/1780 [Ref: M-251 listed the name as "William Purnell (Quipco?)"]. Took the Oath of Allegiance in Worcester County in 1778 in Quepomco Hundred before the Hon. Thomas Purnell [Ref: J-1814 (Box 4)].

PURNELL, William (of John). Took the Oath of Allegiance in Worcester County in 1778 before the Hon. Nathaniel Miller [Ref: J-1814 (Box 4)]. He may have been the William Purnell who was a private in the Worcester Militia, Sinepuxent Bn., Capt. William Purnell's Co., Eighth Class, 1779/1780 [Ref: M-252].

PURNELL, Zadock (c1728-1805). Son of John Purnell and Elizabeth Rackliffe. Served as Co. clerk in Worcester County militia in 1748. Captain by 1767. Lieutenant Colonel, Worcester Militia, 24th Bn., Jan 6, 1776. Colonel, Sinepuxent Bn., Aug 30, 1777 to March 23, 1778; resigned due to advanced age. Served in the Lower House of the Maryland Legislature, 1758-1761, 1768-1770, and attended the Maryland Convention in 1775. Probably never married; died testate in 1805 [Ref: R-667, M-113, O-4, C-350, and C-547 referred to him as "Esq."]. Signed the Association of the Freemen of Maryland on July 26, 1775 [Ref: A-67]. Took the Oath of Allegiance in Worcester County in 1778 in Buckingham Hundred before the Hon. Thomas Purnell [Ref: J-1814 (Box 4)]. Rendered patriotic service by supplying corn for the use of the military on June 14, 1780 and July 10, 1780, and supplying pork on Sep 20, 1781 [Ref: P-296, P-439, G-9]. See "Thomas Purnell, of John" and "Thomas Purnell, of Thomas," q.v.

PURNELL, Zadok. Private, 3rd Maryland Independent Co., Worcester County, Capt. John Watkins' Co., enlisted Feb 7, 1776; muster roll dated Aug 20, 1776, sick at his mother's [Ref: D-21].

PURNELL, Zipporah. See "Thomas Purnell, of John," q.v.

PUSEY, Benjamin. Private, Somerset Militia, Princess Anne Bn., Capt. John Jones' Princess Anne Co., 1780 [Ref: M-219].

PUSEY, David (1754 -   ). son of John and Rebeckah Pusey, born in Coventry Parish on Oct 4, 1754 [Ref: Y-73]. Private, Worcester Militia, Wicomico Bn., Capt. Charles Bennett's Co., First Class, July 15, 1780 [Ref: M-255].

PUSEY, George. Private, Worcester Militia, Wicomico Bn., Capt. Charles Bennett's Co., Seventh Class, July 15, 1780 [Ref: M-255 listed the name as "George Puzey"].

PUSEY, Isaac. Private, Worcester Militia, Wicomico Bn., Capt. Charles Bennett's Co., Eighth Class, July 15, 1780 [Ref: M-255 listed the name as "Isaac Puzey"].

PUSEY, John. See "David Pusey," q.v.

PUSEY, Rebeckah. See "David Pusey," q.v.

QUILLEN, Benjamin. Private, Worcester Militia, Sinepuxent Bn., Capt. John Rackliff's Co., Second Class, 1779/1780 [Ref: M-251 listed the name as "Benjamin Quillin"]. Took the Oath of Allegiance in Worcester County in 1778 in Buckingham Hundred before the Hon. Thomas Purnell [Ref: J-1814 (Box 4) listed the name as "Benjaman Quilling"].

QUILLEN, John. Private, Worcester Militia, Sinepuxent Bn., Capt. John Postly's Co., Fourth Class, 1779/1780 [Ref: M-251].

QUILLEN, Samuel. Private, Worcester Militia, Sinepuxent Bn., Capt. Josiah Dale's Co., Third Class, 1779/1780 [Ref: M-254].

QUINTON, Dixon. Sergeant, 3rd Maryland Independent Co., Worcester County, Capt. John Watkins' Co., enlisted Feb 2, 1776; muster roll dated Aug 20, 1776, absent on furlough 12th instant [Ref: D-21]. Took the Oath of Allegiance in Worcester County in 1778 before the Hon. James Selby [Ref: J-1814 (Box 4)]. See "James Quinton," q.v.

QUINTON, Henrietta. See "John Round (Rounds, Rownds)," q.v.

QUINTON, Jacob. Private, Somerset Militia, Salisbury Bn., Capt. Joseph Venables' Barren Creek Co., 1778/1780 [Ref: M-217].

QUINTON, James (1750/1 -   ). Son of Dixon and Tabitha Quinton, born in Coventry Parish on March 13, 1750/1 [Ref: Y-74]. Second Lieutenant, Worcester Militia, Sinepuxent Bn., Capt. Thomas Purnell's Co., Aug 30, 1777 [Ref: M-253, M-113, and C-350 listed the name as "James Quntan"]. Took the Oath of Allegiance in Worcester County in 1778 before the Hon. Nathaniel

Miller [Ref: J-1814 (Box 4)]. Rendered patriotic service by supplying salt for the use of the military circa 1781-1782 [Ref: P-466].
QUINTON, Mary. See "John Round (Rounds, Rownds)," q.v.
QUINTON, Philip. Captain, Worcester Militia, Wicomico Bn., Aug 30, 1777. Major, June 13, 1782 [Ref: M-113, M-256, C-351, I-190]. Took the Oath of Allegiance in Worcester County in 1778 before the Hon. Nehemiah Holland [Ref: J-1814 (Box 4)].
QUINTON, Philip. Private, Worcester Militia, Wicomico Bn., Capt. Philip Quinton's Co., Second Class, July 15, 1780 [Ref: M-256].
QUINTON, Sally. See "John Round (Rounds, Rownds)," q.v.
QUINTON, Tabitha. See "James Quinton," q.v.
QUINTON, William. Officer (rank not stated), Worcester Militia, May 15, 1781, resigned [Ref: M-113, H-244].
RACKLIFF (RATCLIFF, RACKLIFFE), Charles. Took the Oath of Allegiance in Worcester County in 1778 before the Hon. Nathaniel Miller [Ref: J-1814 (Box 4) listed the name as "Charles Rackliffe"]. Rendered patriotic service by supplying beef for the use of the military on Sep 18, 1780 [Ref: P-318].
RACKLIFF (RATCLIFF, RACKLIFFE), Charles Jr. (c1730-1784). Private, Worcester Militia, Sinepuxent Bn., Capt. Thomas Purnell's Co., Second Class, 1779/1780 [Ref: M-253, V-2407]. Took the Oath of Allegiance in Worcester County in 1778 before the Hon. Nathaniel Miller [Ref: J-1814 (Box 4) listed the name as "Charles Rackliffe, Junr."].
RACKLIFF (RACKLIFFE), Elizabeth. See "Thomas Purnell" and "William Purnell" and "Zadock Purnell," q.v.
RACKLIFF (RATCLIFF, RATLIFF), John. Captain, Worcester Militia, 24th Bn., June 12, 1776. Captain, Sinepuxent Bn., Aug 30, 1777 to Aug 9, 1780, succeeded [Ref: A-286 listed the name as "Capt. Ratcliffe" and M-113, M-251 listed the name as "Captn. Ratliff" and C-350, F-251 listed the name as "John Ratliff"].
RACKLIFF (RATCLIFF), John. Private, Worcester Militia, Sinepuxent Bn., Capt. Thomas Purnell's Co., Sixth Class, 1779/1780 [Ref: M-253]. Took the Oath of Allegiance in Worcester County in 1778 in Buckingham Hundred before the Hon. Thomas Purnell [Ref: J-1814 (Box 4)].
RACKLIFF (RATCLIFF, RACKLIFFE), Nathaniel. Private, Worcester Militia, Sinepuxent Bn., Capt. Thomas Purnell's Co., Eighth Class, 1779/1780 [Ref: M-253]. Took the Oath of Allegiance in Worcester County in 1778 before the Hon. Nathaniel Miller [Ref: J-1814 (Box 4) listed the name as "Nathaniel Rackliffe"]. Rendered patriotic service by supplying beef for the use of the military on Sep 18, 1780 [Ref: P-318].
RADCLIFFE, John. See "John Henry," q.v.
RADISH, Elizabeth. See "Thomas Redish," q.v.
RAILEY, Thomas. Took the Oath of Allegiance in Worcester County in 1778 before the Hon. Nathaniel Miller [Ref: J-1814 (Box 4)].

RAIN, Caleb. Private, Worcester Militia, Wicomico Bn., Capt. John Davis' Co., First Class, July 15, 1780 [Ref: M-254].
RAIN, John. Private, Worcester Militia, Wicomico Bn., Capt. John Davis' Co., Fourth Class, July 15, 1780 [Ref: M-254 listed the name as "John Rane"]. Taken prisoner (among others) by the pirate Joseph Mulliner (who was subsequently executed), John Rain or Rine of Worcester County was paroled on May 31, 1781 and dismissed by the Council of Maryland on October 29, 1781 [Ref: H-538].
RAIN, Phillips. Took the Oath of Allegiance in Worcester County in 1778 before the Hon. Joshua Townsend [Ref: J-1814 (Box 4)].
RAIN, William. Private, Worcester Militia, Wicomico Bn., Capt. John Davis' Co., First Class, July 15, 1780 [Ref: M-254]. Took the Oath of Allegiance in Worcester County in 1778 before the Hon. Joshua Townsend [Ref: J-1814 (Box 4)].
RAMSEY, Mrs. ----. Rendered patriotic service by supplying beef in Worcester County for the use of the military on Oct 13, 1780 [Ref: P-326].
RANDALL, Francis. Private, Worcester Militia, Wicomico Bn., Capt. William Handy's Co., First Class, July 15, 1780 [Ref: M-257].
RANDELL, Sarah. See "Alexander McCready," q.v.
RANKIN, John. Took the Oath of Allegiance in Worcester County in 1778 in Buckingham Hundred before the Hon. Thomas Purnell [Ref: J-1814 (Box 4)].
RANOLDS, Hammond. Private, Worcester Militia, Sinepuxent Bn., Capt. Elisha Purnell's Co., Fifth Class, 1779/1780 [Ref: M-253]. Took the Oath of Allegiance in Worcester County in 1778 in Quepomco Hundred before the Hon. Thomas Purnell [Ref: J-1814 (Box 4) listed the name as "Hammon Runolds"].
RATLIFF, John. See "John Rackliff," q.v.
REA, Francis. Took the Oath of Allegiance in Worcester County in 1778 before the Hon. Joshua Townsend [Ref: J-1814 (Box 4)].
READ, James. Took the Oath of Allegiance in Worcester County in 1778 before the Hon. Joshua Townsend [Ref: J-1814 (Box 4)].
READ, John. Took the Oath of Allegiance in Worcester County in 1778 before the Hon. Joshua Townsend [Ref: J-1814 (Box 4)].
READY, Cornelius. Private, Somerset Militia, Salisbury Bn., Capt. Joseph Venables' Barren Creek Co., 1778/1780 [Ref: M-217].
RECORDS, Ann. On Dec 3, 1782 the Council of Maryland ordered the Treasurer of the Western Shore to "pay Ann Records £19.18.3 specie due her for provision found the recruits in Somerset County." [Ref: I-312].
RECORDS, Archelaus (1760 -   ). Son of Thomas and Sarah Records, born in Stepney Parish on July 2, 1760 [Ref: Y-45]. Private, Somerset Militia, Salisbury Bn., Capt. James Bennett's Salisbury Co., 1778/1780 [Ref: M-218 listed the name as "Archelius Ricords"].

REDDEN, Charles. Private, Somerset Militia, Princess Anne Bn., Capt. James Elzey's Co., 1780 [Ref: M-220].
REDDEN, John. Private, Somerset Militia, Princess Anne Bn., Capt. Isaac Handy's Great Annemessix Co., 1780 [Ref: M-221 listed the name as "John Reddin"].
REDDEN, John. Private, Worcester Militia, Wicomico Bn., Capt. Fisher Walton's Co., Eighth Class, July 15, 1780 [Ref: M-258].
REDDEN, John. Took the Oath of Allegiance in Worcester County in 1778 before the Hon. James Selby [Ref: J-1814 (Box 4) listed the name as "John Readden"].
REDDEN, Nehemiah (c1740-1795). Private, Worcester Militia, Wicomico Bn., Capt. James Patterson's Co., Seventh Class, July 15, 1780 [Ref: M-258, and V-2418 states he married Leah Melvin]. Took the Oath of Allegiance in Worcester County in 1778 before the Hon. James Selby [Ref: J-1814 (Box 4) listed the name as "Nehemiah Readden"].
REDDEN, Peter. Took the Oath of Allegiance in Worcester County in 1778 before the Hon. James Selby [Ref: J-1814 (Box 4) listed the name as "Peter Readden"].
REDDEN, Stephen. Took the Oath of Allegiance in Somerset County in 1778 before the Hon. Levin Wilson [Ref: T-17, N-51].
REDISH, Hiron. Rendered patriotic service by supplying corn for the use of the military in Somerset County on Jan 22, 1780 [Ref: P-264 listed the name as "Hiron Reddish"]. "Hieron Raddish" married Elizabeth Johnson (widow) in Stepney Parish on Oct 10, 1753 [Ref: Y-42]. See "Thomas Redish," q.v.
REDISH, John. Private, Somerset Militia, Salisbury Bn., Capt. Josiah Dashiell's Wicomico Creek Co., 1778/1780 [Ref: M-218].
REDISH, John Jr. Private, Somerset Militia, Salisbury Bn., Capt. Josiah Dashiell's Wicomico Creek Co., 1778/1780 [Ref: M-218].
REDISH, Thomas (1757 -   ). Son of Hieron and Elizabeth Radish *[sic]*, born in Stepney Parish on July 15, 1757 [Ref: Y-42]. Private, Somerset Militia, Salisbury Bn., Capt. Josiah Dashiell's Wicomico Creek Co., 1778/1780 [Ref: M-218].
REED, John. Private, Worcester Militia, Wicomico Bn., Capt. John Davis' Co., Second Class, July 15, 1780 [Ref: M-254].
REED, Levin. Private, Worcester Militia, Snow Hill Bn., Capt. John Parramore's Co., 1777 [Ref: M-250]. Private, Worcester Militia, Wicomico Bn., Capt. Samuel Smyley's Co., Seventh Class, July 15, 1780 [Ref: M-259].
REED, Littleton. Private, Worcester Militia, Snow Hill Bn., Capt. John Parramore's Co., 1777 [Ref: M-250]. Private, Worcester Militia, Wicomico Bn., Capt. Samuel Smyley's Co., Seventh Class, July 15, 1780 [Ref: M-259].
REED, Peirce. Private, Worcester Militia, Wicomico Bn., Capt. Philip Quinton's Co., Fourth Class, July 15, 1780 [Ref: M-256].
REESE, Levi. Private, Maryland Line, whose name appeared on "a list of recruits from and deserters taken up in Somerset County on Oct 20, 1780" [Ref: D-346].

REID, Ballard. Private, Somerset Militia, Princess Anne Bn., Capt. Thomas Irving's Monie Co., 1780 [Ref: M-219]. Took the Oath of Allegiance in Somerset County in 1778 before the Hon. Levin Wilson [Ref: T-17, N-51].

REID, James. Private, Somerset Militia, Princess Anne Bn., Capt. Thomas Irving's Monie Co., 1780 [Ref: M-219].

REID, John. Private, Somerset County, Capt. John Gunby's 2nd Independent Maryland Co.; present on March 9, 1776; mustered on Aug 21, 1776 [Ref: D-641].

REID, Joseph. Took the Oath of Allegiance in Somerset County in 1778 before the Hon. Levin Wilson [Ref: T-17, N-51].

RELPER (RELSEN?), Glyn. Private, Worcester Militia, Wicomico Bn., Capt. John Parramore's Co., Fourth Class, July 15, 1780 [Ref: M-259].

RENCHAR, John. Rendered patriotic service by supplying corn for the use of the military in Somerset County on Feb 26, 1780 [Ref: P-272].

RENCHER, John. Private, Somerset Militia, Salisbury Bn., Capt. William Turpin's Rewastico Co., 1778/1780 [Ref: M-217].

RENCHER, John. Private, Somerset Militia, Salisbury Bn., White Haven Co., 1778/1780 [Ref: M-219].

RENCHER, John. Private, Somerset Militia, Salisbury Bn., Capt. John Span Conway's Nanticoke Point Co., 1778/1780 [Ref: M-216].

RENCHER, Mary. See "Matthias Hobbs," q.v.

RENCHER, Thomas. Private, Somerset Militia, Salisbury Bn., White Haven Co., 1778/1780 [Ref: M-219]. Took the Oath of Allegiance in Somerset County in 1778 before the Hon. John Span Conway [Ref: T-14].

RENDER, Rachael. See "Purnall Truitt," q.v.

REVELL (REVILL), Charles. Private, Maryland Line, whose name appeared on "a list of recruits from and deserters taken up in Somerset County on Oct 20, 1780" [Ref: D-346].

REVELL (REVILL), David. Private, Somerset Militia, Salisbury Bn., White Haven Co., 1778/1780 [Ref: M-218]. Took the Oath of Allegiance in Somerset County in 1778 before the Hon. Levin Wilson [Ref: T-17].

REVELL (REVILL), John. Private, Somerset Militia, Princess Anne Bn., Capt. James Elzey's Co., 1780 [Ref: M-220].

REVELL (REVILL), Levin. Private, Somerset Militia, Princess Anne Bn., Capt. James Elzey's Co., 1780 [Ref: M-220]. Took the Oath of Allegiance in Somerset County in 1778 before the Hon. Levin Wilson [Ref: T-17]. Select Militia, Somerset County, Aug 15, 1781 [Ref: L-35A].

REVELL (REVILL), Randall. Took the Oath of Allegiance in Somerset County in 1778 before the Hon. John Williams [Ref: T-21, N-51].

REVELL (REVILL), William. Took the Oath of Allegiance in Somerset County in 1778 before the Hon. Levin Wilson [Ref: T-17, N-51]. Private, Select Militia, Somerset County, Aug 15, 1781 [Ref: L-35A listed the name as "William Reavel"].

REW, Nancy. See "Horsey Summers," q.v.

RHOADS, Elisha. Private, Somerset Militia, Salisbury Bn., Capt. William Turpin's Rewastico Co., 1778/1780 [Ref: M-217].

RHOADS, William. Private whose name appeared on "a list of recruits from and deserters taken up in Somerset County on Oct 20, 1780" and noted as "deserter belonging to the Delaware State" [Ref: D-346].

RICHARDS, Isaac. Private, Worcester Militia, Sinepuxent Bn., Capt. Matthew Purnell's Co., Eighth Class, July 25, 1780 [Ref: M-252]. Took the Oath of Allegiance in Worcester County in 1778 in Quepomco Hundred before the Hon. Thomas Purnell [Ref: J-1814 (Box 4)].

RICHARDS, John. Private, Worcester Militia, Sinepuxent Bn., Capt. Matthew Purnell's Co., Eighth Class, July 25, 1780 [Ref: M-252].

RICHARDS, Joseph. Ensign, Worcester Militia, Wicomico Bn., Capt. Charles Bennett's Co., Aug 30, 1777 to at least July 15, 1780 [Ref: M-255, M-115, C-351]. Took the Oath of Allegiance in Worcester County in 1778 before the Hon. John Selby [Ref: J-1814 (Box 4)].

RICHARDS, Nathaniel. Private, Worcester Militia, Sinepuxent Bn., Capt. John Coe's Co., First Class, 1779/1780 [Ref: M-251]. Took the Oath of Allegiance in Worcester County in 1778 before the Hon. John Selby [Ref: J-1814 (Box 4)]. Rendered patriotic service by driving cattle for the military on Sep 30, 1781 [Ref: P-442].

RICHARDS, Preston. Recruited by Capt. Levin Handy and enlisted in the Continental Army in Worcester County on April 7, 1780 for the duration of the war, stating he was born in America [Ref: Z-40]. Private, 5th Maryland Line, listed as a recruit among others from Worcester County who were entitled to clothing from the Commissary of Stores on April 24, 1780 [Ref: F-150].

RICHARDS, William. Private, Worcester Militia, Sinepuxent Bn., Capt. Matthew Purnell's Co., Sixth Class, July 25, 1780 [Ref: M-252]. Took the Oath of Allegiance in Worcester County in 1778 before the Hon. Nathaniel Miller [Ref: J-1814 (Box 4)].

RICHARDSON, Alexander. Private, Worcester Militia, Wicomico Bn., Capt. John Parramore's Co., Third Class, July 15, 1780 [Ref: M-259]. Took the Oath of Allegiance in Worcester County in 1778 before the Hon. John Selby [Ref: J-1814 (Box 4)].

RICHARDSON, Ann. See "Whittington Richardson," q.v.

RICHARDSON, Charles (1748-1820). Took the Oath of Allegiance in Worcester County in 1778 in Quepomco Hundred before the Hon. Thomas Purnell [Ref: J-1814 (Box 4)]. Private, Maryland Line, who applied for a pension in Worcester County on June 6, 1818, age 70, stating he had enlisted at Snow Hill and married Nancy Matthews in Somerset County on March 15, 1788. He received $96 per annum effective and died on Jan 22, 1820. His widow applied for a Federal pension (W4320) on May 19, 1842, age 80, stating she had received a State pension after her husband's death. They had three children:

Jesse (b. March 13, 1789; in 1838 lived in Baltimore); Lydia (b. c1792; in 1842 lived in Somerset County); and, Thomas (b. c1794; in 1827 lived in New York City). [Ref: X-44, W-2874].

RICHARDSON, Charles Jr. (c1705-1792/4). Took the Oath of Allegiance in Worcester County in 1778 before the Hon. Joshua Townsend [Ref: J-1814 (Box 4)]. See "Whittington Richardson," q.v.

RICHARDSON, Huldah. See "Whittington Richardson," q.v.

RICHARDSON, James. Took the Oath of Allegiance in Worcester County in 1778 in Bogerternorton Hundred before the Hon. Thomas Purnell [Ref: J-1814 (Box 4)].

RICHARDSON, Jesse. See "Charles Richardson," q.v.

RICHARDSON, John. Second Lieutenant, Worcester Militia, Wicomico Bn., Capt. Elijah Shockley's Co., Aug 30, 1777 to at least July 15, 1780 [Ref: M-115, M-255, C-351]. Took the Oath of Allegiance in Worcester County in 1778 before the Hon. Nehemiah Holland [Ref: J-1814 (Box 4)]. Appointed as one of three Purchasers of Cattle in Worcester County for the use of the Continental Army on Jan 7, 1778 [Ref: C-456]. Rendered patriotic service by supplying beef in 1780 and grazing and driving cattle for the military on Oct 15, 1781 [Ref: P-256, P-448].

RICHARDSON, John. Took the Oath of Allegiance in Worcester County in 1778 before the Hon. William Hopewell [Ref: J-1814 (Box 4)].

RICHARDSON, John (of Robert). Took the Oath of Allegiance in Worcester County in 1778 before the Hon. Joshua Townsend [Ref: J-1814 (Box 4)].

RICHARDSON, Joseph. Private, Worcester Militia, Wicomico Bn., Capt. James Perdue's Co., Fourth Class, July 15, 1780 [Ref: M-256].

RICHARDSON, Levi. Took the Oath of Allegiance in Worcester County in 1778 before the Hon. Joshua Townsend [Ref: J-1814 (Box 4)].

RICHARDSON, Lydia. See "Charles Richardson," q.v.

RICHARDSON, Matthew. Private, Worcester Militia, Wicomico Bn., Capt. James Perdue's Co., Fifth Class, July 15, 1780 [Ref: M-256].

RICHARDSON, Nancy. See "Isaac Mitchell," q.v.

RICHARDSON, Polly. See "Whittington Richardson," q.v.

RICHARDSON, Robert Jr. Took the Oath of Allegiance in Worcester County in 1778 before the Hon. Joshua Townsend [Ref: J-1814 (Box 4)].

RICHARDSON, Robert (of John). Private, Worcester Militia, Snow Hill Bn., Capt. Samuel Smyley's Co., 1777 [Ref: M-250].

RICHARDSON, Robert Martin. Took the Oath of Allegiance in Worcester County in 1778 before the Hon. John Selby [Ref: J-1814 (Box 4)].

RICHARDSON, Sarah Ann. See "Robert Scroggin," q.v.

RICHARDSON, Shadrick. Took the Oath of Allegiance in Worcester County in 1778 before the Hon. John Selby [Ref: J-1814 (Box 4)].

RICHARDSON, Thomas. Private, Worcester Militia, Wicomico Bn., Capt. John Parramore's Co., Fifth Class, July 15, 1780 [Ref: M-259]. Took the Oath of

Allegiance in Worcester County in 1778 before the Hon. Joshua Townsend [Ref: J-1814 (Box 4)]. See "Charles Richardson," q.v.

RICHARDSON, Whittington (c1740-1825). Son of Charles Richardson, Jr. and Ann ---- (second wife). Whittington was born circa 1740, married Polly ----, and their daughter Huldah Richardson (c1780-1842/47) married Lt.Col. John Holston (1770/5-c1828) in 1806 in Worcester County [Ref: Q-23:3 (Summer, 1982), "Ancestor Table of Willis Clayton Tull, Jr.," pp. 247-255]. Private, Worcester Militia, Sinepuxent Bn., Capt. Elisha Purnell's Co., Third Class, 1779/1780 [Ref: M-253]. Took the Oath of Allegiance in Worcester County in 1778 before the Hon. Joshua Townsend [Ref: J-1814 (Box 4)].

RICHARDSON, William. First Lieutenant, Worcester Militia, Snow Hill Bn., Capt. Samuel Smyley's Co., commissioned Aug 30, 1777 [Ref: M-250, C-351, and M-115 mistakenly listed the name as "William Richardon"]. First Lieutenant, Wicomico Bn., Capt. Samuel Smyley's Co., July 15, 1780 [Ref: M-259].

RICHARDSON, William. Private, Worcester Militia, Sinepuxent Bn., Capt. Elisha Purnell's Co., Fifth Class, 1779/1780 [Ref: M-253]. Took the Oath of Allegiance in Worcester County in 1778 before the Hon. Nehemiah Holland [Ref: J-1814 (Box 4)].

RICHARDSON, William. Took the Oath of Allegiance in Worcester County in 1778 in Quepomco Hundred before the Hon. Thomas Purnell [Ref: J-1814 (Box 4) listed the name as "William Richerson"]. Rendered patriotic service by supplying salt for the use of the military on Dec 27, 1781 [Ref: P-464].

RICKER (RICHER?), John. Took the Oath of Allegiance in Worcester County in 1778 before the Hon. William Hopewell [Ref: J-1814 (Box 4)].

RIDER, Charles. Private, Somerset Militia, Salisbury Bn., Capt. Henry Gale's Quantico Co., 1778/1780 [Ref: M-216]. Took the Oath of Allegiance in Somerset County in 1778 before the Hon. William Winder [Ref: T-22].

RIDER, Dorothy. See "John Henry," q.v.

RIDER, John. Took the Oath of Allegiance in Somerset County in 1778 [Ref: N-51].

RIDER, Mary. See "William Moore, Sr.," q.v.

RIDER, William or Willson(?). Took the Oath of Allegiance in Somerset County in 1778 before the Hon. William Winder [Ref: T-22].

RIDLEY, Keziah. See "Solomon Hamblin," q.v.

RIGBY, Eliza. See "Lambert Hyland," q.v.

RIGGEN (RIGGIN), Amia. See "William Riggen," q.v.

RIGGEN (RIGGIN), Anne. See "John Riggen," q.v.

RIGGEN (RIGGIN), Benton (1758 -   ). Son of Teague and Hannah Riggen, born in Coventry Parish on Oct 11, 1758 [Ref: Y-89]. Private, Somerset Militia, Princess Anne Bn., Capt. John Jones' Princess Anne Co., 1780 [Ref: M-219].

RIGGEN (RIGGIN), Charles. See "William Riggen," q.v.

RIGGEN (RIGGIN), Darby. Private, Worcester Militia, Wicomico Bn., Capt. Charles Bennett's Co., Second Class, July 15, 1780 [Ref: M-255]. Took the

Oath of Allegiance in Worcester County in 1778 before the Hon. Joshua Townsend [Ref: J-1814 (Box 4)]. Private, Worcester Militia, Capt. John Martin's Co., 1780/1781 [Ref: J-1814 (Box 12)]. See "Levin Riggen," q.v.

RIGGEN (RIGGIN), Dukes. Private, Somerset Militia, Princess Anne Bn., Capt. Henry Miles' Little Annemessex Co., 1780 [Ref: M-221 listed the name as "Dukies(?) Riggen"]. Dukes Riggen married Martha Sommors (Summers) in Coventry Parish on Jan 28, 1761 [Ref: Y-89].

RIGGEN (RIGGIN), Edith (Ede). See "John Hayman, Jr.," q.v.

RIGGEN (RIGGIN), Eli. Private, Somerset Militia, Princess Anne Bn., Capt. Henry Miles' Little Annemessex Co., 1780 [Ref: M-221].

RIGGEN (RIGGIN), Hannah. See "John Riggen" and "James Riggen" and "Benton Riggen" and "Levin Riggen," q.v.

RIGGEN (RIGGIN), James (1756 -   ). Son of Teague and Hannah Riggen, born in Coventry Parish on May 21, 1756 [Ref: Y-89]. Private, Somerset Militia, Princess Anne Bn., Capt. James Elzey's Co., 1780 [Ref: M-220].

RIGGEN (RIGGIN), James. Took the Oath of Allegiance in Worcester County in 1778 before the Hon. James Selby [Ref: J-1814 (Box 4)]. Private, Worcester Militia, Capt. John Martin's Co., 1780/1781 [Ref: J-1814 (Box 12)].

RIGGEN (RIGGIN), Jemima. See "John Riggen," q.v.

RIGGEN (RIGGIN), John (1756 -   ). Son of Obed and Rebecca Riggen, born in Coventry Parish on June 4, 1756 [Ref: Y-74]. Private, Somerset Militia, Princess Anne Bn., Capt. Henry Miles' Little Annemessex Co., 1780 [Ref: M-221].

RIGGEN (RIGGIN), John (1754 -   ). Son of John and Jemima Riggen, born in Coventry Parish on June 8, 1754 [Ref: Y-74]. Private, Worcester Militia, Wicomico Bn., Capt. Charles Bennett's Co., Fourth Class, July 15, 1780 [Ref: M-255].

RIGGEN (RIGGIN), John (1753 -   ). Son of Perie and Anne Riggin, born in Coventry Parish on June 28, 1753 [Ref: Y-74]. Private, Somerset Militia, Princess Anne Bn., St. Asaph's Co., 1780 [Ref: M-221].

RIGGEN (RIGGIN), John (1753 -   ). Son of Teague and Hannah Riggen, born in Coventry Parish on April 8, 1753 [Ref: Y-74]. Sergeant, Somerset Militia, Princess Anne Bn., Capt. James Elzey's Co., 1780 [Ref: M-220].

RIGGEN (RIGGIN), John (1759 -   ). Son of Teague and Mary Riggen, born in Coventry Parish on Dec 7, 1759 [Ref: Y-74]. Took the Oath of Allegiance in Worcester County in 1778 before the Hon. James Selby [Ref: J-1814 (Box 4)]. See "Frederick Smith," q.v.

RIGGEN (RIGGIN), Jonathan. Private, Worcester Militia, Wicomico Bn., Capt. Samuel Horsey's Co., Fifth Class, July 15, 1780 [Ref: M-257]. Took the Oath of Allegiance in Worcester County on Feb 25, 1778 before the Hon. Ebenezer Handy [Ref: J-1814 (Box 4)]. Drafted from Somerset County on June 20, 1781 to serve in the Continental Army [Ref: L-35C].

RIGGEN (RIGGIN), Joshua. Private, Worcester Militia, Wicomico Bn., Capt. Fisher Walton's Co., Eighth Class, July 15, 1780 [Ref: M-258]. Took the Oath of Allegiance in Worcester County in 1778 before the Hon. Nehemiah Holland [Ref: J-1814 (Box 4)].

RIGGEN (RIGGIN), Levin (1762 -   ). Son of Darby and Hannah Riggen, born in Coventry Parish on Oct 27, 1762 [Ref: Y-89]. Private, Worcester Militia, Sinepuxent Bn., Capt. William Purnell's Co., Fourth Class, 1779/1780 [Ref: M-252]. Private, Somerset Militia, Princess Anne Bn., St. Asaph's Co., 1780 [Ref: M-220].

RIGGEN (RIGGIN), Littleton. Private, Worcester Militia, Wicomico Bn., Capt. Charles Bennett's Co., Fourth Class, July 15, 1780 [Ref: M-255].

RIGGEN (RIGGIN), Mary. See "William Riggen," q.v.

RIGGEN (RIGGIN), Nehemiah (1750 -   ). Son of William and Rhoda Riggin, born in Coventry Parish on April 7, 1750 [Ref: Y-75]. Private, Somerset Militia, Princess Anne Bn., Capt. John Williams' Watkins Point Co., 1780 [Ref: M-222].

RIGGEN (RIGGIN), Obed. See "John Riggen," q.v.

RIGGEN (RIGGIN), Perie. See "John Riggen," q.v.

RIGGEN (RIGGIN), Pierce or Peirce. Private, Worcester Militia, Capt. John Martin's Co., 1780/1781 [Ref: J-1814 (Box 12)].

RIGGEN (RIGGIN), Rebecca. See "John Riggen," q.v.

RIGGEN (RIGGIN), Rhoda. See "Nehemiah Riggen," q.v.

RIGGEN (RIGGIN), Robert. Private, Somerset Militia, Princess Anne Bn., Capt. John Williams' Watkins Point Co., 1780 [Ref: M-222].

RIGGEN (RIGGIN), Stephen. Private, Somerset Militia, Princess Anne Bn., St. Asaph's Co., 1780 [Ref: M-221].

RIGGEN (RIGGIN), Stephen. Private, Somerset Militia, Princess Anne Bn., Capt. John Williams' Watkins Point Co., 1780 [Ref: M-222].

RIGGEN (RIGGIN), Teague. Private, Worcester Militia, Capt. John Martin's Co., 1780/1781 [Ref: J-1814 (Box 12)].

RIGGEN (RIGGIN), Teague Jr. Took the Oath of Allegiance in Somerset County in 1778 before the Hon. John Williams [Ref: T-21, and N-51 listed the name as "Teague Riggins, Jr."]. Private, Somerset Militia, Princess Anne Bn., Capt. James Elzey's Co., 1780 [Ref: M-220 listed the name without the "Jr."].

RIGGEN (RIGGIN), Teague Sr. Took the Oath of Allegiance in Somerset County in 1778 before the Hon. John Williams [Ref: T-21, and N-51 listed the name as "Teague Riggins, Sr."]. See "William Riggen" and "John Riggen" and "James Riggen" and "Benton Riggen," q.v.

RIGGEN (RIGGIN), William (1757 -   ). Son of Teague and Mary Riggen, born in Coventry Parish on March 17, 1757 [Ref: Y-74]. Private, Somerset Militia, Princess Anne Bn., Capt. John Williams' Watkins Point Co., 1780 [Ref: M-222].

RIGGEN (RIGGIN), William (1752 -   ). Son of Charles and Amia Riggen, born in Coventry Parish on April 6, 1752 [Ref: Y-74]. Private, Worcester Militia, Wicomico Bn., Capt. Samuel Horsey's Co., Fifth Class, July 15, 1780 [Ref: M-257].

RIGGEN (RIGGIN), William. See "Nehemiah Riggen," q.v.

RIGGS, Joseph. Private, Worcester Militia, Wicomico Bn., Capt. Samuel Horsey's Co., Second Class, July 15, 1780 [Ref: M-256 listed the name as "Joseph Rigs"]. Took the Oath of Allegiance in Worcester County in 1778 before the Hon. William Hopewell [Ref: J-1814 (Box 4)].

RILEY, Benjamin. Private, Somerset Militia, Salisbury Bn., Capt. James Bennett's Salisbury Co., 1778/1780 [Ref: M-218].

RILEY, Levin. Took the Oath of Allegiance in Worcester County in 1778 before the Hon. Nathaniel Miller [Ref: J-1814 (Box 4)]. Private, Worcester Militia, Sinepuxent Bn., Capt. Thomas Purnell's Co., Seventh Class, 1779/1780 [Ref: M-253 listed the name as "Levin Ryly"].

RITCH, Henry. Drafted from Somerset County on July 30, 1781 to serve in the Continental Army, but was subsequently excused [Ref: L-35C].

RITCHEY, John. Private, Somerset Militia, Salisbury Bn., White Haven Co., 1778/1780 [Ref: M-219].

ROACH, Charles. Private, Worcester Militia, Snow Hill Bn., Capt. Ebenezer Handy's Co., April 9, 1776 [Ref: M-249]. Private, Worcester Militia, Wicomico Bn., Capt. Samuel Horsey's Co., Fourth Class, July 15, 1780 [Ref: M-257]. Took the Oath of Allegiance in Worcester County in 1778 before the Hon. William Hopewell [Ref: J-1814 (Box 4)].

ROACH, James. Private, Worcester Militia, Wicomico Bn., Capt. Samuel Horsey's Co., Third Class, July 15, 1780 [Ref: M-256].

ROACH, John. Private, Somerset Militia, Princess Anne Bn., Capt. Henry Miles' Little Annemessex Co., 1780 [Ref: M-221].

ROACH, John White. Private, Somerset Militia, Princess Anne Bn., Capt. Isaac Handy's Great Annemessix Co., 1780 [Ref: M-221].

ROACH, Jonathan. Private, Somerset Militia, Salisbury Bn., Capt. Sampson Wheatly's Co., 1780 [Ref: M-216].

ROACH, Planner. Private, Somerset Militia, Salisbury Bn., Capt. Sampson Wheatly's Co., 1780 [Ref: M-216].

ROACH, Southy. Recruited from Somerset County by Esau Boston on July 30, 1781 to serve in the Continental Army until Dec 10, 1781 [Ref: L-35C].

ROACH, Stephen. Private, Worcester Militia, Wicomico Bn., Capt. Isaac Layfield's Co., Second Class, July 15, 1780 [Ref: M-257].

ROACH, Stephen. Second Lieutenant, Worcester Militia, June 28, 1777 [Ref: M-116].

ROACH, William. Private, Somerset Militia, Princess Anne Bn., Capt. John Williams' Watkins Point Co., 1780 [Ref: M-222].

ROAN, Joseph. Private, 3rd Maryland Independent Co., Worcester County, Capt. John Watkins' Co., enlisted Feb 3, 1776; muster roll dated Aug 20, 1776, present for duty [Ref: D-22].

ROAN, Matthew. Private, Worcester Militia, Sinepuxent Bn., Capt. John Postly's Co., Fifth Class, 1779/1780 [Ref: M-251].

ROANS, William. Private, Worcester Militia, Sinepuxent Bn., Capt. John Postly's Co., First Class, 1779/1780 [Ref: M-251].

ROBARDS, Levin. Took the Oath of Allegiance in Worcester County in 1778 before the Hon. Joshua Townsend [Ref: J-1814 (Box 4)].

ROBARTS, Thomas. Took the Oath of Allegiance in Somerset County in 1778 before the Hon. John Span Conway [Ref: T-14].

ROBERSON, George. Private, 3rd Maryland Independent Co., Worcester County, Capt. John Watkins' Co., enlisted June 1, 1776; muster roll dated Aug 20, 1776, present for duty [Ref: D-23].

ROBERSON, John. Private, Worcester Militia, Wicomico Bn., Capt. James Patterson's Co., Third Class, July 15, 1780 [Ref: M-258]. Took the Oath of Allegiance in Worcester County in 1778 before the Hon. James Selby [Ref: J-1814 (Box 4)].

ROBERSON, Josiah. Private, Worcester Militia, Wicomico Bn., Capt. Fisher Walton's Co., Sixth Class, July 15, 1780 [Ref: M-258].

ROBERSON, Levi. Private, Worcester Militia, Wicomico Bn., Capt. Fisher Walton's Co., Third Class, July 15, 1780 [Ref: M-258].

ROBERTS, Barkley. Private, Somerset Militia, Princess Anne Bn., Capt. Thomas Irving's Monie Co., 1780 [Ref: M-219].

ROBERTS, Cipher. See "Fisher Roberts," q.v.

ROBERTS, Edward. Private, Somerset Militia, Princess Anne Bn., Capt. Thomas Irving's Monie Co., 1780 [Ref: M-219].

ROBERTS, Fisher (1744-1809). Private, Somerset Militia, Salisbury Bn., Capt. William Turpin's Rewastico Co., 1778/1780 [Ref: M-217]. Took the Oath of Allegiance in Somerset County in 1778 before the Hon. William Winder [Ref: T-22, and N-51 mistakenly listed the name as "Cipher Roberts"].

ROBERTS, George. See "Isaac Henry," q.v.

ROBERTS, John. Private, Somerset Militia, Princess Anne Bn., Capt. Thomas Irving's Monie Co., 1780 [Ref: M-219].

ROBERTS, Levin. Private, Worcester Militia, Wicomico Bn., Capt. Samuel Smyley's Co., Seventh Class, July 15, 1780 [Ref: M-259].

ROBERTS, Thomas. Took the Oath of Allegiance in Somerset County in 1778 [Ref: N-51].

ROBERTS, Underwood. Private, Somerset Militia, Princess Anne Bn., Capt. Thomas Irving's Monie Co., 1780 [Ref: M-219].

ROBERTS, William. Private, Somerset Militia, Salisbury Bn., White Haven Co., 1778/1780 [Ref: M-218]. Took the Oath of Allegiance in Somerset County in 1778 before the Hon. Levin Wilson [Ref: T-17, N-51].

ROBERTSON, Alexander. Rendered patriotic services by supplying bacon for the use of the military in Somerset County on Aug 17, 1780 [Ref: P-310].

ROBERTSON, Edward. On July 30, 1781 he was drafted "by the class" to serve in the Continental Army until Dec 10, 1781 [Ref: L-35C].

ROBERTSON, George. Private, Somerset Militia, Salisbury Bn., Capt. Henry Gale's Quantico Co., 1778/1780 [Ref: M-216].

ROBERTSON, Isaac. Private, Somerset Militia, Salisbury Bn., Capt. Joseph Venables' Barren Creek Co., 1778/1780 [Ref: M-217].

ROBERTSON, Jacob. Private, Somerset Militia, Salisbury Bn., Capt. Joseph Venables' Barren Creek Co., 1778/1780 [Ref: M-217].

ROBERTSON, James. Private, Somerset Militia, Princess Anne Bn., Capt. John Jones' Princess Anne Co., 1780 [Ref: M-220].

ROBERTSON, James. Private, Somerset Militia, Salisbury Bn., Capt. Joseph Venables' Barren Creek Co., 1778/1780 [Ref: M-217].

ROBERTSON, James. Private, Somerset Militia, Salisbury Bn., Capt. Henry Gale's Quantico Co., 1778/1780 [Ref: M-217].

ROBERTSON, James. Took the Oath of Allegiance in Somerset County on March 1, 1778 before the Hon. Joseph Venables [Ref: T-25].

ROBERTSON, John Sr. Took the Oath of Allegiance in Worcester County in 1778 before the Hon. Nehemiah Holland [Ref: J-1814 (Box 4) listed the name as "John Roberson, Senr."]. Drafted from Somerset County on July 30, 1781 to serve in the Continental Army [Ref: L-35C]. Petitioned the Council of Maryland on July 31, 1781, stating he had been drafted, but was incapable of serving due to a disease. His statement was supported by G. R. Brown who certified that "John Robertson hath laboured under a rheumatic complaint upward of four years which appears to be immovable by remedies, and I am of opinion the disease is such as to render him utterly unfit for military duty." [Ref: H-376].

ROBERTSON, John. Private, Somerset Militia, Salisbury Bn., Capt. John Span Conway's Nanticoke Point Co., 1778/1780 [Ref: M-216]. Took the Oath of Allegiance in Somerset County on March 1, 1778 before the Hon. Joseph Venables [Ref: T-25].

ROBERTSON, John (of John). Private, Somerset Militia, Salisbury Bn., Capt. Joseph Venables' Barren Creek Co., 1778/1780 [Ref: M-217].

ROBERTSON, Leah. See "William Melvin," q.v.

ROBERTSON, Levi. Took the Oath of Allegiance in Worcester County in 1778 before the Hon. Nehemiah Holland [Ref: J-1814 (Box 4)].

ROBERTSON, Mary. See "Planner Williams," q.v.

ROBERTSON, Thomas. Took the Oath of Allegiance in Somerset County in 1778 before the Hon. Peter Waters [Ref: T-18].

ROBERTSON, William (1757 -   ). Son of William and Sarah Robertson, born in Stepney Parish on Sep 5, 1757 [Ref: Y-43]. Private, Somerset Militia, Salisbury Bn., Capt. Joseph Venables' Barren Creek Co., 1778/1780 [Ref: M-217].

ROBERTSON, William. Took the Oath of Allegiance in Somerset County on Feb 28, 1778 before the Hon. Joseph Venables [Ref: T-25]. One William Robertson married Sarah Dashiell in Stepney Parish on May 1, 1753 [Ref: Y-43].

ROBINS, Arralanta (Arralantar). See "John Selby Purnell" and "John Purnell Robins," q.v.

ROBINS, Bowdoin Sr. Took the Oath of Allegiance in Worcester County in 1778 before the Hon. Nehemiah Holland [Ref: J-1814 (Box 4) listed the name as "Bowdoin Robins, Senr."].

ROBINS, Bowdoin (c1736-c1786). Took the Oath of Allegiance in Worcester County in 1778 in Bogerternorton Hundred before the Hon. Thomas Purnell [Ref: J-1814 (Box 4)]. Son of Thomas Robins and brother of "John Purnell Robins," q.v.

ROBINS, James. See "John Purnell Robins," q.v.

ROBINS, John Purnell (c1742-1780). Son of Thomas Robins and Arralantar Purnell. He married Anna Spence by 1770 and their children were John Purnell, Littleton, James, Arralantar, and Mary (Polly). John served in the Lower House of the Maryland Legislature from Worcester County between 1771 and 1776; Justice of the Peace, 1777; and, Justice of the Orphans Court from 1777 until his death some time before Dec 1, 1780 [Ref: R-700, R-702, E-249, E-250, C-428]. Major, Worcester Militia, Sinepuxent Bn., Aug 30, 1777 [Ref: M-117, C-350]. Took the Oath of Allegiance in Worcester County in 1778 in Bogerternorton Hundred before the Hon. Thomas Purnell [Ref: J-1814 (Box 4)].

ROBINS, Josiah. Private, Worcester Militia, Wicomico Bn., Capt. Benjamin Dennis' Co., Seventh Class, July 15, 1780 [Ref: M-256]. Took the Oath of Allegiance in Worcester County in 1778 before the Hon. John Selby [Ref: J-1814 (Box 4)]. Josiah Selby and wife Mary (and more) were deposed regarding the Tory activities of others in Worcester County on November 15, 1775 [Ref: B-370, B-371].

ROBINS, Levi. Private, Worcester Militia, Wicomico Bn., Capt. Benjamin Dennis' Co., Fourth Class, July 15, 1780 [Ref: M-255].

ROBINS, Littleton. First Lieutenant, Worcester Militia, Sinepuxent Bn., Capt. William Purnell's Co., Aug 30, 1777. Captain, June 13, 1782 [Ref: M-117, M-252, C-350, I-190]. Took the Oath of Allegiance in Worcester County in 1778 in Bogerternorton Hundred before the Hon. Thomas Purnell [Ref: J-1814 (Box 4)]. Son of Thomas Robins and brother of "John Purnell Robins," q.v.

ROBINS, Mary. See "John Purnell Robins" and William Purnell," q.v.

ROBINS, Thomas. Private, Worcester Militia, Snow Hill Bn., Capt. Samuel Smyley's Co., 1777 [Ref: M-250]. See "John Purnell Robins" and "Littleton Robins" and "Bowdoin Robins," q.v.

ROBINSON, Alexander. Took the Oath of Allegiance in Somerset County in 1778 before the Hon. John Span Conway [Ref: T-14, N-51].

ROBINSON, George. Soldier (rank was not stated) in Capt. Long's Independent Co. of Regulars. On June 14, 1777 the Council of Maryland ordered that his "being made prisoner at the reduction of Fort Washington and discharged by the enemy ... and there being no prospect of a speedy exchange ... [he is] ... therefore discharged from the service of this State." [Ref: C-289]. He was probably the "George Robenson" who took the Oath of Allegiance in Worcester County in 1778 before the Hon. Joshua Townsend [Ref: J-1814 (Box 4)].

ROBINSON, Thomas. Took the Oath of Allegiance in Worcester County in 1778 before the Hon. Joshua Townsend [Ref: J-1814 (Box 4)].

ROCK, Stephen. Took the Oath of Allegiance in Worcester County in 1778 before the Hon. James Selby [Ref: J-1814 (Box 4)].

ROE, Michael. Invalid (disabled) soldier of Somerset County who was pensioned as a private in the Maryland Line at $44 per annum effective Sep 4, 1797 and apparently still living as of April 24, 1816 [Ref: X-18]. However, he is not listed as a soldier or a pensioner in source D-720 or in source W-2931. Additional research will be necessary before drawing conclusions.

ROE, Richard. Private, Somerset Militia, Princess Anne Bn., Capt. Thomas Irving's Monie Co., 1780 [Ref: M-219].

ROLEY (ROWLEY), Arthur. Private, Worcester Militia, Snow Hill Bn., Capt. John Parramore's Co., 1777 [Ref: M-250]. Private, Worcester Militia, Wicomico Bn., Capt. John Parramore's Co., Sixth Class, July 15, 1780 [Ref: M-259].

ROLEY (ROWLEY), Richard. Private, Worcester Militia, Wicomico Bn., Capt. Fisher Walton's Co., Third Class, July 15, 1780 [Ref: M-258]. Took the Oath of Allegiance in Worcester County in 1778 before the Hon. Joshua Townsend [Ref: J-1814 (Box 4) listed the name as "Richard Royley"].

ROLPH, Sarah. See "Benjamin Darby" and "Daniel Darby," q.v.

ROOKES, Mary. See "Joshua Stanford," q.v.

ROUND, Catherine. See "William Morris," q.v.

ROUND, Edward. See "William Morris," q.v.

ROUND (ROWND, ROUNDS), John (c1745-c1785). Private, Somerset Militia, Princess Anne Bn., Capt. James Elzey's Co., 1780 [Ref: M-220, and V-2522 states he married Priscilla (Gilliss) Piper]. Took the Oath of Allegiance in Somerset County on Feb 28, 1778 before the Hon. Joseph Venables [Ref: T-25].

ROUND (ROWND, ROWNDS), John. Took the Oath of Allegiance in Worcester County in 1778 before the Hon. Nathaniel Miller [Ref: J-1814 (Box 4) listed the name as "John Rownd"]. In Worcester County Court in August, 1799, a petition was submitted by John Bratten and Mary, his wife, for a commission to divide the estate of "John Rownds" (grandfather of Mary Bratten) who died leaving considerable real estate. The heirs of John Rownds were Mary Quinton (now wife of John Bratten), Henrietta Quinton (now wife of John Turpin), and

Sally Quinton (minor). [Ref: Article by William D. Patrick in *Maryland Magazine of Genealogy*, Vol. 4, No. 2 (Fall, 1981), p. 77].

ROUND (ROWND, ROUNDS), Samuel Hopkins. First Lieutenant, Worcester Militia, Sinepuxent Bn., Capt. John Rackliff's Co., Aug 30, 1777. Captain, Worcester Militia, Aug 9, 1780. Captain, Select Militia, Aug 23, 1781 [Ref: M-251, M-117, C-350, F-251, G-577 listed the name as "Samuel Hopkins Rounds"]. Took the Oath of Allegiance in Worcester County in 1778 before the Hon. Nathaniel Miller [Ref: J-1814 (Box 4) listed the name as "Samuel H. Rownd"].

ROUND (ROWND, ROUNDS), William. Private, Worcester Militia, Sinepuxent Bn., Capt. John Postly's Co., First Class, 1779/1780 [Ref: M-251]. Rendered patriotic service by supplying corn for the use of the military on June 19, 1780 [Ref: P-297]. Took the Oath of Allegiance in Worcester County in 1778 before the Hon. Nathaniel Miller [Ref: J-1814 (Box 4) listed the name as "William Rownd"]. Rendered patriotic service by supplying corn on July 10, 1780 for the use of the military and by supplying bacon on Sep 20, 1780 [Ref: G-10 listed the name as "William Rownd" and P-319 listed the name as "William Rounds"].

ROUSBY, Gertrude. See "Robert Jenkins Henry," q.v.

ROUSE(?), Joseph. Private, Somerset Militia, Princess Anne Bn., Capt. Isaac Handy's Great Annemessix Co., 1780 [Ref: M-221].

ROW, William. Private, Somerset Militia, Salisbury Bn., Capt. Levin Irving's Black Water Co., 1778/1780 [Ref: M-217].

ROWLEN, Thomas. Private, Worcester Militia, Sinepuxent Bn., Capt. John Rackliff's Co., Fifth Class, 1779/1780 [Ref: M-251].

ROWLEY, Arthur. See "Arthur Roley," q.v.

RUARK, Daniel. Private, Worcester Militia, Wicomico Bn., Capt. Benjamin Dennis' Co., Eighth Class, July 15, 1780 [Ref: M-256].

RUARK, Elget or Elgate (c1756-c1816). Private, Worcester Militia, Wicomico Bn., Capt. Charles Bennett's Co., Third Class, July 15, 1780 [Ref: M-255, V-2529].

RUARK, Ezekiell. Private, Worcester Militia, Wicomico Bn., Capt. Samuel Horsey's Co., Third Class, July 15, 1780 [Ref: M-256].

RUARK, Hezekiah. Private, Worcester Militia, Wicomico Bn., Capt. Charles Bennett's Co., Sixth Class, July 15, 1780 [Ref: M-255].

RUARK, James. Private, Worcester Militia, Wicomico Bn., Capt. William Handy's Co., Fifth Class, July 15, 1780 [Ref: M-257]. Took the Oath of Allegiance in Worcester County in 1778 before the Hon. Nathaniel Miller [Ref: J-1814 (Box 4) listed the name as "James Ruak"].

RUARK, John. Private, Worcester Militia, Wicomico Bn., Capt. Benjamin Dennis' Co., Fourth Class, July 15, 1780 [Ref: M-255]. Took the Oath of Allegiance in Worcester County in 1778 before the Hon. Joshua Townsend [Ref: J-1814 (Box 4) listed the name as "John Ruock"].

RUARK(?), Shadery. Took the Oath of Allegiance in Worcester County in 1778 before the Hon. Nathaniel Miller [Ref: J-1814 (Box 4) listed the name as "Shadery Crook" and then wrote a large "R" over the "C" to make it look like "Rrook" - perhaps to imply the name was "Ruark"?].

RUNNALLS, Eleanor. See "Luke Bowen," q.v.

RUNNALLS, Thomas. See "Luke Bowen," q.v.

RUSSELL (BUSSELL?), John. Private, Worcester Militia, Wicomico Bn., Capt. Charles Bennett's Co., Fifth Class, July 15, 1780 [Ref: M-255].

RUSSELL, Alexander Thomas. Took the Oath of Allegiance in Somerset County on Feb 23, 1778 before the Hon. Joseph Venables [Ref: T-25 listed the name as "Alexr. Thos. Russel"].

RUSSELL, Amelia Catherine. See "Benjamin Darby," q.v.

RUSSELL, Mary. See "Joseph Schoolfield," q.v.

RUSSELL, Price. Sergeant, Somerset Militia, Salisbury Bn., Capt. Henry Gale's Quantico Co., 1778/1780 [Ref: M-216 listed he name as "Pierce (Price, Preist?) Russell"]. Took the Oath of Allegiance in Somerset County in 1778 [Ref: T-22 listed the name as "Price Russele" and N-51 mistakenly listed the name as "Bruce Russell"]. Select Militia, Somerset County, Aug 15, 1781 [Ref: L-35B].

RUSSELL, Thomas. Private, Somerset Militia, Salisbury Bn., Capt. William Turpin's Rewastico Co., 1778/1780 [Ref: M-217 listed the name as "Thomas Russel"].

RYLEY, Thomas. Ensign, Worcester Militia, Sinepuxent Bn., Capt. John Ratliff's Co., Aug 30, 1777 [Ref: M-118, C-350].

RYLY, Levin. See "Levin Riley," q.v.

RYON (RYAN), Valentine. Private, Worcester Militia, Sinepuxent Bn., Capt. John Rackliff's Co., Eighth Class, 1779/1780 [Ref: M-251]. Took the Oath of Allegiance in Worcester County in 1778 before the Hon. Nathaniel Miller [Ref: J-1814 (Box 4) listed the name as "Volentine Ryon"].

SADLER, Thomas. Private, Somerset Militia, Princess Anne Bn., Capt. Isaac Handy's Great Annemessix Co., 1780 [Ref: M-221].

SALISBURY, Joshua. Private, Somerset Militia, Princess Anne Bn., Capt. Henry Miles' Little Annemessex Co., 1780 [Ref: M-221].

SANDERS, Samuel. Private, Somerset Militia, Princess Anne Bn., Capt. James Elzey's Co., 1780 [Ref: M-220].

SASSER, Benjamin. Took the Oath of Allegiance in Somerset County in 1778 before the Hon. Levin Wilson [Ref: T-17, N-51].

SASSER, Benjamin Jr. Private, Somerset Militia, Princess Anne Bn., Capt. Thomas Irving's Monie Co., 1780 [Ref: M-219]. Took the Oath of Allegiance in Somerset County in 1778 before the Hon. Levin Wilson [Ref: T-17 listed the name without the "Jr."].

SASSER, John. Private, Somerset Militia, Princess Anne Bn., Capt. Thomas Irving's Monie Co., 1780 [Ref: M-219 listed the name as "John Sassen"].

SASSER, William. Sergeant, Somerset Militia, Princess Anne Bn., Capt. Thomas Irving's Monie Co., 1780 [Ref: M-219 listed the name as "William Sassen?"].
SASSER, William Jr. Took the Oath of Allegiance in Somerset County in 1778 before the Hon. Levin Wilson [Ref: T-17, and N-51 listed the name as "William Sausser Jr."].
SASSER, William Sr. Took the Oath of Allegiance in Somerset County in 1778 before the Hon. Levin Wilson [Ref: T-17].
SATCHELL, John (1750-1820). Private, Worcester Militia, Snow Hill Bn., Capt. Samuel Smyley's Co., 1777 [Ref: M-250]. Took the Oath of Allegiance in Worcester County in 1778 before the Hon. John Selby [Ref: J-1814 (Box 4)]. "John Satchwell" was born in Maryland in 1750, married Elizabeth Clark, served as a private in Maryland, and died in North Carolina in March, 1820 [Ref: V-2568].
SAUNDERS, George. Private, Somerset Militia, Salisbury Bn., Capt. Henry Gale's Quantico Co., 1778/1780 [Ref: M-216].
SAUNDERS, Samuel. Private, Select Militia, Somerset County, Aug 15, 1781 [Ref: L-35A].
SAUNDERS, Thomas. Took the Oath of Allegiance in Worcester County in 1778 before the Hon. Nathaniel Miller [Ref: J-1814 (Box 4)].
SAVAGE, Ezekiel. Private, Somerset Militia, Princess Anne Bn., Capt. John Jones' Princess Anne Co., 1780 [Ref: M-219].
SAVAGE, Isaac. Private, Worcester Militia, Sinepuxent Bn., Capt. William Purnell's Co., First Class, 1779/1780 [Ref: M-252]. Took the Oath of Allegiance in Worcester County in 1778 in Bogerternorton Hundred before the Hon. Thomas Purnell [Ref: J-1814 (Box 4) listed the name as "Isaac Savige"].
SAVAGE, John. Private, Worcester Militia, Snow Hill Bn., Capt. Samuel Smyley's Co., 1777 [Ref: M-250]. Private, Worcester Militia, Wicomico Bn., Capt. Samuel Smyley's Co., Sixth Class, July 15, 1780 [Ref: M-259]. Took the Oath of Allegiance in Worcester County in 1778 before the Hon. Joshua Townsend [Ref: J-1814 (Box 4)]. See "William Waters," q.v.
SAVAGE, William. See "William Polk," q.v.
SAVAGE, Zorabable. Private, Worcester Militia, Wicomico Bn., Capt. Elijah Shockley's Co., Fifth Class, July 15, 1780 [Ref: M-255].
SCARBOROUGH, John. Took the Oath of Allegiance in Worcester County in 1778 before the Hon. Joshua Townsend [Ref: J-1814 (Box 4)].
SCARBOROUGH, Samuel. Took the Oath of Allegiance in Worcester County in 1778 before the Hon. Nehemiah Holland [Ref: J-1814 (Box 4)].
SCHOOLFIELD, Benjamin. First Lieutenant, Somerset Militia, 17th Bn., Capt. Planner Williams' Co., Feb 24, 1776. Captain, Sep 19, 1776 [Ref: M-118, A-182, B-285]. Appointed by the Council of Maryland to be Inspector of Tobacco at Pocomoke on Aug 30, 1780 [Ref: F-271].
SCHOOLFIELD, Benjamin. Second Lieutenant, Somerset Militia, Princess Anne Bn., Capt. John Williams' Co., Sep 23, 1777. First Lieutenant, Dec 7, 1778,

Capt. Thomas King's Co.. First Lieutenant, St. Asaph's Co., 1780 [Ref: M-220, M-118, C-381, E-260].

SCHOOLFIELD, Bozman. First Lieutenant, Worcester Militia, Wicomico Bn., Capt. Philip Quinton's Co., Aug 30, 1777 to May 20, 1778, resigned [Ref: M-118, C-351].

SCHOOLFIELD, Dolly. See "Levi Houston," q.v.

SCHOOLFIELD, George (c1741-c1798). Second Lieutenant, Somerset Militia, 17th Bn., Sep 19, 1776. First Lieutenant, June 17, 1777 [Ref: M-118, B-285, C-291]. Somerset Militia, Princess Anne Bn., Capt. George Waters' Pocomoke Co., 1780 [Ref: M-220].

SCHOOLFIELD, Henry. Private, Somerset Militia, Princess Anne Bn., Capt. George Waters' Pocomoke Co., 1780 [Ref: M-220].

SCHOOLFIELD, John. Corporal, Somerset Militia, Princess Anne Bn., Capt. George Waters' Pocomoke Co., 1780 [Ref: M-220].

SCHOOLFIELD, John. Private, Worcester Militia, Sinepuxent Bn., Capt. John Rackliff's Co., Sixth Class, 1779/1780 [Ref: M-251].

SCHOOLFIELD, John. Private, Worcester Militia, Sinepuxent Bn., Capt. Matthew Purnell's Co., Fifth Class, July 25, 1780 [Ref: M-252].

SCHOOLFIELD, John. Took the Oath of Allegiance in Worcester County in 1778 before the Hon. Nathaniel Miller [Ref: J-1814 (Box 4)].

SCHOOLFIELD, Joseph. Private, Worcester Militia, Wicomico Bn., Capt. Isaac Layfield's Co., Eighth Class, July 15, 1780 [Ref: M-257]. Took the Oath of Allegiance in Worcester County in 1778 before the Hon. Nehemiah Holland [Ref: J-1814 (Box 4)]. "Joseph L. Scholfield" was a private in the Maryland Line, married Mary Russell (b. 1775 - d. after 1855) on Aug 27, 1812, and died in Washington, D. C. on Sep 19, 1848 [Ref: W-3037].

SCHOOLFIELD, Margaret. See "William Atkinson Selby," q.v.

SCHOOLFIELD, Robert. Private, Worcester Militia, Sinepuxent Bn., Capt. William Purnell's Co., Eighth Class, 1779/1780 [Ref: M-252]. Took the Oath of Allegiance in Worcester County in 1778 before the Hon. John Selby [Ref: J-1814 (Box 4)].

SCHOOLFIELD, Stephen. Private, Somerset Militia, Princess Anne Bn., Capt. George Waters' Pocomoke Co., 1780 [Ref: M-220].

SCHOOLFIELD, William. Ensign, Somerset Militia, 17th Bn., Jan 3, 1776. First Lieutenant, Sep 19, 1776 [Ref: M-118, M-119, B-285].

SCOTT, Benjamin (1744/5-1832). Private, Maryland Line, who married Lotty ---- in Worcester County on Sep 27, 1800 (his first wife had died several years earlier, name not given) and moved to Hamilton County, Ohio where he died on July 15, 1832, age 77 or 78. Lotty Scott married second to George Crestmore on March 26, 1836 and he was run over by a mail stage coach on the Sharonville to Cincinnati Road. Lotty Crestmore married third to Isaac Furgeson on Jan 21, 1838 and he died about 1840. Lotty Furgeson applied for a pension in Hamilton County, Ohio on May 27, 1859, age 84, stating her first husband, Benjamin Scott, had no children, but he had four brothers (not named) who were all deceased [Ref: W-3043].

SCOTT, Christiana. See "Gustavus Scott," q.v.

SCOTT, Day. See "Andrew F. Cheney" and "George D. Scott," q.v.

SCOTT, Elizabeth. See "Gustavus Scott," q.v.

SCOTT, George Day (1736-1796). Son of Day Scott and probably Alice Ballard. George married Elizabeth Handy in 1760 and died without progeny. Served as County Court Justice in 1774-1775 and was a subscriber to Washington College in 1783 [Ref: R-716]. "George Scott" was one of four delegates elected to represent Somerset County at the Maryland Convention in August, 1776 [Ref: O-45]. Captain, Somerset Militia, 1775 [Ref: J-1814 (Box 1)]. Lieutenant Colonel, 1st Bn., Jan 6, 1776. Colonel, Salisbury Bn., Aug 30, 1777 [Ref: M-119, C-351]. Took the Oath of Allegiance in Somerset County in 1778 before the Hon. Peter Waters [Ref: T-18].

SCOTT, Gustavus (1753-1800). Son of Rev. James Scott who immigrated from Scotland circa 1730 to Prince William County, Virginia, and married Sarah Brown, daughter of Dr. Gustavus Brown, of Charles County, Maryland. Gustavus Scott moved to Somerset County circa 1771 and married Margaret Hall Caile, of Dorchester County, on Feb 16, 1777. Children: Robert Caile, John Caile, Gustavus Hall, William Bushrod, Robert James, Elizabeth, Mary Caile, Christiana, and Juliana. Gustavus attended the Maryland Conventions from Somerset County, 1775-1776, and signed the Association of the Freemen of Maryland on July 25, 1775. He served in the Lower House of the Maryland Legislature from Dorchester County, 1780-1784, and was elected a delegate to the Continental Congress, 1784-1785, but did not attend. He was appointed by President George Washington as Commissioner of Washington, D. C. on Aug 23, 1794 and served until his death on Dec 25, 1800. Interred on his farm "Strawberry Vale" in Virginia [Ref: R-717, R-718, O-1, O-4, O-28, P-45, A-67, V-2590].

SCOTT, John. Private, Worcester Militia, Wicomico Bn., Capt. John Davis' Co., Fifth Class, July 15, 1780 [Ref: M-254]. Took the Oath of Allegiance in Worcester County in 1778 before the Hon. Nathaniel Miller [Ref: J-1814 (Box 4)]. First Lieutenant, Worcester Militia, Wicomico Bn., Capt. Long's Co., June 13, 1782 [Ref: M-119, I-190].

SCOTT, John. Private, Worcester Militia, Wicomico Bn., Capt. Philip Quinton's Co., Sixth Class, July 15, 1780 [Ref: M-256]. Took the Oath of Allegiance in Worcester County in 1778 before the Hon. John Selby [Ref: J-1814 (Box 4)]. See "Gustavus Scott," q.v.

SCOTT, John Day. Captain, 7th Co., Maryland Line, Jan 3, 1776 and paid by the Treasurer of the Western Shore on April 11, 1776 [Ref: A-327, D-15]. His county of origin is uncertain, but George Day Scott was a lieutenant colonel in Somerset County at the same time John Day Scott was a captain. Additional research will be necessary before drawing conclusions.

SCOTT, Joseph. Took the Oath of Allegiance in Worcester County in 1778 before the Hon. John Selby [Ref: J-1814 (Box 4)]. Corporal, Worcester Militia, Capt. John Martin's Co., 1780/1781 [Ref: J-1814 (Box 12)].
SCOTT, Juliana. See "Gustavus Scott," q.v.
SCOTT, Lotty. See "Benjamin Scott," q.v.
SCOTT, Mary. See "Andrew F. Cheney" and "Gustavus Scott," q.v.
SCOTT, Peggy. See "Solomon Long," q.v.
SCOTT, Robert. See "Gustavus Scott," q.v.
SCOTT, Thomas. Took the Oath of Allegiance in Worcester County in 1778 before the Hon. Nehemiah Holland [Ref: J-1814 (Box 4)].
SCOTT, William. Took the Oath of Allegiance in Worcester County in 1778 before the Hon. Joshua Townsend [Ref: J-1814 (Box 4)]. See "Gustavus Scott," q.v.
SCROGGIN (SCROGIN), John (1743-1812). Sergeant, Somerset Militia, Salisbury Bn., Capt. Levin Irving's Black Water Co., 1778/1780. Ensign, April 15, 1781 [Ref: M-217, H-195]. Select Militia, Aug 15, 1781 [Ref: L-35B]. Took the Oath of Allegiance in Somerset County on Feb 14, 1778 before the Hon. Joseph Venables [Ref: T-25]. John was born in Maryland on Nov 13, 1743, married Eunice Jane Polk, served as a sergeant during the war, and died in Woodford County, Kentucky on Dec 14, 1812 [Ref: V-2596].
SCROGGIN (SCROGIN), Joseph. Corporal, Somerset Militia, Salisbury Bn., Capt. Levin Irving's Black Water Co., 1778/1780 [Ref: M-217]. Took the Oath of Allegiance in Somerset County on Feb 21, 1778 before the Hon. Joseph Venables [Ref: T-25].
SCROGGIN (SCROGIN), Philip. Ensign, Worcester Militia, Wicomico Bn., Capt. Robert Handy's Co., March 16, 1781 [Ref: M-119, G-353].
SCROGGIN (SCROGIN), Robert. Sergeant, Somerset Militia, Salisbury Bn., Capt. Levin Irving's Black Water Co., 1778/1780 [Ref: M-217 mistakenly listed the name as "Robt. Swggrt(?)"]. Took the Oath of Allegiance in Somerset County on Feb 21, 1778 before the Hon. Joseph Venables [Ref: T-25]. Recommended for promotion to ensign on July 21, 1781 [Ref: J-1814 (Box 8, Dashiell's correspondence) and H-361 listed the name as "Robt. Scrogin"]. Robert Caldwell Scroggin (Scroggins, Scrogin) was born on March 1, 1753 in Maryland, married first to Ann Culber, second to Sarah Ann Richardson, served as an ensign in Maryland, and died in Kentucky after 1790 [Ref: V-2596].
SCROGGIN (SCROGIN), Thomas C. (1764-c1835) Private, Maryland Line, who applied for a pension (S16524) in Franklin County, Kentucky on Jan 9, 1833, stating he was born in Somerset County, Maryland on July 24, 1764 and lived there at the time of his enlistment. After the war he lived in Delaware "for some years" and in 1792 moved to Kentucky, living mostly in Franklin County [Ref: W-3053, and A. W. Burns' abstracts on revolutionary soldiers of Maryland in Kentucky (p. 39) at the Maryland Historical Society]. Private, Maryland Militia, enlisted in August, 1780; pensioned in Franklin County, Kentucky

under the Act of June 7, 1832 at $45.56 per annum effective Feb 11, 1833, age 70; and, not listed among the pensioners in 1840 [Ref: Anderson C. Quisenberry's *Revolutionary Soldiers in Kentucky* (1896), p. 75; Henry C. Peden, Jr.'s *Marylanders to Kentucky* (1991), p. 130].

SEERS, John. Private, Worcester Militia, Sinepuxent Bn., Capt. Matthew Purnell's Co., Third Class, July 25, 1780 [Ref: M-252].

SELBY, Ann. See "Joseph Selby" and "John Selby," q.v.

SELBY, Benjamin. Private, Somerset Militia, Salisbury Bn., Capt. John Span Conway's Nanticoke Point Co., 1778/1780 [Ref: M-216].

SELBY, Betty (Betsy). See "John Selby," q.v.

SELBY, Daniel. Private, Worcester Militia, Snow Hill Bn., Capt. John Parramore's Co., 1777. Private, Worcester Militia, Wicomico Bn., Capt. John Parramore's Co., Second Class, July 15, 1780 [Ref: M-250, M-259].

SELBY, Daniel. Private, Worcester Militia, Wicomico Bn., Capt. Philip Quinton's Co., Second Class, July 15, 1780 [Ref: M-256]. Took the Oath of Allegiance in Worcester County in 1778 before the Hon. Nehemiah Holland [Ref: J-1814 (Box 4)]. Rendered patriotic service by salting beef for the use of the military in 1781 [Ref: P-349].

SELBY, Daniel. See "John Selby" and "Thomas Purnell, of Thomas," q.v.

SELBY, Ezekiel. Private, Worcester Militia, Wicomico Bn., Capt. Philip Quinton's Co., First Class, July 15, 1780 [Ref: M-256]. See "Parker Selby," q.v.

SELBY, George. Private, Worcester Militia, Wicomico Bn., Capt. Fisher Walton's Co., Fifth Class, July 15, 1780 [Ref: M-258].

SELBY, Henry. Private, Somerset Militia, Salisbury Bn., Capt. John Span Conway's Nanticoke Point Co., 1778/1780 [Ref: M-216].

SELBY, Isabell. See "Parker Selby," q.v.

SELBY, James. Justice who administered the Oath of Allegiance in Worcester County in 1778 [Ref: J-1814 (Box 4)]. Justice of the Peace, commissioned on Nov 29, 1777 and Nov 21, 1778 and Jan 17, 1782 [Ref: C-428, E-249, I-46]. Special Commission of Judge of the Court of Oyer and Terminer and Gaol Delivery issued to him and five others in Worcester County by the Governor and Council of Maryland on Dec 10, 1783 [Ref: I-488]. See "John Selby," q.v.

SELBY, James. Private, Worcester Militia, Wicomico Bn., Capt. Philip Quinton's Co., Eighth Class, July 15, 1780 [Ref: M-256].

SELBY, James. Private, Worcester Militia, Wicomico Bn., Capt. William Handy's Co., Second Class, July 15, 1780 [Ref: M-257].

SELBY, James. Private, Worcester Militia, Wicomico Bn., Capt. Isaac Layfield's Co., Third Class, July 15, 1780 [Ref: M-257].

SELBY, James. Private, Worcester Militia, Snow Hill Bn., Capt. John Parramore's Co., 1777 [Ref: M-250].

SELBY, James. Private, 3rd Maryland Independent Co., Worcester County, Capt. John Watkins' Co., enlisted April 30, 1776; muster roll dated Aug 20, 1776, present for duty [Ref: D-22]. Took the Oath of Allegiance in Worcester County in 1778 before the Hon. James Selby [Ref: J-1814 (Box 4)].

SELBY, Jesse. Private, 3rd Maryland Independent Co., Worcester County, Capt. John Watkins' Co., enlisted April 28, 1776; muster roll dated Aug 20, 1776, present for duty [Ref: D-21]. On Oct 19, 1776 "Jesse Selby of Capt. Long's Co. discharged from the service of this State" by the Maryland Council of Safety [Ref: B-369]. Paid for his services on Dec 17, 1782 [Ref: I-323].

SELBY, Jesse. Private, Worcester Militia, Sinepuxent Bn., Capt. Thomas Purnell's Co., Sixth Class, 1779/1780 [Ref: M-253]. Took the Oath of Allegiance in Worcester County in 1778 before the Hon. Joshua Townsend [Ref: J-1814 (Box 4)].

SELBY, John (c1715-1790). Son of Parker Selby and Mary Watts (d. 1776). John married Anne Drummond and their children were: James; Daniel; William; John (d. 1780); Anne (Nancy) married first to her cousin Parker Selby (d. 1789, son of Parker, d. 1773), married second to John Gunby (d. 1801), and died in 1796; Polly; and, Betty (Betsy) married her first cousin William Selby, Jr. (d. 1821). John attended the Maryland Convention in 1776 and served in the Lower House of the Maryland Legislature from Worcester County, 1777 [Ref: O-36, R-719]. Justice who administered the Oath of Allegiance in Worcester County in 1778 [Ref: J-1814 (Box 4)]. Justice of the Peace and Justice of the Orphans Court, commissioned on June 4, 1777 and Nov 21, 1778 and Jan 17, 1782 [Ref: C-274, E-249, I-46]. Commissioned by the Council of Maryland on Aug 19, 1779 to receive subscriptions for the Continental Loan Office [Ref: E-499]. Rendered patriotic service by supplying beef for the use of the military in Worcester County on Oct 10, 1780 [Ref: P-325]. Special Commission of Judge of the Court of Oyer and Terminer and Gaol Delivery issued to him and five others in Worcester County by the Governor and Council of Maryland on Dec 10, 1783 [Ref: I-488]. John was also a lieutenant in the Worcester Militia in 1748, and captain by 1757. He held many offices during the Revolutionary era (as shown above) and was "accused in 1784 by Nehemiah Holland (d. 1788) of Tory sympathies during the war, although Holland's credibility is open to question. Selby's brother, Col. William Selby (d. 1793) of Accomack County, Virginia, also charged in a deposition to the governor and the Council that his brother was a Tory." [Ref: R-720]. Additional research will be necessary before drawing conclusions. See "William Selby, of John" and "Edward Vandame (Vondome)," q.v.

SELBY, John (1754/5 -   ). Son of John and Mary Selby, born in Coventry Parish on Aug 21, 1754 or 1755 [Ref: Y-75]. Private, Worcester Militia, Wicomico Bn., Capt. Philip Quinton's Co., Eighth Class, July 15, 1780 [Ref: M-256]. Private, Worcester Militia, Capt. John Martin's Co., 1780/1781 [Ref: J-1814 (Box 12)].

SELBY, John. Private, Worcester Militia, Wicomico Bn., Capt. John Parramore's Co., First Class, July 15, 1780 [Ref: M-259].

SELBY, John. Second Lieutenant, Worcester Militia, Snow Hill Bn., Capt. John Parramore's Co., Aug 30, 1777 [Ref: M-119, M-250, C-351]. "Capt. John Selby" took the Oath of Allegiance in Worcester County in 1778 before the Hon. John Selby [Ref: J-1814 (Box 4)].

SELBY, John. Sergeant, Somerset Militia, Salisbury Bn., Capt. John Span Conway's Nanticoke Point Co., 1778/1780 [Ref: M-216 listed the name as "John Sibbey (Libbey, etc.?)"].

SELBY, John Jr. (c1740-1780). Son of John Parker and Anne Drummond. John married Leah ---- and died in 1780 [Ref: R-719]. Took the Oath of Allegiance in Worcester County in 1778 before the Hon. Joshua Townsend [Ref: J-1814 (Box 4) listed the name as "John Selby, son of Capt. John"]. Elected Sheriff of Worcester County, commissioned on Oct 25, 1779 and died by Oct 2, 1780 when he was replaced in office [Ref: E-566, and F-310 listed the name without the "Jr."].

SELBY, John Sr. Took the Oath of Allegiance in Worcester County in 1778 before the Hon. Joshua Townsend [Ref: J-1814 (Box 4)].

SELBY, Joseph. On Sep 24, 1776 the Maryland Council of Safety contracted with Joseph Selby "for making 2,000 cartouch boxes, bayonet belts and gunslings, to be delivered one month from this date ..." [Ref: B-297]. On Jan 19, 1781, the Council of Maryland directed "that Mr. John Shaw receive of Mrs. Ann Selby, widow of the late Joseph Selby, all the cartridge boxes which had been finished by Selby and Howard according to their contract with the State" [Ref: G-280].

SELBY, Joshua. Private, Worcester Militia, Wicomico Bn., Capt. Charles Bennett's Co., First Class, July 15, 1780 [Ref: M-255]. Took the Oath of Allegiance in Worcester County in 1778 before the Hon. Joshua Townsend [Ref: J-1814 (Box 4)].

SELBY, Major. Private, Worcester Militia, Wicomico Bn., Capt. Benjamin Dennis' Co., Eighth Class, July 15, 1780 [Ref: M-256].

SELBY, Mary. See "William Atkinson Selby" and "William Purnell" and "John Selby," q.v.

SELBY, Nancy. See "John Selby," q.v.

SELBY, Parker (1761 -   ). Son of Ezekiel and Isabell Selby, born in Coventry Parish on Nov 28, 1761 [Ref: Y-89]. Private, Worcester Militia, Sinepuxent Bn., Capt. Thomas Purnell's Co., First Class, 1779/1780. Private, Worcester Militia, Wicomico Bn., Capt. Samuel Smyley's Co., First Class, July 15, 1780 [Ref: M-253, M-258]. He was probably the Parker Selby who took the Oath of Allegiance in Worcester County in 1778 before the Hon. John Selby although he was not yet 18 years of age, but he was in his 18th year nonetheless [Ref: J-1814 (Box 4)]. See "John Selby," q.v.

SELBY, Parker Sr. Took the Oath of Allegiance in Worcester County in 1778 before the Hon. John Selby [Ref: J-1814 (Box 4)]. Rendered patriotic service by supplying beef for the use of the military on Sep 20, 1781 [Ref: P-439].

SELBY, Parker (of Parker). Private, Worcester Militia, Snow Hill Bn., Capt. Samuel Smyley's Co., 1777 [Ref: M-250]. Took the Oath of Allegiance in Worcester County in 1778 before the Hon. John Selby [Ref: J-1814 (Box 4)]. See "John Selby," q.v.

SELBY, Philip. Private, Worcester Militia, Snow Hill Bn., Capt. John Parramore's Co., 1777. Sergeant, Worcester Militia, Wicomico Bn., Capt. John Parramore's Co., July 15, 1780 [Ref: M-250, M-259]. Took the Oath of Allegiance in Worcester County in 1778 before the Hon. John Selby [Ref: J-1814 (Box 4)].

SELBY, Polly. See "John Parker," q.v.

SELBY, Sarah. See "Dennis Hudson," q.v.

SELBY, Thomas. Private, Worcester Militia, Sinepuxent Bn., Capt. John Rackliff's Co., Fourth Class, 1779/1780 [Ref: M-251]. Ensign, Sinepuxent Bn., Capt. Samuel H. Round's Co., March 16, 1781 [Ref: M-119, G-353]. Took the Oath of Allegiance in Worcester County in 1778 before the Hon. Nathaniel Miller [Ref: J-1814 (Box 4)]. See "William Atkinson Selby," q.v.

SELBY, Thomas Jr. Private, Worcester Militia, Capt. John Martin's Co., 1780/1781 [Ref: J-1814 (Box 12)].

SELBY, William. Private, Worcester Militia, Snow Hill Bn., Capt. Samuel Smyley's Co., 1777. Private, Worcester Militia, Wicomico Bn., Capt. Fisher Walton's Co., Second Class, July 15, 1780 [Ref: M-250, M-258]. Private, Worcester Militia, Capt. John Martin's Co., 1780/1781 [Ref: J-1814 (Box 12)]. See "John Selby," q.v.

SELBY, William Jr. Private, Worcester Militia, Wicomico Bn., Capt. Philip Quinton's Co., Third Class, July 15, 1780 [Ref: M-256]. On Dec 17, 1777 he refused a commission as Sheriff of Worcester County and recommended Benjamin Purnell in his stead [Ref: O-83].

SELBY, William (of John). Served in the Lower House of the Maryland Legislature from Worcester County from June 8 to June 17, 1780. "There was insufficient information to positively identify William Selby, of John. A man by that name owned 350 acres of *Pharsalia* in Mattapony Hundred, Worcester County, in 1783, but the original tract encompassed 2,400 acres which makes it difficult to trace the history of ownership. There was no probate in Worcester County or in neighboring Accomack County, Virginia, for William Selby, of John. John Selby (d. 1790) of Mattapony Hundred, Worcester County, had a son William, but John's will treats this son as if he were incapable of handling his share of the estate, instead creating a trust for him. The will does address the possibility that William might have children at some future date, however, and there is no hint of his specific problem, which would help determine if he had the capacity to hold elective office. There were at least two conveyances of land owned by this William Selby. In one, he and Zadock Selby jointly executed a deed for the sale of property, and in the other the deed was executed by his trustees as named in his father's will." [Ref: R-721]. Additional research will be necessary before drawing conclusions.

SELBY, William (of Parker). Took the Oath of Allegiance in Worcester County in 1778 before the Hon. Joshua Townsend [Ref: J-1814 (Box 4)].

SELBY, William (of William). Second Lieutenant, Worcester Militia, 10th Bn., Capt. James Martin's Co., May 25, 1776 [Ref: M-119, A-444]. Took the Oath of Allegiance in Worcester County in 1778 before the Hon. Joshua Townsend [Ref: J-1814 (Box 4)].

SELBY, William Atkinson (1757-1809). Born on May 28 or Nov 28, 1757, married Sarah White Townsend, served as a private in the Maryland troops, and died on Aug 2, 1809 [Ref: V-2609]. "Son of John Selby of Nassawadux, Pocomoke Hundred, Worcester County, was indicted by the Worcester County Court in June, 1779, for 'going to the enemy.' He was a great-grandson of Thomas Selby (d. 1702) who immigrated to Maryland from Accomack County, Virginia, by 1674, His grandfather was John Selby, son of Thomas (d. 1758), and his wife Margaret Scholfield [Schoolfield]. His mother was Mary Atkinson, daughter of Angelo Atkinson (d. 1766) of Worcester County." [Ref: R-721]. In spite of this allegation, or perhaps because of it, we find William Atkinson Selby as a private in the Worcester Militia, Wicomico Bn., Capt. Philip Quinton's Co., Seventh Class, by July 15, 1780 [Ref: M-256]. William Atkinson Selby, son of John and Mary Selby, was born in Coventry Parish on May 28, 1757 [Ref: Y-75].

SELBY, Zadock. Took the Oath of Allegiance in Worcester County in 1778 before the Hon. John Selby [Ref: J-1814 (Box 4)]. Private, Worcester Militia, Sinepuxent Bn., Capt. John Coe's Co., Sixth Class, 1779/1780 [Ref: M-252]. See "William Selby, of John," q.v.

SELBY, Zadok. Private, Worcester Militia, Snow Hill Bn., Capt. Samuel Smyley's Co., 1777. Sergeant, Worcester Militia, Wicomico Bn., Capt. Samuel Smyley's Co., July 15, 1780 [Ref: M-250, M-259].

SELLEY, James. Rendered patriotic service by hauling corn for the use of the military in Worcester County 1779/1780 [Ref: P-256].

SEON, Thomas. Took the Oath of Allegiance in Somerset County in 1778 (made his "X" mark) before the Hon. Peter Waters [Ref: T-18]. It is interesting to note the following from the Council of Maryland on June 17, 1778: "On examination of Thomas Seon, who appears by his own confession to have been an ensign in the 5th Regiment of the British Troops and to have lately come out of Philadelphia, having as he says resigned his commission in the month of June, 1777. This Board not being satisfied that he is not now in the British service and on some evil design travelling about this State and being of opinion that the truth of this case may be better enquired into in the neighborhood of Philadelphia, especially of General Irvine, Colonel Marbury of Maryland, and Major Giles to whom he refers for a knowledge of his situation in Philadelphia should be released. It is ordered that the said Thomas Seon be kept under guard ... with this commitment in order that due inquiry may be made." Subsequently, on Sep 10, 1778, the Council recorded the following, in part: "In June last Mr.

Thomas Seon was sent from this State to Philadelphia ... Mr. Seon having returned hither and shewing a desire to go to the West Indies, the Council and I [Governor Johnson to General Arnold] have enquired of him whether he is not on paroll, but he says that his discharge was absolute and that you were fully satisfied by Major Giles and others, that the suspicions here entertained of him, were groundless ..." [Ref: E-139, E-198].

SHANIS(?), Mathew. Took the Oath of Allegiance in Somerset County in 1778 before the Hon. William Winder [Ref: T-22].

SHANKS, David. Drafted from Somerset County on June 20, 1781 to serve in the Continental Army and subsequently noted as "dead" (no date was given). [Ref: L-35C].

SHARP, Daniel. Private, Somerset Militia, Salisbury Bn., Capt. Josiah Dashiell's Wicomico Creek Co., 1778/1780 [Ref: M-218].

SHARP, George. Private, Somerset Militia, Salisbury Bn., Capt. Josiah Dashiell's Wicomico Creek Co., 1778/1780 [Ref: M-218 listed the name as "George Sharpe"]. Took the Oath of Allegiance in Somerset County in 1778 before the Hon. Gillis Polk [Ref: T-15, N-51].

SHAW, John. On Dec 19, 1782 the Council of Maryland ordered that John Shaw, Armourer, deliver to Col. Joseph Dashiell one barrel of musket powder and one ream of cartridge paper for the use of the militia of Worcester County [Ref: I-325].

SHEAR, John. Took the Oath of Allegiance in Worcester County in 1778 in Buckingham Hundred before the Hon. Thomas Purnell [Ref: J-1814 (Box 4)].

SHELLIAM(?), Edward. Took the Oath of Allegiance in Somerset County in 1778 before the Hon. William Winder [Ref: T-22].

SHELMAN, David. Took the Oath of Allegiance in Somerset County in 1778 [Ref: N-51].

SHELTON, William. Private, Somerset Militia, Princess Anne Bn., Capt. Thomas Irving's Monie Co., 1780 [Ref: M-219].

SHERMAN (SHURMAN), Charles. Took the Oath of Allegiance in Somerset County in 1778 before the Hon. William Winder [Ref: T-22 listed the name as "Charles Shurman" and N-52 mistakenly listed the name as "Charles Shensman"].

SHERMAN (SHERMON), Temperance. See "Jordan Parsons," q.v.

SHILES, John. Took the Oath of Allegiance in Somerset County in 1778 before the Hon. John Span Conway [Ref: T-14].

SHILES, Thomas. Adjutant, Somerset County Militia, 1775 [Ref: J-1814 (Box 1)].

SHIPHAM, George. Private, Somerset Militia, Princess Anne Bn., Capt. James Elzey's Co., 1780 [Ref: M-220]. Took the Oath of Allegiance in Somerset County in 1778 before the Hon. John Williams [Ref: T-21, and N-51 listed the name as "George Shipman"].

SHIPLEY, Robert. Private, 3rd Maryland Independent Co., Worcester County, Capt. John Watkins' Co., enlisted Feb 15, 1776; muster roll dated Aug 20, 1776, present for duty [Ref: D-21].

SHOCKLEY (SHOCKLY), Benjamin. Private, Worcester Militia, Wicomico Bn., Capt. James Perdue's Co., Third Class, July 15, 1780 [Ref: M-256]. See "George Truitt," q.v.

SHOCKLEY (SHOCKLY), Elijah. Private, Worcester Militia, Wicomico Bn., Capt. Elijah Shockley's Co., First Class, July 15, 1780 [Ref: M-255].

SHOCKLEY (SHOCKLY), Elijah. Captain, Worcester Militia, Wicomico Bn., May 15, 1776 to at least July 15, 1780 [Ref: M-121, A-405, A-466, C-351, M-255]. Took the Oath of Allegiance in Worcester County in 1778 before the Hon. William Hopewell [Ref: J-1814 (Box 4)].

SHOCKLEY (SHOCKLY), John. First Lieutenant, Worcester Militia, Wicomico Bn., Capt. James Perdue's Co., May 27, 1779 to at least July 15, 1780 [Ref: M-121, M-256, E-423].

SHOCKLEY (SHOCKLY), John (c1757-1827). Private, 3rd Maryland Independent Co., Worcester County, Capt. John Watkins' Co., enlisted April 8, 1776; muster roll dated Aug 20, 1776, sick in barracks [Ref: D-21]. Private, Worcester Militia, Wicomico Bn., Capt. Benjamin Dennis' Co., Second Class, July 15, 1780 [Ref: M-255]. Private, Maryland Line, who applied for a pension (S35066) in Somerset County on April 23, 1818, stating he enlisted at Snow Hill [Worcester County]; age 63 in 1820 [Ref: W-3119]. Another source stated he pensioned at $96 per annum effective April 23, 1818, age 70, and died on Feb 6, 1827 in Worcester County [Ref: X-44]. This could be the John Shockley who was a soldier in Capt. Long's Independent Co. of Regulars. On June 14, 1777 the Council of Maryland ordered that his "being made prisoner at the reduction of Fort Washington and discharged by the enemy ... and there being no prospect of a speedy exchange ... [he is] ... therefore discharged from the service of this State." [Ref: C-289].

SHOCKLEY (SHOCKLY), Jonathan. Private, Worcester Militia, Wicomico Bn., Capt. Samuel Horsey's Co., Fourth Class, July 15, 1780 [Ref: M-257]. Private, Worcester Militia, Wicomico Bn., Capt. Elijah Shockley's Co., Fourth Class, July 15, 1780 [Ref: M-255]. One took the Oath of Allegiance in Worcester County in 1778 before the Hon. William Hopewell [Ref: J-1814 (Box 4)]. One was a private in the Maryland line who was discharged on Dec 3, 1781 [Ref: I-11]. One Jonathan Shockley died in Georgia in 1837 [Ref: V-2654]. Since there were possibly two men with this name in the Maryland militia, additional research will be necessary before drawing conclusions.

SHOCKLEY, Lucy. See "Thomas P. Wimbro," q.v.

SHOCKLEY, Kerenhappuck. See "Solomon Hamblin," q.v.

SHOCKLEY, Peter. See "Thomas P. Wimbro," q.v.

SHOCKLEY (SHOCKLY), Richard. Took the Oath of Allegiance in Worcester County in 1778 before the Hon. Joshua Townsend [Ref: J-1814 (Box 4)].

Private, Worcester Militia, Wicomico Bn., Capt. Benjamin Dennis' Co., First Class, July 15, 1780 [Ref: M-255].

SHOCKLEY (SHOCKLY), Richard Jr. Took the Oath of Allegiance in Worcester County in 1778 before the Hon. Joshua Townsend [Ref: J-1814 (Box 4)].

SHOCKLEY (SHOCKLY), Sampson. Private, Worcester Militia, Wicomico Bn., Capt. Elijah Shockley's Co., Second Class, July 15, 1780 [Ref: M-255].

SHOCKLEY (SHOCKLY), Saul. Private, Worcester Militia, Snow Hill Bn., Capt. Ebenezer Handy's Co., April 9, 1776 [Ref: M-249]. Private, Worcester Militia, Wicomico Bn., Capt. Robert Handy's Co., Eighth Class, July 15, 1780 [Ref: M-254].

SHOCKLEY (SHOCKLY), Solomon (c1760-1823). Took the Oath of Allegiance in Worcester County in 1778 before the Hon. Joshua Townsend [Ref: J-1814 (Box 4)]. Private, Worcester Militia, Wicomico Bn., Capt. Benjamin Dennis' Co., Seventh Class, July 15, 1780 [Ref: M-256, V-2654].

SHOCKLEY (SHOCKLY), William. Took the Oath of Allegiance in Worcester County in 1778 before the Hon. Joshua Townsend [Ref: J-1814 (Box 4)]. Private, Worcester Militia, Wicomico Bn., Capt. Benjamin Dennis' Co., Seventh Class, July 15, 1780 [Ref: M-256]. William Shockley was born in Maryland, married Karenhappuch Carey, was a soldier in the revolution, and died circa 1798 in Maryland [Ref: V-2654].

SHORE, Alaner (Claner?). Private, Worcester Militia, Wicomico Bn., Capt. James Perdue's Co., Sixth Class, July 15, 1780 [Ref: M-256].

SHORES, Levin. Private, Somerset Militia, Princess Anne Bn., Capt. Thomas Irving's Monie Co., 1780 [Ref: M-219 mistakenly listed the name as "Levin Shone"]. On July 30, 1781 John Parker recruited Levin Shores from Somerset County to serve in the Continental Army until Dec 10, 1781 [Ref: L-35C].

SHORES, Thomas. Took the Oath of Allegiance in Somerset County in 1778 before the Hon. Levin Wilson [Ref: T-17, N-52].

SHOWELL, Bethewell. Private, Worcester Militia, Sinepuxent Bn., Capt. John Coe's Co., Seventh Class, 1779/1780 [Ref: M-252].

SHOWELL, Eli. Private, Worcester Militia, Sinepuxent Bn., Capt. John Coe's Co., Eighth Class, 1779/1780 [Ref: M-252].

SHOWELL, Elisha. Private, Worcester Militia, Sinepuxent Bn., Capt. Josiah Dale's Co., Seventh Class, 1779/1780 [Ref: M-254].

SHOWELL, John. Private, Worcester Militia, Sinepuxent Bn., Capt. John Coe's Co., Sixth Class, 1779/1780 [Ref: M-252].

SHOWELL, Lemuel. Private, Worcester Militia, Sinepuxent Bn., Capt. Josiah Dale's Co., Third Class, 1779/1780 [Ref: M-254].

SIBBEY (LIBBEY?, SILBEY?), John. Sergeant, Somerset Militia, Salisbury Bn., Capt. John Span Conway's Nanticoke Point Co., 1778/1780 [Ref: M-216].

SIMPSON, Drummond. Private, Somerset Militia, Salisbury Bn., Capt. Joseph Venables' Barren Creek Co., 1778/1780 [Ref: M-217].

SIMPSON, Kendall (Kendal). Private, Worcester Militia, Snow Hill Bn., Capt. Samuel Smyley's Co., 1777. Private, Worcester Militia, Wicomico Bn., Capt. Samuel Smyley's Co., Fourth Class, July 15, 1780 [Ref: M-250, M-259]. Took the Oath of Allegiance in Worcester County in 1778 before the Hon. Joshua Townsend [Ref: J-1814 (Box 4) listed the name as "Kendal Simson"].

SIMPSON, Southy. See "Horsey Summers," q.v.

SIMS (SIMMS), Joseph. Private, Somerset Militia, Princess Anne Bn., Capt. Isaac Handy's Great Annemessix Co., 1780 [Ref: M-221].

SIMS (SIMMS), Sally and Sarah. See "Smith Sims," q.v.

SIMS (SIMMS), Smith. Private, Somerset Militia, Salisbury Bn., White Haven Co., 1778/1780 [Ref: M-219]. Smith Simms, Sr., son of Thomas Simms, married Sarah ---- and died circa 1813 in Somerset County. Their daughter Sally Simms married Littleton Bloodsworth, Sr. on Dec 16, 1810 [Ref: S-2999A].

SIMS (SIMMS), Thomas. See "Smith Sims," q.v.

SKINNER, Thomas. First Lieutenant, Somerset Militia, Salisbury Bn., Capt. James Bennett's Co., May 27, 1779 [Ref: M-121, C-423].

SKIRVEN (SKIRVICE), Margaret. See "Denwood Wilson," q.v.

SLATTERY, Bartholomew. Ensign, Worcester Militia, Wicomico Bn., Capt. John Davis' Co., May 27, 1779 to at least July 15, 1780 [Ref: E-423, M-122 listed the name as "Bartholomew Slatony" and M-254 listed the name as "Battw. Slatter"]. Took the Oath of Allegiance in Worcester County in 1778 before the Hon. Nehemiah Holland [Ref: J-1814 (Box 4)].

SLOCOMB, Riley. Private, Worcester Militia, Wicomico Bn., Capt. Isaac Layfield's Co., Seventh Class, July 15, 1780 [Ref: M-257]. Took the Oath of Allegiance in Worcester County in 1778 before the Hon. James Selby [Ref: J-1814 (Box 4)].

SLOCOMB, Robert. Took the Oath of Allegiance in Worcester County in 1778 before the Hon. John Selby [Ref: J-1814 (Box 4)]. Private, Worcester Militia, Snow Hill Bn., Capt. John Parramore's Co., 1777 [Ref: M-250 listed the name as "Robert Slocam"].

SLOCOMB, Thomas. Private, Worcester Militia, Snow Hill Bn., Capt. John Parramore's Co., 1777 [Ref: M-250 listed the name as "Thomas Slocam"]. Private, Wicomico Bn., Capt. John Parramore's Co., Third Class, July 15, 1780 [Ref: M-259].

SLOCOMB, William. Private, Worcester Militia, Snow Hill Bn., Capt. John Parramore's Co., 1777 [Ref: M-250 listed the name as "William Slocam"]. Private, Wicomico Bn., Capt. John Parramore's Co., Sixth Class, July 15, 1780 [Ref: M-259].

SLONE, Samuel. Took the Oath of Allegiance in Somerset County in 1778 before the Hon. Peter Waters [Ref: T-18].

SLOSS, Mary Stoughton. See "Levin Winder," q.v.

SLOSS, Thomas (c1722-1797). Took the Oath of Allegiance in Somerset County in 1778 before the Hon. Levin Wilson [Ref: T-17, N-52]. Commissioned a

Judge of the Court of Appeals for Somerset County on May 23, 1778 [Ref: E-109]. Rendered patriotic service by supplying bacon for the use of the military on Aug 8, 1780 [Ref: P-308]. Thomas Sloss married Mary Stoughton (b. 1724), daughter of William Stoughton (1692-1759) of Monie Hundred, in 1750 [Ref: R-790].

SLOYD, Sally. See "Kemp Holder," q.v.

SMACK, Elizabeth. See "Henry Dennis," q.v.

SMALL, David. Took the Oath of Allegiance in Somerset County in 1778 (made his "X" mark) before the Hon. Peter Waters [Ref: T-18].

SMASHEY, James. See "James Smoshey," q.v.

SMITH, Abram. Private, 3rd Maryland Independent Co., Worcester County, Capt. John Watkins' Co., enlisted May 1, 1776; muster roll dated Aug 20, 1776, present for duty [Ref: D-23]. Took the Oath of Allegiance in Somerset County on Feb 27, 1778 before the Hon. Joseph Venables [Ref: T-25].

SMITH, Archabald. Private, Worcester Militia, Snow Hill Bn., Capt. Ebenezer Handy's Co., April 9, 1776 [Ref: M-249]. Ensign, Somerset Militia, Princess Anne Bn., Capt. Robert Handy's Co., Sep 22, 1777 to at least July 15, 1780 [Ref: M-122, M-254, C-381]. Ensign, Worcester Militia, Wicomico Bn., Capt. Robert Handy's Co., July 15, 1780 to March 12, 1781, resigned [Ref: M-122, M-254]. "Arch Smith" took the Oath of Allegiance in Worcester County in 1778 before the Hon. William Hopewell [Ref: J-1814 (Box 4)].

SMITH, Archibald. Private, Somerset Militia, Salisbury Bn., Capt. Levin Irving's Black Water Co., 1778/1780 [Ref: M-217].

SMITH, Ayrs. Took the Oath of Allegiance in Worcester County in 1778 before the Hon. Joshua Townsend [Ref: J-1814 (Box 4)].

SMITH, Benjamin. Private, Worcester Militia, Snow Hill Bn., Capt. Ebenezer Handy's Co., April 9, 1776 [Ref: M-249]. Took the Oath of Allegiance in Worcester County in 1778 before the Hon. Joshua Townsend [Ref: J-1814 (Box 4)].

SMITH, Christopher. See "Smith Christopher," q.v.

SMITH, Edward. Private, Somerset Militia, Princess Anne Bn., Capt. John Jones' Princess Anne Co., 1780 [Ref: M-219].

SMITH, Elijah. Private, Worcester Militia, Snow Hill Bn., Capt. Ebenezer Handy's Co., April 9, 1776 [Ref: M-249]. Private, Worcester Militia, Wicomico Bn., Capt. James Perdue's Co., Fifth Class, July 15, 1780 [Ref: M-256].

SMITH, Frederick. On July 30, 1781 John Riggen recruited Frederick Smith from Somerset County to serve in the Continental Army until Dec 10, 1781 [Ref: L-35C].

SMITH, George. Private, Worcester Militia, Wicomico Bn., Capt. James Perdue's Co., Eighth Class, July 15, 1780 [Ref: M-256].

SMITH, George. Sergeant, Worcester Militia, Snow Hill Bn., Capt. Ebenezer Handy's Co., April 9, 1776 [Ref: M-249]. Took the Oath of Allegiance in

Worcester County in 1778 before the Hon. William Hopewell [Ref: J-1814 (Box 4)].

SMITH, George (blacksmith?). Private, Worcester Militia, Wicomico Bn., Capt. Robert Handy's Co., Fifth Class, July 15, 1780 [Ref: M-254 listed the name as "George Smith BP (BS?)"].

SMITH, George (of George). Took the Oath of Allegiance in Worcester County in 1778 before the Hon. William Hopewell [Ref: J-1814 (Box 4)].

SMITH, Henry. Took the Oath of Allegiance in Somerset County in 1778 before the Hon. John Williams [Ref: T-21].

SMITH, Isaiah. Private, Worcester Militia, Snow Hill Bn., Capt. Ebenezer Handy's Co., April 9, 1776 [Ref: M-249].

SMITH, James. Private, Somerset Militia, Salisbury Bn., Capt. Joseph Venables' Barren Creek Co., 1778/1780 [Ref: M-217].

SMITH, James. Private, Somerset Militia, Salisbury Bn., Capt. John Span Conway's Nanticoke Point Co., 1778/1780 [Ref: M-216].

SMITH, James. Private, Worcester Militia, Wicomico Bn., Capt. James Patterson's Co., Eighth Class, July 15, 1780 [Ref: M-258].

SMITH, James. Took the Oath of Allegiance in Worcester County in 1778 before the Hon. John Selby [Ref: J-1814 (Box 4)].

SMITH, James Jr. Took the Oath of Allegiance in Worcester County in 1778 before the Hon. Nehemiah Holland [Ref: J-1814 (Box 4)].

SMITH, Jehu. Private, Worcester Militia, Wicomico Bn., Capt. Robert Handy's Co., First Class, July 15, 1780 [Ref: M-254].

SMITH, Jesse. Private, Worcester Militia, Sinepuxent Bn., Capt. John Coe's Co., Eighth Class, 1779/1780 [Ref: M-252]. Private, Worcester Militia, Wicomico Bn., Capt. John Davis' Co., Third Class, July 15, 1780 [Ref: M-254].

SMITH, John. Private, Worcester Militia, Snow Hill Bn., Capt. Ebenezer Handy's Co., April 9, 1776 [Ref: M-249]. Private, Worcester Militia, Sinepuxent Bn., Capt. Thomas Purnell's Co., First Class, 1779/1780 [Ref: M-253]. Private, Worcester Militia, Sinepuxent Bn., Capt. Matthew Purnell's Co., First Class, July 25, 1780 [Ref: M-252].

SMITH, John. Private, Somerset Militia, Salisbury Bn., Capt. William Turpin's Rewastico Co., 1778/1780 [Ref: M-217].

SMITH, John. Private, Somerset Militia, Salisbury Bn., Capt. Levin Irving's Black Water Co., 1778/1780 [Ref: M-218].

SMITH, John. Private, Somerset Militia, Salisbury Bn., Capt. Henry Gale's Quantico Co., 1778/1780 [Ref: M-216].

SMITH, John. Took the Oath of Allegiance in Worcester County in 1778 before the Hon. Joshua Townsend [Ref: J-1814 (Box 4)].

SMITH, John. Rendered patriotic service by supplying bacon for the use of the military in Somerset County on Sep 6, 1780 [Ref: P-315].

SMITH, John Jr. (1755 -   ). Private, Worcester Militia, Sinepuxent Bn., Capt. Thomas Purnell's Co., Fourth Class, 1779/1780 [Ref: M-253]. Private,

Worcester Militia, Sinepuxent Bn., Capt. Matthew Purnell's Co., Third Class, July 25, 1780 [Ref: M-252]. "John Smith, son of John and Mary Smith" was born in Coventry Parish on March 21, 1755. "John Smith, of John" took the Oath of Allegiance in Worcester County in 1778 before the Hon. Nathaniel Miller [Ref: J-1814 (Box 4)].

SMITH, John, Segr.*[sic]*. Took the Oath of Allegiance in Worcester County in 1778 before the Hon. Nathaniel Miller [Ref: J-1814 (Box 4)].

SMITH, John (of Purnell). Took the Oath of Allegiance in Worcester County in 1778 before the Hon. Nathaniel Miller [Ref: J-1814 (Box 4)].

SMITH, Joshua. Took the Oath of Allegiance in Somerset County in 1778 before the Hon. Levin Wilson [Ref: T-17, N-52]. Select Militia, Somerset County, Aug 15, 1781 [Ref: L-35B].

SMITH, Joshua Jr. Private, Somerset Militia, Princess Anne Bn., Capt. James Elzey's Co., 1780 [Ref: M-220].

SMITH, Levi. Private, Worcester Militia, Snow Hill Bn., Capt. Ebenezer Handy's Co., April 9, 1776 [Ref: M-249]. Private, Worcester Militia, Sinepuxent Bn., Capt. Matthew Purnell's Co., Eighth Class, July 25, 1780 [Ref: M-252].

SMITH, Levin. Private, Worcester Militia, Snow Hill Bn., Capt. Ebenezer Handy's Co., April 9, 1776 [Ref: M-249]. Private, Worcester Militia, Wicomico Bn., Capt. Robert Handy's Co., First Class, July 15, 1780 [Ref: M-254].

SMITH, Marshal. Took the Oath of Allegiance in Worcester County in 1778 before the Hon. William Hopewell [Ref: J-1814 (Box 4)].

SMITH, Mary. See "John Smith, Jr.," q.v.

SMITH, Milby. Private, Worcester Militia, Sinepuxent Bn., Capt. Matthew Purnell's Co., Second Class, July 25, 1780 [Ref: M-252].

SMITH, Purnell. Private, Worcester Militia, Sinepuxent Bn., Capt. Thomas Purnell's Co., Fifth Class, 1779/1780 [Ref: M-253].

SMITH, Richard. Private, Worcester Militia, Sinepuxent Bn., Capt. Thomas Purnell's Co., Fourth Class, 1779/1780 [Ref: M-253].

SMITH, Samuel. Private, Somerset Militia, Princess Anne Bn., Capt. James Elzey's Co., 1780 [Ref: M-220].

SMITH, Samuel. Private, Worcester Militia, Wicomico Bn., Capt. James Patterson's Co., Second Class, July 15, 1780 [Ref: M-258].

SMITH, Samuel. Private, Worcester Militia, Snow Hill Bn., Capt. Ebenezer Handy's Co., April 9, 1776 [Ref: M-249]. Private, Worcester Militia, Wicomico Bn., Capt. Robert Handy's Co., Seventh Class, July 15, 1780 [Ref: M-254].

SMITH, Solomon. Private, Worcester Militia, Wicomico Bn., Capt. Robert Handy's Co., First Class, July 15, 1780 [Ref: M-254].

SMITH, Sophia. See "John Adams," q.v.

SMITH, Thomas. Private, Somerset Militia, Salisbury Bn., Capt. John Span Conway's Nanticoke Point Co., 1778/1780 [Ref: M-216].

SMITH, Thomas. Private, Worcester Militia, Sinepuxent Bn., Capt. Matthew Purnell's Co., Fourth Class, July 25, 1780 [Ref: M-252].

SMITH, Thomas. Took the Oath of Allegiance in Worcester County in 1778 before the Hon. Joshua Townsend [Ref: J-1814 (Box 4)].
SMITH, Walter. Took the Oath of Allegiance in Worcester County in 1778 before the Hon. John Selby [Ref: J-1814 (Box 4)].
SMITH, William. First Lieutenant, Worcester Militia, Snow Hill Bn., Capt. James Patterson's Co., Aug 30, 1777 [Ref: M-123, C-351]. Took the Oath of Allegiance in Worcester County in 1778 before the Hon. William Hopewell [Ref: J-1814 (Box 4)].
SMITH, William. Private, Somerset Militia, Princess Anne Bn., Capt. Thomas Irving's Monie Co., 1780 [Ref: M-219]. Took the Oath of Allegiance in Somerset County in 1778 before the Hon. John Williams [Ref: T-21, N-52].
SMITH, William. Private, Worcester Militia, Wicomico Bn., Capt. John Davis' Co., Sixth Class, July 15, 1780 [Ref: M-254].
SMITH, William. Sergeant, Worcester Militia, Wicomico Bn., Capt. James Patterson's Co., July 15, 1780 [Ref: M-258].
SMOCK, Brittingham. Private, Worcester Militia, Sinepuxent Bn., Capt. John Rackliff's Co., Second Class, 1779/1780 [Ref: M-251].
SMOCK, Elizabeth. See "Henry Dennis," q.v.
SMOCK, Holland. Private, Worcester Militia, Wicomico Bn., Capt. William Handy's Co., Fourth Class, July 15, 1780 [Ref: M-257]. Took the Oath of Allegiance in Worcester County in 1778 before the Hon. William Hopewell [Ref: J-1814 (Box 4)].
SMOCK, John. Private, Worcester Militia, Sinepuxent Bn., Capt. Elisha Purnell's Co., First Class, 1779/1780 [Ref: M-253]. Took the Oath of Allegiance in Worcester County in 1778 in Quepomco Hundred before the Hon. Thomas Purnell [Ref: J-1814 (Box 4)].
SMOCK, John. Took the Oath of Allegiance in Worcester County in 1778 before the Hon. Joshua Townsend [Ref: J-1814 (Box 4)]. Rendered patriotic service by hauling corn for the use of the military on Sep 1, 1781 [Ref: P-432].
SMOCK, Kendall. Private, 3rd Maryland Independent Co., Worcester County, Capt. John Watkins' Co., enlisted Feb 3, 1776; muster roll dated Aug 20, 1776, present for duty [Ref: D-22]. "Kendal Smock who was of Long's Independent Co. having as appears by an affidavit lodged, procured a man to inlist in his room on or about the 14th day of April last which substitute was accepted and hath marched, he the said Kendal Smock is discharged" (proceedings of the Council of Maryland dated July 2, 1777). [Ref: C-306].
SMOCK, McKimmy (McKemmy). Private, Worcester Militia, Sinepuxent Bn., Capt. Thomas Purnell's Co., Second Class, 1779/1780 [Ref: M-253]. Took the Oath of Allegiance in Worcester County in 1778 before the Hon. Joshua Townsend [Ref: J-1814 (Box 4)].
SMOCK, Powell (Powel). Private, Worcester Militia, Sinepuxent Bn., Capt. John Postly's Co., Fourth Class, 1779/1780 [Ref: M-251]. Took the Oath of

Allegiance in Worcester County in 1778 before the Hon. Nathaniel Miller [Ref: J-1814 (Box 4)].

SMOCK, Stephen. Private, Worcester Militia, Sinepuxent Bn., Capt. John Rackliff's Co., Sixth Class, 1779/1780 [Ref: M-251]. Took the Oath of Allegiance in Worcester County in 1778 in Buckingham Hundred before the Hon. Thomas Purnell [Ref: J-1814 (Box 4)].

SMOCK, William. Took the Oath of Allegiance in Worcester County in 1778 before the Hon. Joshua Townsend [Ref: J-1814 (Box 4)].

SMOCK, William. Took the Oath of Allegiance in Worcester County in 1778 in Quepomco Hundred before the Hon. Thomas Purnell [Ref: J-1814 (Box 4)].

SMOSHEY (SMASHEY), James. Took the Oath of Allegiance in Worcester County in 1778 before the Hon. Joshua Townsend [Ref: J-1814 (Box 4)]. Private, Worcester Militia, Sinepuxent Bn., Capt. Thomas Purnell's Co., Fifth Class, 1779/1780 [Ref: M-253 listed the name as "James Smashey"].

SMULLEN (SMULLIN), Edmond. Private, Somerset Militia, Princess Anne Bn., Capt. James Elzey's Co., 1780 [Ref: M-220].

SMULLEN (SMULLIN), John. Private, Somerset Militia, Princess Anne Bn., Capt. John Jones' Princess Anne Co., 1780 [Ref: M-219].

SMULLEN (SMULLIN), Randall. Private, 3rd Maryland Independent Co., Worcester County, Capt. John Watkins' Co., enlisted Feb 13, 1776; muster roll dated Aug 20, 1776, present for duty [Ref: D-21 listed the name as "Randall Smulling"].

SMULLEN (SMULLIN), Saml(?). Private, Worcester Militia, Wicomico Bn., Capt. Charles Bennett's Co., Seventh Class, July 15, 1780 [Ref: M-255].

SMULLEN (SMULLIN), William. Private, Worcester Militia, Wicomico Bn., Capt. Samuel Horsey's Co., Sixth Class, July 15, 1780 [Ref: M-257].

SMULLEN (SMULLIN), William. Private, Worcester Militia, Wicomico Bn., Capt. Charles Bennett's Co., Sixth Class, July 15, 1780 [Ref: M-255].

SMULLEN (SMULLIN), William. Private, Somerset Militia, Princess Anne Bn., Capt. James Elzey's Co., 1780 [Ref: M-220].

SMYLEY, Samuel. Captain, Worcester Militia, Snow Hill Bn., Aug 30, 1777. Captain, Worcester Militia, Wicomico Bn., July 15, 1780 [Ref: M-123, M-250, M-258, C-351]. Took the Oath of Allegiance in Worcester County in 1778 before the Hon. Nehemiah Holland [Ref: J-1814 (Box 4) listed the name as "Capt. Samuel Smyly"].

SNEAD, Henry. Took the Oath of Allegiance in Worcester County in 1778 before the Hon. William Hopewell [Ref: J-1814 (Box 4)]. Private, Worcester Militia, Sinepuxent Bn., Capt. John Rackliff's Co., Fifth Class, 1779/1780 [Ref: M-251 listed the name as "Henry Sneed"].

SNEAD, John. Private, Worcester Militia, Wicomico Bn., Capt. Fisher Walton's Co., First Class, July 15, 1780 [Ref: M-258]. Took the Oath of Allegiance in Worcester County in 1778 before the Hon. Nehemiah Holland [Ref: J-1814 (Box 4)].

SNELLING, Acquilla. Private, Somerset Militia, Princess Anne Bn., Capt. John Jones' Princess Anne Co., 1780 [Ref: M-219].
SOCKWELL (SACKWELL), George. Private, Somerset Militia, Salisbury Bn., Capt. James Bennett's Salisbury Co., 1778/1780 [Ref: M-218]. Drafted from Somerset County into the Continental Army on June 20, 1781, but was subsequently excused [Ref: L-35C].
SOCKWELL (SACKWELL), Samuel. Took the Oath of Allegiance in Somerset County on Feb 28, 1778 (made his "X" mark) before the Hon. Joseph Venables [Ref: T-25].
SOMMORS, Catheron. See "Stephen Summers," q.v.
SOMMORS, Martha. See "Duke Riggen," q.v.
SOMMORS, Mary. See "Stephen Summers" and "Thomas Summers," q.v.
SOPER, John. Took the Oath of Allegiance in Somerset County in 1778 [Ref: N-52].
SPEER, Henry. See "William Speer," q.v.
SPEER, William (1759-c1856). Private, Worcester Militia, Wicomico Bn., Capt. James Perdue's Co., Second Class, July 15, 1780 [Ref: M-256]. One should also see the pension application of a William Speer (S11446) who served in North Carolina as an ensign in the Co. of his brother Capt. Henry Speer, stating he was born on the Eastern Shore of Maryland in 1758 and lived with his father (name not given) in Surry County, North Carolina at the time of his enlistment. William moved to Kentucky in 1801 and to Alabama in 1824. He applied for pension in Jackson County, Alabama on Feb 13, 1856, age 97 [Ref: W-3263].
SPENCE, Anna. See "John Purnell Robins," q.v.
SPENCE, George. Captain, Worcester Militia, Snow Hill Bn., Aug 30, 1777 [Ref: M-124, C-351]. Took the Oath of Allegiance in Worcester County in 1778 before the Hon. Joshua Townsend [Ref: J-1814 (Box 4)].
SPENCE, John. First Lieutenant, Worcester Militia, Snow Hill Bn., Capt. George Spence's Co., Aug 30, 1777 [Ref: M-124, C-351]. Took the Oath of Allegiance in Worcester County in 1778 in Bogerternorton Hundred before the Hon. Thomas Purnell [Ref: J-1814 (Box 4)]. Rendered patriotic service by supplying corn for the use of the military on July 10, 1780 [Ref: G-9].
SPENCER, John. Private, Somerset Militia, Princess Anne Bn., Capt. George Waters' Pocomoke Co., 1780 [Ref: M-220].
SPIRES, William. Private, Worcester Militia, Wicomico Bn., Capt. Isaac Layfield's Co., Seventh Class, July 15, 1780 [Ref: M-257].
STANFORD, David. Sergeant, Somerset Militia, Salisbury Bn., Capt. Josiah Dashiell's Wicomico Creek Co., 1778/1780 [Ref: M-218]. Took the Oath of Allegiance in Somerset County on Feb 21, 1778 before the Hon. Joseph Venables [Ref: T-25].
STANFORD, Jesse. Private, Worcester Militia, Wicomico Bn., Capt. Elijah Shockley's Co., Eighth Class, July 15, 1780 [Ref: M-255].

STANFORD, Jonathan. Private, Worcester Militia, Wicomico Bn., Capt. Charles Bennett's Co., First Class, July 15, 1780 [Ref: M-255].
STANFORD, Joshua. Private, Somerset Militia, Salisbury Bn., Capt. Josiah Dashiell's Wicomico Creek Co., 1778/1780 [Ref: M-218]. Joshua Stanford, Sr. was born in Maryland in 1740, married Mary Rookes [Fookes?], was a soldier in the revolution, and died in Georgia on May 1, 1826 [Ref: V-2774].
STANFORD, Nancy. See "Stephen Stanford," q.v.
STANFORD, Obediah. Private, Somerset Militia, Salisbury Bn., Capt. Henry Gale's Quantico Co., 1778/1780 [Ref: M-216]. Took the Oath of Allegiance in Somerset County on Feb 28, 1778 before the Hon. Joseph Venables [Ref: T-25].
STANFORD, Stephen (c1742-1805). Private, Worcester Militia, Wicomico Bn., Capt. Elijah Shockley's Co., Second Class, July 15, 1780 [Ref: M-255]. Stephen Stanford was born in Maryland circa 1742, married Nancy ----, served as a private in the revolution, and died in Georgia in 1805 [Ref: V-2774].
STANFORD, Thomas (1756-1795). Sergeant, Somerset Militia, Salisbury Bn., Capt. Henry Gale's Quantico Co., 1778/1780 [Ref: M-216]. Took the Oath of Allegiance in Somerset County on Feb 21, 1778 before the Hon. Joseph Venables [Ref: T-25]. Thomas Stanford was born on Dec 28, 1756, married Amelia (Milly) Disharoon, served as a sergeant in the revolution, and died on March 2, 1795 [Ref: V-2774].
STANFORD, William. Sergeant, Somerset Militia, Salisbury Bn., Capt. Henry Gale's Quantico Co., 1778/1780 [Ref: M-216]. Took the Oath of Allegiance in Somerset County in 1778 before the Hon. Levin Wilson [Ref: T-17, N-52].
STAPLES, Helen. See "Gowen Wright," q.v.
STARLING, Aaron. See "Aaron Sterling (of Aaron)," q.v.
STARLING, Captain. See "Horsey Summers," q.v.
STEEL, James. Took the Oath of Allegiance in Worcester County in 1778 before the Hon. Joshua Townsend [Ref: J-1814 (Box 4)].
STEPHENS, George. Private, Select Militia, Somerset County, Aug 15, 1781 [Ref: L-35B].
STEPHENS, Stephen. Took the Oath of Allegiance in Somerset County in 1778 before the Hon. William Winder [Ref: T-22].
STEPHENSON, William. Justice of the Peace for Worcester County, commissioned on Nov 29, 1777 [Ref: C-429].
STERLING, Aaron Sr. (1715 -   ). Took the Oath of Allegiance in Somerset County in 1778 before the Hon. John Williams [Ref: T-21, N-52]. On July 13, 1781 Aaron Sterling petitioned the Council for the Eastern Shore of Maryland through George Dashiell, County Lieutenant, who wrote that "Aaron Sterling is an inhabitant of Annimessix, Somerset County, and is now 66 years of age, that from the beginning of the present contest with Great Britain to the present day he has been a firm friend for the liberties and independence of America, that he was plundered last fall by the British barges and four times this spring

... his houses have been burnt and all the furniture ... he was also wounded, beat and bruised exceedingly ... he has been obliged to remove near seventeen miles from his plantation with his wife and children ... his son Josiah has lately been drafted, that in his present distressed situation his said son is of the greatest service to him ... please take the premises into consideration and discharge the said Josiah Sterling ..." On July 30, 1781 the Council replied that it was "not in our power to relieve him [and] ... advised to apply to General Smallwood ..." [Ref: J-1814 (Box 8, Dashiell's correspondence)]. See "Josiah Sterling," q.v.

STERLING, Aaron. Private, Somerset Militia, Salisbury Bn., Capt. Joseph Venables' Barren Creek Co., 1778/1780 [Ref: M-217]. Corporal, Somerset Militia, Salisbury Bn., Capt. Sampson Wheatly's Co., 1780 [Ref: M-215]. Sergeant, Somerset Militia, Princess Anne Bn., Capt. Henry Miles' Little Annemessex Co., 1780 [Ref: M-221].

STERLING, Aaron (of Aaron). Took the Oath of Allegiance in Somerset County in 1778 before the Hon. John Williams [Ref: T-21, and N-52 listed the name as "Aron Sterling of Aron"]. "Aaron Starling, son of Aaron and Easter Starling" was born in Coventry Parish on Jan 10, 1751 [Ref: Y-75].

STERLING, Aaron (of Henry). Corporal, Somerset Militia, Princess Anne Bn., Capt. Henry Miles' Little Annemessex Co., 1780 [Ref: M-221]. Aaron (Hickory) Sterling, son of Henry Sterling and Grace Toadvine (Todyvn), was born in May, 1738 and died testate by Aug 25, 1835 (date of probate; will was written on Oct 16, 1828) in Somerset County [Ref: S-3368].

STERLING, Easter. See "Aaron Sterling (of Aaron)," q.v.

STERLING, Ephraim (c1758-c1845). Private, Somerset Militia, Princess Anne Bn., Capt. Henry Miles' Little Annemessex Co., 1780 [Ref: M-221]. Ephraim Sterling was born circa 1758, married Esther Polk, served in the revolution, and died after Nov 4, 1845 [Ref: V-2794].

STERLING, Grace. See "Travers Sterling," q.v.

STERLING, Henry (1763-1856). Private, Somerset Militia, Princess Anne Bn., Capt. Henry Miles' Little Annemessex Co., 1780 [Ref: M-221]. Applied for a pension (R10019) in 1852, stating he was born in 1763 in Somerset County and lived there at the time of his enlistment [Ref: W-3318]. Henry Sterling married Mary Ward and died in 1856 [Ref: V-2794]. See "Aaron Sterling (of Henry)," q.v.

STERLING, John. Private, Somerset Militia, Princess Anne Bn., Capt. Henry Miles' Little Annemessex Co., 1780 [Ref: M-221].

STERLING, John. Private, Somerset Militia, Salisbury Bn., Capt. Sampson Wheatly's Co., 1780 [Ref: M-216]. Drafted from Somerset County on July 30, 1781 to serve in the Continental Army [Ref: L-35C].

STERLING, John. Private, Worcester Militia, Wicomico Bn., Capt. Isaac Layfield's Co., Third Class, July 15, 1780 [Ref: M-257].

STERLING, Joseph. Private, Somerset Militia, Salisbury Bn., Capt. Sampson Wheatly's Co., 1780 [Ref: M-216].

STERLING, Josiah. Private, Somerset Militia, Princess Anne Bn., Capt. Henry Miles' Little Annemessex Co., 1780 [Ref: M-221]. In July, 1781, Aaron Sterling, father of Josiah, contacted George Dashiell, County Lieutenant, requesting the discharge of his son for personal family reasons [Ref: J-1814 (Box 8, Dashiell's correspondence)]. See "Aaron Sterling," q.v.

STERLING, Littleton. Private, Somerset Militia, Princess Anne Bn., Capt. Henry Miles' Little Annemessex Co., 1780 [Ref: M-221 listed the name as "Lill. Sterling"].

STERLING, Southey. Private, Worcester Militia, Wicomico Bn., Capt. Isaac Layfield's Co., Third Class, July 15, 1780 [Ref: M-257].

STERLING, Travers (1740-c1826). Private, Somerset Militia, Princess Anne Bn., Capt. Henry Miles' Little Annemessex Co., 1780 [Ref: M-221 listed the name as "Traves Sterling"]. Travers Sterling was born on March 4, 1740, married Grace ----, served as a private in the revolution, and died after Feb 27, 1826 [Ref: V-2794].

STERN, James. Private, Somerset Militia, Salisbury Bn., Capt. Sampson Wheatly's Co., 1780 [Ref: M-216].

STEUART, William. Took the Oath of Allegiance in Somerset County in 1778 [Ref: N-52].

STEVENS, Anna. See "Levi Stevens," q.v.

STEVENS, Archibald. Private, Somerset Militia, Salisbury Bn., Capt. William Turpin's Rewastico Co., 1778/1780 [Ref: M-217].

STEVENS, Benjamin (c1751-1820). Private, Somerset Militia, Salisbury Bn., Capt. James Bennett's Salisbury Co., 1778/1780 [Ref: M-218]. Private, Maryland Line, who applied for a pension (R10138) in Somerset County in April, 1818, age 67, stating he had enlisted at Salisbury. Benjamin died on Feb 14, 1820 and his widow Priscilla (whom he married about 1797) died on April 7, 1821, leaving a son James who was born on July 17, 1799 and in 1857 lived in Somerset County [Ref: W-3320]. Another source stated he pensioned at $96 per annum effective April 21, 1818, age 69, and died on Feb 14, 1820 [Ref: X-41].

STEVENS, Betsy. See "Levi Stevens," q.v.

STEVENS, Betty. See "Denwood Wilson," q.v.

STEVENS, Daniel. Private, Worcester Militia, Wicomico Bn., Capt. John Parramore's Co., Third Class, July 15, 1780 [Ref: M-259].

STEVENS, Daniel (molato). Took the Oath of Allegiance in Worcester County in 1778 before the Hon. Nehemiah Holland [Ref: J-1814 (Box 4)].

STEVENS, David. See "Levi Stevens," q.v.

STEVENS, Eleanor. Rendered patriotic service by storing corn in Worcester County for the use of the military on Oct 10, 1780 and for rental of her house on Oct 15, 1780 [Ref: P-325, P-326].

STEVENS, Ephraim. First Lieutenant, Somerset Militia, Salisbury Bn., Capt. Josiah Dashiell's Wicomico Creek Co., Sep 22, 1777 to at least July 24, 1780

[Ref: M-125, C-382, and M-218 listed the name as "Epp. Stevens"]. Took the Oath of Allegiance in Somerset County in 1778 before the Hon. Peter Waters [Ref: T-18 listed the name as "Ephraim Stevans"]. Appointed as one of three Purchasers of Cattle in Somerset County for the use of the Continental Army on Jan 7, 1778 [Ref: C-456]. Rendered patriotic service by supplying beef for the use of the military on March 15, 1781 [Ref: P-370].

STEVENS, George. Private, Somerset Militia, Salisbury Bn., Capt. James Bennett's Salisbury Co., 1778/1780 [Ref: M-218]. Took the Oath of Allegiance in Somerset County in 1778 before the Hon. Gillis Polk [Ref: T-15, N-52].

STEVENS, Henry. See "Levi Stevens," q.v.

STEVENS, James. See "Benjamin Stevens," q.v.

STEVENS, John. Private, Worcester Militia, Sinepuxent Bn., Capt. John Rackliff's Co., Seventh Class, 1779/1780 [Ref: M-251]. Took the Oath of Allegiance in Worcester County in 1778 in Buckingham Hundred before the Hon. Thomas Purnell [Ref: J-1814 (Box 4) listed the name sa "John Stevence"].

STEVENS, John. Private whose name appeared on "a list of recruits from and deserters taken up in Somerset County on Oct 20, 1780" and noted as "deserter belonging to the Delaware State" [Ref: D-346].

STEVENS, John. See "Levi Stevens," q.v.

STEVENS, Josiah. See "Levi Stevens," q.v.

STEVENS, Joshua. Private, Worcester Militia, Sinepuxent Bn., Capt. John Rackliff's Co., First Class, 1779/1780 [Ref: M-251].

STEVENS, July. See "Levi Stevens," q.v.

STEVENS, Levi (1757-1834). Private, Somerset Militia, Salisbury Bn., Capt. James Bennett's Salisbury Co., 1778/1780 [Ref: M-218]. Private, Maryland Line, who applied for a pension in July, 1833 in Worcester County, stating he was born on June 1, 1757 and lived in Worcester County "during the revolution and afterwards." Levi died on Dec 16, 1834 and his widow Mary applied for a pension (W25147) on April 21, 1841, age 71. Her brother Josiah Furniss, age 67, on July 31, 1841, a resident of Somerset County, stated he was a son of William and Sarah Furniss who had 3 children: John (oldest child, died at age 14), Mary (2nd child), and Josiah (himself, the youngest). Mary Furniss married Levi Stevens in August, 1791 in Worcester County and a William and Littleton Furniss were at the wedding. The children of Levi and Mary Stevens were John (b. Dec 23, 1791, d. a minor), Sally (b. Aug 12, 1794), Anna (b. July --, 1796), William (b. Nov 21, 1797), David (b. Nov 6, 1799), Betsy (b. Oct 3, 1802), Susey (b. Nov 20, 1803), Josiah (b. Dec 20, 1805), July (b. Nov 10, 1808), and Henry (b. Dec 6, 1812). Priscilla Connelly, age 76, resident of Worcester County, also made an affidavit on May 13, 1841 [Ref: W-3326]. Levi Stevens was a pensioner of Maryland in Worcester County at $96 per annum effective April 17, 1818; dropped from roll under Act of May 1, 1820; reinstated at $80 per annum effective March 4, 1831 [Ref: X-52].

STEVENS, Littleton (molato). Took the Oath of Allegiance in Worcester County in 1778 before the Hon. Nehemiah Holland [Ref: J-1814 (Box 4)].
STEVENS, Major (molato). Took the Oath of Allegiance in Worcester County in 1778 before the Hon. Nehemiah Holland [Ref: J-1814 (Box 4)].
STEVENS, Mary. See "Jones Bounds" and "Levi Stevens," q.v.
STEVENS, Priscilla. See "Benjamin Stevens," q.v.
STEVENS, Sally. See "Levi Stevens," q.v.
STEVENS, Stephen. Private, Somerset Militia, Salisbury Bn., Capt. William Turpin's Rewastico Co., 1778/1780 [Ref: M-217].
STEVENS, William. First Lieutenant, Somerset Militia, Princess Anne Bn., Capt. George Waters' Pocomoke Co., Sep 22, 1777 to at least July 24, 1780 [Ref: M-125, C-381, M-220]. Justice of the Peace, commissioned on Nov 25, 1780 and Jan 17, 1782 [Ref: G-225, I-45].
STEVENS, William. Private, Somerset Militia, Salisbury Bn., Capt. John Span Conway's Nanticoke Point Co., 1778/1780 [Ref: M-216].
STEVENS, William. Took the Oath of Allegiance in Somerset County in 1778 before the Hon. Peter Waters [Ref: T-18]. He may be the William Stevens, of Coventry Parish, Somerset County, Maryland, who married "Winefrid Whitwell, daughter of Col. Thomas Whitwell, in Bartie County, North Carolina on May 15, 1760." [Ref: Y-90]. See "Levi Stevens," q.v.
STEVENSON, Adam. Took the Oath of Allegiance in Worcester County in 1778 before the Hon. Joshua Townsend [Ref: J-1814 (Box 4)].
STEVENSON, Benjamin. Ensign, Worcester Militia, Wicomico Bn., Capt. James Patterson's Co., July 15, 1780 [Ref: M-258]. Took the Oath of Allegiance in Worcester County in 1778 before the Hon. Nehemiah Holland [Ref: J-1814 (Box 4)]. Recommended for promotion to second lieutenant on Aug 4, 1780 "as there is a want of officers in Capt. Patterson's Co." [Ref: G-41].
STEVENSON, George. Private, Worcester Militia, Wicomico Bn., Capt. James Patterson's Co., First Class, July 15, 1780 [Ref: M-258]. Took the Oath of Allegiance in Worcester County in 1778 before the Hon. Nehemiah Holland [Ref: J-1814 (Box 4)].
STEVENSON, Hugh. Private, Worcester Militia, Wicomico Bn., Capt. William Handy's Co., Seventh Class, July 15, 1780 [Ref: M-257]. Took the Oath of Allegiance in Worcester County in 1778 before the Hon. Joshua Townsend [Ref: J-1814 (Box 4)]. Rendered patriotic services by processing beef for the use of the military in Worcester County in 1781 [Ref: P-349].
STEVENSON, James. Private, Worcester Militia, Wicomico Bn., Capt. William Handy's Co., Fourth Class, July 15, 1780 [Ref: M-257].
STEVENSON, James. Second Lieutenant, Worcester Militia, Wicomico Bn., Capt. James Patterson's Co., June 28, 1777, and First Lieutenant, July 15, 1780 [Ref: M-125, M-258]. Took the Oath of Allegiance in Worcester County in 1778 before the Hon. John Selby [Ref: J-1814 (Box 4)]. Rendered patriotic service

by butchering cattle for the use of the military on Oct 15, 1781 and also for conveying horses on Nov 8, 1781 [Ref: P-448, P-454].

STEVENSON, James Jr. Private, Worcester Militia, Sinepuxent Bn., Capt. Elisha Purnell's Co., Fourth Class, 1779/1780 [Ref: M-253].

STEVENSON, James Sr. Private, Worcester Militia, Sinepuxent Bn., Capt. Elisha Purnell's Co., Second Class, 1779/1780 [Ref: M-253].

STEVENSON, James (of Joseph). Son of Joseph and Rachel Stevenson, born in Coventry Parish on July 11, 1745 [Ref: Y-90]. Took the Oath of Allegiance in Worcester County in 1778 before the Hon. Nehemiah Holland [Ref: J-1814 (Box 4)].

STEVENSON, James (of Samuel Sr.). Took the Oath of Allegiance in Worcester County in 1778 before the Hon. Joshua Townsend [Ref: J-1814 (Box 4)].

STEVENSON, James (miller). Took the Oath of Allegiance in Worcester County in 1778 before the Hon. John Selby [Ref: J-1814 (Box 4)].

STEVENSON, James (Snow Hill). Took the Oath of Allegiance in Worcester County in 1778 before the Hon. Joshua Townsend [Ref: J-1814 (Box 4)].

STEVENSON, John. Took the Oath of Allegiance in Worcester County in 1778 before the Hon. Joshua Townsend [Ref: J-1814 (Box 4)].

STEVENSON, Jonathan. Ensign, Worcester Militia, Wicomico Bn., Capt. James Patterson's Co., June 28, 1777. Second Lieutenant, July 15, 1780 [Ref: M-125, M-258]. Took the Oath of Allegiance in Worcester County in 1778 before the Hon. Nehemiah Holland [Ref: J-1814 (Box 4)]. Recommended for promotion to first lieutenant on Aug 4, 1780 "as there is a want of officers in Capt. Patterson's Co." [Ref: G-41].

STEVENSON, Joseph. Sergeant, Worcester Militia, Wicomico Bn., Capt. James Patterson's Co., July 15, 1780 [Ref: M-258].

STEVENSON, Joseph Jr. Took the Oath of Allegiance in Worcester County in 1778 before the Hon. James Selby [Ref: J-1814 (Box 4)].

STEVENSON, Joseph Sr. Took the Oath of Allegiance in Worcester County in 1778 before the Hon. James Selby [Ref: J-1814 (Box 4)].

STEVENSON, Rachel. See "James Stevenson (of Joseph)," q.v.

STEVENSON, Samuel. Private, Worcester Militia, Wicomico Bn., Capt. Benjamin Dennis' Co., First Class, July 15, 1780 [Ref: M-255].

STEVENSON, William. First Lieutenant, Worcester Militia, Sinepuxent Bn., Capt. Samuel H. Round's Co., Aug 9, 1780 [Ref: M-125, F-2].

STEVENSON, William. Private, Worcester Militia, Sinepuxent Bn., Capt. John Rackliff's Co., Third Class, 1779/1780 [Ref: M-251].

STEVENSON, William. Took the Oath of Allegiance in Worcester County in 1778 in Buckingham Hundred before the Hon. Thomas Purnell [Ref: J-1814 (Box 4)]. Justice of the Peace for Worcester County, commissioned on Nov 21, 1778 [Ref: E-250].

STEVENSON, Zadock. Took the Oath of Allegiance in Worcester County in 1778 before the Hon. John Selby [Ref: J-1814 (Box 4)].

STEWARD, John. Attended the Maryland Convention in 1775, one of the representatives of Somerset County [Ref: O-4]. Commissioned by the Council of Maryland on Aug 19, 1779 to receive subscriptions for the Continental Loan Office [Ref: E-499].

STEWARD, William. Took the Oath of Allegiance in Somerset County in 1778 before the Hon. John Span Conway [Ref: T-14].

STEWART, Alexander. See "John Stewart," q.v.

STEWART, Jane. See "John Stewart," q.v.

STEWART, John (c1745-1794). Son of Alexander Stewart and Rebecca Dashiell. In 1767 he married his first cousin Elizabeth Dashiell (daughter of William Dashiell) and their children were Jane (b. 1771, d. young) and Alexander (1773-1810; captain). John served in the Lower House of the Maryland Legislature from Somerset County, 1777, 1782-1789; attended the Constitution Ratification Convention in 1788; Justice of the Peace, 1778-1782; Justice of the Orphans Court, 1778-1791; County Court Justice, 1777-1794; Commissioner of the Tax, 1781-1782; and, Agent for Purchasing Provisions for the U. S. Army in Somerset County, appointed March 25, 1778. First Major, Somerset Militia, 1st Bn., Jan 6, 1776. Lieutenant Colonel, Salisbury Bn., Aug 30, 1777, and 23rd Militia Regiment by 1794 [Ref: R-778, R-779, M-125, C-351, C-464, C-551, E-248, I-45]. Justice who administered the Oath of Allegiance in Somerset County in 1778 [Ref: T-19, N-52].

STEWART, John. Captain, Worcester Militia, Snow Hill Bn., Aug 30, 1777 to Feb 23, 1781, resigned [Ref: M-125, C-351]. Rendered patriotic service by supplying bacon for the use of the military on Aug 8, 1780 [Ref: P-308]. Took the Oath of Allegiance in Somerset County in 1778 before the Hon. Levin Wilson [Ref: T-17].

STEWART, John. Took the Oath of Allegiance in Worcester County in 1778 before the Hon. John Selby [Ref: J-1814 (Box 4)]. Rendered patriotic service by driving cattle for the military in Worcester County on Dec 20, 1781 [Ref: P-463].

STEWART, William. Private, Somerset Militia, Capt. George Day Scott's Co., 1775 [Ref: J-1814 (Box 1)]. Ensign, Somerset Militia, Salisbury Bn., Capt. John Span Conway's Nanticoke Point Co., Sep 22, 1777. Second Lieutenant, April 17, 1781. First Lieutenant, Aug 22, 1781 [Ref: M-126, M-216, C-381, G-575, J-1814 (Box 8, Dashiell's correspondence), H-195]. Appointed by the Council of Maryland to be Inspector of Tobacco on Wicomico River at the warehouse near Green Hill Town on Aug 30, 1780 [Ref: F-271].

STEWART, William. Private, Somerset Militia, Princess Anne Bn., Capt. John Jones' Princess Anne Co., 1780 [Ref: M-219].

STEWART, William. Private, Somerset Militia, Salisbury Bn., Capt. Joseph Venables' Barren Creek Co., 1778/1780 [Ref: M-217].

STEWART, William. Private, Somerset Militia, Princess Anne Bn., Capt. Thomas Irving's Monie Co., 1780 [Ref: M-219].

STEWART, William. Took the Oath of Allegiance in Somerset County in 1778 before the Hon. Peter Waters [Ref: T-18].
STILLEY, Ephraim. Private, 3rd Maryland Independent Co., Worcester County, Capt. John Watkins' Co., enlisted Feb 9, 1776; muster roll dated Aug 20, 1776 indicated "deserted 19 July" [Ref: D-22].
STOCKWELL, William. Private, Somerset County, Capt. John Gunby's 2nd Independent Maryland Co.; present on July 26, 1776; mustered on Aug 21, 1776 [Ref: D-642].
STONE, William. Took the Oath of Allegiance in Somerset County on Feb 21, 1778 before the Hon. Joseph Venables [Ref: T-25].
STOUGHTON, Mary. See "Thomas Sloss" and "Levin Winder," q.v.
STOUGHTON, Sarah. See "Levin Wilson," q.v.
STOUGHTON, William. See "Thomas Sloss," q.v.
STRAWBRIDGE, James. See "William Strawbridge," q.v.
STRAWBRIDGE, Mary. See "William Davis Allen," q.v.
STRAWBRIDGE, William (c1730-1796). Son of James Strawbridge and Jane Polk. He married (wife unknown) and had a daughter Jane who died by 1796. William served in the Lower House of the Maryland Legislature from Somerset County, 1777-1779, and was a trustee of Washington Academy in 1779 [Ref: R-791]. Rendered patriotic service by supplying pork for the use of the military on Aug 15, 1780 [Ref: P-309]. Took the Oath of Allegiance in Somerset County in 1778 before the Hon. Peter Waters [Ref: T-18]. "Dr. William Strawbridge" rendered patriotic service by supplying pork in Somerset County for the use of the military on June 4, 1781 [Ref: P-402]. See "John Brereton," q.v.
STRAWBRIDGE, William. Private, Somerset Militia, Princess Anne Bn., Capt. James Elzey's Co., 1780 [Ref: M-220].
STREETS, William. Private, 3rd Maryland Independent Co., Worcester County, Capt. John Watkins' Co., enlisted Feb 9, 1776; muster roll dated Aug 20, 1776, present for duty [Ref: D-23].
STUDER, Charles. Took the Oath of Allegiance in Somerset County in 1778 [Ref: N-52].
STURGIS, Abraham. Private, Worcester Militia, Wicomico Bn., Capt. Fisher Walton's Co., Fifth Class, July 15, 1780 [Ref: M-258]. Took the Oath of Allegiance in Worcester County in 1778 before the Hon. John Selby [Ref: J-1814 (Box 4)]. Rendered patriotic service by collecting cattle for the use of the military on Sep 25, 1781 [Ref: P-440 listed the name as "Abraham Sturges"].
STURGIS, Daniel. Private, Worcester Militia, Wicomico Bn., Capt. Samuel Smyley's Co., Third Class, July 15, 1780 [Ref: M-259]. Took the Oath of Allegiance in Worcester County in 1778 before the Hon. Joshua Townsend [Ref: J-1814 (Box 4) listed the name as "Daniel Stirgis"].

STURGIS, Elijah. Took the Oath of Allegiance in Worcester County in 1778 before the Hon. Joshua Townsend [Ref: J-1814 (Box 4) listed the name as "Elijah Stirgis"].

STURGIS, Elizabeth. See "Levin Sturgis," q.v.

STURGIS, Esther. See "Outten Sturgis, Sr.," q.v.

STURGIS, Jacob. Took the Oath of Allegiance in Worcester County in 1778 before the Hon. Nehemiah Holland [Ref: J-1814 (Box 4)].

STURGIS, John Sr. Took the Oath of Allegiance in Worcester County in 1778 before the Hon. Joshua Townsend [Ref: J-1814 (Box 4) listed the name as "John Stirgis, Sener"].

STURGIS, John. First Lieutenant, Worcester Militia, Wicomico Bn., Capt. Samuel Horsey's Co., Aug 30, 1777 [Ref: M-126, C-351]

STURGIS, John. Private, Worcester Militia, Wicomico Bn., Capt. Samuel Horsey's Co., Fourth Class, July 15, 1780 [Ref: M-257 listed the name as "John Stirgis"]. Rendered patriotic service by processing pork for the use of the military in Worcester County in 1782 [Ref: P-467 listed the name as "John Sturges"].

STURGIS, John (of Thomas). Took the Oath of Allegiance in Worcester County in 1778 before the Hon. Joshua Townsend [Ref: J-1814 (Box 4) listed the name as "John Stirgis, son of Thomas"].

STURGIS, John (Wicciomoco). Took the Oath of Allegiance in Worcester County in 1778 before the Hon. Nehemiah Holland [Ref: J-1814 (Box 4)].

STURGIS, John Outten. Second Lieutenant, Worcester Militia, Snow Hill Bn., Capt. Samuel Smyley's Co., Aug 30, 1777 [Ref: C-351, M-126, M-250 listed the name as "John Outton Sturgiss"]. Second Lieutenant, Worcester Militia, Wicomico Bn., Capt. Samuel Smyley's Co., July 15, 1780 [Ref: M-259]. Took the Oath of Allegiance in Worcester County in 1778 before the Hon. Joshua Townsend [Ref: J-1814 (Box 4) listed the name as "John Outten Stirgis"].

STURGIS, Joshua. Private, Worcester Militia, Wicomico Bn., Capt. Samuel Horsey's Co., Fourth Class, July 15, 1780 [Ref: M-257 listed the name as "Joshua Stirgiss"]. Took the Oath of Allegiance in Worcester County in 1778 before the Hon. William Hopewell [Ref: J-1814 (Box 4) listed the name as "Joshua Stirgis"]. Rendered patriotic service by supplying corn for the use of the military on March 7, 1780 and July 10, 1780 [Ref: P-274, G-10].

STURGIS, Joshua. Private, Worcester Militia, Snow Hill Bn., Capt. John Parramore's Co., 1777 [Ref: M-250 listed the name as "Joshua Stirgiss"]. Private, Worcester Militia, Wicomico Bn., Capt. John Parramore's Co., Fourth Class, July 15, 1780 [Ref: M-259].

STURGIS, Joshua. See "Isaac Houston," q.v.

STURGIS, Joshua Jr. Took the Oath of Allegiance in Worcester County in 1778 before the Hon. Joshua Townsend [Ref: J-1814 (Box 4) listed the name as "Joshua Stirgis, Juner"].

STURGIS, Joshua Sr. Took the Oath of Allegiance in Worcester County in 1778 before the Hon. William Hopewell [Ref: J-1814 (Box 4) listed the name as "Joshua Stirgis, Sener"].

STURGIS, Joshua (of Outten). Son of Outten Sturgis and Martha Purnell. Died by 1798 [Ref: R-793]. Private, Worcester Militia, Wicomico Bn., Capt. Fisher Walton's Co., Sixth Class, July 15, 1780 [Ref: M-258]. See "Outten Sturgis, Sr.," q.v.

STURGIS, Levin (c1743-c1820). Private, Worcester Militia, Snow Hill Bn., Capt. John Parramore's Co., 1777 [Ref: M-250 listed the name as "Levin Sturgiss"]. Sergeant, Worcester Militia, Wicomico Bn., Capt. John Parramore's Co., July 15, 1780 [Ref: M-259]. Took the Oath of Allegiance in Worcester County in 1778 before the Hon. John Selby [Ref: J-1814 (Box 4)]. Levin Sturgis was born circa 1743, married Elizabeth ----, was a sergeant in the revolution, and died after 1820 [Ref: V-2851].

STURGIS, Martha. See "Outten Sturgis, Sr." q.v.

STURGIS, Mary. See "Isaac Houston" and "Outten Sturgis, Sr.," q.v.

STURGIS, Outten Sr. (c1730-1796). He married first to Martha Purnell (d. 1794), daughter of John Purnell (d. c1742), and second to Sarah Atkinson Townsend (widowed twice) who may have been a daughter of William Cord. Children: Thomas Purnell, Joshua, Mary (Polly), Martha, and Esther. Outten served in the Lower House of the Maryland Legislature from Worcester County, 1778-1779; Committee of Observation, 1776; Commissioner of the Tax, 1777-1778; Judge of the Court of Appeals under the Act to Procure Troops, 1778; County Court Justice, 1787-1795; and, died testate by Oct 25, 1796 [Ref: R-793, A-457, and E-112 listed the name as "Outen Sturgis"]. Took the Oath of Allegiance in Worcester County in 1778 before the Hon. Nehemiah Holland [Ref: J-1814 (Box 4)]. Rendered patriotic service by supplying corn for the use of the military on March 8, 1780 and July 10, 1780 [Ref: G-10, P-274 listed the name as "Outton Sturgis"]. See "Benjamin Aydelott" and "Benjamin Gunby," q.v.

STURGIS, Outten. Private, Worcester Militia, Snow Hill Bn., Capt. Samuel Smyley's Co., 1777 [Ref: M-250]. Private, Worcester Militia, Wicomico Bn., Capt. Samuel Smyley's Co., First Class, July 15, 1780 [Ref: M-258 listed the name as "Outton Sturges"]. Took the Oath of Allegiance in Worcester County in 1778 before the Hon. John Selby [Ref: J-1814 (Box 4)].

STURGIS, Richard. Private, Worcester Militia, Snow Hill Bn., Capt. Samuel Smyley's Co., 1777 [Ref: M-250 listed the name as "Richard Sturgiss"]. Private, Worcester Militia, Wicomico Bn., Capt. William Handy's Co., Eighth Class, July 15, 1780 [Ref: M-258]. Private, Maryland Troops, Worcester County, draughted May 1, 1781 [Ref: K-99, D-372]. Took the Oath of Allegiance in Worcester County in 1778 before the Hon. John Selby [Ref: J-1814 (Box 4)].

STURGIS, Stephen. Private, Worcester Militia, Snow Hill Bn., Capt. John Parramore's Co., 1777 [Ref: M-250 listed the name as "Stephen Sturgiss"].

Took the Oath of Allegiance in Worcester County in 1778 before the Hon. Joshua Townsend [Ref: J-1814 (Box 4) listed the name as "Stephen Stirgis"].

STURGIS, Thomas. Private, Worcester Militia, Wicomico Bn., Capt. William Handy's Co., Seventh Class, July 15, 1780 [Ref: M-257]. Took the Oath of Allegiance in Worcester County in 1778 before the Hon. John Selby [Ref: J-1814 (Box 4)]. "Thomas Sturges" was a private in the 5th Maryland Line who enlisted on July 5, 1777 and was reported as "left out" in July, 1778 [Ref: D-244]. "Thomas Purnell Sturgis" died in 1782. See "Outten Sturgis, Sr.," q.v.

STURGIS, William. Private, Worcester Militia, Snow Hill Bn., Capt. Samuel Smyley's Co., 1777 [Ref: M-250 listed the name as "William Sturgiss"]. Sergeant, Worcester Militia, Wicomico Bn., Capt. Samuel Smyley's Co., July 15, 1780 [Ref: M-259].

STURGIS, William. Private, Worcester Militia, Wicomico Bn., Capt. John Parramore's Co., Second Class, July 15, 1780 [Ref: M-259 listed the name as "William Stirgis"].

STURGIS, William. Private, Worcester Militia, Wicomico Bn., Capt. Samuel Horsey's Co., Third Class, July 15, 1780 [Ref: M-256 listed the name as "William Stirgis"].

STURGIS, Zadock. Private, Worcester Militia, Sinepuxent Bn., Capt. William Purnell's Co., Eighth Class, 1779/1780 [Ref: M-252 listed the name as "Zadok Sturges"]. Rendered patriotic service by collecting cattle for the use of the military on Oct 25, 1781 [Ref: P-450 listed the name as "Zadock Sturges"].

SUDLAR, Thomas. Private, Select Militia, Somerset County, Aug 15, 1781 [Ref: L-35A].

SUMMERS, David. Private, Somerset Militia, Salisbury Bn., Capt. Sampson Wheatly's Co., 1780 [Ref: M-216]. See "Stephen Summers" and "Thomas Summers," q.v.

SUMMERS, Elias (1752 -   ). Son of Samuel and Elizabeth Summers, born in Coventry Parish on April 29, 1752 [Ref: Y-75]. Private, Somerset Militia, Princess Anne Bn., St. Asaph's Co., 1780 [Ref: M-221].

SUMMERS, Elizabeth. See "Horsey Summer" and "Elias Summers" and "Richard Summers," q.v.

SUMMERS, George. Private, Somerset Militia, Princess Anne Bn., Capt. John Williams' Watkins Point Co., 1780 [Ref: M-222].

SUMMERS, George. Private, Somerset Militia, Salisbury Bn., Capt. Sampson Wheatly's Co., 1780 [Ref: M-216].

SUMMERS, Horsey (1762-1852). Private, Maryland Line, who applied for a pension (S7664) in Accomack County, Virginia on Sep 12, 1851, age 89, stating he was born in Somerset County, Maryland and lived there at the time of his enlistment. Shortly after the war he moved to Accomack County where he was married [wife was Nancy Rew]. He died on Feb 25, 1852, leaving no widow, but these children: John, Horsey, Mary, Elizabeth, Sally, and William [Ref: W-3389, V-2854]. On Sep 20, 1851, Horsey Summers, age 89, stated he "served in the militia of Somerset County, Maryland from the time he was in his 15th year of age. They were frequently called out to keep guard and suppress the tories, who were frequently trying to discourage them by telling them that 'the British would take us and if they did we should all be hung.' On one occasion Col. Southy Simpson's Co. was ordered from the Virginia side to assist us in destroying the 'Tory Camp' where the tories all collected and were furnished with arms from the British, and in the engagement in which he took part the tories were routed and had to take to the British ships which were then lying in Tangier harbour to blockade the Pocomoke Sound. Colonel Gunbey had command of the militia. He said that he was a private in the various companies of Henry Miles, then Captain Starling, and last Capt. John Cox, and performed service and kept guard at Apes Hold, Summers Cove, and Miles Gum, which was the general place of meeting at which place he swore allegiance to his country against the King of Great Britain. He recollects his Captain Cox told his men to put their names to that paper or they deserved kicking out of the Co.. He was in service more than two years, off from all other employment. He was born in Somerset County, Maryland on the Virginia line and shortly after the close of the war he crossed over onto the Virginia side into Accomack County where he married and has resided ever since." [Ref: Stratton Nottingham's *Soldiers and Sailors of the Eastern Shore of Virginia in the Revolutionary War*, pp. 74-75]. See "Richard Summers," q.v.

SUMMERS, Jacob. Private, Somerset Militia, Princess Anne Bn., Capt. Henry Miles' Little Annemessex Co., 1780 [Ref: M-221].

SUMMERS, James. Private, Somerset Militia, Princess Anne Bn., Capt. Henry Miles' Little Annemessex Co., 1780 [Ref: M-221].

SUMMERS, Jemima. See "Charles Caton," q.v.

SUMMERS, John. Sergeant, Somerset Militia, Princess Anne Bn., Capt. Henry Miles' Little Annemessex Co., 1780 [Ref: M-221]. Select Militia, Somerset County, Aug 15, 1781 [Ref: L-35A listed the name as "John Somers"]. See "Horsey Summers," q.v.

SUMMERS, Jonathan. Private, Somerset Militia, Salisbury Bn., Capt. Sampson Wheatly's Co., 1780 [Ref: M-216].

SUMMERS, Lazarus. Private, Somerset Militia, Salisbury Bn., Capt. Sampson Wheatly's Co., 1780 [Ref: M-216]. See "Stephen Summers," q.v.

SUMMERS, Martha. See "Dukes Riggen," q.v.

SUMMERS, Mary. See "Horsey Summers" and Stephen Summers" and "Thomas Summers," q.v.

SUMMERS, Obadiah. Private, Somerset County, Capt. John Gunby's 2nd Independent Maryland Co.; present on June 26, 1776; mustered on Aug 21, 1776 [Ref: D-641].

SUMMERS, Richard (1759-1850). Private, Somerset Militia, Salisbury Bn., Capt. Sampson Wheatly's Co., 1780 [Ref: M-216]. Applied for a pension (S7663). His widow Elizabeth was first married to George Lewis, a Revolutionary soldier, on Nov 21, 1822 and he died on May 9, 1834. She next married Richard Summers in 1836 in Accomack County, Virginia and he died there on July 7, 1850. Richard had enlisted in Somerset County, Maryland and shortly after the war he moved to Accomack County, Virginia. His brother Horsey Summers served with him and also lived in Accomack County in 1851 [Ref: W-3390]. On Sep 29, 1851 Elizabeth Summers, widow of Richard Summers, made the following declaration. She stated "her former name was Elizabeth Lewis and she married Richard Summers and they lived as husband and wife until his death on 7 July past. She heard him speak of his services in the militia during the war; his brother Horsey Summers served with him. Her husband served, she believes, over two years. Her husband lived on the Virginia (Accomack Co.) - Maryland line during the Revolutionary War on the Maryland side and crossed over into Accomack and was married there by Rev. George H. Ewell and resided there until he died, in his 91st year. Certificate from Rev. Ewell, acquainted with Richard Summers for at least 60 years." [Ref: Stratton Nottingham's *Soldiers and Sailors of the Eastern Shore of Virginia in the Revolutionary War*, p. 74].

SUMMERS, Sally. See "Horsey Summers," q.v.

SUMMERS, Samuel. Took the Oath of Allegiance in Worcester County in 1778 before the Hon. Joshua Townsend [Ref: J-1814 (Box 4)]. See "Elias Summers," q.v.

SUMMERS, Solomon. Private, 5th Maryland Line, enlisted on May 6, 1778 and present for duty on Nov 1, 1780 [Ref: D-245].

SUMMERS, Stephen. Private, Somerset Militia, Princess Anne Bn., Capt. Henry Miles' Little Annemessex Co., 1780 [Ref: M-221]. One Stephen Sommors was the son of David and Mary Sommors, born in Coventry Parish on March 7, 1755, and another Stephen Sommors was the son of Lazarus and Catheron Sommors, born in Coventry Parish on June 1, 1758 [Ref: Y-89, Y-91]. Additional research will be necessary before drawing conclusions.

SUMMERS, Thomas (1762 -   ). Son of David and Mary Sommors *[sic]*, born in Coventry Parish on Feb 4, 1762 [Ref: Y-89]. Corporal, Somerset Militia, Princess Anne Bn., Capt. Henry Miles' Little Annemessex Co., 1780 [Ref: M-221].

SUMMERS, Thomas (1762 -   ). Son of Thomas Sommors *[sic]* and Ann Boston, born in Coventry Parish on Dec 11, 1762 [Ref: Y-89]. Private, Somerset Militia, Salisbury Bn., Capt. Sampson Wheatly's Co., 1780 [Ref: M-216].

SUMMERS, William. Private, Somerset Militia, Princess Anne Bn., Capt. George Waters' Pocomoke Co., 1780 [Ref: M-220]. See "Horsey Summers," q.v.

SURMAN, Charles. Private, Somerset Militia, Salisbury Bn., Capt. Henry Gale's Quantico Co., 1778/1780 [Ref: M-216].

SURMAN, George. Corporal, Somerset Militia, Salisbury Bn., Capt. Josiah Dashiell's Wicomico Creek Co., 1778/1780 [Ref: M-218].

SURMAN, Nicholas. Private, Somerset Militia, Salisbury Bn., Capt. Henry Gale's Quantico Co., 1778/1780 [Ref: M-216].
SWANSTON, Nicholas. Private, Somerset Militia, Salisbury Bn., Capt. John Span Conway's Nanticoke Point Co., 1778/1780 [Ref: M-216].
SWIFT, David. Private, 5th Maryland Line, enlisted on June 6, 1778 and discharged on March 1, 1779 [Ref: D-245].
SWIFT, Gideon. Private, 5th Maryland Line, enlisted on Sep 4, 1777 and reported as "left out" in April, 1778 [Ref: D-244].
SWIFT, Thomas. Took the Oath of Allegiance in Somerset County in 1778 before the Hon. Levin Wilson [Ref: T-17, N-52].
T----, Elizabeth. See "Pierce Dant Hamblen," q.v.
TALL, Levi. Took the Oath of Allegiance in Worcester County in 1778 before the Hon. Nathaniel Miller [Ref: J-1814 (Box 4)].
TAMSON, Black George. Took the Oath of Allegiance in Somerset County in 1778 (made his "X" mark") before the Hon. John Williams [Ref: T-21, N-52].
TARR, Azariah. Private, Worcester Militia, Wicomico Bn., Capt. John Parramore's Co., Eighth Class, July 15, 1780 [Ref: M-259].
TARR, Eleanor. See "John Tarr (of John)," q.v.
TARR, Eli. Private, Worcester Militia, Snow Hill Bn., Capt. John Parramore's Co., 1777. Private, Worcester Militia, Wicomico Bn., Capt. John Parramore's Co., Seventh Class, July 15, 1780 [Ref: M-250, M-259].
TARR, Eli Jr. Took the Oath of Allegiance in Worcester County in 1778 before the Hon. John Selby [Ref: J-1814 (Box 4)].
TARR, Eli (of Eli). Private, Worcester Militia, Wicomico Bn., Capt. Fisher Walton's Co., First Class, July 15, 1780 [Ref: M-258]. Took the Oath of Allegiance in Worcester County in 1778 before the Hon. Nehemiah Holland [Ref: J-1814 (Box 4) listed the name as "Elie Tarr, of Elie"].
TARR, Eli (of Michael). Private, Worcester Militia, Snow Hill Bn., Capt. Samuel Smyley's Co., 1777 [Ref: M-250].
TARR, Elijah. Private, Worcester Militia, Snow Hill Bn., Capt. Samuel Smyley's Co., 1777. Private, Worcester Militia, Wicomico Bn., Capt. Samuel Smyley's Co., Fifth Class, July 15, 1780 [Ref: M-250, M-259]. Took the Oath of Allegiance in Worcester County in 1778 before the Hon. John Selby [Ref: J-1814 (Box 4)].
TARR, Elisha. Private, Worcester Militia, Snow Hill Bn., Capt. Samuel Smyley's Co., 1777 [Ref: M-250]. Took the Oath of Allegiance in Worcester County in 1778 before the Hon. John Selby [Ref: J-1814 (Box 4)].
TARR, Israel. Private, Worcester Militia, Snow Hill Bn., Capt. John Parramore's Co., 1777. Private, Worcester Militia, Wicomico Bn., Capt. John Parramore's Co., Seventh Class, July 15, 1780 [Ref: M-250, M-259]. Took the Oath of Allegiance in Worcester County in 1778 before the Hon. John Selby [Ref: J-1814 (Box 4)]. See "John Tarr (of John)," q.v.

TARR, James. Private, Worcester Militia, Wicomico Bn., Capt. Philip Quinton's Co., First Class, July 15, 1780 [Ref: M-256]. Took the Oath of Allegiance in Worcester County in 1778 before the Hon. Joshua Townsend [Ref: J-1814 (Box 4)].

TARR, John. Three men by this name (in addition to the four John Tarr's listed below) took the Oath of Allegiance in Worcester County in 1778 before the Hon. John Selby [Ref: J-1814 (Box 4)].

TARR, John Jr. Private, Worcester Militia, Snow Hill Bn., Capt. John Parramore's Co., 1777. Private, Worcester Militia, Wicomico Bn., Capt. John Parramore's Co., First Class, July 15, 1780 [Ref: M-250, M-259].

TARR, John (of John). Took the Oath of Allegiance in Worcester County in 1778 before the Hon. John Selby [Ref: J-1814 (Box 4)]. John Tarr, son of John Tarr (d. 1730) and Mary Webb, was born between 1720 and 1730, married Sarah Holland and died testate in Worcester County by Jan 28, 1785, leaving children Israel Tarr, Nehemiah Tarr, Tabitha Bradford, Sarah Harper, and Eleanor Dewey Latchum. On Aug 15, 1780, John Tarr, Benjamin Holland and James Collins petitioned the Council of Maryland with a proposal to manufacture salt in Worcester County for the use of the State [Ref: G-48 indicated he made his "X" mark on the petition]. This is probably the John Tarr who married the aforementioned Sarah Holland. Their daughter Eleanor or Eleanora Tarr was born on Jan 30, 1770, married Macajah or Micajah Latchum on Jan 7, 1789, and he died March 30, 1827. She died on March 30, 1848 in Worcester County [Ref: *Maryland and Delaware Bible Records*, by Raymond B. Clark, Jr. (1990), p. 28; *Provincial Families of Maryland, Volume I*, by Vernon L. Skinner, ed. (1998), pp. 90-91, citing Worcester Wills Liber MH#27, ff. 284-285].

TARR, John (of Michael). Private, Worcester Militia, Snow Hill Bn., Capt. Samuel Smyley's Co., 1777 [Ref: M-250].

TARR, John (of Samuel). Private, Worcester Militia, Wicomico Bn., Capt. John Parramore's Co., Seventh Class, July 15, 1780 [Ref: M-259].

TARR, Joshua. Private, Worcester Militia, Wicomico Bn., Capt. John Parramore's Co., Fifth Class, July 15, 1780 [Ref: M-259].

TARR, Michael Jr. Private, Worcester Militia, Snow Hill Bn., Capt. John Parramore's Co., 1777 [Ref: M-250 listed the name as "Mickail Tarr, Jr."]. Took the Oath of Allegiance in Worcester County in 1778 before the Hon. John Selby [Ref: J-1814 (Box 4)].

TARR, Michael Sr. Took the Oath of Allegiance in Worcester County in 1778 before the Hon. Nehemiah Holland [Ref: J-1814 (Box 4)].

TARR, Michael (of Michael). Private, Worcester Militia, Wicomico Bn., Capt. John Parramore's Co., Third Class, July 15, 1780 [Ref: M-259].

TARR, Michael (of Samuel). Private, Worcester Militia, Snow Hill Bn., Capt. John Parramore's Co., 1777. Private, Worcester Militia, Wicomico Bn., Capt. John Parramore's Co., Fourth Class, July 15, 1780 [Ref: M-250, M-259].

TARR, Nehemiah. Private, Worcester Militia, Snow Hill Bn., Capt. John Parramore's Co., 1777. Private, Worcester Militia, Wicomico Bn., Capt. John Parramore's Co., First Class, July 15, 1780 [Ref: M-250, M-259]. Took the Oath of Allegiance in Worcester County in 1778 before the Hon. John Selby [Ref: J-1814 (Box 4)]. See "John Tarr (of John)," q.v.

TARR, Samuel Sr. Private, Worcester Militia, Snow Hill Bn., Capt. John Parramore's Co., 1777 [Ref: M-250]. Took the Oath of Allegiance in Worcester County in 1778 before the Hon. Joshua Townsend [Ref: J-1814 (Box 4)].

TARR, Samuel. Private, Worcester Militia, Wicomico Bn., Capt. Fisher Walton's Co., Fourth Class, July 15, 1780 [Ref: M-258].

TARR, Samuel (of Michael). Took the Oath of Allegiance in Worcester County in 1778 before the Hon. John Selby [Ref: J-1814 (Box 4)].

TARR, William. Private, Worcester Militia, Snow Hill Bn., Capt. John Parramore's Co., 1777. Private, Worcester Militia, Wicomico Bn., Capt. William Handy's Co., Third Class, July 15, 1780 [Ref: M-250, M-257]. Took the Oath of Allegiance in Worcester County in 1778 before the Hon. John Selby [Ref: J-1814 (Box 4)].

TAWS, John. See "John Laws," q.v.

TAYLO(?), William. Private, Somerset Militia, Salisbury Bn., Capt. Sampson Wheatly's Co., 1780 [Ref: M-216].

TAYLOR, Abraham. Private, Somerset Militia, Princess Anne Bn., Capt. John Jones' Princess Anne Co., 1780 [Ref: M-219]. Drafted from Somerset County on July 30, 1781 to serve in the Continental Army, but was subsequently excused [Ref: L-35C].

TAYLOR, Alexander. Private, Worcester Militia, Sinepuxent Bn., Capt. John Rackliff's Co., Third Class, 1779/1780 [Ref: M-251 listed the name as "Alexander Tayler"]. Took the Oath of Allegiance in Worcester County in 1778 before the Hon. Nathaniel Miller [Ref: J-1814 (Box 4)].

TAYLOR, Ann. See "William Adams" and "Charles Taylor," q.v.

TAYLOR, Barkley. Private, Somerset Militia, Salisbury Bn., Capt. Joseph Venables' Barren Creek Co., 1778/1780 [Ref: M-217].

TAYLOR, Bartholomew (1755 -   ). Private, Maryland Line, who applied for a pension (S31411) in Bracken County, Kentucky on May 19, 1834, stating he was born in Somerset County, Maryland on Feb 17, 1755 and lived there at the time of his enlistment in 1778. He moved to Kentucky in 1796 [Ref: W-3425, and A. W. Burns' abstracts on revolutionary soldiers of Maryland in Kentucky (p. 13) at the Maryland Historical Society].

TAYLOR, Belitha. Private, 3rd Maryland Independent Co., Worcester County, Capt. John Watkins' Co., enlisted Feb 5, 1776; muster roll dated Aug 20, 1776, present for duty [Ref: D-21].

TAYLOR, Bundick. See "Brittingham Henderson," q.v.

TAYLOR, Charles. Private, Worcester Militia, Sinepuxent Bn., Capt. John Coe's Co., Second Class, 1779/1780 [Ref: M-251 listed the name as "Charles

Tayler"]. In Worcester County Court, in November, 1796, a petition was submitted to divide the real estate of Charles Taylor who died possessed of a tract called *Turner's Hall* and left the following heirs at law: William Taylor (of full age), and Griffin, James, Fulton (listed as "Tulla W." in February, 1797), and Anne Taylor (minors). Hannah Taylor was appointed guardian to the minors in November, 1796, and Stephen Purnell was appointed guardian in February, 1797 [Ref: Article by William D. Patrick in *Maryland Magazine of Genealogy*, Vol. 4, No. 1 (Spring, 1981), p. 4].

TAYLOR, Coalburn. Private, Somerset Militia, Salisbury Bn., Capt. Sampson Wheatly's Co., 1780 [Ref: M-216].

TAYLOR, David. Private, Worcester Militia, Sinepuxent Bn., Capt. John Rackliff's Co., Fourth Class, 1779/1780 [Ref: M-251]. Took the Oath of Allegiance in Worcester County in 1778 before the Hon. Nathaniel Miller [Ref: J-1814 (Box 4)].

TAYLOR, David. Took the Oath of Allegiance in Worcester County in 1778 before the Hon. Nathaniel Miller [Ref: J-1814 (Box 4)].

TAYLOR, Dennis. Private, Somerset Militia, Princess Anne Bn., Capt. John Williams' Watkins Point Co., 1780 [Ref: M-222].

TAYLOR, Elias. Private, Worcester Militia, Wicomico Bn., Capt. William Handy's Co., Seventh Class, July 15, 1780 [Ref: M-257]. Took the Oath of Allegiance in Worcester County in 1778 before the Hon. Joshua Townsend [Ref: J-1814 (Box 4)].

TAYLOR, Elias. Took the Oath of Allegiance in Worcester County in 1778 before the Hon. John Selby [Ref: J-1814 (Box 4)].

TAYLOR, Elisha. Private, Somerset County, Capt. John Gunby's 2nd Independent Maryland Co.; present on May 22, 1776; mustered on Aug 21, 1776 [Ref: D-641]. Private, Worcester Militia, Snow Hill Bn., Capt. Samuel Smyley's Co., 1777 [Ref: M-250]. Took the Oath of Allegiance in Worcester County in 1778 before the Hon. Joshua Townsend [Ref: J-1814 (Box 4)].

TAYLOR, Ezekiel. Private, Somerset Militia, Salisbury Bn., Capt. William Turpin's Rewastico Co., 1778/1780 [Ref: M-217]. On June 20, 1781 Levin Wilson recruited Ezekiel Taylor from Somerset County to serve in the Continental Army for 3 years [Ref: L-35C].

TAYLOR, Frederick. Recruited from Somerset County "by the class" to serve in the Continental Army until Dec 10, 1781 [Ref: L-35C].

TAYLOR, Fulton. See "Charles Taylor," q.v.

TAYLOR, George. Private, Worcester Militia, Sinepuxent Bn., Capt. John Rackliff's Co., Second Class, 1779/1780 [Ref: M-251 listed the name as "George Tayler"].

TAYLOR, George. Private, Worcester Militia, Sinepuxent Bn., Capt. Thomas Purnell's Co., Sixth Class, 1779/1780 [Ref: M-253 listed the name as "George Tayler"].

TAYLOR, George. Took the Oath of Allegiance in Worcester County in 1778 before the Hon. Nathaniel Miller [Ref: J-1814 (Box 4)]. Private, Worcester Militia, Capt. John Martin's Co., 1780/1781 [Ref: J-1814 (Box 12)].
TAYLOR, Griffin. See "Charles Taylor," q.v.
TAYLOR, Hannah. See "Charles Taylor," q.v.
TAYLOR, Hessey. See "Nevil (Nevit) Taylor," q.v.
TAYLOR, Isaac. Private, Worcester Militia, Sinepuxent Bn., Capt. John Rackliff's Co., Second Class, 1779/1780 [Ref: M-251].
TAYLOR, Isaac. Private, Somerset Militia, Salisbury Bn., Capt. Joseph Venables' Barren Creek Co., 1778/1780 [Ref: M-217].
TAYLOR, Jacob. Private, Somerset Militia, Salisbury Bn., Capt. Joseph Venables' Barren Creek Co., 1778/1780 [Ref: M-217]. Drafted from Somerset County "by the class" on July 30, 1781 to serve in the Continental Army until Dec 10, 1781 [Ref: L-35C].
TAYLOR, Jacob. Private, Worcester Militia, Snow Hill Bn., Capt. John Parramore's Co., 1777 [Ref: M-250].
TAYLOR, James. See "Charles Taylor," q.v.
TAYLOR, Jehu. Private, Worcester Militia, Wicomico Bn., Capt. James Patterson's Co., Sixth Class, July 15, 1780 [Ref: M-258].
TAYLOR, Jeremiah. Took the Oath of Allegiance in Worcester County in 1778 before the Hon. James Selby [Ref: J-1814 (Box 4)]. Jeremiah Taylor married Mary Townsand in Coventry Parish on June 15, 1760 [Ref: Y-90].
TAYLOR, John. Private, Worcester Militia, Sinepuxent Bn., Capt. John Rackliff's Co., Sixth Class, 1779/1780 [Ref: M-251].
TAYLOR, John. Private, Worcester Militia, Wicomico Bn., Capt. Samuel Horsey's Co., First Class, July 15, 1780 [Ref: M-256].
TAYLOR, John. Private, Somerset Militia, Princess Anne Bn., Capt. George Waters' Pocomoke Co., 1780 [Ref: M-220].
TAYLOR, John. Private, Somerset Militia, Salisbury Bn., Capt. Joseph Venables' Barren Creek Co., 1778/1780 [Ref: M-217].
TAYLOR, John. Took the Oath of Allegiance in Worcester County in 1778 before the Hon. James Selby [Ref: J-1814 (Box 4)].
TAYLOR, John. Took the Oath of Allegiance in Worcester County in 1778 in Buckingham Hundred before the Hon. Thomas Purnell [Ref: J-1814 (Box 4)].
TAYLOR, John. Took the Oath of Allegiance in Worcester County in 1778 before the Hon. John Selby [Ref: J-1814 (Box 4)].
TAYLOR, Joseph. Private, Worcester Militia, Sinepuxent Bn., Capt. Matthew Purnell's Co., Sixth Class, July 25, 1780 [Ref: M-252]. Took the Oath of Allegiance in Worcester County in 1778 before the Hon. Nathaniel Miller [Ref: J-1814 (Box 4)].
TAYLOR, Joshua. Private, Worcester Militia, Snow Hill Bn., Capt. John Parramore's Co., 1777 [Ref: M-250]. Private, Worcester Militia, Wicomico Bn., Capt. John Parramore's Co., Sixth Class, July 15, 1780 [Ref: M-259].

TAYLOR, Joshua. Private, Somerset Militia, Salisbury Bn., Capt. Joseph Venables' Barren Creek Co., 1778/1780 [Ref: M-217]. Private, Somerset Militia, Princess Anne Bn., Capt. John Jones' Princess Anne Co., 1780 [Ref: M-219].

TAYLOR, Kendal. Private, Maryland Troops, Worcester County, draughted May 1, 1781 [Ref: K-99, D-372].

TAYLOR, Levin (1752-1827). Private, Virginia Line, who applied for a pension (S35058) in Worcester County on Sep 12, 1818, age 66, subsequently received $96 per annum, and died on Sep 3, 1827 [Ref: W-3435, X-44].

TAYLOR, Levin. Private, Somerset Militia, Princess Anne Bn., St. Asaph's Co., 1780 [Ref: M-221].

TAYLOR, Littleton. Private, Worcester Militia, Wicomico Bn., Capt. Isaac Layfield's Co., Fourth Class, July 15, 1780 [Ref: M-257]. "Littleton Tylor, son of Thomas and Jemima Tylor" was born in Coventry Parish on Feb 8, 1751 [Ref: Y-75].

TAYLOR, Matthias. Took the Oath of Allegiance in Worcester County in 1778 in Buckingham Hundred before the Hon. Thomas Purnell [Ref: J-1814 (Box 4)].

TAYLOR, Nancy. See "Brittingham Henderson," q.v.

TAYLOR, Nevil or Nevit or Knevit (c1754-c1833). Private, Virginia Line, who applied for a pension (S35094) in Worcester County, Maryland on April 10, 1818, age 65, but in 1820 he gave his age as 64 [Ref: W-3436 listed the name as "Nevil or Nevit or Knevit Taylor"]. "Nevil Taylor" received a pension in Worcester County of $96 per annum in 1818 [Ref: X-44]. "Knevit Taylor, soldier in the Virginia Continental Line in the Revolutionary War, died intestate; Hessey Taylor is his only heir at law. Selby Taylor, soldier in the Virginia Continental Line in the Revolutionary War, died intestate; Hessey Taylor is his only heir at law. 28 Jan 1834." (Court Orders, 1832-1836, p. 145). [Ref: Stratton Nottingham's *Soldiers and Sailors of the Eastern Shore of Virginia in the Revolutionary War*, p. 46].

TAYLOR, Obediah (Obed). Private, Worcester Militia, Snow Hill Bn., Capt. John Parramore's Co., 1777 [Ref: M-250]. Private, Worcester Militia, Wicomico Bn., Capt. John Parramore's Co., Fifth Class, July 15, 1780 [Ref: M-259]. Took the Oath of Allegiance in Worcester County in 1778 before the Hon. James Selby [Ref: J-1814 (Box 4)].

TAYLOR, Peter. Took the Oath of Allegiance in Somerset County in 1778 before the Hon. John Williams [Ref: T-21].

TAYLOR, Richard. Private, Worcester Militia, Snow Hill Bn., Capt. John Parramore's Co., 1777 [Ref: M-250]. Took the Oath of Allegiance in Worcester County in 1778 before the Hon. Joshua Townsend [Ref: J-1814 (Box 4)]. Rendered patriotic service by supplying beef for the use of the military on Sep 26, 1781 [Ref: P-441].

TAYLOR, Samuel. Corporal, Somerset Militia, Princess Anne Bn., Capt. John Jones' Princess Anne Co., 1780 [Ref: M-219].

TAYLOR, Samuel. Private, Somerset Militia, Princess Anne Bn., Capt. George Waters' Pocomoke Co., 1780 [Ref: M-220].
TAYLOR, Samuel. Took the Oath of Allegiance in Somerset County in 1778 before the Hon. Levin Wilson [Ref: T-17, N-52].
TAYLOR, Samuel Jr. Private, Worcester Militia, Sinepuxent Bn., Capt. John Rackliff's Co., Fourth Class, 1779/1780 [Ref: M-251 listed the name as "Samuel Tayler, Jr."].
TAYLOR, Samuel Sr. Took the Oath of Allegiance in Worcester County in 1778 before the Hon. Nathaniel Miller [Ref: J-1814 (Box 4)].
TAYLOR, Sarah Ann. See "William Adams," q.v.
TAYLOR, Selby. See "Nevil (Nevit) Taylor," q.v.
TAYLOR, Solomon. Private, 3rd Maryland Independent Co., Worcester County, Capt. John Watkins' Co., enlisted Feb 9, 1776; muster roll dated Aug 20, 1776, present for duty [Ref: D-21]. Private, Somerset Militia, Salisbury Bn., Capt. Josiah Dashiell's Wicomico Creek Co., 1778/1780 [Ref: M-218].
TAYLOR, Stephen. Private, Worcester Militia, Sinepuxent Bn., Capt. Matthew Purnell's Co., Sixth Class, July 25, 1780 [Ref: M-252 listed the name as "Stephen Tayler"]. Took the Oath of Allegiance in Worcester County in 1778 before the Hon. Nathaniel Miller [Ref: J-1814 (Box 4) listed the name as "Steven Taylor"].
TAYLOR, Stephen. Private, Somerset Militia, Salisbury Bn., Capt. Josiah Dashiell's Wicomico Creek Co., 1778/1780 [Ref: M-218].
TAYLOR, Thomas. Private, Worcester Militia, Snow Hill Bn., Capt. Ebenezer Handy's Co., April 9, 1776 [Ref: M-249]. Private, Worcester Militia, Wicomico Bn., Capt. Robert Handy's Co., Eighth Class, July 15, 1780 [Ref: M-254].
TAYLOR, Thomas. Sergeant, Worcester Militia, Wicomico Bn., Capt. John Parramore's Co., July 15, 1780 [Ref: M-259].
TAYLOR, Thomas. Took the Oath of Allegiance in Worcester County in 1778 before the Hon. John Selby [Ref: J-1814 (Box 4)].
TAYLOR, Tulla W. See "Charles Taylor," q.v.
TAYLOR, William. Private, Worcester Militia, Wicomico Bn., Capt. Isaac Layfield's Co., Eighth Class, July 15, 1780 [Ref: M-257].
TAYLOR, William. Private, Somerset Militia, Salisbury Bn., Capt. William Turpin's Rewastico Co., 1778/1780 [Ref: M-217].
TAYLOR, William. Private, Worcester Militia, Wicomico Bn., Capt. Elijah Shockley's Co., First Class, July 15, 1780 [Ref: M-255]. See "Charles Taylor," q.v.
TAYLOR, William. Second Lieutenant, Worcester Militia, Sinepuxent Bn., March 16, 1781 [Ref: M-128, G-353].
TAYLOR, William. Took the Oath of Allegiance in Somerset County in 1778 before the Hon. Peter Waters [Ref: T-18].
TAYLOR, William Sr. Private, Somerset Militia, Salisbury Bn., Capt. William Turpin's Rewastico Co., 1778/1780 [Ref: M-217].

TAYLOR, Zadock. Private, Somerset Militia, Salisbury Bn., Capt. Josiah Dashiell's Wicomico Creek Co., 1778/1780 [Ref: M-218].

TEAGUE, Jacob. Private, Worcester Militia, Sinepuxent Bn., Capt. William Purnell's Co., Seventh Class, 1779/1780 [Ref: M-252 listed the name as "Jacob Teage"]. Took the Oath of Allegiance in Worcester County in 1778 in Bogerternorton Hundred before the Hon. Thomas Purnell [Ref: J-1814 (Box 4)].

TEAGUE, Laban. Private, 3rd Maryland Independent Co., Worcester County, Capt. John Watkins' Co., enlisted Feb 9, 1776; muster roll dated Aug 20, 1776, present for duty [Ref: D-22].

TEAGUE, Samuel. Private, Worcester Militia, Snow Hill Bn., Capt. Samuel Smyley's Co., 1777 [Ref: M-250]. Took the Oath of Allegiance in Worcester County in 1778 before the Hon. James Selby [Ref: J-1814 (Box 4)].

TEBREW, Richard. Private, Somerset Militia, Salisbury Bn., Capt. William Turpin's Rewastico Co., 1778/1780 [Ref: M-217].

THOMAS, George. Private, Somerset Militia, Princess Anne Bn., Capt. James Elzey's Co., 1780 [Ref: M-220].

THOMAS, John J. (1760 -   ). Private, Maryland Line, who applied for a pension (S37488) in Bracken County, Kentucky on Feb 5, 1821, age 61, stating he was born on Somerset County, Maryland in 1760 and lived in Elkton [Cecil County], Maryland at the time of his enlistment on April 15, 1778. After the war he moved to Kentucky. His wife (name not given) died before 1821 at which time their children were Nancy and Priscilla (twins, age 17), Margaret (age 11), and William (age 14, a very sickly child). [Ref: W-3466, and A. W. Burns' abstracts on revolutionary soldiers of Maryland in Kentucky (p. 13) at the Maryland Historical Society].

THOMAS, Rachel. See "William Covington, Sr.," q.v.

THOMASON, Ezekiel (c1760-1824). Private, Maryland Line, who applied for a pension (S35100) in 1818 in Worcester County. In 1820 he stated he was aged 60 with a wife about age 50 and he had 2 girls and 5 boys "of which one lived at home age 13" [Ref: W-3470]. Another source stated he pensioned in Worcester County at $96 per annum effective April 29, 1818, age 64, and died on Aug 8, 1824 [Ref: X-44].

THOMPSON, James. First Lieutenant, Worcester Militia, Wicomico Bn., Capt. Elijah Shockley's Co., from Aug 30, 1777 to at least July 15, 1780 [Ref: C-351, M-129, M-255 listed the name as "James Thomson"]. Took the Oath of Allegiance in Worcester County in 1778 before the Hon. William Hopewell [Ref: J-1814 (Box 4) listed the name as "James Thomson"].

THOMPSON, Letitia. See "Minos Cannon," q.v.

TIGNAL, Southey. Took the Oath of Allegiance in Worcester County in 1778 before the Hon. William Hopewell [Ref: J-1814 (Box 4)]. Private, Worcester Militia, Wicomico Bn., Capt. Samuel Horsey's Co., Second Class, July 15, 1780 [Ref: M-256 listed the name as "Sothy Tignol"].

TILGHMAN, Aaron. Private, Somerset Militia, Princess Anne Bn., Capt. George Waters' Pocomoke Co., 1780 [Ref: M-220]. See "Samuel Tilghman," q.v.

TILGHMAN, Caleb. See "Samuel Tilghman," q.v.

TILGHMAN, Isaiah. Took the Oath of Allegiance in Somerset County in 1778 before the Hon. Peter Waters [Ref: T-18].

TILGHMAN, Jabez. Sergeant, Somerset Militia, Princess Anne Bn., Capt. James Elzey's Co., 1780 [Ref: M-220].

TILGHMAN, James. See "Samuel Tilghman," q.v.

TILGHMAN, John (1760-1848). Private, Worcester Militia, Capt. John Martin's Co., 1780/1781 [Ref: J-1814 (Box 12) listed the name as "John Tilman"]. He appears to have been the "John Tilghman, born 1760, made home here in 1782, born to him 6 sons and 4 daughters, died 1848" as inscribed on his tombstone in the John Tilghman Family Graveyard (of which his is the only tombstone recorded) on the east side of Johnson Schoolhouse Road, 1.2 miles south of the intersection with Layfield Road in Wicomico County [Ref: *Graveyards and Gravestones of Wicomico*, by John E. Jacob (1996), p. 59].

TILGHMAN, Joseph. Sergeant, Somerset Militia, Princess Anne Bn., Capt. James Elzey's Co., 1780 [Ref: M-220]. Took the Oath of Allegiance in Somerset County in 1778 before the Hon. John Williams [Ref: T-21, N-52].

TILGHMAN, Mary. See "Samuel Tilghman," q.v.

TILGHMAN, Samuel (1752-1796). Private, Worcester Militia, Wicomico Bn., Capt. Charles Bennett's Co., Seventh Class, July 15, 1780 [Ref: M-255]. "Samuel Tillman, son of Aaron and Hannah" was born in Coventry Parish on July 29, 1752, married Nancy Dreaden [Dryden], and died before March 11, 1796 [Ref: Y-75, V-2942]. In Worcester County Court, in November, 1796, a petition to divide the real estate of Samuel Tilghman was submitted by Sarah Tilghman (being of lawful age) and Caleb, Mary, and James Tilghman (minors), children and coheirs of Samuel Tilghman, their father, who died intestate and seized of tracts called *Porter's Security* and *Shockley's Purchase*. Thomas R. Handy was appointed guardian to the minors [Ref: Article by William D. Patrick in *Maryland Magazine of Genealogy*, Vol. 4, No. 1 (Spring, 1981), p. 4].

TILGHMAN, Sarah. See "Samuel Tilghman," q.v.

TILGHMAN, William. Private, Somerset Militia, Princess Anne Bn., Capt. Isaac Handy's Great Annemessix Co., 1780 [Ref: M-221].

TILLMAN, Aaron. See "Samuel Tilghman," q.v.

TILLMAN, Hannah. See "Samuel Tilghman," q.v.

TIMMONS, Benjamin. Private, Worcester Militia, Sinepuxent Bn., Capt. Matthew Purnell's Co., Fourth Class, July 25, 1780 [Ref: M-252].

TIMMONS, Elijah (1736-c1811). Private, Worcester Militia, Sinepuxent Bn., Capt. Matthew Purnell's Co., Fourth Class, July 25, 1780 [Ref: M-252]. Took the Oath of Allegiance in Worcester County in 1778 before the Hon. Nathaniel Miller [Ref: J-1814 (Box 4)]. Elijah Timmons was born on Sep 19, 1736, married Martha ----, served in the militia, and died before Sep 11, 1811 [Ref: V-2945].

TIMMONS, Elisha. Private, Worcester Militia, Wicomico Bn., Capt. John Davis' Co., Third Class, July 15, 1780 [Ref: M-254 listed the name as "Elisha Timons"].

TIMMONS, Isaac. Took the Oath of Allegiance in Worcester County in 1778 in Buckingham Hundred before the Hon. Thomas Purnell [Ref: J-1814 (Box 4)].

TIMMONS, Joseph. Private, Worcester Militia, Sinepuxent Bn., Capt. Matthew Purnell's Co., Seventh Class, July 25, 1780 [Ref: M-252].

TIMMONS, Levan. Took the Oath of Allegiance in Worcester County in 1778 before the Hon. Nathaniel Miller [Ref: J-1814 (Box 4)].

TIMMONS, Littleton. Private, Somerset Militia, Princess Anne Bn., Capt. Thomas Irving's Monie Co., 1780 [Ref: M-219 listed the name as "Lill. Timmons"].

TIMMONS, Martha. See "Elijah Timmons," q.v.

TIMMONS, Michael. Private, Somerset Militia, Princess Anne Bn., Capt. Thomas Irving's Monie Co., 1780 [Ref: M-219].

TIMMONS, Nehemiah. Private, Worcester Militia, Wicomico Bn., Capt. John Davis' Co., Fifth Class, July 15, 1780 [Ref: M-254].

TIMMONS, Samuel. Private, Worcester Militia, Sinepuxent Bn., Capt. Matthew Purnell's Co., Fifth Class, July 25, 1780 [Ref: M-252].

TIMMONS, Stephen. Private, Worcester Militia, Sinepuxent Bn., Capt. Matthew Purnell's Co., Fifth Class, July 25, 1780 [Ref: M-252].

TIMMONS, William. Private, Worcester Militia, Wicomico Bn., Capt. John Davis' Co., First Class, July 15, 1780 [Ref: M-254 listed the name as "William Timons"].

TIMMONS, Zadock. Private, 3rd Maryland Independent Co., Worcester County, Capt. John Watkins' Co., enlisted Feb 9, 1776; muster roll dated Aug 20, 1776, present for duty [Ref: D-22].

TINDALL, John. Private, Worcester Militia, Snow Hill Bn., Capt. John Parramore's Co., 1777 [Ref: M-250].

TINDALL, Nehemiah. Private, Somerset Militia, Princess Anne Bn., Capt. George Waters' Pocomoke Co., 1780 [Ref: M-220 listed the name as "Nehemiah Tindal"].

TINGLE, James. Private, Worcester Militia, Sinepuxent Bn., Capt. John Postly's Co., First Class, 1779/1780 [Ref: M-251].

TITTEL, Thomas. Private, Worcester Militia, Sinepuxent Bn., Capt. John Rackliff's Co., Fourth Class, 1779/1780 [Ref: M-251].

TOADVINE, Arnold (1755 -   ). Son of Thomas and Mary Todvine *[sic]*, born in Stepney Parish on Jan 29, 1755 [Ref: Y-45]. Private, Worcester Militia, Wicomico Bn., Capt. Samuel Horsey's Co., Fifth Class, July 15, 1780 [Ref: M-257]. Took the Oath of Allegiance in Worcester County in 1778 before the Hon. William Hopewell [Ref: J-1814 (Box 4)].

TOADVINE, Betty (Bettey). See "William Cottingham," q.v.

301

TOADVINE, Dixon. Took the Oath of Allegiance in Worcester County in 1778 before the Hon. John Selby [Ref: J-1814 (Box 4)].

TOADVINE, Grace. See "Aaron Sterling (of Henry)," q.v.

TOADVINE, Henry. Private, Worcester Militia, Wicomico Bn., Capt. Samuel Horsey's Co., Sixth Class, July 15, 1780 [Ref: M-257]. Took the Oath of Allegiance in Worcester County in 1778 before the Hon. William Hopewell [Ref: J-1814 (Box 4)].

TOADVINE, Henry. Took the Oath of Allegiance in Somerset County on Feb 28, 1778 (made his "O" mark) before the Hon. Joseph Venables [Ref: T-25].

TOADVINE, John. Private, Worcester Militia, Wicomico Bn., Capt. Samuel Horsey's Co., Sixth Class, July 15, 1780 [Ref: M-257]. Took the Oath of Allegiance in Worcester County in 1778 before the Hon. Joshua Townsend [Ref: J-1814 (Box 4)].

TOADVINE, Mary. See "Stephen Toadvine" and "Arnold Toadvine," q.v.

TOADVINE, Priscilla. See "William Toadvine," q.v.

TOADVINE, Stephen or Steven (1753 -   ). Son of Thomas and Mary Toadvine, born in Stepney Parish on Jan 18, 1753 [Ref: Y-42 listed the name as "Stevan Todvine"]. Private, Somerset Militia, Salisbury Bn., Capt. James Bennett's Salisbury Co., 1778/1780 [Ref: M-218]. Took the Oath of Allegiance in Somerset County on Feb 28, 1778 before the Hon. Joseph Venables [Ref: T-25].

TOADVINE, Thomas. See "Stephen Toadvine" and "Arnold Toadvine," q.v.

TOADVINE, William (c1760-1804). Private, Worcester Militia, Wicomico Bn., Capt. Samuel Horsey's Co., Second Class, July 15, 1780 [Ref: M-256]. William Toadvine was born circa 1760, married Priscilla Toadvine, served as a private in the war, and died before Dec 4, 1804 [Ref: V-2949, S-1445].

TOLCHETT, Thomas. See "Thomas Felchett (Fitchett)," q.v.

TOMERLSON(?), Samuel. Private, Somerset Militia, Princess Anne Bn., Capt. John Williams' Watkins Point Co., 1780 [Ref: M-222].

TOWNSEND, Absolom (of Joshua). Private, Worcester Militia, Wicomico Bn., Capt. Charles Bennett's Co., Second Class, July 15, 1780 [Ref: M-255].

TOWNSEND, Alexander. Private, Worcester Militia, Snow Hill Bn., Capt. Samuel Smyley's Co., 1777 [Ref: M-250].

TOWNSEND, Barkley or Bartley (c1737-1795). Son of Jeremiah Townsend and brother of "Joshua Townsend," q.v. Barkley or Bartley Townsend was born circa 1737, married Mary ----, and died on April 3, 1795 [Ref: R-838, V-2963]. First Lieutenant, Worcester Militia, Snow Hill Bn., Capt. John Stewart's Co., Aug 30, 1777. Captain, March 16, 1781 [Ref: M-130, C-351, G-353]. Took the Oath of Allegiance in Worcester County in 1778 before the Hon. Joshua Townsend [Ref: J-1814 (Box 4)].

TOWNSEND, Beletha. Private, Worcester Militia, Sinepuxent Bn., Capt. John Coe's Co., Second Class, 1779/1780 [Ref: M-251].

TOWNSEND, Charles. Private, Worcester Militia, Wicomico Bn., Capt. Philip Quinton's Co., Eighth Class, July 15, 1780 [Ref: M-256].
TOWNSEND, Charlotte. See "Joshua Townsend," q.v.
TOWNSEND, Danford. Took the Oath of Allegiance in Worcester County in 1778 before the Hon. John Selby [Ref: J-1814 (Box 4)]. Private, Worcester Militia, Wicomico Bn., Capt. Philip Quinton's Co., Seventh Class, July 15, 1780 [Ref: M-256]. See "William Townsend (of Danford)" and "Ephraim Townsend," q.v.
TOWNSEND, Daniel. Took the Oath of Allegiance in Worcester County in 1778 before the Hon. James Selby [Ref: J-1814 (Box 4) listed the name as "Dannel Townsen"].
TOWNSEND, Elias. Private, Worcester Militia, Wicomico Bn., Capt. Philip Quinton's Co., Fifth Class, July 15, 1780 [Ref: M-256].
TOWNSEND, Elijah. Private, Worcester Militia, Wicomico Bn., Capt. James Patterson's Co., Seventh Class, July 15, 1780 [Ref: M-258]. Took the Oath of Allegiance in Worcester County in 1778 before the Hon. James Selby [Ref: J-1814 (Box 4) listed the name as "Elijah Townsen"].
TOWNSEND, Elizabeth. See "William Townsend (of Danford)" and "Ephraim Townsend" and "Zadock Townsend," q.v.
TOWNSEND, Ephraim (1758 -   ). Son of Danford and Elizabeth Townsand, born in Coventry Parish on July 26, 1758 [Ref: Y-76]. Private, Worcester Militia, Wicomico Bn., Capt. Charles Bennett's Co., First Class, July 15, 1780 [Ref: M-255]. Took the Oath of Allegiance in Worcester County in 1778 before the Hon. Joshua Townsend [Ref: J-1814 (Box 4)].
TOWNSEND, Israel Jr. Private, Worcester Militia, Sinepuxent Bn., Capt. John Coe's Co., Seventh Class, 1779/1780 [Ref: M-252].
TOWNSEND, James. Private, Somerset County, Capt. John Gunby's 2nd Independent Maryland Co.; present for duty on July 15, 1776; discharged on Aug 21, 1776 [Ref: D-642].
TOWNSEND, James. Private, Worcester Militia, Wicomico Bn., Capt. Isaac Layfield's Co., Fourth Class, July 15, 1780 [Ref: M-257].
TOWNSEND, James. Private, Worcester Militia, Wicomico Bn., Capt. Robert Handy's Co., Second Class, July 15, 1780 [Ref: M-254]. Private, Worcester Militia, Capt. John Martin's Co., 1780/1781 [Ref: J-1814 (Box 12)].
TOWNSEND, James. Private, Worcester Militia, Wicomico Bn., Capt. Charles Bennett's Co., Eighth Class, July 15, 1780 [Ref: M-255].
TOWNSEND, James. Justice of the Peace for Worcester County, commissioned on Nov 29, 1777 and Nov 21, 1778 [Ref: C-429, E-250].
TOWNSEND, James. Second Lieutenant, Worcester Militia, Wicomico Bn., Capt. Philip Quinton's Co., July 6, 1776. First Lieutenant by July 15, 1780. Captain, March 16, 1781 [Ref: M-130, M-256, A-553, C-351, I-190].
TOWNSEND, James. Took the Oath of Allegiance in Worcester County in 1778 before the Hon. James Selby [Ref: J-1814 (Box 4) listed the name as "James Townsen"].

TOWNSEND, James (shoemaker). Took the Oath of Allegiance in Worcester County in 1778 before the Hon. John Selby [Ref: J-1814 (Box 4)].

TOWNSEND, James (of Danford). Took the Oath of Allegiance in Worcester County in 1778 before the Hon. Joshua Townsend [Ref: J-1814 (Box 4)].

TOWNSEND, Jemima. See "Levin Townsend," q.v.

TOWNSEND, Jeremiah. Private, Worcester Militia, Sinepuxent Bn., Capt. Matthew Purnell's Co., Eighth Class, July 25, 1780 [Ref: M-252]. Took the Oath of Allegiance in Worcester County in 1778 before the Hon. Nathaniel Miller [Ref: J-1814 (Box 4)].

TOWNSEND, Jeremiah Sr. (d. 1784). Took the Oath of Allegiance in Worcester County in 1778 before the Hon. John Selby [Ref: J-1814 (Box 4)]. See "Joshua Townsend," q.v.

TOWNSEND, John. First Lieutenant, Worcester Militia, Wicomico Bn., Capt. Benjamin Dennis' Co., June 21, 1776 to at least July 15, 1780 [Ref: A-506, M-130, and M-255 listed the name as "John Townsand"].

TOWNSEND, John. Private, Worcester Militia, Snow Hill Bn., Capt. Samuel Smyley's Co., 1777. Private, Worcester Militia, Wicomico Bn., Capt. Samuel Smyley's Co., Second Class, July 15, 1780 [Ref: M-250, M-259].

TOWNSEND, John. Private, Worcester Militia, Wicomico Bn., Capt. William Handy's Co., Seventh Class, July 15, 1780 [Ref: M-257]. Private, Worcester Militia, Capt. John Martin's Co., 1780/1781 [Ref: J-1814 (Box 12)].

TOWNSEND, John. Took the Oath of Allegiance in Worcester County in 1778 before the Hon. James Selby [Ref: J-1814 (Box 4) listed the name as "John Townsen"]. Rendered patriotic service by driving cattle for the military on Nov 30, 1781 [Ref: P-458].

TOWNSEND, John (of John). Took the Oath of Allegiance in Worcester County in 1778 before the Hon. Joshua Townsend [Ref: J-1814 (Box 4)].

TOWNSEND, Joshua (1744-1794). Son of Jeremiah Townsend (d. 1784). He married first to Nancy Brittingham and second to Mary Houston Purnell, widow of Matthew Purnell and daughter of James Houston. Children: Littleton, William Bartley, Charlotte, Nancy, and Sarah. Joshua served in the Lower House of the Maryland Legislature, 1784, 1792; Justice of the Peace, 1777-1782; Justice of the Orphans Court, 1779, 1782-1785; Sheriff of Worcester County, 1785-1788; Justice of the Court of Oyer and Terminer and Gaol Delivery, 1783; Collector of the Tax, 1786; and, County Court Justice, 1777-1784, 1791-1794. Second Lieutenant, Worcester Militia, Snow Hill Bn., Capt. William Handy's Co., Aug 30, 1777. Second Lieutenant, Wicomico Bn., Capt. William Handy's Co., July 15, 1780 [Ref: R-838, M-130, M-257, E-249, C-428, I-46, I-488]. Justice who administered the Oath of Allegiance in Worcester County in 1778 [Ref: J-1814 (Box 4)]. Rendered patriotic service by killing cattle and providing provisions for the use of the military in 1781 [Ref: P-349, P-442]. He died testate before Nov 24, 1794 [Ref: R-839].

TOWNSEND, Lazarous. Private, Worcester Militia, Snow Hill Bn., Capt. Samuel Smyley's Co., 1777 [Ref: M-250]. Took the Oath of Allegiance in Worcester County in 1778 before the Hon. John Selby [Ref: J-1814 (Box 4)].

TOWNSEND, Leah. See "Major Townsend," q.v.

TOWNSEND, Levin or Leven (1755 -   ). Son of William and Jemima Townsand, born in Coventry Parish on Aug 2, 1755 [Ref: Y-76]. Took the Oath of Allegiance in Worcester County in 1778 before the Hon. Joshua Townsend [Ref: J-1814 (Box 4)]. Private, Worcester Militia, Wicomico Bn., Capt. Benjamin Dennis' Co., Seventh Class, July 15, 1780 [Ref: M-256]. Rendered patriotic service by driving cattle for the military on Nov 30, 1781 [Ref: P-458].

TOWNSEND, Littleton. See "Joshua Townsend," q.v.

TOWNSEND, Major (c1750-1795). Son of Jeremiah Townsend and brother of "Joshua Townsend," q.v. Major Townsend married Leah ---- and died in 1795 [Ref: R-838]. Took the Oath of Allegiance in Worcester County in 1778 before the Hon. Joshua Townsend [Ref: J-1814 (Box 4)].

TOWNSEND, Margaret. See "John Cottingham," q.v.

TOWNSEND, Marshall. Private, Worcester Militia, Capt. John Martin's Co., 1780/1781 [Ref: J-1814 (Box 12)].

TOWNSEND, Mary. See "Jeremiah Taylor" and "Barkley Townsend," q.v.

TOWNSEND, Nancy. See "Joshua Townsend," q.v.

TOWNSEND, Rives. Private, Worcester Militia, Sinepuxent Bn., Capt. Matthew Purnell's Co., Fifth Class, July 25, 1780 [Ref: M-252].

TOWNSEND, Samuel. First Lieutenant, Somerset Militia, 1st Bn., Capt. John McClester's Co., May 15, 1776 [Ref: M-130, A-426].

TOWNSEND, Sarah. See "Joshua Townsend" and "Outten Sturgis" and "William Atkinson Selby," q.v.

TOWNSEND, Saul. Quartermaster, Worcester Militia, Capt. John Martin's Co., 1780/1781 [Ref: J-1814 (Box 12)].

TOWNSEND, Solomon. Private, Worcester Militia, Wicomico Bn., Capt. Charles Bennett's Co., Third Class, July 15, 1780 [Ref: M-255].

TOWNSEND, Solomon. Private, Worcester Militia, Wicomico Bn., Capt. Philip Quinton's Co., Seventh Class, July 15, 1780 [Ref: M-256]. See "Zadock Townsend," q.v.

TOWNSEND, Susannah. See "John Dashiell," q.v.

TOWNSEND, Thomas. Private, Worcester Militia, Sinepuxent Bn., Capt. Matthew Purnell's Co., Fifth Class, July 25, 1780 [Ref: M-252].

TOWNSEND, William. Private, Worcester Militia, Sinepuxent Bn., Capt. John Rackliff's Co., Fifth Class, 1779/1780 [Ref: M-251]. Private, Worcester Militia, Sinepuxent Bn., Capt. John Coe's Co., Third Class, 1779/1780 [Ref: M-252].

TOWNSEND, William. Private, Worcester Militia, Wicomico Bn., Capt. Charles Bennett's Co., Third Class, July 15, 1780 [Ref: M-255].

TOWNSEND, William. Private, Worcester Militia, Wicomico Bn., Capt. Charles Bennett's Co., First Class, July 15, 1780 [Ref: M-255].

TOWNSEND, William (of Danford). Took the Oath of Allegiance in Worcester County in 1778 before the Hon. Joshua Townsend [Ref: J-1814 (Box 4)]. "William Townsand, son of Danfort and Elizabeth Townsand" was born in Coventry Parish on Oct 13, 1754 [Ref: Y-75].

TOWNSEND, William (of Dickson). Private, Worcester Militia, Wicomico Bn., Capt. Charles Bennett's Co., Third Class, July 15, 1780 [Ref: M-255].

TOWNSEND, William. See "Levin or Leven Townsend," q.v.

TOWNSEND, William Bartley. Private, Worcester Militia, Capt. John Martin's Co., 1780/1781 [Ref: J-1814 (Box 12) listed the name as "Wm. Bart. Townsend"]. See "Joshua Townsend," q.v.

TOWNSEND, Zadock (1757 -   ). Son of Solomon and Elizabeth Townsand, born in Coventry Parish on June 23, 1757 [Ref: Y-76]. Private, Worcester Militia, Wicomico Bn., Capt. Philip Quinton's Co., Second Class, July 15, 1780 [Ref: M-256].

TRADER, Henry. Private, Somerset Militia, Salisbury Bn., Capt. James Bennett's Salisbury Co., 1778/1780 [Ref: M-218].

TRADER, James. Private, Somerset Militia, Salisbury Bn., Capt. Joseph Venables' Barren Creek Co., 1778/1780 [Ref: M-217].

TRADER, Richard. Private, Somerset Militia, Salisbury Bn., Capt. Levin Irving's Black Water Co., 1778/1780 [Ref: M-218].

TRADER, Staten. Private, Worcester Militia, Wicomico Bn., Capt. Fisher Walton's Co., Eighth Class, July 15, 1780 [Ref: M-258]. Took the Oath of Allegiance in Worcester County in 1778 before the Hon. Nehemiah Holland [Ref: J-1814 (Box 4)].

TRAIN, James. Private, Somerset Militia, Salisbury Bn., Capt. William Turpin's Rewastico Co., 1778/1780 [Ref: M-217].

TRAVERS, John. Private, Worcester Militia, Wicomico Bn., Capt. Samuel Smyley's Co., Eighth Class, July 15, 1780 [Ref: M-259]. Took the Oath of Allegiance in Worcester County in 1778 in Bogerternorton Hundred before the Hon. Thomas Purnell [Ref: J-1814 (Box 4)].

TREHEARN, Cyrus. Private, Somerset Militia, Princess Anne Bn., Capt. John Williams' Watkins Point Co., 1780 [Ref: M-222].

TREHEARN, James. Private, Somerset Militia, Princess Anne Bn., Capt. John Williams' Watkins Point Co., 1780 [Ref: M-222]. Took the Oath of Allegiance in Somerset County in 1778 before the Hon. Levin Wilson [Ref: T-17, N-52 listed the name as "James Trahearn"].

TREHEARN, Obediah (Obed). Private, Somerset Militia, Princess Anne Bn., Capt. John Williams' Watkins Point Co., 1780 [Ref: M-222]. Took the Oath of Allegiance in Somerset County in 1778 before the Hon. Peter Waters [Ref: T-18].

TREHEARN, Samuel. Private, Somerset Militia, Princess Anne Bn., Capt. John Williams' Watkins Point Co., 1780 [Ref: M-222].

TRUITT (TRUETT), Benjamin. Private, Worcester Militia, Sinepuxent Bn., Capt. William Purnell's Co., Sixth Class, 1779/1780 [Ref: M-252].

TRUITT (TRUETT), Ebenezer (Eben). Private, Worcester Militia, Wicomico Bn., Capt. John Davis' Co., Second Class, July 15, 1780 [Ref: M-254].

TRUITT (TRUETT), Eli (Ely). Private, Worcester Militia, Sinepuxent Bn., Capt. William Purnell's Co., Second Class, 1779/1780 [Ref: M-252]. Rendered patriotic service by driving cattle for the military on Nov 20, 1781 [Ref: P-456]. Took the Oath of Allegiance in Worcester County in 1778 in Bogerternorton Hundred before the Hon. Thomas Purnell [Ref: J-1814 (Box 4) listed the name as "Ely Trueitt"].

TRUITT (TRUETT), George Sr. Took the Oath of Allegiance in Worcester County in 1778 before the Hon. Joshua Townsend [Ref: J-1814 (Box 4) listed the name as "George Truett, Sener"].

TRUITT (TRUETT), George Sr. Took the Oath of Allegiance in Worcester County in 1778 before the Hon. Joshua Townsend [Ref: J-1814 (Box 4) listed the name as "George Truett, Sener"].

TRUITT (TRUETT), George Sr. Took the Oath of Allegiance in Worcester County in 1778 before the Hon. John Selby [Ref: J-1814 (Box 4)].

TRUITT (TRUETT), George. Private, 3rd Maryland Independent Co., Worcester County, Capt. John Watkins' Co., enlisted Feb 2, 1776; muster roll dated Aug 20, 1776, sick at his father's [Ref: D-22]. See "James Dale," q.v.

TRUITT (TRUETT), George. Private, Worcester Militia, Wicomico Bn., Capt. John Davis' Co., Fifth Class, July 15, 1780 [Ref: M-254].

TRUITT (TRUETT), George. Private, Worcester Militia, Wicomico Bn., Capt. James Perdue's Co., Second Class, July 15, 1780 [Ref: M-256].

TRUITT (TRUETT), George. Took the Oath of Allegiance in Worcester County in 1778 before the Hon. Joshua Townsend [Ref: J-1814 (Box 4)]. One George Truitt was commissioned Sheriff of Worcester County due to the resignation of Edward Vandome on Feb 3, 1781. It was reported to the Council of Maryland on Feb 11, 1781 that Sheriff Truett, while in "the collection of taxes, a certain Benjamin Shockley, an old offender, tryed all in his power to kill the sheriff, the other day, in the execution of his office, the sheriff has resigned his commission, I realy beleave for fear of losing his life, by sum of those enimyes to our country and its government." [Ref: H-63, H-64].

TRUITT (TRUETT), George (of Jacob). Private, Worcester Militia, Wicomico Bn., Capt. James Perdue's Co., Second Class, July 15, 1780 [Ref: M-256].

TRUITT (TRUETT) Henry. Private, Worcester Militia, Wicomico Bn., Capt. William Handy's Co., Sixth Class, July 15, 1780 [Ref: M-257]. Took the Oath of Allegiance in Worcester County in 1778 before the Hon. Joshua Townsend [Ref: J-1814 (Box 4)]. Rendered patriotic service by slaughtering beef for the use of the military on April 24, 1781 [Ref: P-386].

TRUITT (TRUETT), James. Private, 3rd Maryland Independent Co., Worcester County, Capt. John Watkins' Co., enlisted Feb 18, 1776; muster roll dated Aug

20, 1776, sick at his mother's [Ref: D-21]. Took the Oath of Allegiance in Worcester County in 1778 before the Hon. Joshua Townsend [Ref: J-1814 (Box 4)].

TRUITT (TRUETT), Jebediah. Private, Worcester Militia, Wicomico Bn., Capt. John Davis' Co., Seventh Class, July 15, 1780 [Ref: M-255].

TRUITT (TRUETT), Job. Took the Oath of Allegiance in Worcester County in 1778 before the Hon. Joshua Townsend [Ref: J-1814 (Box 4)].

TRUITT (TRUETT), John Jr. Took the Oath of Allegiance in Worcester County in 1778 before the Hon. Joshua Townsend [Ref: J-1814 (Box 4) listed the name as "John Truett, Juner"].

TRUITT, Martha. See "James Dale," q.v.

TRUITT (TRUETT), Nehemiah (1757 -   ). Private, Worcester Militia, Sinepuxent Bn., Capt. John Postly's Co., Fifth Class, 1779/1780 [Ref: M-251]. Took the Oath of Allegiance in Worcester County in 1778 before the Hon. Nathaniel Miller [Ref: J-1814 (Box 4) listed the name as "Nemiah Truit"]. Born in Worcester Parish on Feb 13, 1757 [Ref: Y-28].

TRUITT (TRUETT), Outton. Private, Worcester Militia, Sinepuxent Bn., Capt. Elisha Purnell's Co., Third Class, 1779/1780 [Ref: M-253]. Took the Oath of Allegiance in Worcester County in 1778 in Quepomco Hundred before the Hon. Thomas Purnell [Ref: J-1814 (Box 4) listed the name as "Outten Trueitt"].

TRUITT (TRUETT), Patty Jr. Took the Oath of Allegiance in Worcester County in 1778 before the Hon. Joshua Townsend [Ref: J-1814 (Box 4) listed the name as "Patey Truett, Juner"].

TRUITT (TRUETT), Patty. Private, Worcester Militia, Sinepuxent Bn., Capt. Matthew Purnell's Co., Fifth Class, July 25, 1780 [Ref: M-252].

TRUITT (TRUETT), Purnall (1757-1838). Born in Worcester County on Feb 26, 1757, married first to Polly Godfrey, second to Rachael Render, served as a private in Delaware during the revolution, and died before September, 1838 in Georgia [Ref: V-2982].

TRUITT (TRUETT), Rounds. Private, Worcester Militia, Sinepuxent Bn., Capt. William Purnell's Co., Seventh Class, 1779/1780 [Ref: M-252]. Took the Oath of Allegiance in Worcester County in 1778 in Bogerternorton Hundred before the Hon. Thomas Purnell [Ref: J-1814 (Box 4) listed the name as "Rownd Truett"].

TRUITT (TRUETT), Samuel. Private, 3rd Maryland Independent Co., Worcester County, Capt. John Watkins' Co., enlisted April 1, 1776; muster roll dated Aug 20, 1776, present for duty [Ref: D-22]. Took the Oath of Allegiance in Worcester County in 1778 before the Hon. John Selby [Ref: J-1814 (Box 4)].

TRUITT (TRUETT), Samuel Jr. Took the Oath of Allegiance in Worcester County in 1778 before the Hon. Joshua Townsend [Ref: J-1814 (Box 4) listed the name as "Samuel Truett, Juner"].

TRUITT (TRUETT), Samuel (of G.). Private, Worcester Militia, Wicomico Bn., Capt. John Davis' Co., First Class, July 15, 1780 [Ref: M-254].

TRUITT (TRUETT), Thomas. Private, Worcester Militia, Wicomico Bn., Capt. James Perdue's Co., Fourth Class, July 15, 1780 [Ref: M-256].
TRUITT (TRUETT), William. Private, Worcester Militia, Sinepuxent Bn., Capt. John Postly's Co., Second Class, 1779/1780 [Ref: M-251].
TRUITT (TRUETT), William. Took the Oath of Allegiance in Worcester County in 1778 before the Hon. Nathaniel Miller [Ref: J-1814 (Box 4) listed the name as "William Trewit"].
TRUITT (TRUETT), William. Took the Oath of Allegiance in Worcester County in 1778 in Bogerternorton Hundred before the Hon. Thomas Purnell [Ref: J-1814 (Box 4) listed the name as "William Trueitt"].
TRUITT (TRUETT), William. Took the Oath of Allegiance in Worcester County in 1778 in Bogerternorton Hundred before the Hon. Thomas Purnell [Ref: J-1814 (Box 4) listed the name as "William Trueitt"].
TRUITT (TRUETT), William Sr. Private, Worcester Militia, Sinepuxent Bn., Capt. William Purnell's Co., Sixth Class, 1779/1780 [Ref: M-252].
TRUITT (TRUETT), William Jr. Private, Worcester Militia, Sinepuxent Bn., Capt. William Purnell's Co., First Class, 1779/1780 [Ref: M-252].
TRUITT (TRUETT), William Powell. Private, Worcester Militia, Sinepuxent Bn., Capt. Matthew Purnell's Co., First Class, July 25, 1780 [Ref: M-252]. Took the Oath of Allegiance in Worcester County in 1778 before the Hon. Nathaniel Miller [Ref: J-1814 (Box 4) listed the name as "William Powel Trewit"].
TUBES, James. See "John Tubbs" and "Joseph Tubbs," q.v.
TUBES, Levinah. See "John Tubbs" and "Joseph Tubbs," q.v.
TUBBS, David. Private, Worcester Militia, Sinepuxent Bn., Capt. John Coe's Co., Sixth Class, 1779/1780 [Ref: M-252].
TUBBS, Henry. See "Thomas P. Wimbro," q.v.
TUBBS (TUBES), John. Private, Worcester Militia, Sinepuxent Bn., Capt. John Rackliff's Co., First Class, 1779/1780 [Ref: M-251]. John Tubes, son of James and Levinah Tubes, was born in Worcester Parish on Feb 1, 1757 [Ref: Y-29].
TUBBS (TUBES), Joseph. Private, Worcester Militia, Sinepuxent Bn., Capt. John Rackliff's Co., Third Class, 1779/1780 [Ref: M-251]. Joseph Tubes, son of James and Levinah Tubes, was born in Worcester Parish on Sep 27, 1762 [Ref: Y-29].
TUBBS, Sarah. See "Thomas P. Wimbro," q.v.
TULL, Benjamin. Private, Worcester Militia, Wicomico Bn., Capt. Fisher Walton's Co., Fifth Class, July 15, 1780 [Ref: M-258]. Took the Oath of Allegiance in Worcester County in 1778 before the Hon. Nehemiah Holland [Ref: J-1814 (Box 4)].
TULL, Eleanor. See "Handy Tull," q.v.
TULL, Elijah. Took the Oath of Allegiance in Somerset County in 1778 before the Hon. Peter Waters [Ref: T-18].
TULL, George. Ensign, Somerset Militia, 1st Bn., Capt. Robert Hitch's Co., commissioned April 11, 1776 [Ref: M-131, A-327].

TULL, George. Private, Somerset Militia, Salisbury Bn., Capt. Henry Gale's Quantico Co., 1778/1780 [Ref: M-216]. Private, Somerset Militia, Princess Anne Bn., Capt. Isaac Handy's Great Annemessix Co., 1780 [Ref: M-221]. Drafted from Somerset County into the Continental Army on June 20, 1781, but was subsequently excused [Ref: L-35C].

TULL, Handy. Private, Worcester Militia, Wicomico Bn., Capt. Isaac Layfield's Co., First Class, July 15, 1780 [Ref: M-257]. Handy Tull was born in Maryland, married Eleanor ----, served in the revolution, and died before Aug 1, 1796 in Kentucky [Ref: V-2988].

TULL, Hannah. See "John Goslee," q.v.

TULL, Jacob. Private, Worcester Militia, Wicomico Bn., Capt. Samuel Horsey's Co., Seventh Class, July 15, 1780 [Ref: M-257]. In Worcester County Court in February, 1800, a petition was submitted for a commission to divide the estate of Jacob Tull by Samuel Tull, Levin Tull, Elizabeth Wilson and Job Wilson her husband, Leah Mills and Jonathan Mills her husband, and Sarah Tull. Jacob Tull died intestate and seized of tracts of land near Dividing Creek called *Little Profit, Grate Profit*, and *Fortitude*. The petitioners were sons, sons-in-law, and daughters of Jacob Tull and they asked the court to appoint a guardian to James Tull (minor), in which case Levin Tull was so appointed [Ref: Article by William D. Patrick in *Maryland Magazine of Genealogy*, Vol. 4, No. 2 (Fall, 1981), pp. 79-80].

TULL, James Sr. Took the Oath of Allegiance in Worcester County in 1778 before the Hon. James Selby [Ref: J-1814 (Box 4)].

TULL, James (1754-1795). Son of Stephen Tull and Sarah Hall, born in Coventry Parish on April 19, 1754, married Elizabeth Porter, and died before Oct 16, 1795 [Ref: Y-75, V-2988]. Sergeant, Worcester Militia, Wicomico Bn., Capt. James Patterson's Co., July 15, 1780 [Ref: M-258]. See "John Tull" and "Jacob Tull," q.v.

TULL, John (c1748-1792). First Lieutenant, Worcester Militia, Sinepuxent Bn., Capt. John Coe's Co., Aug 30, 1777. Captain, March 16, 1781 [Ref: M-131, M-252, C-350, G-353]. John Tull was born circa 1748, married Hannah Collins, and died on March 2, 1792 [Ref: V-2988].

TULL, John (1752-1810/20). Son of James Tull (c1722-c1761) and Rachel White. He was born on Dec 12, 1752 in Somerset County, married Martha Woods (b. Feb 3, 1757), and their son John was born circa 1785/90, married Susan ----, and died circa 1819/20 [Ref: Q-23:3 (Summer, 1982), "Ancestor Table of Willis Clayton Tull, Jr.," pp. 247-255]. Private, Capt. John Gunby's 2nd Independent Maryland Co.; present on March 2, 1776; mustered on Aug 21, 1776 [Ref: D-641]. Corporal, Capt. Solomon Long's (later Lt. John Gassaway's) Co., Col. Thomas Price's 2nd Maryland Regiment of Foot, Maryland Continental Line [Ref: Q-23:3, *Ibid.*]. He may have been the John Tull who was a sergeant in the Somerset Militia, Princess Anne Bn., Capt. John Williams'

Watkins Point Co., in 1780 [Ref: M-221]. Since there were other men by this name, additional research will be necessary before drawing conclusions.

TULL, John. Private, Somerset Militia, Princess Anne Bn., Capt. James Elzey's Co., 1780 [Ref: M-220].

TULL, John. Took the Oath of Allegiance in Somerset County in 1778 before the Hon. Peter Waters [Ref: T-18].

TULL, Jonathan. Private, Somerset Militia, Princess Anne Bn., Capt. George Waters' Pocomoke Co., 1780 [Ref: M-220]. Took the Oath of Allegiance in Somerset County in 1778 before the Hon. Peter Waters [Ref: T-18]. Select Militia, Somerset County, Aug 15, 1781 [Ref: L-35A].

TULL, Joshua. Took the Oath of Allegiance in Somerset County in 1778 before the Hon. Peter Waters [Ref: T-18].

TULL, Levin. Private, Somerset Militia, Princess Anne Bn., Capt. Isaac Handy's Great Annemessix Co., 1780 [Ref: M-221].

TULL, Levin. Private, Somerset Militia, Princess Anne Bn., Capt. John Williams' Watkins Point Co., 1780 [Ref: M-222]. See "Jacob Tull," q.v.

TULL, Nicholas. Took the Oath of Allegiance in Somerset County in 1778 before the Hon. Peter Waters [Ref: T-18].

TULL, Samuel. See "Jacob Tull," q.v.

TULL, Sarah. See "James Tull," q.v.

TULL, Solomon. Private, Somerset County, Capt. John Gunby's 2nd Independent Maryland Co.; present on April 5, 1776; mustered on Aug 21, 1776 [Ref: D-641].

TULL, Stephen. Took the Oath of Allegiance in Somerset County in 1778 (made his "X" mark) before the Hon. Peter Waters [Ref: T-18]. See "James Tull," q.v.

TULL, Thomas. Private, Somerset Militia, Princess Anne Bn., Capt. John Williams' Watkins Point Co., 1780 [Ref: M-222].

TULL, Thomas. Private, Somerset Militia, Princess Anne Bn., Capt. Isaac Handy's Great Annemessix Co., 1780 [Ref: M-221].

TULL, Thomas. Took the Oath of Allegiance in Somerset County in 1778 before the Hon. Peter Waters [Ref: T-18].

TULL, William. Private, Somerset Militia, Princess Anne Bn., Capt. Isaac Handy's Great Annemessix Co., 1780 [Ref: M-221]. Drafted from Somerset County on July 30, 1781 to serve in the Continental Army [Ref: L-35C].

TULLEY, Benjamin. Private, Somerset Militia, Salisbury Bn., Capt. William Turpin's Rewastico Co., 1778/1780 [Ref: M-217].

TULLEY, James. Private, Somerset Militia, Salisbury Bn., Capt. Joseph Venables' Barren Creek Co., 1778/1780 [Ref: M-217 listed the name as "James Tully"]. Took the Oath of Allegiance in Somerset County on Feb 28, 1778 before the Hon. Joseph Venables [Ref: T-25].

TULLEY, John. Private, Somerset Militia, Salisbury Bn., Capt. William Turpin's Rewastico Co., 1778/1780 [Ref: M-217].

TULLEY, Joseph. Private, Somerset Militia, Salisbury Bn., White Haven Co., 1778/1780 [Ref: M-219].

TULLEY, Richard. Private, Somerset Militia, Salisbury Bn., Capt. William Turpin's Rewastico Co., 1778/1780 [Ref: M-217].

TURBURT, Peter. Private, Somerset Militia, Salisbury Bn., White Haven Co., 1778/1780 [Ref: M-219].

TURNER, George. Private, Worcester Militia, Wicomico Bn., Capt. Benjamin Dennis' Co., Eighth Class, July 15, 1780 [Ref: M-256]. Private, Maryland Troops, Worcester County, draughted May 1, 1781 [Ref: K-99, D-372]. Took the Oath of Allegiance in Worcester County in 1778 before the Hon. Joshua Townsend [Ref: J-1814 (Box 4)].

TURNER, Henry. Private, Worcester Militia, Wicomico Bn., Capt. James Perdue's Co., Sixth Class, July 15, 1780 [Ref: M-256].

TURNER, Jackson. Private, Worcester Militia, Wicomico Bn., Capt. Benjamin Dennis' Co., Second Class, July 15, 1780 [Ref: M-255].

TURNER, John. Took the Oath of Allegiance in Worcester County in 1778 in Buckingham Hundred before the Hon. Thomas Purnell [Ref: J-1814 (Box 4)].

TURNER, Levin. Private, Worcester Militia, Snow Hill Bn., Capt. Ebenezer Handy's Co., April 9, 1776 [Ref: M-249]. Private, Worcester Militia, Wicomico Bn., Capt. Robert Handy's Co., Sixth Class, July 15, 1780 [Ref: M-254].

TURNER, Osburn. Private, Maryland Line, from Somerset County, who was discharged on Dec 3, 1781 [Ref: I-11].

TURNER, William. Private, Worcester Militia, Snow Hill Bn., Capt. Samuel Smyley's Co., 1777 [Ref: M-250]. Took the Oath of Allegiance in Worcester County in 1778 before the Hon. John Selby [Ref: J-1814 (Box 4)]. Private, Worcester Militia, Wicomico Bn., Capt. John Davis' Co., Seventh Class, July 15, 1780 [Ref: M-255].

TURNER, Zadock. Private, Worcester Militia, Wicomico Bn., Capt. James Perdue's Co., Sixth Class, July 15, 1780 [Ref: M-256].

TURPIN, Denwood. Took the Oath of Allegiance in Somerset County in 1778 before the Hon. Peter Waters [Ref: T-18]. Private, Select Militia, Somerset County, Aug 15, 1781 [Ref: L-35B].

TURPIN, Handy. Private, Somerset Militia, Salisbury Bn., Capt. James Bennett's Salisbury Co., 1778/1780 [Ref: M-218].

TURPIN, John (1745-c1795). First Lieutenant, Somerset Militia, Princess Anne Bn., Capt. John Williams' Watkins Point Co., Dec 7, 1778 to at least July 24, 1780 [Ref: M-131, M-221, E-260]. Took the Oath of Allegiance in Somerset County in 1778 before the Hon. John Williams [Ref: T-21, N-52]. John Turpin was born on Nov 22, 1745, married Sarah Dixon, served as a first lieutenant in the revolution, and died before Jan 19, 1795 [Ref: V-2995].

TURPIN, John. Private, Somerset Militia, Princess Anne Bn., Capt. Isaac Handy's Great Annemessix Co., 1780 [Ref: M-221]. Select Militia, Somerset County, Aug 15, 1781 [Ref: L-35A]. See "John Round (Rounds, Rownds)," q.v.

TURPIN, Joshua. Private, Somerset Militia, Princess Anne Bn., Capt. Isaac Handy's Great Annemessix Co., 1780 [Ref: M-221]. Took the Oath of Allegiance in Somerset County in 1778 before the Hon. John Williams [Ref: T-21, N-52].

TURPIN, Nehemiah. Private, Somerset Militia, Princess Anne Bn., Capt. James Elzey's Co., 1780 [Ref: M-220]. Took the Oath of Allegiance in Somerset County in 1778 before the Hon. John Williams [Ref: T-21]. One Nehemiah Turpin married Orpha Brittingham in Coventry Parish on July 14, 1762 [Ref: Y-91].

TURPIN, Nehemiah Jr. Took the Oath of Allegiance in Somerset County in 1778 before the Hon. John Williams [Ref: T-21, N-52]. Private, Select Militia, Somerset County, Aug 15, 1781 [Ref: L-35A listed the name without the "Jr."].

TURPIN, Sally. See "Joshua Wright," q.v.

TURPIN, Whittey. Took the Oath of Allegiance in Somerset County in 1778 before the Hon. Peter Waters [Ref: T-18 listed the name as "Whittey Turpen"].

TURPIN, William. Captain, Somerset Militia, Salisbury Bn., Rewastico Co., Sep 22, 1777 to at least July 24, 1780 [Ref: M-131, M-217, C-382, E-173]. See "Huet Nutter," q.v.

TURPIN, William. Sergeant, Somerset Militia, Princess Anne Bn., Capt. Isaac Handy's Great Annemessix Co., 1780 [Ref: M-221].

TWIFORD, Bartholomew. Private, Somerset Militia, Princess Anne Bn., Capt. John Williams' Watkins Point Co., 1780 [Ref: M-222].

TWIFORD, Sarah. See "Benjamin Darby," q.v.

TWIGG, William. Private, Worcester Militia, Wicomico Bn., Capt. Elijah Shockley's Co., Sixth Class, July 15, 1780 [Ref: M-255].

TWILLEY, George (1743-1801). Private, Somerset Militia, Salisbury Bn., Capt. William Turpin's Rewastico Co., 1778/1780 [Ref: M-217]. George Twilley was born in 1743, married Ann Bradley, served as a private in the revolution, and died on March 13, 1801 [Ref: V-2999].

TWILLEY, Joseph. Private, Somerset Militia, Salisbury Bn., Capt. William Turpin's Rewastico Co., 1778/1780 [Ref: M-217].

TWILLEY, Stephen. Private, Somerset Militia, Salisbury Bn., Capt. William Turpin's Rewastico Co., 1778/1780 [Ref: M-217].

TWILLEY, William. Private, Worcester Militia, Wicomico Bn., Capt. James Perdue's Co., Third Class, July 15, 1780 [Ref: M-256 listed the name as "William Twilly"].

TYE, Elizabeth Hamblin Powers. See "Solomon Hamblin," q.v.

TYLER, David. Private, Somerset Militia, Princess Anne Bn., Capt. Henry Miles' Little Annemessex Co., 1780 [Ref: M-221 listed the name as "David Tylor"].

TYLER, John. See "Henry Waggaman," q.v.

TYLER, Littleton. See "Littleton Taylor," q.v.

TYLER, Martha Jefferson. See "Henry Waggaman," q.v.

TYLER, Spencer. Private, Somerset Militia, Princess Anne Bn., Capt. Henry Miles' Little Annemessex Co., 1780 [Ref: M-221].
TYLER, Thomas. Private, Worcester Militia, Wicomico Bn., Capt. Isaac Layfield's Co., Fifth Class, July 15, 1780 [Ref: M-257]. See "Littleton Taylor," q.v.
TYNDALL, Violetta. See "Daniel Fooks," q.v.
UPSHUR, Susanna. See "Henry Dennis," q.v.
VALLANCE, Nicholas. Took the Oath of Allegiance in Worcester County in 1778 before the Hon. Joshua Townsend [Ref: J-1814 (Box 4)].
VANCE, David. Second Lieutenant, Somerset Militia, Salisbury Bn., Capt. James Bennett's Co., May 27, 1779 [Ref: M-131, E-423]. Rendered patriotic service by supplying corn for the use of the military on Jan 25, 1780 [Ref: P-265]. Took the Oath of Allegiance in Somerset County on Feb 14, 1778 before the Hon. Joseph Venables [Ref: T-25].
VANCE, George. Private, Worcester Militia, Snow Hill Bn., Capt. Ebenezer Handy's Co., April 9, 1776 [Ref: M-249].
VANCE, William. Private, Worcester Militia, Wicomico Bn., Capt. Samuel Horsey's Co., Second Class, July 15, 1780 [Ref: M-256].
VANDOME (VONDOME), Edward. Recommended on Sep 29, 1780 to be appointed Sheriff of Worcester County due to the death of Sheriff John Selby. Commissioned on Oct 2, 1780 by the Council of Maryland as Sheriff of Worcester County "in the room of John Selby, dead, and in consequence of the refusal of Jesse Bennett." Resigned from office on Feb 3, 1781 [Ref: G-125 listed the name as "Edward Vandame" and F-310 listed the name as "Edward Vondome" and H-40 listed the name as "Edward Vandome"].
VAUGHAN (VAUGHN), Charles. Private, Somerset Militia, Princess Anne Bn., Capt. John Jones' Princess Anne Co., 1780 [Ref: M-219]. Took the Oath of Allegiance in Somerset County in 1778 before the Hon. Levin Wilson [Ref: T-17].
VAUGHAN, Mary. See "William Polk, Sr.," q.v.
VEAZEY, Charles. Private, Worcester Militia, Wicomico Bn., Capt. Fisher Walton's Co., Fourth Class, July 15, 1780 [Ref: M-258 listed the name as "Charles Veazy"]. Took the Oath of Allegiance in Worcester County in 1778 before the Hon. John Selby [Ref: J-1814 (Box 4)].
VEAZEY, John. Private, Worcester Militia, Snow Hill Bn., Capt. John Parramore's Co., 1777 [Ref: M-250 listed the name as "John Veasey"]. Private, Worcester Militia, Wicomico Bn., Capt. John Parramore's Co., Third Class, July 15, 1780 [Ref: M-259 listed the name as "John Veazy"]. Took the Oath of Allegiance in Worcester County in 1778 before the Hon. John Selby [Ref: J-1814 (Box 4)].
VEAZEY, Southey. Private, Worcester Militia, Snow Hill Bn., Capt. John Parramore's Co., 1777 [Ref: M-250 listed the name as "Sothey Veasey"]. Took the Oath of Allegiance in Worcester County in 1778 before the Hon. John Selby [Ref: J-1814 (Box 4)].

VENABLES, Benjamin. First Lieutenant, Somerset Militia, Salisbury Bn., Capt. Joseph Venables' Barren Creek Co., Sep 22, 1777 to at least July 24, 1780 [Ref: M-132, M-217, C-381]. Took the Oath of Allegiance in Somerset County in 1778 [Ref: N-52].
VENABLES, Benjaman Sr. Took the Oath of Allegiance in Somerset County on Jan 26, 1778 before the Hon. Joseph Venables [Ref: T-25].
VENABLES, Benjaman Jr. Took the Oath of Allegiance in Somerset County on March 1, 1778 before the Hon. Joseph Venables [Ref: T-25].
VENABLES, Benjaman 3rd. Took the Oath of Allegiance in Somerset County on Feb 23, 1778 before the Hon. Joseph Venables [Ref: T-25].
VENABLES, Joseph. Captain, Somerset Militia, Salisbury Bn., Barren Creek Co., Sep 22, 1777 to at least July 24, 1780 [Ref: M-132, M-217, C-381]. Justice who administered the Oath of Allegiance in Somerset County in 1778 [Ref: T-25]. Justice of the Peace, commissioned on Jan 7, 1778 and Nov 21, 1778 and Nov 25, 1780 and Jan 17, 1782 [Ref: E-248, G-225, C-464, I-45].
VENABLES, Joseph. Took the Oath of Allegiance in Somerset County in 1778 before the Hon. William Winder [Ref: T-22].
VENABLES, Samuel. Private, Somerset Militia, Salisbury Bn., Capt. Joseph Venables' Barren Creek Co., 1778/1780 [Ref: M-217]. Select Militia, Somerset County, Aug 15, 1781 [Ref: L-35B].
VENABLES, Thomas. Private, Somerset Militia, Salisbury Bn., Capt. Joseph Venables' Barren Creek Co., 1778/1780 [Ref: M-217]. Select Militia, Somerset County, Aug 15, 1781 [Ref: L-35B].
VENABLES, William. Ensign, Somerset Militia, Salisbury Bn., Capt. Robert Dashiell's Co., Jan 7, 1778. Second Lieutenant, April 20, 1778 [Ref: M-131, C-457, E-42]. Took the Oath of Allegiance in Somerset County on Feb 9, 1778 before the Hon. Joseph Venables [Ref: T-25].
VENABLES, William. Sergeant, Somerset Militia, Salisbury Bn., Capt. Henry Gale's Quantico Co., 1778/1780 [Ref: M-216]. Select Militia, Somerset County, Aug 15, 1781 [Ref: L-35B].
VENABLES, William Jr. Took the Oath of Allegiance in Somerset County on Feb 21, 1778 before the Hon. Joseph Venables [Ref: T-25].
VENABLES, William (of Purkins). Took the Oath of Allegiance in Somerset County on Feb 14, 1778 before the Hon. Joseph Venables [Ref: T-25].
VESSELS, James C. Private, Somerset Militia, Princess Anne Bn., Capt. James Elzey's Co., 1780 [Ref: M-220].
VESTRY, Hugh. Private, Worcester Militia, Wicomico Bn., Capt. Charles Bennett's Co., Third Class, July 15, 1780 [Ref: M-255].
VICTOR, James. Private, Worcester Militia, Wicomico Bn., Capt. Benjamin Dennis' Co., Fifth Class, July 15, 1780 [Ref: M-256]. Took the Oath of Allegiance in Worcester County in 1778 before the Hon. Joshua Townsend [Ref: J-1814 (Box 4)].

VICTOR, John (c1756-1791). Second Lieutenant, Worcester Militia, Wicomico Bn., Capt. Benjamin Dennis' Co., from Aug 30, 1777 to at least July 15, 1780 [Ref: M-132, M-256, C-351]. Took the Oath of Allegiance in Worcester County in 1778 before the Hon. Nehemiah Holland [Ref: J-1814 (Box 4)]. John Victor was born before 1756, married Hannah Bruington, served as a second lieutenant in the revolution, and died in April, 1791 [Ref: V-3052].

VICTOR, Thomas. Private, Worcester Militia, Wicomico Bn., Capt. Benjamin Dennis' Co., First Class, July 15, 1780 [Ref: M-255]. Took the Oath of Allegiance in Worcester County in 1778 before the Hon. Joshua Townsend [Ref: J-1814 (Box 4)].

VICTOR, Thomas Jr. Took the Oath of Allegiance in Worcester County in 1778 before the Hon. Joshua Townsend [Ref: J-1814 (Box 4)].

VIGEROUS, Armwell. Private, Worcester Militia, Sinepuxent Bn., Capt. John Coe's Co., Fifth Class, 1779/1780 [Ref: M-252].

VINCENT, Isaac. Private, Somerset Militia, Salisbury Bn., Capt. Levin Irving's Black Water Co., 1778/1780 [Ref: M-218].

VINSON, Elijah. Took the Oath of Allegiance in Somerset County on Feb 14, 1778 before the Hon. Joseph Venables [Ref: T-25].

VINSON, Elisha. Private, Worcester Militia, Wicomico Bn., Capt. James Perdue's Co., Eighth Class, July 15, 1780 [Ref: M-256].

VIRDIN (VIRDEN), James. Private, Worcester Militia, Wicomico Bn., Capt. James Patterson's Co., Seventh Class, July 15, 1780 [Ref: M-258]. Took the Oath of Allegiance in Worcester County in 1778 before the Hon. John Selby [Ref: J-1814 (Box 4)].

WABERTON, Thomas. See "Thomas Warbleton," q.v.

WADDEY (WADDY), William. Captain, Somerset Militia, Princess Anne Bn., Aug 22, 1781 [Ref: M-132, G-575].

WADDEY (WADDY), William. Private, Somerset Militia, Princess Anne Bn., Capt. George Waters' Pocomoke Co., 1780 [Ref: M-220].

WAGGAMAN, Elizabeth. See "Henry Waggaman," q.v.

WAGGAMAN, George Augustus. See "Henry Waggaman," q.v.

WAGGAMAN, Henry (1753-1809). Son of Henry Waggaman and Mary Woolford. He married Sarah Ennalls on May 3, 1780 and their children were Thomas Ennalls (married Martha Jefferson Tyler, sister of President John Tyler), George Augustus (senator), Henry Pierpont (physician), and Elizabeth. Henry attended the Maryland Convention in 1774 and served in the Lower House of the Maryland Legislature from Somerset County, 1781-1782, from Dorchester County, 1785, from Somerset County, 1788, and from Dorchester County, 1793. He was also a Justice of the Orphans Court of Somerset County in 1791. He died on May 26, 1809 at *Fairview* near Cambridge in Dorchester County [Ref: R-852, R-853, V-3065]. Took the Oath of Allegiance in Somerset County in 1778 before the Hon. John Span Conway [Ref: N-52, and T-14 listed the name as "Henry Waggamen"].

WAGGAMAN, Sarah. See "Isaac Outten (Outton)," q.v.
WAGGAMAN, Thomas. See "Henry Waggaman," q.v.
WAGGAMAN, William Elliott. Took the Oath of Allegiance in Somerset County in 1778 before the Hon. John Span Conway [Ref: N-52, and T-14 listed the name as "William Elliot Waggamen"].
WAILES (WAILS, WALES), Benjamin. One Benjamin Wales or Wailes was born in Maryland on Jan 2, 1727, married Sarah Howard, rendered patriotic service during the revolution, and died in 1789 [Ref: V-3073]. Another Benjamin Wales or Wailes was born in Maryland on Feb 14, 1756, married Anne Handy, rendered patriotic service during the revolution, and died circa 1810-1812 [Ref: V-3073]. One took the Oath of Allegiance in Somerset County on Feb 2, 1778 [Ref: T-25, N-52]. One rendered patriotic service by storing corn in Worcester County for the use of the military on Oct 10, 1780 [Ref: P-325]. Additional research will be necessary before drawing conclusions. One should consult "The Wailes Family of Eastern Maryland and Some of Their Relatives on the Eastern and Western Shores," by Ernest C. Allnutt, Jr., Lt.Col. AUS-Ret. [Ref: Q-36:2 (Spring, 1995), pp. 146-196, and the Christopher Johnston Collection at the Maryland Historical Society Library].
WAILES (WAILLS), Betty. See "Joseph Wailes," q.v.
WAILES (WAILS), Charles. Private, Somerset Militia, Salisbury Bn., Capt. Levin Irving's Black Water Co., 1778/1780 [Ref: M-217].
WAILES (WAILLS), Daniel. See "Joseph Wailes," q.v.
WAILES (WALES), Elijah. Private, Worcester Militia, Wicomico Bn., Capt. James Perdue's Co., Third Class, July 15, 1780 [Ref: M-256].
WAILES (WAILS), George. Took the Oath of Allegiance in Somerset County on Feb 28, 1778 before the Hon. Joseph Venables [Ref: T-25]. Appointed by the Council of Maryland to be Inspector of Tobacco on Nanticoke River at the head of Barren Creek on Aug 30, 1780 [Ref: F-271]. Captain, Somerset Militia, 1st Bn., Feb 10, 1776 or May 11, 1776, resigned (both dates were given). [Ref: A-327, M-132]. For additional information about this family, see Ref: Q-36:2 (Spring, 1995), "The Wailes Family of Early Maryland and Some of Their Relatives on the Eastern and Western Shores," by Ernest C. Allnutt, Jr., Lt.Col. AUS-Ret., pp. 145-196].
WAILES (WAILS), John. Took the Oath of Allegiance in Somerset County on Feb 6, 1778 before the Hon. Joseph Venables [Ref: T-25].
WAILES (WAILLS), Joseph (1753 -   ). Son of Daniel and Betty Waills *[sic]*, born in Stepney Parish on Sep 15, 1753 [Ref: Y-42]. Ensign, Somerset Militia, Salisbury Bn., Capt. Henry Gale's Quantico Co., 1780/1781 [Ref: M-216, H-195]. Took the Oath of Allegiance in Somerset County in 1778 before the Hon. John Stewart [Ref: T-19]. See "Abraham Dogan," q.v.
WAILS (WAILES), Nelly (Eleanor). See "William Horsey," q.v.
WAILS (WAILES), William. Private, Somerset Militia, Salisbury Bn., Capt. Levin Irving's Black Water Co., 1778/1780 [Ref: M-218].

WAINWRIGHT, Cannon (c1745-c1820). Private, Somerset Militia, Salisbury Bn., Capt. John Span Conway's Nanticoke Point Co., 1778/1780 [Ref: M-216 listed the name as "Cannon Winwright"]. Private, Worcester Militia, Wicomico Bn., Capt. Charles Bennett's Co., Fifth Class, July 15, 1780 [Ref: M-255 listed the name as "Cannon Wainright"]. Cannon Wainwright was born circa 1745, married (name of wife unknown), was a private in the revolution, and died after 1820 in Maryland [Ref: V-3067].

WAINWRIGHT, Evans. Private, Somerset Militia, Salisbury Bn., Capt. John Span Conway's Nanticoke Point Co., 1778/1780 [Ref: M-216 listed the name as "Evans Winwright"].

WAINWRIGHT, George. Private, Worcester Militia, Sinepuxent Bn., Capt. Thomas Purnell's Co., First Class, 1779/1780 [Ref: M-253]. Took the Oath of Allegiance in Worcester County in 1778 before the Hon. William Hopewell [Ref: J-1814 (Box 4) listed the name as "George Wainright"]. Rendered patriotic service by hauling corn for the use of the military on Sep 30, 1780 [Ref: P-322 listed the name as "George Whanright"].

WAINWRIGHT, Solomon (1740-c1801). Private, Somerset Militia, Salisbury Bn., Capt. John Span Conway's Nanticoke Point Co., 1778/1780 [Ref: M-216 listed the name as "Solomon Winright"]. Solomon Wainwright was born on Jan 9, 1740, married (name of wife unknown), was a private in the revolution, and died before Oct 5, 1801 in Maryland [Ref: V-3067].

WAITE, William. Private, Worcester Militia, Sinepuxent Bn., Capt. Elisha Purnell's Co., First Class, 1779/1780 [Ref: M-253]. Select Militia, Somerset County, Aug 15, 1781 [Ref: L-35B].

WALKER, Dovey. See "Ebenezer Hearn," q.v.

WALKER, John. Private, Worcester Militia, Sinepuxent Bn., Capt. Thomas Purnell's Co., Third Class, 1779/1780 [Ref: M-253]. Took the Oath of Allegiance in Worcester County in 1778 before the Hon. Nathaniel Miller [Ref: J-1814 (Box 4)].

WALKER, William. Took the Oath of Allegiance in Somerset County in 1778 before the Hon. Peter Waters [Ref: T-18]. Second Lieutenant, Somerset Militia, Salisbury Bn., Capt. John McClester's Nanticoke Point Co., by July, 1781 [Ref: J-1814 (Box 8, Dashiell's correspondence)].

WALLACE, David. Private, Somerset Militia, Princess Anne Bn., Capt. Thomas Irving's Monie Co., 1780 [Ref: M-219].

WALLACE, James. Private, Somerset Militia, Princess Anne Bn., Capt. Thomas Irving's Monie Co., 1780 [Ref: M-219]. See "Henry Walston Miles," q.v.

WALLACE, Richard. Private, Somerset Militia, Princess Anne Bn., Capt. Thomas Irving's Monie Co., 1780 [Ref: M-219].

WALLER, Ebenezer. Private, Somerset Militia, Salisbury Bn., Capt. Levin Irving's Black Water Co., 1778/1780 [Ref: M-218]. Took the Oath of Allegiance in Somerset County on Feb 28, 1778 before the Hon. Joseph Venables [Ref: T-25]. See "Clarkson Cox," q.v.

WALLER, John. Took the Oath of Allegiance in Worcester County on Feb 25, 1778 before the Hon. Ebenezer Handy [Ref: J-1814 (Box 4)].
WALLER, Joseph. Private, Worcester Militia, Snow Hill Bn., Capt. Ebenezer Handy's Co., April 9, 1776 [Ref: M-249].
WALLER, Thomas. Private, Somerset Militia, Salisbury Bn., Capt. Levin Irving's Black Water Co., 1778/1780 [Ref: M-218].
WALLER, Thomas. Private, Somerset Militia, Salisbury Bn., Capt. Levin Irving's Black Water Co., 1778/1780 [Ref: M-217].
WALLER, William. Ensign, Somerset Militia, 17th Bn., Sep 19, 1776. Second Lieutenant, Salisbury Bn., Capt. John McCloster's Co., July 21, 1781 [Ref: M-132, B-285, G-575, H-361]. Took the Oath of Allegiance in Somerset County in 1778 before the Hon. John Span Conway [Ref: T-14, N-52].
WALLER, William. Sergeant, Somerset Militia, Salisbury Bn., Capt. John Span Conway's Nanticoke Point Co., 1778/1780 [Ref: M-216]. Ensign, April 17, 1781 [Ref: H-195].
WALLS, Charles. Private, Worcester Militia, Wicomico Bn., Capt. John Parramore's Co., Sixth Class, July 15, 1780 [Ref: M-259].
WALLS, John. Private, Somerset Militia, Salisbury Bn., Capt. William Turpin's Rewastico Co., 1778/1780 [Ref: M-217].
WALLY (WALLEY), Charles. Private, Worcester Militia, Sinepuxent Bn., Capt. Josiah Dale's Co., Third Class, 1779/1780 [Ref: M-254].
WALLY (WALLEY), Seth. Private, Worcester Militia, Sinepuxent Bn., Capt. Josiah Dale's Co., Second Class, 1779/1780 [Ref: M-254].
WALLY (WALLEY), Thomas. Private, Worcester Militia, Sinepuxent Bn., Capt. Josiah Dale's Co., Eighth Class, 1779/1780 [Ref: M-254].
WALLY (WALLEY), Zedekiah. Rendered patriotic service by supplying brandy for the use of the military in Worcester County on Aug 1, 1781 [Ref: P-418]. Earlier, a Committee from Worcester County wrote to the Governor and Council of Maryland on March 21, 1781 to inform them that Capt. Zeekiah *[sic]* Walley, in order to defend the inhabitants of this part of the State and "who has been kind enough to offer us the following plan, is not only well acquainted with his duty as a sea officer, but whose integrity attachment and unexceptionable character renders him in our judgment a proper person to carry it into execution, proposes to build a barge about 50 feet by the keel, to carry about 60 men, and a 24 pounder in her head ..." as a necessary defensive measure [Ref: H-140, H-141].
WALSTON, Bathsheba. See "Boas or Boaz Walston," q.v.
WALSTON, Benjamin. Ensign, Worcester Militia, Capt. Handy's Co., Feb 16, 1777 [Ref: M-133, C-140].
WALSTON, Boas or Boaz (1757-1823). Private, Somerset Militia, Princess Anne Bn., Capt. James Elzey's Co., 1780 [Ref: M-220 listed the name as "Boas Walston"]. Boaz Walston was born in 1757, married Bathsheba ----, served as a private in the revolution, and died in 1823 [Ref: V-3088].

WALSTON, Boaz. Ensign, Worcester Militia, Snow Hill Bn., Capt. Ebenezer Handy's Co., April 9, 1776 or May 15, 1776 (both dates were given). [Ref: M-133, M-249, A-426]. Ensign(?), Worcester Militia, Wicomico Bn., Capt. James Perdue's Co., Fourth Class, July 15, 1780 [Ref: M-256].

WALSTON, Charles. Private, Somerset Militia, Princess Anne Bn., Capt. Isaac Handy's Great Annemessix Co., 1780 [Ref: M-221].

WALSTON, Henry (Dames Quarters). Private, Somerset Militia, Princess Anne Bn., Capt. Thomas Irving's Monie Co., 1780 [Ref: M-219 listed the name as "Henry Walston (DQ)"]. He may be the Henry Walston who was born circa 1740, married (name of wife not known), served as a private in the revolution, and died in 1796 in Maryland [Ref: V-3088].

WALSTON, Jesse. Private, Somerset Militia, Princess Anne Bn., Capt. John Jones' Princess Anne Co., 1780 [Ref: M-219]. Took the Oath of Allegiance in Somerset County in 1778 before the Hon. Peter Waters [Ref: T-18].

WALSTON, Joseph. Private, Somerset Militia, Princess Anne Bn., Capt. Thomas Irving's Monie Co., 1780 [Ref: M-219].

WALSTON, Levin. Private, Somerset Militia, Princess Anne Bn., Capt. Isaac Handy's Great Annemessix Co., 1780 [Ref: M-221].

WALSTON, Obediah. Private, Somerset Militia, Princess Anne Bn., Capt. Isaac Handy's Great Annemessix Co., 1780 [Ref: M-221].

WALSTON, Peter. Private, Somerset Militia, Princess Anne Bn., Capt. James Elzey's Co., 1780 [Ref: M-220].

WALSTON, Thomas. Private, Somerset Militia, Princess Anne Bn., Capt. Isaac Handy's Great Annemessix Co., 1780 [Ref: M-221].

WALTAM, Fisher. See "Fisher Walton," q.v.

WALTER, Daniel. Corporal, Somerset Militia, Salisbury Bn., Capt. John Span Conway's Nanticoke Point Co., 1778/1780 [Ref: M-216].

WALTER, James. Private, Somerset Militia, Salisbury Bn., Capt. John Span Conway's Nanticoke Point Co., 1778/1780 [Ref: M-216].

WALTER, John. Private, Worcester Militia, Sinepuxent Bn., Capt. Josiah Dale's Co., Seventh Class, 1779/1780 [Ref: M-254].

WALTER, Joseph. Took the Oath of Allegiance in Worcester County in 1778 before the Hon. William Hopewell [Ref: J-1814 (Box 4)]. Rendered patriotic service by supplying salt for the use of the military on Dec 20, 1781 [Ref: P-463 listed the name as "Joseph Walters"].

WALTER, Levin. Corporal, Somerset Militia, Salisbury Bn., Capt. John Span Conway's Nanticoke Point Co., 1778/1780 [Ref: M-216].

WALTER, Robert. Private, Somerset Militia, Salisbury Bn., Capt. John Span Conway's Nanticoke Point Co., 1778/1780 [Ref: M-216].

WALTON, Fisher. First Lieutenant, Worcester Militia, Snow Hill Bn., Capt. William Holland's Co., Aug 30, 1777. Captain, Wicomico Bn., May 27, 1779 to at least July 15, 1780 [Ref: C-351, M-133, M-258, and C-423 listed the name as "Fisher Waltam"]. Took the Oath of Allegiance in Worcester County in 1778 before the Hon. Nehemiah Holland [Ref: J-1814 (Box 4)].

WALTON, Job. Took the Oath of Allegiance in Worcester County in 1778 before the Hon. Nehemiah Holland [Ref: J-1814 (Box 4)].

WALTON, William. Private, Worcester Militia, Wicomico Bn., Capt. John Parramore's Co., Fifth Class, July 15, 1780 [Ref: M-259 listed the name as "William Waltom"]. Took the Oath of Allegiance in Somerset County in 1778 before the Hon. Levin Wilson [Ref: T-17 listed the name as "William Waltom" and N-52 listed the name as "William Walton"]. See "William Delastatious," q.v.

WAMBLIN, Joseph. Took the Oath of Allegiance in Worcester County in 1778 before the Hon. Nathaniel Miller [Ref: J-1814 (Box 4)].

WARBLETON (WABERTON), Thomas. Private, Somerset Militia, Salisbury Bn., White Haven Co., 1778/1780 [Ref: M-219 listed the name as "Thomas Warbleton"]. Drafted from Somerset County on July 30, 1781 to serve in the Continental Army, but was subsequently excused [Ref: L-35C listed the name as "Thomas Waberton"].

WARD, Cornelius. Corporal, Somerset Militia, Salisbury Bn., Capt. Sampson Wheatly's Co., 1780 [Ref: M-215].

WARD, Cornelius. Private, Somerset Militia, Princess Anne Bn., Capt. Henry Miles' Little Annemessex Co., 1780 [Ref: M-221].

WARD, Ezekiel (1750/1 -   ). Son of John and Rachel Ward, born in Coventry Parish on Feb 4, 1750/1 [Ref: Y-76]. Private, Somerset Militia, Princess Anne Bn., Capt. Henry Miles' Little Annemessex Co., 1780 [Ref: M-221].

WARD, Isaac (1754 -   ). Son of Matthias and Margaret Ward, born in Coventry Parish on Feb 12, 1754 [Ref: Y-76]. Private, Somerset Militia, Princess Anne Bn., Capt. John Williams' Watkins Point Co., 1780 [Ref: M-222].

WARD, Jacob. Private, Somerset Militia, Salisbury Bn., Capt. Sampson Wheatly's Co., 1780 [Ref: M-216].

WARD, James. Private, Somerset Militia, Princess Anne Bn., Capt. Henry Miles' Little Annemessex Co., 1780 [Ref: M-221].

WARD, James. Private, Somerset Militia, Salisbury Bn., Capt. Sampson Wheatly's Co., 1780 [Ref: M-216].

WARD, James. Private, Worcester Militia, Wicomico Bn., Capt. Benjamin Dennis' Co., First Class, July 15, 1780 [Ref: M-255]. Took the Oath of Allegiance in Worcester County in 1778 before the Hon. Joshua Townsend [Ref: J-1814 (Box 4)].

WARD, James. Drafted from Somerset County on June 20, 1781 to serve in the Continental Army [Ref: L-35C].

WARD, James Jr. Private, Somerset Militia, Princess Anne Bn., Capt. Henry Miles' Little Annemessex Co., 1780 [Ref: M-221].

WARD, Jesse. Private, Somerset Militia, Princess Anne Bn., Capt. John Jones' Princess Anne Co., 1780 [Ref: M-219].

WARD, Jesse. Private, Somerset Militia, Princess Anne Bn., Capt. George Waters' Pocomoke Co., 1780 [Ref: M-220].
WARD, Jesse. Drafted from Somerset County on June 20, 1781 to serve in the Continental Army [Ref: L-35C].
WARD, John. Private, Somerset Militia, Princess Anne Bn., Capt. Henry Miles' Little Annemessex Co., 1780 [Ref: M-221]. See "Ezekiel Ward," q.v.
WARD, Joseph. Private, Somerset Militia, Princess Anne Bn., Capt. John Jones' Princess Anne Co., 1780 [Ref: M-219].
WARD, Joseph. Private, Somerset Militia, Princess Anne Bn., Capt. Henry Miles' Little Annemessex Co., 1780 [Ref: M-221].
WARD, Joseph. Private, Somerset Militia, Salisbury Bn., Capt. Sampson Wheatly's Co., 1780 [Ref: M-216].
WARD, Josiah. Private, Worcester Militia, Wicomico Bn., Capt. Philip Quinton's Co., Seventh Class, July 15, 1780 [Ref: M-256].
WARD, Levi. Private, Somerset Militia, Princess Anne Bn., Capt. John Jones' Princess Anne Co., 1780 [Ref: M-219].
WARD, Levi. Private, Somerset Militia, Princess Anne Bn., Capt. John Williams' Watkins Point Co., 1780 [Ref: M-222].
WARD, Matthew. Private, Somerset Militia, Princess Anne Bn., Capt. John Jones' Princess Anne Co., 1780 [Ref: M-219]. Took the Oath of Allegiance in Somerset County in 1778 before the Hon. Levin Wilson [Ref: N-52, and T-17 listed the name as "Mathews Ward"].
WARD, Margaret. See "Isaac Ward," q.v.
WARD, Matthias. See "Isaac Ward," q.v.
WARD, Rachel. See "Ezekiel Ward," q.v.
WARD, Samuel. Private, Somerset Militia, Salisbury Bn., Capt. Sampson Wheatly's Co., 1780 [Ref: M-216].
WARD, Sarah. See "Esau Boston" and "Solomon Long," q.v.
WARD, Saul. Took the Oath of Allegiance in Somerset County on Feb 28, 1778 before the Hon. Joseph Venables [Ref: T-25].
WARD, Solomon. Private, Somerset Militia, Princess Anne Bn., Capt. John Jones' Princess Anne Co., 1780 [Ref: M-219].
WARD, Stephen. Private, Worcester Militia, Sinepuxent Bn., Capt. William Purnell's Co., Fifth Class, 1779/1780 [Ref: M-252].
WARD, Stephen. Private, Somerset Militia, Princess Anne Bn., Capt. Henry Miles' Little Annemessex Co., 1780 [Ref: M-221].
WARD, Stephen. Private, Somerset Militia, Princess Anne Bn., Capt. Henry Miles' Little Annemessex Co., 1780 [Ref: M-221].
WARD, Stephen. Private, Somerset Militia, Princess Anne Bn., Capt. John Williams' Watkins Point Co., 1780 [Ref: M-222].
WARD, Stephen. Took the Oath of Allegiance in Somerset County on Feb 28, 1778 before the Hon. Joseph Venables [Ref: T-25]. Rendered patriotic service

by supplying pork in Somerset County for the use of the military on May 1, 1781 [Ref: P-389].

WARD, Stephen (of Jacob). Took the Oath of Allegiance in Somerset County in 1778 before the Hon. John Williams [Ref: T-21, N-52].

WARD, Thomas. Private, Somerset Militia, Princess Anne Bn., Capt. Henry Miles' Little Annemessex Co., 1780 [Ref: M-221]. Took the Oath of Allegiance in Somerset County in 1778 before the Hon. John Williams [Ref: T-21, N-52].

WARD, William. Private, Somerset Militia, Princess Anne Bn., Capt. George Waters' Pocomoke Co., 1780 [Ref: M-220].

WARD, William. Private, Somerset Militia, Princess Anne Bn., Capt. Henry Miles' Little Annemessex Co., 1780 [Ref: M-221].

WARREN, Ananias (Annanias). Private, Worcester Militia, Sinepuxent Bn., Capt. John Postly's Co., Sixth Class, 1779/1780 [Ref: M-251 listed the name as "Annanias Warran"]. In Worcester County Court in August, 1798, a petition by Ananias Warren was submitted for a commission to divide the estate of his father Thomas (son of Nicklus Warren who died testate). Thomas Warren died leaving land which the petitioner Ananias Warren thinks cannot be divided. His heirs were Ananias, Matthias, Caty, Nelly, Sally, and Mary Warren, and Ezekiah (Ezekiel?) Crapper, and Pheme Boulds [Ref: Article by William D. Patrick in *Maryland Magazine of Genealogy*, Vol. 4, No. 2 (Fall, 1981), pp. 76-77].

WARREN, Caty. See "Ananias Warren," q.v.

WARREN, Isaac. Private, Worcester Militia, Sinepuxent Bn., Capt. John Postly's Co., Sixth Class, 1779/1780 [Ref: M-251 listed the name as "Isaac Warran"]. Took the Oath of Allegiance in Worcester County in 1778 before the Hon. Joshua Townsend [Ref: J-1814 (Box 4) listed the name as "Isaac Warraen"].

WARREN, John. Private, Worcester Militia, Sinepuxent Bn., Capt. Matthew Purnell's Co., Sixth Class, July 25, 1780 [Ref: M-252]. Took the Oath of Allegiance in Worcester County in 1778 before the Hon. John Selby [Ref: J-1814 (Box 4)]. One John Warren was a private in the 5th Maryland Line who enlisted on April 23, 1777 and was discharged on Oct 12, 1779 [Ref: D-254].

WARREN, Mary. See "Ananias Warren," q.v.

WARREN, Matthias. See "Ananias Warren," q.v.

WARREN, Nelly. See "Ananias Warren," q.v.

WARREN, Pharoh. Took the Oath of Allegiance in Worcester County in 1778 before the Hon. Nathaniel Miller [Ref: J-1814 (Box 4) listed the name as "Pharoh Warran"].

WARREN, Sally. See "Ananias Warren," q.v.

WARREN, Thomas. See "Ananias Warren," q.v.

WARRICK (WARWICK), Arthur. Private, Somerset Militia, Princess Anne Bn., Capt. James Elzey's Co., 1780 [Ref: M-220]. Took the Oath of Allegiance in Somerset County in 1778 before the Hon. Peter Waters [Ref: T-18 listed the name as "Arthur Warwick"].

WARRICK (WARWICK), Josiah. Private, Somerset Militia, Princess Anne Bn., Capt. George Waters' Pocomoke Co., 1780 [Ref: M-220].

WARRICK (WARWICK), William. Private, Somerset Militia, Princess Anne Bn., Capt. James Elzey's Co., 1780 [Ref: M-220]. Took the Oath of Allegiance in Somerset County in 1778 before the Hon. Peter Waters [Ref: T-18 listed the name as "William Wawick"].

WARRINGTON, Alexander. Private, Worcester Militia, Sinepuxent Bn., Capt. Josiah Dale's Co., Fourth Class, 1779/1780 [Ref: M-254].

WASHBOURN, Ruben. Private, Somerset Militia, Salisbury Bn., Capt. James Bennett's Salisbury Co., 1778/1780 [Ref: M-218]. On July 30, 1781, William Evans recruited Ruben Washbourn from Somerset County to serve in the Continental Army until Dec 10, 1781 [Ref: L-35C].

WASHINGTON, George. See "George Gale" and "Gustavus Scott," q.v.

WATERS, Abraham. Private, 5th Maryland Line, who enlisted on May 20, 1778 and was reported dead on July 29, 1778 [Ref: D-255].

WATERS, Edward. Took the Oath of Allegiance in Somerset County in 1778 before the Hon. Peter Waters [Ref: T-18].

WATERS, Elizabeth. See "John Waters," q.v.

WATERS, Francis. See "John Waters," q.v.

WATERS, George. Captain, Somerset Militia, Princess Anne Bn., Pocomoke Co., Sep 22, 1777 to at least July 24, 1780 [Ref: M-134, M-220, C-381]. Took the Oath of Allegiance in Somerset County in 1778 before the Hon. Peter Waters [Ref: T-18]. Justice of the Peace, commissioned on Nov 25, 1780 and Jan 17, 1782 [Ref: G-224, G-225, I-45]. In Somerset County there was a George Waters (1741/2-1801), son of William Waters, Sr. (d. 1781), and a George Nicholas Severn Waters (1738-c1784), son of John Waters (d. 1761) and brother of John and Peter Waters [Ref: R-866]. Additional research will be necessary before drawing conclusions. See "William Waters, Sr.," q.v.

WATERS, James. Sergeant, Somerset Militia, Princess Anne Bn., Capt. Isaac Handy's Great Annemessix Co., 1780 [Ref: M-221].

WATERS, Jesse. Private, Worcester Militia, Sinepuxent Bn., Capt. William Purnell's Co., Fourth Class, 1779/1780 [Ref: M-252]. Took the Oath of Allegiance in Worcester County in 1778 in Bogerternorton Hundred before the Hon. Thomas Purnell [Ref: J-1814 (Box 4) listed the name as "Jesse Watous"].

WATERS, John (c1727-1784). Son of John Waters (d. 1761) and Mary Elizabeth Hack. He married Elizabeth Hutchins or Hutchings circa 1763 and their children were Francis Hutchings, Elizabeth, and Sarah. John attended the Maryland Conventions in 1774-1775 from Somerset County and signed the Association of the Freemen of Maryland on July 26, 1775. He was elected to the Lower House of the Maryland Legislature in 1777, but did not attend due to the election being voided on March 5, 1777 because thirty armed men had intimidated the voters at the time of the election [Ref: R-866, O-4, A-67]. See "Peter Waters" and "George Waters" and "Richard Waters, Jr.," q.v.

WATERS, John Jr. Private, Somerset Militia, Salisbury Bn., Capt. Henry Gale's Quantico Co., 1778/1780 [Ref: M-217].

WATERS, Joseph. Private, Worcester Militia, Sinepuxent Bn., Capt. John Rackliff's Co., First Class, 1779/1780 [Ref: M-251]. Took the Oath of Allegiance in Worcester County in 1778 before the Hon. Nathaniel Miller [Ref: J-1814 (Box 4)].

WATERS, Margaret. See "William Waters, Sr.," q.v.

WATERS, Patrick. Private, Worcester Militia, Wicomico Bn., Capt. William Handy's Co., Seventh Class, July 15, 1780 [Ref: M-257]. Took the Oath of Allegiance in Worcester County in 1778 before the Hon. John Selby [Ref: J-1814 (Box 4)].

WATERS, Peter (1744/5-1806). Son of John Waters (d. 1761) and Mary Elizabeth Hack. Peter was born Jan 8, 1774/5, never married, and died before Oct 9, 1806. He served in the Lower House of the Maryland Legislature from Somerset County, 1773-1774, attended the Maryland Conventions, 1774-1776, and served on the Committee of Observation for Somerset County, 1775-1776 [Ref: R-866, O-1, O-28]. Lieutenant Colonel, Somerset Militia, 17th Bn., June 6, 1776. Lieutenant Colonel, Princess Anne Bn., Oct 24, 1780, resigned [Ref: M-134]. Justice who administered the Oath of Allegiance in Somerset County in 1778 [Ref: T-18]. Took the Oath of Allegiance in 1778 before the Hon. Levin Wilson [Ref: T-17, N-52]. Justice of the Orphans Court and Justice of the Peace, commissioned on Jan 7, 1778 and Nov 21, 1778 [Ref: C-464, E-248]. See "George Waters," q.v.

WATERS, Richard. Took the Oath of Allegiance in Somerset County in 1778 before the Hon. Peter Waters [Ref: T-16, N-52].

WATERS, Richard Jr. Son of William Waters, Sr. (d. 1781) and Rose Ann Harmanson. Richard married Elizabeth Waters Maddux, widow of ---- Maddux and daughter of John Waters (d. 1784); children, if any, unknown. He lived in Somerset County until 1787, Dorchester County until 1812, and was living in Baltimore City in 1813. He owned land in Alleghany County, Dorchester County and Harford County. Richard was second lieutenant, First Maryland Line, 1777; first lieutenant, 1778; captain, 1779; transferred to Third Maryland Line, 1781; retired, 1783; and, was an original member of the Society of the Cincinnati. He also served in the Lower House of the Maryland Legislature from Somerset County, 1784-1785 [Ref: R-866, R-867]. See "William Waters, Sr.," q.v.

WATERS, Sarah. See "John Waters" and "William Waters, Sr.," q.v.

WATERS, Thomas. Private, Somerset Militia, Salisbury Bn., White Haven Co., 1778/1780. Ensign, Salisbury Bn., Capt. Joseph Cottman's Co., Aug 22, 1781 [Ref: M-134, M-218, G-575].

WATERS, Thomas. Private, Select Militia, Somerset County, Aug 15, 1781 [Ref: L-35B]. See "William Waters, Sr.," q.v.

WATERS, Tubman. Private, Somerset Militia, Princess Anne Bn., Capt. Isaac Handy's Great Annemessix Co., 1780 [Ref: M-221].

WATERS, William. "There were two William Waters of age and from legislator families who were eligible to serve in the Conventions from Somerset County, 1774-1776. An extensive search of the records has failed to produce positive identification of which man actually served in 1775." [Ref: R-867]. There was a William Waters (c1736-1815), a William Waters (1740-1804), and a William Waters (c1717-1781) in Somerset County during the revolutionary era. There was also one or two men named William Waters (of William), and even though this appears illogical, the dates and events do not line up for just one person by that name (see below). Additional research will be necessary before drawing conclusions [Refer to source R-867 and R-868 for more information].

WATERS, William Sr. (c1717-1781). Took the Oath of Allegiance in Somerset County in 1778 before the Hon. Peter Waters [Ref: T-18]. He married Rose Ann Harmanson circa 1739 and their children were William (1740-1804), George (1741/2-1801), Thomas, Richard Jr., Margaret (married John Savage), and Sarah (married first to Dr. John Done and second to David Wilson). [Ref: R-868, Y-91].

WATERS, William. Private, Worcester Militia, Wicomico Bn., Capt. James Patterson's Co., Eighth Class, July 15, 1780 [Ref: M-258]. Took the Oath of Allegiance in Worcester County in 1778 in Bogerternorton Hundred before the Hon. Thomas Purnell [Ref: J-1814 (Box 4) listed the name as "William Watous"]. Rendered patriotic service by loading tobacco for the use of the military in 1781 [Ref: P-405].

WATERS, William (of John). Son of John Waters (d. 1761) and Mary Elizabeth Hack. William was born circa 1736, married Sarah Waters, and died by April 15, 1815 (will probated in Somerset County). Children: Levin Denwood, William Gillis, and Ann Hack. He attended the Maryland Convention in 1775, one of the representatives of Somerset County. He wa a captain in the Somerset Militia, Great Annamessex Co., Princess Anne Bn., Sep 22, 1777. Colonel, 1780 (resigned his commission due to his residence in Baltimore). [Ref: M-134, G-575, O-4]. Took the Oath of Allegiance in Somerset County in 1778 before the Hon. Peter Waters [Ref: T-18].

WATERS, William (of William). Captain, Somerset Militia, St. Asaph Co., Princess Anne Bn., Sep 22, 1777 to Aug 22, 1781, succeeded [Ref: M-134, C-381, G-575]. Took the Oath of Allegiance in Somerset County in 1778 before the Hon. Peter Waters [Ref: T-18].

WATERS, William (of William). Second Major, Somerset Militia, 17th Bn., Jan 6, 1776. Lieutenant Colonel, Princess Anne Bn., Oct 20 (28?), 1780 [Ref: M-134, C-381, J-1814 (Box 6), G-155].

WATKINS, John. Captain, 3rd Maryland Independent Co., Worcester County, commissioned Jan 5, 1776; muster roll dated Aug 20, 1776, present for duty [Ref: D-21].

WATSON, Jesse. Private, Worcester Militia, Wicomico Bn., Capt. Charles Bennett's Co., Fourth Class, July 15, 1780 [Ref: M-255].

WATSON, John. Private, Worcester Militia, Sinepuxent Bn., Capt. John Postly's Co., Third Class, 1779/1780 [Ref: M-251]. Took the Oath of Allegiance in Worcester County in 1778 before the Hon. Nehemiah Holland [Ref: J-1814 (Box 4)]. Private, Worcester Militia, Wicomico Bn., Capt. Fisher Walton's Co., Sixth Class, July 15, 1780 [Ref: M-258].

WATSON, Jonathan West (c1730/35-c1800/1805). Took the Oath of Allegiance in Worcester County in 1778 before the Hon. James Selby [Ref: J-1814 (Box 4) listed the name as "Jonathan West Wattson"]. Jonathan married Sarah ---- (first wife) and their daughter Rebecca married "Edward Joynes III," q.v.

WATSON, Joseph. Took the Oath of Allegiance in Worcester County in 1778 before the Hon. Nathaniel Miller [Ref: J-1814 (Box 4)].

WATSON, Levin. Private, Worcester Militia, Snow Hill Bn., Capt. John Parramore's Co., 1777 [Ref: M-250]. Private, Worcester Militia, Wicomico Bn., Capt. Samuel Smyley's Co., Second Class, July 15, 1780 [Ref: M-259]. Took the Oath of Allegiance in Worcester County in 1778 before the Hon. John Selby [Ref: J-1814 (Box 4)].

WATSON, Major. Private, Worcester Militia, Wicomico Bn., Capt. James Patterson's Co., Sixth Class, July 15, 1780 [Ref: M-258].

WATSON, Nathan. Private, Worcester Militia, Snow Hill Bn., Capt. Samuel Smyley's Co., 1777 [Ref: M-250]. Took the Oath of Allegiance in Worcester County in 1778 before the Hon. Nehemiah Holland [Ref: J-1814 (Box 4)].

WATSON, Parker. Private, Worcester Militia, Snow Hill Bn., Capt. John Parramore's Co., 1777 [Ref: M-250]. Took the Oath of Allegiance in Worcester County in 1778 before the Hon. Nehemiah Holland [Ref: J-1814 (Box 4)].

WATSON, Rebecca. See "Jonathan West Watson" and "Edward Joynes," q.v.

WATSON, Sarah. See "Jonathan West Watson," q.v.

WATTERS, James. Private, Worcester Militia, Sinepuxent Bn., Capt. John Rackliff's Co., Eighth Class, 1779/1780 [Ref: M-251]. Took the Oath of Allegiance in Worcester County in 1778 in Buckingham Hundred before the Hon. Thomas Purnell [Ref: J-1814 (Box 4)].

WATTERS, William. Took the Oath of Allegiance in Worcester County in 1778 before the Hon. Joshua Townsend [Ref: J-1814 (Box 4)].

WATTS, Mary. See "John Selby," q.v.

WATTS, William. Private, Worcester Militia, Sinepuxent Bn., Capt. Thomas Purnell's Co., Fifth Class, 1779/1780 [Ref: M-253]. Took the Oath of Allegiance in Worcester County in 1778 before the Hon. Nathaniel Miller [Ref: J-1814 (Box 4)].

WAYNE, Colonel. See "Moses Greer," q.v.

WEATHERLY, Charles. Private, Somerset Militia, Salisbury Bn., Capt. Joseph Venables' Barren Creek Co., 1778/1780 [Ref: M-217]. Took the Oath of

Allegiance in Somerset County on March 1, 1778 before the Hon. Joseph Venables [Ref: T-25].

WEATHERLY, Constant. Sergeant, Somerset Militia, Salisbury Bn., Capt. William Turpin's Rewastico Co., 1778/1780 [Ref: M-217].

WEATHERLY, James. Private, Somerset Militia, Salisbury Bn., Capt. William Turpin's Rewastico Co., 1778/1780 [Ref: M-217].

WEATHERLY, Jesse. Private, Somerset Militia, Salisbury Bn., Capt. Joseph Venables' Barren Creek Co., 1778/1780 [Ref: M-217].

WEATHERLY, John. Second Lieutenant, Somerset Militia, Salisbury Bn., Capt. Joseph Venables' Barren Creek Co., Sep 22, 1777 to 1780 [Ref: M-134, M-217, C-381, which latter source listed the name as "John Weatherby"].

WEATHERLY, Richard Trane. Private, Somerset County, Capt. John Gunby's 2nd Independent Maryland Co.; present on May 28, 1776; mustered on Aug 21, 1776 [Ref: D-641].

WEBB, Elias. Private, Worcester Militia, Sinepuxent Bn., Capt. Matthew Purnell's Co., Second Class, July 25, 1780 [Ref: M-252].

WEBB, Elisha. Private, Worcester Militia, Sinepuxent Bn., Capt. John Coe's Co., Third Class, 1779/1780 [Ref: M-252].

WEBB, Israel. Private, Worcester Militia, Wicomico Bn., Capt. Fisher Walton's Co., Fifth Class, July 15, 1780 [Ref: M-258]. One "Israel Lane Webb" was born in Coventry Parish on April 5, 1762, a son of Solomon and Mary Webb [Ref: Y-92].

WEBB, Jeptha. Private, Worcester Militia, Sinepuxent Bn., Capt. Matthew Purnell's Co., Seventh Class, July 25, 1780 [Ref: M-252].

WEBB, John. Private, Worcester Militia, Sinepuxent Bn., Capt. Matthew Purnell's Co., Eighth Class, July 25, 1780 [Ref: M-252].

WEBB, Mary. See "Israel Webb" and "John Tarr (of John)," q.v.

WEBB, Scarborough. Private, Worcester Militia, Sinepuxent Bn., Capt. John Coe's Co., Eighth Class, 1779/1780 [Ref: M-252].

WEBB, Solomon. Private, Worcester Militia, Wicomico Bn., Capt. Isaac Layfield's Co., Seventh Class, July 15, 1780 [Ref: M-257]. See "Israel Webb," q.v.

WEBB, William. Private, Somerset Militia, Princess Anne Bn., Capt. Thomas Irving's Monie Co., 1780 [Ref: M-219].

WEBB, William. Private, Worcester Militia, Sinepuxent Bn., Capt. John Coe's Co., Eighth Class, 1779/1780 [Ref: M-252].

WEBB, Zepheniah. Private, Worcester Militia, Sinepuxent Bn., Capt. Matthew Purnell's Co., Seventh Class, July 25, 1780 [Ref: M-252].

WEBSTER, Jabez. Private, Somerset Militia, Princess Anne Bn., Capt. Thomas Irving's Monie Co., 1780 [Ref: M-219].

WEBSTER, John. Private, Somerset Militia, Princess Anne Bn., Capt. Thomas Irving's Monie Co., 1780 [Ref: M-219].

WEBSTER, Mesheck. Private, Somerset Militia, Princess Anne Bn., Capt. Thomas Irving's Monie Co., 1780 [Ref: M-219].

WEBSTER, William. Private, Somerset Militia, Princess Anne Bn., Capt. Thomas Irving's Monie Co., 1780 [Ref: M-219].
WEDGER, John. Private, Worcester Militia, Sinepuxent Bn., Capt. Josiah Dale's Co., First Class, 1779/1780 [Ref: M-253].
WELCH, George. Drafted "by the class" from Somerset County on July 30, 1781 to serve in the Continental Army until Dec 10, 1781 [Ref: L-35C].
WELLER, William. Took the Oath of Allegiance in Somerset County in 1778 [Ref: N-52].
WELLS, John. Private, Worcester Militia, Wicomico Bn., Capt. Charles Bennett's Co., Eighth Class, July 15, 1780 [Ref: M-255].
WELLS, Risdon. Took the Oath of Allegiance in Worcester County in 1778 before the Hon. Joshua Townsend [Ref: J-1814 (Box 4)].
WELSH, William. Rendered patriotic service by supplying corn for the use of the military in Somerset County on Feb 26, 1780 [Ref: P-272].
WEST, James. Private, Somerset Militia, Salisbury Bn., Capt. William Turpin's Rewastico Co., 1778/1780 [Ref: M-217].
WEST, Mary. See "Anthony Murphy," q.v.
WEST, William. See "Anthony Murphy," q.v.
WHALEY, Nathaniel. Private, Worcester Militia, Wicomico Bn., Capt. Elijah Shockley's Co., Second Class, July 15, 1780 [Ref: M-255 listed the name as "Nathaniel Whaly"].
WHALEY, William. Private, Somerset Militia, Salisbury Bn., Capt. Sampson Wheatly's Co., 1780 [Ref: M-216].
WHALLEN, Thomas. Private, Somerset Militia, Salisbury Bn., Capt. Josiah Dashiell's Wicomico Creek Co., 1778/1780 [Ref: M-218].
WHARTON, Phila. See "James Atkinson," q.v.
WHARTON, Revil. Private, Worcester Militia, Snow Hill Bn., Capt. Ebenezer Handy's Co., April 9, 1776 [Ref: M-249].
WHEATLEY, Michael. Private, Somerset Militia, Princess Anne Bn., Capt. John Williams' Watkins Point Co., 1780 [Ref: M-222].
WHEATLEY, Sampson. Captain, Somerset Militia, Salisbury Bn., 1780 [Ref: M-215].
WHEATLEY, Sampson. Private, Somerset Militia, Princess Anne Bn., Capt. John Williams' Watkins Point Co., 1780 [Ref: M-222].
WHEATLEY, William. Ensign, Somerset Militia, Salisbury Bn., Capt. Sampson Wheatly's Co., 1780 [Ref: M-215].
WHEATLEY, William. Private, Somerset Militia, Princess Anne Bn., Capt. John Williams' Watkins Point Co., 1780 [Ref: M-222]. Drafted from Somerset County on July 30, 1781 to serve in the Continental Army [Ref: L-35C].
WHEELER, Elisha. Private, Worcester Militia, Sinepuxent Bn., Capt. Matthew Purnell's Co., Sixth Class, July 25, 1780 [Ref: M-252].
WHEELER, John. Private, Worcester Militia, Sinepuxent Bn., Capt. William Purnell's Co., Seventh Class, 1779/1780 [Ref: M-252].

WHEELER, Jonathan. Private, Somerset Militia, Salisbury Bn., Capt. Sampson Wheatly's Co., 1780 [Ref: M-216 listed the name as "Jonathan Whealer"].

WHEELER, Nathaniel (c1750-1825). Private, 2nd Maryland Line, who was wounded at the Battle of Eutaw Spring. On Dec 20, 1784 he appeared on a "return of disabled soldiers who have been allowed by the Orphans Court of Somerset County on account their half pay, etc." from Jan 1, 1783; settled up to Dec 1, 1784, £43.2.6 [Ref: D-634, D-635]. He died on Nov 5, 1825 [Ref: X-18].

WHEELER, Southey (Sowthey). Took the Oath of Allegiance in Worcester County in 1778 in Buckingham Hundred before the Hon. Thomas Purnell [Ref: J-1814 (Box 4)].

WHEELER, Zadock (c1743-1809). Private, Somerset Militia, Princess Anne Bn., St. Asaph's Co., 1780 [Ref: M-220]. Took the Oath of Allegiance in Somerset County in 1778 before the Hon. John Williams [Ref: N-52, and T-21 listed the name as "Zadok Wheeller"].

WHEELTON, Daniel. Private, 3rd Maryland Independent Co., Worcester County, Capt. John Watkins' Co., enlisted Feb 24, 1776; muster roll dated Aug 20, 1776, present for duty [Ref: D-23].

WHEELTON, Joshua. Private, 3rd Maryland Independent Co., Worcester County, Capt. John Watkins' Co., enlisted Feb 24, 1776; muster roll dated Aug 20, 1776, present for duty [Ref: D-22].

WHEELTON(?), William. Private, 3rd Maryland Independent Co., Worcester County, Capt. John Watkins' Co., enlisted April 17, 1776; muster roll dated Aug 20, 1776, present for duty [Ref: D-22 listed the name as "Wm. ----ton"].

WHEYLAND, William. See "John Henry," q.v.

WHITCAR, George. Private, Somerset Militia, Capt. George Day Scott's Co., 1775 [Ref: J-1814 (Box 1)].

WHITE, Barkley (Barclay). Private, Worcester Militia, Wicomico Bn., Capt. Benjamin Dennis' Co., Fourth Class, July 15, 1780 [Ref: M-255]. Took the Oath of Allegiance in Worcester County in 1778 before the Hon. Joshua Townsend [Ref: J-1814 (Box 4)].

WHITE, Betsey. See "William White," q.v.

WHITE, Betty. See "James Bruff," q.v.

WHITE, Elias. See "Stephen (Steven) White," q.v.

WHITE, Elisabeth. See "William Bell White," q.v.

WHITE, Elizabeth. See "William White," q.v.

WHITE, Francis. Private, Somerset Militia, Princess Anne Bn., Capt. Thomas Irving's Monie Co., 1780 [Ref: M-219]. Drafted from Somerset County on July 30, 1781 to serve in the Continental Army [Ref: L-35C].

WHITE, Henry. Private, Worcester Militia, Sinepuxent Bn., Capt. Thomas Purnell's Co., Second Class, 1779/1780 [Ref: M-253]. Took the Oath of Allegiance in Worcester County in 1778 before the Hon. Nathaniel Miller [Ref: J-1814 (Box 4)]. Rendered patriotic service by herding and grazing cattle for the use of the military in September, 1781 [Ref: P-431]. In Worcester County Court, on August 16, 1797, a petition to divide the real estate of Henry White was submitted by James Collins and Molly his wife, and Sally White. Henry White had died possessed of land called *Buckingham*, it falling by descent upon the petitioners, all of age [Ref: Article by William D. Patrick in *Maryland Magazine of Genealogy*, Vol. 4, No. 1 (Spring, 1981), p. 7].

WHITE, Isaac. Corporal, Somerset Militia, Salisbury Bn., Capt. Josiah Dashiell's Wicomico Creek Co., 1778/1780 [Ref: M-218]. Took the Oath of Allegiance in Somerset County on Feb 28, 1778 before the Hon. Joseph Venables [Ref: T-25]. Drafted from Somerset County on July 30, 1781 to serve in the Continental Army, but was subsequently excused [Ref: L-35C].

WHITE, James (of J.). Private, 3rd Maryland Independent Co., Worcester County, Capt. John Watkins' Co., enlisted Feb 10, 1776; muster roll dated Aug 20, 1776, present for duty [Ref: D-22].

WHITE, James (of William). Private, 3rd Maryland Independent Co., Worcester County, Capt. John Watkins' Co., enlisted Feb 6, 1776; muster roll dated Aug 20, 1776, present for duty [Ref: D-22].

WHITE, John. Private, Worcester Militia, Sinepuxent Bn., Capt. Thomas Purnell's Co., Fifth Class, 1779/1780 [Ref: M-253]. Private, Worcester Militia, Capt. John Martin's Co., 1780/1781 [Ref: J-1814 (Box 12)].

WHITE, John. Sergeant, Somerset Militia, Salisbury Bn., Capt. Sampson Wheatly's Co., 1780 [Ref: M-215]. Took the Oath of Allegiance in Worcester County in 1778 before the Hon. Nathaniel Miller [Ref: J-1814 (Box 4)].

WHITE, John Jr. Private, Somerset Militia, Princess Anne Bn., Capt. Thomas Irving's Monie Co., 1780 [Ref: M-219]. There were at least two John White, Jr.'s born in Coventry Parish: John White, son of John and Mary, was born on April 3, 1751, and John White, son of John and Mary, was born on Nov 8, 1756 [Ref: Y-76, Y-92]. Additional research will be necessary before drawing conclusions.

WHITE, Joshua. Private, Worcester Militia, Wicomico Bn., Capt. Benjamin Dennis' Co., Seventh Class, July 15, 1780 [Ref: M-256]. Took the Oath of Allegiance in Worcester County in 1778 before the Hon. Joshua Townsend [Ref: J-1814 (Box 4)].

WHITE, Littleton. See "William White," q.v.

WHITE, Major. Private, Worcester Militia, Wicomico Bn., Capt. Philip Quinton's Co., Fourth Class, July 15, 1780 [Ref: M-256]. Took the Oath of Allegiance in Worcester County in 1778 before the Hon. Joshua Townsend [Ref: J-1814 (Box 4)]. Rendered patriotic service by killing beef for the use of the military in 1781 [Ref: P-442].

WHITE, Michel. Took the Oath of Allegiance in Somerset County on Feb 28, 1778 (made his "X" mark) before the Hon. Joseph Venables [Ref: T-25].

WHITE, Peter. Took the Oath of Allegiance in Worcester County in 1778 before the Hon. Joshua Townsend [Ref: J-1814 (Box 4)].

WHITE, Philip. Private, Worcester Militia, Sinepuxent Bn., Capt. John Coe's Co., Third Class, 1779/1780 [Ref: M-252].
WHITE, Rachel. See "John Tull," q.v.
WHITE, Sally. See "Henry White," q.v.
WHITE, Samuel. Private, Worcester Militia, Wicomico Bn., Capt. Samuel Horsey's Co., Fourth Class, July 15, 1780 [Ref: M-257].
WHITE, Sarah. See "Stephen (Steven) White," q.v.
WHITE, Stephen. Corporal, Somerset Militia, Princess Anne Bn., St. Asaph's Co., 1780 [Ref: M-220].
WHITE, Stephen (Steven). Took the Oath of Allegiance in Worcester County in 1778 before the Hon. Joshua Townsend [Ref: J-1814 (Box 4)]. Private, Worcester Militia, Wicomico Bn., Capt. Benjamin Dennis' Co., Second Class, July 15, 1780 [Ref: M-255 listed the name as "Steven White"]. One "Stevens White" was a son of Elias and Sarah White, of Coventry Parish, born on Nov 14, 1760 [Ref: Y-91].
WHITE, Stephen (of John). Private, Worcester Militia, Sinepuxent Bn., Capt. Thomas Purnell's Co., Eighth Class, 1779/1780 [Ref: M-253].
WHITE, Stevens. See "Stephen (Steven) White," q.v.
WHITE, Thomas. Private, Somerset Militia, Princess Anne Bn., Capt. Thomas Irving's Monie Co., 1780 [Ref: M-219].
WHITE, Thomas. Private, Worcester Militia, Wicomico Bn., Capt. James Perdue's Co., Sixth Class, July 15, 1780 [Ref: M-256].
WHITE, Thomas. Sergeant, Somerset Militia, Salisbury Bn., Capt. Sampson Wheatly's Co., 1780 [Ref: M-215].
WHITE, William. First Lieutenant, Worcester Militia, Sinepuxent Bn., Capt. Matthew Purnell's Co., Aug 30, 1777 [Ref: M-136, C-350].
WHITE, William. Private, Worcester Militia, Wicomico Bn., Capt. Benjamin Dennis' Co., Third Class, July 15, 1780 [Ref: M-255].
WHITE, William. Private, Worcester Militia, Sinepuxent Bn., Capt. John Postly's Co., Sixth Class, 1779/1780 [Ref: M-251]. Took the Oath of Allegiance in Worcester County in 1778 before the Hon. Nathaniel Miller [Ref: J-1814 (Box 4)].
WHITE, William. Surgeon's Mate in the Virginia Navy during the Revolutionary War who "was a resident of Worcester County, Maryland at the time of his death. Littleton S. White and Elizabeth A. White are the only heirs at law of William White, formerly of Accomack County ... said Elizabeth A. White is an infant and Betsey T. White is the widow of the said William White. Oct 26, 1830." (Court Orders, 1829-1832, p. 192). [Ref: Stratton Nottingham's *Soldiers and Sailors of the Eastern Shore of Virginia in the Revolutionary War*, p. 16].
WHITE, William (blacksmith). Took the Oath of Allegiance in Worcester County in 1778 before the Hon. Joshua Townsend [Ref: J-1814 (Box 4)].
WHITE, William (corker). Took the Oath of Allegiance in Worcester County in 1778 before the Hon. Joshua Townsend [Ref: J-1814 (Box 4)].

WHITE, William Bell. Son of William White (d. 1789) and wife Elisabeth [Ref: *Provincial Families of Maryland, Volume I*, by Vernon L. Skinner, ed. (1998), pp. 109-110]. Private, Somerset Militia, Princess Anne Bn., Capt. George Waters' Pocomoke Co., 1780 [Ref: M-220].

WHITE, William Stevens. Took the Oath of Allegiance in Somerset County in 1778 before the Hon. John Williams [Ref: T-21, N-52].

WHITHEARS, George. Took the Oath of Allegiance in Somerset County in 1778 before the Hon. Levin Wilson [Ref: T-17 listed the name as "George Whithears" and N-52 listed the name as "George Whithen"].

WHITTINGHAM, Heber. Sergeant, Somerset Militia, Princess Anne Bn., Capt. John Jones' Princess Anne Co., 1780 [Ref: M-219]. Took the Oath of Allegiance in Somerset County in 1778 before the Hon. Peter Waters [Ref: T-18].

WHITTINGTON, Betty. See "Benton Harris," q.v.

WHITTINGTON, Isaac (1730-1815). Took the Oath of Allegiance in Somerset County in 1778 before the Hon. John Williams [Ref: T-21, N-52]. Isaac Whittington was born in 1730 in Somerset County, married Elizabeth Wishart, and died in 1815. Their son Thomas Wishart Whittington (1763-1818) married Sarah S. Conner (1767-1839) on March 4, 1799 [Ref: S-3004].

WHITTINGTON, James. Corporal, Somerset Militia, Princess Anne Bn., Capt. John Williams' Watkins Point Co., 1780 [Ref: M-222].

WHITTINGTON, Joseph. Private, 5th Maryland Line, enlisted in June, 1778 and was reported as "left out" in July, 1778 [Ref: D-255].

WHITTINGTON, Mary. See "William Davis Allen," q.v.

WHITTINGTON, Southy (c1732-1785/6). Took the Oath of Allegiance in Worcester County in 1778 before the Hon. Nehemiah Holland [Ref: J-1814 (Box 4)]. Southey Whittington was born circa 1732, married Esther Nairne, rendered patriotic service during the revolution, and died in 1785 or 1786 in Maryland [Ref: V-3204].

WHITTINGTON, Thomas. See "Isaac Whittington," q.v.

WHITTINGTON, William (c1740-c1815). Corporal, Somerset Militia, Princess Anne Bn., Capt. John Williams' Watkins Point Co., 1780 [Ref: M-222]. Took the Oath of Allegiance in Somerset County in 1778 before the Hon. John Williams [Ref: T-21, N-52]. William Whittington was born circa 1740, married Priscilla Polk, was a corporal in the revolution, and died after Dec 29, 1815 [Ref: V-3204]. See "Benton Harris" and "William Whittington, Sr.," q.v.

WHITTINGTON, William Jr. Took the Oath of Allegiance in Somerset County in 1778 before the Hon. John Williams [Ref: T-21, N-52].

WHITTINGTON, William Sr. Corporal, Somerset Militia, Princess Anne Bn., Capt. John Williams' Watkins Point Co., 1780 [Ref: M-222]. See "William Whittington," q.v.

WHITWELL, Thomas and Winefrid. See "William Stevens," q.v.

WILEY, William. Took the Oath of Allegiance in Somerset County in 1778 before the Hon. Levin Wilson [Ref: T-17, N-52].
WILKINS, Isaac. Private, Somerset Militia, Salisbury Bn., Capt. James Bennett's Salisbury Co., 1778/1780 [Ref: M-218].
WILKINS, John. Private, Somerset Militia, Princess Anne Bn., Capt. John Jones' Princess Anne Co., 1780 [Ref: M-219].
WILKINS, Major. Private, Worcester Militia, Wicomico Bn., Capt. James Perdue's Co., First Class, July 15, 1780 [Ref: M-256]. Took the Oath of Allegiance in Worcester County in 1778 before the Hon. Nehemiah Holland [Ref: J-1814 (Box 4)].
WILKINS, Samuel. Took the Oath of Allegiance in Somerset County in 1778 before the Hon. Peter Waters [Ref: T-18].
WILLETT, Ambrose. Private, Worcester Militia, Wicomico Bn., Capt. Fisher Walton's Co., First Class, July 15, 1780 [Ref: M-258].
WILLETT, Henry. Private, Worcester Militia, Snow Hill Bn., Capt. John Parramore's Co., 1777 [Ref: M-250 listed the name as "Henry Willit"]. Private, Worcester Militia, Wicomico Bn., Capt. Samuel Smyley's Co., Fifth Class, July 15, 1780 [Ref: M-259].
WILLIAMS, Amelia. See "John Gale," q.v.
WILLIAMS, Arthur. Private, Somerset Militia, Salisbury Bn., Capt. Sampson Wheatly's Co., 1780 [Ref: M-216].
WILLIAMS, Benjamin. Private, Somerset Militia, Princess Anne Bn., Capt. Henry Miles' Little Annemessex Co., 1780 [Ref: M-221]. Took the Oath of Allegiance in Somerset County in 1778 before the Hon. John Williams [Ref: T-21, N-52].
WILLIAMS, Charles. Drafted from Somerset County on July 30, 1781 to serve in the Continental Army [Ref: L-35C].
WILLIAMS, Charles N. Private, Worcester Militia, Sinepuxent Bn., Capt. John Postly's Co., Sixth Class, 1779/1780 [Ref: M-251].
WILLIAMS, David. Ensign, Somerset Militia, Princess Anne Bn., Capt. John Williams' Co., Sep 22, 1777 [Ref: M-137, C-381]. Took the Oath of Allegiance in Somerset County in 1778 before the Hon. John Williams [Ref: T-21, N-52].
WILLIAMS, David. Private, Worcester Militia, Sinepuxent Bn., Capt. John Postly's Co., Seventh Class, 1779/1780 [Ref: M-251]. Took the Oath of Allegiance in Worcester County in 1778 before the Hon. Joshua Townsend [Ref: J-1814 (Box 4)].
WILLIAMS, Esau (1747-1799). Ensign, Worcester Militia, Sinepuxent Bn., Capt. William Purnell's Co., Aug 30, 1777. Ensign(?), Worcester Militia, Sinepuxent Bn., Capt. John Postly's Co., Third Class, 1779/1780. First Lieutenant, March 16, 1781, Capt. Isaac Evans' Co. [Ref: G-353, M-137, M-251, and C-350 listed the name as "Esaw Williams, Ensign"]. Took the Oath of Allegiance in Worcester County in 1778 before the Hon. Nathaniel Miller [Ref: J-1814 (Box 4)]. Esau Williams was born on Jan 3, 1747, married Mary Jones, was an ensign in the revolution, and died before Sep 11, 1799 [Ref: V-3227].

WILLIAMS, Isaac. Private, Worcester Militia, Sinepuxent Bn., Capt. Thomas Purnell's Co., Second Class, 1779/1780 [Ref: M-253].
WILLIAMS, Isaac. Private, Worcester Militia, Sinepuxent Bn., Capt. John Rackliff's Co., Third Class, 1779/1780 [Ref: M-251].
WILLIAMS, Isaac. Took the Oath of Allegiance in Worcester County in 1778 before the Hon. Nathaniel Miller [Ref: J-1814 (Box 4)].
WILLIAMS, Ismeal (Ishmel). Private, Worcester Militia, Sinepuxent Bn., Capt. John Postly's Co., Seventh Class, 1779/1780 [Ref: M-251]. "Ishmel William" took the Oath of Allegiance in Worcester County in 1778 before the Hon. Joshua Townsend [Ref: J-1814 (Box 4)].
WILLIAMS, Jacob. Private, Worcester Militia, Capt. John Martin's Co., 1780/1781 [Ref: J-1814 (Box 12)].
WILLIAMS, James. Private, Worcester Militia, Wicomico Bn., Capt. Philip Quinton's Co., Fifth Class, July 15, 1780 [Ref: M-256].
WILLIAMS, Jesse. Private, Worcester Militia, Sinepuxent Bn., Capt. John Postly's Co., Fifth Class, 1779/1780 [Ref: M-251]. Took the Oath of Allegiance in Worcester County in 1778 before the Hon. Joshua Townsend [Ref: J-1814 (Box 4)].
WILLIAMS, John Sr. Took the Oath of Allegiance in Somerset County in 1778 before the Hon. John Williams [Ref: T-21, N-52]. See "Littleton Williams," q.v.
WILLIAMS, John. Captain, Somerset Militia, Princess Anne Bn., Watkins Point Co., from Sep 22, 1777 to at least July 24, 1780. Captain, Select Militia, Aug 23, 1781 [Ref: M-137, M-221, C-381, G-577]. Justice who administered the Oath of Allegiance in Somerset County in 1778 [Ref: T-21]. Justice of the Peace, commissioned on Jan 9, 1778 and Nov 21, 1778 and Jan 17, 1782 [Ref: C-464, E-248, I-45].
WILLIAMS, John. Private, 3rd Maryland Independent Co., Worcester County, Capt. John Watkins' Co., enlisted Feb 27, 1776; muster roll dated Aug 20, 1776, present for duty [Ref: D-21]. Soldier in Capt. Long's Independent Co. who was permitted by the Council of Safety on Oct 4, 1776 to go to Worcester County for the recovery of his health [Ref: B-318]. Took the Oath of Allegiance in Worcester County in 1778 before the Hon. John Selby [Ref: J-1814 (Box 4)].
WILLIAMS, John. Private, Worcester Militia, Sinepuxent Bn., Capt. Matthew Purnell's Co., Third Class, July 25, 1780 [Ref: M-252]. Took the Oath of Allegiance in Worcester County in 1778 before the Hon. Nathaniel Miller [Ref: J-1814 (Box 4)].
WILLIAMS, John (1755 -   ). Son of John Williams and Sarah Davis, born in Coventry Parish on June 30, 1755 [Ref: Y-77]. Private, Somerset Militia, Princess Anne Bn., Capt. Isaac Handy's Great Annemessix Co., 1780 [Ref: M-221]. Took the Oath of Allegiance in Somerset County in 1778 [Ref: N-52]. Select Militia, Somerset County, Aug 15, 1781 [Ref: L-35A].

WILLIAMS, John. Drafted from Somerset County on July 30, 1781 to serve in the Continental Army [Ref: L-35C].
WILLIAMS, Levin. Private, Somerset Militia, Princess Anne Bn., St. Asaph's Co., 1780 [Ref: M-221].
WILLIAMS, Littleton (1754 -   ). Son of John Williams and Sarah Davis, born in Coventry Parish on March 23, 1754 [Ref: Y-76]. Private, Somerset Militia, Princess Anne Bn., Capt. Isaac Handy's Great Annemessix Co., 1780 [Ref: M-221 listed the name as "Litt(?) Williams"].
WILLIAMS, Nathaniel. Took the Oath of Allegiance in Worcester County in 1778 before the Hon. Nathaniel Miller [Ref: J-1814 (Box 4)].
WILLIAMS, Planner (c1735 -   ). Captain, Somerset Militia, 17th Bn., Feb 24, 1776 [Ref: M-137, A-182]. Justice of the Orphans Court for Somerset County, commissioned on June 4, 1777 [Ref: C-274]. Planner Williams married Mary Robertson in Coventry Parish on Jan 1, 1760 [Ref: Y-92].
WILLIAMS, Planner (1762 -   ). Son of Planner Williams and Mary Robertson, born in Coventry Parish on March 3, 1762 [Ref: Y-92]. Private, Somerset Militia, Salisbury Bn., White Haven Co., 1780 [Ref: M-218].
WILLIAMS, Rebeccah. See "Hope Hull," q.v.
WILLIAMS, Richard. Private, Somerset Militia, Salisbury Bn., Capt. Joseph Venables' Barren Creek Co., 1778/1780 [Ref: M-217]. Took the Oath of Allegiance in Somerset County on Feb 21, 1778 before the Hon. Joseph Venables [Ref: T-25].
WILLIAMS, Samuel, Segr.*[sic]*. Took the Oath of Allegiance in Worcester County in 1778 before the Hon. Nathaniel Miller [Ref: J-1814 (Box 4)].
WILLIAMS, Samuel. Private, Somerset Militia, Salisbury Bn., Capt. James Bennett's Salisbury Co., 1778/1780 [Ref: M-218]. Took the Oath of Allegiance in Somerset County in 1778 [Ref: N-52].
WILLIAMS, Sarah. See "Littleton Williams," q.v.
WILLIAMS, Thomas. Ensign, Somerset Militia, 17th Bn., Capt. Planner Williams' Co., Feb 24, 1776 to at least Jan 1, 1778 [Ref: M-137, C-458, A-182]. Took the Oath of Allegiance in Somerset County in 1778 [Ref: N-52]. Rendered patriotic service by supplying pork for the use of the military on May 1, 1781 [Ref: P-389].
WILLIAMS, Thomas. Private, Somerset Militia, Princess Anne Bn., Capt. Isaac Handy's Great Annemessix Co., 1780 [Ref: M-221].
WILLIAMS, Thomas. Private, 3rd Maryland Independent Co., Worcester County, Capt. John Watkins' Co., enlisted April 15, 1776; muster roll dated Aug 20, 1776, absent on furlough [Ref: D-22].
WILLIAMS, Thomas. Second Lieutenant, Somerset Militia, Princess Anne Bn., Capt. William Waters' Co., Sep 22, 1777 [Ref: M-137, C-381]. Took the Oath of Allegiance in Somerset County in 1778 before the Hon. John Williams [Ref: T-21].

WILLIAMS, William (schoolmaster). Took the Oath of Allegiance in Worcester County in 1778 before the Hon. John Selby [Ref: J-1814 (Box 4)].

WILLIAMS, William. Private, Somerset County, Capt. John Gunby's 2nd Independent Maryland Co.; present on April 9, 1776; mustered on Aug 21, 1776 [Ref: D-641]. Private, Somerset Militia, Salisbury Bn., Capt. Sampson Wheatly's Co., 1780 [Ref: M-216].

WILLIAMS, William. Took the Oath of Allegiance in Worcester County in 1778 before the Hon. John Selby [Ref: J-1814 (Box 4)].

WILLIN (WILLEN), Clement. Private, Somerset Militia, Salisbury Bn., Capt. John Span Conway's Nanticoke Point Co., 1778/1780 [Ref: M-216].

WILLIN (WILLEN), Elijah. Private, Somerset Militia, Salisbury Bn., Capt. John Span Conway's Nanticoke Point Co., 1778/1780 [Ref: M-216].

WILLIN (WILLEN), George. Corporal, Somerset Militia, Salisbury Bn., Capt. John Span Conway's Nanticoke Point Co., 1778/1780 [Ref: M-216].

WILLIN (WILLEN), George. Corporal, Somerset Militia, Salisbury Bn., Capt. John Span Conway's Nanticoke Point Co., 1778/1780 [Ref: M-216].

WILLIN (WILLEN), James. Private, Somerset Militia, Salisbury Bn., Capt. John Span Conway's Nanticoke Point Co., 1778/1780 [Ref: M-216]. Select Militia, Somerset County, Aug 15, 1781 [Ref: L-35B].

WILLIN (WILLEN), John Jr. Private, Somerset Militia, Salisbury Bn., Capt. John Span Conway's Nanticoke Point Co., 1778/1780 [Ref: M-216].

WILLIN (WILLEN), Levin. Private, Somerset Militia, Salisbury Bn., Capt. John Span Conway's Nanticoke Point Co., 1778/1780 [Ref: M-216].

WILLIN (WILLEN), Levin Jr. (1758-c1840). Private, Somerset Militia, Salisbury Bn., Capt. John Span Conway's Nanticoke Point Co., 1778/1780 [Ref: M-216]. Private, Maryland Line and Maryland Sea Service, who applied for a pension (S7921) stating he was born in 1758 in Dorchester County, Maryland and lived in Somerset County at the time of his enlistment [Ref: W-3875 listed the name without the "Jr."]. Another source stated he was a private and seaman in the U. S. Navy who pensioned at $42 per annum effective March 4, 1831, age 76 [Ref: X-50]. "Levin Willing, age 84" was a pensioner in 1840 and head of household in the 1st Division of Somerset County [Ref: Q-28:4 (1987), p. 446].

WILLIN (WILLEN), Samuel. Private, Somerset Militia, Salisbury Bn., Capt. John Span Conway's Nanticoke Point Co., 1778/1780 [Ref: M-216].

WILLIN (WILLEN), Thomas. Private, Somerset Militia, Salisbury Bn., Capt. John Span Conway's Nanticoke Point Co., 1778/1780 [Ref: M-216].

WILLIN (WILLEN), William. Took the Oath of Allegiance in Somerset County in 1778 before the Hon. Gillis Polk [Ref: T-15].

WILLIS, Abel. Private, Worcester Militia, Wicomico Bn., Capt. Elijah Shockley's Co., Fourth Class, July 15, 1780 [Ref: M-255].

WILLIS, Benjamin. Private, Worcester Militia, Snow Hill Bn., Capt. Ebenezer Handy's Co., April 9, 1776 [Ref: M-249]. Private, Worcester Militia, Wicomico Bn., Capt. Elijah Shockley's Co., Seventh Class, July 15, 1780 [Ref: M-255].

WILLIS, David. Private, Worcester Militia, Sinepuxent Bn., Capt. Thomas Purnell's Co., First Class, 1779/1780 [Ref: M-253].
WILLIS, Jabez. Private, Worcester Militia, Wicomico Bn., Capt. Philip Quinton's Co., Fifth Class, July 15, 1780 [Ref: M-256].
WILLIS, James. Private, Somerset Militia, Princess Anne Bn., Capt. Isaac Handy's Great Annemessix Co., 1780 [Ref: M-221]. Drafted from Somerset County on July 30, 1781 to serve in the Continental Army, but was subsequently excused [Ref: L-35C].
WILLIS, John. Private, Worcester Militia, Sinepuxent Bn., Capt. Thomas Purnell's Co., Third Class, 1779/1780 [Ref: M-253].
WILLIS, William. Private, Worcester Militia, Wicomico Bn., Capt. Philip Quinton's Co., First Class, July 15, 1780 [Ref: M-256].
WILLIS, William. Private, Worcester Militia, Wicomico Bn., Capt. Elijah Shockley's Co., Third Class, July 15, 1780 [Ref: M-255].
WILLIS, William. Private, Worcester Militia, Wicomico Bn., Capt. Robert Handy's Co., Sixth Class, July 15, 1780 [Ref: M-254].
WILLIT, Henry. See "Henry Willett," q.v.
WILSON, --?--. Ensign, Somerset Militia, 1st Bn., April 11, 1776, resigned [Ref: M-138, A-327].
WILSON, Ann. See "Levin Wilson," q.v.
WILSON, Betty. See "Ephraim Wilson" and "Denwood Wilson" and "Samuel Wilson," q.v.
WILSON, David. Captain, Somerset Militia, Princess Anne Bn., Back Creek Co., Sep 22, 1777 [Ref: M-138, C-381]. Took the Oath of Allegiance in Somerset County in 1778 before the Hon. Levin Wilson [Ref: T-17, N-52]. See "William Waters, Sr." and "Ephraim Wilson" and "Denwood Wilson" and "Samuel Wilson" and "Jacob Ker" and "William Morris," q.v.
WILSON, Denwood (1740-1803). Son of David Wilson (1704-1750) and first wife Betty ----. Denwood married first to Margaret Skirven or Skirvice on Aug 31, 1758 and second to Betty Stevens in 1803 [Ref: R-897]. Took the Oath of Allegiance in Somerset County in 1778 before the Hon. Levin Wilson [Ref: T-17, N-52]. Rendered patriotic service by hauling corn on April 18, 1780 and supplying bacon for the use of the military on July 1, 1780 [Ref: P-285, P-299].
WILSON, E. K. See "Levin Handy," q.v.
WILSON, Elizabeth. See "Henry Jackson" and "George Handy" and "Jacob Tull," q.v.
WILSON, Ephraim. Private, Somerset Militia, Salisbury Bn., Capt. James Bennett's Salisbury Co., 1778/1780 [Ref: M-218].
WILSON, Ephraim. Private, Somerset Militia, Salisbury Bn., Capt. Joseph Venables' Barren Creek Co., 1778/1780 [Ref: M-217].
WILSON, Ephraim (1726-1778). Son of David Wilson (1704-1750) and first wife Betty ----. Ephraim was an attorney in Somerset County and married Mary ----

[Ref: R-897]. Took the Oath of Allegiance in Somerset County in 1778 before the Hon. Levin Wilson [Ref: T-17].

WILSON, Esther. See "Jacob Ker" and "William Morris," q.v.

WILSON, George. Captain, Somerset Militia, Salisbury Bn., White Haven Co., Sep 22, 1777 to Aug 22, 1781, succeeded [Ref: M-138, C-382, G-575]. Took the Oath of Allegiance in Somerset County in 1778 before the Hon. William Winder [Ref: T-22, N-52].

WILSON, George. Private, Somerset Militia, Salisbury Bn., Capt. James Bennett's Salisbury Co., 1778/1780 [Ref: M-218]. Private, Somerset Militia, Princess Anne Bn., Capt. John Williams' Watkins Point Co., 1780 [Ref: M-222]. Took the Oath of Allegiance in Somerset County in 1778 before the Hon. Levin Wilson [Ref: T-17]. See "Levin Wilson," q.v.

WILSON, Hannah. See "Levin Wilson," q.v.

WILSON, Henrietta. See "Arnold Elzey," q.v.

WILSON, James (doctor). Took the Oath of Allegiance in Worcester County in 1778 before the Hon. John Selby [Ref: J-1814 (Box 4)].

WILSON, James. Private, Somerset Militia, Salisbury Bn., Capt. Joseph Venables' Barren Creek Co., 1778/1780 [Ref: M-217]. Private, Somerset Militia, Princess Anne Bn., Capt. James Elzey's Co., 1780 [Ref: M-220].

WILSON, James. Private, Worcester Militia, Sinepuxent Bn., Capt. Thomas Purnell's Co., First Class, 1779/1780 [Ref: M-253]. Rendered patriotic service by supplying bacon for the use of the military on July 9 and July 29, 1780 [Ref: P-300, P-305].

WILSON, James Jr. Private, Select Militia, Somerset County, Aug 15, 1781 [Ref: L-35B].

WILSON, James Sr. Took the Oath of Allegiance in Somerset County in 1778 before the Hon. Levin Wilson [Ref: T-17]. Rendered patriotic service by supplying pork in Somerset County for the use of the military on March 20, 1781 [Ref: P-372 listed the name without the "Sr."].

WILSON, Job. See "Jacob Tull," q.v.

WILSON, John. Private, Somerset Militia, Salisbury Bn., Capt. Joseph Venables' Barren Creek Co., 1778/1780 [Ref: M-217]. Private, Somerset Militia, Princess Anne Bn., Capt. James Elzey's Co., 1780 [Ref: M-220].

WILSON, John Jr. Private, Somerset Militia, Princess Anne Bn., Capt. Isaac Handy's Great Annemessix Co., 1780 [Ref: M-221].

WILSON, John Sr. Private, Somerset Militia, Princess Anne Bn., Capt. Isaac Handy's Great Annemessix Co., 1780 [Ref: M-221].

WILSON, John (of John). Private, Somerset Militia, Princess Anne Bn., Capt. John Williams' Watkins Point Co., 1780 [Ref: M-222].

WILSON, John (of Samuel). Private, Select Militia, Somerset County, Aug 15, 1781 [Ref: L-35A].

WILSON, John Custis. See "Samuel Wilson," q.v.

WILSON, Levin (1735-1791). Son of Samuel Wilson (d. 1748) and Martha Woolford. Levin married Sarah Stoughton on May 21, 1771 and they had a daughter Ann (b. 1773). Served in the Lower House of the Maryland Legislature from Somerset County, 1777-1778 [Ref: R-900]. Justice who administered the Oath of Allegiance in Somerset County in 1778 [Ref: T-17]. Justice of the Orphans Court and Justice of the Peace for Somerset County, 1778-1785. Commissioner of the Tax, 1777-1782 [Ref: C-464, E-248, I-45, R-900]. See "Ezekiel Taylor," q.v.

WILSON, Levin. Took the Oath of Allegiance in 1778 in Somerset County before the Hon. Peter Waters [Ref: T-18]. "Levin Willson" was born in Stepney Parish on Feb 11, 1757, the son of George and Phiriba Willson, and "Levin Wilson" was born in Coventry Parish on Sep 19, 1750, the son of George and Hannah Wilson [Ref: Y-76]. Additional research will be necessary before drawing conclusions.

WILSON, Mary. See "Ephraim Wilson," q.v.

WILSON, Milcah. See "Samuel Wilson," q.v.

WILSON, Nancy. See "Levin Handy," q.v.

WILSON, Phiriba. See "Levin Wilson," q.v.

WILSON, Robert. Private, Somerset Militia, Salisbury Bn., Capt. John Span Conway's Nanticoke Point Co., 1778/1780 [Ref: M-216].

WILSON, Samuel (1735-1790). Son of David Wilson (1704-1750) and first wife Betty ----. He married first to Peggy (Margaret) Custis and second to Mary Gale. Children: John Custis, Samuel, and Milcah Gale. Samuel served in the Lower House of the Maryland Legislature from Somerset County, 1758-1774, attended the Maryland Convention, 1774, was a Senator, Eastern Shore, 1776-1781, and served on the Council of Safety, Eastern Shore, 1776-1777 [Ref: R-897]. Rendered patriotic service by supplying corn, brandy, and fodder for the use of the military on Aug 21, 1781 [Ref: P-427]. See "Henry Jackson" and "Levin Wilson," q.v.

WILSON, William. Private, Somerset Militia, Princess Anne Bn., Capt. Henry Miles' Little Annemessex Co., 1780 [Ref: M-221].

WILSON, William. Private, Somerset Militia, Princess Anne Bn., Capt. John Williams' Watkins Point Co., 1780 [Ref: M-222].

WILSON, William. Private, Worcester Militia, Wicomico Bn., Capt. Samuel Horsey's Co., Seventh Class, July 15, 1780 [Ref: M-257].

WILTEN, Charles. Private, Somerset Militia, Salisbury Bn., Capt. John Span Conway's Nanticoke Point Co., 1778/1780 [Ref: M-216].

WIMBRO, Thomas P. (c1750-1831). Private, 2nd Maryland Line, who pensioned in Worcester County at $80 per annum effective Oct 22, 1828 (his representative was J. R. Nourse, attorney). [Ref: X-54]. Thomas P. Wimbro or Wimbrow received bounty land warrant #2267-100 and "also pensioned under Act of 15 May 1828 at which time he was living in Worcester County, Maryland and he was living there when he died (no date given). On 4 Nov 1839 soldier's son Peter Wimbro or Wimbrow applied in Somerset County, Maryland on behalf of himself and his brothers and sisters, to wit: Elijah and Thomas Wimbro or Wimbrow, Henry Tubbs' widow (her name was not given) and Lucy, the wife of Peter Shockley or Shockly." [Ref: W-3900]. Thomas P. Wimbrow or Wimbrough married Leah ---- in 1790, served in the 1st Maryland Regiment between Aug 1, 1780 and Nov 15, 1783, and died on March 28, 1831. His son Peter Wimbrow (1793-1875) married Sarah Tubbs (1794-1874) on Jan 16, 1816 [Ref: S-1446, S-1448].

WINDER, Charles. See "William Winder, Jr.," q.v.
WINDER, Charlotte. See "William Winder, Jr.," q.v.
WINDER, Dorothy. See "William Winder, Jr.," q.v.
WINDER, Edward. See "Levin Winder," q.v.
WINDER, Esther. See "William Winder," q.v.
WINDER, Jane. See "Henry Handy" and "William Winder," q.v.
WINDER, John (1745-1822). Son of William Winder and Esther Gillis [Ref: R-903, R-904]. Took the Oath of Allegiance in Somerset County in 1778 before the Hon. Levin Wilson [Ref: T-17]. See "William Winder," q.v.
WINDER, Leah. See "William Winder" and "William Morris," q.v.
WINDER, Levin (1757-1819). Son of William Winder (1714/5-1792) and Esther Gillis. Levin was born on Sep 4, 1757 in Somerset County, married Mary Stoughton Sloss (1765-1822) on May 13, 1790, and died on July 1, 1819 in Baltimore City (where he had been taken for medical treatment). He was initially interred in the First Presbyterian Church Cemetery in Baltimore and later reinterred on his estate at Monie Creek near Princess Anne in Somerset County. His children were William Sidney, Edward Stoughton, and Mary Ann. Levin served in the Lower House of the Maryland Legislature, 1789-1790, 1791-1792 (speaker), 1793 (speaker) 1806-1807, 1808-1809 (speaker), and was Governor of Maryland, 1812-1816. He was a member of Masonic Lodge No. 37 and was Grandmaster of the Grand Lodge of Maryland, 1814-1815. During the Revolutionary War, he served as first lieutenant, 5th Co., Gen. Smallwood's Regiment, January, 1776; captain, 1st Maryland Line, December, 1776; major, 4th Maryland Line, 1777; was wounded and taken prisoner at the Battle of Camden, South Carolina on Aug 16, 1780; exchanged in 1781; lieutenant colonel, 2nd Maryland Line, 1781; transferred to the 1st Maryland Line; and, discharged in 1783. He was commissioned major general of the 2nd Division, Maryland Militia, 1794, served as presidential elector (for George Washington) in 1792, and senate elector in Somerset County in 1796, 1801, 1806, and 1811 [Ref: R-902, V-3256]. See "William Winder," q.v.
WINDER, Mary Ann. See "Levin Winder," q.v.
WINDER, Priscilla. See "William Winder," q.v.
WINDER, Rider. See "William Winder, Jr.," q.v.
WINDER, Thomas. See "William Winder," q.v.

WINDER, William (1714/5-1792). Son of John Winder (1676-1716) and Jane (Jean) Dashiell. William was born on March 16, 1714/5, married first to Esther Gillis (1724-c1770), second to Mary Denwood (widow of Thomas), and died on Oct 24, 1792. His children were John, William Jr., Levin, Jane, Leah, Esther, Priscilla, and possibly Thomas (lost at sea early in life). William was a mariner by 1743, master and co-owner of the sloop *Polly* in 1749 and the schooner *Betty* in 1750, and ship captain by 1777. He served as a Justice of Somerset County, 1756-1788 (quorum, 1762-1788); Justice of the Court of Oyer and Terminer and Gaol Delivery, 1770; Justice of the Orphans Court, 1777; Judge of the Court of Appeals, 1778-1782; Commissioner of the Tax, 1777-1779; Justice of the Peace, 1778-1782; Associate Justice, 4th District, 1789-1791 [Ref: R-903, E-109, E-248, C-274, C-464, I-45]. Took the Oath of Allegiance in Somerset County on Feb 28, 1778 before the Hon. Joseph Venables [Ref: T-25 listed the name as "William Winder, Sr."]. Justice who administered the Oath of Allegiance in Somerset County in 1778 [Ref: T-22]. Commissioned by the Council of Maryland on Aug 19, 1779 to receive subscriptions for the Continental Loan Office [Ref: E-499]. Rendered patriotic service by storing corn and pork for the use of the military on Oct 7, 1780 [Ref: P-324]. See "John Henry" and "William Winder, Jr." and "Levin Winder" and "William Polk" and "James Rownd Morris," q.v.

WINDER, William Jr. (c1750-1808). Son of William Winder (d. 1792) and Esther Gillis. He married Charlotte Henry (daughter of John Henry, d. 1781) and their children were William Henry (1775-1824, General, War of 1812), Rider Henry, Charles H., Dorothy Arietta, and Charlotte Henry. William served in the Lower House of the Maryland Legislature from Somerset County, 1777-1778; Commissioner of the Tax for Somerset County, appointed in 1783; and, Senator, Eastern Shore, 1793-1795 [Ref: R-904]. First Lieutenant, Somerset Militia, Salisbury Bn., Capt. Robert Dashiell's Co., Sep 22, 1777. Captain, April 20, 1778 to May 27, 1779, succeeded [Ref: M-139, C-382, E-42, E-423]. Appointed as one of three Purchasers of Cattle in Somerset County for the use of the Continental Army on Jan 7, 1778 [Ref: C-456]. Took the Oath of Allegiance in Somerset County in 1778 before the Hon. Gillis Polk [Ref: T-15, N-52]. Also served as Commissioner of the Navy Board of the Middle Department, 1778-1780; Commissioner of Accounts for the State of Delaware, 1782-1787; District Commissioner for the Settlement of State Accounts with the Confederation Government after the Revolution, appointed 1787; Accountant of the Navy, appointed in July, 1798 and resigned in January, 1780 [Ref: R-904]. See "William Winder," q.v.

WINDER, William Henry. See "William Winder, Jr.," q.v.

WINDER, William Sidney. See "Levin Winder," q.v.

WINDSOR, James. Private, Somerset Militia, Salisbury Bn., Capt. John Span Conway's Nanticoke Point Co., 1778/1780 [Ref: M-216].

WINDSOR, John Jr. Private, Somerset Militia, Princess Anne Bn., Capt. Thomas Irving's Monie Co., 1780 [Ref: M-219].
WINDSOR, William. Private, Somerset Militia, Princess Anne Bn., Capt. Thomas Irving's Monie Co., 1780 [Ref: M-219].
WINGATE, Henry. Private, Somerset Militia, Princess Anne Bn., Capt. Thomas Irving's Monie Co., 1780 [Ref: M-219].
WINGATE, Henry. Private, Somerset Militia, Princess Anne Bn., Capt. Thomas Irving's Monie Co., 1780 [Ref: M-219].
WINGATE, Phil. Private, Somerset Militia, Princess Anne Bn., Capt. Thomas Irving's Monie Co., 1780 [Ref: M-219].
WINTERS, John. Private, Worcester Militia, Wicomico Bn., Capt. Fisher Walton's Co., Third Class, July 15, 1780 [Ref: M-258].
WISE, John. Took the Oath of Allegiance in Worcester County in 1778 before the Hon. Nathaniel Miller [Ref: J-1814 (Box 4)]. Register of Wills for Worcester County, commissioned on Aug 16, 1782 in the room of William Morris, deceased [Ref: I-235].
WISE, Samuel. Took the Oath of Allegiance in Worcester County in 1778 before the Hon. Joshua Townsend [Ref: J-1814 (Box 4)].
WISE, William. Ensign, Worcester Militia, Snow Hill Bn., Capt. William Handy's Co., Aug 30, 1777. Ensign, Wicomico Bn., Capt. William Handy's Co., July 15, 1780 [Ref: M-139, M-257, C-351]. Took the Oath of Allegiance in Worcester County in 1778 before the Hon. Nehemiah Holland [Ref: J-1814 (Box 4)]. Appointed as one of three Purchasers of Cattle in Worcester County for the use of the Continental Army on Jan 7, 1778 [Ref: C-456]. He wrote to the Governor of Maryland on March 11, 1781 stating that "being informed that a quantity of corn and lumber is proposed to be sent by this State to New York for the support of the American prisoners ... I have a vessel about 800 bushels burthen and corn ready purchased and would engage to transport any quantity that may be necessary as the vessel can do it." [Ref: H-118].
WISHART, Elizabeth. See "Isaac Whittington," q.v.
WITHERS, George. See "George Whithears," q.v.
WONNELL (WONNALL), James (1751 -   ). Son of James and Sarah Wonnall, born in Coventry Parish on Sep 8, 1751 [Ref: Y-76]. Private, Worcester Militia, Wicomico Bn., Capt. Charles Bennett's Co., Sixth Class, July 15, 1780 [Ref: M-255].
WOOD, William (captain). On March 30, 1780, Joseph Dashiell, Commissary for Purchases in Worcester County, issued a certificate to Capt. William Wood for hauling corn [Ref: P-280].
WOOD, William. Private(?), Somerset Militia, Princess Anne Bn., St. Asaph's Co., 1780 [Ref: M-220].
WOODGATE, Mary. See "William Polk," q.v.
WOODLEY, Gavily. Private, Worcester Militia, Wicomico Bn., Capt. John Davis' Co., Fifth Class, July 15, 1780 [Ref: M-254].

WOODS, Martha. See "John Tull," q.v.
WOOLEN, Edward. See "Thomas Harris," q.v.
WOOLEN, Johnston. See "Thomas Harris," q.v.
WOOLEN, Nancy. See "Thomas Harris," q.v.
WOOLFORD, John. Corporal, Somerset Militia, Princess Anne Bn., Capt. Thomas Irving's Monie Co., 1780 [Ref: M-219].
WOOLFORD, Levin. Appointed as one of three Purchasers of Cattle in Somerset County for the use of the Continental Army on Jan 7, 1778 [Ref: C-456]. Took the Oath of Allegiance in Somerset County in 1778 before the Hon. Levin Wilson [Ref: T-17, N-52]. Justice of the Orphans Court and Justice of the Peace, commissioned on Jan 9, 1778 and Nov 21, 1778 and Nov 25, 1780 and Jan 17, 1782 [Ref: C-464, E-248, G-224, G-225, I-45]. Coroner, resigned in 1783 [Ref: I-420].
WOOLFORD, Levin Jr. Private, Select Militia, Somerset County, Aug 15, 1781 [Ref: L-35A].
WOOLFORD, Martha. See "Levin Wilson," q.v.
WOOLFORD, Mary. See "Henry Waggaman," q.v.
WOOLFORD, Thomas. Private, Select Militia, Somerset County, Aug 15, 1781 [Ref: L-35A].
WOOLSEY, Daniel. Took the Oath of Allegiance in Worcester County in 1778 before the Hon. Nathaniel Miller [Ref: J-1814 (Box 4)].
WORRING, Richard. Took the Oath of Allegiance in Worcester County in 1778 in Buckingham Hundred before the Hon. Thomas Purnell [Ref: J-1814 (Box 4)].
WRIGH (WEIGK?), Joseph. Private, Somerset Militia, Salisbury Bn., Capt. William Turpin's Rewastico Co., 1778/1780 [Ref: M-217].
WRIGHT, Betty. See "Isaac Wright" and "Joshua Wright," q.v.
WRIGHT, Elizabeth. See "Zadock Wright," q.v.
WRIGHT, Gowen or Gowan (1732-1805). Ensign, Somerset Militia, Princess Anne Bn., Capt. Thomas Irving's Monie Co., Sep 22, 1777 to at least July 24, 1780 [Ref: M-219, M-140, and C-381 mistakenly listed the name as "Gavin Wright"]. Took the Oath of Allegiance in Somerset County in 1778 before the Hon. Levin Wilson [Ref: T-17, N-52]. On May 23, 1783 "Gowen Wright" was commissioned one of the coroners of Somerset County in the room of Levin Woolford who had resigned [Ref: I-420]. "Gowan Wright" was born on Jan 9, 1732, married Helen Staples, served as an ensign in the revolution, and died on Dec 26, 1805 [Ref: V-3307].
WRIGHT, Handy. Private, Somerset Militia, Salisbury Bn., Capt. Joseph Venables' Barren Creek Co., 1778/1780 [Ref: M-217].
WRIGHT, Henrietta. See "Isaac Wright," q.v.
WRIGHT, Hetty. See "Zadock Wright," q.v.
WRIGHT, Hezekiah. See "Zadock Wright," q.v.

WRIGHT, Isaac (1761-1814). Son of Jacob and Betty Wright, born in Stepney Parish on May 25, 1761. Isaac married Henrietta Dashield or Dashiell, was a private in the revolution, and died in 1814 [Ref: Y-46, V-3307]. Private, Somerset Militia, Salisbury Bn., Capt. Joseph Venables' Barren Creek Co., 1778/1780 [Ref: M-217]. Isaac Wright died in January, 1814, aged about 50 (inscription on his tombstone) and is buried in the Isaac Wright Family Graveyard on the north side of Snethen Road, a quarter mile southeast of Cross Road in Wicomico County. The tombstone inscription for his wife Henrietta reads exactly the same [Ref: *Graveyards and Gravestones of Wicomico*, by John E. Jacob (1996), p. 85].

WRIGHT, Isaiah. Private, Worcester Militia, Snow Hill Bn., Capt. Ebenezer Handy's Co., April 9, 1776 [Ref: M-249]. Private, Worcester Militia, Wicomico Bn., Capt. Robert Handy's Co., Third Class, July 15, 1780 [Ref: M-254].

WRIGHT, Jacob. See "Isaac Wright" and "Joshua Wright," q.v.

WRIGHT, Jesse. Private, 3rd Maryland Independent Co., Worcester County, Capt. John Watkins' Co., enlisted Feb 21, 1776; muster roll dated Aug 20, 1776, present for duty [Ref: D-22].

WRIGHT, John. Corporal, Somerset Militia, Princess Anne Bn., Capt. Thomas Irving's Monie Co., 1780 [Ref: M-219]. Took the Oath of Allegiance in Somerset County in 1778 before the Hon. Levin Wilson [Ref: T-17]. See "Zadock Wright," q.v.

WRIGHT, Joshua (1757-1814). Son of Jacob and Betty Wright, born in Stepney Parish on Oct 13, 1757. Joshua married Sally Turpin, was a private in Maryland during the revolution, and died in Delaware on June 10, 1814 [Ref: Y-46, V-3309]. Private, Somerset Militia, Salisbury Bn., Capt. Joseph Venables' Barren Creek Co., 1778/1780 [Ref: M-217].

WRIGHT, Josiah. Took the Oath of Allegiance in Worcester County in 1778 before the Hon. William Hopewell [Ref: J-1814 (Box 4) listed the name as "Josiah Right"].

WRIGHT, Levin. Private, Somerset Militia, Salisbury Bn., Capt. William Turpin's Rewastico Co., 1778/1780 [Ref: M-217].

WRIGHT, Obadiah. Took the Oath of Allegiance in Worcester County in 1778 before the Hon. Nathaniel Miller [Ref: J-1814 (Box 4)].

WRIGHT, Sally. See "Zadock Wright," q.v.

WRIGHT, Stephen. Private, Somerset Militia, Salisbury Bn., Capt. Joseph Venables' Barren Creek Co., 1778/1780 [Ref: M-217]. Took the Oath of Allegiance in Somerset County on Feb 28, 1778 (made his "X" mark) before the Hon. Joseph Venables [Ref: T-25].

WRIGHT, Thomas. Took the Oath of Allegiance in Worcester County in 1778 before the Hon. Nehemiah Holland [Ref: J-1814 (Box 4)].

WRIGHT, Zadock. Took the Oath of Allegiance in Worcester County in 1778 before the Hon. Joshua Townsend [Ref: J-1814 (Box 4) listed the name as "Zadock Right"]. In Worcester County Court, in August, 1797, a petition by

Hezekiah Wright was submitted for a commission to divide the real estate of "Zadok Wright" who died possessed of sundry tracts and parts of tracts, leaving the petitioner, and a certain John Wright, Jr., Elizabeth Wright, Sally Wright, and Hetty Wright his children and heirs, all of whom excepting the petitioner, were under the age of twenty-one [Ref: Article by William D. Patrick in *Maryland Magazine of Genealogy*, Vol. 4 No. 1 (Spring, 1981), p. 7].

WYATT, Caleb. Private, Worcester Militia, Sinepuxent Bn., Capt. Josiah Dale's Co., Fourth Class, 1779/1780 [Ref: M-254 listed the name as "Caleb Wayatt"].

WYATT, Edward. Private, Somerset Militia, Princess Anne Bn., Capt. John Williams' Watkins Point Co., 1780 [Ref: M-222]. Took the Oath of Allegiance in Somerset County in 1778 before the Hon. John Williams [Ref: T-21, N-52].

YOUNG, Anthony. Took the Oath of Allegiance in Somerset County in 1778 (made his "X" mark) before the Hon. John Williams [Ref: T-21, N-52].

YOUNG, Daniel (Dannel). Private, Worcester Militia, Wicomico Bn., Capt. Isaac Layfield's Co., Second Class, July 15, 1780 [Ref: M-257]. Took the Oath of Allegiance in Worcester County in 1778 before the Hon. James Selby [Ref: J-1814 (Box 4)].

YOUNG, Ephraim. Private, Worcester Militia, Wicomico Bn., Capt. Isaac Layfield's Co., Sixth Class, July 15, 1780 [Ref: M-257].

YOUNG, Ezekiel. Private, Worcester Militia, Wicomico Bn., Capt. Isaac Layfield's Co., First Class, July 15, 1780 [Ref: M-257]. Took the Oath of Allegiance in Worcester County in 1778 before the Hon. James Selby [Ref: J-1814 (Box 4)].

YOUNG, George. Private, Select Militia, Somerset County, Aug 15, 1781 [Ref: L-35B].

YOUNG, John. Private, Worcester Militia, Wicomico Bn., Capt. Isaac Layfield's Co., Fourth Class, July 15, 1780 [Ref: M-257]. Took the Oath of Allegiance in Somerset County in 1778 (made his "X" mark) before the Hon. Peter Waters [Ref: T-18].

YOUNG, Milby. Private, Worcester Militia, Wicomico Bn., Capt. Isaac Layfield's Co., Fourth Class, July 15, 1780 [Ref: M-257].

YOUNG, William. Private, Worcester Militia, Wicomico Bn., Capt. James Patterson's Co., Sixth Class, July 15, 1780 [Ref: M-258].

--?--, Elihu. Private, Somerset Militia, Salisbury Bn., Capt. John Span Conway's Nanticoke Point Co., 1778/1780 [Ref: M-216].

--?--, Hudson (of Truitt). Private, Worcester Militia, Snow Hill Bn., Capt. Samuel Smyley's Co., 1777 [Ref: M-250].

--?--, James. Private, Somerset Militia, Princess Anne Bn., Capt. Henry Miles' Little Annemessex Co., 1780 [Ref: M-221].

--?--, John. Private, Somerset Militia, Salisbury Bn., Capt. John Span Conway's Nanticoke Point Co., 1778/1780 [Ref: M-216].

--?--, John. Private, Somerset Militia, Salisbury Bn., Capt. Henry Gale's Quantico Co., 1778/1780 [Ref: M-216].

--?--, Richard. Private, Somerset Militia, Salisbury Bn., Capt. James Bennett's Salisbury Co., 1778/1780 [Ref: M-218].

--?--, Roger. Private, Somerset Militia, Salisbury Bn., Capt. John Span Conway's Nanticoke Point Co., 1778/1780 [Ref: M-216].

--?--, Samuel. Private, Somerset Militia, Salisbury Bn., Capt. John Span Conway's Nanticoke Point Co., 1778/1780 [Ref: M-216].

Other books by the author:

A Closer Look at St. John's Parish Registers [Baltimore County, Maryland], 1701-1801
A Collection of Maryland Church Records
A Guide to Genealogical Research in Maryland: 5th Edition, Revised and Enlarged
Abstracts of the Ledgers and Accounts of the Bush Store and Rock Run Store, 1759-1771
Abstracts of the Orphans Court Proceedings of Harford County, 1778-1800
Abstracts of Wills, Harford County, Maryland, 1800-1805
Baltimore City [Maryland] Deaths and Burials, 1834-1840
Baltimore County, Maryland, Overseers of Roads, 1693-1793
Bastardy Cases in Baltimore County, Maryland, 1673-1783
Bastardy Cases in Harford County, Maryland, 1774-1844
Bible and Family Records of Harford County, Maryland Families: Volume V
Children of Harford County: Indentures and Guardianships, 1801-1830
Colonial Delaware Soldiers and Sailors, 1638-1776
Colonial Families of the Eastern Shore of Maryland
Volumes 5, 6, 7, 8, 9, 11, 12, 13, 14, and 16
Colonial Maryland Soldiers and Sailors, 1634-1734
Dr. John Archer's First Medical Ledger, 1767-1769, Annotated Abstracts
Early Anglican Records of Cecil County
Early Harford Countians, Individuals Living in Harford County, Maryland in Its Formative Years
Volume 1: A to K, Volume 2: L to Z, and Volume 3: Supplement
Harford County Taxpayers in 1870, 1872 and 1883
Harford County, Maryland Divorce Cases, 1827-1912: An Annotated Index
Heirs and Legatees of Harford County, Maryland, 1774-1802
Heirs and Legatees of Harford County, Maryland, 1802-1846
Inhabitants of Baltimore County, Maryland, 1763-1774
Inhabitants of Cecil County, Maryland, 1649-1774
Inhabitants of Harford County, Maryland, 1791-1800
Inhabitants of Kent County, Maryland, 1637-1787
Joseph A. Pennington & Co., Havre De Grace, Maryland Funeral Home Records:
Volume II, 1877-1882, 1893-1900
Maryland Bible Records, Volume 1: Baltimore and Harford Counties
Maryland Bible Records, Volume 2: Baltimore and Harford Counties
Maryland Bible Records, Volume 3: Carroll County
Maryland Bible Records, Volume 4: Eastern Shore
Maryland Deponents, 1634-1799
Maryland Deponents: Volume 3, 1634-1776
Maryland Public Service Records, 1775-1783: A Compendium of Men and Women of Maryland Who Rendered Aid in Support of the American Cause against Great Britain during the Revolutionary War
Marylanders to Carolina: Migration of Marylanders to North Carolina and South Carolina prior to 1800

Marylanders to Kentucky, 1775-1825
Methodist Records of Baltimore City, Maryland: Volume 1, 1799-1829
Methodist Records of Baltimore City, Maryland: Volume 2, 1830-1839
Methodist Records of Baltimore City, Maryland: Volume 3, 1840-1850 (East City Station)
More Maryland Deponents, 1716-1799
More Marylanders to Carolina: Migration of Marylanders to North Carolina and South Carolina prior to 1800
More Marylanders to Kentucky, 1778-1828
Outpensioners of Harford County, Maryland, 1856-1896
Presbyterian Records of Baltimore City, Maryland, 1765-1840
Quaker Records of Baltimore and Harford Counties, Maryland, 1801-1825
Quaker Records of Northern Maryland, 1716-1800
Quaker Records of Southern Maryland, 1658-1800
Revolutionary Patriots of Anne Arundel County, Maryland
Revolutionary Patriots of Baltimore Town and Baltimore County, 1775-1783
Revolutionary Patriots of Calvert and St. Mary's Counties, Maryland, 1775-1783
Revolutionary Patriots of Caroline County, Maryland, 1775-1783
Revolutionary Patriots of Cecil County, Maryland
Revolutionary Patriots of Charles County, Maryland, 1775-1783
Revolutionary Patriots of Delaware, 1775-1783
Revolutionary Patriots of Dorchester County, Maryland, 1775-1783
Revolutionary Patriots of Frederick County, Maryland, 1775-1783
Revolutionary Patriots of Harford County, Maryland, 1775-1783
Revolutionary Patriots of Kent and Queen Anne's Counties
Revolutionary Patriots of Lancaster County, Pennsylvania
Revolutionary Patriots of Maryland, 1775-1783: A Supplement
Revolutionary Patriots of Maryland, 1775-1783: Second Supplement
Revolutionary Patriots of Montgomery County, Maryland, 1776-1783
Revolutionary Patriots of Prince George's County, Maryland, 1775-1783
Revolutionary Patriots of Talbot County, Maryland, 1775-1783
Revolutionary Patriots of Washington County, Maryland, 1776-1783
St. George's (Old Spesutia) Parish, Harford County, Maryland: Church and Cemetery Records, 1820-1920
St. John's and St. George's Parish Registers, 1696-1851
Survey Field Book of David and William Clark in Harford County, Maryland, 1770-1812
The Crenshaws of Kentucky, 1800-1995
The Delaware Militia in the War of 1812
Union Chapel United Methodist Church Cemetery Tombstone Inscriptions, Wilna, Harford County, Maryland

www.ingramcontent.com/pod-product-compliance
Lightning Source LLC
Chambersburg PA
CBHW071953220426
43662CB00009B/1118